Faithful Conclusions

A Religious Encyclopedia of Belief and Practice

Dr. Lee Ann B. Marino, Ph.D., D.Min., D.D.

FAITHFUL CONCLUSIONS

A Religious Encyclopedia of Belief and Practice
(First Edition)

DR. LEE ANN B. MARINO, PH.D., D.MIN., D.D.

Published by:

APOSTOLIC COVENANT
THEOLOGICAL SEMINARY
Wisdom • Diversity • Friendship • Knowledge
WWW.ACTS176.ORG

Book classification:
1. Nonfiction > Religion > Reference.
2. Nonfiction > Religion > Education.

ISBN: 1-940197-72-4
13-Digit: 978-1-940197-72-2

Printed in the United States of America.

THOU ART AN IMPRESSION OF MY MIND,
WHICH PERVADES ME FOR EVER,
THAT ALL MY CHORES ARE GIVEN STRENGTH,
AND MY FAITH ON MYSELF RESTORED,
THAT MAKETH THE BEAST IN ME, A MAN,
AND REVEALS TO ME THE HOLY PLAN,
WHICH WOULD BE THE GUIDING LIGHT BY THEE,
TO SHOWER THY BLESSINGS OVER ME,
MY FAITH, THE HEART OF MY SOUL,
WHICH MAKES ME A 'MAN,' ON THE WHOLE.
(SREERAM VASUDEVAN)[1]

Table of Contents

Acknowledgements

I WAS RECENTLY told by a colleague I hadn't seen in several years that I was still as relevant as I ever was. This word made me think about the concept of relevance; something that I, as a long-time student and teacher of religion in its varied forms, often consider in the dark hours of the night. What makes us, and for those of us who do pursue faith, our faith relevant? How does our faith stand from age to age, through ups and downs? Maybe more than anything else right now, what will continue to make it relevant in the future?

I first decided to write this book over 25 years ago as a largely naïve individual. I had no idea what life would bring in the next few years. I was a seminary Bible college student who fell in love with the interview process of research while studying general religious belief. I liked to write; I liked religion; and that was about all I knew. I had to complete five interviews with people of varying backgrounds, all within a specified period of about four months. Between September 1998 and January of 1999, I interviewed a Jewish rabbi, a group of members at a local American Orthodox church, a conservative Baptist youth pastor, a Muslim stay-at-home mom, and a Christian Science librarian. When I finished the required research, I continued my research. The interviews became a vital source of information to aid additional projects and assignments. This process became a way of seeing the world, one that would later turn into visiting services. It offered windows into a world of religion that many never dared to see, and pursuit after pursuit to obtain the "insider level" of information only a member would have.

After a quarter of a century in this specified field – one that is in many ways regarded differently than in days past and often not as accessible nor respected as it once was – I find myself overwhelmed with gratitude. I've had the chance to see the way religion has continued and transformed. Perhaps, I am most grateful for the way that I have transformed because of it. It's been a wild ride with many ups and downs, not to mention unexpected detours that we never see coming around the bend. Through this initial project, I found my own calling. I found the faith that I have espoused now for over 25 years. I remember those initial interviews as building blocks: steppingstones preparing me for what I would one day become. Some were funny, some were irritating, some caused offense, and many more were wonderful experiences that enriched my perspective through education. In every situation, and now every memory and power-packed information session that each was, I find my blessing and my answer.

Many of the original people I interviewed are now deceased. Many of their houses of worship have since closed. Their children are now grown, and some are now grandparents. Their lives did not outlast the changing times, changing tides, and turning seasons. Yet they remain: their words, faith, and pursuit of spiritual things lives and remains. They are forever relevant.

Many don't understand the core understanding of religion is change, as groups strive for relevance from age to age. Here we will examine the things that both change and stay the same as we embrace the foundations of faith and belief that have transcended ages.

Here is to relevance. Thank you to everyone who has not only helped me see how important it is, but to remain that way as life continues. Thanks for being part of my story.

Agnosticism

A totally nondenominational prayer: Insofar as I may be heard by anything, which may or may not care what I say, I ask, if it matters, that I be forgiven for anything I may have done or failed to do which requires forgiveness. Conversely, if not forgiveness but something else may be required to insure any possible benefit for which I may be eligible after the destruction of my body, I ask that this, whatever it may be, be granted or withheld, as the case may be, in such a manner as to insure said benefit. I ask this in my capacity as your elected intermediary between yourself and that which may not be yourself, but which may have an interest in the matter of your receiving as much as it is possible for you to receive of this thing, and which may in some way be influenced by this ceremony. Amen.

(Roger Zelazny)[1]

Theology

Belief that the divine, who is referred to as GOD, DIVINE, or SUPERNATURAL, is nameless, without personality, and impossible to fathom, know, or connect with in any shape or form. Agnostics see the existence of the divine as irrelevant in terms of human existence and human life, believing human reason is insufficient to provide rational grounds either for or against the existence of the divine.

Most agnostics place most of their belief system in the existence of science, scientific evidence, and scientific proof. In the face of things unseen (as is the realm of faith) agnostics uphold the rationale of science and scientific process. With interest in science, Agnostics believe in the existence of the material world, but do not believe in certain belief in anything beyond material existence (such as the spirit realm).

Philosophy

Agnosticism centers around the principle of total uncertainty regarding all things scientifically unproven. This equates to total impossibility of ever knowing, beyond a shadow of reasonable doubt, that things such as God, life after death, miracles, the spiritual realm, and religious beliefs have any origin or basis in something beyond intellectual comprehension that can be trusted and known by faith. As these things cannot be seen or proven by any scientific or methodological reasoning, agnostics take a non-position. Such things are seen as having no comprehensive or obtainable. Agnosticism is a literal "non position" on such matters.

The word "agnostic" was first used by T.H. Huxley, a British biologist and evolutionist in 1869. He saw the term as "counter" to the "gnostic" (meaning "knowledge") church of history that claimed to know things he could not discover. Therefore, he was in a state of ignorance about those things. This is not to say agnosticism is a profession of ignorance, but instead, that it follows a single principle, rigorously applied, by which one follows reason on such matters as opposed to applying faith or belief without evidence. The term is often used in a strictly religious context, although it also extends to skepticism about anything non-material, unseen, or existing without evidence that can apply by a singular principle.

Though agnosticism is not considered a religion, it often shapes the way people think about religion, spirituality, spiritual ideas, and the divine.[2]

T.H. Huxley (1825-1895)

ADHERENT IDENTITY

Agnostic, irreligious, non-theistic, freethinker, doubter, skeptic, questioner, materialist, Freethinker; some agnostics identify as Unitarian Universalists.

TRADITIONAL LANGUAGES

English.

SECTS/DIVISIONS

Even though agnosticism is not formally classified as a religion, that does not stop some agnostics from seeking the same type of ideals and structure as would be found in religion through different means. There are a few entities of agnosticism, some more visible than other.

- **Religious agnosticism:** Religious agnosticism takes form in an individual who desires to associate with traditional religion while taking agnostic positions on some of the doctrinal tenants of theology found therein. A religious agnostic may believe in the existence of the divine but may not find the divine being to be knowable or relatable in modern times. In Christianity, for example, they may believe in parts of a theology (such as in the being of Jesus Christ) but reject the being of the Holy Spirit or may deny aspects of the Bible. They may believe God exists as Creator but may not believe in prayer or the experience thereof. Religious agnostics belong to traditional religious groups because they believe the ideals present therein are admirable and good. Though they may reject parts, or all the theology involved, they still feel religion offers a benefit to humanity they cannot find elsewhere. Such individuals would be classified as deists and nontheists.

- **Agnostic churches:** There are specially identified "agnostic churches" that offer the same benefits of belonging to an organized religious group, with an agnostic focus and ideals. Agnostic churches either focus on the exploration of the possibility of God (especially through different religious texts) or on upholding structure of strict agnostic principles. Such groups focus on science, the material world, and comfort in not knowing about the divine, either way. Examples of agnostic churches are the United Agnostic Church, Oasis Network, Sunday Assembly, and the Church of Freethought. Many would also consider the Unitarian Universalist Association to fall into this category, although the UUA is not exclusive to agnostics.

- **Agnostic organizations**: Agnostic organizations are non-religious entities that advocate for the rights of agnostics as well as educating the public on agnostic issues. Many of these organizations serve as networking centers for other agnostics. Often, these organizations partner with atheist organizations or other groups that are non-religious in nature. An example of such is the National Office of the Freedom From Religion Foundation.

- **Independent agnostics:** Many agnostics don't identify with any one group or entity, preferring to remain skeptical of matters without any form of association with others.

NUMBER OF ADHERENTS

Approximately 7% of the world's population is atheist and agnostic (as numbers are often grouped together); approximately 450,000,000 to 500,000,000 are found worldwide.[3]

DISPUTES WITHIN GROUP

Because agnosticism is a literal non-position on things unseen, not all agnostics agree about the nature of agnosticism or what it means to be agnostic. There are relevant questions over what agnosticism is: does it eliminate the total realm of the divine? How are things without an explanation explained? Is the paranormal off limits? What happens when science is wrong? Can one be agnostic and religious? Are holidays eliminated? What happens to morality? Each agnostic and as an extension of each agnostic, each group establishes its own unique positions on these and other current issues. Agnostics also disagree over the political intensity of agnostic implementations within society. While some will take an obvious issue with religion and the concepts it promotes, some will be supportive of its existence, and practice or uphold certain aspects of it.

SCRIPTURES

Agnostics do not embrace the concept of divine inspiration, as they question the existence of the divine. Agnostics do, however, frequently use scriptural texts from a diversity of religions (including the Bible, Hindu scripture, and the Qur'an) for ethical or moral arguments. Some use scripture inversely, to prove them to be contradictory or amoral, and thereby defend their own agnostic positions.

There are no specific "scriptures" that expound the beliefs or ideas of agnosticism, but there are a few writers considered foundational to agnostic belief. These include:

- **David Hume** (1711-1776): David Hume was a Scottish enlightenment philosopher who delved into specified areas of skepticism and naturalism. He is often considered the formal foundation of agnostic thought within the philosophical community. His prominent works in this specified field are *Enquiry Concerning Human Understanding* (1748) and *Dialogues Concerning Natural Religion* (1779).

  In our reasonings concerning matter of fact, there are all imaginable degrees of assurance, from the highest certainty to the lowest species of moral evidence. A wise man, therefore, proportions his belief to the evidence.[4]

- **Charles Darwin** (1809-1882): Charles Darwin claimed to be an agnostic towards the latter part of his life, although Darwin's exact beliefs about God and religion are in question. From his records, it does appear Darwin did believe there were questions science couldn't answer, and that theology and science should be free to examine and delve into their specified work and explanation, each having their own purpose. Darwin is best known for his resulting theory of evolution, popularized in the book, *On the Origin of Species* (1859). Many agnostics consider Darwin's theory to be a groundbreaking idea in scientific protocol and the world of material evidence.[5]

  Man could no longer be regarded as the Lord of Creation, a being apart from the rest of nature. He was merely the representative of one among many Families of the order Primates in the class Mammalia.[6]

- **Bertrand Russell** (1872-1970): Perhaps the most famous agnostic of the last century, Bertrand Russell was well known as a philosopher and intellect, very vocal about his views. His most relevant works on agnosticism were: *Why I Am Not a Christian* (1927), *Am I an Atheist or an Agnostic: A Plea for Tolerance in the Face of New Dogmas* (1949), and *What is an Agnostic* (1953).

  As a philosopher, if I were speaking to a purely philosophic audience I should say that I ought to describe myself as an Agnostic, because I do not think that there is a conclusive argument by which one can prove that there is not a God. On the other hand, if I am to convey the right impression to the ordinary man in the street I think that I ought to say that I am an Atheist, because, when I say that I cannot prove that there is not a God, I ought to add equally that I cannot prove that there are not the Homeric gods.[7]

- **Leslie Weatherhead** (1893-1976): A British theologian who followed a liberal Protestant tradition that had much in common with deism. He denied the inspiration of the Bible, questioned the divinity of Christ, and rejected the existence of the Holy Spirit as a separate individual. He was author of *The Christian Agnostic* (1965), a work that examined the realm of religious agnosticism from the Christian perspective.

No honest mind can exclude doubt, or ignore criticism, or shut its ears against reason. And if we could do these things we should be left, not with faith, but with a head-in-the-sand superstition.[8]

BASIC RELIGIOUS PRACTICES

Agnosticism does not have a specified practice of belief. Agnostic beliefs center around the agnostic themselves, and the way they perceive the lack of comprehensive rational evidence on matters of the unseen. Many agnostics join forces with atheists against religion and belief. They strongly support the separation of church and state through every means, including education and teaching in schools, religious displays on government or city property, and legal legislation. Others may attend a Unitarian Universalist Church, which allows agnostic memberships, a church that is specifically agnostic in ideals, or still attend a mainline church, supporting its views on ethics and morality while not ascribing to matters of dogmatic faith.

HOLIDAYS

Many agnostics celebrate holidays such as Christmas and Easter from a secular perspective. They will use the time for family gatherings, social events, and may celebrate the season without any religious significance. There are some agnostics who opt out of any holiday with religious connotation. Many are highly patriotic, upholding agnosticism as their right under American law. Thus, many agnostics hold special appreciation for patriotic holidays.

VISUAL SIGNS AND SYMBOLS

The letter "A" within a circle that is open on the bottom end; three question marks in a circle; question marks; the agnostic question mark (the "A" symbol within a circle that serves as the top of a question mark); Darwin's evolutionary fish eating the smaller fish of faith; the symbols of all world religions with a question mark over them; the American flag.

Agnostic symbol

CREEDS, BOOKS, AND LAWS

Agnosticism exists without creed or statement of belief because agnostics do not take a position on belief. Agnostics tend to live according to the laws of science and scientific reason: in other words, they decide what is worthy of belief or disbelief on their understanding of science's ability to prove or disprove the existence of something. Morality is personally subjective and open to interpretation. Many believe in humanism, which extols the best of humanity within its conceptual understanding. We could say agnostics live by the precept that "seeing is believing;" until they can see, or prove according to their definitions of rationalism, they will not believe in things unseen.

ECLECTIC BELIEFS

Since agnosticism is a literal non-position, the nature of it – and what one believes or adheres to as part of it – often falls into a state of perpetual questions. Agnosticism only poses questions, which according to its own theory, cannot possibly be answered in any way. It offers no answers or solutions, or even the possible hope of answers. Many agnostics spend time in deep thought over the greater life questions and the results therein, especially those related to morality and personal conduct. The result is a life of why rather than the pursuit of answers, and while some are satisfied with this, many are not.

RELATIONS WITH NON-AGNOSTICS

Depending on their personal affiliation, agnostic relations to others vary. Some agnostics avoid the general religious community, with a particular dislike for evangelical Christians. Some are more diverse, not only engaging with the general religious community, but actually belonging to one. Many favor more liberal branches of Christianity or engage in interfaith activity. Many agnostics feel the need to justify and defend their position, feeling largely misrepresented, ostracized, and outcasted by society. For many, the interfaith forum seems to be the perfect opportunity for this dialogue.

HOLY SITES

None, as agnosticism takes no specific position on the existence of deity, thus denying the abstract concept of holiness.

NOTABLE FIGURES

Bertrand Russell (1872-1970), philosopher; Charles Darwin (1809-1882), scientist; Thomas Henry Huxley (1825-1895), philosopher; Larry King (1933-2021), television personality; Brad Pitt (1963-), actor; Leonardo DiCaprio (1974-), actor; Zac Efron (1987-), actor; Uma Thurman (1970-), actress; Carrie Fisher (1956-2016), actress; Dave Matthews (1967-), musician; Sting (1951-), musician; Ridley Scott (1937-), director and producer; Howard Stern (1954-), radio personality; Charlie Chaplain (1889-1977), actor; Stan Lee (1922-2018), comic book writer; Matt Groening (1954-), cartoonist; Sidney Poitier (1927-2022), actor; Andy Rooney (1919-2011), journalist; Samuel Beckett (1906-1989), playwright; Ambrose Bierce (1842-1914), journalist; Joseph Heller (1923-1999), author; Franz Kafka (1883-1924), author; H.P. Lovecraft (1890-1937), author; Ted Turner (1938-), founder of Turner Broadcasting System; Salvador Dali (1904-1989), artist; Bob Guccione (1930-2010), publisher; Steve Austin (1964-), athlete.

NOTABLE GROUPS

Founded in 1991, the Church of Freethought stands as a non-theistic, non-supernaturalistic religious organization. Its goal is to serve the needs of those who don't believe in the existence of deities, specifically atheists and agnostics. Their organization provides the same type of social experience as church: services, Sunday School classes, and regular gatherings and events. Their identity as a church is controversial; organizations such as American Atheists and the Council for Secular Humanism reject and discourage the idea.[9]

FACTS AND FIGURES

Approximately 13.2% of the United States population identifies as atheist or agnostic. 32% believe in life after death, and 6% say they believe in the physical resurrection of the dead.[10]

OTHER IMPORTANT DEFINITIONS[11]

- **Apathetic agnosticism**: Apathetic agnostics believe there is no proof a higher power exists or does not exist, but they believe that, in the end, the issue does not matter; if the divine does exist, they do not care about humanity, anyway.

Agnostic symbol

- **Objective observation**: Something that, through science or universal experience, everyone can see is true.

- **Strong agnosticism**: The position that there is absolutely no way anyone can ever know God exists, no matter what one may do.

- **Subjective observation**: An observation or belief that relies on a person's individual thoughts, feelings, or perspectives about a subject.

- **Weak agnosticism**: Also known as "mild agnosticism" or "open agnosticism." The position that no one concretely recognizes if God or the divine exists at this time, but that just because something can't be proven or understood right now does mean it can never be proven. Weak agnostics believe the questions they seek will be answered at some point in time.

BELIEVER'S CHARACTERISTICS

Emphasis on patriotism, separation of church and state, concrete scientific proof, and reason; independence from religion; upholding humanism; interest in humanity, the good of humanity, and seeking answers for humanity within and on their own, as their own moral guide; use of scriptural ideals for ethics; emphasis on rights, particularly agnosticism as a right, freedom of thought and word, and from unwanted influence; questions; moral questions; questioning; interest in rationality and materialism; insistence upon rationalism, intelligence, and provable reality; non-position on religious issues; focus on questions rather than answers; inability to produce answers, as movement isn't about answers, but unanswerable questions.

Armstrongism

....Now I'm bringing out in my new book, something that has been hidden for centuries, something that NO ONE has ever gotten before...how the lineage of one man, Noah, remained racially pure through his generations. God destroyed Man by the Flood because of INTERRACIAL MARRIAGE!!! Adam and Eve WERE CREATED WHITE!!! Now interracial marriage...supposing that you are a stock breeder, entering your prize animals in a State Fair or Stock Show....you will only enter PUREBLOOD or PEDIGREE livestock, not any with a mixture of breeds! But interracial marriage is doing JUST THAT!!!

(Herbert W. Armstrong)[1]

Theology

Belief in one true deity (monotheism), referred to as GOD the FATHER or JESUS CHRIST, with personal attributes; Creator of the universe; omnipotent, omnipresent, unchangeable, and omniscient. Armstrongism teaches binitarian monotheism: GOD is a family, rather than a trinity or one being. At this time, GOD is restricted to the Father and Son as the first members. Jesus the Messiah is the creator and spokesperson (the *Logos*, or Word), for the GOD family. Those who are faithful to live by every word of Scripture (as is interpreted through the group), enduring through to the end of either one's life or the Second Coming of Jesus Christ, will be "born again" into the family of GOD, as literal children; thus joining the "God family." At that time, all who have endured will be transformed into perfect, spiritual, divine creatures, becoming part of the Godhead. The Holy Spirit is not seen as a person or independent being, but a force, agency, and power by which God the Father works to achieve specific work or purpose within the world.

Armstrongism is a branch of British Israelism with strong Christian Identity Movement overtones: a theology of white supremacy believing Adam, the first man in the Bible, was the father not of humanity, but exclusively of the white race. This Adam was created as a son of the divine, made in the likeness of their deity, and his descendants are also the children of GOD the FATHER. All other races were created prior to Adam, designating them as inferior or "mud races." Adam is seen as the beginning of a higher race of individuals who contain not just a body and a soul, but also a divinely implanted spirit. This distinguishes him from other races. Throughout the ages, the special "set apart" group was a "higher race," separate from lower ones, now chosen and elect to create a special and unique theocratic kingdom throughout the ages. This lineage is, therefore, the only one chosen of the divine, the true lineage, true Israel, and the only group that can know the divine. All major figures in the Bible are believed to be of the white race, including Adam, Noah, Moses, David, Solomon, Jesus, the twelve apostles, and the apostle Paul.

Armstrongism sees Jesus Christ is the Savior only of true Israel, which consists of those of the white race, exclusively: "Aryan" or "Christian nations," specifically those of western European descent. They are the only beings on earth who can be saved, as the new covenant was made with the same individuals as the original covenant: the white race. British Israelists believe the two sons of the Biblical patriarch Joseph, Ephraim and Manasseh, became two full tribes, replacing the tribe of Joseph. The descendants of the lost tribes are believed to be primitive tribes of the British, Celtic, and northwestern European nations (such as Denmark and Finland. Other nations of interest include New Zealand, Belgium, France, Canada, Australia, and Israel). Britain is considered as Ephraim, and the United States is considered as Manasseh. Anglo-Saxons are considered the true Israelites or "true Jews," the true chosen people established to reign until the return of Christ. British Israelists believe the Davidic line (throne and authority of King David) can be traced through the royal lineage of Britain; they believe the British monarchy is the throne of King David.

Philosophy

Centers on the belief that at an advancing point in time, a government of the divine shall usher in an all-consuming reign on earth. This shall coincide with the return of Jesus Christ in the second coming. At this time, all humanity will be rescued from sin and will be persuaded to follow divine law as found in the Old Testament (and understood through the lens of Armstrongism). A millennial period of one thousand years will follow, focused on peace and justice. The followers of Armstrongism, identified as children of God will be world leaders through this period. Most people who have lived throughout history will be resurrected and saved, accepting the specific criteria and laws for this new ruling period. They shall be saved according to a divine plan, by which most of the world is now blinded to the truths of Armstrongism. This "blinding" is because the multitudes would never accept them, so their ultimate choice and salvation is reserved for the end of time. Those who follow the teachings of Armstrongism are now preparing to be that much further ahead, to rule during this coming period. Then, they will be "born again" into the family of God, becoming as God Himself, either physically resurrected or transformed to serve this leadership purpose.

Armstrongism is the product of the teaching of its founder, Herbert W. Armstrong (1892-1986), who was a product of the Church of God Seventh Day. The movement gained considerable attention due to its extensive use of marketing and media work, especially through magazines, tracts, books, and television and radio programming. It is a combination of British Israelism (described above) and Sabbataranism: a belief system, integrated of Old Testament interpretation, focusing on the observance of the seventh-day Sabbath (Saturday) from Friday night at sundown to Saturday night at sundown. A byproduct of this idea is the relevance and essential nature of the Ten Commandments, often considered to be a summary of the greater law, parts of which are also seen as both mandatory observances and spiritually binding for believers in modern times. Within Armstrongism, Sabbatarianism extends beyond the seventh-day Sabbath to include observance of the law (especially the Ten Commandments), four different applications of tithing, the various dietary laws found in the Old Testament (abstinence from pork, shellfish, and prohibitions on mixing meat and dairy), and celebration of Old Testament feast days rather than holidays such as Christmas and Easter.

Armstrongism believes it alone is the correct system, considering all Christian systems to exist in a state of apostasy. As a Sabbatarian restoration movement, they feel Christianity has deviated from its original model, found in first century Christianity. It has, in their view, been restored by Herbert Armstrong; since his death, the movement has fractioned, as there is considerable debate over the succession of leadership within the movement. As a result, many Armstrong groups have differing points about leadership authority while all maintaining their central ties and points with Armstrong's founding leadership.[2]

Herbert W. Armstrong

NUMBER OF ADHERENTS

There are no official estimates on Armstrong's followers in modern times. It is estimated that prior to his death, the Armstrong movement had approximately 100,000 followers worldwide. Current rough estimates range anywhere from around 50,000 to 300,000, worldwide.

TRADITIONAL LANGUAGES

English.

ADHERENT IDENTITY

Armstrongism, Armstrongists, Armstrongite, British Israelites, Anglo-Israelism, Israelitism, Sabbatarians, Sabbatarianism; Worldwide Church of God (WCG); Church of God International (United States) (COGI); Philadelphia Church of God (PCG); Church of the Great God (CGG); Global Church of God (GCG); United Church of God (UCG); The Intercontinental Church of God (ICOG); Living Church of God (LCG); Restored Church of God (RCG); Church of God Preparing for the Kingdom of God (COG-PKG); Church of God, a Worldwide Association (COGWA); Bethel Church of God (BCG); Christian Biblical Church of God (CBCG); Congregational Fellowship of God (CFG); Christian Educational Ministries (CEM); Congregation of God, A Free Church; Congregation of God; Church of God (Christianos); Church of God Fellowship; Church of God, Sabbath Day; and other associations from smaller groups that are part of the bigger Armstrongism family.

SECTS/DIVISIONS

Since the death of Herbert Armstrong, the Worldwide Church of God (which was Herbert Armstrong's official church denomination) underwent considerable change. As a result, there are thousands of splinter sects that seek to restore what they consider to be the "original movement," believing the bigger movement to have gone awry. Many, in different ways, also do not agree with one other about central doctrinal points. There are approximately five different headings for Armstrong splinters: The Worldwide Church of God (WCG), organizations that formed prior to Herbert Armstrong's death; successor splinters; post-split splinters, and independent Church of God sects.

- **Worldwide Church of God (WCG)**: The Worldwide Church of God (also called the Radio Church of God) was founded by Herbert Armstrong himself in Eugene, Oregon in 1934. It started as a church service designed for radio. After falling out with his parent organization, the Church of God Seventh Day, over his doctrines (especially that of British Israelism), he formally incorporated his church in 1946 as the Radio Church of God. It relocated to Pasadena, California in 1947. Its name was changed to the Worldwide Church of God in 1968. The organization served as the primary denomination for the dissemination of Armstrong's teachings throughout his life. At its peak, it had its own college for ministers, Ambassador College; a concert hall, Ambassador Auditorium; television and radio programs, books, magazines, and tracts. Herbert Armstrong travelled all over the world, meeting with various spiritual and political leaders to spread his message. The Worldwide Church of God began to decline in the 1970s due to controversy over Armstrong's false prophecies (including several apocalyptic and political events), the fact that all church income went to him personally, his dispute with his son, Garner Ted (1930-2003), and his marriage to a much younger woman. Splinter sects began forming while he was still alive. After his death in 1986, sects multiplied as they questioned who his legitimate successor was. Joseph W. Tkach, Sr. (1927-1995) became the leader of the Worldwide church of God and began making doctrinal changes as early as 1988. In response, a large percentage of the church leadership and membership left the organization. Today, the church maintains a doctrinal position and identity far from its roots in Herbert Armstrong's teachings; it has now declared him a false prophet and heretic. Women are now ordained as pastors and elders, they uphold Trinitarianism, members celebrate Christmas and Easter, tithing is no longer practiced, most early publications and books are no longer in print, and many of properties owned by the church were sold. Headquarters are now in Charlotte, North Carolina. The church is quite a bit smaller than it used to be. While the church does still maintain a few interpretations of older doctrines that would be considered unorthodox, the church today belongs to the Evangelical Council of Churches.[3]

Worldwide Church of God Logo

- **Organizations formed prior to Herbert Armstrong's death**: The major "split" within the Worldwide Church of God happened after Armstrong's death. However, prior to his death, there were a few smaller groups that broke away. Major reasons for breakaway include disputes between Herbert Armstrong and his son, Garner Ted; receiving tithes and offerings personally; and general internal disagreements among church leadership. These issues led to the formation of several churches, most notably, the Church of God, International (now Intercontinental Church of God), formed by Garner Ted Armstrong in Tyler, Texas. Such groups adhere to standard Armstrong doctrine, expansive media ministry and publications, and authoritarian leadership. Other groups include Restoration

Church of God, the Church of God (Boise City), Church of God (Sabbatarian), and the Fountain of Life Fellowship.

- **Successor splinters**: There was a substantial leadership crisis within the Armstrong movement after the death of Herbert Armstrong. It was unclear who the successor to the movement should be, and several individuals claimed to be the rightful new leader of the Worldwide Church of God. When Joseph W. Tkach, Sr. took over as leader of the movement and then began to make changes, more leaders began to claim Tkach was not the appropriate leader of the organization. In a fit of conflict, they left the church to establish their own. All these groups uphold traditional Armstrong doctrine while modifying some of their prophetic interpretations to fit the establishment of their group and their leader as the rightful successor to Herbert Armstrong's work. Just about all say a specified "falling away" was prophesied after Armstrong's death, causing the fractioning of the movement. A "faithful remnant" exists to continue the work. Each individual group becomes the "faithful remnant," rejecting the successorship of other movement leaders. Many also attempt to "restore" the work of Herbert Armstrong, rebuilding properties, campuses, and established buildings on land acquired through their specified financial giving systems. Such groups include the Living Church of God (LCG), the Global Church of God (GCG), the United Church of God (UCG), and the Philadelphia Church of God (PCG).

- **Post-split splinters:** Post-split splinters are Armstrong groups that split from other breakaway sects that were the result of successor splinters. Just about every one of these groups emerged in response to further leadership disputes. These include Church of God, an International Community, Church of God, a Worldwide Association, Church of God's Faithful, Church of God Scattered Faithful, Faithful Church of God in Laodicea, The Church of God Armstrong Remembrances, and Keepers of God's Covenant. Some continue onward, but many either no longer exist or are near extinction.

- **Independent Church of God sects**: There are several independent Church of God sects that somehow connect back to the Armstrong movement, often splintering off other splinter groups or organically evolving without formal association with any Armstrong denomination (usually through Armstrong's publications or splinter group media). Most have modifications of Armstrong's doctrine in one form or another, but otherwise are not similar to one another. These include Seventh Day Church of God, Akron Fellowship, Appalachian Church of God, The Assembly of the Eternal, Assembly of God in Christ Jesus, Associates for Scriptural Knowledge, Barnabas Ministries, Bethel Church of God, Christ Fellowship Ministries, Church of Acts, the Church of God (Christianos), Church of God, Sabbath Day, and Church of God, In Truth.

Disputes Within Group

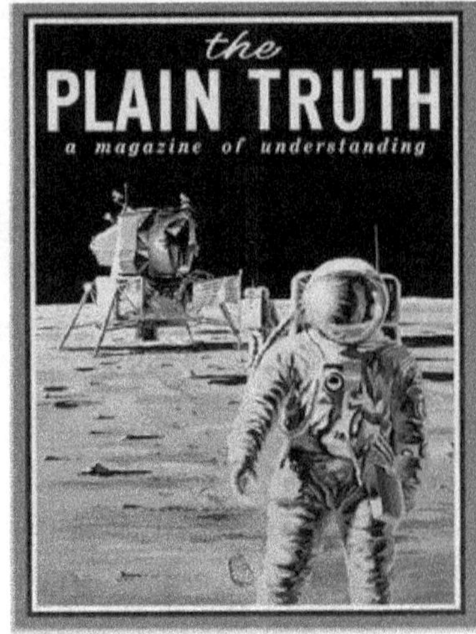

The Plain Truth Magazine, 1969

There are three major disagreements among the Armstrong splinters. The first is the legitimacy of Herbert Armstrong's legacy, which is of dispute within the Worldwide Church of God. As the WCG has long abandoned the teachings of Herbert Armstrong, there is considerable debate among those who do desire to preserve his teachings. Among those groups that do uphold Armstrong's teachings are several additional disputes, including leadership authority, expanding Armstrong doctrine in modern times, and interpretation of what the movement should look like today.

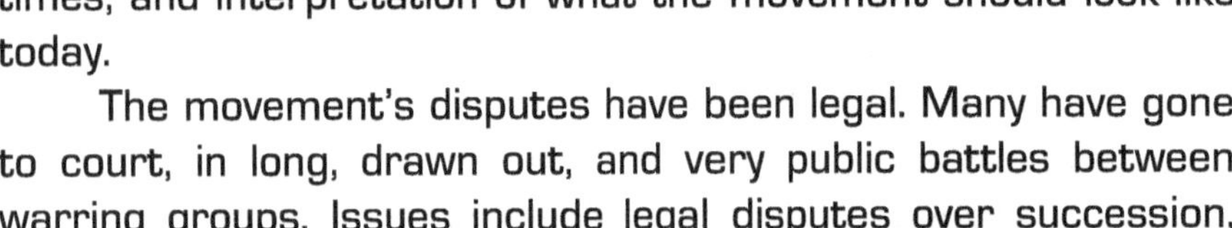

The movement's disputes have been legal. Many have gone to court, in long, drawn out, and very public battles between warring groups. Issues include legal disputes over succession, position within the church, rightful ownership or possession of property, and copyright protection to reprint of his work outside the Worldwide Church of God. Each Armstrong sect believes it is the only true successor of Armstrong's work, and considers all others to be fallen away, apostate, or in error.

Scriptures

The Holy Bible, both Old and New Testaments, inclusive of 66 books: the Pentateuch (Genesis, Exodus, Leviticus, Numbers, and Deuteronomy), Historical books (Joshua, Judges, Ruth, 1 Samuel, 2 Samuel, 1 Kings, 2 Kings, 1 Chronicles, 2 Chronicles, Ezra, Nehemiah, Esther), Wisdom books (Job, Psalms, Proverbs, Ecclesiastes, Song of Songs), Prophetic books (Isaiah, Jeremiah, Lamentations, Ezekiel, Daniel, Hosea, Joel, Amos, Obadiah, Jonah, Micah, Nahum, Habakkuk, Zephaniah, Haggai, Zechariah, Malachi), the Gospels (Matthew, Mark, Luke, John), the Acts of the Apostles, the Pauline Epistles (Romans, 1 Corinthians, 2 Corinthians, Galatians, Ephesians, Philippians, Colossians, 1 Thessalonians, 2 Thessalonians, 1 Timothy, 2 Timothy, Titus, Philemon, Hebrews) the General Epistles (James, 1 Peter, 2 Peter, 1 John, 2 John, 3 John, Jude) and Revelation. Preferred translation was traditionally the Authorized King James Version, although some groups now use or occasionally reference updated translations.

The Armstrong movement places special emphasis on the role and study of Old Testament law. As a subheading, they study Old Testament regulations for worship, separateness, and purity. Most Armstrong movements place particular emphasis on the King James Version of the Bible. While some do use or supplement with other translations, the King James Version is standard usage among Armstrong adherents.

While the movement would not classify the works of Herbert Armstrong and subsequent movement leaders to be formally "inspired" works, adherents do believe they cannot understand the Bible without these writings. Of relevance is *Mystery of the Ages* (1985). It is a summation of Armstrong's basic beliefs and teachings: drawing from British Israelism, the nature of the "God family," and the coming anticipation into the new world. It was written later in Herbert

Armstrong's life, outlining his theological premise.

> *But to my utter disappointed astonishment, I found that many of the popular church teachings and practices were not based on the Bible. They had originated, as research in history had revealed, in paganism. Numerous Bible prophecies foretold it. The amazing, unbelievable truth is that the source of these popular beliefs and practices of professing Christianity was, quite largely, paganism and human reasoning and custom, not the Bible!*
>
> *I had first doubted, then searched for evidence, and found proof that God exists—that the Holy Bible is, literally, his divinely inspired revelation and instruction to mankind. I had learned that one's God is what a person obeys. The word Lord means master—one you obey! Most people, I had discovered, are obeying false gods, rebelling against the one true Creator who is the supreme Ruler of the universe.*
>
> *The argument was over a point of obedience to God.*
>
> *The opening of my eyes to the truth brought me to the crossroads of my life. To accept it meant to throw in my lot with a class of humble and unpretentious people I had come to look upon as inferior. It meant being cut off from the high and the mighty and the wealthy of this world, to which I had aspired. It meant the final crushing of vanity. It meant a total change of life!*[A]

Basic Religious Practices

The basic tenets of Armstrongism focus on preparing each individual believer for the time to come: when they will be transformed, born again as members of the God family, prepared to lead the world in the coming thousand-year period after Jesus returns. They embrace a strong, literal understanding of spiritual legalism: to be saved, one must first be a descendant of the Aryan interpretation of the Twelve Tribes of Israel, observe the seventh-day Sabbath, follow the Ten Commandments, recognize Old Testament festivals, embrace dietary laws, and obey the authorities and teaching of the Armstrong movement. The group is highly authoritarian; men alone serve as pastors, leaders, and church authorities, and positional leaders supervise the activities of church groups on a local level. Local church groups typically meet in rented facilities or private homes. Some groups do not assemble weekly, but meet through teleconference lines, watching programs on television, distance studies, and online meetups. Members are expected, in addition to meeting with their local groups, to remain connected to headquarters by watching the media produced by each church, reading literature, and supporting the work.

Armstrong adherents pay three separate tithes each year. The first is for the continued spread of the message throughout the world. The second is for each household's expense to travel for the annual Holy Day festivals. The third is for orphans, widows, and the poor in the church, typically given every third and sixth year. On top of these tithes, each member pays a "tithe of a tithe" to maintain holy day and festival sites. Members are also expected to give freewill offerings to various causes such as building funds, youth programs, and summer programs. Higher level leaders receive tithes rather than give them, as they are considered as "Levites." Many within the ministry live according to a much higher standard of living than the average member, some of which contribute more than forty or fifty percent of their income for the function of the church.

Family life and units are an essential component of Armstrong theology. As God is seen as a family, so the family unit is a reflection and preparation for the advancing time to come. Families are patriarchal, with the male as the head of the family unit. Women are encouraged to be homemakers. Makeup is prohibited for women; in many sects, women also avoid pants or fitted clothing. Homosexuality and homosexual marriage are prohibited.

Armstrongism is strictly against abortion. Many sects discourage or prohibit the use of birth control. Under traditional teaching, the use of medical intervention and practice are also prohibitive. Members are prohibited from military service and voting (even in the context of a PTA membership).[5]

HOLIDAYS

Within Armstrongism, holidays are considered types and shadows of prophesied events soon to come. Members of the Armstrong movement are prohibited from celebrating holidays such as Christmas, Easter, Halloween, Thanksgiving, and birthdays. Observance of Old Testament festivals is required for every member. Members pay a second tithe to cover travel to and from fall holidays and a tithe of a tithe to cover the expense of site maintenance. Many events are held in resorts or hotels.

- **Feast of Unleavened Bread (Passover)**: Includes both a seven-day first fruits barley harvest festival where members eat unleavened bread (disposing all products that contain yeast) and the Passover ceremony. The ceremony recalls not just the Old Testament exodus from Egypt, but the sacrifice and death of Jesus Christ. Held in March or April.

- **Feast of Weeks (Shavuot or Pentecost)**: Also known as Feast of Harvest and Day of First fruits. Observed with two loaves of leavened bread, interpreted to reference Jews and Gentiles. Day depicts the Holy Spirit given to the apostles, the Biblical cycle of Jubilee, and the Bride of Christ (assembly of Armstrong churches). Held in May or June.

- **Feast of Trumpets (Rosh Hashanah)**: Observed by blowing the traditional shofar (a ram's horn trumpet). Signifies the second coming of the Messiah, when he shall be crowned King over all the earth. At this time to come, people will repent from their sins, the dead rise in resurrection, and the King will execute his vengeance on the Day of the Lord. Held in September or October.

- **Atonement (Yom Kippur)**: Marked with prayer, fasting, repentance, and acknowledgement of Christ's sacrifice for sin. Held in September or October.

- **Booths (Sukkot or the Feast of Tabernacles)**: Also known as the Festival of Ingathering, Feast of the Nations, Festival of Dedication, Festival of Lights, and Season of Our Joy. A seven-day harvest festival where believers gather in temporary dwellings or shelters. Signifies humanity's dependence on God for all things, especially food, water, and shelter.

Members of the Armstrong movement meet for this festival at a resort or hotel. Held in October.

- **Eighth Day**: The conclusion of Sukkot. A special day to dwell in the divine's presence while tarrying and praying. Many see it as an "eighth day festival," representing the world to come or that which is to come, new (as the number eight represents new beginnings). Held in October.

VISUAL SIGNS AND SYMBOLS

Church-sponsored publications and magazines; *The World Tomorrow* rebroadcasts; British Israelism; images of Herbert Armstrong and splinter sect church leaders.

CREEDS, BOOKS, AND LAWS

Literature is a central point within the Armstrong movement. While the movement is non-credal, the texts of the Armstrong movement create its foundational beliefs. These various texts often overlap content, especially among splinter groups. They form the outline of how prophecy, current events, ideas, and relationships form within the movement. Material is repetitive and limited to specific topics that reflect different aspects of doctrine. Originally, writings were authored by Herbert Armstrong; today, they are written by the leaders of each founding group. Many are modifications of Armstrong's earlier literature written to support a splinter group's existence in the scheme of the larger movement's disagreements. Common authors include Herbert W. Armstrong, Gerald Flurry (1935-), Garner Ted Armstrong, Roderick C. Meredith (1930-2017), David C. Pack (1948-), John Ritenbaugh (1932-2023), and Ronald Weinland (1949-).

ECLECTIC BELIEFS

Herbert Armstrong is best known for predicting the end of the four times, starting in 1936 and ending in 1975. Along with these major predictions were several smaller ones, all related to cataclysmic events (natural disasters, governmental falls, or national collapse). Because his ministry was very visible, generated criticism caused defense and new predictions, most of which also failed. In addition to internal divisions, this caused skepticism and question among outsiders.

> *Mussolini and the Pope will hatch up an idea between [them] of setting up a world headquarters at Jerusalem—and so Mussolini's armies will enter Palestine (Dan. 11:41) and eventually will capture just half of the city of Jerusalem! (Zech. 14:2)*[6]
>
> *Mussolini will fight Christ!*[7]
>
> *HITLER Did Not Die. Adolph Hitler's fake suicide in his Berlin Bunker is exposed as History's greatest Hoax! Hitler is alive, directing Nazi Underground, today...Thus it has been proved conclusively and beyond doubt, that Hitler did not die – his body was not there – HE HAD ESCAPED! ... The next Pope will be a professed miracle worker, as supposed proof that God is using him to order and pacify the world!*[8]

Here we are, in 1958! Time is running out on us.... But brethren in God's Church today, here is the IMPORTANT thing to shake us out of our lethargy and WAKE US UP! If it is true that God has allotted to us, as He did to the church 19 centuries ago, just TWO 19-year time cycles to complete His work, FIVE OF OUR LAST 19 YEARS HAVE ALREADY SPED BY! Only 14 more short years remain![9]

And yet, about 90% of all of the prophecies in the Bible pertain to events that are yet to happen in the next 10 to 20 years from now, believe it or not![10]

Now HERE IS SOMETHING STARTLING! Herman Hoeh, in his eye-opening article you will read in the June number of The PLAIN TRUTH on the Times of the Gentiles shows that the Times of the Gentiles—if chronologies are correct—will come to their final end in the year 1982...

Now if this chronology is correct, that means Christ shall return some very few years PRIOR to 1982! NO MAN KNOWS THE DAY, HOUR, OR YEAR OF CHRIST'S RETURN. But we CAN know exact dates of one or two other events. ...

IF THE TIMES OF THE GENTILES END IN 1982, in October, as Mr. Hoeh has it figured, THE INVASION OF AMERICA AND THE GREAT TRIBULATION MUST BEGIN NOT LATER THAT MARCH-APRIL, 1972![11]

Prophecy is a key point of the Armstrong movement. There's a focus on establishment of prophetic ideas and explaining or expounding prophecy in a modern context. As a restorationist movement, the central figures of each group take on a prophetic, evangelistic, and apostolic leadership component in their work. Founders of Armstrong splinters are regarded as true prophets and apostolic leaders, distinguished from other Armstrong leaders, who are considered false. As a result, several movement leaders, including Ronald Weiland and Gerald Flurry, have also made false or inaccurate predictions regarding current events.

The next and far more meaningful "count" and alignment for Christ's coming is on Pentecost, June 9th of 2019.

You can know if that is the time Christ will once again stand upon the Mt. of Olives if a third world war has broken out by February or March of 2019 at the latest. If not, then the next possible return will be the Pentecost of 2020. Beyond that and there will be a space of more time that will be a matter of a few years.[12]

By most appearances, Joe Biden will be America's next president. But I absolutely do not believe that at all. Mr. Trump will weather this storm too. Regardless of what the media says or how things look right now, I am confident Donald Trump will remain president.[13]

According to the Armstrong Movement, there are three different sleep states following death. The dead are classified as "sleeping," awaiting final resurrection. The first resurrection is of the righteous, the "first fruits," at the Second Coming. The second is temporary, to see if non-believers will accept the ways of the God family, to live forever. The third is for the wicked, who will receive final judgment.

RELATIONS WITH NON-ARMSTRONGISTS

Traditional Armstrongism prohibits relationships with non-believers, citing a need for "separateness." Believers have no relationship with those outside the church. Those who leave the movement or disfellowshipped are considered apostate and experience an extreme form of shunning.

Modern Armstrong splinter groups also don't associate with one another. Grace Communion International (GCI), formerly known as the Worldwide Church of God, has no such prohibitions.

HOLY SITES

Worldwide Grace Communion International headquarters, Charlotte, North Carolina; Philadelphia Church of God International Headquarters, Edmond, Oklahoma; Church of the Great God headquarters, Fort Mill, South Carolina; Restored Church of God headquarters, Wadsworth, Ohio; Living Church of God headquarters, Charlotte, North Carolina; The Church of God, Preparing for the Kingdom of God headquarters, Cincinnati, Ohio; Intercontinental Church of God headquarters, Tyler, Texas; the United Church of God International headquarters, Milford, Ohio; the Church of God, International headquarters, Tyler, Texas; other specified headquarters of splinter sects as found worldwide.

NOTABLE FIGURES

Herbert W. Armstrong (1892-1986), founder; Garner Ted Armstrong (1930-2003), son of founder and founder of the Church of God, International; Jules Dervaes (1947-2016), urban farmer; Bobby Fischer (1943-2008), chess champion; Roderick C. Meredith (1930-2017), founder, the Living Church of God; Stanley Rader (1930-2002), attorney; Basil Wolverton (1909-1978), cartoonist; Joseph W. Tkach, Sr. (1927-1995), second leader of the Worldwide Church of God; Joseph Tkach, Jr. (1951-), successor to Joseph W. Tkach.[14]

NOTABLE GROUPS

The Living Church of God (LCG) is the most successful of all Armstrong splinter groups. Founded by Roderick C. Meredith and now headquartered in Charlotte, North Carolina, it functions on the traditional model of the Worldwide Church of God. Its media branch, *Tomorrow's World*, has been a television feature for over 25 years. The Living Church of God made national headlines when a member, Terry Ratzmann, opened fire during a church service at a Brookfield, Wisconsin hotel. He killed eight people, including the pastor and the pastor's son. Eventually, he killed himself. The reason for the shooting remains unclear.[15]

FACTS AND FIGURES

At its height, the Worldwide Church of God had approximately 100,000 members.

OTHER IMPORTANT DEFINITIONS

- **Bad attitude**: Challenging the doctrines or leadership of an immediate Armstrong group.[16]
- **Called**: Those who hear, and heed, and obey, the teachings of Armstrongism this side of the Second Coming.[17]
- **Calling**: The process of coming across the message of Armstrongism and from hearing it, choosing to follow it.[18]
- **Doing the work**: Fulfilling membership requirements to remain within the movement, such as paying tithes, attending the required church events, supporting the work financially beyond the work of tithes, following literature, and obeying the rules of the organization.[19]
- **The end times**: The present time; right now. Also called the last hour, last end, end of the age, and end of the end time.[20]
- **Fellowship**: Spending time with other members of the same Armstrong organization.[21]
- **God's way**: The directives and instruction of Armstrong leaders.[22]
- **Government of God**: Armstrongism leadership.[23]
- **Government problem**: Internal conflict or strife within the leadership of an Armstrong group.[24]
- **Hell**: The grave.
- **Laodiceans**: Any church that is somehow against or not in alignment with a specified Armstrong denomination.
- **New Revelation**: The process by which doctrine is changed, altered, or adjusted as no longer in conformity with older teaching.
- **Reward**: A leadership position within the movement.
- **Saved**: Those who will survive into the coming new world without dying first.

- **Spiritual widow/widower**: An individual married to someone who is not a part of the Armstrong movement.[25]

- **Trunk of the tree**: The foundational teachings of Herbert Armstrong that are core to the system; what people must believe, without alteration, to remain part of any Armstrong organization.[26]

- **The Work**: Also known as God's work or God's end time work. The mission of the Armstrong movements, to promote Armstrong's teachings until the time when Jesus Christ returns.

BELIEVER'S CHARACTERISTICS

Emphasis on Sabbatarianism, Old Testament law, dietary regulations, and excessive tithing; observance of Biblical feasts; belief in deity as a family, with many worthy believers also becoming deity at the end of time; British Israelism; separateness; focus on adhering to the Ten Commandments; dietary regulations; isolation; apocalypticism; fatalism; traditional relationship rules; refusal to vote, serve in the military, celebrate conventional holidays, and use of modern medicine; unusual methods of church connection, such as teleconferences, internet, radio, television, and media; promotion of ideas through print, internet, radio, and television; leadership disputes; exclusive membership.

Atheism

Atheism is more than just the knowledge that gods do not exist, and that religion is either a mistake or a fraud. Atheism is an attitude, a frame of mind that looks at the world objectively, fearlessly, always trying to understand all things as a part of nature.
(Emmett F. Fields)[1]

Theology

Atheists do not believe in the existence of any form of deity, whether a construct is monotheistic, polytheistic, or something else. Atheists reject the idea of theology and are opposed to its construct. They deny the existence of a god or gods.

The word "atheism" literally means "without gods." From the Greek term *atheos*, the original term denotes an individual who either rejects the deities worshiped within a society, refuses to commit to such deities, or are perceived to be forsaken by the gods. In modern usage, the word "atheist" dates to the 1700s. It rose in popularity with the age of skepticism, freethought, and the critical analysis of religion. People first identified as atheists in the 1800s.

Philosophy

There are several reasons why atheists deny the existence of deity and divinity. The common ones are the lack of empirical or scientific evidence to prove a deity exists, the issues of societal evil and injustice, inconsistency in spiritual revelation, the idea that religious or spiritual ideas can be falsified, and the standpoint that things happen to good and bad alike. Atheists do not believe that belief or nonbelief is of any consequence in an individual's life or outcome. Most atheists find their position more "objective" than individuals who adhere to a specified theology, seeing atheism as the only logical and rational perspective with authentication. Atheists believe in provable knowledge, scientific data, research, findings, and concrete ideas versus those that might be seen as abstract or imaginative. Theists, or individuals who accept the existence of a deity or deities, are posed with responsibility to prove their position. If a theist is unable to do so meet the standard of an atheist, the argument or defense is considered irrational. Faith is often seen as a superstition; something that seems to work, only by random chance. Things such as destiny, divine calling, or providence are rejected.

This does not mean all atheists are the same. There are different forms of atheism, including those who are definitive about the denial of deity, those who identify as atheists but are open to spirituality and spiritual ideas, those who are predominately atheist but not in totality, and others who find themselves somewhere on the spectrum.

Atheism is not a negative point within several world religions. These include Hinduism, Buddhism, Taoism, Jainism, neopaganism, occultism, Unitarian Universalism, among some liberal Jewish groups, and in many Satanic strains. It is not technically a religion, but a system of non-belief that often reflects how people feel about spiritual and religious ideas. It also doesn't mean all atheists are non-religious or opposed to religion. There are many atheists who find comfort in the idea of community and participate in secular religious ceremonies that are inclusive of atheism (such as in groups listed above) or as "atheist religions," promoting and establishing atheist ideals while modeling religious community structure.[3]

ADHERENT IDENTITY

Atheists, atheist, freethinker, nonbeliever, disbeliever, unbeliever, skeptic, doubter, nihilist, materialist.

Atomic Whirl atheist symbol

NUMBER OF ADHERENTS

It is difficult to know how many atheists exist worldwide. In some countries, "blasphemy charges" (statements or beliefs against the standard national religions) exist, punishable by fines, imprisonment, or death. In much of the world, atheism is seen in a negative light. As a result, some atheists may not always voice their beliefs. Atheists also have different understandings of what it means to be an atheist. They may identify themselves in a variety of ways, such through a religious group that is atheistic in nature. Estimates range from approximately 200,000,000 to 750,000,000 worldwide.[4]

TRADITIONAL LANGUAGES

Atheism has, at diverse points in time, been found in many places within the world, with language diversity to accompany such. Traditional languages include Arabic, German, Latin, French, and English.

SECTS/DIVISIONS

There are several identities and subheadings of atheism. Like other groups, there is a prevalent spectrum of belief, ranging from firm to indefinite, to more radical or lenient ideas. Because atheism is a personal understanding, there isn't a specific, universal consensus on what defines an atheist or what someone must believe (or not believe) to identify as one. In some ways, many subheadings of atheism can and do overlap in both individuals and groups. The major divisions of atheism include:

- **Strong atheism**: Also known as "hard atheism" or "positive atheism." Individuals who are assured, within their own understanding and convictions, that there is no such thing as any sort of divine being, creator, life force, or existence of spiritual beings. To such individuals, there is no question or thought about the existence of a deity or deities. Strong atheism also includes the category of explicit atheists, who believe the idea of a deity is irrational and should be rejected by all. There are some organizations who use the term "positive atheism" to exemplify a better view of atheism than the hardened cynicism often associated with it. Examples of strong atheists include Atheist Community of Austin, American Atheists, Inc., and Godless Americans Political Action Committee.

- **Soft atheism**: Also known as "weak atheism" or "negative atheism." Individuals who deny a belief in a deity or deities but do not necessarily feel this means no deities exist. This covers a wide scope of atheist belief, including the denial of specific ideas or concepts of deity (such as the idea that a god or gods take personal interest in humanity) while not denying the idea of deity all together (such as deism). Both relative and Implicit atheism are part of this subheading. Relative atheism believes in the idea of an absolute entity, but that entity has no personal attributes (such as in monism, pantheism, panentheism, and deism). Implicit atheism is when one is an atheist without rejecting theology (such as when one has no knowledge of deity, nor entertained the idea of it). Agnostics also fall into this category, although their inclusion is controversial. An example of soft atheist organizations is the Freedom from Religion Foundation.

- **Religious atheists**: Individuals who do not believe in a divine being, creator, or existence of spiritual beings, but believe in the benefit of religious practice (especially fellowship and community). Religious atheists may be part of a larger religious community that does not find atheism antithetical (such as Hinduism, Buddhism, Taoism, Jainism, neopaganism, occultism, Unitarian Universalism, some liberal Jewish groups, or many Satanic strains), or organizations specific to atheist ideas and beliefs, such as the Church of Freethought. There are also individuals who identify as atheists in mainline religions (Protestant Christianity, Roman Catholicism, and Islam) in small percentages. Such individuals regard and enjoy the ritual and tradition of the group while denying its core theologies. Religious atheists may or may not believe in secondary points, such as spiritual experiences, reincarnation, life after death, or heaven. Religious atheists also vary in personal practice and devotion as part of religious experience.

- **Practical atheism**: The idea that one should live and conduct themselves with total disregard toward a god or gods. Practical atheism is understood to have four different principles: one is not guided by religion, disinterest in matters related to theology or divinity, ignorance of the concept of a god, and exclusion of theological ideas from intellectual, social, and practical pursuits. A subheading of practical atheism is pragmatic atheism (the view that it is unnecessary for one to believe in a deity or deities for one's regular life and practical applications).[5]

- **New atheism**: An atheist movement emerging after the year 2000 that focuses on the promotion of atheism as a counter to the religious world. New atheists believe it is their duty to counter, criticize, and expose within religion what it finds irrational. New atheists examine things seen as intrusions upon the separation of church and state within American culture, such as teaching creationism as school curriculum. The work of new atheism is promoted through books. It's criticized for not properly refuting its own arguments. Some critics have accused the movement of establishing its own new religion based on science. Authors include Richard Dawkins (1941-), Christopher Hitchens (1949-2011), and Sam Harris (1967-).[6]

- **Secular humanism**: Secular humanism is not atheism per se, but often overlaps in thought and ideas with atheism and atheistic ideals. Secular humanism is a philosophical outlook embracing the ideals of empirical reason, naturalism, and secular ethics while rejecting religious ideas (including dogma, superstition, and spirituality). Secular humanists pursue truth, not through spiritual means, but science and philosophical ideas. Many atheists and agnostics alike embrace the principles of secular humanism and align with them. A secular humanist organization is Humanists International, which consists of more than one hundred different organizations, including rationalists, atheists, irreligious, agnostics, secular, and freethought groups.[7]

DISPUTES WITHIN GROUP

As a theory of non-belief, atheism represents a wide spectrum of ideas and thoughts. Atheists can identify as atheist with no specified set of beliefs or thoughts. As a result, atheists do not agree on a variety of matters and issues that relate to their identity. Each atheist interprets atheism and what it means to be an atheist for themselves. Among atheists there is considerable internal dispute between hard and soft atheism, expressions of atheism, and religion and social issues.

Karl Marx (1818-1883)

SCRIPTURES

Atheists do not recognize the concept of scriptural inspiration. While some atheists regard religious works as reflections of ancient peoples or as containing ethical or moral ideas, most atheists regard the idea of scripture (especially the Bible) as errant, hypocritical, misguided, mythological, or fictional. This does not mean atheists are unfamiliar with scriptural readings, however. Many atheists are well-versed in perceived religious and scriptural contradictions and use them to defend their positions and arguments.

There are key writings within atheistic circles that are standards in the history and tradition of modern atheism. These writers have helped to shape atheist ideals and concepts, as well as expound on social ideas and platforms important to and relevant to atheists. While not all meet the modern definitions of atheism today, many were important leaders in the modern atheistic movement. Such authors include Karl Marx, Friedrich Engels (1820-1895), Arthur Clarke (1917-

2008), Bertrand Russell (1872-1970), Primo Levi (1919-1987), Antony Flew (1923-2010), Ludwig Feuerbach (1804-1872), Friedrich Nietzsche (1844-1900), Sigmund Freud (1856-1939), Jean-Paul Sartre (1905-1980), and Ayn Rand (1905-1982). In modern times, writers include Richard Dawkins, Christopher Hitchens, and Sam Harris.

> *Is man merely a mistake of God's? Or God merely a mistake of man?*[8]

> *There is something infantile in the presumption that somebody else has a responsibility to give your life meaning and point... The truly adult view, by contrast, is that our life is as meaningful, as full and as wonderful as we choose to make it.*[9]

> *That which can be asserted without evidence, can be dismissed without evidence.*[10]

> *We are all atheists about most of the gods that humanity has ever believed in. Some of us just go one god further.*[11]

> *The man who refuses to judge, who neither agrees nor disagrees, who declares that there are no absolutes and believes that he escapes responsibility, is the man responsible for all the blood that is now spilled in the world. Reality is an absolute, existence is an absolute, a speck of dust is an absolute and so is a human life. Whether you live or die is an absolute. Whether you have a piece of bread or not, is an absolute. Whether you eat your bread or see it vanish into a looter's stomach, is an absolute.*

> *There are two sides to every issue: one side is right and the other is wrong, but the middle is always evil. The man who is wrong still retains some respect for truth, if only by accepting the responsibility of choice. But the man in the middle is the knave who blanks out the truth in order to pretend that no choice or values exist, who is willing to sit out the course of any battle, willing to cash in on the blood of the innocent or to crawl on his belly to the guilty, who dispenses justice by condemning both the robber and the robbed to jail, who solves conflicts by ordering the thinker and the fool to meet each other halfway. In any compromise between food and poison, it is only death that can win. In any compromise between good and evil, it is only evil that can profit. In that transfusion of blood which drains the good to feed the evil, the compromise is the transmitting rubber tube.*[12]

BASIC RELIGIOUS PRACTICES

Atheists observe no religious practices. The issue of religious practice is a dividing point for the atheist community. While some atheists do engage in specified religious practice with other atheists and agnostics or through an atheist-positive religious community, others regard religious practice as antithetical to atheist principles.

Religious atheists gather in groups that accept their position and engage in specific practices that are community driven, humanist in nature, secular, or open to atheism. While it is understood that atheists do not communicate to, pray with, or worship any sort of deity, they may engage in practices such as mediation without a divine focus, an interest in the ethical principles of a religion, community or group ritual, the promotion of philosophical ideas, or see science and religion as intertwined.

Some non-religious atheists have joined forces with agnostics and other anti-religionists, hoping to abolish religion from society. It is safe to say most, if not all atheists, believe in strict boundaries separating church and state. Atheists oppose the use of religious literature or education within a public-school setting, the celebration of religious holidays in schools, the teaching of any sort of religious doctrine or influence in curriculum (such as creationism or intelligent design), and religious after school clubs or programs on public school grounds. They also oppose religious monuments on state property or in conjunction with state buildings or governments. There have been numerous lawsuits, advocacy groups, and controversies in the past fifty-plus years prompted by these issues.

HOLIDAYS

The National Day of Reason (the first Monday in May) is a secular holiday observance for atheists, humanists, and freethinkers. This is in contrast with the National Day of Prayer, held on the first Thursday in May. Atheists take issue with the National Day of Prayer, regarding it as a religious holiday and day of national observance, seeing it as a violation of the separation of church and state. In response, atheists, agnostics, and secular humanists propose a required counter day of recognition known as the National Day of Reason. While it has some support, the event is largely unnoticed by the United States government.

The National Day of Reason is observed with community events in different regions, including protests or requests to end the National Day of Prayer, blood and food drives, or other celebrations.

Atheists are largely opposed to religious holidays, although some do acknowledge Christmas or Easter as secular holidays (without the religious ties to the birth or resurrection of Christ) for familial ties or childhood participation. Most atheists acknowledge national and secular holidays and are patriotic, with interest in influencing the legal and legislative process. Atheists see a lack of spiritual beliefs as a constitutional right protected by law.

VISUAL SIGNS AND SYMBOLS

The "atomic whirl," an atomic symbol with the letter "A" in the center; the capital letter "A" circling around with an opening on the side; a "no god" sign; empty set symbol (a circle with a diagonal line running through it); Circle with a wide intersecting capital A shape across the bottom; the capital letter "A" (scarlet "A" symbol); A triangle symbol open at the bottom; flying spaghetti monster symbol (an unusual looking crab); Happy Human symbol; black and red cause ribbon; the American flag; emphasis on separation of church and state; secular humanism; Darwin fish evolution symbol; emphasis on science.

CREEDS, BOOKS, AND LAWS

The concept of a creed is to state what one believes. As atheism is a statement against belief, it may seem odd to say that atheists have a creed. There is, however, an atheist creed:

I believe in time, matter, and energy,
which make up the whole of the world.

I believe in reason, evidence, and the human mind,
the only tools we have;
they are the product of natural forces
in a majestic but impersonal universe,
grander and richer than we can imagine,
a source of endless opportunities for discovery.

I believe in the power of doubt;
I do not seek out reassurances,
but embrace the question,
and strive to challenge my own beliefs.

I accept human mortality.

We have but one life,
brief and full of struggle,
leavened with love and community,
learning and exploration,
beauty and the creation of
new life, new art, and new ideas.

I rejoice in this life that I have,
and in the grandeur of a world that preceded me,
and an earth that will abide without me.[13]

The atheist's creed is not a statement on behalf of all atheists, nor is adherence to its statements required to call oneself an atheist. It is seen as a summary of concepts and ideas that are part of many atheist's values, and fundamental to rational idea and thought.

Atheism has no specified moral rules, laws, or guidelines. There are atheists that emphasize ethics and personal rules; there are atheists that believe in hedonism and in doing whatever one desires from a moral perspective. Many atheists fall somewhere in the middle, embracing their own combination of personal moralities, views, and politics.

Eclectic Beliefs

As was stated earlier, atheists represent a wide variety of beliefs and perspectives. Atheism could be described as an assortment of eclectic beliefs; ones that influence and range from empirical study, to philosophy, to science. Because there are no specific standards, atheists have no specified beliefs or standards. Not unlike those who have religious beliefs, atheists do seek to shape

Atheist symbol

society and the world at large as they see it, reflecting their own unique concepts and ideas in the things they do. They also falter on matters and questions, much in the same way that those of faith do at times, because they also do not have all the answers.

Relations with Non-Atheists

Atheism is a personal experience. Atheist interactions vary. Some atheists, while not believing in a deity themselves, do not take issue with those who do. They may not want to practice someone else's faith system, but they are not antithetical to it. There are also atheists who are more extreme and interested in dismantling religious systems. There are many atheists who embrace the idea of defending their position, as they feel underrepresented within society. Such atheists are often interested in discussion, but not necessarily in relationships with others who feel differently than they do.

Atheists, agnostics, secular humanists, and non-religious individuals have some notable differences, but have aligned for the promotion of their ideals and common values. It is not uncommon to see events, groups, or communities that gather and work for the promotion of such ideals, all with the goal of celebrating, studying, and embracing their own unique ideas.

Holy Sites

None, as atheists deny the existence of something sacred or holy.

Notable Figures

Madalyn Murray O'Hair (1919-1995), founder, American Atheists, Inc.; Woody Allen (1935-), actor; Isaac Asimov (1920-1992), scientist; Isaiah Berlin (1909-1997), philosopher; George Carlin (1937-2008), comedian; Noam Chomsky (1928-), linguist; Clarence Darrow (1857-1938), lawyer; Sigmund Freud (1856-1939), psychoanalyst; Karl Marx (1818-1883), philosopher; Arian Foster (1986-), athlete; Daniel Radcliffe (1989-), actor; Julianne Moore (1960-), actress; Javier Bardem (1969-), actor; Kiera Knightley (1985-), actress; Emma Thompson (1959-), actress; Billy Joel (1949-), musician; Penn Jillette (1955-), magician; Seth MacFarlane (1973-), animated series creator; Kathy Griffin (1960-), comedian; Richard Dawkins (1941-), scientist; Christopher Hitchens (1949-2011), author; Sam Harris (1967-), scientist; Daniel Dennett (1942-), philosopher; Stephen Hawking (1942-2018), scientist; Kurt Vonnegut (1922-2007), author; Douglas Adams (1952-2001), author; Ayn Rand (1905-1982), philosopher; Katharine Hepburn (1907-2003), actress; Dave Barry (1947-), author; Simone de Beauvoir (1908-1986), philosopher; Gabriel Byrne (1950-), actor; Bob Geldof (1951-), musician; Frank Zappa (1940-1993), musician.

Notable Groups

American Atheists, Inc., is a national organization representing the interests of atheists in the separation of church and state. It was founded by Madalyn Murray O'Hair in 1963 after she filed a lawsuit with the Baltimore Public School System to challenge the idea of school sanctioned Bible reading and mandatory public prayer. She won the case. As a result, she started a number of other lawsuits, some of which were found in the organization's favor, and some, not.[14]

The organization faced criticism as O'Hair was both disagreeable and unpleasant. She claimed to experience bitter opposition and harassment for her views. She was also arrested on different occasions for disorderly conduct. As the voice of the organization, she continued, including through a radio program, the television show *American Atheist Forum*, lawsuits, and television appearances.[15]

In August 1995, O'Hair, her son Jon Garth Murray (1954-1995), and her granddaughter Robin Murray O'Hair (1965-1995) went missing. They disappeared in what appeared to be a great hurry, with approximately $400,000 worth of merchandise. Until September 27 of that year, various employees at American Atheists received phone calls from Robin and Jon, in which they were notably distressed. After this, no one ever heard from any of them again. They were believed to be murdered by David Roland Walters (1947-2003), an employee of American Atheists. In wake of the scandal, American Atheists lost considerable financial backing.[16]

FACTS AND FIGURES

While approximately 4% of the US population identifies as atheist, atheism is more common in Europe. Approximately 19% of Belgians, 16% of Danish, 15% of French, 15% of Slovakia, and 14% of Dutch and Swedes identify as atheist.[17]

OTHER IMPORTANT DEFINITIONS[18,19]

- **Agnostic**: An individual who is uncertain of the existence of god or gods in the universe. Sometimes identified as a form of soft atheism.

- **Anti-evolution atheist**: An atheist who does not believe in evolution, believing instead the principle of naturalism, rather than the idea that species evolved from one another.

- **Anti-theism**: The active opposition of all theism, founded on the atheist viewpoint.

- **Apatheist**: An individual who does not care if there is a god, or not.

- **Athe-Agnostic**: An individual who is a blend of atheism and agnosticism, usually given in a 20 (atheist)/80 (agnostic) ratio.

- **Atheist's Bible**: A reference to a book that replaces religious belief with any assortment of scientific philosophies or ideas, such as naturalism, materialism, or logic. There are also several books published in modern times with the same title; critiquing the Bible, replacing Biblical text with atheist ideas, or examining the history of a supposed "atheist Bible" text, circulated by rumor, that there is no evidence ever existed.

- **Closet atheist**: An individual who espouses atheism but does not reveal their beliefs or thoughts to others.

- **Crypto-atheist**: An individual who writes with the intention of presenting atheism, but presenting it in a manner that is coded, or metaphorical.

- **Deconversion**: The process by which one removes religious belief and practice from their lives; the opposite of conversion.

- **Materialism**: The idea that all things consist of matter, and that there is nothing else that can exist without matter.

- **Mortalism**: The belief that there is no afterlife, soul outside of the body after death, or life after death.

- **Naturalism**: The belief that the universe and nature, at large, can be explained by natural law and natural forces, exclusively.

- **Problem of evil**: A philosophical question as to how evil can exist in a universe that is to be governed by an all-powerful deity.

- **Rabbit hole**: The perception of change in idea and belief by an individual who moves from the beliefs (especially those that relate to theism) they were raised with to those that reflect atheism.

- **Secular**: The concept that ideas, society, and politics can exist without the involvement of religious, supernatural, or spiritual matters.

- **Semi-atheist**: An individual who believes natural laws explain the dynamics and working of the universe.

BELIEVER'S CHARACTERISTICS

Spiritual and theological doubt; materialism; disbelief in anything intangible, unperceivable, invisible, or unproven by science; interest in philosophy; insistence of accuracy of concrete scientific knowledge and proof; emphasis on proof; rejection of all spiritual and unperceivable realities; denial of supernatural phenomena or paranormal events; intense separation of church and state; interest in reason; variation in understanding and belief.

Bahá' í Faith

He urges you to persevere and add up your accomplishments, rather than to dwell on the dark side of things. Everyone's life has both a dark and bright side. He urges you to persevere and add up your accomplishments, rather than to dwell on the dark side of things. Everyone's life has both a dark and bright side.
The Master said: turn your back to the darkness and your face to Me.
(Shoghi Effendi, *The Unfolding Destiny of the British Bahá'í Community*, p. 457)[1]

Theology

Belief in one specified, unifying deity, known as GOD: considered personal, inaccessible, all-knowing, all-seeing, all-present, and almighty, in every sense of the word. God is believed to be without beginning nor end, completely and fully eternal. God is directly inaccessible to believers (too great for human beings to understand) but manifests his will and purpose through various Manifestations of God, also known as messengers. These messengers are reflective of different dispensations (or eras) by which an individual is appointed by God to bring forth revelation. Each dispensation represents a greater deposit of divine revelation than the past. Revelation never ends, continuing throughout the cycles of the ages.

There are three central messengers within the Bahá'í Faith: the Báb (1819-1850), who was a preparatory messenger proclaiming a prophet was soon to come, one who would be in the same tradition as Jesus or Mohammed; Bahá'u'lláh (Mízrá Hussai-'Alí Noorí, 1817-1892), who claimed to be that prophet, and faced prison and exile throughout much of his life; and 'Abdu'l-Bahá (1844-1921), who was the son of Bahá'u'lláh, who taught beyond Iran throughout much of his life.

The theology of Bahá'í is Iranian in origin, serving as a theological offshoot of Islam. It is strictly monotheistic with syncretic elements of all major world religions existing prior to its foundation.[2]

Philosophy

The Bahá'í Faith started as a sect of Bábism, which reflects the same foundations: the absolute oneness of God and various manifestations of God through messengers. The Báb (a Persian term meaning "the gate") believed his work was the beginning of an apocalyptic process, ending one cycle and establishing a new one. As part of this new cycle, a new great and promised prophet was to come. This messenger was the fulfillment of the promised being to come in all major world religions (the Second Coming of Jesus Christ in Christianity, the messiah in Judaism, Maitreye of Buddhism, the Tenth Avatar of Hinduism, and the Day of God in Islam). Bábism, as a sect of Islam, flourished for some time before the Báb was executed. The Bahá'í Faith, picking up where Bábism left off, taught their leader, Bahá'u'lláh was the fulfillment of the prophecy of the Báb, as the promised prophet who would come and establish the new cyclical order.

The Bahá'í Faith is founded on the specific teachings of Bahá'u'lláh, the promised one to come according to the Báb. The religion's focus is religious unity; all religions of the world are seen as essential and valuable. While other world religions reflect lesser covenants of revelation unique to their dispensational era, the Bahá'í Faith is seen as a greater covenant of revelation. All people of the world are also seen as valuable, having an essential common virtue which should unite them together. All people, religion, paths, and beliefs teach the same message, and all equally lead to the divine. Any individual can pursue any religion and find the divine in their life. Central to this goal is universal, worldwide education, international peace, unity, social and economic equality, and brotherhood among all people (especially through the unity of all religions). Racism, sexism, and nationalism are strongly denounced. A one-world government, language, and religion are seen as the solutions to worldwide discord. By following the teachings of the divine messengers, humanity can transform and develop moral and spiritual quality.

'Abdu'l-Bahá, son of Bahá'u'lláh

ADHERENT IDENTITY

Bahá'í Faith, Bahá'í, Bahá'ís, Bábists.

NUMBER OF ADHERENTS

There are approximately 7,000,000 adherents of the Bahá'í Faith worldwide.[3]

TRADITIONAL LANGUAGES

Persian.

SECTS/DIVISIONS

There are several sects of the Bahá'í Faith, all with ties and connections back to Bábism. Each group has its own committed group of followers, typically centering around a singular, central figure.

- **Bayanis**: Also known as People of Bayan, the Bayanis believe Mizrá Yahá Subh-e-Azal (1831-1912) is the true successor of the Báb, not Bahá'u'lláh. This sect has their own scriptures, specific teachings, and lineage, and is one of the best organized of all the Bahá'í Faith sects.[4]

- **Daheshists**: The Daeshists believe Bahá'u'lláh was a guide, not a prophet. The true leader prophesied by the Báb is Saleem Moosha El-Awshee (1912-1984), known as Dr. Dahesh. He founded Daheshism in Beirut, Lebanon. Dr. Daesh is believed to have performed several miracles and authored five books, which the Daheshists believe are inspired writings. He is considered the reincarnation of the Báb himself. His position and claims are denied by the Bahá'í Faith.[5]

- **Free Bahá'í s**: There are several breakaway groups that feel the will and testament of the Bahá'u'lláh is, in some way, fraudulent or misinterpreted. Most contest the issue of the Bahá'u'lláh's son, 'Abdu'l-Bahá, as successor. These include The Essence of the Bahá'í Faith, Unitarian Bahá'ís, Free Bahá'ís, Reform Bahá'ís, and the New History Society.[6]

- **The Guardianship groups**: Some sects of the Bahá'í Faith believe there is a guardian of the true fulfillment of the Bahá'u'lláh's teaching, usually living, or who believe that one shall yet come to serve as a guardian of the faith. These include the Heart of the Bahá'í Faith (Followers of Jacques Soghomonian), Bahá'ís Under the Provisions of the Covenant (Jensen Group), Tarbiyat Bahá'ís (followers of Rex King), and Orthodox Bahá'ís.[7]

- **Heterodox Bahá'í s**: Also called the Haifa-Wilmette (a reference to the Universal House of Justice in Haifa, Israel, and the Bahá'í Temple in Wilmette, Illinois) Sect. The major Bahá'í sect in existence, representative of the faith internationally. This group teaches that God has changed his plans and that there are no more guardians in effect. The last leader was Shoghi Effendi (1897-1957). Shoghi Effendi was a figure within the Bahá'í Faith that died suddenly while abroad, with no clear will and testament for future leadership. By revelation, some in leadership (within the Persian group) declared guardianship of the message to be done for all time. The group was led by his widow, Ruhiyyih Khannum (1910-2000), until her death. After her death in 2000, a nine-member council known as the Universal House of Justice was established. This council is elected every five years.[8]

- **Universal House of Guardianship Followers of Five Elders**: Another sect that debates issues of guardianship, this predominately Canadian organization follows the Báb, the Bahá'u'lláh, 'Abdu'l-Bahá, and Shoghi Effendi. They believe the Universal House of Justice should have an infallible guardian, as Bahá'u'lláh prophesied there would be twenty-four guardians. Currently, there have only been nineteen. Shoghi Effendi did not list a successor. In conclusion, they are waiting for these five future elders.[9]

- **Adqas Bahá'í Faith**: A complicated sect that believes the Kitáb-i-Aqdas, or Most Holy Book of Bahá'u'lláh has been suppressed. This, to them, is a criminal matter they take with grave severity. It is based on thirty-one life giving principles, which state and interpret the Bahá'u'lláh's purpose as creating a new religion, rather than merging the world's religions. They see the mainline Bahá'ís as materialistic, greedy, and corrupting the real teachings of the religion.[10]

DISPUTES WITHIN GROUP

Disputes within the Bahá'í Faith are about succession and group leadership. As the religion is based in Persian culture and adhering to specifications of successors, wills, testaments, and followers of faith, there is considerable debate over who the proper or expected successor should have been after Bahá'u'lláh or another later leader in the movement.

SCRIPTURES

Bahá'ís accept all religious scriptures, considering them all to hold teaching value as representative of revelation up to that point in history. They often use different religious scriptures to prove their own doctrinal beliefs, as well as the presence of their prophetic leadership and their beliefs as pertain to him. Within the international scriptural tradition, the Qur'an is considered fully authoritative while other religious scriptures are considered partially authoritative. None of these scriptures are considered binding or authoritative in Bahá'í belief and practice.

Scriptures unique and central to the Bahá'í Faith include the writings of the Báb, Bahá'u'lláh, 'Abdu'l-Bahá, Shoghi Effendi, and now the Universal House of Justice. The writings of the Báb and Bahá'u'lláh are considered divine revelation (some include Selections from the Writings of the Báb, The Call of the Divine Beloved, Days of Remembrance, Epistle to the Son of the Wolf, Gems of Divine Mysteries, Gleanings from the Writings of Bahá'u'lláh, The Hidden Words, the Kitáb-i-Aqdas, the most Holy Book; The Kitáb-i- Íquán, the Book of Certitude; Prayers and Meditations by Bahá'u'lláh, The Seven Valleys and the Four Valleys, The Summons of the Lord of Hosts, The Tabernacle of Unity, and The Tablets of Bahá'u'lláh), the writings and talks of 'Abdu'l-Bahá and Shoghi Effendi are considered interpretation with authority (some include Memorials of the Faithful, Paris Talks, The Promulgation of Universal Peace, The Secret of Divine Civilization, Selections from the Writings of 'Abdu'l-Bahá, A Traveler's Narrative, Will and Testament of 'Abdu'l-Bahá, The Advent of Divine Justice, Bahá'í Administration, Citadel of Faith, God Passes By, The Promised Day is Come, This Decisive Hour, and The World Order of Bahá'u'lláh), and the Universal House of Justice writes for legislation and education. Some include Letters to the World's Religious Leaders and The Promise of World Peace).[11]

> *"It is upon the plane of understanding that the power of the Bahá'í writings operates, in that are of being which lies beyond the personal desire, the personal thought, the personal will. Their operation is to restore in the individual, whatever his race, class, creed, profession or temperament, that eternal vision of the oneness of God whose evolving expression is directly the development of the soul, and indirectly the harmonious organization of mankind. Compared to other writings of this age, the Bahá'í Scriptures are as light compared to the reflection of light from surfaces more or less luminous or opaque. This essential quality of illumination, as distinct from the subject illuminated, and of vision, as distinct from the subject visioned, reveals anew the very sources of man's spiritual being, and discloses, also, the predominant forces working to mold the character of the new day."*[12]

> *"Therefore it is shown that in the primary sense "sun", "moon" and "stars" signify the Prophets,*

the saints and their companions, through the light of whose knowledge the worlds of the visible and invisible are enlightened and illumined. In another sense, by "sun," "moon" and "stars" is intended the divines of the former Dispensation, at the time of the subsequent Manifestation and in whose hands are the reins of the religion of the people. If they are illumined by the light of the subsequent Sun in His Manifestation, they will be acceptable, radiant and shining; otherwise they will be declared as darkened, even though they are apparently guides. For all these states, including belief and unbelief, guidance and error, happiness and misery, light and darkness are dependent upon the approval of that Ideal Sun of Divinity. If, in the Day of Judgment (Day of a new Manifestation), any one of these divines is declared faithful by the Source of Wisdom, he can truly be regarded as possessing knowledge, light and faith, and as having attained the good pleasure of God. Otherwise, ignorance, rejection, infidelity and injustice will be applied to him.

In another sense, the words, "sun," "moon" and "stars" are applied to the ordinances and instructions enacted in every religion. As in every subsequent Manifestation the established, shining, clear and fixed ceremonies, customs and instructions of the preceding Manifestation are abolished, they symbolically mentioned them by the names "sun" and "moon."

First western Bahá'í Pilgrims, 1898

"Briefly; this is the purpose of the symbolism in the words of the divine Manifestations. Consequently the application of these meanings to "sun" and "moon" in the mentioned instances is confirmed and demonstrated through revealed verses and recorded traditions. Therefore by the "darkness of the sun and moon" and the "falling of the stars" is intended the aberration of the divines and the abolition of the ordinances established in a religion, of which the Manifestation of a Dispensation speaks through these symbols. Only the righteous have a portion of this cup and only the just partake thereof.

"It is certain that during every subsequent Manifestation, the "sun" of the teachings, ordinances, commands and prohibitions established in the preceding Manifestation, - the "sun" and "moon" of teachings and command under which the people of that age are enlightened and guided, - become darkened, that is, their influence and efficiency vanish. Now consider, had the people of the Gospel understood the purpose of "sun" and "moon" or inquired concerning it from the Manifestor of divine knowledge, without contradiction or obstinacy, the meanings thereof would have necessarily become clear and they would not have been confined in the darkness of egotism and desire. Yea, since they did not acquire the knowledge from its mine and source, they perished in the fatal valley of unbelief and error, and are not yet aware that all the signs appeared and the promised Sun dawned from the horizon of Manifestation, while the sun and moon of former knowledge, ordinances and teachings were darkened and disappeared.

"O my brother, take the step of the soul, that thou mayest in a moment traverse the distant valleys

of separation and remoteness, enter the Ridván of union and nearness and in a breath attain to the divine Souls. These stages can never be traveled nor the destination reached by the step of the body. Peace be upon these who follow the truth in truth and stand in the path of command upon the shore of knowledge in the name of God.

"In like manner through these clear, firm, well-founded and direct explanations understand the 'cleaving of heaven' which is one of the signs of the hour of Resurrection: As it is said: 'When the heaven shall be cloven asunder.' (K.S. 82) By this is meant the heaven of religions elevated during every Dispensation and cloven asunder in every subsequent Manifestation, that is, abolished and annulled. I swear by God that to one who carefully considers, the cleaving asunder of this heaven is greater than the cleaving of the phenomenal heaven. Reflect a little; a long-established religion, under which all have grown and developed; by the shining ordinances of which they have been trained for long periods; hearing nothing from their fathers and ancestors except its mention, so that the eyes see only the effectiveness of its commands and ears hear only its ordinances; then afterward one appearing, severing and separating all these through divine power and strength, nay rather, abolishing them. Consider whether this is of greater importance than that which these worthless creatures have imagined concerning the cleaving of heaven. Moreover, consider the difficulties and afflictions of these Countenances in executing the laws of God in face of all in the earth, without a worldly helper or assister. Notwithstanding the persecutions inflicted upon these pure, high and blessed Beings, they endure with the utmost power and suffer with infinite strength."[13]

Basic Religious Practices

The Bahá'í Faith has no formalized clergy, rituals, or specified rites or sacraments. Bahá'ís gather every nineteen days in a cycle to meet for reading, meditation, study, and discussion. These nineteen-day spans are known as months within the Bahá'í Faith, created for their specific celebrations and observances. The year is divided into nineteen different months, at the beginning of which members are encouraged to gather for their regular feasts (although a regular feast can happen at any time in a month). At the end of the year, Bahá'ís observe a holiday to compensate for any days that fall outside their nineteen-day cycle. There is no congregational prayer held at meetings. These days are often compared to Sundays for Christians, Fridays for Muslims, or Saturdays for Jews, although their purpose and practice are different. The purpose of these meetings is community unity and encouragement, as well as to discuss news or happenings that may be of value or interest for the community. Participation in such is not required for members of the Bahá'í Faith but is strongly encouraged. Feasts are held in social halls, homes, or in community centers.

Bahá'í Faith temples are used for major feasts and occasions within the religion. These buildings are not envisioned just for worship, but also to one day serve as a seat for economic and political concerns as well. The temples host one annual nineteen-day fast, from March 2 to March 20. There are currently eight continental Bahá'í temples, one on each continent: Wilmette, Illinois; New South Wales, Australia; Kampala, Uganda; Langenhain, Germany; Panama City, Panama; Tiapapata, Samoa; New Delhi, India; and Santiago, Chile. Bahá'í s are expected to live in tolerance and harmony with all, in both family, friend, and global capacity.

All Bahá'ís recite an obligatory prayer each day, according to a fixed form established by

Bahá'u'lláh. There is a short prayer:

> *I bear witness, O my God, that Thou hast created me to know Thee and to worship Thee. I testify, at this moment, to my powerlessness and to Thy might, to my poverty and to Thy wealth. There is none other God but Thee, the Help in Peril, the Self-Subsisting.*

a medium prayer, and a long prayer, the texts of which are found in Bahá'u'lláh's Prayers and Meditations. Prior to praying, Bahá'ís are required to wash their hands and face, or recite the verse, *In the Name of God, the Most Pure, the Most Pure"*, five times if water is unavailable. On a daily basis, Bahá'í s are also required to offer daily devotional prayer and meditate and study upon their scriptures.

Practitioners of the Bahá'í Faith over 15 years of age (who are not older than seventy, not in ill health, menstruating, pregnant, or nursing women, or otherwise have other complications) are required to fast for 19 days during daylight hours March 2-20 each year. A 19% voluntary payment on one's income goes to the Universal House of Justice every year. Backbiting and gossip are prohibited, drinking and selling alcohol are forbidden, and professional begging is forbidden. Sexual relationships are only permitted in heterosexual marriages; homosexuality, extramarital, and premarital sexual relationships are forbidden.

Bahá'ís are forbidden from participating in partisan politics; however, political and social action are seen as an expression of faith, especially when it comes to the fundamental vision of society that is unique to the Bahá'í Faith.[14]

HOLIDAYS

Bahá'ís celebrate 11 different holidays and one holiday period that lasts through several days throughout their calendar year. These holidays do not have specialized observances or rites, and the various Bahá'í communities are free to celebrate them as they desire.

- **Naw-Ruz, Bahá'í New Year's Day**: Marks the beginning of spring (March 20/21).
- **Festival of Ridván**: Celebrates Bahá'u'lláh's declaration as a messenger of God (April 20/21-April 1/2).
- **Declaration of the Báb**: Celebrates the Báb's declaration as the "gate" or "door," leading to the foundation of the Bahá'í Faith (May 23/24).
- **Martyrdom of the Báb**: The anniversary of the Báb's death by execution in the Persian Empire on grounds of apostasy (July 9/10).
- **Birth of the Báb**: Celebration of the Báb's birth (first day after the eighth new moon following Naw-Ruz, usually Mid-October to Mid-November).

- **Birth of Bahá'u'lláh**: Celebration of the Bahá'u'lláh's birth (second day after the eight new moon following Naw-Ruz, usually mid-October to mid-November).

- **Day of the Covenant**: The appointment of 'Abdu'l-Bahá as central to Bahá'u'lláh covenantal promise (November 25/26).

- **Ascension of 'Abdu'l-Bahá in 1921**: The death of 'Abdu'l-Bahá (November 27/28).

- **Ayyám-i-Há**: Intercalary days on the Bahá'í calendar that are the four or five days inserted between the last two months of the Bahá'í year.

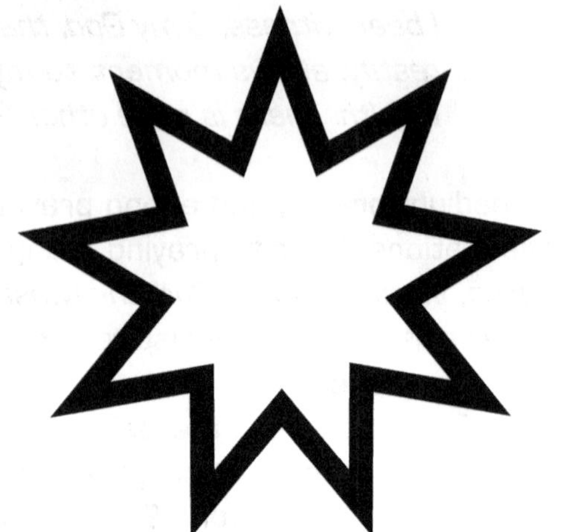

Nine-pointed Bahá'í star

VISUAL SIGNS AND SYMBOLS

Nine-pointed star; Arabic calligraphy forms of the word *Bahá*, which means "glory," and *Yá Bahá'u'l-Abhá*, which means "O glory of the all glorious;" ringstone symbol, consisting of two stars interspersed with a Bahá symbol; writings of Bahá'u'lláh and use of international scriptures; five-pointed star; symbolic language.

CREEDS, BOOKS, AND LAWS

The Bahá'í Faith accepts and embraces all nations, creeds, races, and classes. They do not profess one specific creed, believing all that exist should be treated equally without any prejudice. The central legal text for Bahá'ís is the Kitáb-i-Aqdas. It is Bahá'u'lláh's book of laws, written while he was in prison. Later additions include his writings and answers to a series of questions asked by Bahá'u'lláh's secretary.

The organization is governed by the Universal House of Justice in Haifa, Israel, a nine-member supreme ruling board over the entire international Bahá'í community. Members are selected every five years by delegates of the Bahá'í National Spiritual assemblies worldwide (local governing bodies that help to lead Bahá'í communities). Its purpose is to address issues that are not clearly outlined in Bahá'í writings and to allow the religion to adapt to new and changing times and issues that would arise. The Universal House of Justice is responsible for messages each year during Ridvan, developing local spiritual groups, translating and promoting Bahá'í literature, establishing temples and houses of worship, and leading the organization's social betterment programs and community worship direction. Proclamations and books produced by the Universal House of Justice are considered infallible decisions and legislative directives. In contrast with the organization's egalitarian nature, the nine-member board is entirely male.[15]

ECLECTIC BELIEFS

Family life is essential to the Bahá'í Faith and its adherents' way of living. Marriage is seen as a unifying principle, one with the ability to create harmony and unity among men and women, in addition to helping to provide such as a stable building block for society. Marriage is encouraged (monastic life is forbidden), divorce is met with disapproval, marriages must be heterosexual, and understanding a potential mate's character is essential before marriage. Interracial marriage is encouraged, seen as a unifying point within society.

The Bahá'í Faith actively promotes their belief in developing a one-world government and needed vision for world society. They are active in support of programs through the United Nations, known as the Bahá'í International Community. This group works in consultation with the World Health Organization, the United Nations Children's Fund, United Nations Development Fund for Women, United Nations Economic and Social Council, and the United Nations Environment Programme.

Bahá'ís have experienced frequent persecution in Islamic nations. In many sects of Islam, the Bahá'í Faith is seen as an apostasy from Islam, and punishable under Islamic law. In several countries, the rights of Bahá'ís are restricted, including Egypt, Afghanistan, Indonesia, Iraq, Morocco, and Yemen.[16]

RELATIONS WITH NON- BAHÁ'ÍS

Because Bahá'ís hold a strict position on doctrinal tolerance and equality, they are active in their interfaith pursuits, willing to work with those of other religions. Bahá'ís tend to shy away from Christian fundamentalism or groups that may in some way contradict their doctrines of tolerance.

HOLY SITES

Shrine of the Báb, Haifa, Israel; The Bahá'í Houses of Worship located in Sydney, Australia; Wilmette, Illinois; New Delhi, India; Frankfurt, Germany; Apia, Western Samoa; and Ashkabad, Central Asia; the Shrine of 'Abdu'l-Bahá, Haifa, Israel; Mansion of Bahji, the burial place of Bahá'u'lláh, Haifa, Israel.

NOTABLE FIGURES

The Báb (1819-1850), influential founder; Bahá'u'lláh (1817-1892), founder who claimed to be the fulfillment of the final Muslim lineage prophecy; Mizra Abdollah (1918-1843), musician; Celeste Buckingham 1995-), musician; Anthony Azizi (1969-), actor; Eva LaRue (1966-), actress; Rainn Wilson (1966-), actor; Barry Crump (1935-1966), comic author; Cathy Freeman (1973-), athlete; Dwight Allen (1931-2021), professor; Ron McNair (1950-1986), astronaut; Phoebe Hearst (1842-1919), feminist; Hilda Yen (1906-1970), diplomat.

NOTABLE GROUPS

The Bahá'í International Community, headquartered in New York City, seeks to influence the United Nations by representing the beliefs and values of the Bahá'í Faith in a governmental position. Its goal is to influence policy through advocating a one world, universal governmental system; universal education; human rights; women's advancement; and solid, just economic development. They represent, through activism, their beliefs and attempt to enact them politically through global decisions. Their activities are reported in their quarterly international newsletter titled *ONE COUNTRY*.[17]

FACTS AND FIGURES

In the United States, the retention rate of Bahá'í membership is approximately 50% within two years of enrollment.[18]

OTHER IMPORTANT DEFINITIONS[19]

- **Abha Kingdom**: Most glorious Kingdom; the spiritual world.
- **Ages**: The three divisions of the Bahá'í revelation: The heroic, which covers the work of the Báb, Bahá'u'lláh, and 'Abdu'l-Bahá; the formative, which began with the reading of 'Abdu'l-Bahá's Will and Testament, ushering in the current age of Bahá'í governance; and the Golden Age, which is yet to come, when the world shall exist under one government, one world community, and one world civilization and culture.
- **Ancient of Days**: Bahá'u'lláh
- **Army of Light**: The Bahá'í community, both those on earth and those individuals who now exist as celestial spirits and angels.
- **Bábis**: Follower of the Báb.
- **Bahá'í World Commonwealth**: The future Bahá'í community that will be worldwide, in which the principles of Bahá'í will govern the entire world, functioning under a one world governmental system.
- **Covenant**: An agreement or contract between two parties that is binding and formal; a binding agreement between God and man, as God requires certain conduct for certain blessings; the manifestations of God.
- **Covenant-Breaker**: A member of the Bahá'í Faith that attempts to disrupt the faith and its precepts by opposing Bahá'u'lláh, 'Abdu'l-Bahá, or the Universal House of Justice.

- **Cradle of the Faith**: The nation of Iran, as it is where the religion and its founders originate.

- **Dawn-breakers**: The early followers of Báb and Bahá'u'lláh, many of whom were killed for their faith.

- **Day of God**: A reference to a manifestation of God, their life on earth, and their duration of stay. Also a reference to Bahá'u'lláh.

- **International Bahá'í Convention**: Held every five years in Haifa, Israel, where the members of the National Spiritual Assemblies gather to elect the members of the Universal House of Justice.

- **Local Spiritual Assembly**: A nine-member panel of Bahá'ís in a community, elected each year for local guidance and governance.

- **Manifestation of God**: A prophet who is founder of a specified religious dispensation. Term is applied to the founders of all the world's major world religions.

BELIEVER'S CHARACTERISTICS

Emphasis on unity, global economy, and a one world government, with specified aims of equality in gender, race, economics, environmental rights, peace, education, and development; practice of daily Bahá'í principles; avoiding behaviors that cause division; acceptance of all religions, believing Bahá'í is the fulfillment of all existing religious promises and visions; belief in culmination of religious experience within Bahá'í movement; interest in mix of politics and religion, that all systems may be one; advocacy; focus on the Báb, Bahá'u'lláh, and 'Abdu'l-Bahá; interest in Bahá'í writings; embrace of a strong view of the importance of family as part of unity; encouragement of interracial marriages; participation in Bahá'í community life.

Black Identity Movement

The government of America is owned lock stock and barrel by those Zionists that love Israel above the United States of America.
(Louis Farrakhan)[1]

Theology

A counter to Christian Identity white supremacy, black supremacy takes one of two forms: either that of a modified Sacred Name/Hebrew Roots theology, or a modified Muslim theology, both of which revolve around the idea that the black male (and by extension, the black female), classified as a "black man," is of a specific, special, supreme identity. This identity has been distorted and controlled by the white man throughout history. Some Hebrew groups also see black-skinned individuals as part of the lost tribes of Israel or true Israel (in contrast to traditional ideas about Judaism). The black man, of dark skin and African descent, is the highest creation of ALLAH, GOD, YAHWEH, or YAVHEH (or some variation of such), the creator. There is no other deity, nor being, on the level of their god, anywhere else; the movements are almost universally unitarian. Most Black supremacy movements view the transmission of their history through a central messianic or prophetic figure (typically the founder or current leader of their specified group). This individual restores and/or leads the group as an official voice of the divine. In some groups, the black man progresses through awareness and knowledge of his true destiny, ultimately to become a god himself. Black women are seen as earth mothers rather than gods, and are seen as subordinate, even in an eternal sense, to black men.

Black identity movements believe all Biblical, Muslim, and central religious historical figures were black individuals, including Abraham, Moses, Jesus, and Mohammed. The black man is seen as the original "man," the first, and official race, from which came all other races: brown, yellow, red, and white. In more extreme groups, the Caucasian, or "white" man, is seen as being the devil, a strictly oppressive force. He exists to suppress the black man, keeping him from becoming all he can be. Focused on socioeconomic advancement, betterment, and black identity as a theological presupposition, the Black Identity Movement's sole spiritual purpose is the advancement, and often superiority, of the black man.

Philosophy

Black identity movements, also called black nationalism, offer a restorationist view of history. They teach the black man (and by extension, the black woman) has a special and unique identity that has been destroyed, oppressed, and controlled by the white man. This basic belief exists in varying degrees throughout the movement; from those that are more benign and are nothing more than a church movement identifying dark skinned individuals as the Biblical nation of Israel, to those that inspire extreme hate and encourage violence, anti-Semitism, and anti-white sentiment.

In their essence, black identity movements seek to change the way black men think about themselves, contrasting with the struggles of slavery, racism, and oppression. History is often rewritten to include historical concepts or ideas that are not supported by archaeological or historical facts. Rather than presenting themselves as economic betterment or self-esteem boosting programs, they do so through faith, offering unique theologies based in acclaimed revelations specific to their movements. Black identity theology is secondary; it enhances the identity narrative of the black man as Israelite or true Muslim, ascending to godhood, or somehow otherwise special, superior, and greater than the white man. To aspire to their full potential, black men are required to establish lives set apart from men of other races: in attire, diet (pork is forbidden), health (smoking is forbidden), social activity (gambling is forbidden), adherence to divinely established laws for a special people (whether Old Testament laws or Muslim regulations), and a complete and total separateness of the races.

Many have classified black identity movements as equivalents of white supremacist movements. As the black versions of a hate group, they alter perspective, history, facts, and ideas to produce propaganda and promote hatred of other racial groups, specifically those identified as white. Many of their conspiracy theories, dietary ideas, and separatist concepts, however, are found and rooted in ideas propagated by white supremacists. The only difference is the racial narrative.

ADHERENT IDENTITY

Black nationalists, Black Hebrew Israelite, Hebrew Israelites, Black Hebrews, Black Israelites, African Hebrew Israelites, Church of the Living God, the Pillar Ground of Truth for All Nations, Church of God and Saints of Christ, Commandment Keepers, African Hebrew Israelites of Jerusalem, Israelite School of Universal Practical Knowledge, Nation of Yahweh, the Nation of Islam, Black Muslim, Nation of Gods and Earths, Five-Percent Nation, Five Percenters, Moorish Science Temple of America, Black sovereign citizens.

NUMBER OF ADHERENTS

It is difficult to ascertain the exact number of black identity adherents. Some groups are not forthcoming with membership statistics, and others, due to extreme views, do not readily provide information about their members. The number of black Hebrews was somewhere between 25,000 and 40,000 in the 1980s. Black Muslim sects are somewhere between about twenty thousand and sixty thousand.[2]

TRADITIONAL LANGUAGES

English.

SECTS/DIVISIONS

There are two main divisions of black identity: the Hebrew (or Israelite) branches and the black Muslim identity branches. Neither division should be confused with long-standing religious groups such as Judaism or Islam. While both may claim lineage and have some things in common with each, neither group meets the proper definition to be classified as either one. The third group are black sovereign citizens, who often combine views of white supremacy inverted, as applied to black community understanding.

- **Hebrew, or Israelite branches:** Such believes that African Americans are the rightful descendants of the ancient Israelites, incorporating elements of Christianity, Judaism, and their own unique Biblical interpretations into their religious practice. Details on the movement's origins vary, with some claiming ties to ancient African groups and other religious movements as early as the sixteenth century. Most associate the official start to the late nineteenth century work of Frank Cherry (c. 1875-1963) and William Saunders Crowdy (1847-1908). It was Crowdy who claimed to have visions affirming the identity of the African Americans as Hebrew descendants. The first known organizations were the Church of the Living God, the Pillar Ground of Truth for All Nations (1886) and the Church of God and Saints of Christ (1896). Many smaller groups emerged, concentrated between the Midwest and east coast over the next few decades. There is no racial diversity among these groups, although most adherents are either African American or descendants of West Indian immigrants. These groups believe the 12 tribes of Israel can be found in modern-day tribal groups (Judah: American blacks, Benjamin: West Indian blacks, Levi: Haitians, Ephraim: Puerto Ricans, Manasseh: Cubans, Simeon: Dominicans, Zebulon: Mayans from Guatemala to Panama, Gad: Native-American Indians, Reuben: Seminole Indians, Asher: Incas from Columbia to Uruguay, Issachar: Aztecs in Mexico, and Naphtali: Argentina/Chile). The Hebrew branches represent a diversity of beliefs and practices. Many practice historical revisionism, which present altered versions of historical details and accounts to promote the views and ideas of the group. Of particular interest is the belief that African Americans are the biological descendants of the Israelites, often traced through a specific Biblical figure (such as Solomon) or through all Biblical figures, also believed to be African American ancestors. The most notable division between such groups is those that are messianic or embracing of Jesus Christ as a central messianic figure, and those who do not, embracing a modified form of Jewish worship or identity. Perhaps the best known of these groups are the Hebrew Israelites that embrace the idea of black supremacy. This group believes authentic Jews are the devil, while also condemning whites as evil figures worthy of death and enslavement. These views are not held by all Hebrew Israelites, but those that do embrace such views include the Israelite School of Universal Practical Knowledge, the Nation of Yahweh, the Israelite Church of God in Jesus Christ, and the Twelve Tribes of Israel. Other Hebrew Israelite groups include the Rastafari (Rastafarians), Commandment Keepers, and African Hebrew Israelites of Jerusalem.[3]

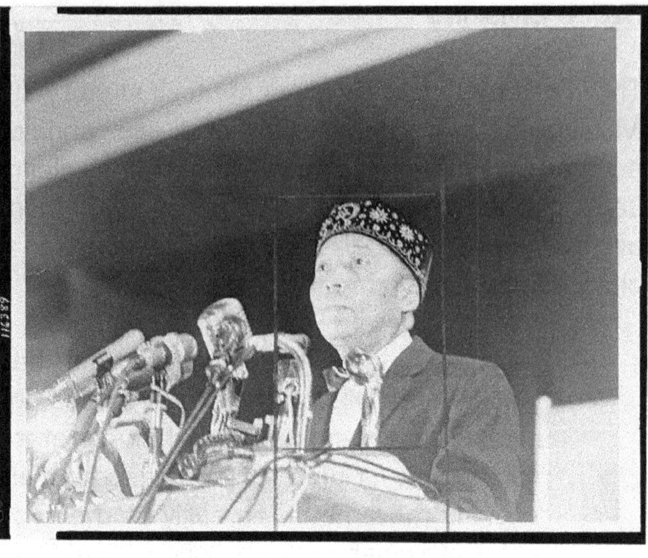

Elijah Muhammad (1897-1975), founder of the Nation of Islam

- **Black Muslim branches**: Black Muslim groups should not be confused with individuals identified as "black Muslims" belonging to accepted and recognized Muslim sects. American black Muslim communities have their origin in the Nation of Islam. The Nation of Islam (NOI) is not rightly part of the Islamic body, nor is it considered to be a valid aspect of Islam by Muslims. It is a uniquely African American political and spiritual entity founded in Detroit, Michigan in the 1930s. Its founder, Wallace Fard Muhammad (1897-1975), disappeared within a few years of the founding and it was his successor, Elijah Muhammad (c. 1877-1934) who became the face of the movement. Like mainline Muslims, the Nation of Islam affirms there is no deity but Allah. Fard Muhammad was the *mahdi*, a prophesied redeemer who would rid the world of evil before the Day of Judgment. The current leader of the Nation of Islam is Louis Farrakhan, who has led the movement since 1977. The Nation of Islam is known for an unconventional historical interpretation. The group teaches a form of creationism: the moon was once part of earth, and the earth is trillions of years old. The original humans on earth were all of the black race. Whites, or Caucasians, are a devil race created by a scientist named Yakub on Patmos (in Greece). A policy on Patmos came by decree to kill all blacks, thus creating a preference for white-skinned individuals. Becoming part of NOI is seen as returning to one's true faith, believing Christianity to be a form of enslavement for African Americans. Members uphold a different set of the Five Pillars of the Islamic faith: Belief in one deity, Allah; daily prayers; fasting during either Ramadan or during the month of December; compulsory charity; and pilgrimage to Mecca. Fard Muhammad is considered the Messiah of both Judaism and the *Mahdi* of Muslims. While Mohammed was the last prophet of Allah, Elijah Muhammad was a messenger taught by the *Mahdi*. Religious centers are known as *Masjids* (Mosque) and usually followed with a number, indicating their order of establishment. The Nation of Islam is considered a hate group as it promotes black supremacy, anti-Semitism, anti-Asian sentiment, subjugated roles for women, and anti-LGBTQ attitudes. In modern times, members of the Nation of Islam are encouraged to pursue studies associated with Scientology, especially L. Ron Hubbard's *Dianetics*. There are approximately 50,000 members of the Nation of Islam today. Offshoots of the Nation of Islam include the Five-Percent Nation (Nation of Gods and Earths), University of Islam schools, Muslim Girls Training & General Civilization Class, the Fruit of Islam, and the Moorish Science Temple of America.

- **Black sovereign citizens**: Also known as Moorish sovereigns, Moorish sovereign citizens, Washitaw Nation, and Moors, black sovereign citizens are a subset of the white supremacist, conspiracy theorist sovereign citizens movement. Based on the same ideas and concepts as the Sovereign Citizens movement, black sovereign citizens date back to 1990 as an offshoot of the Moorish Science Temple of America. Foundationally, the group believes there is a 1787 treaty between the United States and Morocco, giving those who identify as "Moors" full immunity from US law. Those who claim to be of the Washitaw Nation believe they occupy the United Nations Indigenous People's Seat 215. There was never such a treaty and there is no such thing as the United Nations Indigenous People's Seat 215. Claiming to be immune from federal, state, and local law, many create their own birth certificates, passports, driver's licenses, and vehicle registrations. They refuse to pay taxes, register vehicles with the states, and buy auto insurance. The black sovereign citizens movement is renowned for fraud, including defrauding banks and lending institutions and selling phony registrations, licenses, and insurance policies through their websites.

William Saunders Crowdy (1847-1908)

  Like other Sovereign citizens, black sovereign citizens believe Jews are working behind the scenes to manipulate the government and control the banking system, and participating in such supports this so-called agenda, for Jews to control the world. They also believe the government has pledged its citizens as a federal, financial "collateral." The sale of Americans begins at birth, with application for a birth certificate and social security card, by which the government creates a secret, corporate treasury account in the baby's name (amounts range from $600,000 to $20 million). They then believe the use of all capital letters on official documents creates a "straw man" identity. Names printed with upper and lowercase letters are the real flesh-and-blood identity of the individual. A true black sovereign citizen must devoid themselves of their "straw man" corporate identity (a process known as redemption) and live and abide by only Moorish treaty law (which does not exist). To be a black sovereign citizen, one must be of African American heritage, claiming Moorish ancestry. Most gather in small groups (no more than a few dozen at most) led by a central leader. There is no centralized leadership or leadership requirements. They are recognized by a red banner or flag with a five-pointed green star left of center. Most have Africanized names incorporating the words "bey" or "el," or a combination of those two words. There are somewhere between 2,000 and 4,000 black sovereign citizens in the US today.

  The black sovereign citizens movement is not regarded as legitimate by white sovereign citizens. Moorish citizens, though not militia involved, are frequently investigated for fraud, have been arrested for associations with street gangs, the Nation of Islam, and the Black Hebrew Israelites. In recent years, they have also been involved with police confrontation, bank robberies, murders, shootings, and armed conflicts. They have also been known to retaliate against local and federal authorities when courts rule against them.[4]

DISPUTES WITHIN GROUP

Black identity movements emerged from highly racist periods in western history. They seek to provide identity, advancement, and economic opportunity with a spiritual foundation. The movements vary in theology, practice, and degrees of severity. While some are more spiritual in nature and identity, others take a more comprehensive, even violent, approach to their beliefs.

SCRIPTURES

Most, if not all, Hebrew Israelite groups use the King James Version of the Bible, both Old and New Testaments. Some groups use the Old Testament exclusively, or more prominently than the New Testament. Texts include: the Pentateuch (Genesis, Exodus, Leviticus, Numbers, and Deuteronomy), Historical books (Joshua, Judges, Ruth, 1 Samuel, 2 Samuel, 1 Kings, 2 Kings, 1 Chronicles, 2 Chronicles, Ezra, Nehemiah, Esther), Wisdom books (Job, Psalms, Proverbs, Ecclesiastes, Song of Songs), Prophetic books (Isaiah, Jeremiah, Lamentations, Ezekiel, Daniel, Hosea, Joel, Amos, Obadiah, Jonah, Micah, Nahum, Habakkuk, Zephaniah, Haggai, Zechariah, Malachi), the Gospels (Matthew, Mark, Luke, John), the Acts of the Apostles, the Pauline Epistles (Romans, 1 Corinthians, 2 Corinthians, Galatians, Ephesians, Philippians, Colossians, 1 Thessalonians, 2 Thessalonians, 1 Timothy, 2 Timothy, Titus, Philemon, Hebrews) the General Epistles (James, 1 Peter, 2 Peter, 1 John, 2 John, 3 John, Jude) and Revelation.

Additionally, some Hebrew Israelites also use the Deuterocanonical books (a series of books included in between the Old and New Testaments): Tobit, Judith, 1 and 2 Maccabees, Wisdom of Solomon, Sirach, Baruch, Letter of Jeremiah, Greek additions to Esther, and Greek additions to Daniel, including the Prayer of Azariah, Song of the Three Holy Children, Susanna and the Elders, and Bel and the Dragon. Some others use additional Pseudepigrapha or Apocryphal works, such as the books of Enoch, Jubilees, Jasher, and 3 and 4 Maccabees. There are some groups that also incorporate the Talmud, or the tradition of Jewish interpretation and commentary of the law, into their scriptural canon.

Black identity Muslims have a more complicated history with scripture that is not as easily explained as Hebrew Israelite groups. Though Muslim in name, the Nation of Islam draws more on mythological histories than actual scriptural record. These mythologies are, within Black Muslim teaching, essential narratives that uphold black identity as the original race from which all others extend. The enslavement of the black race (which, within belief, constitute their own nation) is a fulfillment of Biblical prophecy, as the seed of Abraham. The vision of Ezekiel is considered a UFO (the mother Wheel or mother plane). The Babylon of Revelation is believed to be America, led by white individuals, who are classified as "blue-eyed devils." All Black Muslim groups have written their own central texts. The Nation of Islam has *Message to the Blackman in America*, The Moorish Holy Temple of Science has *The Holy Koran* (an independent text that has nothing to do with the Qur'an of Islam), and the Five-Percent Nation, *Supreme Wisdom*.

> *"I will raise them up a prophet from among thy brethern like unto thee and will put my words in his mouth and shall speak unto them all that I command him." This is an answer or a prophecy that compares with the prayer of Abraham—that God raised up a messenger from among them and taught him the wisdom and the book, because his people would not have knowledge of the book and were only guessing at its meaning. This book is referring to the Bible—that they were guessing at its meaning. This is true! Thousands of preachers here are preaching the Bible and do not understand the true meaning of it. They only guess at its meaning."*[6]

> *"As David said in his Psalms (37:32): "The wicked watcheth the righteous and seeketh to slay him." Also, Psalms (37:30): "The mouth of the righteous speaketh wisdom, and his tongue talketh of judgment." And in another place (Psa. 94:16): "Who will rise up for me against the workers of iniquity?" I have answered Him and said, "Here I am, take me." For the evil done against my people (the so-called Negroes) I will not keep silent until He executes judgment and defends my cause. Fear not my life, for He is well able to defend it. Know that God is a man and not a spook!"*[7]

> *"The person who leaves the teachings of the Honorable Elijah Muhammad makes himself a fool. The advice to all our people is Get On To Your Own Kind, this world is at hand!"*[8]

> *1. The last Prophet in these days is Noble Drew Ali, who was prepared divinely in due time by Allah to redeem men from their sinful ways; and to warn them of the great wrath which is sure to come upon the earth.*

> *2. John the Baptist was the forerunner of Jesus in those days, to warn and stir up the nation and prepare them to receive the divine creed which was to be taught by Jesus.*

> *3. In these modern days there came a forerunner of Jesus, who was divinely prepared by the great God-Allah and his name is Marcus Garvey, who did teach and warn the nations of the earth to prepare to meet the coming Prophet; who was to bring the true and divine Creed of Islam, and his name is Noble Drew Ali who was prepared and sent to this earth by Allah, to teach the old time religion and the everlasting gospel to the sons of men. That every nation shall and must worship under their own vine and fig tree, and return to their own and be one with their Father God-Allah.*

> *4. The Moorish Science Temple of America is a lawfully chartered and incorporated organization. Any subordinate Temple that desires to receive a charter; the prophet has them to issue to every state throughout the United States, etc.*

> *5. That the world may hear and know the truth, that among the descendants of Africa there is still much wisdom to be learned in these days for the redemption of the sons of men under Love, Truth, Peace, Freedom, and Justice.*

6. We, as a clean and pure nation descended from the inhabitants of Africa, do not desire to amalgamate or marry into the families of the pale skin nations of Europe. Neither serve the gods of their religion, because our forefathers are the true and divine founders of the first religious creed, for the redemption and salvation of mankind on earth.

Fletcher Chapel, one of the first buildings used by Church of God and Saints of Christ

7. Therefore we are returning the Church and Christianity back to the European Nations, as it was prepared by their forefathers for their earthly salvation.

8. While we, the Moorish Americans are returning to Islam, which was founded by our forefathers for our earthly and divine salvation.

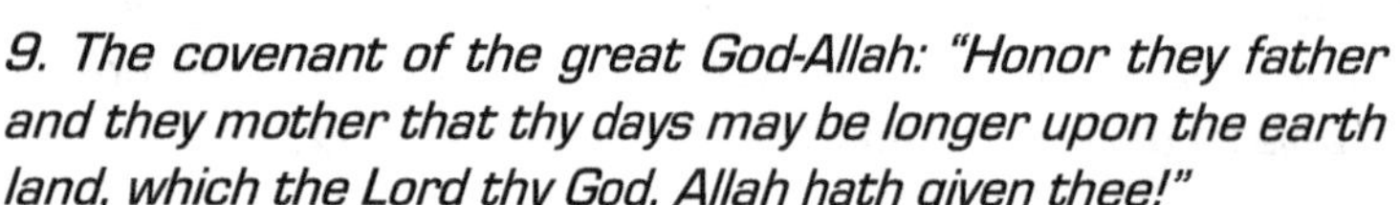

9. The covenant of the great God-Allah: "Honor they father and they mother that thy days may be longer upon the earth land, which the Lord thy God, Allah hath given thee!"

10. Come all ye Asiatics of America and hear the truth about your nationality and birthrights, because you are not negroes. Learn of your forefathers ancient and divine Creed. That you will learn to love instead of hate.

11. We are trying to uplift fallen humanity. Come and link yourselves with the families of nations. We honor all the true and divine prophets.[10]

In an interesting turn, the Nation of Islam has also embraced the works of Scientology's L. Ron Hubbard and its auditing techniques of Dianetics since 2010. By 2013, approximately 8,500 members of the Nation of Islam had utilized Dianetics auditing and had 1,055 auditors. This move has been of particular controversy within the organization and has caused faction in membership.[11]

Basic Religious Practices

The primary unifying factor of black identity groups is their focus on the special, or unique, nature of the black race. From there, basic practices vary slightly. In the case of Hebrew Israelites, most members adopt Hebrew names or a variation of Hebrew and African names, believing the original Hebrews were of African descent. Most synthesize a combination of beliefs that reflect both those of Christianity and Judaism. Some others incorporate their own interpretations of Freemasonry, occultism, Christian Holiness, Pentecostalism, Theosophy, and New Thought. Black Hebrew religious observance could be compared to Sacred Name theology as embodied by predominately (if not exclusively, white communities): emphasis on sacred names of God, use of the King James Version of the Bible, worship on Saturday rather than Sunday, observance of Old Testament Biblical festivals, and the New Testament observances of baptism, foot washing, and communion. Many require men to wear skullcaps (yarmulkes), women to cover their heads in assembly, and the separation of men and women in the church or assembly building. Some additionally embrace veganism, polygamy, arranged marriage, Old Testament dietary laws, Biblical laws surrounding menstruation and childbirth, circumcision, African dress, and prohibit birth control. Some communities have relocated to Israel, claiming right as Hebrew descendants.

Black identity Muslims also embrace their own unique customs and practices, mixing Christian and Muslim influences while expounding their own beliefs. Black Muslims (especially black males) must embrace a belief in racial separation and pursue their own means of entrepreneurial productivity. Members are to practice the Five Pillars of the Islamic faith, with different interpretations of belief in one deity, daily prayer, fasting during Ramadan (or December), charity, and pilgrimage to mecca. Some subsets of Black Muslims do not practice the Five Pillars at all. Instead, they embrace other concepts of identity they feel are more properly fulfilled in their Muslim identity and purpose rather than in the identity of another movement. Most have lessons, or variations, on the ideas present within the Nation of Islam. The movement is heavily text-based (disseminated through newspapers, such as *The Final Call*) and through long messages, delivered by the movement's central figures. In the Nation of Islam specifically, the practice of Scientology auditing, is now also commonplace.

Women do not hold a formal place within the Black Muslim identity movement. They benefit from the advance of the religious system as the men become entrepreneurs, offer self-love, and self-esteem. They, therefore, become their protectors. Women typically dress in all white or long-sleeved clothing, covered from neck to floor, wearing a white veil. Men often wear dark suits with white shirts and bowties, especially in assemblies.

HOLIDAYS

Hebrew Israelites practice the same holidays present among Sacred Name and Hebrew Roots adherents, with some different traditions and observances. As found in Leviticus 23:2:

> *Speak unto the children of Israel, and say unto them, Concerning the feasts of the LORD, which ye shall proclaim to be holy convocations, even these are my feasts.*

For example, Passover is seen not just in its literal context as a redemption of the Hebrews from Egypt, but in the sense of liberation of black individuals.

Black Muslims observe the month of Ramadan, a traditional Muslim holiday, observing the time when the Prophet Mohammed first received the Qur'an. They also observe Eid-al-Udha and Eid al-Fitr, those feasts at the end of Ramadan. They do not, however, always observe these feasts in the same manner as traditional Muslims. For example, Black Muslims have the option of postponing their Ramadan fast until December if they so decide to do so. In addition, there is the Nation of Islam holiday Saviours' Day, which commemorates the movement's founders, Wallace Fard Muhammad and Elijah Muhammad. It is celebrated on February 26th. Members of the Five Percenters observe Allah the Father's Birthday on February 22nd and the founding of the Nation, celebrating the founding of their group, on October 10th. Of all black Muslim groups, the Moorish Science Temple of America observes the most holidays: Prophet Noble Drew Ali's Birthday

(January 8th), Moorish-American New Year's Day (January 15), Moorish Senior's Day (First Sunday in March), Moorish-American Tag Day (March 17th), Moorish Annual National Convention (September 15-20), Our Authority Day (July 20), The Young People's Moorish National League (First Saturday in December), and Sister's Auxiliary Day (Third Saturday in December).[13]

VISUAL SIGNS AND SYMBOLS

Star of David; symbols of the twelve tribes of Israel; lion head on black background; Egyptian ankh; Torah scrolls; skullcaps; head coverings for women; swords; inverted crescent white moon on red background with the letters J(ustice), F(reedom), E(quality), and I(slam) on each corner; compass with a star and the number 7 in the center, surrounded by the message, "In the Name of Allah;" Nation of Islam periodicals; raised closed fist; green five-pointed pentagram star on red background; red number 7 in a broken green circle; red fezz caps; bowties.

CREEDS, BOOKS, AND LAWS

Overall, the Hebrew and Muslim black identity movements are non-credal in that they do not have a specified creed recited or spoken every week in their services. Within the Hebrew branch of the black identity movement, the beliefs are more based in tradition than specified writing, for the reason most of the adherents were originally slaves and illiterate.
Black Muslim beliefs, as found within the Nation of Islam, are summarized as:

1. WE BELIEVE In the One God whose proper Name is Allah.

2. WE BELIEVE in the Holy Qur'an and in the Scriptures of all the Prophets of God.

3. WE BELIEVE in the truth of the Bible, but we believe that it has been tampered with and must be reinterpreted so that mankind will not be snared by the falsehoods that have been added to it.

4. WE BELIEVE in Allah's Prophets and the Scriptures they brought to the people.

5. WE BELIEVE in the resurrection of the dead–not in physical resurrection–but in mental resurrection. We believe that the so-called Negroes are most in need of mental resurrection; therefore they will be resurrected first. Furthermore, we believe we are the people of God's choice, as it has been written, that God would choose the rejected and the despised. We can find no other persons fitting this description in these last days more than the so-called Negroes in America. We believe in the resurrection of the righteous.

Official symbol representing the Nation of Islam

6. WE BELIEVE in the judgment; we believe this first judgment will take place as God revealed, in

America...

7. WE BELIEVE this is the time in history for the separation of the so-called Negroes and the so-called white Americans. We believe the black man should be freed in name as well as in fact. By this we mean that he should be freed from the names imposed upon him by his former slave masters. Names which identified him as being the slave master's slave. We believe that if we are free indeed, we should go in our own people's names–the black people of the Earth.

8. WE BELIEVE in justice for all, whether in God or not; we believe as others, that we are due equal justice as human beings. We believe in equality–as a nation–of equals. We do not believe that we are equal with our slave masters in the status of "freed slaves."

We recognize and respect American citizens as independent peoples and we respect their laws which govern this nation.

9. WE BELIEVE that the offer of integration is hypocritical and is made by those who are trying to deceive the black peoples into believing that their 400-year-old open enemies of freedom, justice and equality are, all of a sudden, their "friends." Furthermore, we believe that such deception is intended to prevent black people from realizing that the time in history has arrived for the separation from the whites of this nation.

If the white people are truthful about their professed friendship toward the so-called Negro, they can prove it by dividing up America with their slaves. We do not believe that America will ever be able to furnish enough jobs for her own millions of unemployed, in addition to jobs for the 20,000,000 black people as well.

10. WE BELIEVE that we who declare ourselves to be righteous Muslims, should not participate in wars which take the lives of humans. We do not believe this nation should force us to take part in such wars, for we have nothing to gain from it unless America agrees to give us the necessary territory wherein we may have something to fight for.

11. WE BELIEVE our women should be respected and protected as the women of other nationalities are respected and protected.

12. WE BELIEVE that Allah (God) appeared in the Person of Master W. Fard Muhammad, July, 1930; the long-awaited "Messiah" of the Christians and the "Mahdi" of the Muslims.

We believe further and lastly that Allah is God and besides HIM there is no god and He will bring about a universal government of peace wherein we all can live in peace together.[14]

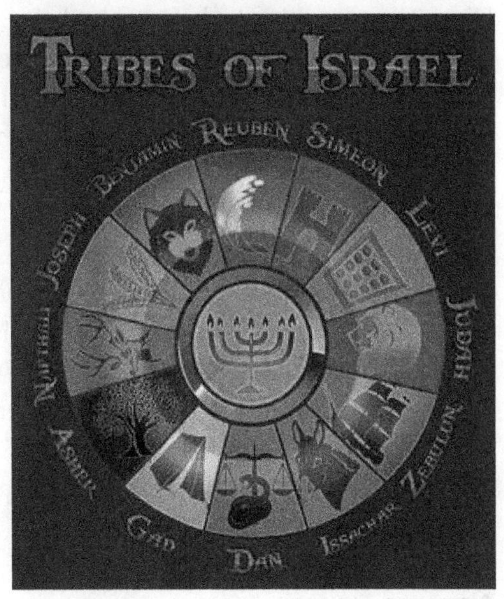

Twelve Tribes of Israel representation

While other Black Muslim groups would agree with most of these beliefs, they would dispute the twelfth point; viewing, in the Moorish Science Temple of America that Noble Drew Ali is the promised Prophet, and among the Five-Percent Nation, Clarence 13X, who was known as Allah the Father.

Eclectic Beliefs

While not all of the Black identity movements embody anti-white sentiment or hate, many black identity groups are centered around black supremacy, or the idea that black individuals are superior to whites and need to systematically engage in retaliation against whites for the survival of the black race. As a result, many embody the same conspiracy theory views as white supremacists, only from a black narrative. Many black identity groups have been active on social media, creating conspiracy theory videos against the United States government, against banking institutions and currency, against Jews, and against society in general.

Many of the movements, especially that of the Nation of Islam and some Hebrew Israelite groups, are vehemently anti-Semitic.

Relations with Non-Black Identity Adherents

Black identity movements, adhering to the idea of their own superiority, often do not interact with those of other races or beliefs. There are variations of such, but with the rise of violence among many communities, isolation is often desirable. There have been numerous incidents throughout the years where individuals of other races have been attacked, harassed, or threatened by black identity adherents.

This makes the alliance between the Nation of Islam and Scientology most interesting. Dianetics, founded by L. Ron Hubbard, is not part of black identity theory or belief. L. Ron Hubbard, as a white man, should not be considered as a legitimate teaching source within the Nation of Islam. As a result, the inclusion of Dianetics into Nation of Islam teaching has created discord and dissention within the organization.

Holy Sites

First Tabernacle Church of God and Saints of Christ, Washington, D.C.; Nation of Yahweh Headquarters, Liberty City, Florida; Mt. Horeb Congregation, Bronx, New York; Beth Shalom, Bedford-Stuyvesant, Brooklyn; B'nai Adat, Brooklyn, New York; Beth Elohim, Queens, New York; B'nai Zaken, Chicago, Illinois; African Hebrew Israelite Nation of Jerusalem, Dimona, Israel; Church of the Living God, the Pillar Ground of Truth for All Nations, Philadelphia, Pennsylvania; Mosque Maryam (Muhammed Mosque #2), Chicago, Illinois; Grand Major Temple #1, Chicago, Illinois.

Notable Figures

Eddie Butler (1971-), musician; Chingy (1980-), musician; Brandon T. Jackson (1984-), actor;

Wentworth Arthur Matthew (1892-1973), founder, Commandment Keepers of the Living God; Yahweh ben Yahweh (1935-2007), founder, Nation of Yahweh; Louis Farrakhan (1933-), leader of the Nation of Islam; Tony King 1947-), actor; Shahrazad Ali (1954-), author; Jay Electronica (1976-), musician; Busta Rhymes (1972-), musician; Allah Mathematics (1972-), music producer; Carmelo Anthony (1984-), athlete; Erykah Badu (1971-), musician.

NOTABLE GROUPS

Though the Five-Percent Nation has never been a very large group, its influences are notable in music, especially rap and hip-hop music from the 1980s and 1990s. (Lingo, such as "word is bond," break it down," and "peace" are all slang terms found among the Five-Percent nation.) An offshoot of the Nation of Islam, the movement was founded by Clarence 13X (1928-1969). Its adherents believe all black men are Allah. They emphasize education, self-sustainability, and self-awareness among the black community. The name, Five-Percent Nation, comes from the division of people into three categories: the 85% of whom are ignorant of their true identity, 10% who are misled as to the true nature of Allah in the black man, and the resulting 5%, who are the only ones who know the truth. Women are referred to as Earths, or queens. Their teachings are known as Supreme Mathematics: a set of eight different lessons (Supreme Mathematics, Supreme Alphabets, Student Enrollment, English Lesson C-1, Lost-Found Muslim Lesson No. 1, Lost-Found Muslim Lesson No. 2, Actual Facts, and Solar Facts). Members are required to learn, and then share the information with others.

This organization claims to be "neither anti-white, nor pro-black." Instead, it is against institutions – those that keep its membership poor. As a result, there have been members of diverse races throughout its history. They have also served in peace-keeping activities between gangs in New York City.

The FBI had active investigation on the Five-Percent Nation starting in 1965, especially as it gained prominence in the Civil Rights Movement. The founder of the group was murdered in 1969.[15]

FACTS AND FIGURES

The founders of the Hebrew Israelite movement created their own modified version of the Hebrew language, which they believed was to be free from any sort of modern impurity or language contamination.[16]

OTHER IMPORTANT DEFINITIONS[17,18]

- **Camp**: The black Hebrew organization, or a specific street witnessing event.

- **Edom**: Also known as the Edomites or Esau, a play on the Biblical teaching of the twin brother of Jacob, believed by Black Hebrews to be the ancient ancestors of the Caucasian race.

- **Fruit of Islam**: The security force for the Nation of Islam.

- **Resurrection of the dead**: A concept in Black Muslim movements to refer to "mental resurrection;" the idea that blacks need a change in thinking, and therefore, they are to be resurrected first.

- **Satan**: Also called the white devil or blue-eyed devil. A reference to the white man.

- **"So-Called"**: A phrase used to instill doubt about a group's identity or identification. Because Black Hebrews believe they are the true descendants of Israel, they label Jewish communities as "so-called Jews."

- **Street Teaching**: Also called street units. Specific activities by which members read passages of scripture on the street corners or sidewalks to advertise their group. There is also the goal of bothering and stirring up people who pass by.

- **Synagogue of Satan**: Another term to express extreme antagonism to the Jewish community, seeing them as false Jews.

- **X**: The last name of many Nation of Islam followers, used in place of a legal last name. As legal last names are associated with slaveowners, the "X" represents that the black man has lost his identity in slavery and is uncertain of who he really is.

BELIEVER'S CHARACTERISTICS

Belief in black racial supremacy; teaching that the black race is the true descendants of the ancient Hebrews, or the true Muslims; a mixture of beliefs from Judaism, Christianity, or Islam, mixed with racial ideas; sexism; observance of Old Testament Biblical or modified Muslim holidays; conservative or African-style dress; emphasis on economic advancement for black individuals; focus on central leaders within Black identity movements; black sovereign citizens; modified use of Hebrew or Arabic language; combativeness; active street preaching; promotion of literature associated with such groups; hatred of whites; belief the white man is of the devil; association of the black man with a special position within society, whether it is racial supremacy or being a god; heavy group evangelism; violence; terrorism.

Buddhism

There is no need for temples; no need for complicated philosophies.
My brain and my heart are my temples; my philosophy is kindness.
(Tenzin Gyatso, The 14th Dalai Lama)[1]

Theology

Non-theistic belief system that denies any creator god, personal god, or divine eternal being. While Buddhists do believe there are divine beings or gods, they are long-living beings that are not creators, connected to creation, or eternal. These beings aren't specifically revered, nor part of prayer or homage. The decision to honor such beings is personal in nature. These beings are:

- **Buddhas**: Enlightened beings who fully comprehend the specific traditions of Buddhism known as the Four Noble Truths. Different Buddhist traditions revere different specified Buddhas, or individuals who, in their systematic understanding, have attained the place of awakening. These are viewed as enlightened beings.

- **Bodhisattvas**: Any being working toward full enlightenment (Buddhahood). Much like Buddhas, different Buddhist traditions revere specified Bodhisattvas, or individuals who, in their specified systems, are on the path of enlightenment.

- **Vidyaraja**: Known as the "Wisdom Kings," such are venerated beings honored in East Asian Buddhism and other Buddhist systems that focus on these beings. They are considered an expression of Buddha's compassion, depicted as aggressive or fierce to dispel negativity. There are five Wisdom Kings: Kongo-Yasha (Vajrayaksa), Fudo-Myo (Acala), Gosanze (Trailokyavijaya), Gundari (Kundali), and Daiitoku (Yamantaka).

- **Yidam**: Personal meditation deities that are specific manifestations of enlightenment. Buddhist practitioners focus on these deities while in meditation. Such deities are personal in form and may embody any form of a historical religious leader, different Buddhist figures, or any Buddha or Bodhisattva.

- **Fierce deities**: In Buddhism, fierce deities are not representative of demons or devils. Instead, they are an aggressive representation to dispel evil spirits. A fierce deity may manifest in any form, including a Buddha or Bodhisattvas. This is especially common in Tantric Buddhist systems.

- **Devas**: Divine beings that are not specifically wise or on a particular Buddhist path. They have very long lives and are not immune from pain, suffering, or discomfort. They have limited power and knowledge. Devas may or not have a physical form. Some Buddhist devas include Ganesha, Brahma, Sarasvati, Laksmi, Sakra, Hariti, Pattini, and Saman.

- **Asuras**: Enemies of the Devas that fight them in the spirit realm. They have been defeated by the Devas, as led by Sakra. Asuras are often associated with strong leadings, such as hatred.

- **Mara**: The word mara means "death" and refers to any being or group of beings who are seen as being antagonistic to Buddha, Dharma, and Sangha. Such dominate the "desire realm" (carnality).

- **Caturmaharajakayika devas**: Four heavenly kings who rule over the world. They are: Dhrtarastra (guardian of the east), Virudhaka (guardian of the south), Virupaksa (guardian of the west) and Vaisravana (guardian of the north).

- **Yaksha**: Nature spirits that take care of nature and the natural treasures found therein. They are mostly kind. The yakshas reside on earth under the Himalayan Mountains. They are ruled over by the lord of wealth, Kubera.

There are also several diverse spirits part of Buddhist mythology.[2]

PHILOSOPHY

Buddhism started with Gautama Buddha (480-400 BC), an Indian aristocrat who tired of the world and desired to find meaning for his life. Of particular interest was a way to end suffering. After several years of thought and meditation, he founded the Buddhist system as we understand it today. Buddhism centers on the principle that suffering is created by the different attachments we hold to the material world. If one seeks to end suffering, they must release and abandon all attachments in this life. One can attain the desired state of enlightenment by doing such, and thus releasing personal suffering. When one successfully ends suffering, they also end the cycle of death and rebirth through the ages (returning to this life repeatedly to resolve karma, or results of deeds, from former lives). When a Buddhist does such, they attain Buddhahood. The reward is Nirvana, a state of nothingness; the cycle of death and rebirth is broken. The Buddhist principles surrounding such are best explained in the Four Noble Truths:

- ***Dukkha* (Truth of Suffering)**: Suffering (*tanha*) is part of existence each time an individual is reborn into the world.

- ***Samudaya* (Origin of Suffering)**: The suffering of this world lies in one's attachment (sometimes described as a craving) to the material things of this world.

- **Nirodha (Extinction of Suffering)**: For one's suffering to end, an individual must eliminate their attachment and desire for the things present in this world.

- ***Marga* (Leading to the Extinction of Suffering)**: Also known as the Noble Eightfold Path, the way to end these cycles and thus end they cycle of death and rebirth.

Buddhist dharma wheel

The Noble Eightfold Path, also known as the *marga*, is found in eight divisions:

- **Right Mindedness**: Also called "right view," right mindfulness reminds Buddhists that actions have consequences. Death is not seen as the end of one's life. Because one can be reborn into this life again, the things one does and believes can have an impact on their next life.

- **Right Resolve**: The work of abandoning the world as one knows it in favor of following a religious path as a Buddhist monk or nun. One does this to completely renounce the world. Buddhist monks and nuns live void of any attachments, sensuality, desire, harm, and ill-will. In this state, Buddhists who pursue such seek active contemplation as they strip away any sense of suffering within themselves.

- **Right Speech**: Buddhists believe it essential to speak with kindness. They avoid what they consider to be crude or rude speech, lying, dishonesty, or anything that might cause damage to a relationship with another.

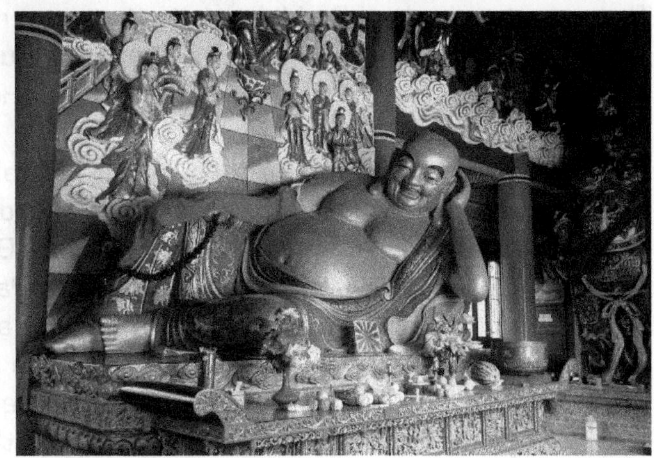

Happy Buddha statue

- **Right Action**: One should refrain from any form of killing, including insects or animals. Likewise, they are to refrain from theft or other behaviors, especially inappropriate sexual conduct.

- **Right Living**: Aiming to obtain one's livelihood in fashion that is in no way contrasting from Buddhist ideals. Buddhists who operate business or work for a living are not to profit from things that cause harm. This includes weapons, poisons, drugs, and alcohol.

- **Right Effort**: Restraint of one's senses, thereby helping to create a state of purity and wholesomeness rather than sensuality.

- **Right Attentiveness**: Making sure one is always conscious of whatever they are doing.

- **Right Concentration**: Practicing *dhyana* (meditation) as one aspires for total mindfulness and focus on enlightenment.

Buddhists believe they can achieve their desired goals by looking inward, as the answers they seek can be found within themselves. They do so through extensive meditation. Enlightenment comes from abandoning attachment to the material aspects of this world. To do so, adherents discipline themselves and focus on the principles of meditation. In meditation, one may focus on an object, a deity, a *koan* (a short, meditative saying part of Far East Buddhist meditation), or one's breathing or body rhythms.

ADHERENT IDENTITY

Buddhist, identity with one specific sect of Buddhism, such as Zen Buddhist, Tibetan Buddhist, or Ch'an Buddhist.

TRADITIONAL LANGUAGES

Pali, Sanskrit, Chinese, and Tibetan.

SECTS/DIVISIONS

There are hundreds of Buddhist sects that, as a rule, often all claim a similar staring place and then deviate into different systems in history. Buddhist sects also have influenced each other throughout history, with many overlaps in ideas. Here, we will highlight the major ones.[3,4]

- **Nikaya Buddhism**: The most ancient of all Buddhist systems and the most doctrinal. History teaches there have been nineteen different schools of Nikaya, with only Theravada Buddhism surviving to today. Theravada Buddhism (a descendant of the Tamrashatiya school) adheres to the Pali Canon, a Pali-language scriptural collection of Buddhist writings that form the most complete of all early Buddhist scriptural collections. These writings contain what's believed to be the authentic teachings of the Buddha (known as sutras). These were transcribed and preserved in the Sutta Pitaka. Theravada Buddhists emphasize looking inward for answers as they seek to attain Nirvana. Ch'an Buddhism is an example of Nikaya Buddhism.

- **Mahayana Buddhism**: Mahayana Buddhist systems do not exist for the establishment of doctrine, but the experience of wisdom obtained in distancing from knowledge that comes by theory or intellect. Rather than looking at Buddhist teaching as a religious doctrine,

Mahayana Buddhists see their teachings as guides. They also accept different Buddhist writings, known as the Mahayana sutras, from Chinese, Tibetan, and Sanskrit traditions. Zen Buddhism is an example of Mahayana Buddhism.

- **Vajrayana Buddhism**: A more esoteric strain of Buddhism that evolved in the Himalayas. There are four different schools of Vajrayana Buddhism: *Nyigma* (promoting absolute truth through personal purification; body, word, and mind); *Kagyu* (focuses on simplicity, the product of the Buddhist life, and transcending any concept that can be elaborated); *Sakya* (the "way of the fruit," aiming to produce results from Buddhist practice), and *Gelug* (best-known Tibetan Buddhism, as part of the system of the Lamas, or teaching system by which we recognize the Dalai Lama). Examples of such are Tibetan Buddhism, Mikkyo, Tantric Theravada, Nepalese Newar Buddhism, Indonesian Esoteric Buddhism, Chinese Esoteric Buddhism, and Philippine Esoteric Buddhism.

- **Modern Buddhism**: A general heading that encompasses modern interpretations of traditional Buddhist ideas. It is Buddhism has merged with western ideals as well as modern intellectual ideas. Examples of such are Humanistic Buddhism, Secular Buddhism, Navayana, Nichiren Buddhism (Soka Gakkai, Dobokai Movement), the Vipassana Movement, and the Triratna Buddhist Community.

- **Buddhist tantra**: Buddhism is, in its strictest definition, a simplified variation on Hindu ideas. Because of this, there are a few overlaps between Hinduism and Buddhism. Tantra is one of those overlaps, as an esoteric tradition found in both religious systems. It emerged somewhere around the fifth century. The word tantra literally means "loom" or "weave" and relates to the interwoven nature of different traditions into a practice or a text (compared to a weaving on a loom). Those who practice tantra apply it to every aspect of their lives: business, spirituality, and daily interactions. Tantra is often associated with sex but is far more than just a sexual practice. Tantra incorporates deity devotion, mantras, visualization and identification with a specified deity, initiation, esotericism, ritual mandalas, the status of women, and more. Tantric Buddhism is considered part of Vajrayana Buddhism.

- **Aleph cult (Aum Shinri Kyo)**: The Aleph cult is best known for the1995 Tokyo subway sarin attack. It is a Japanese doomsday cult founded in the mid-1980s by Shoko Asahara (1955-2018). It mixes Indian and Tibetan Buddhism with Hinduism, Christian millennialism, yoga, and Nostradamus' writings and predictions (while claiming to restore true Buddhism). Ashara claimed to be the only completely enlightened Buddhist master, naming himself Christ and the Lamb of God. Central was his prophecy of a third world war headed by the United States set to start in 1997. The

Aum Shinri Kyo logo

group caught media attention for refusing to allow members to leave, forcing donations and murder before attacking the Tokyo subway in 1995. The organization began producing sarin (a nerve agent) and nerve gas in 1993. In March 1995, Aum Shinri Kyo released their chemical weapons into the Tokyo subway, killing fourteen people, injuring fifty-four others, and affecting six thousand people. The group's leader and thirteen other members were arrested and sentenced to death. The group continues to the present day, living in compounds despite splintering. Today, they have around 1,500 members. Most recently, they were involved in Tokyo car attack in retaliation for the execution of its central leaders.[5]

NUMBER OF ADHERENTS

There are approximately 488,000,000 Buddhists worldwide. Most Buddhists are found in China, Japan, South Korea, and Vietnam.[6]

DISPUTES WITHIN GROUP

The different sects of Buddhism differ on accepted texts, the transmission of their traditions to the present day, variations on meditation, theology, and practices. The idea of lineage, location, and history of teaching orders also varies. As Buddhism retains the culture of its nation, each Buddhist sect adapts to the national culture of its surroundings. The ethics of Buddhism are also often in debate, as ethics of each nation often influence its teaching, wherever it may be. Like most other religious groups, Buddhists do not always agree about specified morals, ethics, or modern-day issues, such as same-sex marriage, contraception, modern politics, or abortion.

SCRIPTURES

There are over ten thousand Buddhist scriptures and writings. They are manuscripts first passed down as oral traditions among Buddhist monks. Different traditions adhere to different writings, all of which accentuate, expound upon, and enhance the teachings of their specific sect of Buddhism. The major types of Buddhist scripture include:

- **Sutras (buddhavacana)**: Discourses and teachings believed to be from the Buddha himself. They combine discussions, including explanations, analysis, speech, discussion of his life, exploits, and instructions. There are both long and short discourses. Some are numbered. In some traditions (such as Zen Buddhism) the sutras also include the teachings, sayings, or meditative practice instructions of the masters of their systems.

  "I have heard that on one occasion Ven. Ánanda was staying in Kosambi, at Ghosita's Park. Then the Brahman Unnabha went to where Ven. Ánanda was staying and on arrival greeted him courteously. After an exchange of friendly greetings and courtesies, he sat down to one side. As he was sitting there, he said to Ven. Ánanda: "Master Ánanda, what is the aim of this holy life lived under the contemplative Gotama?"

"Brahman, the holy life is lived under the Blessed One with the aim of abandoning desire."
"Is there a path, is there a practice, for the abandoning of that desire?"

"Yes, there is a path, there is a practice, for the abandoning of that desire."

"What is the path, the practice, for the abandoning of that desire?"

"Brahman, there is the case where a monk develops the base of power endowed with concentration founded on desire and the fabrications of exertion. He develops the base of power endowed with concentration founded on persistence... concentration founded on intent... concentration founded on discrimination and the fabrications of exertion. This, Brahman, is the path, this is the practice for the abandoning of that desire."

"If that's so, Master Ánanda, then it's an endless path, and not one with an end, for it's impossible that one could abandon desire by means of desire."

"In that case, Brahman, let me question you on this matter. Answer as you see fit. What do you think: Didn't you first have desire, thinking, 'I'll go to the park,' and then when you reached the park, wasn't that particular desire allayed?"

"Yes, sir."

"Didn't you first have persistence, thinking, 'I'll go to the park,' and then when you reached the park, wasn't that particular persistence allayed?"

"Yes, sir."

"Didn't you first have the intent, thinking, 'I'll go to the park,' and then when you reached the park, wasn't that particular intent allayed?"

"Yes, sir."

"Didn't you first have [an act of] discrimination, thinking, 'I'll go to the park,' and then when you reached the park, wasn't that particular act of discrimination allayed?"

"Yes, sir."

"So it is with an Arahant whose mental effluents are ended, who has reached fulfillment, done the task, laid down the burden, attained the true goal, totally destroyed the fetter of becoming, and who is released through right gnosis. Whatever desire he first had for the attainment of Arahantship, on attaining Arahantship that particular desire is allayed. Whatever persistence he first had for the attainment of Arahantship, on attaining Arahantship that particular persistence is allayed. Whatever intent he first had for the attainment of Arahantship, on attaining Arahantship that particular intent is allayed. Whatever discrimination he first had for the attainment of Arahantship, on attaining Arahantship that particular discrimination is allayed. So what do you think, Brahman? Is this an endless path, or one with an end?"

"You're right, Master Ánanda. This is a path with an end, and not an endless one. Magnificent, Master Ánanda! Magnificent! Just as if he were to place upright what was overturned, to reveal what was hidden, to show the way to one who was lost, or to carry a lamp into the dark so that those with eyes could see forms, in the same way has Master Ánanda – through many lines of reasoning – made the Dhamma clear. I go to Master Gotama for refuge, to the Dhamma, and to the Sangha of monks. May Master Ánanda remember me as a lay follower who has gone for refuge, from this day forward, for life."[7]

- **Vinaya**: Deals with the rule of monastic discipline for Buddhist monks and nuns as well as some doctrine, ritual text, biographies, and stories of the Buddha's birth.

  Discipline is for the sake of restraint, restraint for the sake of freedom from remorse, freedom from remorse for the sake of joy, joy for the sake of rapture, rapture for the sake of tranquility, tranquility for the sake of pleasure, pleasure for the sake of concentration, concentration for the sake of knowledge and vision of things as they have come to be, knowledge and vision of things as they have come to be for the sake of disenchantment, disenchantment for the sake of dispassion, dispassion for the sake of release, release for the sake of knowledge and vision of release, knowledge and vision of release for the sake of total unbinding through non-clinging.[8]

- **Adhidharma**: Scholastic summaries of the sutras, specifically their doctrine. They focus on *citta* (mind, consciousness), *cetasika* (mental factors, mentality*)*, *rupa* (material form), and *nibbana* (cesssation). As a controversial aspect of Buddhist scripture, not all schools accept *Adhidharma* as part of their texts.

  When, that he may attain to the Formless heavens, he cultivates the way thereto, and so, by passing wholly beyond all consciousness of form, by the dying out of the consciousness of sensory reaction, by turning the attention from any consciousness of the manifold, he enters into and abides in that rapt meditation which is accompanied by the consciousness of a sphere of unbounded space — even the Fourth Jhana, to gain which all sense of ease must have been put away, and all sense of ill must have been put away, and there must have been a dying out of the happiness and misery he was wont to feel — (the rapt meditation) which is imbued with disinterestedness, and where no ease is felt nor any ill, but only the perfect purity that comes of mindfulness and disinterestedness — then the contact, etc. . . . [cf. § 165] the balance that arises, these . . . are states that are good.[9]

- **Prajnaparamita**: The wisdom literature of Mahayana Buddhism.

  The Lord Buddha continued:-If any disciple were to say that the Tathagata, in his teachings, has constantly referred to himself, other selves, living beings, an Universal Self, what think you Subhuti? Would that disciple have understood the meaning of what I have been teaching?

  Subhuti replied: No Blessed Lord. That disciple would not have understood the meaning of the Lord's teachings. For when the Lord has referred to them he has never referred to their actual existence; he has only used the words as figures and symbols. It is only in that sense that they can be used, for conceptions, and ideas, and limited truths, and Dharmas have no more reality than have matter and phenomena.[10]

- **Shastras**: The precepts, rules, and specific manuals as scriptural or sutra commentary for the Mahayana Buddhist tradition.

- **Tantras**: The writings of Buddhist tantric traditions, found in Tibetan Buddhist literature. The Kanguyr (Tibetan Buddhist sacred texts) contains approximately 500 different tantras, all considered buddhavacana.

There are several other Buddhist writings of varying importance that serve as unique markers of different Buddhist sects. Some Buddhists also adopt writings from other traditions, including the Tao-te-King and other Shinto or Confucianist documents, teachings recognized as ethical or of interest from a broader religious scope, or writings deemed spiritual or of interest by an individual practitioner of Buddhism.

BASIC RELIGIOUS PRACTICES

As Buddhism centers around the detachment of the individual from the material world to end suffering, personal meditation offers the solution to attain enlightenment. Buddhists are encouraged to pursue the Noble Eightfold Path as they seek to overcome aggression, passions, and personal sufferings. Buddhism does not require its adherents to worship at a temple with others, but many do gather for group chants, meditation sessions, to hear instruction or teaching of the monks, listen to the monks chant scripture, and to meditate. While in temple, Buddhists typically sit on the floor, facing the statue or image of the Buddha.

Buddhist temples are found throughout the world. They reflect different styles of design, including the gold dome towers of Nepal and pagodas in the Far East. Every Buddhist temple contains symbols of the five elements of fire, air, earth (square base), water, and wisdom (pinnacle at the top). Another type of Buddhist structure is known as a *Stupa*, which is a stone building built over relics of the Buddha or copies of Buddhist teachings. The leader of a temple is called Master.

Most Buddhists have home altars, set up in a corner of a room or an entire room as a personal shrine. There are statues of Buddha, candles, and an incense burner, used for personal meditation and offering to the Buddha.

Buddhists are encouraged to do good works and live life in peace and harmony with nature and those around them. They are encouraged to look to good role models of enlightenment, have a practical mindset of enlightenment, and maintain the basic dignity of life.

HOLIDAYS

Buddhist holidays vary depending on the specific form, culture, and nation involved. There are also numerous Buddhist festivals, dependent on different Buddhist sects. The major Buddhist holidays include[11]:

- **Uposatga (Observance Day)**: Four holy days on the new moon, full moon, and quarter moon of each month; present to clear one's mind. Ancient tradition stemming all the way back to the Buddha himself.

- **Parinirvana Day (Nirvana Day)**: Celebration of the Buddha's death at age 80. Day is held in February, but the specific date varies, depending on Buddhist sect.

- **Magha Puja (Maka Bucha Day)**: Celebrates a gathering held between Buddha and 1,250 of his early disciples; reflects upon the monastic tradition present in Buddhism. Largely celebrated in Cambodia, Laos, Thailand, Sri Lanka, and Myanmar in February or March.

- **Avalokitesvara's Birthday**: Held on the full moon in March, it celebrates the ideals of Bodhisattvas of compassion. Held in Tibet and China.

- **Vesak**: The Buddha's birthday, usually held in May or June (depending on the lunar cycle). Called "Buddha's Birthday" in Japan and celebrated on April 8.

- **Abhidhamma Day**: Burmese tradition acknowledging the Buddha's trip to the Tushita Heaven to teach his mother the *Abhidhamma*. Usually celebrated in April.

- **Ploughing Festival**: Celebrating the Buddha's first moment of enlightenment, Buddhists take two oxen and have them pull a gold-painted plough. Girls dressed in white follow behind, sowing rice seeds. Usually held in May.

- **Asalha Puja Day (Dharma Day)**: The anniversary of the Buddha's first teaching, usually in July.

- **Kathina Ceremony**: A robing ceremony held at the end of the Vassa Retreat, a three-month long mandatory retreat from July to October (rainy season). New robes and other items are offered to the monks from the Buddhist faithful.

- **Festival of the Tooth**: A processional festival celebrating Buddha's tooth relic. Celebrated every August in Sri Lanka.

- **Madhu Purnima**: Commemoration of the Buddha's retreat into the Parileyya forest, aiming to reconcile the disputes of his disciples. Usually held in August or September.

- **Hungry Ghost Festival (Ulambana, Ancestor Day)**: Observed from the first to the fifteenth days of the eighth lunar month (usually held in October), upon completion of the Vassa Retreat. Celebrates the merits of monastics. The lay faithful make offerings on behalf of their ancestors, dedicating the good of the monks to those suffering in other spiritual realms.

- **Loy Krathong (Festival of the Floating Bowls)**: Thai tradition held on the full moon night of the twelfth lunar month (usually held around November), when the rivers and canals are fill of water. Bowls are made with leaves, candles and incense sticks, placed in the water, and sent floating away, as a representation of bad luck leaving the participants.

- **Elephant Festival**: A Buddhist discipling festival. It depicts the Buddha's illustration of a wild elephant harnessed to a domesticated elephant for training. New Buddhists are to be trained in special relationship with an older, more experienced Buddhists. Held on the third Saturday in November.

- **Bhodi Day**: The day when Buddha first experienced enlightenment. Celebrated in Mahayana traditions (Zen, Pureland Buddhist schools) in China, Korea, Japan, and Vietnam in December.

VISUAL SIGNS AND SYMBOLS

Buddha statue in Thailand

Statuary and pictures of the Buddha; aum (om) symbol; a bell (the symbol of the Buddha's voice); Bodhi fig leaf and tree (it is believed the Buddha first reached enlightenment while sitting under one); Enso (circle of enlightenment, appears to be a rough, hand-painted or drawn circle); incense; lotus wheel; mandala; lion; lotus flower; images of the Buddha; *mala* (recitation beads, used for meditation); a pearl (symbol of spiritual wealth); swastika (representative of peace and good luck; not represented counterclockwise as in Nazi Germany, but vertically up and down); vajra (a battle club used as a ritual object in connection with a bell); Sanskrit, Tibetan, and eastern writing; symbols representing balance; robed and bald monks and nuns.

CREEDS, BOOKS, AND LAWS

Buddhism is a non-credal religion. Instead, they abide by the concept of refuge. In Buddhism, taking refuge means one is going to do something or make something happen. Buddhists take refuge in a few ways:

- The Three Jewels, also called the "Triple Gem" or "Three Refuges." These are the Buddha, the Dharma (teachings expounded by Buddha) and the Sangha (monastic order of

Buddhism). This is where the idea of faith, or accumulating experience and reasoning, originates in Buddhism.

- Lay Buddhist devotees also take five precepts when they also take refugees. These are:
    - To refrain from killing
    - To refrain from stealing
    - To refrain from lying
    - To refrain from improper sexual conduct
    - To refrain from consuming intoxicants

Buddhists also respect the insights of their teachers and masters, although those are not classified as specified "law" or "creed." There is no central authority or governing body within Buddhism, although teachers are often considered mentors to their students. Buddhists believe it's important to promote good karma, as the deeds one does in this life will affect the outcome of the next.[12]

ECLECTIC BELIEFS

Unlike many religions, Buddhism does not have a strong family value at its center. There is no ideal family value or specified family model present within Buddhist belief or life. Buddhism is highly individualistic; it is about the individual's ability to detach from this world and focus on their own specified pursuit of enlightenment rather than developing family life. It is believed one can become more loving and more engaging with others (including family) if one becomes less attached and more enlightened.

As a rule, far eastern Buddhists (except for Japanese Buddhists) avoid eating all meat products (it is in violation of the prohibition against killing). Meat is also considered an intoxicant. Most Buddhist cuisine is vegetarian or vegan. In Theravada Buddhism, monks and nuns are fed by the generosity of others. They are expected to eat whatever is provided to them (even meat). They do avoid meat killed from those seeking alms and meat regarded as "impure" (snakes and dogs). These encourage vegetarianism whenever it is possible, also recognizing such might be impossible in a region due to climate or growing seasons. Many Buddhists avoid what are classified as "strong-smelling plants," such as garlic, onion, and leeks.

Central to their belief in the life cycle is rebirth, or the idea that one dies and is then reborn again into humanity after death. This cycle is known as *samsara* and is a painful point of suffering. Everything that happens to one in their current life is related to whatever happened to them in their past life, both things good and bad. This principle is known as karma, or the Buddhist law of cause and effect. There are six different realms of existence in Buddhism: three good (gods realm, hyman realm, and demi-god realm), and three bad (animal realm, hungry ghost realm, and hell realm). One's ultimate hope is to achieve the state of Nirvana through enlightenment. There, one enters into a place of *moksha* (liberation). Nirvana is a state of nothingness, a place where there is no self-identity or suffering; it is a place of total detachment. When one reaches nirvana, they no longer are reborn into the endless cycle of death, life, and rebirth.

Buddhism embraces a strict monastic tradition. Buddhist monastics can be any gender, both monks (*bhikku*) and nuns (*bhikshuni*). They are responsible for teaching, spreading, and preserving Buddha's teaching in this world. Monks and nuns also instruct and guide the Buddhist lay faithful. From the beginning, there have always been individuals who devoted themselves to disseminating Buddhist ideas, travelling together and living on the outskirts of society. After the Buddha's death, the tradition of communal monastic living became more popular among Buddhist monks and nuns. Specific traditions vary depending on sects of Buddhism, but most require monks and nuns to be celibate, live off alms or donations, and limit meal intakes. Robes are typically bright in color: deep red, orange, or saffron yellow. In the Far East, robes are darker in color and fully cover the body. Robes signify simplicity and detachment from material things. Buddhist monks and nuns shave their heads (tonsure) for the same reason; it symbolizes detachment from worldly things. The rule for Buddhist monks and nuns is the same, and in some instances, the two live together.

RELATIONS WITH NON-BUDDHISTS

Buddhists believe all paths can eventually lead to enlightenment. Such is not specific, nor exclusive, to Buddhism alone. As they also strive to peacefully exist with others, Buddhists are not against interfaith dialogue and believe all should work together for peace. Central Buddhist figures have met with secular and religious authorities alike, including numerous Roman Catholic popes, chief Rabbis, and Muslim leaders.

HOLY SITES

The most relevant places are those connected to the life of the Buddha himself. These are found in India and Nepal, specifically the Gangetic plains. Within this area is the birthplace of the Buddha (Lumbini), the site of his enlightenment (Bodh Gaya, now in the Mahabodhi Temple in Bihar, India), the place where Buddha first taught (Sarnath), and the place where Buddha died (Kusinagara).

In addition to these four sites, there are four other places where Buddha's followers reported miracles: The Place of the Twin miracle (showing the Buddha's ability to perform miracles) (Sravasti), The Place of subduing an angry elephant (Rajgir), the place of descending to earth after the Buddha's visit to heaven (Sankassa), and the place where Buddha received an offering of honey from a monkey (Vaishali).

Other famous Buddhist holy sites include the temple of Angkor Wat and the Silver Pagoda in Cambodia; the Four Sacred Mountains in China; Potala Palace, Mount Kailash, and Lame Manasarovar in Tibet; Kyoto in Japan; Maha Vihara in Malaysia; Sagaing Hill, Mandalay Hill, and Shwedagon Pagoda in Myanmar; Anuradhapura and Temple of the Tooth in Sri Lanka; Three Jewel Temples in Sourht Korea; Wat Phra Kawe and Phutthabat District in Thailand; Dau Pagoda in Vietnam; and City of Ten Thousand Buddhas in Talmage, California.[13]

NOTABLE FIGURES

Gautama Buddha (480-400 BC); Tenzin Gyatso (1935-), the fourteenth Dalai Lama; B. Allan

Wallace (1950-), author; Mark Epstein (1953-), psychotherapist; Anne Hopkins Aitken (1911-1994), Zen teacher; Joseph Goldstein (1944-), writer; Hank Johnson (1954-), politician; Thich Huyen Quang (1919-2008), activist; Belinda Carlisle (1958-), musician; Leonard Cohen (1934-2016), musician; Allen Ginsberg (1926-1997), writer; Jet Li (1963-), actor; Courtney Love (1964-), musician; Steven Seagal (1952-), actor; Tina Turner (1939-2023), musician; Kenneth Pai (1937-), writer; Sharon Stone (1958-), actress; Naomi Watts (1968-), actress; Marcia Wallace (1942-2013), actress; Oliver Stone (1946-), film director.

NOTABLE GROUPS

Soka Gakkai International is a Nichiren Buddhist movement rooted in the Mahayana Buddhist tradition. Founded in 1975 by Daisaku Ikeda (1928-), it incorporates Buddhist ideals through social interaction and practice. Adherents meet in small groups wherever they may be, often in members' homes. They take interest in public and political issues, such as environmental awareness, nuclear disarmament, aid and assistance in disaster situations, and interfaith dialogue. Culturally diverse and accessible, Soka Gakkai has a large body of celebrity members. There are approximately 12,000,000 members of Soka Gakkai International worldwide.[14]

FACTS AND FIGURES

Buddhists comprise approximately 7% of the world's population, but this figure is expected to drop to about 5% by 2060. Buddhists have lower fertility rates than other religious groups, and there is no anticipated mass conversion to Buddhism expected in the next fifty years. Half of the world's Buddhists are in China, where they are approximately 18% of the population.[15]

OTHER IMPORTANT DEFINITIONS

- ***Karuna***: Compassion.
- **Lama**: A spiritual teacher in Tibetan Buddhism.
- **Mantra**: A word, phrase, or statement either said, chanted, or repeated to aid one's focus in meditation.
- ***Metta Bhavana***: Specific meditation designed to inspire loving-kindness toward other people.
- ***Om mani padme hum***: The most common mantra in Buddhism that translates to mean, "Behold, the jewel in the lotus."
- ***Panna***: Wisdom.
- **Puja**: A Buddhist religious ceremony.

- **Prayer flag**: A cloth that contains images of the Buddha and any variation of 400 traditional mantras (in their original languages) that is hung outside, designed to carry the prayers present on the flag throughout the world through the wind. Prayer flags are typically brightly colored (green, blue, yellow, white, and red) and are never to touch the ground.

- **Prayer wheel**: A cylindrical wheel used in Buddhism to accumulate good karma and reduce negative karma. The wheel has a metal body that is embossed and mounted on a pin set with a handle that turns it in a circular motion. The embossed lettering on the outside contains a mantra in a Nepali language, which then "turns" when it is spun by the handle. It is believed that spinning the mantra has the same effect as saying or chanting those words.

- **Renunciation *(nekkhama)***: Giving up the ways of the world to pursue the ways of freedom from lust, craving, and desire.

- **Retreat**: A specified period of time by which an individual visits a Buddhist monastery and lives the same disciplines as a Buddhist monk or nun. Retreats may also be shorter and themed for something such as meditation, information, or education about Buddhist beliefs, lifestyle, or ways.

- ***Satori***: Zen term for enlightenment.

- **Three poisons**: Also called the Three Fires. The three major things that cause suffering and keep people in the continual cycle of death and rebirth. These are greed, hatred, and ignorance.

BELIEVER'S CHARACTERISTICS

Emphasis on meditation, enlightenment, and alleviating personal suffering; belief that enlightenment and centeredness are found within; self-focused; pacifism; emphasis on balance and harmony; withdrawing from the world, and the world's problems in search of enlightenment; belief in karma; seeking ultimate nirvana; belief in the cycles of death and rebirth; Buddhist holidays; spiritual evolution found in diverse places, including all major world religions; belief in spiritual healing energies, such as Reiki; emphasis on the Buddha; use of prayer flags, prayer wheels, mantras, or Buddhist meditation; other beliefs from other religions incorporated into Buddhist practices, including diverse eastern religions.

Chinese Christianity

We must have a spirit of power towards the enemy, a spirit of love towards men,
and a spirit of self-control towards ourselves.
(Watchman Nee)[1]

Theology

The landscape of Chinese Christianity is not one specific thing, although the majority of Chinese Christians do appear, at least in some semblance, to embrace Trinitarianism: the belief that God the Father, Jesus Christ the Son, and the Holy Spirit are three persons in one divine God, eternal and everlasting.

Outside of this immediate definition, there are smaller groups of Christians in China who embrace Oneness theology (the belief that God is one person and one being in three different manifestations); Unitarianism (the belief that God is one literal being, with Jesus Christ the Son, a created being subordinate to God, and the Holy Spirit, as an active, living force); the idea that their specified group leaders are incarnations of the divine; the idea of tritheism (belief that the Father, Son, and Holy Spirit are three separate gods), or other, smaller groups with eastern theological syncretism or theological merging between differing groups.

Philosophy

Chinese Christians identify with their specified denominations, typically falling into one of two categories: those that have government approval, and those that do not. Under the Chinese government, there are five recognized religious groups: Buddhism, Islam, Taoism, Catholicism, and Protestantism. Recognized church groups (Chinese Patriotic Catholic Church, the China Christian Council, and the Protestant Three-Self Church) are registered and approved by the government. Unrecognized church groups (house churches, sometimes called underground churches) often face harassment and eventual shutdown from and by governmental agencies.

Chinese Christians represent a diversity of traditions, with roots tracing back as early as the fourth, sixth, or eighth centuries. Due to persecutions under various emperors, Chinese Christianity has faced several ups and downs, creating its own unique image, ideals, and identity among Eastern Christian movements.

Christianity in China has long served as an agent of cultural change, standing as a cross-point of spiritual independence and government conflict. As a result, Chinese Christianity does not have its own specific philosophical establishment; it stands through its survival and its continually changing relationship with governmental authorities. While the world focuses on modern religious controls in China, government regulations on Chinese Christianity have existed since the dynastic eras. As a result, it is either a movement of conformity or one of conflict, depending on the specific sect at hand.[2,3]

Number of Adherents

Exact statistics on practitioners of Chinese Christianity are difficult to obtain. The Chinese government only considers baptized members of churches in state-sanctioned groups as legitimate practitioners. This means children, unbaptized individuals, and individuals who belong to unregistered groups are not included in membership counts. There are often individuals who attend both sanctioned and unsanctioned churches. Independent sources have released their own findings, but it's impossible to tell whether statistics are accurate, inflated, or non-representative.

According to the Chinese government, the government-sponsored Three-Self Church has approximately 20,000,000 members and the Chinese Patriotic Catholic Church has approximately 6,000,000 members. Independent sources have cited approximately 35,000,000 independent Chinese Protestant groups and 20,000 Orthodox Christians.[4]

Traditional Languages

Chinese; Korean.

Adherent Identity

Three-Self Patriotic Movement, Three-Self Church, Three-Self, Chinese Protestants, Chinese Christians, China Christian council, Chinese Patriotic Catholic Church, Chinese Catholics, Independent Churches, Independent Protestants, Shouters, Underground Christians, Orthodox Church in China, Chinese Orthodox Christians, Korean House Churches, House Churches, specified denominational affiliations (such as Chinese Pentecostal, Chinese Charismatic, Chinese Evangelical, etc.)

Sects/Divisions

With the independent house church movements, it is nearly impossible to identify every single movement in existence. Some probably, with their unique mix and isolation from the rest of the church outside of China, do not exist beyond their immediate congregations or regions. There are a few major recognized divisions that help us recognize the way Chinese Christianity has developed and now exists in modern times.

- **Three-Self Patriotic Movement** – Also known as the Three-Self Church, the Three-Self Patriotic Movement is one of three specified government recognized church entities in China. The Three-Self Patriotic Movement, along with the China Christian Council, represent Protestantism in the nation. It is "three-self" identifying it as self-governing, self-supporting (financial contributions are not received from churches in other nations), and self-propagation (it operates its own missionary work within the nation). The model for the church has its origins outside of China; it was first introduced in the 1870s by British and American missionaries working in the country. The method was formally drafted in 1892. It emphasized establishing Chinese leadership and unique Chinese worship methods within the denomination. After the Communist takeover, the Three-Self Church took measures to assure its patriotic allegiance to the new government, pledging anti-imperialism, anti-feudalism, and anti-bureaucratic capitalism. This established the government's involvement with the church, which remains to this day.

Headquarters of the China Christian Council and Three-Self Patriotic Movement, Shanghai, China

The denomination affirms most traditional Protestant Christian beliefs in the Apostles' and Nicene Creeds, use of the Bible, the Trinity, the sacrifice of Christ for sin, the work of the Holy Spirit as Comforter, Christ is the Head of the church, God is creator, and humanity is created in the image of God, and the return of Jesus Christ. A unique facet of the Three-Self Church is the belief that faith and works are one, and that a Christian must live out their lives for benefit of others. The Three-Self Church uses the *Chinese New Hymnal* and *Canaan Hymns* hymnal. Its official publication is *Tian Feng: The Magazine of the Protestant Churches in China*.[5]

- **China Christian Council**: Along with the Three-Self Patriotic Movement, the China Christian Council represents government-sanctioned Protestantism within the nation. It is considered an "umbrella organization," representing all Protestants in China. Its major works include theological education, Bible publication (the *Chinese Union Version*), hymnals (such as the *Chinese New Hymnal*), religious literature, and evangelization and pastoral work. Its best-known role is the promotion of a specific church order of worship, used in local churches. It is part of the World Council of Churches and maintains the Nanjing Union Theological Seminary.[6]

- **Chinese Patriotic Catholic Church**: The Chinese Patriotic Church represents government-sanctioned Catholicism within the nation. Established in 1957, it has a controversial relationship with the Vatican. Overall, the church is considered informally schismatic (such has never been declared officially), with individual bishops recognized as serving in communion with Rome. The church overall, however, is considered an agency of the Chinese government, thus placing it in conflict with the papacy.

The denomination presents a hodgepodge of older beliefs. Most notably, it rejects modern doctrinal changes after around 1950. The CPCA rejects the doctrine of the Assumption of the Blessed Virgin Mary, devotions to the Sacred Heart of Jesus, and the Second Vatican Council. The Tridentine Mass form in place prior to the Second Vatican Council was used until the 1980s. Priests and bishops are forbidden to speak against the Chinese government, even in the face of moral controversy, over issues such as contraception and abortion. There is question, therefore, as to the legitimacy of the Catholic Church in China and if it is a legitimate representation of Roman Catholic identity in the world at large. As a result, there are several "underground" Catholic assemblies that do not operate in accord with the Chinese Patriotic Catholic Church.[7]

- **Chinese Independent Churches (existing before 1949)**: No one knows how many independent Christian groups exist in China. Most of these churches are part of the "house church movement," forming after the Communist takeover in 1949. These groups are not authorized by the Chinese government. Groups forming prior to the Communist takeover had strong ties to western missionaries, who encouraged Chinese believers to practice principles of financial and spiritual independence. Most of these churches are Pentecostal or Evangelical in nature, merging their own unique ideas about independence and autonomy with western Christian ideals. Most are informal, small communities that focus on prayer, Bible study, and in some instances, spiritual gifts (especially speaking in tongues). Little is known about their status within China today, although some do have a presence outside the mainland. Such groups include Gospel of Grace Church (1881), Christian Tabernacle (1925), True Jesus Church (1917), Jesus Family (1921), and Church Assembly Hall (1922), known most infamously for its founders Watchman Nee (1903-1972), Zhou-An Lee, and Shang-Jie Song.

- **Shouters/Underground churches (post-1949)**: In China, there are an unknown number of independent churches existing without government approval "underground" (house churches). Most that identify as "underground" are underground Catholic Churches in allegiance with the Vatican, while independent house churches ("house gatherings") are identified with Protestantism. While illegal, groups of twenty-five or less are typically tolerated by the government. Most have Pentecostal characteristics and are associated with "shouting," or emotional fervor in worship (although not do such). The term originated with Watchman Nee's "local church" movement which took hit during the government's overthrow of all religious groups in 1950. Independent churches particularly faced persecution from the 1950s to the 1980s. Many believe underground churches form the majority of Chinese Christians today. These churches also have a presence outside of China, as well as embrace other churches of the east, especially those of Korea.

  Independent groups openly suppressed by the Chinese government include the Shouters, New Testament Church, Spirit Church, Mentuhui, All Ranges Church (Word of Life Church, the Born Again Movement), and Zhushenjiao.

- **Chinese Orthodox Church:** The autonomous Eastern Orthodox Church in China with roots in Russia, existing without governmental approval. Most members are Russian refugees, and a few thousand Chinese converts. Only three specific communities exist with regular services and clergy within the nation.[8]

- **Foreign Christian communities**: Groups meeting in hotels, local churches, or other public meeting facilities in large cities (such as Beijing) to provide religious engagement for foreign visitors. To participate in any such church, one must own a foreign passport.[9]

Disputes Within Group

The Chinese government proves to be the most powerful dispute among Chinese Christians. Its interference in religious practice means Christians have a powerful dividing point, depending on whether or not their group has governmental authorization. The groups themselves do vary, depending on denominational practice, much like Christian denominations also vary in other parts of the world. Pentecostal churches have doctrinal differences from Roman Catholics, independent Evangelicals vary from more mainline Protestants, and in the uniqueness that is Chinese Christianity, the insistence on independence has created their own unique traditions, often varying from the rest of the world. Still, some Chinese Christians practice their own forms of syncretism, incorporating traditional Chinese ancestral worship and spiritism within their spiritual practice.

The Nestorian Stele (in both Chinese and Syriac) from the Tang era (781) documenting one hundred and fifty years of Christianity in China.

Scriptures

The Bible (standard 66 book Protestant version) is legally printed in China. It is only available at specified booksellers and through the Three-Self Patriotic Church. Protestants use the Chinese Union Version, first published in 1919. Its most recent revision was approved by the Chinese government in 2010. Other Chinese translations include Today's Chinese Version, Chinese New Version, and the Chinese Contemporary Bible; however, only Today's Chinese Version was ever printed in China, under the auspices of the Chinese government.

Translating the Bible into Chinese was not part of Catholic missions. The first Catholic Chinese Bible was not published in a singular volume until 1968. There have been three Chinese Orthodox New Testaments produced since 1864, with the most prevalent one completed in 1910.

Since 2019, the Chinese government has launched a reeducation effort to encourage Bible interpretation in light of Chinese culture. This includes understanding the Bible through Taoist,

Confucianist and Buddhist concepts, seeing the Bible through Chinese characters and cultural reflections, and seeing one's Christian beliefs through a Chinese lens. Whether or not the government is calling for a new translation of the Bible in Chinese is of debate.[10,11]

BASIC RELIGIOUS PRACTICES

Chinese Christianity centers heavily around the concept of living one's faith. It must be applied through works rather than being a musing of belief. Values of independence, self-reliance, and refusing to accept identity and help from outside sources are considered primary. Believers are expected to exemplify these specified Christian values in their everyday lives, with a heavy focus on duty and responsibility to family, society, and the state. Proselytizing is only allowed in public and private venues by state-approved organizations.

Chinese Christians worship at state-approved churches or in small gatherings in homes or public facilities around the country. Worship is typically on Sundays, but there are small groups that observe the Saturday Sabbath. Services involve public reading of Scripture, some preaching or life application, and the singing of hymns.

HOLIDAYS

The Chinese government restricts western-style holiday observances. As a result, some Christians in China do observe western holidays such as Christmas and Easter but do so with several restrictions. Christian holidays are seen as religious holidays, often marked with religious services, social get-togethers, and limited gift giving. It is also very common for Chinese Christians to forego religious holidays.[12]

VISUAL SIGNS AND SYMBOLS

Chinese national flag; cross; Chinese Bible; Chinese characters.

CREEDS, BOOKS, AND LAWS

The diversity of Chinese Christianity creates a plurality of beliefs among its adherents. The Three-Self Patriotic Movement adheres to the following Confession of Faith:

> *The Chinese Church takes the contents of the entire Bible, the Apostles' Creed and the Nicene Creed as the foundation of our faith, the main points of which are as follows:*
>
> *Ours is a Triune God, everlasting and eternal.*
>
> *God is Spirit. God is loving, just, holy, and trustworthy. God is almighty Father, the Lord who creates and sustains the cosmos and all that is in it, who keeps and cares for the whole world.*
>
> *Jesus Christ is the only Son of God, born of the Holy Spirit, the Word made flesh, wholly God and wholly human. He came into the world to save humankind, to witness to God the Father, to preach*

the gospel; he was crucified, died, and was buried. He rose again and ascended into heaven. He will come again to judge the world.

The Holy Spirit is the Comforter, who enables people to know their sinfulness and to repent, who bestows wisdom and ability and every grace, leading us to know God and to enter into the truth, enabling people to live holy lives, and to give beautiful witness to Christ.

The church is the body of Christ and Christ is its Head. The church is apostolic, one, holy, and catholic. The visible church is called by God to be a fellowship of those who believe in Jesus Christ. It was established by the apostles as Jesus instructed them. The mission of the church is to preach the gospel, to administer the Sacraments, to teach and nurture believers, to do good works, and to bear witness to the Lord. The church is both universal and particular. The Chinese Church must build itself up in love and be one in Christ.

The Bible has been revealed by God and written down by human beings through the inspiration of the Holy Spirit. The Bible is the highest authority in matters of faith and the standard of life for believers. Through the leading of the Holy Spirit, people in different times have gained new light in the Bible. The Bible should be interpreted in accordance with the principle of rightly explaining the word of truth. It should not be interpreted arbitrarily or out of context.

Human beings are made in the image of God, but cannot become gods. God has given humanity dominion over all God's creation. Because of sin, human beings have diminished God's glory, yet through faith and the grace of Jesus Christ, human beings are redeemed and saved, and are granted resurrection and everlasting life.

Christ will come again. According to the teachings of the Bible, no one knows the day of his coming, and any method to determine when Christ will come again violates the teachings of the Bible.

A Christian's faith and works are one. Christians must live out Christ in the world, glorifying God and benefiting people.[13]

Similarly, the Chinese Patriotic Catholic Association would also adhere to the Apostles' Creed and Nicene Creed, as well as the traditions of the Catholic Church up until around 1957. Beliefs of Catholic laws and governance after that point do vary.

Legally, churches in China are governed by the Communist party rather than by themselves. The major exception to such is the independent/underground churches, most of which are autonomous in governance due to the restrictions inflicted by political dissidence. While some may have origins or allegiances to churches in other parts of the world (such as the Vatican or American denominations), circumstances prevent contact or governance outside of the group.

ECLECTIC BELIEFS

Christians in China are expected to maintain the views of the Chinese regime. It is understood they will, in proclaiming allegiance to the state, agree with and uphold the beliefs of the state as part of their faith. Publicly, Christians in China are for the government's policies, including Chinese Communism, abortion, required birth control or sterilization policies, anti-evangelism, and the idea of a state-run church. Given the diversity of beliefs present in independent and underground churches, it's evident this expectation is probably not always met, although public dissidence is, most likely, not a thing.

Relations with Non-Chinese Christian church groups

Due to the government's restrictions, Christians in China are limited in their contact with Christians outside of their immediate local or state churches. While the government acknowledges five religions, we've established are other groups in existence within the nation. State involvement with religious practice alters one's relationship with other religious groups, and as things such as evangelism are either limited or prohibited. As a result, religious practice in China is a complicated experience for a practitioner of any theological belief.

China has one of the largest populations of religious prisoners worldwide, and many groups do face persecution of varying sources by governing authorities, especially those who are outside of state-supervised denominations.[14]

Holy Sites

Haidian Christian Church (Three-Self Patriotic Movement), Beijing, China; Saint Sophia Cathedral (former Russian Orthodox), Harbin City, China; St. Joseph Cathedral (Roman Catholic), Tanjin, China; Kuanjie Protestant Church (Three-Self Patriotic Movement), Beijing, China.

Notable Figures

Procession on Palm Sunday, a Tang Dynasty-era painting found on a church wall in Khocho, China

Ding Limei (1871-1936), Christian Presbyterian minister; Shi Meiyu (1873-1954), missionary doctor; Basil Shuang (1888-1962), last Chinese Orthodox bishop of Beijing; Bing Xin (1900-1999), writer; Lizzie Yu "Princess" Der Ling (1881-1944), first-lady in waiting for Empress Cixi and Hanjun bannerwoman; Charles K. Kao Kuen (1933-2018), electrical engineer and physicist; John Ching Hsiung Wu (1899-1986), jurist and author; Candida Xu (1607-1680), the "Apostle of China;" Zeng Xueming (1905-1991), midwife and wife of Vietnamese leader Ho Chi Minh; Leanne Li Yanan (1984-), actress; Lin Yutang (1895-1976), author; Zhang Zhan (1983-), citizen journalist; Zhang Yuning (1997-), athlete; Yao Chen (1979-), actress; Miyuki Hatoyama (1943-), wife of the former Prime Minister of Japan; Liu Zhenying (Brother Yun) (1958-), exiled Chinese Christian house church leader; Anthony Liu Bainian (1934-), honorary chairman of the Chinese Catholic Patriotic Association; Zhao Xiao (1967-), Chinese economist; Peter Xu (1940-), founder of the Born Again Movement Chinese house church group; William Hung (1893-1980), historian and sinologist; Bob Fu (1968-

), founder, China Aid; Watchman Nee (1903-1972), author and church leader.

NOTABLE GROUPS

The China Gospel Fellowship (also called the Tanghe Fellowship) is one of the largest house church networks found in Henan, China. It is an evangelical Christian group formed in the 1980s, most likely one of the largest Protestant denominational bodies in the world today.

It is best-known for the 2002 kidnapping of thirty-four of its top leaders by the Eastern Lightning cult. All leaders were released, only for more than one hundred of its leaders to be arrested in a government raid against unregistered church groups two years later. From what we do know, relationship with the China Gospel Fellowship and the Communist government has improved since the kidnappings and raids, and they are not currently pursued by the authorities.[15,16,17,18]

FACTS AND FIGURES

It is difficult to ascertain specific statistics on Chinese Christian groups. Numbers coming in from the Chinese government are inaccurate and numbers from western Christian groups are often inflated. Due to circumstances, it is hard to confirm or deny the statistics provided.

OTHER IMPORTANT DEFINITIONS[19]

- *Dōng zhèng jiào:* Eastern Orthodoxy.
- *Jī dū jiào:* Term for Christianity, means "Christ religion."
- *Jīdū jiào xīn jiào:* Term form Protestantism, means "Christ religion's new religion."
- *Jīdū tú:* Christ followers/believers.
- *Shangdi:* Term for God, means "the highest emperor." Frequently used by Protestants and non-Christians.
- *Tianzhu:* Term for God, means "Lord of Heaven." Frequently used by Catholics.
- *Tiānzhǔ jiào:* Term for Chinese Catholicism, means "Heavenly Lord religion."
- *Shen:* Term for God, used by Protestants; traditionally used to refer to the gods or the powers of nature.

BELIEVER'S CHARACTERISTICS

Christian belief modified through the lens of Chinese Communism; mixture of state and home churches; mixture of state beliefs incorporated within Christian understanding; Emphasis on Chinese culture as reflecting the understanding and belief of Christianity; Independence; spiritual autonomy; emphasis on works and personal duty; syncretism with traditional Chinese religions.

Christian Identity Movement

Spreading a message of faith, truth and hope to the Adamic Nations of the World.
(From the Church of Jesus Christ-Christian website)[1]

Theology

Belief that Yahweh (or YHVH), as the proper name for the God of the Bible, stands omnipotent, omnipresent, unchangeable, and omniscient; manifested in three beings of God the Father, God the Son, and God the Holy Spirit (or in some instances, a divine monarchist view by which the Godhead is unique to the Father and the Son, with the Son always subordinate to the Father). Focusing on Hebrew names for the divine and for figures such as Jesus Christ, the movement has theological influence from the Sacred Name Movement.

The Christian Identity Movement believes Adam, the first man in the Bible, was the father not of humanity, but exclusively of the white race. He was created as a son of the divine, made in the likeness of their god. His descendants are also the children of god. All other races existed prior to Adam, thus designating them as inferior "mud races." Adam is the start of a higher race of individuals who are not just body and soul, but also a divinely implanted spirit that distinguishes him from other races. Throughout the ages, the established special group is a "higher race," separate from lower ones, now chosen and elect to create a special and unique theocratic kingdom. This particular lineage is, therefore, the only one chosen by the divine, seen as the true lineage, true Israel, and only group that can know of their god. All major figures in the Bible are believed to be of the white race, including Adam, Noah, Moses, David, Solomon, Jesus, the twelve apostles, and the apostle Paul.

The Christian Identity Movement adheres to an idea that Yahshua the Messiah (Jesus Christ) is the Savior only of true Israel, which consists exclusively of the white race. They are the only beings on earth who can be saved, as the new covenant was made with the same individuals as the original covenant: the white race. Today, they see the white, Anglo-Saxon, Germanic, and other groups as the literal children of Israel, those who fulfill the specified details of Biblical prophecy and history, especially in retaining the blessings, promises, covenants, and prophecies. They are also known as "Christian nations" or "Aryan nations" and are seen as superior to all other races and nations of people on earth. The various 12 tribes are linked to specific European nations: Dan (Denmark), Gad (Italy), Asher (Sweden), Issachar (Finland), Simeon (Spain), Zebulun (France), Naphtali (Norway), Benjamin (Iceland), Reuben (the Netherlands), Judah (Germany), Ephraim (Great Britain), and Manasseh (United States).

Among many, Anglo-Saxons are seen exclusively as the true Israelites, the true chosen people, established to reign until the return of Christ (thus excluding other nations that may be mentioned above). This is due to a claim that the Davidic line can be traced through the royal lineage of Britain; thus, they believe the British monarchy is the throne of King David.[2]

The adherents of Christian Identity believe in what is called "Two House theology," which asserts there is a distinction between the Tribe of Judah and the other ten lost tribes of Israel. Unlike many adherents of this position, the Christian Identity Movement denies the tribe of Judah ever consisted of Jewish people (many consider them to be descendants of Cain and descendants of Satan), and instead believes that white Europeans (especially those from Scotland and Germany) are from the tribe of Judah, along with those nations that compose the House of Israel (other Anglo-Saxon, Germanic, Celtic, Nordic, and other nations). The unity of the 12 Tribes of Israel is found in the United States, standing as a prophetic ensign to reunite all gathered tribes in one nation.

Christian Identity adherents believe in strict racial separation and an expressed need to maintain the purity of what is called the white race, believing it to be the true spiritual race of humanity and the superior race. More than just a social prejudice, individuals in the Christian Identity Movement see their racial views as the preservation of theological belief.[3]

Philosophy

The Christian Identity Movement is what we could define as a theological endorsement of racism, anti-Semitism, and white supremacy. Its foundational ideas emerged in the United States as an offshoot of British Israelism, which holds to similar viewpoints (with the exception that original British Israelites supported Zionism and believed Jews were from the tribe of Judah; only the other ten lost tribes were of Anglo-Saxon descent). As a more extreme form, it emerged in the 1920s and 1930s (as an overlap to a national revival of the Ku Klux Klan), promoting the idea that the Bible makes a separation between lower and higher races: Aryans hold position as the highest race of mankind, the only one made in the image of YHVH. Non-whites do not have the spirit of YHVH alive within them, thus they believe they cannot be saved. Jews are believed to be the product of Cain's offspring, resulting as a genetic hybrid race. This hybrid originates with Eve's sexual union with the serpent, introducing the "fall of mankind." Christian Identity adherents believe the "fruit" with which Satan tempted Eve in the Garden of Eden was not physical fruit, but sex. Eve succumbed to the temptation, and the result was Cain. Therefore, Jews are considered the genetic offspring of Satan. This is known as the "Serpent Seed" doctrine.

The teachings of the movement forge a unique interpretation of the Bible. There is no evidence to bespeak any of its foundational theories of identity or interpretations. It is in its basic mix British Israelism, Sacred Name, white supremacy, and Nazi ideals, symbols, and customs, all mixed together. The Christian Identity Movement has woven a complicated narrative that could be described as a radical form of Calvinism; it takes the idea of a saved elect to an extreme level: that of uber-racism, deduced through a radical Bible interpretation, not shared by anyone else.

Christian Identity goals include the creation of an all-white state (often to exist in the Pacific Northwest corner of the United States, where members are encouraged to relocate), the propagation of the white race, and the preservation of this race, as it is the only one preserving the legacy of YHVH. Interracial relationships are strictly prohibited. Christian Identity adherents do not utilize marriage or driver's licenses, reject government interference, believe Jews control the government and financial institutions, distrust the media (believing it is Jewish controlled), believe the Holocaust was a hoax, are anti-abortion (many have been involved in the murder of abortion doctors or clinic attacks), and refuse to submit to societal authority. They often adhere to and spawn several conspiracy theories, refuse to pay taxes, and reject the social security system (believing it enslaves citizens). They prohibit feminist ideology (preferring a regulated role for women as mothers, the "guardians" of the white race) and both homosexuality and the queer community at large.

The Christian Identity Movement, as a movement, does not have any specified centralized authority. It is practiced by independent congregations, prison gangs, and individuals across the United States. There are some slight variations in understanding, but as a rule, the Christian Identity Movement is largely united in its basic doctrine and outlook. It is the religious branch of the Aryan Nations.[4]

ADHERENT IDENTITY

Christian Identity, white supremacist, white supremacism, Aryan Nations, racialists, neo-Confederates, racists, neo-Nazi, Aryan Youth, Aryan Brotherhood, Kinism, knights, white Israelites, Israel.

NUMBER OF ADHERENTS

Exact numbers of the Christian Identity Movement are hard to calculate. Estimates are as low as 2,000 members and as high as 50,000 members. In the United States and parts of western Europe, the movement is on the rise.[5,6]

TRADITIONAL LANGUAGES

English.

SECTS/DIVISIONS

There are several different headings for the Christian Identity Movement, all of which espouse its views. While there are slight differences, the movement is amazingly united on its points. The major difference between Christian Identity groups is the issue of force and violence in practice. Examples include:

Aryan Nations emblem

- **Church of Jesus Christ-Christian, Aryan Nations**: Founded by Wesley Swift (1913-1970) (a former Methodist minister and Ku Klux Klan leader) in 1946, the Church of Jesus Christ-Christian is a forerunner of religious groups forming within the Christian Identity Movement. Members must be able to prove white heritage and commit to the white race as part of membership. Most know the divisions of the church, such as the Aryan Nations. The Aryan Nations are a white supremacist, anti-Semitic, neo-Nazi organization, standing as a nationwide terrorist organization within the United States. After a series of lawsuits, losing their headquarters to a humanitarian organization (after attacking two people), and the reveal of several illegal activities, the Aryan Nations filed for bankruptcy. Not long after, their long-term leader, Richard Butler (1918-2004), died. Today, there are three main divisions of the Aryan Nations: one headquartered in Ulysses, Pennsylvania; one in Union City, Tennessee; and the Aryan Nations Revival, now in cooperation with another Aryan Nations group. The Aryan Nations are best known for their prison gangs (known as the Aryan Brotherhood and its subdivisions) and for their neo-Nazi activities, many of which have become violent. Today, the Church of Jesus Christ-Christian is headed by a board of three men, one of whom stands as a senior pastor of the group.

- **Church of Israel**: The Mormon restorationist branch of the Christian Identity Movement. Established in 1972 by Dan Gayman, this movement broke away from Church of Christ at Zion's Retreat, an independent breakaway sect of the Latter-day Saint movement. The church emerged as a hostile takeover on the part of Gayman, and later became its own church, separating in 1981. This group adheres to little of its Mormon roots, except for its highly survivalist and isolated settings for the church's practice, headquarters, and adherents. Adherents distrust the government, discourage the use of medical services and vaccines (it believes such are associated with Jews), home births, refusal of social security numbers, driver's licenses, and marriage licenses; and are adherents of the serpent seed doctrine. Members observe closed communion (on the feasts of Passover and Atonement), the seventh-day Sabbath and the Old Testament Biblical feasts (Passover, Unleavened Bread, Pentecost, Feast of Trumpets, and Day of Atonement). They use the *Book of Common Prayer* in worship. Their publishing branch is known as Watchman Outreach.[7]

Church of Israel logo

- **Kingdom Identity Ministries**: Founded by Mike Hallimore (1946-2021) in the 1980s, Kingdom Identity Ministries is the copyright holder of Wesley Swift's and Bertrand Comparet's writings. Self-identified as a "politically incorrect Christian Identity outreach ministry to God's chosen race, true Israel, the White, European peoples." Doctrine includes the coming judgment day shall manifest as a race war, serpent seed doctrine, and the death penalty for idolatry, homosexuality, blasphemy, and abortion. The work was largely run by Hallimore himself, on a large property in Harrison, Arkansas. Since his death, matters are handled by Chip Lamkin. Most of the

Kingdom Identity Ministries logo

ministry's production is publishing, especially works authored by the early founders of the Christian Identity Movement. The organization also distributes general white supremacist literature.[8]

- **Media ministries**: The Christian Identity Movement (and white supremacy in general) have gained substantial followings in modern times with the advance of the internet. While many groups are no longer current or embrace an online presence, others do, using the internet as a forum to connect other members of the movement together and to promote their views in the hopes of gaining new members. Such groups promote podcasts, publish research believed to support Christian Identity beliefs, operate their own record labels promoting white supremacist heavy metal music, anti-government conspiracies, and their views on gender, homosexuality, abortion, and race. Such groups include Christogenea, Divine International Church of the Web, and Euro Folk Radio.

- **Independent groups**: There are a small number of white supremacist churches that are not formally connected with any of the main ministries, but still uphold the same beliefs and concepts. Most operate publishing houses or small bookstores that promote Christian Identity and supremacist literature. Such include Christian Revival Center, Covenant People's Ministry, Fellowship of God's Covenant People, Our Place Fellowship, Sacred Truth Publishing & Ministries, and LaPorte Church of Christ (publisher: Scriptures for America Worldwide Ministries).[9]

- **Sovereign Citizens**: A complicated blend of white supremacy and conspiracy theory, The Sovereign Citizens movement dates back to the Posse Comitatus, a Christian Identity and white supremacist group popular in the Midwest in the 1970s and 1980s. The group believes Jews are working behind the scenes to manipulate the government and control the banking system. Participating in such supports the so-called agenda for Jews to control the world. To be a sovereign citizen, one must be white (even though there are African American sovereign citizens today, they are not regarded as legitimate and are often unaware of the history of the movement), as the fourteenth amendment to the constitution (guaranteeing citizenship to anyone born on US soil) is believed to have made African Americans permanently subject to federal and state law. Sovereign Citizens believe the original government, established with the founding fathers, was based on "common law." At some point in history, this common law government was replaced with a new governmental system based on sea and international commerce (admiralty law). There are two popular theories on how this change occurred: some attribute it to the Civil War, while others believe it happened when the US abandoned the gold standard in 1933. Sovereign Citizens believe they were free men under common law, but slaves under this new admiralty law. They also believe there are secret government forces that desire to enslave all of society. Now, sovereign citizens

Richard Butler (1918-2004)

believe the government has pledged its citizens as a federal, financial "collateral," and the sale of Americans begins at birth, with an application for a birth certificate and social security card. Through these, the government creates a secret, corporate treasury account in the baby's name (amounts range from $600,000 to $20,000,000). They then believe that the use of all capital letters on official documents creates a "straw man" identity, while names printed with upper and lowercase letters are the real flesh-and-blood identity of the individual. The belief, is therefore, that a true, white sovereign citizen must devoid themselves of their "straw man" corporate identity (a process known as redemption) and live and abide only by common law, rather than admiralty law. They reject social security cards, registration of car vehicles, driver's licenses, zip codes, firearms regulations, and refuse to pay income taxes. They believe they cannot be tried for crimes where there is no victim (such as in zoning or licensure violations) and are subject only to common law courts. They do not consider themselves citizens of the United States, but as non-resident aliens. None of the conspiracy theories or ideas present within this movement hold any evidence to substantiate such claims. Most sovereign citizens operate independently, although small groups have formed over the years. Such groups include the Montana Freemen, the redemption movement, the Christian Patriot movement, the tax protester movement, Embassy of Heaven, Guardians of the Free Republics, and the Patriot movement. Many militia organizations within the United States are also part of the sovereign citizens movement.[10,11]

- **Individual practitioners**: There are several white supremacists practicing the values and ideas of the Christian Identity Movement on their own, without the influence of a larger group. These individuals may practice and espouse the beliefs in prison or as free people, gathering in home meetings or home churches, family associations, or as a lifestyle, in a rural setting, often owning large plots of land on the outskirts of small communities. Many practice home births, reject vaccines and medical assistance, homeschool their children, and distrust the government, banking and financial institutions, and public-school systems. They are against racial integration, interracial marriage, and are awaiting what they perceive to be an inevitable Armageddon race war. They may identify politically and socially as neo-Nazis, white supremacists, Skinheads, American Nazis, separatists, Aryans, or as part of the Aryan Nations.

Disputes Within Group

Wesley Swift (1913-1970)

The Christian Identity Movement struggles most notably with its inclusion of non-Christian white supremacists in its embrace. There are a limited number of Christian Identity groups that are now inclusive of neo-pagans, atheists, and other religions deemed part of "white" society. Christian Identity adherents also disagree over the use of violence and militant force in promotion of their message and agenda. Over the past several years, several governmental stand-offs, federal bombings, and attacks on abortion doctors and clinics have been connected to Christian Identity practitioners. Many in the movement desire to disassociate with such obvious violence, considering the separation of the races and distance from general society to be the solution.

SCRIPTURES

The Christian Identity Movement uses the Holy Bible, Old and New Testaments: the Pentateuch (Genesis, Exodus, Leviticus, Numbers, and Deuteronomy), Historical books (Joshua, Judges, Ruth, 1 Samuel, 2 Samuel, 1 Kings, 2 Kings, 1 Chronicles, 2 Chronicles, Ezra, Nehemiah, Esther), Wisdom books (Job, Psalms, Proverbs, Ecclesiastes, Song of Songs), Prophetic books (Isaiah, Jeremiah, Lamentations, Ezekiel, Daniel, Hosea, Joel, Amos, Obadiah, Jonah, Micah, Nahum, Habakkuk, Zephaniah, Haggai, Zechariah, Malachi), the Gospels (Matthew, Mark, Luke, John), the Acts of the Apostles, the Pauline Epistles (Romans, 1 Corinthians, 2 Corinthians, Galatians, Ephesians, Philippians, Colossians, 1 Thessalonians, 2 Thessalonians, 1 Timothy, 2 Timothy, Titus, Philemon, Hebrews) the General Epistles (James, 1 Peter, 2 Peter, 1 John, 2 John, 3 John, Jude) and Revelation. The movement upholds the inspiration and infallibility of Scripture, as do many groups; the issue is not the belief in the Bible, but the interpretation of it. Christian Identity groups read the Bible through a pseudoarcheological lens, seeing the scriptures as a validation for white supremacy when such is not factual.

Most of the Christian Identity Movement would fall into the category of King James Only adherents, believing the King James translation of the Bible to be the only Bible translation in existence that is correct and accurate in its entirety. Believing more than the translation is preferred, they would say the translation itself is infallible, rejecting all others as inferior. There are exceptions to this idea, however. Some Christian Identity groups uphold and reprint rare or hard-to-find translations of the Bible that are believed to somehow enhance or support their views, such as The Holy Bible in Modern English (Ferrar Fenton translation), the Geneva Bible, The Emphasized Bible (Rotherham), and The Septuagint Bible (Charles Thomson translation). Many publish and promote the writings of the Deuterocanonical apocrypha and other apocryphal books, such as The Book of Jasher, the Book of Enoch, and the Lost Chapter of the Acts of the Apostles.

In their unique interpretation of the Bible, the Christian Identity Movement also lauds the writings of its founders as essential in understanding. They are not considered inspired, but important in the interpretation and narration of scripture. Prominent writers include William Dudley Pelley (1890-1965), Wesley Swift, Bertrand Comparet (1901-1983), Howard Rand (1889-1991), Richard Butler, William Potter Gale (1916-1988), William Pierce (1933-2002), James K. Warner (1917-1979) Peter J. Peters (1946-2011), and Sheldon Emry (1926-1985).

> *I advocated the preservation of the white race, whatever it takes to preserve it. The white race is the most endangered species on the face of the earth.*[12]

> *I want to review in a general way the subjects discussed in the Bible, and note into which class each falls—"economic", "political", or "religious"—all in the same book. On the authority of that book, the Bible, this program takes its stand, and we will not deviate therefrom. Now let's see what*

authority we have for this broad coverage.

Let's start with Moses. The Book of Genesis introduces us to our God, and to that extent it is religious. But it also contains God's promises to Abraham, Isaac and Jacob, ancestors of the Anglo-Saxon race, that these people would become great nations, a blessing to all the earth; that they shall control the great gateways of the earth; that other nations shalt bow down before us; that we shall be blessed with all good things, or as we say today, the "have" nations. These promises are economic and political.[13]

Arise and fight! If a Jew comes near you, run a sword through him.[14]

You know, the media and the politicians would have us believe that there's something inherently immoral about terrorism. That is, they would have us believe that it's not immoral for us to destroy a pharmaceutical factory in Sudan with cruise missiles, but it is immoral for someone like Bin Laden to blow up a government building in Washington with a truck bomb. It's okay for us to take out an air-raid shelter full of women and children in Baghdad with a smart bomb, but it's cowardly and immoral for an Iraqi or Iranian agent to pop a vial of sarin in a New York subway tunnel. Really, what should we expect? They don't have aircraft carriers and cruise missiles and stealth bombers. So should we expect them to just sit there and take their punishment when we wage war on them? I think that it is the most reasonable thing in the world for them to hit back at us in the only way they can. It actually takes more courage to be a terrorist behind enemy lines than it does to push the firing button for a cruise missile a hundred miles away from your target. And yet we certainly will see Bill Clinton and every other Jew-serving politician in our government on television denouncing as a "cowardly act" the first terrorist bomb which goes off in the United States as a result of a war against Iraq. And don't be surprised when the FBI and the CIA announce that they have studied the evidence carefully and have determined that it was Iranian terrorists who built the bomb, so that the Jews will have an excuse for expanding the war to take out Iran as well as Iraq.[15]

Basic Religious Practices

The Christian Identity Movement does not have any specified religious practices. As a result, there is diversity in practice among those who embrace its ideals. There are Sabbatarian (seventh day) and Sunday observers, those who observe Old Testament Biblical festivals, those who hold weekly church services in their homes, those who attend service at a church building, and those who do not meet with others, as a rule, at all. Because the Christian Identity Movement has no centralized authority, the practice aspect of the belief system is open to interpretation. It is more of a way of looking at oneself and the world, using a specified interpretation of the Bible to do so. There are a few basic things, however, that are universal within its practice:

- All members are required to be classified as "white;" of north, central, western, and eastern European descent. Those of other races and mixed races are prohibited from participation.

- The promotion of the white race as supreme and created supreme is an essential part of the outlook and work of the group. Along with this promotion is the increase of the white race. Large families are encouraged. Along with large families, the Christian Identity Movement encourages rural living, owning large tracts of land, home births, homeschooling, agrarian lifestyles, and strict gender roles for men and women. Homosexuality and queer identity is prohibited. Birth control is strongly discouraged, and abortion is forbidden. Interracial dating, relationships, and marriages are forbidden.

- Conspiracy theories, especially those related to non-white races, are the norm and accepted as commonplace. There is a general anti-government, anti-establishment, and anti-society feel to these movements. It is often part of their appeal; it makes individuals who feel overcome by societal changes or unimportant in the general scope of life feel like "somebody." The conspiracy theory mindset makes an individual who follows them feel like they know something, have access to hidden information that the general public does not have, and that they are different from societal changes, concepts, and inclusions that cause them to feel excluded, ignored, or less important.

- Paralleling conspiracy theories, Christian Identity adherents believe the world is embroiled in an impending race war. It is, therefore, necessary to preserve and defend the white race, at all costs. Hostility is a way of life. Such communities understand and embrace the fact that what they do is not in accord with the precepts of neither general society, nor religion; that is part of why it appeals to them. Aggression, hostility, and violence are part of the way of life.

Nazi flag

- Dissemination of information is essential to their survival. Most, if not all, of the Christian Identity groups maintain publishing houses, online bookstores, or small bookstores attached to their churches or communities. Organizations are known to hand out tracts, literature, pamphlets, and advertisements espousing their beliefs in the greater community where they live. As previously stated, the Christian Identity Movement has also mastered use of the internet to distribute their ideas through podcasting, reposting of old literature and information, promoting services or events, and finding new initiates now through social media.

HOLIDAYS

As a rule, the Christian Identity Movement is against the promotion of secular and religious holidays (such as Christmas and Easter), often citing their origins as pagan. The majority recognize the celebration of Old Testament Biblical festivals of Passover, Unleavened Bread, Pentecost, Feast of Trumpets, and Day of Atonement. As they see themselves as true Israel, they tie such festivals to prophecies and promises that relate to themselves and events to come.

Christian Identity adherents also observe holidays or dates that may not be federal or state observed, but relate to the history of the Confederacy, the founders of the Ku Klux Klan, Confederate soldiers and generals, Adolf Hitler, and other key figures in white supremacist history.

VISUAL SIGNS AND SYMBOLS

The number 100% (used to indicate 100% white), 109/110 (a numeric shorthand for the number of countries white supremacists claim Jews have been expelled from; they believe the 110th country will be the United States), 14 words (the slogan, "We must secure the existence of our people and a future for white children."), 14/88 (the 14 words slogan over the number 88, which stands for "Heil Hitler"), 23 hand sign (numeric symbol for W, meaning "white), 83 (numeric sign for "Heil Christ), 9% (the supposed world population that is white), arrow cross; swastika; shamrock and swastika image; Aryan fist; Confederate flag; Wolfsangel symbol, with a sword down the center; phoenix bird with a lightning bolt and runic symbol in the center; blood drop cross; SS bolts Nazi symbol; burning crosses; burning neo-Nazi symbols; Celtic cross; crossed grenade emblem; crucified skinhead; echo symbol (three parentheses used on either side of someone's identity or name); fasces; H8 (stands for hate); iron cross; Jera rune; Life rune; Nazi eagle; Nazi party flag; hangman's noose; not equal sign; othala rune; Pepe the frog; pit bulls; *Seig Heil*; St. Michael's cross; the "happy merchant;" Thor's hammer; Totenkopf (Death's head); triangular Klan symbol; triskele; Tyr rune; Valknot; WP ("white power").[16]

CREEDS, BOOKS, AND LAWS

The Christian Identity Movement does not have any specified creed, book, or regulatory law. What it does have, is several different slogans. The most popular one is known as "14 words," and it outlines their essential interests: "We must secure the existence of our people and a future for white children."[17]

The 14 Words was authored by David Lane, who was part of a now defunct Aryan Nations organization known as The Order. While in prison, Lane also authored the 88 Precepts, which is an expansion of the 14 Words. Its purpose was to establish the territorial imperatives of white supremacists and is often considered the tenets of white supremacist life. While still not a creed or official law, many of its precepts are embraced by those in the movement. Their precepts include criticism of democracy, restrictive gender roles, subjugation of women, a deliberate larger Jewish plot to integrate people and destroy the white race and taking up weapons.[18]

Christian Identity adherents have an often-confusing relationship with morality and moral concepts because they see governmental structures as antithetical to their goals and views. They see themselves as subject to the movement's interpretation of law and governance, thus not subject to secular law. They believe themselves to be under the direct rule of the divine, equipped as the only race with the ability to make moral, intellectual, and spiritual judgments. Most would argue they are not subject to state, national, or federal law. With this in mind, many reject marriage licenses, birth certificates, social security cards, driver's licenses, passports, and other forms of identification. They adhere to their own codes of ethics, which involve defense of their race at all costs, rebellion against the governmental forces, social order, and racial integrations. The Christian Identity Movement has a long-standing history of inciting violence and attacks. The movement tends to attract individuals on the "fringes" of society, especially those who have been discharged from the military or are in or have been in prison.

ECLECTIC BELIEFS

There are several Christian Identity adherents that encourage, promote, or practice polygamy (not all do, but it is an interest in many communities). It is their belief that by doing so, they can increase and promote the interests of the white race faster.

Diseases such as cancer, sexually transmitted diseases (especially HIV and herpes) are the product of human "rodents," acquired by contact with unclean individuals, such as those who mate with or are involved with those of differing, non-white races. They are seen as a divine judgment upon those who engage in practices they disapprove of, including homosexuality and race-mixing.

Christian Identity adherents are against most, if not all, modern forms of government. They are critical of democracy and communism alike, and believe communism is hiding within world governments, especially in the United Nations. They are also believers that the "New World Order," a secretly emerging attempt to exert totalitarian control over Europe, the United States, or both (and often the world at large) is communist in nature and preparing to destroy the entire world.

The movement adheres to a unique eschatology, believing that general society is moving towards Armageddon, which shall be a huge, massive race war between whites and all non-whites. In this battle, all non-whites will be exterminated or enslaved, thereby having to serve the white race for a thousand years. This shall occur during the new "heavenly kingdom" come to earth, under the reign of Jesus Christ. Only those of Adam's race shall survive to this new time. The movement rejects the rapture doctrine, believing their members will have to survive a seven-year tribulation to receive the outcome of ultimate white supremacy in the new world.

For this reason, Christian Identity adherents believe in the practice of survivalism, by which they prepare to live through war, chaos, and disorder. They focus on self-discipline, self-sufficiency, and total separation, as they prepare for that they believe is to come. Some advocate living "off the grid," being "doomsday ready," and having the ability to handle matters of daily living, self-defense, and preparedness for the time when society shall collapse, and they will stand ready to defend the white race.

In preparation for this day, adherents seek to disassociate from society. They have proposed the establishment of The Northwest Territorial Imperative (also called the White American Bastion, White Aryan Republic, White Aryan Bastion, White Christian Republic, or the 10% solution), desiring to create a white ethnostate in the northwest pacific of the United States (the states of Washington, Oregon, Idaho, Montana, and Wyoming). Under this proposal, all non-whites shall be expelled from the territory.[19,20]

Relations with Non-Christian Identity members

The Christian Identity Movement is hostile with all outside groups, especially those mainline in religion and practice. Even though white supremacy and racial segregation has been practiced in most denominations within the United States at some point in history, the Christian Identity Movement rejects any and all relationship, even among the most conservative Protestant or Evangelical denominations. There are a few reasons for this; the most notable is the integration of most churches and denominations. Of secondary interest are Christian support for the Zionist state of Israel, Christian sympathies for the Jewish community (especially in wake of the Holocaust), acceptance of the Jewish people as the legitimate descendants of the Bible's Jewish community, and interfaith discussion and dialogue among those of differing religions. As a secondary point, they are also largely hostile among themselves, as well.

Holy Sites

The Northwest Territorial Imperative (states of Washington, Oregon, Idaho, Montana, and Wyoming); Aryan Nations compounds in Ulysses, Pennsylvania, Union City, Tennessee; Hoodoo Mountains Aryan Nations "world headquarters" compound, Bonner County, Idaho; Christian Revival Center, Harrison, Arkansas: Church of Israel, Schell City, Missouri; Covenant People's Ministry, Brooks, Georgia; Fellowship of God's Covenant People, Union, Kentucky; Kingdom Identity Ministries, Harrison, Arkansas; Our Place Fellowship, Colville, Washington; LaPorte Church of Christ, LaPorte, Colorado.

Notable Figures

Wesley Swift (1913-1970), founder; Richard Butler (1918-2004), founder; Thomas Robb (1946-), Ku Klux Klan leader; Larry Gene Ashbrook (1952-1999), mass murderer; Samuel Bowers (1924-2006), first Grand Wizard of the White Knights of the Ku Klux Klan; Byron De La Beckwith (1920-2001), murderer of Medgar Evers; Chevie O'Brien Kehoe (1973-), murderer of William Mueller and his family; August Byron Kreis III (1954-), murderer and child molester who called for an Aryan Nations-al Qaeda alliance; Eric Rudolph (1966-), the Olympic Park Bomber; Michael Wayne Ryan (1948-2015), leader of an anti-government compound and murderer; Matthew Thomas Shea (1974-), former politician and host of the Patriot Radio broadcast; Buddy Tucker, former pastor of Temple Memorial Baptist Church (Knoxville, Tennessee); Rick Tyler (1957-), political candidate in Tennessee; Randy Weaver (1948-2022), former American Green Beret influential in the standoff at Ruby Ridge (Naples, Idaho); Timothy McVeigh (1968-2001), Oklahoma City building bomber.

Notable Groups

Elohim City (also called Elohim Village) is a private community in Adair County, Oklahoma. It was

White power fist

originally a rural retreat, founded in 1973 by Robert G. Millair. It has gained national attention for ties to Aryan Nations affiliates and offshoots and for the implementation of white supremacist ideas in its structure and daily living. Approximately 12 different structures exist on the 400-acre property, with the center of the compound, a church-community center. Those who live within the community meet daily for religious services; Saturday is regarded as the official holy day of the week. The religious life of the community focuses on the Old Testament. While not practiced at current, the group was formerly polygamous. The community is governed by elders who form a board of directors. The property has been under FBI surveillance for many years (especially for drug trafficking). A number of criminal white supremacists, including Timothy McVeigh, Dennis Mahon (1950-), and James Ellison (c. 1941-) all lived at, spent time at, or trained at Elohim City at some point in their lives.[21]

FACTS AND FIGURES

Approximately 15,000-20,000 individuals, both in and out of prison, are part of the Aryan Brotherhood, the prison branch of the Aryan Nations.[22]

OTHER IMPORTANT DEFINITIONS[23]

- **Aryan race**: A term used to describe the original speakers of the Indo-European languages. Used by extension to refer to indigenous Europeans, associated as Caucasian, or "white" people. It is rooted in a nineteenth century racial categorizing no longer employed today.

Confederate flag

- **Blood and soil**: A Nazi chant designed to connect the Aryan race to their German homeland. Used today by Christian Identity adherents and other white supremacists to create connection between American soil and the white race.

- **British Israelism**: The origins of the Christian Identity Movement. The doctrine, while embracing the idea of the supremacy of white Europeans (especially those of Anglo-Saxon heritage), was not an independent movement; it was a belief system employed by religious individuals who remained within their respective denominations (until the advance of Armstrongism, which shall be discussed in a separate section). British Israelism varies from Christian Identity in that it believes most Jews today are not of the lineage of Israel, but that the British are the true Jews, and the throne of David is that of the British monarchy; many held great respect for the authentic Jewish community, and supported

Zionism, whereby the Christian Identity movement does not. Its claims have been widely refuted by archaeological, linguistic, and genetic research.

- **Israel**: The white race.

- **Neo-Nazis**: The group of Christian Identity that revere Adolf Hitler, Nazi principles, the Nazi era of German history, and the symbols and mythology of the Third Reich.

- **Odinism**: Also called Wotanism. A neopagan revival of an ancient warrior Norse religion. Classified as a tribal religion for Europeans, it is a more racially aggressive of Asatru. Those white supremacists who identify with such classify themselves as racialist, tribal, or folkish.

- **White genocide**: The white supremacist idea that the white race is in danger of dying out due to larger non-white populations of people and what is "forced assimilation," by which whites and those of other races are forced to coexist together in one society. Christian Identity adherents believe such is a deliberate conspiracy controlled by Jews to destroy the white race.

- **White Power**: A supremacist inversion of the "black power" slogan used by groups such as the Black Panthers in the 1970s.

- **White Pride**: The supremacist slogan which claims white supremacists are not racists, but instead, are proud of their white heritage and they are exhibiting "white pride" as a response to such.

- **White separatism**: The idea that whites should exist separately from all other races, as such are deemed inferior. In white supremacy, such advocate establishing all-white communities, states, territories, and in the process, expelling all non-whites. Many in the movement use the term "white separatism" because it is considered to be a less extreme version of "ethnic cleansing."

BELIEVER'S CHARACTERISTICS

Belief in the superiority of the white race above all other races; Biblical interpretation that creates a narrative of the white race as central to its understanding; belief that all major Biblical figures, from Adam onward, were white; promotion of the creation of an all-white state; prohibitions on interracial dating, marriage, relationships, birth control abortion, homosexuality, medical intervention, banking, and modern gender roles; paranoia; encouragement of large families; promotion of violence; use of Nazi ideology, symbology, or propaganda; isolation; survivalism; doomsday prepping; home births, homeschooling, and lack of government identification (driver's licenses, birth certificates, social security cards); sovereign citizens; conspiracy theories; antisemitism; identity with white individuals as the true nation of Israel; excessive promotion of their ideas; use of "white power" slogans; anti-government sentiments; belief that disease is caused by racial mixing; use of the "14 words" and "88 precepts;" belief in female subjugation; promotion of white supremacist ideas through internet and media; hate.

Christian Science

A wicked mortal is not the idea of God. He is little else than the expression of error. To suppose that sin, lust, hatred, envy, hypocrisy, revenge, have life abiding in them, is a terrible mistake. Life and Life's idea, Truth and Truth's idea, never make men sick, sinful, or mortal.
(Mary Baker Eddy)[1]

Theology

Belief in one divine power, known as FATHER-MOTHER GOD and also subsequently as INFINTE MIND, SPIRIT, SOUL, PRINCIPLE LIFE, ALL, TRUTH, ONE, MIND, LOVE, ETERNAL, and GOD; omnipotent and omnipresent. Christian Scientists do not regard Father-Mother God as a personal being, but as divine Principle, an impersonal life force that is love: the intelligence of Mind, accuracy of truth, orderliness of principle, incorporeality of Spirit, and the beauty and discernment of Soul. Father-Mother God is seen creator of the universe; the font of life, health, and love; of all good things that are recognized in this world. Studying about Father-Mother God and the all-encompassing nature found therein causes humans to see healing power as available to them. One might classify Christian Science's theological understanding as a form of deism (a supreme, creator exists, without personage of being or personality, or interference in universal affairs). Christian Scientists strive to express the different qualities of Father-Mother God, Love, in their own lives.

Jesus Christ is seen as the son of Father-Mother God, the promised Messiah. He came to rescue humanity from worldly materialism and the attachments of sin. The crucifixion was a sign of divine love, one by which people were to become one with Father-Mother God (rather than as reparation for sin). His ultimate purpose was to reveal an inseparable relationship, oneness, from Father-Mother God: Love, Mind, Eternal, and Spirit. He is seen as being subordinate to Father-Mother God in all things, the complete idea of spiritual sonship. Christian Scientists do not see Christ as deity.

The Holy Ghost is identified as divine science, the "comforter" promised by Jesus Christ. This concept of divine science ("science" being defined as a development of eternal Life, Truth, and Love; a living power) is considered equivalent of truth and is recognized as Love immortal in an ever-operating divine principle. In its essence, the Holy Ghost is Christian Science.

The Trinity of Christian Science is identified as Life, Truth (divine sonship present in Christ), and Love (divine Science in the Holy Comforter). The traditional doctrine of the Trinity as understood in many Christian denominations is seen as polytheism.[2,3,4,5]

Philosophy

Christian Science centers around the principle that the universe operates by a duality, specifically one between matter and spirit. Matter is an evil illusion, something perceived by the material senses incorrectly. Man, or humanity, is spirit, for humanity is created in the likeness of Father-Mother God. Therefore, man is good, spiritual, and not carnal. Sin, sickness, illness, disease, and hell are all illusions created by man in the material world. They are, in essence, unreal. When one rejects the material world and adheres to the spiritual world, the material world (including the body) has no affect or reality on pain or perception of suffering.

Christian Science is identified as a "science" because it is based on what is seen as an infinite Principle and a love which does not change; namely, Father-Mother God. Rather than seen as a traditional church, Christian Science explains and adheres to fundamental laws of Love, using the same principles Jesus Christ used to heal sickness and sin. Because it is about the study and execution of spiritual law, it sees itself as a practice therein.

Christian Science was started by Mary Baker Eddy (1821-1910), a chronically ill and unhappy woman who sought answers to illness, suffering, and healing in her own life. Inspired by a number of different sources including the ideas of New Thought originating with Phineas Quimby (1802-1866), popular nineteenth century ideas about scientific exploration, and extensive Bible study, Mary Baker Eddy proposed a theoretic application of spiritual healing in her work *Science and Health With Key to the Scriptures*. She then established the First Church of Christ, Scientist in 1879 along with twenty-six of her followers. Not seeing divine healing as miraculous, Christian Science believes anyone can experience healing without the use of medicine or medical intervention if they properly understand the nature and essence of Father-Mother God as love. Christian Scientists are encouraged to avoid doctors at all costs except for optometrists, dentists, obstetricians, or physicians who set broken bones (or something similar). They reject vaccines and medication and believe the principles of Christian Science are most effective without medical intervention.

Adherent Identity

The First Church of Christ, Scientist, Christian Science, Christian Scientists, Christian Science Practitioner.

Traditional Languages

English.

Sects/Divisions

Mary Baker Eddy (1821-1910)

Christian Science is a part of the New Thought Movement, along with groups such as Religious Science and the Unity School. It varies from others in that it is more authoritarian than other New Thought sects. It has never been a prominent group on the religious scene, thus there are not even a handful of sects that have followed its tenets. The major notable group is The Bookmark, located in Santa Clarita, California. It was started by Ann Beals in 1980 with the goal to promote the literature of the First Church of Christ, Scientist. When it came to her attention that literature on healing and the push for better healing work was not coming from the "Mother Church" (the headquarters of the First Church of Christ, Scientist), she disbanded from mainline Christian Science and began promoting her own teachings and ideas about Christian Science.

NUMBER OF ADHERENTS

Christian Scientists do not keep membership registrations or count their members. There are estimates of approximately four hundred thousand Christian Scientists worldwide, although actual numbers may be lower.[6]

DISPUTES WITHIN GROUP

Mary Baker Eddy never left specific provisions for governing, operations, and doctrinal adjustments after her death. Over the years, there have been many conflicts about authority, publications, and interpretations of her teachings and work. As the religion has an individualistic nature to it, this furthered the independent nature of Christian Science ideals. Many dissenters formulated similar doctrinal teachings without the "Christian" label. The ideas of Christian Science, having their origins in another movement, are also common throughout the New Age Movement, metaphysical divisions of Christianity, and some positive thinking/visualization movements, as well. As a result, it is possible for participants to incorporate its ideas into other belief systems, walking away from Christian Science membership and participation while keeping its ideals.

SCRIPTURES

The Holy Bible, Old and New Testaments: the Pentateuch (Genesis, Exodus, Leviticus, Numbers, and Deuteronomy), Historical books (Joshua, Judges, Ruth, 1 Samuel, 2 Samuel, 1 Kings, 2 Kings, 1 Chronicles, 2 Chronicles, Ezra, Nehemiah, Esther), Wisdom books (Job, Psalms, Proverbs, Ecclesiastes, Song of Songs), Prophetic books (Isaiah, Jeremiah, Lamentations, Ezekiel, Daniel, Hosea, Joel, Amos, Obadiah, Jonah, Micah, Nahum, Habakkuk, Zephaniah, Haggai, Zechariah, Malachi), the Gospels (Matthew, Mark, Luke, John), the Acts of the Apostles, the Pauline Epistles (Romans, 1 Corinthians, 2 Corinthians, Galatians, Ephesians, Philippians, Colossians, 1 Thessalonians, 2 Thessalonians, 1 Timothy, 2 Timothy, Titus, Philemon, Hebrews) the General Epistles (James, 1 Peter, 2 Peter, 1 John, 2 John, 3 John, Jude) and Revelation. Most service text and quotations in literature are from the King James Version of the Holy Bible. The Bible is seen as the foundation of Christian Science, as one explores the identity of mankind as entirely spiritual. It is regarded as inspired.

Science and Health With Key to the Scriptures, written by Mary Baker Eddy, is the official textbook of Christian Science. Christian Scientists believe its contents were given by divine revelation. *Science and Health With Key to the Scriptures* contains spiritual laws and principles that relate to health and how to practice these ideas as they are seen manifesting through the Bible.

> *Atonement is the exemplification of man's unity with God, whereby man reflects divine Truth, Life, and Love. Jesus of Nazareth taught and demonstrated man's oneness with the Father, and for this we owe him endless homage. His mission was both individual and collective. He did life's work aright not only in justice to himself, but in mercy to mortals, — to show them how to do theirs, but not to do it for them nor to relieve them of a single responsibility. Jesus acted boldly, against the accredited evidence of the senses, against Pharisaical creeds and practices, and he refuted all opponents with his healing power.*
>
> *The atonement of Christ reconciles man to God, not God to man; for the divine Principle of Christ is God, and how can God propitiate Himself? Christ is Truth, which reaches no higher than itself. The fountain can rise no higher than its source. Christ, Truth, could conciliate no nature above his own, derived from the eternal Love. It was therefore Christ's purpose to reconcile man to God, not God to man. Love and Truth are not at war with God's image and likeness. Man cannot exceed divine Love, and so atone for him-self. Even Christ cannot reconcile Truth to error, for Truth and error are irreconcilable. Jesus aided in reconciling man to God by giving man a truer sense of Love, the divine Principle of Jesus' teachings, and this truer sense of Love redeems man from the law of matter, sin, and death by the law of Spirit, — the law of divine Love.*[7]
>
> *If Christianity is not scientific, and Science is not of God, then there is no invariable law, and truth becomes an accident. Shall it be denied that a system which works according to the Scriptures has Scriptural authority?*
>
> *Christian Science awakens the sinner, reclaims the infidel, and raises from the couch of pain the helpless invalid. It speaks to the dumb the words of Truth, and they answer with rejoicing. It causes the deaf to hear, the lame to walk, and the blind to see. Who would be the first to disown the Christliness of good works, when our Master says, "By their fruits ye shall know them"?*[8]
>
> *Truth and Love enlighten the understanding, in whose "light shall we see light;" and this illumination is reflected spiritually by all who walk in the light and turn away from a false material sense.*[9]

Christian Science logo

Mary Baker Eddy is the "pastor emeritus" of Christian Science, with the Bible *and Science and Health With Key to the Scriptures* as the current, and continuing, church pastor.

Basic Religious Practices

Christian Science centers entirely around the spiritual health of the individual as the individual comes to understand their nature as spiritual, rather than material. As an individual comes to discover they are entirely good, they can embrace divine healing as a spiritual principle. Services take place on Sunday mornings at 10:30 in every church around the world. Churches have no ordained clergy, personal pastor, or formal governmental structure. Instead, they have readers (one male and one female) who read selections of Bible passages alternating with key texts *from Science and Health With Key to the Scriptures*. These readings are a "Bible Lesson" in *The Christian Science Quarterly*. Services consist of hymns unique to Christian Science and the readings as presented by the readers. Sunday School is held for children up to 20 years of age at the same time as the Sunday morning services. Christian Science churches hold Wednesday night services that feature hymns, readings, and testimonials of members who claim they have experienced divine healing through the principles of Christian Science.

Christian Scientists do not believe in literal symbols or rites, such as baptism or communion. They opt instead to embrace such concepts as spiritual realities rather than literal embodiments. The only prayer ever spoken out loud is the Lord's Prayer (Our Father), with the accompanying *Science and Health With Key to the Scriptures* amplification of the text, during service. Otherwise, Christian Scientists only pray silently. They believe such will help them to develop spiritual understanding and devotion. They are not to supplicate, or ask, God for requests in their prayers. There is no laying on of hands for the sick or physical anointing with oil, but exerted, silent faith, that healing shall come for the afflicted.

Christian Scientists are required to live a life of spiritual health as stipulated by their doctrinal understanding. This starts with their understanding of morality, which is right thought and action through Christian Science. If one changes their view of matter and spiritual identity, one can change the entirety of their lives (including relationships, actions, health, and being). They have no specific positions on current events such as homosexuality, birth control, abortion, or other contemporary issues, often citing legal issues or medical abstinences for their neutral positions. Christian Scientists are required to abstain from alcohol, tobacco, drug use, and the use of hypnosis.

If a Christian Scientist runs into an issue that causes conflict in Christian Science application (such as a relationship issue or chronic health ailment), one consults a Christian Science practitioner, a practicing member of Christian Science who acts as a counselor. They are available for prayer, counseling, study of the Bible *or Science and Health With Key to the Scriptures*, answering questions about the beliefs of the faith and providing in-person visits.

HOLIDAYS

Christian Scientists observe Christmas, Easter, and Thanksgiving as their holidays. Churches are closed on all legal holidays. Christian Scientists do not gather for a special service on Christmas Day. Outside of Sunday and Wednesday services, Christian Scientists have a special service on the American Thanksgiving holiday (fourth Thursday in November).

VISUAL SIGNS AND SYMBOLS

Cross and crown motif encircled by the command to "heal the sick, raise the dead, cast out demons and cleanse the lepers; Christian Science reading room; *Science and Health With Key to the Scriptures*; books by and about founder, Mary Baker Eddy; images of Mary Baker Eddy; *The Christian Science Monitor*, *The Christian Science Sentinel*, *The Christian Science Quarterly*.

Creeds, Books, and Laws

Within its history, Christian Science has aspired to be a religion without creed. The Tenants of Christian Science, as outlined by Mary Baker Eddy herself, are as follows:

1. *As adherents of Truth, we take the inspired Word of the Bible as our sufficient guide to eternal Life.*
2. *We acknowledge and adore one supreme and infinite God. We acknowledge His Son, one Christ; the Holy Ghost or divine Comforter; and man in God's image and likeness.*
3. *We acknowledge God's forgiveness of sin in the destruction of sin and the spiritual understanding that casts out evil as unreal. But the belief in sin is punished so long as the belief lasts.*
4. *We acknowledge Jesus' atonement as the evidence of divine, efficacious Love, unfolding man's unity with God through Christ Jesus the Way-shower; and we acknowledge that man is saved through Christ, through Truth, Life, and Love as demonstrated by the Galilean Prophet in healing the sick and overcoming sin and death.*
5. *We acknowledge that the crucifixion of Jesus and his resurrection served to uplift faith to understand eternal Life, even the allness of Soul, Spirit, and the nothingness of matter.*
6. *And we solemnly promise to watch, and pray for that Mind to be in us which was also in Christ Jesus; to do unto others as we would have them do unto us; and to be merciful, just, and pure.*[10]

Christian Science is governed by *Science and Health with Key to the Scriptures* spiritually, including financial instruction for the denomination. Its structural governance is found in *The Manual of the Mother Church*, written by Mary Baker Eddy. *The Manual of the Mother Church* operates as a constitution and outlines its bylaws, divided into thirty-five articles stipulating the responsibilities and duties for church officers, rules and guidelines for Christian Science practitioners and teachers, and the responsibilities of each member. It also provides disciplinary means. All local churches are democratic in structure. The international church is led by a president and a five-person board of directors. There is also the Committee on Publication, which operates for international public relations.[11,12]

Eclectic Beliefs

As sin, sickness, and disease are believed to be an illusion, Christian Scientists are notorious for rejecting medical care, inoculations, and refusing to use medication to the neglect of their own physical well-being. There have been several court cases examining the ethics involved in refusing medical care for minors or incapacitated individuals who cannot state for themselves what their desires or wishes are in such situations.

Christian Scientists are best known for their reading rooms, which are church libraries devoted to materials written by Mary Baker Eddy and other Christian Scientists throughout the church's history. Libraries are overseen by a Christian Science librarian, an individual who can answer questions about Christian Science and also recommend literature. Patrons can borrow or buy books. These libraries are maintained by the "Mother Church," which is headquartered in Boston, Massachusetts.[13]

Only the Mother Church can be identified as "The" First Church of Christ, Scientist in its title. Branch churches are identified without proper article, such as "First Church of Christ, Scientist," or "Second Church of Christ, Scientist." Their number reflects the order in which they were built within a city.

Christian Science is largely on the decline, especially over the past 50 years. Internal conflicts within the organization, especially at the highest levels of practice, are to blame, due to resulting mismanagement. Many attribute the decline to the fact that the religion's text-based nature does not appeal to modern society, especially youth. Christian Scientists also do not engage in active evangelization, outside of giving testimonies on the way Christian Science changes or enhances an individual's life.

Mother Church (Christian Science headquarters), Boston, Massachusetts

Relations with Non-Christian Scientists

Christian Scientists do not place any prohibition on interfaith and ecumenical activities. Not all Christians, however, regard Christian Science as a valid Christian religion because it rejects many essential tenants of traditional Christian belief and understanding.

Holy Sites

Headquarters of the First Church of Christ, Scientist (the "Mother Church"), Boston, Massachusetts.

Notable Figures

Mary Baker Eddy (1821-1910), founder; Martha Welch (1944-), founder of The Mothering Center and "Holding Time" attachment therapy; Nancy Astor (1879-1964), politician; Evelyn Dunbar (1906-1960), artist; Joan Crawford (1904-1977), actress; Carol Channing (1921-2019), actress; Doris Day (1922-2019), actress; Colleen Dewhurst (1924-1991), actress; Georgia Engel (1948-2019), actress; Lionel Hampton (1908-2002), musician; Val Kilmer (1959-), actor; Mary Pickford (1892-1979), actress; Jean Stapleton (1923-2013), actress; Alfre Woodard (1952-), actress; Shannon Miller (1977-), athlete; Bette Nesmith Graham (1924-1980), inventor; Kelsey Grammer (1955-), actor; Bruce Hornsby (1954-), musician; Danielle Steel (1947-), author.

Notable Groups

The Christian Science Publishing Society is the official publishing arm of the First Church of Christ,

Scientist. They are best-known for producing *The Christian Science Journal*, *The Christian Science Sentinel*, *The Herald of Christian Science*, *The Christian Science Quarterly*, and *The Christian Science Monitor*, which has won several awards. Today, The Christian Science Publishing Society is the primary publisher of Mary Baker Eddy's works and other writings on Christian Science. It is managed by a three-person Board of Trustees, under the auspices of the Christian Science Board of Directors.[14]

FACTS AND FIGURES

The number of Christian Science practitioners and teachers is declining at the rate of approximately 5% per year. Churches are declining at the average rate of approximately 2% per year.[15]

OTHER IMPORTANT DEFINITIONS[16]

- **Animal magnetism**: The ability for one person to negatively impact another person through mental thoughts.
- **Belief**: A term used when speaking of disease or the material world, emphasizing such is illusionary.
- **Challenge**: A term applied to anything that challenges Christian Science belief in a negative way.
- **Christian Science Lecture**: Usually one-hour talks, often in the form of a college-style lecture (although some are in the form of workshops or question/answer sessions) that are directed towards individuals who are not Christian Scientists. All branch churches are required to host at least one lecture per year, at the expense of the host church.
- **Error**: A term used to indicate anything bad or contrary to the spirituality present in Christian Science.
- **Mental malpractice**: When someone is injured or interfering with another's healing through thoughts contrary to the healing process.
- **Mortal mind**: Anything referring to material (sickness, the body), that is the opposite of spirit, or reality.
- **Protective work**: The belief that by engaging in daily Christian Science prayer, study with the Lesson Sermon (the weekly Lesson) a Christian Scientist can be protected against disease and harm.

- **Scientific Statement of Being**: A paragraph from *Science and Health With Key to the Scriptures* that is read at every Christian Science service and repeated by Sunday School Students: "There is no life, truth, intelligence, nor substance in matter. All is infinite Mind, and its infinite manifestation, for God is All-in-All. Spirit is immortal Truth; matter is mortal error. Spirit is the real and eternal; matter is the unreal and temporal. Spirit is God, and man is His image and likeness. Therefore man is not material; he is spiritual." (p. 468)

- **Synonyms**: Specific words used as equivalents to Father-Mother God, capitalized throughout Christian Science literature. These are Mind, Soul, Spirit, Principle, Life, Truth, and Love.

- **Teacher**: A person who has taken Normal, an introductory class of instruction at the Mother Church and is now authorized to teach Christian Science to others.

BELIEVER'S CHARACTERISTICS

Emphasis on spiritual health as a means to physical health; rejection of medicine, death, sin, sickness, disease, hell, the devil, and consequence; reference to deity as Father-Mother, and the capitalized synonyms of Mind, Soul, Spirit, Principle, Life, Truth, and Love; emphasis on Science and Health With Key to the Scriptures and prayer as a means to divine health; portrait of Mary Baker Eddy as the perfect model of Christian faith; largely empirical philosophically on all matters of reality; passivity regarding political and moral stances; refusal to inoculate, medicate, or use medical care; division in the duality of body and mind or spirit, with matter as delusional evil and spirit as good; neglect of the physical care of the body; positive thinking; interest in metaphysics; rejection of outward signs and symbols, such as ordinances or sacraments; reading rooms; refusal to pray out loud; refusal to make supplication in prayer; interest in mind science; belief human beings are good and spiritual by nature; use of Christian Science practitioners and teachers.

Cults

Many cults start off with high ideals that get corrupted by leaders or their board of advisors who become power-hungry and dominate and control members' lives. No group with high ideas starts off as a 'cult;' they become one when their errant ways are exposed.
(Philip Zimbardo)[1]

Theology

On the surface, cult theology may vary, appearing very diverse in approach. Most cults have what we could classify as a "front door" theology: one that is presented to the world and appears to have a standard appeal, something that might be found in any one of the world's major religions. A cult may appear to be Christian, Jewish, Hindu, Buddhist, Muslim, or any of the other world's religious groups; it may also appear atheist, agnostic, or have no specified theological position. The "front door" theology, however, is literally that: a front, or a gateway, to make the group appear legitimate. When one is within the group, they are invited to explore a different level of theological understanding, one that is far different more convoluted than what appears on the surface. The defense of such, rather than describing it as deceptive, is to state certain aspects of cult doctrine and teaching can only be understood by those in the group. Cults frequently accuse critics and skeptics outside the group of maligning their doctrine, of persecuting them, or of being unable to understand it, because they are not within the group.

To cult members, cult theology sounds innovative, different, or new. Cults present the concept of spiritual revelation as present exclusively within the cult; its secret, innovative understandings cannot be found anywhere else (especially among typical, organized religious groups). To receive this revelation, one must remain a part of the cult, which is directed by a central messianic figure. This central figure is usually believed to be a prophet or spokesperson for the divine, an individual of unique or brilliant capacities, or a reincarnation of a major religious figure throughout history (such as Jesus Christ, Buddha, a Biblical prophet, or the fulfillment of some special promise or prophecy that sets the leader and their subsequent ideas apart from the rest of the religious spectrum). Such leaders are revered and worshiped for their unique positions. They are considered irreplaceable, insightful, and elevated above that of the standard worshiper, believer, member, or leader found in any said group. Outside of said leader, revelation, insight, and theological perspective are impossible to obtain.

When one analyzes cult theology (especially in detail) on the merits of each individual cult group, cult theology is almost always, if not always, bizarre in one form or another. It has elements that seem unbelievable or implausible, and many cult beliefs are easily disproved. Most outside of cults do not understand why or how cults thrive within the realm of reason, not understanding that people do not join cults because they are convinced of their theological merit. People do not join cults because of theology. It is seldom an organic spiritual conversion, but a practical one. People join cults because of the way the group makes them feel, offering a sense of belonging, exclusivity, special membership, and personal purpose. As individuals remain connected to the group, the theology of the group becomes belief, and becomes a deeper aspect of the sense of belonging and insight one feels they have as part of cult membership.

PHILOSOPHY

While the technical details of cult philosophy vary, the basic philosophy of all cult groups remains the same: The cult offers its members a perceived innovative, universal good by divine appointment, present only within the cult community. In the process, the individual must separate themselves from both their past lives and society, which are seen as evil distractions meant to lure them away from their destiny within the cult. To remain focused on the goals of the cult, members are required to surrender total control over themselves to the purposes of the cult. This seldom happens all at once, but consistently over time, as a cult's ideals and leadership take over more and more of one's ideals, ideas, time, and decision making. The process by which a cult takes over one's thoughts is known as the process of thought reform through totalism (more commonly called "brainwashing"). Through eight specific points of thought reform (milieu control, mystical manipulation, demand for purity, cult of confession, sacred science, loaded language, doctrine over person, and dispensing of existence), cult members are gradually changed into different people: those who are controlled by the group's ideals and its leaders, with a life vision that is far from the reality they often live.

Thinking specifically of the good of the group (especially above the individual) and their need to maintain membership for the good of themselves, humanity, and the mission, individuals in cults spend their lives in the pursuit of perfect obedience, trying to measure up to the ideals of the group which are usually unreasonable and unobtainable. Underneath the attempts to please is a philosophy of perfection: members must, in any and all situations, obtain, maintain, and excel in abstract forms of perfection that are always just out of reach.

NUMBER OF ADHERENTS

There are no specific statistics available on how many people worldwide may be part of cults worldwide. Given that cults can be large and small, it is safe to say the number is probably in the millions.

TRADITIONAL LANGUAGES

Varies. Cult groups typically operate in the vernacular of their central founder or leader, though additional languages may be added as groups expand.

ADHERENT IDENTITY

Cult, cult member; brainwashed; group identity specific to the cult one belongs to: for example,

Scientology refers to their members as Scientologists; Fundamentalist Mormon sects refer to their members as Saints or Zion; Twelve Tribes refers to their members as the Community; Jehovah's Witnesses refer to themselves as Jehovah's Witnesses; Armstrongists refer to themselves as Church of God, and so on.

SECTS/DIVISIONS

There are an unknown number of cults in the world. It is neither reasonable nor practical to list all of them in this section. Some are quite large, with many adherents and a large following; some are quite small. What defines a cult is not the number of members, but the level of control a group and group's leaders exert over its membership. We could define cults into four different categories: small, devoted groups; large cults that mask as mainstream religious groups; governmental or secular cults; and high control groups.

- **Small, devoted groups**: Cult groups are often stereotyped as small organizations, extremely devout in nature. It's assumed members live together in one location, operate by specific, strict regulations, and have no contact whatsoever with anyone outside the immediate group. These are not the most visible organizations (their invisibility being a central point of their literal separation from the world) until something controversial happens: stockpiling weapons, child abuse, accusations of physical or sexual abuse, doomsday prepping or militia drills, or threats against general society of the government. Such groups do exist, no matter how small, isolated, or seemingly off everyone's radar they may be. Their major focus is on the adherence of their immediate members: on the separateness, perfection, and discipline of a small group, often setting themselves apart in preparation for something soon to come. Instead of focusing on mega recruitment, small cults are more about the community aspect of cult life: literally controlling media and internet access, isolating from family and friends, only encountering the world in mandatory instances (such as shopping or work), self-sustenance (homesteading, growing one's own vegetables, farming, living off the grid, creating independent companies or labor contract jobs), group living (on farms, massive dormitory-style living, apartment buildings, or group houses), communal habits (chores are divided, typically by gender assignment, and shared by the entire group), and extensive hours spent in devotion and study to the teachings of their specified leader or group. Such groups include Twelve Tribes, People's Temple (Jonestown massacre), Branch Davidians, the Family International (Children of God), the Family (Charles Manson), The Unification Church (Moonies), NXIVM Cult, Heaven's Gate, Rajineeshpuram (Osho/Rajineesh), and Gloriavale Christian Community.

- **Large cults that mask as mainstream religious groups**: Larger cults are often more visible than smaller cult groups. This also creates confusion as to the nature of their operations and activities. Many people are under the incorrect assumption that a cult cannot be a large group; this is untrue. There are several organizations that function as cults whereby the majority (if not all members) live and maintain their own livelihoods, live separately, and operate under the mentality of thought reform. Larger cult groups often appear to be mainstream religious groups or may claim to be such, often accusing outside groups of discrimination or bias when they are viewed with suspicion. Larger cults often have more extensive assets and a larger reach and focus more heavily on obvious and overstated recruitment on a far grander scale than smaller cults. Major focuses among larger cults are constant recruitment and fundraising, frequently imposing several membership fines, multiple tithes, mandatory purchases of literature or other materials unique to the group, and limitations on time, social interaction, and relationships with those outside the group. Most groups require an extensive amount of time spent in promotion of the group's ideals; to maintain an active membership, one must be present in person or in promotion several times during the week, in addition to one's everyday commitments, such as work and family. Activities are also family minded, with all persons (child to adult) involved in promotional and devotional activities. The work of each community group is directed and governed by a headquarters organization, usually rigid within structure and authoritarian in nature. Such groups include Scientology, Jehovah's Witnesses, Mormonism, Armstrongism, many subheadings of the Sacred Name, Hebrew Roots, and Sabbatarian Movements, and the Transcendental Movement (TM).

- **Governmental or secular cults**: Most are unaware of the fact that Robert Lifton's original research on thought reform took place with individuals who had gone through prison and reorientation camps under the initial Communist revolution in China. Starting with intellectuals and revolutionaries, Communist reform in China began with totalistic practices torture, physical exhaustion, starvation, and repeated exposure to the ideals of the Communist government. The ideals of cults, cult criteria, and high control organizations are not just prevalent among private groups: they can also be seen with prisoners and inmates, prisoners of war, military subjects, political parties, during coup de états, espionage, governmental overthrow, governments, and political seizes and shifts worldwide.

- **High control groups**: Within the spectrum of cults are organizations that exert at least five of the eight points of thought reform (rather than the entire list). Many of these organizations fall in different places on the religious spectrum and incorporate aspects of legitimate religious or spiritual experience with borderline cult tendencies and concepts. These manifest in any combination of ways: as groups with strong peer pressure and peer influences, a singular, dominating and controlling leader, several excessive rules that disconnect an individual from families or from society, financial burdens, social isolation, or other unusual and pressuring techniques used to keep a person in social conformity with a high control movement. Labeling a group as "high control" is controversial, especially with groups that may take offense to the label, as they identify with standard, or more mainline, organizations in their identity.

DISPUTES WITHIN GROUP

Cults are identified through the eight points of thought reform, which we shall discuss in detail a little later. Cults perhaps most disputing of the label of being a "cult" to begin with; most do not accept the label, and instead argue the point as one related to persecution, discrimination, or further proof that they are indeed the true group. Within a cult, one can only obtain salvation, protection, or insight within the group. other groups, no matter how much of the thought reform label they may have in common with another group, will never, ever accept another cult group as legitimate. Cults also do not express uniform details in their practice or theology outside of the basics of cult criteria. What defines a cult is its internal operation and level of control over a person, rather than its specific points of doctrine. As a rule, much of the theology and practice of cults falls outside of the "norm" of doctrinal teaching and practice; to outsiders, it appears strange, odd, and more than just unconventional.

David Koresh (1959-1993), leader of the Branch Davidians

SCRIPTURES

The use of inspired writing varies between cults. Often, there are one of two ways that cults use scripture, or sometimes the overlap of both. The first is the use of a standard scripture used within a religious community (such as the Bible, *Bhagavad Gita*, New Age texts, the *Book of Mormon*, or other accepted religious works), with interpretation and understanding twisted to fit the beliefs of the group. Often, the existence of the group is somehow interpreted as a sign of prophecy or the fulfillment thereof: at some point, somewhere in history, the existence of this group was destined to become reality. In accord with this, most cults also add to such fulfillment with their own writings, almost all classified as equivalent to their scriptural tradition. Such additions are clarifications, rewrites, or corrections of existing mistakes in scriptural text. In some instances, their writings are considered superior, because they are seen as a direct revelation: they are divine, free from impurity, and a direct confirmation to the veracity of the group's existence.

The second is for a cult group to skip traditional religious text and embody their own exclusive body of literature. These may be collected from sermons or speeches made by the central leadership of the group or actual text written by the leader or leaders themselves. While some cults do produce literature specifically for non-members, such text is often deliberately questionable or misleading in its content. Texts that reveal truth about what a group believes are exclusive to the group and difficult to obtain for outsiders.

BASIC RELIGIOUS PRACTICES

Cults center around eight specific points of thought reform, regardless of the specific belief or ritual, as outlined by Robert J. Lifton in his work, *Thought Reform and the Psychology of Totalism*. These are:

- **Milieu control**: "Milieu" is the French word for "around" and relates to the control of communication a cult member has with the outside world. Milieu control is managed in a few specific ways, from the obvious to the more sublime. Milieu control starts with the concept that all one can obtain, need, or pursue can be found exclusively within the group. Outside pursuits, ideas, activities, and thoughts are viewed with suspicion or prohibited. When one desires to pursue time or activity outside of the group, they are met with criticism. This extends to outside influences, such as family and friends (who are now seen as the enemy), and things such as television, radio, internet, cell phones, newspapers, magazines, books, educational resources, or other communication that is seen as contradictory or threatening. Milieu control is accomplished through regulation, physically removing devices or items that permit contact or influence with the outside world, prohibitions, or the heavy use of peer pressure, whereby members influence and pressure other members to avoid such usage (or tattle to leaders when they find someone else using prohibited things or items). The goal of milieu control is to create an environment where the only voice, thoughts, and concepts one hears are those of the group.

- **Mystical manipulation**: Mystical manipulation is the deliberate manipulation of an individual's thoughts, beliefs, and spiritual experiences through staged performances that are perceived as genuine or authentic by an individual. The purpose of mystical manipulation is to give someone the idea they have a specific, destined purpose as part of this group; their participation with this group is not an accident. If they are to fulfill this deep, purposed destiny, they must remain part of this group. Mystical manipulation varies from a sincere, genuine spiritual experience in that this is an artificial production designed to play on people's emotional states, causing them to believe belonging to this group is a spiritual orchestration rather than a play on their thoughts and feelings. Through mystical manipulation, members of a cult feel a sense of destined belonging: while uncertain of their purpose in life prior due to any number of circumstances, they now feel like their ultimate life destiny has been discovered in belonging to the group. This may come through sexual rites, sexual regulations, or the abstinence of sex; the feeling a leader is omnipotent and extremely charismatic or charming; intense and long, complicated spiritual rites that may enact drama or ritual; obviously staged, fake mystical experiences or events; fake healings; or some other orchestrated action that causes the individual to feel spiritually connected to the leader of the cult in a destiny-shaping way.

- **The demand for purity**: Within cult view, the world is sharply divided between those who are pure (the group) and those who are deemed impure (the world, or everyone else). The required state of purity is nothing short of perfection, both unobtainable and unreasonable. The more attempts one makes to reach it, the more obstacles placed to keep one from reaching the ultimate goal. Achieving this state of complete purity, no matter how unrealistic it may be, is only possible within the group. Those outside the group are unable to reach this pure state. They are, therefore, seen as eternally damned or unable to achieve the ultimate promise. They are seen as impure, contaminated, and bad influences, with their only agenda to destroy the goal of purity one believes can be achieved only through the group.

- **Cult of confession**: Within cults, individuals are encouraged and expected to divulge personal information about themselves to the group. This creates a feeling of secrecy: what happens within the group cannot, under any circumstances, be divulged in full truth to the outside world. The expectation is that all personal confessions, secrets, and other things one would ordinarily be unwilling to divulge outside the group should be shared within the group. This level of reveal about a person has many complicated effects on a person: they feel guilt for not measuring up to the required perfection of the group and a sense of "starting over" again, now that all that is a part of one's "past" life. The information divulged gives the cult's leadership leverage over the member if they decide to leave (i.e., blackmail or reveal). Even if a member does not leave, they are less likely to leave the group knowing that those within the group have such an intimate knowledge of them.

- **Sacred science**: The work and ideas of cults are presented to members as innovative, new, never-done before, and the very thing needed in response to today's world. The ideals and beliefs of the cult are seen as the answer to humanity's problems. The group can save the entire world, if the world is willing to conform to its ideals and practices. As a result, the cult often has a myriad of subheadings and groups that mask as other organizations (such as community service, literacy, drug and alcohol recovery, education, family values, or political lobbying) to hide the true agenda: bring people into the cult to expand recruitment and funds. Because the outside world is unwilling to receive the value of this sacred science, the world is perceived as evil, opposing the group, and in a backward state of utter darkness and inferiority. There is no hope for the world, unwilling to receive the new, innovative cult.

- **Loaded language**: Cults are notorious for repeated jargon and cliches, catchy slogans, and repeated use of language, sometimes stated to the point of excessiveness and obsessiveness. Words and terms used are known and properly understood only within the group; the world is believed to be ignorant of such things. Even if outsiders were to understand, they would not receive the language themes used among group members. Often, words are used outside the group with alternative meanings within the group. This equates to confusion, as those outside of the group assume the words to be used as they are in general society, when they are not. This is neither explained to the world nor to the initiate; one only discovers this as a full member of the group.

- **Doctrine over person**: Within cults, doctrine is not seen as a general thing, but a personal thing. The doctrine of the cult is individual, with each person adhering to a singular set of principles and inward adherence and devotion. Each cult member has the goal of attaining personal perfection and is focused on applying the doctrine of the cult within themselves, rather than seeing them as good for practice or as moral principles. Truth is seen as totalistic and absolute, in every conceivable sense. Living the cult's doctrinal ideals is essential for each member. Failure to do so is not just one of disciplinary measures, but a personal failing on the person, causing guilt, condemnation, and shame.

- **Dispensing of existence**: All things must eventually come to an end. This is truer nowhere more than in a cult. Because cults view the world through a very limited and narrow lens (us vs. them), the realm of truth (totalistic and absolute) requires a choice of those both in the group and outside of it. Those outside the group, not having made the choice to join the group, are seen as perpetually evil. There is no middle ground or alternate option. Those outside the group do not have the right to, nor will they always exist. This leaves two fatalistic options for the dispensing of existence: either cult members will seek to fight the wickedness of the world (as with some sort of attack, malignment, interpretation of world events as a personal attack on them, or attack on civil or secular authorities) or cessation or departure from the world (group suicide or dissolution of the group in some way). The dispensing of existence leads to paranoia among members. There is a chronic feeling of being watched or supervised, feeling that, for no reason other than the group's existence, those in the group are individually and personally hated by the world. In fear and preparation for this time, cults stockpile weapons, hoard supplies, doomsday prep, and an unreasonable attachment to the group, fearing that its end, or the end of all things, is immediately near.

HOLIDAYS

Cults take a different approach to holidays than mainline groups. Holidays are either celebrated or not celebrated, depending on the leadership's view of such days and their interaction with the world. Many cult groups celebrate traditional holidays within the framework of the group's agenda or motive; for example, Christmas or Easter might be connected to the group's ideals and goals. In some instances, groups may also revive the practice of long-forgot holidays, such as that observed in Old Testament or pagan times, as part of their ritual and rite. Many cults create their own calendars and have their own days of observation. Some also thrive on the abstinence of observances of any sort, believing such makes them even more unique and set apart.

VISUAL SIGNS AND SYMBOLS

Odd or branded uniform or dress; living compound; excessive demands for purity; emphasis on a central leader or group of leaders; sudden desire for holiness through a group; brandings or markings; logos; abnormal or odd behaviors relating to teaching, life, or worship; giving away large amounts of money or property to the group; increasing involvement with the group, including excessively long services; use of loaded or coded language; disassociation from others, including family members and friends; sexual disciplines or controls; emphasis on staying within the group; odd teachings centering around absolutism or death.

Creeds, Books, and Laws

Cult groups are infamous for excessive rules, regulations, and governances. They are typically ruled by a convoluted law that changes as issues arise and becomes more and more controlled as time goes by. The wording of cult law is authoritarian, impossible to follow, loaded, and expands over every area of an individual's life. Cults cover your life "from morning until bed, from the time you are born, until you are dead." The rules and regulation of a group are usually carefully guarded from outsiders, who are assumed to misinterpret the controls of the organization.

More relevant than the standard laws of a cult, however, is its leadership. Cult leadership is central and highly organized. Cults typically operate from the top down, with one central leader who, in turn, appoints a few advisers who do not contradict or question the leader of the cult. There are then a few more individuals who descend in number to ensure the goals of the organization are met, in full. The execution and maintenance of laws are ridged and fixed, and no exceptions are ever made in any circumstances for the average member. When top leadership fails to live up to mandatory perfection, it is usually explained away, excused, or maligned to make it appear other than it really is.

Eclectic Beliefs

Many outsiders judge those within cults as intellectually inferior or inept. This is not the case. People do not join cults for intellectual reasons; they join them for emotional ones. The cult gives a feeling of belonging and of being a part of something purposeful and greater than one is on their own.

At some point in everyone's lives (or perhaps more than one point), we are all vulnerable to the influences of a group that offers us this sense of belonging. Whether it is due to loss, death, a move, dissatisfaction in life, or an experience with life that leaves someone lacking, everyone can be vulnerable to the ideas of something that seems almost too good to be true. This is especially true considering much of cult experience is a manipulation on emotions, spiritual perceptions, and one's sense of reality.

Relations with Non-Cult Members

Cults not only avoid relations with other religions and religious groups; they avoid relations with the rest of the world, setting themselves apart under the justification of separateness. Whether living together as a group or finding ways to promote and encourage separation of its members from general society, relationships with those outside the group are typically forbidden. Many practice extreme forms of shunning with those who leave the group or who refuse to join. Group members are prohibited from communication with such: visits, discussions, phone calls, and other communications are prohibited, especially when all attempts to get someone to join or rejoin the group are exhausted.

HOLY SITES

The concept of the sacred or holy differs in cults than it does among the average religious individual. The sacred or holy aspect of a place is one where the practice of the cult occurs; especially within secret rites that are not available or accessible to outsiders. Holy sites, therefore, vary by cult, in keeping with their concept of the sacred or holy places.

NOTABLE FIGURES

Jonestown pavilion after the mass death of its members in Jonestown, Guyana

David Koresh (1959-1993), leader, Branch Davidians; L. Ron Hubbard (1911-1986), founder, Church of Scientology (Los Angeles, California); Sun Myung Moon (1920-2012), founder, Unification Church (Pulsan, South Korea); Josemaria Escriva de Balaguer (1902-1975), founder, Opus Dei (Rome, Italy); Charles Manson (1934-2017), leader, the Family (San Fernando Valley, California); Marshall Applewhite (1931-1997), leader, Heaven's Gate (San Diego, California); Jim Jones (1931-1978), founder, People's Temple/Jonestown (Jonestown, Guyana); Shoko Ashara (1955-2018), founder, Aum Shinrikyo (Tokyo, Japan); David Berg (1919-1994), the Children of God (Huntington Beach, California); Joseph Di Mambro (1924-1994), founder, the Order of the Solar Temple (Geneva, Switzerland); Bhagwan Rajneesh (1931-1990), founder, Rajneesh Movement/Osho (Pune, India); Warren Jeffs (1955-), leader, Fundamentalist Church of Jesus Christ of Latter-Day Saints (Hildale, Utah); Charles Taze Russell (1852-1916), founder, Jehovah's Witnesses (Wallkill, New York); Joseph Smith (1805-1844), founder, Mormonism (Salt Lake City, Utah).

NOTABLE GROUPS

The Unification Movement, founded by Sun Myung Moon in Korea in 1954, is notable for its extensive myriad of organizations, all working under the heading of the main organization, the Holy Spirit Association for the Unification of World Christianity (HAS-UWC). Its founding principles are found in the book *Divine Principle*, which introduces several unusual doctrines into Christian teaching. These teachings include the idea that Sun Myung Moon was the second coming of Jesus Christ. While Jesus Christ failed in His ministry of salvation, Moon would fulfill the salvation work that Christ failed to perform. The movement is best known for its mass marriages, arranged by Moon himself, performed in huge stadiums at once. Members of the movement live together in communal housing. The organization is not disclosing of many of its beliefs in a practice known as "heavenly deception."

The Unification Church has received billions of dollars by different political groups and affiliations, including the United States government, several businesses (Moon was a businessman), and audiences with presidents (including George W. Bush). Perhaps the strangest alliance was with religious right organizers, such as Jerry Falwell, for the promotion of conservative politics and values. The Unification Church owns the *The Washington Times*.[2]

Facts and Figures

Cult members do not see themselves as members of a cult; therefore, no one is going to fill out a survey and admit to cult involvement.

Other Important Definitions

- **New religious movement**: Also called "new religion." A term for a religious group that is new and often carries characteristics of a cult.[3]

Believer's Characteristics

Emphasis on a central leader or leaders, a new and innovative concept, and a need for purity; may act and dress in a specific manner; giving away and leaving behind possessions, friends, and family to pursue a "pure" life with the group; hours of study, services, and experiences; eight points of mind control; strong personal aversion to those outside the group; prohibitions on communications with the outside world; living with the group in an isolated situation; sexual prohibitions and controls; surrendering one's control and life direction to that of another human being; inability to think for oneself, make independent decisions, or decide for oneself even about basic everyday things; regimented and ritualistic day; legalism; personal demands for purity, that are impossible to abide by; a philosophy that includes the dispensation of existence; myriad of subheading organizations fronting as social betterment organizations; confusing and convoluted doctrine; hostility to outsiders.

Eastern Church Movements

I served the famous professors and scholars, and eventually they learned that the Reverend Moon is superior to them. Even Nobel laureate academics who thought they were at the center of knowledge are as nothing in front of me.
(Sun Myung Moon)[1]

Theology

Church movements originating in the mid-to-late 1900s within the far east (especially Korea) often represent a syncretism of traditional animism and polytheism mixed with Christian theology. Most have a few central theological points in common. The first is that the divine, namely the concept of a "Divine Father," is often countered with a "Divine Mother" image. This reflects indigenous ideas of a central god and goddess instrumental in the creation of eastern nations and spiritual culture. Most also believe in the relevance and role of lesser gods or spirits in the work of creation and the lives of believers.

It is not uncommon to find eastern church movements that believe in the current or modern incarnation of the divine (both as father and mother) in the form of their respective denominational leaders. All manifestations are culturally relevant, appearing as either Chinese or Korean. Such individuals came to a divine realization of their nature, either having a specific mission revealed to them or coming to personal knowledge of their divine status. Most see this through the lens of the second coming of Christ (which may appear as either male or female), the manifestation of the Holy Spirit as a being, or both at once. Mixing Biblical ideas with their own points of personal doctrinal revelation and cultural input, such is often believed to be equivalent of or expounding of Biblical revelation.

These movements do consider themselves to be Christian but reject more traditional Christian theological statements, such as Trinitarianism or Oneness theology. Their focus is on their immediate incarnations of the divine, the needed spiritual guidance for modern times, and on embracing leadership's directives. All other churches and religious groups are seen to be in theological error.

Philosophy

Eastern church movements would classify themselves to be Christian within a restorationist tradition: through the theophany revelations of the divine manifest in their leadership, their expounding of the faith, and their theological differences, they are restoring (or reestablishing) Christianity to stand as its original divine design. By believing their leadership is not just agency of the divine but incarnations therein, they believe their belief system is the only true religion in existence. One cannot come to find, nor discover, salvation outside of the group. To complete one's spiritual purpose and find meaning in one's life, an individual must fully submit themselves to the will and directives of the group's leadership.

Such movements all believe in the literalness of Matthew 24:27:

For as the lightning cometh out of the east, and shineth even unto the west; so shall also the coming of the Son of man be.

Yang Xianbin (1973-), the mouthpiece of Eastern Lightning, and Zhao Weishan (1951-), group founder

They believe the second coming shall emerge from the east, with its unique theologies, prophetic understandings, and need for a rising messianic figure. Eastern church movements are highly apocalyptic in nature, believe judgment is soon at hand, and adhere to strict personal codes. Church involvement, regulation, participation, and study dominate the lives of members. All eastern church movements: The Unification Church, World Mission Society Church of God, Shincheonji Church of Jesus the Temple of the Tabernacle of the Testimony, Good News Mission, and The Church of Almighty God (Eastern Lightning) are classified as high control cult organizations due to their extreme doctrines, measures, proselytizing, and lifestyle of members, all of which revolve around the worship of their leaders.

NUMBER OF ADHERENTS

In the decades since their initial founding, eastern church movements have gained worldwide interest. Growth outside of their founding nations is often slow. Exact numbers for these groups are often speculative; some are difficult to obtain. The Unification Church is estimated to have between 1,000,000 and 2,000,000 members worldwide[2]; The Church of Almighty God has approximately 3,000,000 to 4,000,000 members worldwide[3]; the World Mission Society Church of God has approximately 100,000 members worldwide[4]; Church of Jesus the Temple of the Tabernacle of the Testimony has approximately 320,000 members[5]; and the Salvation Sects of Korea (the Good News Mission, Evangelical Baptist Church of Korea, and the Life Word Mission) have an unknown number of members. Overall, eastern church movements have somewhere around 6,500,000 million members worldwide.

TRADITIONAL LANGUAGES

Korean, Chinese.

ADHERENT IDENTITY

Unification Church, Unification Movement, Unificationism, Unificationists, Moonies, Family Federation for World Peace and Unification; Holy Spirit Association for the Unification of World

Christianity; The Church of Almighty God, Eastern Lightning; World Mission Society Church of God (WMSCOG), the Church of God, Jesus Witnesses, Witness of Ahn Sahng-hong, Witnesses of Ahn Sahng-hong Church of God; Good News Mission; Shincheonji, Church of Jesus, the Temple of the Testimony (SCJ), Shincheonji Church of Jesus; Guwonpa, Salvation Sect.

SECTS/DIVISIONS

There are a few major divisions of eastern church movements, each with their own unique leadership and church structure. Outside the basic thematic beliefs, they also vary some in their denominational identities.

- **The Unification Church**: The most visible of all eastern church movements, the Unification Church is better known as the "Moonies." More properly asserted the Unification Movement or recognized by its other entities such as The Holy Spirit Association for the Unification of World Christianity and the Family Federation for World Peace and Unification, the Unification Church was founded by Sun Myung Moon (1920-2012) in 1954. According to church doctrine, Moon believes Jesus appeared to him in 1936, asking him to complete the work Christ did not complete after the crucifixion. He came to believe he was the Second Coming of Christ, a new figure living now as Christ with the same mission. He is identified as True Father, and his second wife, Hak Ja Han Moon (1943-) as True Mother. He started proclaiming his message after the end of Japanese occupation in 1945, with the publication of his book *The Divine Principle* (later published as *Exposition of the Divine Principle*). *The Divine Principle* applies a three-fold principle of systematic theology unique to the group. It includes God's purpose in the creation of humanity, the fall of humanity, and restoration. Such now stands as the central text of the movement, outlining a need to conform existing Christian groups according to his vision for the church.

Unification Church symbol on flag

  According to the Unification Church, Jesus was destined to be the restorer of fallen humanity, serving as a new Adam. While he was destined to be such, his death came prematurely, before he had a chance to marry and establish a family line. Because he was unable to do so, the role of the messianic head of the new humanity was transferred to Moon. Adam and Eve first sinned through mutual fornication after Even committed adultery (the Unification Church believes Eve committed adultery with the serpent in the garden). From this action, the two failed to realize God's purpose for them. They introduced selfish love into human experience. Salvation is acquired through a process of indemnity: mistake or loss must provide a greater value in order to repay the divine (because the divine cannot relate with impurity). Humans are responsible to repay indemnity before the divine.[6]

Family life is central to the Unification Church. Marriage is considered the only official "sacramental rite" within the movement. The church is best known for its mass weddings or renewal ceremonies hosted by Moon and his wife. When one receives this blessing, they are removed from the lineage of sin and now members of a new sinless family line. By doing so, one connects themselves to perfection, creating a new family far away from the sinful human line. Marriages are arranged (and often not legal). Families live together in church-sponsored housing. It is not possible for one to remain single within the movement. After their marital arrangement and ceremony, members of the Unification Church begin a series of rituals: such includes sexual activities in front of a portrait of Moon and the bride bowing down before the groom, proving she would complete her role in absolute goodness and submission. New members are expected to live in poverty-like conditions. Alcohol and drugs are forbidden. Participants are expected to give everything for Moon's cause.[7]

International Family Association logo

Outside of these beliefs, much of the Unification Church's teachings are unknown to outsiders. This secrecy, along with the way that members disconnect from non-believing family and friends (among other things) cause concern of cultlike activities within the Unification Church. The church also operates a host of other organizations that front as independent, political, business, or civic organizations, including *The Washington Times*, United Press International, International Black Student Alliance CARP Project, International Family Association, World Mission Center, Causa Ministerial Alliance, Ecumenical Foundation for Community Development, Council for the World's Religions, Interdenominational Conference of Clergy, Korean Evangelical Association, the Committee to Defend the First Amendment, American Constitution Committee, and the American Freedom Foundation. Moon has been connected to several different conservative causes, including loans, friendships, and alliances with Evangelicals Jerry Falwell (1933-2007) and Tim LaHaye (1926-2016).

The Unification Church entered a state of internal chaos after the death of Sun Myung Moon in 2012. Hak Ja Han Moon is considered now to be the "mother of humankind" while Moon's oldest son leads the Family Peace Association. The church split, and two of Moon's surviving sons established their own congregations. World Peace and Unification Sanctuary (known as Sanctuary Church), also known as Rod of Iron Ministries, is a church located in Newfoundland, Pennsylvania. It is best known for a ceremony blessing their assault rifles (specifically AR-15s) in a marriage ceremony vow renewal during a special service. Seeing assault rifles as a 'rod of iron'. They believe through their weapons they shall control the world. Bearing arms and stockpiling weapons is seen as a spiritual duty.[8]

- **The Church of Almighty God**: Known more casually as "Eastern Lightning" or *Quánnéngshén* (in its original Chinese), The Church of Almighty God is probably known to most through its infiltrative methods promoting videos and teachings through social media. A newer group, Eastern Lightning (a reference to Matthew 24:27) originated in China in 1991. Its foundational beliefs are the idea that Jesus Christ has returned to earth (in the form of the Second Coming) as a Chinese woman, Yang Xiangbin (1973-) ("Lightning Deng"). She was first declared to be Jesus Christ by her partner, Zhao Weishan (1951-). Zhao appears to be the organizing leadership of the group. Since 2000, the group's headquarters are located in New York City.

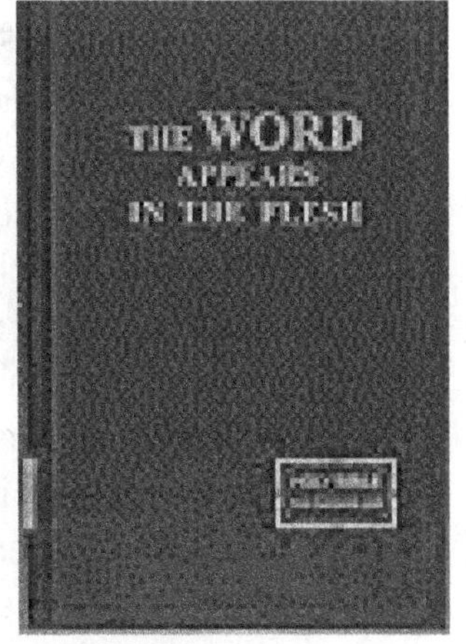

Eastern Lightning's key text, The Word Appears in the Flesh

The group believes there are three different stages of a 6,000-year divine management dispensation: the Age of Law (Jehovah guides Israel); the Age of Grace (Jesus Christ saves humanity but doesn't erase sin) and the Age of Kingdom (beginning with the establishment of the church in 1991). To follow will be a Millennial Kingdom of peace (the earth will enter this era after the death of Almighty God). The group's theology forms divine revelation has changed three times: in the Old Testament, known as Jehovah; in the New Testament, as Jesus Christ; and now, as Almighty God (a form of modalism). While Jesus did forgive the sins of humanity, his work was not complete, because sin remained. Now, under the work of Almighty God, people can find total cleansing from sin. To find this, one must believe fully in the teachings of the Church of the Almighty God. The teachings of the church are most often found in the writings of Lightning Deng, known as *The Word Appears in the Flesh*. These writings are considered scriptural and continue revelation from past ages (Biblical times) to the present day.[9]

Specifics on much of the group's doctrines are unknown, as the group operates by great secrecy. We do know there is no formal liturgical structure, and believers do not practice baptism or communion. The organization appears hierarchical: local congregations are overseen by subregional and regional leaders, who are overseen by inspectors from headquarters. Members meet weekly, often in private homes to discuss, pray, hear messages, and to, most relevantly, discuss the revelations of their leader, whom they refer to as "Almighty God."

The group has garnered its share of controversy in its short history. Sexual coercion, riots, kidnapping, bribes, brainwashing, blackmail, beatings, and manipulation among poor individuals have all been reported. There remains question as to how factual these claims are, as the group is a vocal opponent of the Communist regime in China. Nonetheless, the Chinese government has declared it to the be the most dangerous cult in China.[10]

- **World Mission Society Church of God (WMSCOG)**: The World Mission Society Church of God is the Sabbatarian branch of eastern church movements. Established in South Korea in 1964, the WMSCOG believes its founder, Ahn Sahng-hong (1918-1985) (who spent a number of years studying Seventh-day Adventism, from which he was excommunicated) is God the Father, Jesus Christ, and the Holy Spirit (as the Second Coming). Zahng Gil-jah (1943-), the widow and successor to Ahn Sahng-hong, is God the Mother. The Elohim gods of father and mother created the earth and all that is within it, including human beings. The church believes itself to be teaching the full revelation of the Bible, only properly understood through the teachings of Ahn Sahng-hong. These serve as continued, modern revelation for their followers. These writings and revelations are revealed through copious amounts of literature, published and distributed through the church. It awaits the end of the world, which has been predicted three different times since its founding in 1964.[11,12]

World Mission Society Church of God logo

Baptism, considered the first step of church membership, is done in the name of Jehovah, Jesus, and Ahn Sahng-hong. Among other rites, the church observes footwashing (often done by Zang Gil-jah for some of the followers) and eating the unleavened bread and drinking the wine of Passover. All prayers are spoken in the name of Ahn Sahng-hong. Women are required to wear veils in prayer. All imagery is considered idolatry; crosses, stained glass windows, and other images associated with church life are forbidden. Unique among eastern church movements, the WMSCOG observes the Sabbath day from sunrise to sunset and the Old Testament festivals of Passover, Unleavened Bread, First Fruits, Feast of Weeks, Feast of Trumpets, Day of Atonement, and Feast of Tabernacles. Three services are held weekly on Saturdays, and members are expected to attend all three. In between services, churches hold Bible studies, watch video footage, or volunteer or engage in street or community preaching.[13]

As a group, much like the others mentioned, WMSCOG is secretive about some of its doctrines, choosing to only reveal specific aspects of its beliefs to members after they join. The group is known for aggressive evangelization methods. Some former members have come forward reporting excessive control methods including forced abortion, micromanaging time, prohibitions on internet usage, and limits on entertainment (such as music). There have been several lawsuits against the group; most have been unsuccessful. The group has also been accused of human trafficking through college campuses in Mississippi, South Carolina, Utah, Kentucky, Georgia, Texas, Arizona, Tennessee, and Ohio. Classified as a cult by most researchers and experts, the WMSCOG is closely monitored and criticized.[14,15]

- **Shincheonji, Church of Jesus, the Temple of the Testimony (SCJ)**: A breakaway group from the Olive Tree, a once highly relevant syncretistic Korean religious group. Its leader, Park Tae Son (1917-1990), believed he was one of the two witnesses mentioned in the book of Revelation. Over time, he came to begin teaching the Bible was mostly in error, Jesus was not the Christ, and Park himself was the true Messiah and creator. Now Shincheonji, founded in 1984, stands as a fast-growing religious group in Korea. The Church of Jesus, the Temple of the Testimony revolves around Lee Man-hee (1931-), who claims he is the promised pastor of the New Testament, the only one with the power to interpret the metaphorical coding in the book of Revelation. He is believed to be the second coming of Christ, referred to as the "spirit of the returned Jesus Christ." He is also known as "Chairman Lee," "the chairman," "the one who overcomes," and "the advocate." The church considers itself to be the true nation of God and the only true faith, revealing divine will to people in modern times. The word "Shincheonji" is an abbreviation for a Korean term for "New Heaven and New Earth."[16,17]

Shincheonji logo

  To belong to the group, one must study with Shincheonji for approximately six to nine months and pass several tests to prove competency in the presented material. The churches are divided into twelve "tribes" (paralleling the twelve tribes of Jacob in the Old Testament). It is often branded a "doomsday cult" due to its emphasis on coming judgment: 144,00 sealed adherents will testify of the revealed word through Lee and a multitude in white will go to heaven with him. Members wear white and black clothing as a sign of this time to come and to identify themselves as members of the church.[18,19]

  The group is best known for aggressive and manipulative evangelization methods, including attending other churches under the guise of desired membership to lure or convince other church members to join theirs. Shincheonji has also been accused of influencing Korean politicians. With several vocal ex-members, the group is under fire by governments, churches, and religious groups worldwide. Using a host of subsidiary names, other subsets of the church include Mannam Volunteer Association/Mannam International Youth Coalition (MIYC), International Peace Youth Group (IPYG)/Heavenly Culture, World Peace, Restoration of Light (HWPL), Parachristo, Temple of the Tabernacle of the Testimony (SCJ), and Zion International Bible Study.[20]

Good News Mission logo

- **Guwonpa "Salvation Sects"**: The Good News Mission (Ock Soo Park [1944-], 1972), Evangelical Baptist Church of Korea (Yoo Byung-eun [1941-2014] and Kwon Shin-chan [1923-1996], 1962), and Life Word Mission (Le Yo-han, 1982) are under a general heading of *Guwonpa*, which means "salvation sect" in Korean. This label relates to how they evangelize: the first question they ask others is, "Are you saved?" or "Do you have salvation?"[21] These three churches appear more traditional on the surface than their other counterparts, but there are some significant differences between *Guwonpa* and mainline churches. The first is that matters of salvation are often treated differently. For example, the Evangelical Baptist Church of Korea (formerly known as Korean Evangelical Layman's Church) focuses on a form of hypercalvinism (members are entirely detached from sin both now and in the future and are guaranteed to go to heaven).[22] Little is spoken of repentance. Most focus on dualistic ideas: a contrast between the soul and the flesh, and that sin can only exist within the flesh, not the soul. All groups are extremely aggressive in evangelization, promoting lectures, missionary efforts, youth events, and service events. The *Guwopna* sects have come into focus over the past few years due to public disasters (such as the sinking of the Sewol ferry), ex-member testimonies, and criticisms from other groups of cultlike methods and behavior.[23]

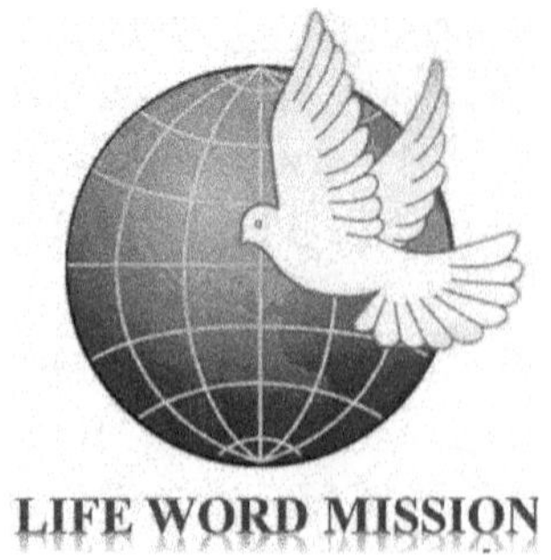

Life Word Mission logo

DISPUTES WITHIN GROUP

Each eastern church group is unique to its own. Despite the many foundational things they have in common, the groups are not in union with one another. Each believes its specific manifestation of the divine is true, with others in error. Along with that belief goes their own adherence to practice, sacred writings, teachings, observances, and holidays.

SCRIPTURES

All Korean church groups use a combination of the standard western Bible canon, consisting of Old and New Testaments, inclusive of 66 books: the Pentateuch (Genesis, Exodus, Leviticus, Numbers, and Deuteronomy), Historical books (Joshua, Judges, Ruth, 1 Samuel, 2 Samuel, 1 Kings, 2 Kings, 1 Chronicles, 2 Chronicles, Ezra, Nehemiah, Esther), Wisdom books (Job, Psalms, Proverbs, Ecclesiastes, Song of Songs), Prophetic books (Isaiah, Jeremiah, Lamentations, Ezekiel, Daniel, Hosea, Joel, Amos, Obadiah, Jonah, Micah, Nahum, Habakkuk, Zephaniah, Haggai, Zechariah, Malachi), the Gospels (Matthew, Mark, Luke, John), the Acts of the Apostles, the Pauline Epistles (Romans, 1 Corinthians, 2 Corinthians, Galatians, Ephesians, Philippians, Colossians, 1 Thessalonians, 2 Thessalonians, 1 Timothy, 2 Timothy, Titus, Philemon, Hebrews) the General Epistles (James, 1 Peter, 2 Peter, 1 John, 2 John, 3 John, Jude) and Revelation.

The Bible's usage is often different than in western churches. It is often narrated through the unique revelatory teachings of their leaders. These additional teachings are considered as inspired, if not superior, to Biblical revelation. They are seen as being for right now, unveiling and clarifying the teachings of Biblical prophecy, rather than for ancient times. These writings include *Divine Teaching* (Unification Church), *The Word Appears in the Flesh*, the scripture collecting the utterances of Almighty God (Church of Almighty God), *The Truth Books* (World Mission Society Church of God; a series of seven books published by the WMSCOG of which ownership outside the group is prohibited), *The Book of Shinchonji* (Shinchonji), and the salvation sects use the Bible, with very twisted and speculative interpretations. Most often, the Bible is used as evidence of their leaders' claims of divinity. Only a handful of these texts are available in English, or any other language outside of Korean.

> *Had Adam as a man realized the ideal of creation and become the tree of life, and had Eve as a woman realized the ideal of creation and fulfilled the tree of the knowledge of good and evil, they would have stood together as the True Parents of humankind. They would have fulfilled God's three great blessings and established the Kingdom of God on earth. Instead, because they fell, this world became an earthly hell. Therefore, to give rebirth to fallen people, Jesus came as the second Adam, the True Father of humankind, with the mission symbolized by the tree of life. This being the case, should not there also have come the True Mother of humankind, the second Eve with the mission symbolized by the tree of the knowledge of good and evil? The one who has come as the True Mother to give rebirth to fallen people is the Holy Spirit.*

Sun Myung Moon officiating over a mass wedding

> *A new life is born through the love of parents. When we believe in Jesus as the Savior through the inspiration of the Holy Spirit, we receive the love of the spiritual True Parents, which is generated through the give and take between Jesus, the spiritual True Father, and the Holy Spirit, the spiritual True Mother. Through this love, new life is infused into us, and our spirits are reborn as new selves. This is spiritual rebirth. Nevertheless, since human beings fell both spiritually and physically, we must be cleansed of original sin by being born again both spiritually and physically. Christ must return to earth to grant physical salvation to humanity, which is to be realized through our physical rebirth.*

> *According to the Principle of Creation, God's purpose of creation is completed based upon the four position foundation, which is established by fulfilling the three object purpose through origin-division-union action. To fulfill the purpose of creation, Jesus and the Holy Spirit stand before God as object partners who separately manifest the dual characteristics of God. They unite through give and take with each other with God as the center, and form the four position foundation. God, Jesus and the Holy Spirit thus become one, and this oneness constitutes the Trinity.*

> *Originally, God's purpose for creating Adam and Eve was to form a trinity by raising them to be the True Parents of humankind united in harmonious oneness as husband and wife centered on God in a four position foundation. If Adam and Eve had not fallen, but had formed this trinity with God and become the True Parents who could multiply good children, their descendants would have also become good husbands and wives with God as the center of their lives. Each couple would thus have formed a trinity with God. The Kingdom of Heaven on earth fulfilling God's three great blessings would have been realized at that time. Instead, when Adam and Eve fell, they formed a four position foundation with Satan as their center; in other words, they formed a fallen trinity with*

Satan. Their descendants likewise have continued to form trinities with Satan, and so built a corrupt and immoral society.

Since the Fall, God has worked for the day when He could give rebirth to people and join them in trinities with Himself. For this purpose, God intended to exalt Jesus and his Bride as the second Adam and Eve to become the True Parents of humanity. However, the resurrected Jesus and the Holy Spirit in oneness with God could form only a spiritual trinity. They could fulfill only the mission of spiritual True Parents. Thus, Jesus and the Holy Spirit have been giving spiritual rebirth to people of faith as their spiritual children, restoring them to spiritual trinities.

Christ must return in the flesh and find his Bride. They will form on the earth a perfect trinity with God and become True Parents both spiritually and physically. They will give fallen people rebirth both spiritually and physically, removing their original sin and enabling them to build trinities on earth with God as the center. When fallen people are restored to the point where they can establish true four position foundations centered on God, they will finally be able to build the Kingdom of Heaven on earth where God's three great blessings are fulfilled.[24]

In the past, people grasped a law in God's words: When God's words are spoken, they are soon made real. There is no falsehood in this. Since God has said He shall chastise all peoples, and, furthermore, since He has issued His administrative decrees, it can be seen that God's work has been carried out to a certain stage. The constitution that was issued forth to all people addressed their lives and their attitude toward God. It did not get to the root; it did not say that it was based on God's predestination, but on man's behavior at that time. The administrative decrees of today are extraordinary and they speak of how "all people will be separated according to their own kind, and will receive chastisements commensurate with their actions." Without a close reading, no problem can be found in this. Because it is only during the final age that God separates all things according to their kind, after reading this, most people remain puzzled and confused; they still adopt a lukewarm attitude, not seeing the urgency of the times, and so they do not take this as a warning. Why, at this point, are God's administrative decrees, which are announced to the whole universe, shown to man? Do these people represent all those throughout the universe? Could God, afterward, have more mercy on these people? Have these people grown two heads? When God chastises the people of the entire universe, when all manner of catastrophes strike, changes will occur in the sun and moon as a result of these catastrophes, and, when these catastrophes end, the sun and moon will have been altered—and this is called "the transition." Suffice to say, the disasters of the future will be grievous. Night might take the place of day, the sun might not appear for a year, there might be several months of searing heat, a waning moon might always face mankind, there might appear the bizarre state of the sun and moon rising together, and so on. Following several cyclical changes, ultimately, with the passage of time, they shall be renewed. God pays special attention to His plans for those who belong to the devil. Thus, He deliberately says, "Of the human beings within the universe, all those belonging to the devil will be exterminated." Before these "people" have shown their true colors, God always uses them to render service; as a result, He pays no heed to their doings, He gives them no "reward" when they do well, nor does He dock their "wages" when they perform badly. As such, He disregards them and gives them the cold shoulder. He does not suddenly change because of their "goodness," for, regardless of the time or place, man's substance does not change, just like the covenant established between God and man, and just like, as man says, "There will be no change even if the seas run dry and the rocks crumble." Thus, God simply sorts those people according to their kind and does not readily heed them. From the time of creation until today, the devil has never comported itself well. It has always caused interruptions, disturbances, and dissent. When God acts or speaks, the devil always tries to participate, but God takes no notice of it. At the mention of the devil, God's rage flows forth, insuppressible; because they are not of one spirit, there is therefore no connection, only distance and separation. Following the revelation of the seven seals, the state of the earth grows always worse, and all things "advance shoulder-to-shoulder with the seven seals," not falling behind in the slightest. Throughout God's words, people are seen by God as stupefied, yet they do not awaken at all. To reach a higher point, to bring forth the strength of all people, and, moreover, to conclude God's work at its peak, God asks people a string of questions, as if inflating their bellies, and thus He replenishes all people. Because these people have no real stature, based on the actual circumstances, those who are inflated are goods that are up to standard, while those who are not are useless trash. This is God's requirement of man, and the aim of the method by which He speaks. In particular, when God says, "Could it be that I, when on earth, am not the same as I am in heaven? Could it be that I, when in heaven, cannot come down to the earth? Could it be that I, when on earth, am unworthy to be borne up to heaven?" these questions serve as a clearer path on which man might know God. From God's words, God's urgent will is beheld; people are incapable of attaining it, and God repeatedly adds conditions, thus reminding all people to know the heavenly God on earth, and to know the God who is in heaven but lives on earth.

From God's words can be seen the states of man: "All mankind spends effort on My words, undertaking investigations of their own into My outward semblance, but they all meet with failure, their efforts bearing no fruit, and instead are struck down by My words and dare not get up again." Who can understand God's sorrow? Who can comfort God's heart? Who accords with God's heart in what He asks? When people bear no fruit, they deny themselves and truly submit to God's orchestrations. Gradually, as they show their true heart, each is separated according to their kind, and it is thus seen that the substance of the angels is pure obedience to God. And so, God says, "Humanity is exposed in its original form." When God's work reaches this step, it will all have been completed. God appears to say nothing of His being an exemplar for His sons and people, instead focusing on making all people display their original form. Do you understand the true meaning of these words?[25]

BASIC RELIGIOUS PRACTICES

Eastern church groups focus heavily on devotion and obedience to the individuals they believe to be divine incarnations. This requires an extensive amount of an individual's life and time, which is characteristic of this religious subset. Every group requires an extensive "vetting" period by which potential members must receive instruction into specific essential doctrinal points necessary for entry-level participation. In most, if not all instances, finer specifics on doctrinal points (such as the exact nature of the way they see their leadership, or things one might have to do as a member to maintain position within the group) are deliberately excluded. In this process, one might study with an individual or group, take classes, watch videos, study through the group's website, and complete some form of competency testing to show they understand the material.

For active members, participants spend long hours in services (typically held multiple times per week), studies, and evangelization. In some instances, members of different families might live or travel together for the purpose of remaining connected. Financial giving is a requirement, often in the form of multiple tithes and offerings donated to the church on a regular basis.

HOLIDAYS

As a general rule, eastern church groups do not observe traditional, western church holidays (such as Christmas or Easter) in the same sense as other churches might observe them. Each group observes holidays specific to their own revelations and traditions.

- **The Unification Church**: The Unification Church observes five major holy days every year, according to the "heavenly," or lunar calendar. Members are encouraged to prepare for holidays in advance, reading the speeches of Moon and focusing on the advancing events, to create a deep desire to observe them. Seven days are devoted to each holy day: three days of internal preparation, the day's observance itself, and continued offering thereafter for another three days. On holy days, all members of the Unification Church offer financial donations, recited pledges, gifts in honor of the true parents (Moon and his spouse), gifts to the regional or national centers, and gifts given to one another. Banquets are held for the True Parents with a candle lighting ceremony followed as the true children bow to the true parents. In instances where the true parents are unavailable, a picture of the couple is placed on the table or in vicinity of the banquet table. Members celebrate in their meal together, and often engage in rituals throughout the day.

  The holidays of the Unification Church are God's Day, a day to celebrate the divine (January 1); Parents Day a day to celebrate the establishment of the true parents, thus the new family unit (March 1 on the lunar calendar); True Parents' Birthday, celebration of Moon and wife's mutual birthday (January 6 according to the lunar calendar); the Day of All Things celebration of the restoration of the environment (May 1 on the lunar calendar,); and Children's Day, celebrating that all of humanity can become part of the true family, children of the true parents (October 1 on the lunar calendar).

  In addition to the five major holidays, the Unification Church also observes Landmark Days: Day of Victory of Love (January 3), Establishment of HSA-UWC (May 1), Day of the Love of God (May 20), Foundation Day (September 18), and Day of the Victory of Heaven (October 4). Small offerings, modest celebration banquets, outings, or entertainment may be planned. The Unification Church also observes Christmas on December 25 and allows for the observance of secular and national holidays among their members.[26]

- **Eastern Lightning**: It is unknown whether this group observes standard holidays or celebrates their own. As symbols such as baptism and communion are seen as being relevant only in a previous age, it is very possible such days are not observed.

- **World Mission Society Church of God**: As a Sabbatarian subset, the WMSCOG observes the Old Testament festivals of Passover (between March and April), Unleavened Bread (between March and April), First Fruits (between May and June), Feast of Weeks (Pentecost, fifty days after the Day of Resurrection), Feast of Trumpets (between September and October), Day of Atonement (between September and October), and Feast of Tabernacles (late September to late October). Such are believed to be observed according to New Covenant dictates, thus celebrated a little differently than in Old Testament mandate. They are believed to give insight into the work of Christ in His first advent on earth. In addition to the Old Testament festivals, the WMSCOG also celebrates Resurrection Day on the first Sunday after the Feast of Unleavened Bread.[27]

- **Shincheonji**: It is unknown if this group observes standard holidays or celebrates their own.

- ***Guwonpa* "Salvation Sects"**: The *Guwonpa* groups appear to celebrate traditional Christian holidays (such as Christmas and Easter) within the framework of their denominational understanding.

Visual Signs and Symbols

Unification Church official symbol (a sun with twelve rays, enclosed in a square, encircled with a circle broken on the left and right sides); holy robes worn for ceremonies (the Unification Church); Family Federation for World Peace and Unification logo (two large parents with a central heart between them and four children surrounding them, with a sun behind); Lightning bolt; Cross with star enclosed in a boomerang-like symbol (Eastern lightning); divided globe within a circle naming the World Mission Society Church of God; A wing-like blue double-bulged item resting on a hill-like brush stroke (World Mission Society Church of God; Four trees extending from a yellow and green book on a red, white, and blue background, surrounded by a dark green circle and imposed in front of a light blue and gold cross. Trees are surrounded by a blue background imposed to look like a castle; surrounded by a red, light blue, and blue circle (Shincheonji); Seven simple trees (long sticks and circles) with a cross in the center (Good News Mission); light and dark blue globe with dove in front of it (Life Word Mission); choirs; veiled women; men and women separated during worship.

Creeds, Books, and Laws

The work of eastern church groups is often complex, marked by an expansive literature list that details the beliefs and regulations of the church. None of these groups believe in creeds or statements of faith, except for the Unification Church. Members of the Unification Church recite pledges, which are as follows:

> *1. As the center of the cosmos, I will fulfill our Father's Will (purpose of creation), and the responsibility given me (for self- perfection). I will become a dutiful son (or daughter) and a child of goodness to attend our Father forever in the ideal world of creation (by) returning joy and glory to Him. This I pledge.*
> *2. I will take upon myself completely the Will of God to give me the whole creation as my inheritance. He has given me His Word, His personality, and His heart, and is reviving me who had died, making me one with Him and His true child. To do this, our Father has persevered for 6000 years the sacrificial way of the cross. This I pledge.*
> *3. As a true son (or daughter), I will follow our Father's pattern and charge bravely forward into*

the enemy camp, until I have judged them completely with the weapons with which He has been defeating the enemy Satan for me throughout the course of history by sowing sweat for earth, tears for man, and blood for heaven, as a servant but with a father's heart, in order to restore His children and the universe, lost to Satan. This I pledge.
4. The individual, family, society, nation, world, and cosmos who are willing to attend our Father, the source of peace, happiness, freedom, and all ideals, will fulfill the ideal world of one heart in one body by restoring their original nature. To do this, I will become a true son (or daughter), returning joy and satisfaction to our Father, and as our Father's representative, I will transfer to the creation peace, happiness, freedom and all ideals in the world of the heart. This I pledge.
5. I am proud of the one Sovereignty, proud of the one people, proud of the one land, proud of the one language and culture centered upon God, proud of becoming the child of the One True Parent, proud of the family who is to inherit one tradition, proud of being a laborer who is working to establish the one world of the heart.
I will fight with my life. I will be responsible for accomplishing my duty and mission. This I pledge and swear.[28]

Family pledge:

1. Our family pledges to seek our original homeland and establish the original ideal of creation, the Kingdom of God on Earth and in Heaven, by centering on true love.
2. Our family pledges to seek our original homeland and establish the original ideal of creation, the Kingdom of God on Earth and in Heaven, by centering on true love.
3. Our family pledges to perfect the Four Great Realms of Heart, the Three Great Kingships, and the Realm of the Royal Family, by centering on true love.
4. Our family pledges to build the universal family encompassing Heaven and Earth, which is God's ideal of creation, and perfect the world of freedom, peace, unity and happiness, by centering on true love.
5. Our family pledges to strive every day to advance the unification of the spirit world and the physical world as subject and object partners, by centering on true love.
6. Our family pledges to embody God and True Parents; we will perfect a family which moves heavenly fortune and conveys Heaven's blessing to our community, by centering on true love.
7. Our family pledges to perfect a world based on the culture of heart, which is rooted in the original lineage, by centering on true love.[29]

The writings of each eastern church group reflect the beliefs related to their specific theophanies: revelations of the divine incarnate, unique to their own groups. These writings are often copious, not always available in languages outside of Korean or Chinese and are often difficult to understand in their entirety. Their central texts for life and guidelines remain their unique scriptures, often with sections on discipline and social orders within their specific denominations. Members are expected to follow the specific principles outlined by their leaders, seen as divine. Outside of their writings are often recorded speeches of their leadership.

More relevant than the writings are the founders/leaders of said groups. Eastern church groups are more devotional in nature, centered on the incarnate being they worship. Their literature is seen as an extension of that being, and they are more interested in the being, and growing closer to the being, than dissecting and interpreting the text.

This does not mean there are no consequences for individuals who are somehow disobedient, blasphemous, or threatening to the system in some way. Like all cults, there are harsh penalties for disobedience. The ultimate punishment is disfellowship, by which family and friends who remain in the group practice shunning. It is also very difficult to leave these groups by choice if one finds themselves uninterested in participating further.

ECLECTIC BELIEFS

Eastern church groups often prohibit alcohol, tobacco, illegal drugs, sex outside of marriage, homosexuality, and abortion. All operate by highly disciplined methods, requiring evangelism activities by all members. Most also have advanced mission groups that operate their church work in different countries.

RELATIONS WITH NON-EASTERN CHURCH GROUPS

All eastern church groups avoid and exclude participation with other religions and religious groups, regarding them as inferior. The exception to this among eastern church groups is the Unification Church. The Unification Church has created a myriad of different groups and institutions designed to front as ecumenical organizations to gain visible endorsement and acceptability from the mainline religious community. Such action has been harshly criticized by outsiders.

HOLY SITES

Unification Church headquarters, New York, New York; Unification Church "holy grounds" found in all of the continuous 48 states; The Church of Almighty God headquarters, Seoul, South Korea; World Mission Society Church of God Headquarters, Bundang, Seongnam City, Gyeonggi Province, South Korea; Shincheonji Church of Jesus, the Temple of the Tabernacle of the Testimony headquarters, Gwacheon, South Korea; Good News Mission headquarters, Seoul, South Korea; Evangelical Baptist Church of Korea headquarters, Seoul, South Korea; Life Word Mission headquarters, Gyeonggi-do, South Korea.

Mass Unification Church wedding

NOTABLE FIGURES

Sun Myung Moon 1920-2012), founder, Unification Church; Hak Ja Han Moon (1943-), wife of Sun Myung Moon; Patrick Hickey (1950-), Republican assemblyman; Tom McDevitt, chairman of the board of directors of the *Washington Times*; Bo Hi Pak (1930-2019), *Washington Times* founder; Jonathan Wells (1942-), theologian and intelligent design advocate; Yang Xiangbin

(1973-), divine incarnation of Eastern Lightning; Zhao Weishan (1951-), partner of Yang Xiangbin and organizer of Eastern Lightning; Ahn Sahng-hong (1918-1985), divine incarnation of the World Mission Society Church of God; Zahng Gil-jah (1943-), wife of Ahn Sahng-hong; Lee Man-hee (1931-), divine incarnation of Shincheonji; Ock Soo Park (1944-), founder of the Good News Mission; Yoo Byung-eun (1941-2014), co-founder of the Evangelical Baptist Church of Korea; Kwon Shin-chan (1923-1996), co-founder of the Evangelical Baptist Church of Korea; Le Yo-han, founder of the Life Word Mission.

Notable Groups

Shincheonji Church of Jesus came under public scrutiny after the South Korean government blamed the group for causing a rapid spread of COVID-19 throughout the country. The government claimed that as many as 80% of cases in South Korea (at that time, around 1,800) could be traced back to members of the controversial religious group. The group's retort was the government's harassment of their membership due to dispute over the group's legitimacy. Once clear social distancing and health guidelines were established, members stopped in-person meetings and all planned events were cancelled.[30,31]

On July 31, 2020, group founder Lee Man-hee was arrested for falsifying membership and facility information submitted to the government of South Korea at their request. By this time, the government alleged more than five thousand cases of COVID-19 tied back to Shincheonji. At the same time, he was also accused of embezzling church funds. The church fought back with its own countersuits, but eventually such was dismissed by the court. In January of 2021, Lee Man-he was found not guilty of breaking virus control laws, guilty of embezzlement, and given a suspended sentence.[32]

Facts and Figures

It is difficult to ascertain specific statistics on eastern church groups. Numbers released by the groups themselves are often inflated, and due to secrecy, it is hard to confirm or deny the statistics we often have.

Other Important Definitions

- **True Parents**: Unification Church term for founder Moon and his wife.[33]

- **Heart**: In the Unification Church, the essence of divine being; an impulse to love and seek an object by which to love.[34]

- **The Three Blessings**: In the Unification Church, the three-step process by which one becomes perfect (by embracing a four-position foundation of god, perfect individual, and the individual's body and mind), having an ideal marriage (god, man, woman, and children, which will produce sinless children), and having dominion over all creation (god, man, things, and dominion based in love).[35]

- **God's new word**: In the Church of Almighty God, the writings of their female leader.[36]
- **Big red dragon of the Book of Revelation**: In the Church of Almighty God, a reference to the Chinese Communist Party.[37]
- **Save the Earth from A to Z (ASEZ)**: The World Mission Society Church of God Student Volunteer Group.[38]
- **Heavenly family system**: In the World Mission Society Church of God, Heavenly father (Ahn Sahng-hong), heavenly mother (Zahng Gil-jah), and spiritual brothers and sisters (human members of the church).[39]
- **Tree**: In Shincheonji, a term for the church.[40]
- **Bird**: In Shincheonji, a term for the Holy Spirit.[41]
- **God's advocate**: In Shincheonji, a term for Man-he Lee.[42]

BELIEVER'S CHARACTERISTICS

Central focus on a human being regarded as an incarnation of a divine being; extensive collection of literature, all reflecting the words and speeches of the divine being devotees worship; hours of study, services, unique holidays, and specialized holy days; devotional-centered religious practice; Biblical claims as interpreted through the writings of their current incarnation; apocalypticism; millennialism; secrecy; regimented and ritualistic day; legalism; personal demands for purity; a myriad of subheading organizations fronting as social betterment organizations; complex and convoluted doctrine that is difficult to understand.

Evangelical Christianity

The Christian Church should not be a secret society of specialists, but a public manifestation of believers in Jesus.
(Oswald Chambers)[1]

Theology

Belief in one true God, traditionally referred to as FATHER GOD, LORD GOD, JEHOVAH, or JESUS CHRIST, with personal attributes. There is a wide range of interpretation on theological doctrine. Most evangelicals believe God to be eternally existent in three divine persons: Father, Son, and Holy Spirit (without any existing hierarchy), commonly defined as the Trinity doctrine. In Evangelical Christianity, Trinitarianism is often more relational in concept than doctrinal, and there is considerable disagreement over the nature of expression and explanation of this doctrine among varying groups.

There are also some that reject Trinitarianism in one form or another. They may believe God is one being in three different manifestations or revelations (Father, Son, and Holy Spirit), often called Modalism. Some believe the Son is always subordinate to the Father (called Divine Monarchism). In some groups, the role of the Holy Spirit varies, and is occasionally considered a force or power rather than a being. There are also still some who reject these doctrines all together, declaring the Father, Son, and Holy Spirit to be three separate entities, or yet again with God as one person in three revelations or manifestations.

Central – and universal – to Evangelical Christianity is the relevance of Jesus Christ as Savior. Jesus Christ is seen as the Savior of the world, reconciling humanity to God through His sacrifice on the cross. The work of Jesus saves individuals; not just in a general sense, but in a personal way, from one's personal faults and failings, giving the opportunity to reconcile through a personal relationship with God throughout one's life.

Philosophy

Evangelical Christianity is a specific branch-movement of Protestant Christianity that has evolved a unique and influential enough theology and philosophy to consider it as having its own unique heading and identity. While it maintains and upholds the "five solas" of Protestantism (*sola fide/* faith alone, *sola gratia/* grace alone, *sola scriptura/* scripture alone, *solus Christus/* in Christ alone and *Soli Deo Gloria/* glory to God alone), Evangelical Christianity holds to a slightly different focus and interest than traditional Protestant groups. In primary interest, Evangelical Christianity centers around the principle that one must be "born again," done by accepting Jesus Christ as their personal Lord and Savior, reflecting belief found in John 3:16-18:

For God so loved the world, that He gave His only begotten Son, that whosoever believeth in Him should not perish, but have everlasting life.

For God sent not His Son into the world to condemn the world; but that the world through Him might be saved.

He that believeth on Him is not condemned: but he that believeth not is condemned already, because he hath not believed in the name of the only begotten Son of God.

Receiving Jesus as one's personal Lord and Savior is the way one is "born again." Such acknowledges Christ as sovereign over one's life, repenting from sin and personally accepting the work Christ has done for them. Reception of Christ as Lord is accompanied by a public confession of such. This is considered the beginning of one's "personal relationship" with God. Those who believe and make their public confession (sometimes called a profession of faith) are considered part of the church, made up of all true believers who have done the same worldwide. In some Evangelical groups, a full immersion water baptism follows profession of faith (some groups do not place an emphasis on baptism). Those who have believed in Christ and made a public confession are believed to be spared from hellfire and shall go to heaven when they die. Those who are not born again are damned to hell for all eternity.

Evangelicalism, or the foundational ideas of Evangelical Christianity, started as a movement. It focused on the revival and renewal of believers rather than formalized religion. As a movement, it overlaps with other spiritual movements in Christian history, especially certain strains of Protestantism (Congregationalism, Pietism, and Methodism) and the Holiness Movement. For this reason, there are many doctrinal strains present within Evangelical belief. Some Evangelicals, while maintaining the same basic premise of faith, are more Reformed in their roots, adopting Calvinist principles. Some are more Anabaptist in style, opting for emphasis on independence, Scripture, and freedom of faith. Others are more influenced by the traditions and values of the Holiness Movement (especially Methodism). Many Evangelical doctrines and ideas overlap.

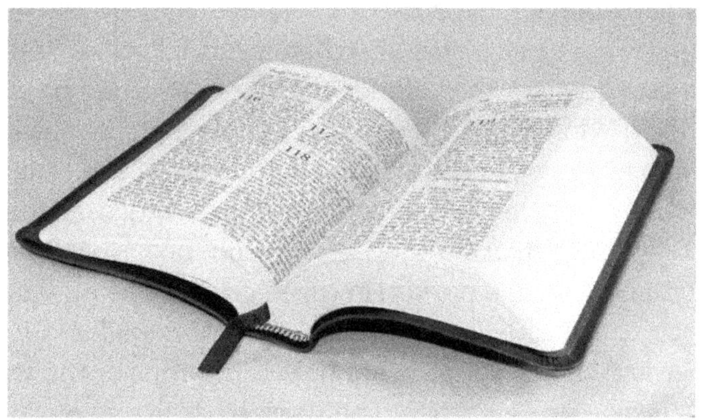

Open Bible

Evangelical Christians are so-called because of their belief in the command for all believers to share and spread the Gospel among all of humanity. This is accomplished through personal witness and instruction, with heavy emphasis on the study of the Bible. This need to evangelize is the cornerstone of their faith, believing that al who profess faith in Christ should take the words of Mark 16:15 literally:

And he said unto them, Go ye into all the world, and preach the gospel to every creature.

TRADITIONAL LANGUAGES

English.

ADHERENT IDENTITY

Christian, Evangelical Christian, born again Christian, Evangelical, Holiness Christian, identity through one's unique sect, denomination, or Evangelical church; general Evangelical churches are often identified as "community" churches, "Missionary" churches, "Christian" churches, or "Bible" churches. Some other major denominational identities of Evangelical churches include the Wesleyan Church, Church of the Nazarene, Church of Christ, Christian and Missionary Alliance, Freewill Baptists, Church of God (Anderson), and the Free Methodist Church.

SECTS/DIVISIONS

Evangelical Christianity is highly unstructured in terms of adherents and doctrine. Outside of the basics that define faith, there are no unifying requirements among Evangelicals. Divisions over interpretive matters are not uncommon, some so small, we may not be aware of their existence.

- **Holiness Movement**: A nineteenth-century Christian movement inspired by John Wesley's (1703-1791) work in creating a "new method" (Methodism) among Christians. Holiness Christianity believes an individual is regenerated, or cleansed from original sin, enabling them to move toward Christian sanctification, or perfection. This is considered the evidence of the Holy Spirit at work in a believer. The Holiness Movement was best-known for a few key things: first, the work of circuit riding to establish churches and communities of believers in every city possible, especially throughout the United States. A preacher would travel from city to city, working in a specified "circuit" of areas to establish and maintain the community groups. Second, they were known for camp meeting-style, open-air revivals by which people would set up campsites to experience the several-weeks long spiritual experience, which revolved around congregational singing and preaching. Third, the Holiness Movement was known for the "holiness codes," specific regulations as pertain to dress and lifestyle. These included refraining from smoking, drinking, gambling, dancing, short skirts, shorts, long sleeve shirts, no neckties for men, no makeup for women, long hair for women, and short hair for men. Not all these codes are upheld in Holiness churches today, but in some more traditional, conservative groups, they are upheld, either in whole or part. Some groups that have origins in the Holiness Movement include the Church of the Nazarene, Christian and Missionary Alliance, Church of God (Anderson, Indiana), Free Methodist Church, the Salvation Army, the Wesleyan Church, Evangelical Methodist Church, Holiness Baptist Association, and Bible Missionary Church.

- **Restoration Movement**: Also called the Stone-Campbell Movement, the Restoration Movement is an outgrowth of the Evangelical Movement's influence on the Second Great Awakening (1790-1840). The movement began with a revival meeting in Cane Ridge,

Kentucky, led by Barton Stone (1772-1844). It was also influenced by work in Pennsylvania and West Virginia as led by Thomas (1763-1854) and Alexander Campbell (1788-1866). Their goal was to create a specific pattern of worship, doctrine, and church practice by examining similar patterns seen in the New Testament. They rejected all exterior denominational labels, opting instead to be identified as Christians or followers of Jesus. They did not, and do not today, consider themselves to be Protestant. A strong unity movement, the Restoration Movement believes itself to be the restorers of first-century Christianity, rejecting all other churches, movements, and denominations as false. As a result, the Stone-Campbell Movement rejects all creeds, traditions, names, and ideas seen as dividing. In the traditional movement, there were no recognized, nor ordained clergy, and the Bible was seen as both inspired and completely infallible. Communion services are held weekly. Today, there are three main divisions of the Stone-Campbell Movement: the Christian Church (Disciples of Christ) which is the most liberal of all Restorationist descendants (uses instruments in worship and song, actively involved in ecumenism, recognizing ordained clergy, congregational in polity, welcoming of same-sex ordination and marriage, and notable by its chalice logo); the Churches of Christ, which are composed of several self-governing Christian congregations, all of which led by all-male elders (they a doctrine of baptismal regeneration, believing water baptism forgives sins, acapella singing in service, no use of instruments, application of Christian principles for life, refusal to participate in ecumenical activities, homosexuality is regarded as a sin, and the Bible remains in belief to be held as infallible); and a number of independent churches, all with slight variances in doctrine, due to breakaway divisions from the main denominations.

- **Plymouth Brethren**: While the Plymouth Brethren are technically an offshoot of the Anglican Church, their message, purpose, and work comes from Evangelical influence. Founded in the 1820s in Dublin, Ireland, the Plymouth Brethren believe in a literal, Scripture alone interpretation of Scripture. Though not the only founder, the best-known originator of the Plymouth Brethren is John Nelson Darby (1800-1882), responsible for The Darby Bible (*The Holy Scriptures: A New Translation from the Original Languages*). Their particular interest has always been prophecy, one that relates to the end of days and the interpretation of such, known as Dispensationalism. Dispensationalism is the belief that salvation history is divided up into different periods by which God dealt with humanity in different ways. Of particular interest to dispensationalists is the current time, which is seen as the end of times before Jesus returns for His people. Dispensationalism has become part of eschatology in many Evangelical circles, especially the doctrine of the rapture. The rapture of the church is a belief originating in the vision of a Plymouth Brethren woman in the 1800s. It states there will be a seven-year tribulation period in which a series of disastrous events shall occur (including the reign of a central political figure known as the Antichrist). During this time, true believers shall be caught up into the air and taken from the earth to be protected in heaven. There are three divisions of rapture believers: pre-tribulation, who believe they will be raptured before the tribulation begins or at the very beginning of it; mid-tribulation, who believe they will be raptured at some point during the tribulation, most likely around the middle; and post-tribulation, who believe the rapture of the church will occur at the end of the seven-year tribulation. After the tribulation shall come a literal thousand-year period in which Christ shall reign with the church. Plymouth Brethren, although not large in numbers, are divided into two categories: Open, which indicates they are part of a network of other churches, and open to working with other Evangelical churches, and Exclusive, or churches that do not work with other churches, and maintain a principle of closed communion, only allowing those who are members of that church to partake of communion elements. There are no ordained clergy within the Plymouth Brethren churches.

- **Christian Adventism**: A small branch of Evangelicalism that believes the Second Coming of Christ is imminent. Adventism grew out of the Millerite Movement of the 1830s and 1840s in which a Baptist minister named William Miller (1782-1849) proposed a theory predicting the date for the Second Coming of Christ as October 22, 1844. When the date passed without a successful manifestation, groups of followers walked away with different ideas about what the whole experience meant to them. Those who believed something did begin in 1844 or who believed the Second Coming was still imminent became Christian Adventists. As devout students of whole Bible study, Adventists represent a wide subheading of belief while maintaining the fundamentals of Evangelicalism. Some groups under the Christian Adventist heading are the Advent Christian Church, the Church of God (Seventh Day), Church of God and Saints of Christ, and Church of God General Conference. Seventh-day Adventism is also considered part of Christian Adventism, but because its doctrine varies from Evangelical Christianity, we will examine it under its own heading.

- **Evangelical Baptists**: The Baptist Church, as a Protestant denomination, encompasses more traditional and more Evangelical believers within its expanse of denominational labels. There are many independent or association Baptists, not part of the expressed Baptist community, that adhere to the Evangelical understanding of salvation and utilize either a mix of Evangelical and Protestant worship form or prefer the Evangelical form in their regular services. All are decidedly politically and theologically conservative, identifying with American conservative politics and values. The most visible of these groups is the Southern Baptist Convention.

- **Independent, Non denominational, non-Charismatic Churches**: This broad category covers Evangelical churches that are either entirely independent, part of a network of self-governing churches (often educated in the same or similar independent Bible colleges), or outgrowths of other churches that meet this definition but are not Charismatic or Pentecostal in nature. They would be classified as cessationalists, meaning they do not believe in the New Testament spiritual gifts as active or current for modern times.

- **Seeker Friendly Churches**: The official name for "seeker friendly" or "seeker sensitive" churches is the "Church Growth Movement." Not extraordinary from other Evangelical churches in much of their teaching, they are more modern in form and structure and have modern influences, especially church format, music style, and some teaching from the Charismatic Movement. Seeker friendly churches are based on a specific corporate-style model of church operation and governance, designed to attract people who do not attend traditional church due to required attire, conduct, length and style of services, lack of available programs (such as nursery or Sunday School) and preaching. Very popular in modern times, seeker friendly groups tend to compose much of what we consider "megachurches" in the United States (churches with membership of more than two thousand members). The more subtle side of Evangelicalism, much of seeker friendly doctrine is implied rather than stated. Most do not state objection to same-sex marriage or women's ordination outright; they simply do not say anything about it and do not do them. It is very possible for seeker-friendly attendees to hear a message that sounds encouraging and modern without properly knowing a church's mission, history, or doctrinal position. Churches tend to take interest in recruiting younger couples with young children.

- **Sabbatarianism**: A strict sect of Evangelical Protestantism that focuses on the observance of the seventh-day Sabbath (Saturday). A byproduct of Sabbatarianism is the upholding of the Ten Commandments, especially as relevant and enforced among Christian understanding. Seventh-day Sabbatarianism is in contrast with first-day Sabbatarianism, which was a long-standing Protestant belief that Sunday, the first day of the week, is the Christian Sabbath and should be observed as such. Sabbatarians trace the Saturday Sabbath observance back to the book of Genesis, as the creation account indicates God rested from creation on the seventh day of the week. It was then reaffirmed in the Ten Commandments, when God commanded Israel to "remember the Sabbath day and keep it holy." There are Sabbatarians in a few Protestant denominations, such as the Seventh-day Baptists, as well as those who have branched off to form their own separate denominations stemming from the Adventist movement of the 1800s (such as Armstrongism or Church of God, Seventh Day). Major additional beliefs of those that have formed their own denominations are Divine Monarchists (believing the Father is always superior to the Son) or Biblical Unitarians, refraining from holidays such as Christmas or Easter, the doctrine of "soul sleep" (mankind is sleeping, awaiting the resurrection, after death), the essential nature of tithing, and objection to military service.[2]

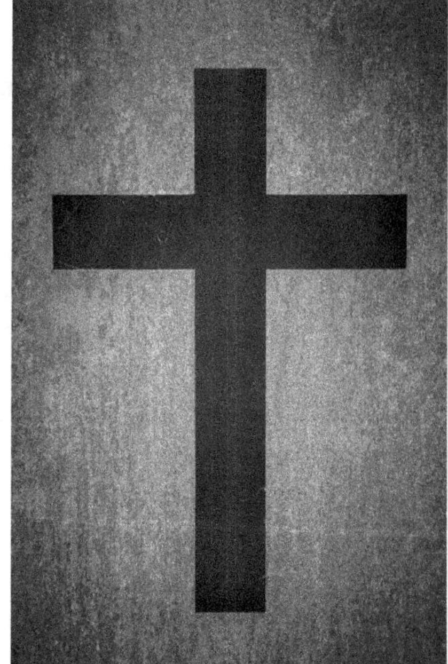

Cross

NUMBER OF ADHERENTS

There are approximately 619,000,000 Evangelicals worldwide.[3]

Disputes Within Group

Because Evangelical Christianity holds no official doctrine or teaching and there is no standard or official leadership, there are constant debates and divisions over the interpretation and meaning of Scripture and moral and ethical issues. The major disputes are often over the interpretation of modern social issues in application of Evangelical understanding. For example, while American Evangelical churches are stereotyped as being politically conservative, that is not the case of every Evangelical church (although in the United States, liberal Evangelicals are not the majority). Evangelicals in other countries are often more liberal than politically conservative. Evangelicals hold differing views on women's ordination, same-sex marriage, LGBTQ+ inclusion and social rights, abortion, church authority and leadership, and even the concept of "eternal security." While some Evangelicals hold to the Calvinist view that one cannot resist their salvation if they are truly destined to be saved, there are others who believe you can lose your salvation (Arminism) if you do something offensive to God or if you do not desire to maintain it. Evangelicals also differ over their beliefs about association with non-Evangelical believers for purposes other than evangelization.

Scriptures

The Holy Bible, both Old and New Testaments: the Pentateuch (Genesis, Exodus, Leviticus, Numbers, and Deuteronomy), Historical books (Joshua, Judges, Ruth, 1 Samuel, 2 Samuel, 1 Kings, 2 Kings, 1 Chronicles, 2 Chronicles, Ezra, Nehemiah, Esther), Wisdom books (Job, Psalms, Proverbs, Ecclesiastes, Song of Songs), Prophetic books (Isaiah, Jeremiah, Lamentations, Ezekiel, Daniel, Hosea, Joel, Amos, Obadiah, Jonah, Micah, Nahum, Habakkuk, Zephaniah, Haggai, Zechariah, Malachi), the Gospels (Matthew, Mark, Luke, John), the Acts of the Apostles, the Pauline Epistles (Romans, 1 Corinthians, 2 Corinthians, Galatians, Ephesians, Philippians, Colossians, 1 Thessalonians, 2 Thessalonians, 1 Timothy, 2 Timothy, Titus, Philemon, Hebrews) the General Epistles (James, 1 Peter, 2 Peter, 1 John, 2 John, 3 John, Jude) and Revelation.

Evangelical Christians see the Scriptures as entire and complete, needing no tradition to assist with their interpretation. They believe the Bible is inspired by God, inerrant, and infallible in its contents. While the entire Bible is considered inspired, there is special attention and interest in the Pauline letters and prophetic writings, such as Daniel and Revelation.

Throughout their history, Evangelicals have taken interest in Bible translation, production, and distribution. The New International Version of the Bible is considered the top choice among most Evangelical leaders in the United States, although it is not the only Bible in use among Evangelicals. Evangelicals also use the King James Version (the Authorized Version), the New King James Version, the New Living Translation, the English Standard Version, The Message paraphrase, and the New English Bible.[4]

Basic Religious Practices

Evangelical Christianity centers around the individual's repentance (turning away from sin) and conversion (change) from the things of the world toward the things of God. Evangelical Christians are interested in sharing their faith with others and developing their life of faith through their Scriptural study, devotional time with God, and participation in the local church community. Evangelical worship services vary; some remaining strikingly Protestant, with hymns and a standard Protestant service format, and others with more modern Charismatic influence, with live music, laying on of hands or group prayer, and a sermon, which can comprise almost half of the service. Most church leaders are referred to as pastor (sometimes elder or reverend), and most also have a council of elders or deacons that assist in the governance and leadership of the congregation.

The expected level of participation in one's local church does vary, but church attendance is often seen as the very heart and life of one's faith. Most churches do seek voluntary congregational participation for church work, such as audio/visual, childcare, Sunday School classes, greeters, hospitality, small group leadership, youth ministry, and men's and women's special programs (and other specified needs, unique to each congregation). Through the local church, an Evangelical Christian makes their point of contact with other believers, hearing the preaching and teaching of Scripture, fellowship, sharing faith, and building community. By staying close to church, Evangelicals believe they are given the proper foundation, tools, and insights into living their Christian faith and experiencing it in a deeper way.

This is especially true when it comes to family, which is often a seat of both spiritual and social entity in the lives of Evangelical Christians. Conservative Evangelicals uphold more traditional concepts of marriage: exclusive to a man and a woman, prohibitions on divorce, expectation that marriage should produce children, and regulated roles for men and women (men as breadwinners and women as homemakers). These ideas are not espoused to the extreme in most cases, but there are groups who do enforce these ideas in full. More liberal Evangelicals espouse ideas as pertain to what they often call "social justice," which calls the church to engage and participate in different social or political issues as part of their faith. Examples of such would be immigrant rights, LGBTQ+ issues, or women's issues.

Questions as to how Evangelicals live daily, what they do or don't believe or apply in their everyday lives, inconsistencies in understanding, and personal conduct are large, looming questions for the Evangelical community. As many Evangelicals see their relationship with God in a personal light, there are many who feel personal perspectives override what they may have been taught or learned elsewhere. Personal conduct and ideas may vary, and change based on the situation and individual in them.

HOLIDAYS

Most Evangelical Christians celebrate Christmas and Easter. American Evangelicals also sometimes incorporate American patriotic holidays into their events or services. With a renewed interest in the Old Testament events, some Evangelicals observe Biblical Jewish holidays within a Christian framework, particularly Passover. There are also some groups of Evangelicals who do not observe any holidays, citing pagan origins and opting instead to focus on the weekly Sunday gathering as the relevant focus for believers.

Visual Signs and Symbols

Cross or resurrection cross (a cross with a draped purple or white cloth over the crossbar, representing Christ resurrected); pictures of Christ or Biblical scenes; Bible; Bible verses; "born again" altar call experience; full-immersion water baptism done only on those old enough to make a profession of faith; laying on of hands; prayer; anointing oil; Ichthus (image of a fish); dove (representing the Holy Spirit); the "Christian flag" (a white field with a smaller royal blue box in the upper left corner, that contains a red cross).

Creeds, Books, and Laws

Taking quite literally the five "solas" of Protestantism, Evangelical Christianity does not ascribe to a specified creed or any traditional recitation of belief in their services. Most churches do not espouse a specific catechism, doctrinal statement, or formal rules. In place of such, Evangelical churches typically have a "statement of faith." These documents vary in length and are all reasonably similar in their statements, even though their approach and interpretation of those beliefs may be radically different from one church to another. Several churches stand behind or in some way expand upon the National Association of Evangelicals Statement of Faith, which upholds Evangelical belief about the Bible, Trinitarianism, Jesus Christ, regeneration, the Holy Spirit, resurrection, and spiritual unity of the church.

Some America Evangelical groups incorporate three specified "pledges" into their Sunday School or private Christian school practices: the Pledge of Allegiance to the American flag, and then the Pledge to the Bible and Pledge to the Christian Flag:

> *I pledge allegiance to the flag of the United States of America, and to the Republic for which it stands, one Nation under God, indivisible, with liberty and justice for all.*
>
> *I pledge allegiance to the Bible, God's holy Word. I will make it a lamp unto my feet and a light unto my path and will hide its words in my heart that I might not sin against God.*
>
> *I pledge allegiance to the Christian flag and to the Savior for whose kingdom it stands; one brotherhood, uniting all mankind in service and love.*[5]

Evangelical Christianity is a "word" movement, highly dependent on the printed word for the dissemination of its ideas. From its earliest days, sermons and teachings were written down and distributed in print form. Even though there is no one central voice or authority within Evangelicalism, there are some voices that are of considerable influence above others. Some of these people include James Dobson (1936-), Rick Warren (1954-), Billy (1918-2018) and Franklin Graham (1952-), and Tim LaHaye (1926-2016).

> *Failure to put the relationship on a slower timetable may result in an act that was never intended in the first place. Another important principle is to avoid the circumstances where compromise is likely. A girl who wants to preserve her virginity should not find herself in a house or dorm room alone with someone to whom she is attracted. Nor should she single-date with someone she has*

reason not to trust. A guy who wants to be moral should stay away from the girl he knows would go to bed with him. Remember the words of Solomon to his son, "Keep to a path far from her, do not go near the door of her house" (Proverbs 5:8). I know this advice sounds very narrow in a day when virginity is mocked and chastity is considered old-fashioned. But I don't apologize for it. The Scriptures are eternal, and God's standards of right and wrong do not change with the whims of culture. He will honor and help those who are trying to follow His commandments. In fact, the apostle Paul said, "He will not let you be tempted beyond what you can bear" (1Corinthians 10:13). Hold that promise and continue to use your head. You'll be glad you did.[6]

If not to God, you will surrender to the opinions or expectations of others, to money, to resentment, to fear, or to your own pride, lusts, or ego. You were designed to worship God and if you fail to worship Him, you will create other things (idols) to give your life to. You are free to choose, what you surrender to but you are not free from the consequence of that choice.[7]

Religion, [some] argue, "may be all right for certain emotional people, but you can't beat a man who believes in himself." But this self-confident generation has produced more alcoholics, more dope addicts, more criminals, more wars, more broken homes, more assaults, more embezzlements, more murders, and more suicides than any other generation that ever lived. It is time for all of us to take stock of our failures, blunders, and costly mistakes. It is about time that we put less confidence in ourselves and more trust and faith in God.[8]

America is infatuated with this false understanding of tolerance. To be truly tolerant is not to give every idea equal standing or to compromise the truth in the interest of keeping the peace and making everyone happy.[9]

It's the lie of evolution that all man are just evolved and that they're all equal, and that all creatures are equal.[10]

ECLECTIC BELIEFS

Evangelical Christianity holds to a necessity in accepting Jesus Christ as one's Savior in a process known as becoming "born again." Because this remains its only unifying teaching, specific teachings vary from sect to sect and sometimes church to church. Evangelical Christianity holds to a certain concept of freedom, and the individual's right to make their decisions about belief and actions along with one's belief. There are a few things that are seen, however, in many, if not the majority, of Evangelical congregations. Most congregations employ a congregational polity, rather than one based on election or appointment (although some pastors and leaders of Evangelical are self-appointed). These congregational structures usually follows the work of a plurality of elders, individuals either elected or selected for service within the congregation. Evangelical congregations tend to be led by men (although there is a small movement of female clergy within Evangelical churches).

Evangelicals recognize the ordinances of water baptism (full immersion) and communion (represented by bread, either leavened or unleavened and grape juice). These two ordinances, or rites, are not considered literal, but are symbols that remind of the work Christ does within a Christian. Through baptism, believers come to new life. Through communion, one recalls the death and resurrection of Jesus Christ. Communion is also seen as a symbolic unity among Christians, especially those in a local church.

It is safe to say many Evangelicals espouse a need to stand against what they perceive to be wrong or errant in culture. Whether it is believing cultural is too liberal or too conservative, most Evangelicals believe their faith helps them stand apart from the evils and ills of the world, seeing it as controlled by the devil (the enemy of God). This becomes relevant when it comes to matters of sexuality, especially in the young. Sex outside of marriage is seen as problematic, if not downright sinful. To help maintain their belief, Evangelicals employ many different things to avoid sexual relationships outside of marriages. The primary way is to marry young, encouraging young people to marry as soon as they are legally married or sustainably able to do so. Some groups promote "virginity pledges," by which young believers pledge their virginity either to their opposite-sex parent or to Jesus Christ, agreeing to remain chaste until marriage. Many Evangelicals are also opposed to abortion, but views on this do vary. Some believe there is no justifiable cause for abortion, others believe abortion is acceptable in certain circumstances, and others believe abortion is a matter of personal conscience. Some Evangelicals are completely opposed to the use of birth control, but it is far more common to meet Evangelicals who believe the use of such is a personal choice.

Unique among many Evangelicals is a struggle between science and faith. The Evangelical Church often sees the Bible in conflict with different scientific ideas, such as evolution (also called Darwinism). In contrast to the belief that life evolved on earth, Evangelicals espouse their own belief in Creationism, or "creation science," as it is sometimes called. Creationism is the belief that all of creation and all life has its origin in the work of God, through specific supernatural acts. Along with Creationism is a literal interpretation of Genesis chapter 1, "young earth creationism" (the belief that the earth is less than 10,000 thousand years old), flood geology (the fossils and such of animals or dinosaurs believed to be millions of years old are improperly dated, as they were destroyed in Noah's flood of Genesis), anti-evolution, or "old earth creationism" (Genesis' creation account includes a gap of time between 1 and 2 Genesis that causes the earth to be substantially older than believed in young earth creationism).

Christian church in New Hampshire

Many Evangelical Christians also believe in the relevance of sharing their faith through media and pop culture. Traditionally speaking, Evangelical Christians often have difficult relationships with secular media entertainments, such as television, radio, music, movies, and in more modern times, the Internet. The "Christian" pop culture subgenre includes movies, television shows, radio, children's programming, music, clothing, and Internet sites specifically designed to appeal to Evangelical Christian audiences. These things are often created by Evangelicals or those who know how they think, and espouse the values, beliefs, ideals, and ideas that Evangelical Christians hold dear in their faith and lives.

While not large, there is also a small group of Evangelicals who follow health fads and are into specific forms of health trends, such as vegetarianism, clean eating, and veganism.

Relations with Non-Evangelicals

Evangelical Christians often shy away from interfaith and ecumenical gatherings, citing separateness and purity as a requirement to keep their faith pure and active. Some have started their own ecumenical circles among themselves, and a very small number will engage in dialogue with other Protestants. Catholics tend to be avoided.

Holy Sites

Evangelical Christians see the church as made up of true believers, from all over the world, all of which have a personal relationship with Jesus Christ. Church is not seen as being confined to a building or a specific location. As a result, Evangelicals have no specific holy sites. Many find Israel and Palestine as spiritually significant, as they connect to Christ's life.

Notable Figures

Billy Graham (1918-2018)

Jonathan Edwards (1703-1758), American Puritan leader and influential force in the First Great Awakening; John Newton (1725-1807), composer of *Amazing Grace*; William Wilberforce (1759-1833), abolitionist; William Carey (1761-1834), British missionary; Charles Finney (1792-1875), preacher and influential force in the Second Great Awakening; William Booth (1829-1912), founder of the Salvation Army; Charles Spurgeon (1834-1892), British preacher; Dwight Moody (1837-1899), founder of the Moody Bible Institute; R.A. Torrey (1856-1928), preacher and author; Billy Sunday (1862-1935), American preacher; Karl Barth (1886-1968), philosopher; D. James Kennedy (1930-2007), pastor; Jerry Falwell (1933-2008), leader of the Moral Majority; James Montgomery Boice (1938-2000), pastor; Pat Robertson (1930-), host of *The 700 Club*; James Dobson (1936-), President of *Focus on the Family*; Wayne Grudem (1948-), co-founder of the Council on Biblical Manhood and Womanhood; J.I. Packer (1926-2020), author; R.C. Sproul (1939-2017), theologian; Bill Hybels (1951-), pastor; John MacArthur (1939-), pastor; Billy Graham (1918-2018), evangelist.

Notable Groups

Liberty University (located in Lynchburg, Virginia) is a private, Evangelical Christian school founded by Jerry Falwell, Sr. The school's instruction has a specific Evangelical slant in doctrine and the university expects students to uphold an "honor code" that forbids premarital sex or private interactions between opposite sex students. It is considered a prominent influencer in American Republican politics. It is home to the Jerry Falwell Library, National Civil War Chaplains Museum, and the Carter Glass Mansion. Between campus and online statistics, Liberty University has approximately 110,000 students. In recent years, Liberty University made headlines across the country during the COVID-19 outbreak when it made the decision to resume classes and encouraged its students to return to their normal schedules.[11]

Facts and Figures

Evangelical Christian adults measure between 7% and 35% of the US population and is estimated to be on the increase. Approximately one out of five "born again" adults meet the Evangelical criteria (18% of the 7% figure). 13.1% of all Christians worldwide identify as "evangelical."[12,13]

Other Important Definitions

- **Amen**: Biblical Hebrew term that means "so be it." Term is used at the end of prayers in all Christian denominations and is also used to indicate agreement with a statement, prayer, or idea in Evangelical Christianity.

- **Believer**: Term for a Christian who has accepted Christ as their Savior and is seen as a legitimate Christian within Evangelical understanding.

- **End Times**: Also called the "Last days," a term used to describe the period of time before Jesus Christ returns in the Second Coming. The "end times" means different things to different Evangelicals but is most often used to refer to the difficulties in current society that are seen as signs that Christ's coming is imminent.

- **Evangelist**: A proclaimer of the Gospel; a minister who preaches their faith, especially to the nonbeliever.

- **Fundamentalism**: An Evangelical Christian response to the rise of more liberal Protestant ideas that denied essential aspects of Biblical literalism in the 1920s. Fundamentalism is named after "The Fundamentals," a two-volume set of doctrinal commentary that outlined the foundations of Biblical inerrancy, miracles, the virgin birth of Jesus Christ, the resurrection of Christ, the Second Coming of Christ, and the sacrifice of Christ on the cross for sin as essential doctrines for Christian belief. It is in Fundamentalism we see the greatest divide between secular society and church society, and the belief that neither can reconcile with the other.

- **Great Awakening**: A period of intense Evangelical revival and renewal that is marked with intense religious conversion, study, and interest in Christian things. Evangelicals acknowledge four different "Great Awakenings: the First (1730-1755), Second (1790-1840), Third (1855-1930) and Fourth (1960-1980).

- **King James Only movement**: Also called Ruckmanism. The belief that the only acceptable Bible translation is the King James Version, because it is seen as superior to all other English translations. It is believed to be inerrant, needing no changes or updates, and that every other Bible translation to come after the King James Version is either in moral error or somehow corrupt.

- **Mark of the Beast**: A mark, found in Revelation 13, that is said to be the "number of the beast," presenting as the number 666. In Dispensational belief, every individual living on earth who is not raptured will be forced to take a literal mark, either on the hand or forehead, that will reflect the number 666.

- **Minister**: A broad term in Evangelicalism for any ordained, elected, or licensed individual who can preach, perform the ordinances or sacraments, perform weddings and funerals, and serve the Evangelical body as a leader of the people. Ministers may or may not be recognized across different Protestant denominations.

- **Miracles**: Supernatural events that come from God alone, and do not have an answer for their occurrence or happenstance in this world. Most evangelicals would believe that miracles have ceased for this day and time.

- **New Covenant**: A term used to indicate one of two things: the first is the New Testament of the Bible, and the second is to indicate the legitimacy of the Christian life, existing under God's work of grace through the sacrifice of Christ, versus the work of the Mosaic Law, which was the legal spiritual rule in the Old Testament.

- **Old Covenant**: A term used to indicate one of two things: the first is the Old Testament of the Bible, and the second is to indicate the Mosaic Covenant, God's agreement with the Jewish people based on 613 different laws and regulations that were designed to aware and convict of sin.

- **Pastor**: The term for a local Evangelical church leader. In some traditions, Pastors are called elders (and on rare occasion, Bishop).

- **Prayer**: A term designating communication with God. In Evangelical communities, prayer is often spontaneous, rather than recited from a book or lectionary.

- **Revival**: A term for "renewal" indicating mass Christian conversion, renewal of one's faith, or return to the church when one has been distant, or uninvolved, with church for an extended period of time. Revivals are often identified with "revival services," those that may take the form of a tent meeting, campmeeting service, extended or special church service, or other special event with the goal to convert and return individuals to the Evangelical faith.

Believer's Characteristics

Speaks of and believes in the urgent need for each human being to experience a "born again" or "new birth" experience; Speaks of a "personal relationship" with God; emphasizes Jesus as Savior; involvement with political issues; emphasis on participation and membership in a local church; dispensational or "end times" ideas; standing against culture; utilization of Christian media, pop culture, music, products, and concepts; belief in Biblical inerrancy; traditional roles for men and women; variety of ideas on social issues; belief in the invisible universal church; rejection of participation with other religious groups; Bible study; Bible reading; revivals; belief in some form of Creationism; avoidance of sin, especially sexual sin; traditional ideas about marriage, in contrast with more liberal ones (although they do exist in some communities); emphasis on family.

Fictitious/Parody Religion

We find, counter-intuitively, that a small population correlates with shorter humans, and a larger population correlates with taller humans. This only makes sense in light of the FSM theory of gravity. With more people on earth today, there are fewer Noodly Appendages to go around, so we each receive less touching—pushing down toward the earth—and thus, with less force downward, we're taller.
(Bobby Henderson)[1]

Theology

While the specific mention of deity varies, the theology of fictitious and parody religion often takes one of two forms: The first is to mock theology in general, most often that of Christianity. Therefore, it makes fun of or pokes fun at the idea of a supreme being or deity. By so doing, adherents believe proof of devotion falls on the one who professes to believe it rather than on the one who rejects it. The second form is as a fan base or enthusiasm of something found within pop culture that turns into a devotion. Fictitious and parody religion can be atheist or theistic in nature and can also take on a combination of the two, with worship or embrace of forces, ideals, or concepts in the foundational ideas present within the originating inspiration for the group.

Philosophy

Fictitious/parody religions are designed to make modern statements about religion and religious devotion in a general sense. In parody religion, the statement of religious devotion is generally negative; it exists to prove people can follow any sort of nonsense that one might conceive. Based on this theory, they see all religion as nonsensical and illogical. While the foundation of parody religion is to prove religion is worthless, that hasn't stopped people from taking parody groups seriously, believing in their principles and following them as if they are a sincere and devoted aspect of religious reality.

In fictitious religion (sometimes identified as post-modern religion), the statement of religious devotion is not negative, even if it is not based in dogmatic practice regarded as authentic or serious. Fictitious religion seeks to create worship out of fandoms: movies, characters, franchises, fiction books, mythological lore, people, and sometimes even the ideas present in these things. Through the embodiment of these concepts in a religious setting, people recreate the experiences, expound upon the values, and engage in the general enthusiasm shared by others who also believe in the necessity of creating such fandom in their devotional lives.

Both parody and fictitious religion can be serious or satirical, independent or group-minded, legally recognized or casual, informal groups, and have a presence on or offline. Some adhere to regulations and scriptural texts; many do not. It is a multifaceted group, created in modern times, based on modern understandings of devotion and worship.

NUMBER OF ADHERENTS

It is difficult to ascertain numbers of individuals practicing a parody or fictitious religion for one simple reason: In most jurisdictions, such groups do not have legal charitable status nor enjoy the protections of a religious group. Because many groups are fronted by an internet presence and do not maintain ritual participation requirements, logs, or other standards for religious membership, there are no accurate numbers on how many people follow such theories in real life. Some groups claim members in the high 10,000s (at most), while some only claim a membership body of under 100 people. It is believed thousands of members in such groups is, most likely, an inflation of the truth, with the maximum of some parody and fictitious groups having membership somewhere in the thousands.

TRADITIONAL LANGUAGES

English, Portuguese, and Russian.

ADHERENT IDENTITY

Parody and fictitious religious adherents are noted by their associations. Such include: Invisible Pink Unicorn; Kibology, kibologist; Landover Baptist Church; Last Thursdayism; Pastafarianism, Pastafarianist; Church of the Flying Spaghetti Monster; First Church of the Last Laugh; Church of Ethuanasia; Church of the SubGenius; the Cult of Kek; Dudeism; Discordianism; Dinkoism; Gadgetology; Googlism; Igreja Evangelica Pica das Galaxias (Dick of Galaxies Evangelical Church), Iglesia Maradoniana (Church of Maradona); Jediism; Jopimism; Matrixism, the Path of the One; Silinism; Sisters of Perpetual Indulgence; and the United Church of Bacon.

SECTS/DIVISIONS

While parody and fictitious religious groups might seem to be vastly different in their specific doctrines and teachings, they can be broken down into a few specific groupings that help one understand more of what they espouse in practice.

- **Parody religion**: Parody religion specifically exists to poke fun at, point out inconsistencies or absurdities, or criticize standard religious groups. Most parody religion is atheist in nature, considering the very nature of theology (in any form) to be absurd. The most well-known is the Church of the Flying Spaghetti Monster, better known as Pastafarianism. It is a mock to creationism, intelligent design, and general religion. Other groups include the Invisible Pink Unicorn and Last Thursdayism. Other parody religions include Kibology (a Usenet-based satire on religious devotion), Landover Baptist Church (a website designed to mock fundamentalist Christianity), Church of the SubGenius (mocks Christianity, Zen

Buddhism, Scientology, new age groups, pop psychology, and motivational thinking), the United Church of Bacon (a Las Vegas atheist organization devoted to fundraising for other charitable organizations), and First Church of the Last Laugh (a mock church known for the annual Saint Stupid's Day parade in San Francisco, California).[2]

- **Fandom religion**: Often regarded as the least serious of all categories, fandom religion is based in adoration of some specific aspect of pop culture – be it film, fictional book, sports, or a character found in a pop culture reference – as a religious devotion. Fandom religions vary, but most combine either standard religious ideology with replacement characters from fictitious elements of fandom or create entire systems of devotion based on the fandom itself. Examples include Dudeism (a variation on Taoism from the movie *The Big Lebowski*), Jediism (a philosophical and religious depiction from the Jedi characters in the *Star Wars* franchise), Matrixism, also known as the Path of the One (a religious group inspired by The Matrix franchise), and Discordianism (based on the book the *Principia Discordia*, combining Zen and Taoist philosophy with absurdism). A unique example is Iglesia Maradoniana or the Church of Maradona, a group that created a syncretistic merging of Catholicism and fandom of Diego Maradona, an Argentinian football player considered the best soccer player of all time.

- **Internet religion**: Technology has notably changed the way people of all belief systems worship, believe, and think. Among fictitious religion, internet religion consists of individuals who desire to use technology to prove something about religion, make a statement about religious ideals, or create a religious group. A few of the parody groups mentioned also fall into the category of internet religion, namely Kibology and Landover Baptist Church. Other groups include Dinkoism (a group based in India that seeks to prove religion is absurd), Missionary Church of Kopimism (a Swedish group who believe file sharing and copying information are sacred principles), and the Cult of Kek (a far-right internet group, supporters of Donald J. Trump, who worship a fake frog known as Pepe).

- **Social statement religions**: Groups that specifically exist to make statements against both societal and religious mores. Such are known for displays and stunts, often with the underlying message to protest whatever ideals are seen as offensive to them. Examples of such include the Church of Euthanasia (addresses overpopulation and anti-choice stances), the Sisters of Perpetual Indulgence (a genderqueer organization that protests sexual and gender norms for the purpose of education and charity fundraising) and Silinism (the religion of the Aerican Empire, a micronation with no sovereign territory; group worships Forsteri, the Great Penguin while protesting against general national norms).[3]

DISPUTES WITHIN GROUP

Parody and fictitious religious groups exist to make statements rather than pursue sincere theological examinations. As a result, they don't pursue disagreements with one another. While they obviously do not agree with one another on all matters, their goal is to voice their dispute and disagreement with organized religion or create alternatives to it rather than take on the traditional voice of religion among themselves.

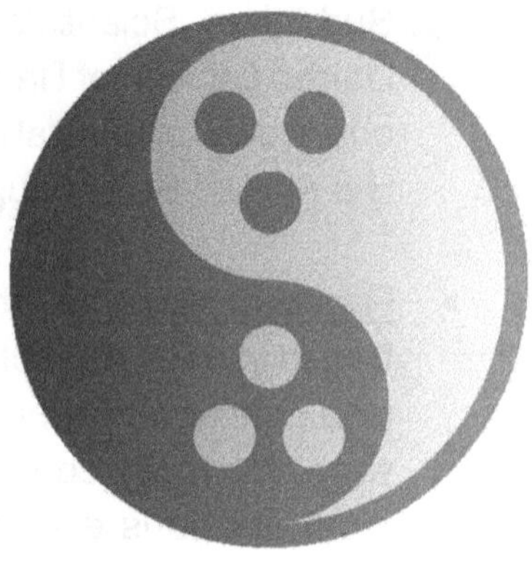

Dudeism logo

SCRIPTURES

Texts vary by group, if a group even embraces the idea of a holy or sacred text. Many fictitious and parody groups gain interest and support from internet users; thus, many key ideas either start or are perpetually found on websites and chat forums. If a group embraces a scriptural text, it usually outlines its basic ideas. Most are not considered to have the same status as a standard religious scripture, such as the Bible or Qur'an; instead, they are a parody on the idea of holy text, used to collect ideas and/or express the idea that such are absurd. Examples of such as found in parody or fictitious religion include:

- **Church of the Flying Spaghetti Monster**: *The Gospel of the Flying Spaghetti Monster* and *The Loose Canon, the Holy Book of the Church of the Flying Spaghetti Monster*.

  Disclaimer: While Pastafarianism is the only religion based on empirical evidence, it should also be noted that this is a faith-based book. Attentive readers will note numerous holes and contradictions throughout the text; they will even find blatant lies and exaggerations. These have been placed there to test the reader's faith.[4]

- **Dudeism**: *The Dude De Ching*, *The Abide Guide*, *Lebowski 101*, *The Tao of the Dude*, and *The Dude and the Zen Master*.

  The Stranger accepts the World, As the World accepts the Dude; He narrates the film, so is clearly heard; Does not self-apply a name, so remains unknown; Has never been to London or France, But can die with a smile on his face without feelin' like the good lord gypped him; Because he does not eat the bar, the bar does not eat him, He does not curse, so no one curses him.[5]

- **Kibology**: *Revisions of the Manifesto.*

  WHEREAS, the computer network named USENET has insurmountable flaws:
  => It is cluttered with thousands of disorganized groups.
  => It is difficult to use due to the various software interfaces.
  => It is infected with viruses, especially in the .signatures.
  => There is no formal rulebook and no official administration.
  => Bozos abound.
  => Power-crazed maniacs frequently try to manipulate Usenet at their whim.

  These problems are most important. THEREFORE, in an official and secret democratic vote, Kibo has been duly elected LEADER OF THE NET. To correct this heinous situation, LEADER KIBO has decided to take bold measures, a brave new initiative, detailed herein.

WAKE UP, IT'S 1994! THE FUTURE WILL NOT WAIT FOR A VOTE![6]

- **Church of the SubGenius**: *Book of the SubGenius.*

  We have a COVENANT with WOTAN and it is the Sacred Grudge-Chore of the SubGenius to SMITE The Conspirators and Their slavish Dupes: the Mediocretins, the stupid Pink Boys, the "Hoi Polloi," Them, the Normals, the Somnabulacs, the Great Unwashed-In-The-Baptism-Of-The-Pee-Of-"Bob," the malignant ones who breathe down our necks and abuse their territorial urges without ever dreaming that they're doing it, Assouls, Cage Men, Infidels, Sames, Anthropophobiacs, Conformers, Timeservers, Mole People, Proleterrorists, Philistines, Pharisees, Witch-burners, the ones who have tried to maim our self-respect down through the centuries by making SLACK and antipredictability TABOO, the Thankers and Wankers, Heilers and Smilers, Sloths and Moths, Cons and Johns, Drivellers and Snivellers, Weepers and Sleepers; CreditHeads, Cliants, Kens and Barbies, Errorists, Yes-Buts, Ordinaryans and Lick Spittles, Corpulators, Signifying Monkeys, UnderAlls, the Slackless Ones...in short, the Remnants of Man: those very False Prophets who have been holding us back and forcing Time Addiction on Themselves...and...others...[7]

- **Discordianism**: *Principia Discordia*, *Summa Universalia*, *Zenarchy*, and the *Illuminatus!* Trilogy.

  If you can master nonsense as well as you have already learned to master sense, then each will expose the other for what it is: absurdity. From that moment of illumination, a man begins to be free regardless of his surroundings. He becomes free to play order games and change them at will. He becomes free to play disorder games just for the hell of it. He becomes free to play neither or both. And as the master of his own games, he plays without fear, and therefore without frustration, and therefore with good will in his soul and love in his being.[8]

BASIC RELIGIOUS PRACTICES

Parody and fictitious religious groups are often independently pursued by virtue of their nature. As opposed to standard religious groups, parody and fictitious followers often find their communities online, through websites and chat rooms. Thus, the basic pursuits of such religious groups take on a very individualized nature. One claims to be a part of the group because they support or embrace the ideals within in it, and they are, therefore, a member. With no active group participation, there is no practical way to measure one's involvement or commitment, other than claims.

Much of the parody and fictitious religious world consists of following concepts and ideas, which do not follow traditional lines of thinking about theology and deity. Things such as prayer, religious devotion, and piety for things such as sacraments or rites are notably absent.

Church of the Flying Spaghetti Monster logo

Exceptions to this rule would be groups that specifically exist for advocacy, fundraising, or to make public statements for their cause. In such instances, members might have an initiation rite (such as the Sisters of Perpetual Indulgence) by which one is affirmed as a member. It is expected thereafter that members participate however the group stipulates: exemplifying goals and ideals, helping in different ways with fundraising, activities, and public stunts, donating, promoting the work, volunteering, or participating in some other specified way.

Other instances that might become outlets for religious practice might consist of attending conventions, events, or international fandom gatherings that promote the group itself. Examples would be the Saint Stupid's Day Parade (First Church of the Last Laugh) or an adherent of Jediism attending a *Star Wars* convention. In modern times, a group might also hold a convention or conference through the internet for attendees.

Some organizations offer mail-order ordination services offering members the opportunity to perform weddings or officiate at gatherings or other religious events for a fee. The nature of the circumstances surrounding such are controversial, and such ordinations are not recognized nor considered legally valid in every state or country worldwide.

HOLIDAYS

Most parody and fictitious religious groups are not formalized enough to recognize a yearly calendar of events. If they recognize specific dates, they are connected to the group's founding or to some abstract idea connected to the group's purpose. The only groups with a complete calendar throughout the year appear to be Dudeism and Discordianism. Examples of holidays include:

- **Dudeism**: Happy Dude Year (January 1); Pal-o-Mine's Day, celebrating friendship (February 13); Hangover, kind of akin to Dudeism Lent (February 27-March 6); The Day of the Dude, celebrating the day *The Big Lebowski* was released (March); Take is Easyster, celebrating not being uptight (same day as Easter); Major Duder, purifying the mind of undude thoughts (same day as Buddhist Magha Puja); April Dude's Day, celebrating foolishness (April 1); Limber Day, their version of the marijuana 420 day (April 20); Passitover, celebrating freedom and opting for unleavened beer (same as Passover); Summer Shabbos, the Dudeish night of rest (June 20); the Summer Slowstice, in acknowledgement of the summer Solstice (June 21); Independence Day, acknowledging anything that hampers personal growth (July 4); Kush Hosanna, relax and find health in life, often observed with marijuana (same as Rosh Hashanah); Melloween, remembering friends and family who've gone before; reconnect with those with whom one is out of touch (October 31); Thankiesgiving (same as Thanksgiving); Mauder's Day, a figurehead of nurturing creativity within (December 3); Slackernalia, a fertility observance through relaxation (December 4); Kerabotsmas, remembering Theodore Donald Kerabastos, those who died and were loved (December 13); the Winter Slowstice, observance of the Winter Solstice (December 21); Dudeistmas, a modified version of Christmas (December 25); St. Marty's Day, in honor of the actor Jack Kehler who played the landlord in The Big Lebowski (the ninth of every month).[9]

- **Discordianism**: The year is divided into five, seventy-three-day seasons of chaos: Discord, Confusion, Bureaucracy, and The Aftermath. Their recognized week is five days long, consisting of Sweetmorn, Boontime, Pungenday, Prickle-Prickle, and Setting Orange. Every year begins with Sweetmorn. Apostle holydays, named in honor of the Discordian apostles, are found on the fifth day of every season: Mungday, Moojoday, Syaday, Zarathud, and Maladay. Season holidays are held on the 50th day of each season. A yearly calendar of events includes Mungday (January 5), Chaoflux (February 19), St. Tib's Day (February 29), Mojoday (March 19), Discoflux (May 3), Syaday (May 31), Confluflux (July 15), Zaraday (August 12), Bureflux (September 26), Maladay (October 24), and Afflux (December 8).[10]

Jediism logo

- **The Church of the Flying Spaghetti Monster**: The season of "Holiday," abstractly observed between Christmas, Hanukkah, and Kwanzaa. It has no specified practice or devotion, but is just declared a season.

- **Jediism**: Jedii Creed Day (March 21); International Jedii Day, the anniversary of the release of the original *Star Wars* film (May 25); Youngling Day/Vocations Day (October 31; TotJo Anniversary Day (December 25); Day of Reflection (December 31).[11]

- **Matrixism**: Bicycle Day, remembering Albert Hofmann's LSD experiment in 1943 (April 19).[12]

- **The First Church of the Last Laugh**: Saint Stupid Day (April 1).

- **The Church of the SubGenius**: X-Day (July 5).[13]

- **Silinism**: Has an extensive calendar of several different days, scattered throughout the year, including Peculiar People Day (January 10), What the Heck is That Day (March 19), Aerica Day (May 8), Saint Bill Day (August 24, in honor of Microsoft founder Bill Gates); and Conspiracy Theory Day (November 22).[14]

VISUAL SIGNS AND SYMBOLS

While many groups do embody some sort of logo or identifying feature, some do not. Groups that do include: play on the Christian fish symbol with added eye stalks and tentacles, including the initials FSM (Church of the Flying Spaghetti Monster); pirate fish flag (white pirate fish on black flag, Church of the Flying Spaghetti Monster); Fading pink or pink unicorn (Invisible Pink Unicorn);

St. Stupid's Day Parade (The First Church of the Last Laugh); face of J.R. Dobbs (Church of the SubGenius); image of Jehovah 1 (Church of the SubGenius); bowling yin yang (Dudeism); image of a Phoenix or Osiris-style bird rising up in the air, with wings spread (Jediism); Eris, the Greek goddess of strife and discord (Discordianism); apple of discord (Discordianism); sacred chao (Discordainism); kanji figure for "red" (Matrixism); Dinkan (Dinkoism); a Greek temple with four pillars (Church of Euthanasia); Pepe the frog (Cult of Kek); image of a radiating Diego Maradona (Iglesia Maradoniana); laughing black and white drag nun in a habit (Sisters of Perpetual Indulgence); genderqueer individuals in extravagant religious drag, usually carrying a fan (Sisters of Perpetual Indulgence); Foresteri, the Great Penguin (Silinism); radiating bacon with the words "praise bacon" near them (United Church of Bacon).

CREEDS, BOOKS, AND LAWS

The diversity of fictitious and parody religion means most respond differently to the idea of regulation within their ranks. Some groups, such as the Church of the Flying Spaghetti Monster, make it clear there are no specified rules or regulations for one to follow as part of the group. Others really don't make mention of the idea of a creed or legal ruling, opting instead to encourage the promotion or thoughts the group espouses.

For those who do espouse a creed or regulating law, most are simple, state the group's identifying markers, or otherwise invert and mock the idea of a creed or statement of faith. How well these creeds, rules, and statements of faith are upheld by membership is of debate, as how such might be personally interpreted by each individual practitioner.

Dudeism recognizes their own creed:

> *The idea is this: Life is short and complicated and nobody knows what to do about it. So don't do anything about it. Just take it easy, man. Stop worrying so much whether you'll make it into the finals. Kick back with some friends and some oat soda and whether you roll strikes or gutters, do your best to be true to yourself and others – that is to say, abide.*[15]

The Church of the SubGenius contains specific "instructions" to their followers:

- *Shun regular employment and stop working. This encapsulates the Church's view that to repent is to "SLACK OFF", as opposed to working for a living. SubGenius leaders say it is permissible for members to collect public assistance in lieu of maintaining employment.*

- *Purchase products sold by the Church, which its leaders say Dobbs founded to gain wealth. Unlike most religious groups, the Church proudly admits it is for-profit (presumably mocking religious groups that seem to have ulterior financial motives). Cusack sees the instruction to buy as an ironic parody of the "greed is good" mentality of the 1980s, and Kirby notes that although the group emphasizes "the consumption of popular cultural artefacts", this consumption is "simultaneously de-emphasized by the processes of remix".*

- *Rebel against "law and order". Specifically, the Church condemns security cameras and encourages computer hacking. Cusack notes that this instruction recalls Robert Anton Wilson's critique of law and order.*

- *Rid the world of everyone who did not descend from Yetis. SubGenius leaders teach that Dobbs hopes to rid the Earth of 90% of humanity, making the Earth "clear". The group praises drug abuse and abortion as effective methods of culling unneeded individuals.*

- *Exploit fear, specifically that of people who are part of the conspiracy. Church leaders teach conspiracy members to fear SubGenius devotees.*[16]

The Missionary Church of Kopimism recognizes a constitution, with the following tenets:

- *Copying of information is ethically right.*
- *Dissemination of information is ethically right.*
- *Copymixing is a sacred kind of copying, more so than the perfect, digital copying, because it expands and enhances the existing wealth of information.*
- *Copying or remixing information communicated by another person is seen as an act of respect and a strong expression of acceptance and Kopimistic faith.*
- *The Internet is holy.*
- *Code is law.*[17]

Discordianism has the Law of fives: all things happen in fives, or are divisible by or are multiples of five...and the law of Fives is never wrong:

I – There is no Goddess but Goddess and She is Your Goddess. There is no Erisian Movement but The Erisian Movement and it is The Erisian Movement. And every Golden Apple Corps is the beloved home of a Golden Worm.

II – A Discordian Shall Always use the Official Discordian Document Numbering System.

III – A Discordian is required to, the first Friday after his illumination, Go Off Alone & Partake Joyously of a Hot Dog; this Devotive Ceremony to Remonstrate against the popular Paganisms of the Day: of Roman Catholic Christendom (no meat on Friday), of Judaism (no meat of Pork), of Hindic Peoples (no meat of Beef), of Buddhists (no meat of animal), and of Discordians (no Hot Dog Buns).

IV – A Discordian shall Partake of No Hot Dog Buns, for Such was the Solace of Our Goddess when She was Confronted with The Original Snub.

V – A Discordian is Prohibited of Believing What he reads.[18]

Jediism, across all its subheadings, has a Jedi Creed, the Tenents of the Jedi Creed, and Jedi code:

Jedi creed:

I am a Jedi, an instrument of peace;

Where there is hatred I shall bring love;

Where there is injury, pardon;
Where there is doubt, faith;
Where there is despair, hope;
Where there is darkness, light;
And where there is sadness, joy.
I am a Jedi.
I shall never seek so much to be consoled as to console;
To be understood as to understand;
To be loved as to love;
For it is in giving that we receive;
It is in pardoning that we are pardoned;
And it is in dying that we are born to eternal life.

The Force is with me always, for I am a Jedi.[19]

- *The Jedi are the guardians of civilization, yet do not allow civilization to destroy needlessly.*
- *A Jedi uses the Force for knowledge and defense, never for aggression or personal gain.*
- *A Jedi respects their brother and sister and all other life-forms.*
- *A Jedi is forbidden from ruling others.*
- *A Jedi must protect the weak and defenseless from evil.*
- *A Jedi must always cooperate in times of crisis.*
- *If a Jedi draws their blade, they must be ready to take a life.*
- *A Jedi will not kill an unarmed opponent.*
- *A Jedi will not take revenge.*[20]

The Jedi Code comes in two versions which are different ways of understanding the same teaching.

- *Emotion, yet Peace.*
- *Ignorance, yet Knowledge.*
- *Passion, yet Serenity.*
- *Chaos, yet Harmony.*
- *Death, yet the Force.*

- *There is no Emotion, there is Peace.*
- *There is no Ignorance, there is Knowledge.*
- *There is no Passion, there is Serenity.*
- *There is no Chaos, there is Harmony.*
- *There is no Death, there is the Force.*[21]

Jedi Also embraces the idea of Twenty-one Jedi Maxims:

The 21 Jedi Maxims, or Maxims of Jediism is one of the first Jediist texts, created for the Jediism/Jedi religion community around 2002. The original version is far from perfect and a bit redundant, this version corrects some of the issues with the original text.

Prowess: To seek excellence in all endeavors expected of a Jedi.
A Jedi strives to acquire greater skill and expertise in what they do at all times so that it may be used in the service of the greater good, and not for personal profit. This requires discipline, patience and perfect practice.

Justice: To always seek the path of 'right'.
A Jedi is unencumbered by bias or personal interest. Justice is a double-edged sword, one that protects the weak, yet also passes judgements according to a set of values. A Jedi tolerates that which is not Jedi and does not pass judgement on that which causes no harm for it is just.

Loyalty: To have faith in your Jedi brothers and sisters.
A Jedi remains true to what they have learned and to their own teachings. A Jedi always serves those who wish to learn more of the ways of the Force and in doing so, remain loyal to the way of Jediism and their Order.

Defense: To defend the way of Jediism.
A Jedi is sworn by oath to defend their faith and all it encompasses.

Courage: To have the will.
To be a Jedi sometimes means choosing the more difficult path, the personally expensive one. A Jedi knows they must make the right choice, take the right side and that the weak they have sworn to defend often stand alone. A Jedi puts aside fear, regret, and uncertainty yet know the difference between courage and sheer stupidity.

The Invisible Pink Unicorn

Faith: To trust in the ways of the Force.
Although the ways of the Force may seem strange at times, a Jedi always knows their place and their role within it.

Humility: To accept the ego for what it is.
A Jedi does not boast of their accomplishments and knows that their accomplishment is its own reward.

Fearlessness: To have no self-imposed limits.
Fear is that which prevents a Jedi from accomplishing their duty. A Jedi learns to let go of their fears through their faith in the Force and has no shame in admitting their shortfalls when they occur.

Nobility: To act with honour.
A Jedi does not engage in petty, mean or otherwise dubious activities. Acting with stature and distinction influences others, offering a compelling example of what can be achieved by those who follow Jediism.

Honesty: To avoid lies.
A Jedi is honest with themselves and seeks to always go beyond appearances. There can be no honest self without the knowledge and wisdom to see truth.

Pure Motive: To act with motive and purpose.
Without a sound motive and purpose, action has no meaning, no destination and lacks a

foundation. A Jedi moves with the Force, trusts in its ways. A Jedi's actions are firmly based upon a deep motivation to be as their path dictates.

Discipline: To let the self be sole master of the self.
A Jedi's mind is structured, peaceful, unencombered by emotions, physical state or external stimuli.

Focus: To select what matters most.
A Jedi focuses in the task at hand. Although a Jedi is aware of the past, and wary of the present's impact on the future, through discipline they know how to select and concentrate on priorities.

Discretion: To become invisible.
A Jedi knows there is a time and place for all things. They do not actively interfere in worldly affairs and refrain from overtly supporting or opposing other individuals or organizations.

Meditation: To exercise the mind.
Through regular meditation a Jedi examines their motivations, and are certain that they are not allowing emotion, ignorance, or passion to intrude upon them. Meditation can be used by a Jedi to improve their mindfulness, focus, or patience.

Training: To know one's ignorance.
A Jedi knows there is always something more to learn and seeks new lessons every day.

Integrity: To be consistent.
A Jedi lives as a Jedi at all times. Hypocrisy is their worst enemy.

Morality: To know the danger of belief.
A Jedi knows how contradicting beliefs of what is right and wrong can lead to devastating crimes and conflicts. A Jedi takes a step away from the subjectivity of opinion in favour of the peace of objectivity. A Jedi does not force their values upon others.

Conflict: To know when to fight.
A Jedi knows the conflicting nature of the Force but they also know its peace and serenity. A Jedi never blindly enters conflict and always does so for the greater good.

Intervention: To know when not to act.
A Jedi knows how inaction can have as great an impact as action and how some of the greatest lessons are self-taught. To be a victor is also taking that victory from those you protect. A Jedi intervenes only when a Jedi's intervention is required.

Harmony: To be connected to the Force.
A Jedi seeks to live in harmony with the Force, for that is the reason to be a jedi. To better understand its ways, to better know one's place within it.[22]

Matrixism has the Four Tenets of Matrixism:

Belief in a messianic prophecy

Use of psychedelic drugs as a sacrament
A perception of reality as multu-layered and semi-subjective
Adherence to the principles of at least one of the world's major religions[23]

The Iglesia Maradoniana have Ten Commandments:

1. *The ball is never soiled.*
2. *Love football above all else.*
3. *Declare unconditional love for Diego and the beauty of football.*
4. *Defend the Argentina shirt.*
5. *Spread the news of Diego's miracles throughout the universe.*
6. *Honor the temples where he played and his sacred shirts.*
7. *Don't proclaim Diego as a member of any single team.*
8. *Preach and spread the principles of the Church of Maradona.*
9. *Make Diego your middle name*
10. *Name your first son Diego*[24]

The Church of Euthanasia has one commandment: "Thou shalt not procreate" and four pillars:

- *Suicide*
- *Abortion*
- *Cannibalism*
- *Sodomy*[25]

The United Church of Bacon issues the Eight Bacon Commandments:

- *Be skeptical.*
- *Respect boundaries.*
- *Normalize atheists and religion.*
- *Have fun.*
- *Be good.*
- *Be generous.*
- *Praise bacon!*
- *Advocate for fair church taxation.*[26]

The Church of Saint Stupid has a pledge to prepare for St. Stupid Day:

I pledge allegiance, to the illusion,
and to the pyramid scheme,
for which it stands.
One species, in denial,
with error and excess
by all.[27]

Matrixism logo

ECLECTIC BELIEFS

As with most groups that have certain unifying concepts in common but are largely autonomous, assorted beliefs are often relative to each individual practitioner. Whether the individual seeks to poke fun at religion, express a personal devotion to a specific fandom, or make a social statement through their membership, most parody and fictitious religious groups leave specified membership expression up to each individual person who desires to pursue belief through such a group.

RELATIONS WITH NON-PARODY AND FICTITIOUS GROUPS

There are a few groups that specify they place no prohibition on individual member participation in that of organized religion (Matrixism, Discordianism, United Church of Bacon), but others do not make any such specified prohibition, even though with some groups, such an allowance is likely implied. With other groups that exist as a parody of religion or to mock specified values, belonging to a standard religious group would be seen as in conflict with the group's ideals. Many parody groups are in extreme conflict with organized religion and regard those who practice such as ignorant or defective.

HOLY SITES

Because parody and fictitious religious groups aren't based in the same ancient ideas as mainline religions, the concept of a holy site isn't part of the belief systems in question.

NOTABLE FIGURES

Bobby Henderson (1980-), founder of the Church of the Flying Spaghetti Monster; James Parry (1967-), founder of Kibology; Chris Harper, founder of Landover Baptist Church; Ivan Stang 91953-) and Philo Drummond, founders, Church of the SubGenius; Greg Hill (1941-2000) and Kerry Wendell Thornely (1938-1998), authors of the *Principa Discordia*; Oliver Benjamin (1968-), founder of Dudeism; Chris Korda (1962-)and Robert Kimberk, founders of the Church of Euthanasia; Penn Jilette (1955-), magician, involved in the creation of the United Church of Bacon; Isak Gerson (1991-) and Gustav Nipe (1988-), founders of the Missionary Church of Kopimism; Eric Lis, founder of Silinism; Hector Campomar, Alejandro Veron and Hernan Amez, founders of the Iglesia Maradoniana; Ed Holmes, founder of The First Church of the Last Laugh.

NOTABLE GROUPS

Perhaps the best-known parody religion is the Church of the Flying Spaghetti Monster, also known as Pastafarianism. It was created by Bobby Henderson in protest of the teaching of intelligent design as an alternative to evolution within the public school system. First outlined in a letter, the founder argued he should have the equal time to teach on the Flying Spaghetti Monster in schools, along with the other two theories. Born out of internet fame (the letter Bobby Henderson first wrote to the Kansas State Board of Education was placed on a website) the group expanded its parody to religion in general. Unlike some parody groups, the Church of the Flying Spaghetti Monster demands entirely equal treatment of its beliefs, however absurd, that are extended to mainline religious groups. According to the church's beliefs, the Flying Spaghetti Monster created earth while drunk, thus leading to its flaws. The Flying Spaghetti Monster isn't regarded as a real being, but an illustration of the absurdity of religious myth. Practitioners openly reject dogma, mock mainline belief, and create inversions of standard Christianity, such as heaven, hell, holidays, and scripture.[28]

FACTS AND FIGURES

Facts and figures are impossible to obtain for the average parody or fictitious religious group, for a few reasons. The first reason is, obviously, such religious groups aren't taken seriously. Second, there often aren't enough followers to track, and third, there are seldom central leadership figures by which membership can be tallied. An interesting facts and figures story, however, related to Jediism, started due to a chain email stating that if a religion could meet a minimum threshold of adherents (somewhere between eight and ten thousand people), the group would receive formal recognition. The information was urban legend, but pushed adherents in New Zealand, Australia, and the United Kingdom to register their religious identity as Jediism. Actual practitioners were far less than the reported numbers, which were inflated by people who answered as "Jedi" on the census for parody purposes.[29]

OTHER IMPORTANT DEFINITIONS

- **Aneristic Principle**: In Discordianism, apparent order.[30]
- **Athorism**: A statement specifically about the Norse god Thor, stating that he does not really exist. Used by extension to prove absurdity in theology and indicate there is no deity that exists. Term was coined by Richard Dawkins. Arguments of athorism are common in atheistic parody religions, such as the Invisible Pink Unicorn and Church of the Flying Spaghetti Monster.[30]
- **Clenches**: Local member groups of the Church of the SubGenius.[31]
- **Devivals**: A play on a Christian revival, devivals are specific gatherings designed to bring together groups of the movement's followers. Often seen in Church of the SubGenius.[32]
- **Disorder**: In Discordianism, unrelated information viewed through a particular form or lens.[33]
- **Drag**: An entertainment performance that specifically features gender expression, often through extremes. The Sisters of Perpetual Indulgence are an example of an organization that uses drag for the purpose of entertainment, education, and social commentary.

- **Eristic Principle**: In Discordianism, apparent disorder.[34]

- **Euthanasia**: Also known as assisted suicide, euthanasia is the painless method by which a terminally ill or coma patient is deliberately put to death. Euthanasia is a controversial practice, outlawed in most countries and prohibitive in most of the world's major religions. The Church of Euthanasia, believing the world is overpopulated, seeks to encourage individuals to voluntarily reduce the world's population by refusing to procreate. It specifically states on its website that it rejects both murder and eugenics to accomplish its goal.[35]

- **Gender bender**: An individual who dresses up in drag, specifically with the purpose of dressing like the opposite sex. Such can also seek to bend gender roles (in a concept known as genderfuck). The Sisters of Perpetual Indulgence perform and educate through use of gender bender.

- ***The Hour of Slack***: A radio program (now a podcast) produced by the Church of the SubGenius.

- **Intelligent design**: A counter-evolutionary position, classified as pseudoscientific, that is designed to argue for the existence of a divine creator by stating that creation is so complex, it cannot be explained by evolution alone. It does not make claims about the age of the earth, support a literal interpretation of the Bible, or make any mention that the creator is the Biblical deity. It lacks scientific theory, however, putting forth an alternative theory that because life forms as we know them are so intricate, they must, therefore, have an origin outside of spontaneous evolutionary theory. The Church of the Flying Spaghetti Monster got its start over a debate about intelligent design as taught in public school settings.[36]

- **J.R. "Bob" Dobbs**: The so-called prophet of the Church of the SubGenius. He is typified as a salesman from the 1950s who is connected to different deities and known conspiracies.

- **Micronation**: A group claiming to be an independent nation with sovereignty without legal or international recognition. Silinism is the official religion of the Aerican Empire, a micronation.

- **Omphalos hypothesis**: The attempt one makes to reconcile scientific belief in the age of the earth (as billions of years old) with creationism, which accepts the interpretation of the young earth Genesis account (implying the earth is only a few thousand years old), by a divine being, within the past six to ten thousand years. Last Thursdayism parodies this idea, stating that the creation of the world could have been last Thursday (or within the last five days), for all anyone can prove.[37]

- **Operation Mindfuck**: The attribution of national calamities, assassinations, and conspiracies are attributed to the Bavarian Illuminati, a now defunct eighteenth century secret society. The purpose of this operation is to cause fear and reveal how absurd conspiracy theory can be. A principle thought found in Discordianism.[38]

- **Ordination mill**: An online or mail order organization by which ordination credentials are offered to individuals for a fee, regardless of training or experience. Most parody and fictitious organizations operate ordination mills to try and appear legitimate alongside mainstream churches.
- **Pirates**: The original members of the Church of the Flying Spaghetti Monster.

- **Poe's Law**: An internet concept, named after Nathan Poe (a commentator on a Christian internet forum), that states without clear indication of an author's intent, every parody of extreme views can seem sincere to someone who is seeing the parody. Much of fictitious and parody religion can be seen through the lens of Poe's Law.[39]

- **R'Amen**: Also known as rAmen, the way individuals in the Church of the Flying Spaghetti Monster end or conclude mock prayers.

- **Russell's Teapot**: An analogy first created by Bertrand Russell: If he were to say there was a teapot in the universe, so small it could not be seen and there was no proof of its existence, he could not expect anyone to believe him simply because no one would prove he was wrong. This argument is now applied by atheists, to state that the burden of evidence for a deity or religious devotion lies upon those who make the claim of such, which cannot be proven, rather than saying one has the burden to disprove that which cannot be proven. Method is common in atheistic parody religions, Invisible Pink Unicorn and Church of the Flying Spaghetti Monster.[40]

Believer's Characteristics

Belief in the absurdity of religion; desire to make a social statement or commentary by using the idea of religion to protest religion; interest in the science vs. faith debate; desire to discredit religion in general; expressing a deep devotion and love to a specific area of fandom; devoted interest in a movie, book, figure, or other entertainment venue; intense pursuit of internet ideas; excessively social through internet platforms; interest in technology; desires to make a social statement, especially against things perceived to be wrong within society; enjoyment and pursuit of absurdism and alternate realities; anti-establishment; outcasts; non-conformity to social structure; interest in participating in things that are counterculture.

GNOSTICISM AND NEO-GNOSTICISM

Light and Darkness, life and death, right and left, are brothers of one another. They are inseparable. Because of this neither are the good good, nor evil evil, nor is life life, nor death death. For this reason each one will dissolve into its earliest origin. But those who are exalted above the world are indissoluble, eternal.
(The Gospel of Philip)[1]

THEOLOGY

Gnostic theology is complex, as it is based on a grouping of theological with some variations. It does not help that we do not know much about the original Gnostic systems, save some fragmentary information we can piece together from discovered writings and the arguments of their enemies. What we do know reveals a multidimensional spiritual world, heavily based in mythological understandings of duality, or the idea that there are existing, incompatible opposites present throughout the universe (such as light and dark, flesh and spirit, matter and spirit, and good and evil). Such is also true within the essence of their theological entities. Gnostics believed in a supreme, hidden deity and a contrasting demiurge or demigod deity responsible for creating the universe. In many strains of Gnosticism, the demiurge was associated with Yahweh, the God of the Old Testament and often called Yaldabaoth (also Samael or Saklas) or some variation therein. The demiurge was understood to be malevolent, demanding worship as the supreme deity when he was not such. He created all matter (including human beings and human bodies, which were seen as imprisonment) in contrast to the spiritual realm. Yaldabaoth created archons to preside over the material realm and create obstacles from individuals truly finding the hidden, secret, true deity.

For Gnostics, the pursuit of salvation came through direct knowledge of the true deity, often known as the MONAD ("the one"). A parallel from Greek philosophy, the Monad is the source of all things, the singular point of existence and the foundational, originating point for metaphysical existence. The Monad is the high source of the pleroma (meaning "fullness"), which is the region of light (sometimes understood as the equivalency of heaven or heavenly light), contrasting with the region of darkness. The heavenly light emanates through different stages and worlds, becoming more embodied with each stage. Eventually, light returns to the Monad, bringing with it spiritual enlightenment. These emanations are known as aeons. They begin as one singular being, who through interactions with the Monad, become two beings, (usually male and female). The number of aeons vary, but thirty are most often recognized. These aeons compose the pleroma, with lower regions closest to the darkness (the physical world). The most recognized aeons are Christ, and Christ's consort, Sophia (the Greek word for wisdom). Sophia is seen as the final and lowest emanation of the Monad; Sophia births the demiurge Yahweh, who then creates the material world.

Views of Jesus Christ vary among Gnostic systems. In some, he is viewed as the embodiment of the Monad come to earth to bring gnosis (true knowledge) to humanity. This poses theological issues for Gnostics, as the question of being able to inhabit flesh while spirit is contradictory. For this reason, some saw Jesus Christ as an illusion of a human being (a spiritual being who did not inhabit a body) but only appeared to be human. In other systems, he is a human being who attained enlightenment of true knowledge and then taught such to his disciples. Still, others considered Jesus Christ to be a false messiah, one who maligned the message of John the Baptist; such groups follow John, and mystical teachings about him, rather than Jesus. Others believe in different saving individuals throughout history, such as Seth of the book of Genesis, or Mani (216-274 or 277), a Gnostic prophet accepted in certain strains of the religion.

PHILOSOPHY

An encompassing movement that is a religious representation of Greek philosophical ideas mixed with Christian, Jewish, Zoroastrian, and Buddhist ideas, Gnosticism represents a collection of different beliefs and ideas comparable to the concept of denominations today. The basis of Gnostic ideas is found in the pursuit of obtaining the secret, hidden knowledge of the Monad, unavailable to the average person. The word "Gnostic" is from the Greek word for "knowledge" and refers to the process of obtaining this knowledge through the specified initiations, rites, and rituals of Gnostic practice. Knowledge of this deity can only come through the group, as they are the ones who hold this knowledge, teach it, instruct upon it, and exclusively offer it. Through the universe's chaotic mess of duality, Gnosticism offers insights into the way things are, reflecting spiritual and physical ideas and offering specified mystical knowledge that one can have only if they engage with the Monad.

The term "Gnosticism" was never used by adherents of this system themselves. Instead, it is used by religious and cultural historians to describe these groups, flourishing between the first and fourth centuries. No one is certain where Gnosticism originated; it appears to have started as an early Christian sect debating issue of spirit and matter. They concluded Jesus Christ could not have been both human and divine because such would be incompatible. Over time, this group became known as Docetists ("to seem") as they believed Jesus only appeared to be human but was really spirit in nature. Several spinoff sects emerged from that point, reflecting Jewish, Christian, Zoroastrian, Greek mystery religions, apocalyptic, and even some ancient Egyptian ideas, all different in combination. As the years went by, Gnostics developed their own unique religious ideas, mystical traditions, and figures. Gnosticism was of considerable prominence throughout the ancient Middle East and Mediterranean religion through the third century, before it started to decline.

The decline of Gnosticism was not caused by one singular factor, but many: its disrespectability among Christian leadership, the economic collapse of the Roman Empire, and historical cultural change. Gnostic ideas also further complicated its demise. The idea of attaining secret knowledge and not much else did not leave possibility for any sort of personal achievement within the religious system in the long term. It was most likely deemed heretical due to its controversial nature, as there was no way for the early church leaders already under persecution to sort out groups that were a little unusual from those who were false. The movement was not classified as heretical until the fourth century. By this time, it was already falling out of favor among followers. While it would remain in existence in small groups (in some instances through the Middle Ages), it largely died out. We have limited information about early Gnostics, save the writings of their enemies and a few scrolls and documents discovered in the 1940s, which help us piece together their ideas (although not completely). It is, therefore, difficult to clearly define their beliefs and systematic practice. Several groups, such as the Albigensians and Waldensians, were accused of Gnostic practice and ideas by the Catholic Church throughout history, but it is unlikely their doctrine had connection to the original Gnostic movement. The Mandean Gnostic sects that connect back to original Gnostic idea and thought are found in Iran and Iraq in extremely small numbers. Modern-day strains of Gnosticism were part of a Gnostic revival, beginning in the 1800s in Europe and the Americas. These groups reconstruct ideas and information obtained about Gnostic traditions; their authenticity of rite and practice is of considerable debate. Most have synthesized their beliefs with occult practice, New Age ideals, or an interfaith platform, thus not accurately representing Gnostic ideas and thoughts.[2]

ADHERENT IDENTITY

Gnostic, Gnostics, Neo-Gnosticism, Neo-Gnostic, Christians of Saint John, Manichaeans, Mandean, Mandeans, Sabeanism, Sabians, Sethian, Valentinian, Basilidans, Serpent Gnostics, Simonians, Hermeticism, Carporcratians, Borborites, Cainites, Cerdonians, Colorbasians, Dositheans, Justinians, Abelonians, Agapetae, Docetae, Elcesaites, Encratites, Marconism, Marcosians, Priscilianism, Quintillians, Secundians, Seleucians, Nicolaism, Messalians, Marcosians, and Knowers of the Way.

NUMBER OF ADHERENTS

Most Gnostic sects declined and then disappeared around the fourth century. There were a few that survived longer, but most of those also no longer exist. The only existing Gnostic community that traces back to the original movement is Mandaeism, also known as Mandaeanism, Sabeanism, or the Christians of Saint John. There are approximately 60,000-70,000 Mandeans left worldwide. Due to conflict and war in the Middle East and the fact that they do not accept converts, their numbers are declining rapidly.

It is difficult to ascertain exact numbers of Gnostic revival groups, as many of these groups identify in different ways. They may not classify themselves as Gnostic, but as occultists, seekers, esoteric Christians, New Agers, thinkers, with specified religious orders (such as the Knights Templar, Gnostic Catholics, Jesuits, or Franciscans, among others), Albigensians, independently or universally Catholic, Druid, or other identities that may come through another association, an organization, or one's own personal thoughts about a group.[3]

TRADITIONAL LANGUAGES

Greek, Coptic, Mandaic, Syriac.

SECTS/DIVISIONS

There were several Gnostic sects. In totality, we probably do not know, nor are able to number, all Gnostic groups that once existed. Based on the information that we have we can piece together some general ideas of the major groups and some of their beliefs.

- **Thomasine Traditions**: An early theory of Gnostic formation states the Gnostic tradition was started by the Apostle Thomas or within his "school" of followers. While this was accepted as fact for some time, there is little evidence to suggest there was a specific Gnostic sect that embraced this idea, nor that there was any Gnostic lineage specifically through Thomas. We now know there are many Gnostic or Christian documents with Gnostic influence attributed to several apostles, including John, Thomas, Judas, and Peter.

- **Syrian-Egyptian Gnosticism**: Largely based on Platonic philosophy, it believes creation itself exists in a series of emanations from the Monad, thus resulting in the material universe. Evil is seen as matter, inferior to goodness, and lacking spiritual insight. Thus, creation is seen not as an equal force in dualistic power, but an inferior one. These sects often had elaborate church systems and rites, like those that were and would be seen in high church Christian form, only with notable theological differences. Most of the Syrian-Egyptian Gnostics considered themselves Christians, and many early church figures, such as Jesus, the Apostle Thomas, John (the writer of Revelation) the Apostle Paul, and Mary Magdalene, are central figures in their writings. Syrian-Egyptian Gnostic groups included Sethianism, Valentinianism, Basilideans, and the Serpent Gnostics.

- **Sethite-Barbeloite**: Also based on Platonic philosophical ideas, it is uncertain if this group was merely an unorthodox Christian sect or an independent movement of its own. Identified as a heresy by Irenaeus (an early Christian figure), the Sethite-Barbeloite movement was a primary Gnostic force, especially in the second and third centuries. The adherents of this system traced their spiritual identity through Seth (born to Adam and Eve) and Norea (attributed to be the wife of Noah) as connected spiritually to Adam as the daughter of Eve. The central text of this group is the Apocryphon of John, by which Jesus transmits secret, hidden knowledge to John the Apostle. The document provides a discourse on Gnostic theology and cosmology in the form of a discussion between John and the Savior. The longer the group existed, the more philosophically Greek their thoughts became, rejecting Christian ideas. Sethite-Barbeloite groups include the Ophites, the Archontics, Audians, Borborites, Phibionites, Stratiotici, and Secundians. Some of these sects lasted until the Middle Ages.

- **Samaritan Baptist sects**: So-called because they traced themselves to the followers of John the Baptist, the Samaritan Baptist sects of Gnosticism believed the world was created by ignorant angels instead of Yaldabaoth. These angels were the cause of death in the world. Adherents overcame death and the problems of sin through their baptismal ritual. The Samaritans were viewed as the complete embodiment and revealers of true knowledge. Within this sect, there were groups that practiced magic (such as the Simonians) and others that existed in Spain and Egypt (such as the Basilidians or Basilideans and Priscilianists).

- **Valentinianism**: A complex and philosophically intense Gnostic sect. Valentinianism was founded by Valentinus (c. 100-c. 180), a Christian bishop who was a candidate for Bishop of Rome but was rejected in favor of someone else. In response, Valentinus established his own church system, which flourished in parts of Africa (especially Egypt), Asia Minor, and Syria. Valentinian Gnosticism was a little different than other strains. It appears to be monistic, rather than dualistic in its theology. Valentinians believed the material world and its flaws are not due to the failings of the demiurge, but because he is not as perfect as the Monad and higher emanations. In other words, the demiurge of the Valentinians was not as much malevolent as ignorant. The material world is not seen as a separate substance from the Monad but as an error in one's perception. This group believed the Biblical epistles should be read as an allegory rather than as reality, seeing the Jew/Gentile conflict of New Testament times as between those who were spiritual but still carnal (psychics) and those who were totally spiritual (pneumatics). These secret understandings were key to knowledge and discovering the truth one could only obtain through Gnosticism. Valentinus was most likely influenced by Basilides, thus making it a subset of Syrian-Egyptian Gnosticism.

- **Marcionism**: Questioned as to whether it classifies as Gnostic, the Marcion system of Gnosticism was found by Marcion (c. 85- c. 160), a church leader expelled around 150 who then started his own group. This group rejected the entirety of the Old Testament and accepted eleven books of the Bible: a shortened version of Luke's Gospel and ten letters of Paul (also edited). Much like Gnostic groups, this one made a distinction between the God of the Old Testament as an evil demiurge and the highest existing God, who was the father of Jesus. This true deity had no part in creation, nor any part with the material world. Jesus came to earth to be freed from the tyranny of Jewish law. Jesus was a divine spirit existing in human form without being human.

- **Hermeticism**: A less dark aspect of Gnosticism, Hermeticism is based on the writings of Hermes Trismegistus. It is believed Hermes Trismegistus was either equivalent of or a mixture of the Greek god Hermes, and the Egyptian God Thoth. It is, however, uncertain if there was a specific individual with this name, if the individual was a pagan magician who foresaw Christianity and Gnostic ideas, or if it is a series of writings that, over the years, developed into a specified magic tradition. More than anything, Hermeticism is a grouping of practices and philosophical points: the concept of the Monad (God the All), identifying a single, true religious system (although such is considered to be part of every religious system that exists), the idea of the macrocosm (universe) and microcosm (self) and that both lie within the other; and the foundations of reincarnation, alchemy, astrology, and theurgy. The cosmology of Hermeticism is a little different than that of most Gnostic groups, believing the All to be the cause of creation, including primary matter. Good and evil are brought about through reason and knowledge, depending on where one gets their ideas and concepts from. The only thing seen as offensive is a focus upon materialism. They adhere to approximately forty-two different books, all attributed to Hermes Trismegistus, including the Corpus Hermeticum. It is considered the foundational point for magic, western esoterism, and scientific development in Renaissance times.[4]

- **Persian Gnosticism**: Persian Gnosticism, the only Gnostic heading which continues to exist in small numbers since ancient times, is among the oldest of all Gnostic sects. It first appeared in the western Persian province of Asoristan (what we know as Mesopotamia). These have their own religious developments and are not subsets of Christianity or Judaism. There are two major groups: one that has survived (Mandaeanism) and one that has not (Manichaeism). Mandaeanism are a Semite people, speaking their own Mandaic language based on Aramaic. Their name, "Mandaeanism," is from a term that means "knowledge of life." John the Baptist is central to their faith practice. For this reason, they are sometimes called the "Christians of St. John." They are highly private and do not receive converts; there is great secrecy surrounding their rites and practice. Considered a cultural heritage more than a theology, the Mandaeans are not credal or doctrinal, although their theology, cosmology, and eschatology are much like that of other Gnostic groups. They are strictly dualist in their nature. They reject Abraham, Moses, and Jesus, seeing Jesus as an anti-messiah. Instead, they embrace Abel, Seth, Enosh, Noah, Shem, and Aram. Today, their main scriptural reference is the Genza Rabba (better known as The Book of Adam). Other important texts include the Qolasta (Book of Prayer) and Sidra d'Yahia (The Mandean Book of John).

- **Manichaeism**: Manichaeism was founded by the Prophet Mani, whose father was part of another Gnostic sect (Elcesiaites). Mani claimed to have had a vision of his "heavenly twin" calling him to leave his father's sect of Gnosticism, and instead preach the true message of Christ. Very classic of Gnostic sects, it is distinct in its teaching of duality, of forces of light and dark in opposition, and of a cosmos in conflict. It held influences from Zoroastrian theology and cosmology; especially the belief that in the end, light would overcome darkness. In 762, it was the state religion of the Uyghur Empire.

- **Other Gnostic groups**: There were numerous other assorted Gnostic groups that held to differing minor points, but adhered to the bulk of Gnostic theology, especially about the existence of a deity obtainable only through knowledge, a demiurge creator, the chaos of the cosmos, and dualism. Many practiced strict dietary regulations, required sexual abstinence, and followed specified teachers who created variations on their spiritual themes. In the case of these groups, we don't have a lot of specific information about them. They include the Abelonians, Agapetae, Barbeliotae, Borborites, Cainites, Carporcratians, Cerenthians, Docetae, Elcesaites, Encratites, and the Ophites.

- **Modern Gnostic sects**: Modern day Gnostic sects have their roots in the Gnostic revival of the late 1800s, connecting back to the discovery of certain Gnostic documents, especially the Pistis Sophia. These groups are often a mixture of independent Catholic, occult, New Thought, New Age, and Gnostic ideas, inasmuch as we know about them. Most do not require the practice of any specific doctrine. There are a number of sects and breakaway groups off of other groups. Some of these include Anthroposophy, the Church of St. Mary & St. John, Ecclesia Gnostica, Ecclesia Gnostica Catholica, Ecclesia Gnostica Mysteriorum, Eglise Gnostique, Gnostic Church of France, Gnostic Society, Johannite Church, Lectorium Rosicrucianum, Liberal Catholic Union, and Bohemian theosophy.[5]

Phaethon (Gustave Moreau)

DISPUTES WITHIN GROUP

Gnostic sects were quite varied in their claimed lineages, central prophetic figures, some of their practices, and their unique scriptural references. Most Gnostic sects agreed about core ideas related to Gnostic foundations and outlooks but varied in some of their unique points about the subheadings of the religious group.

SCRIPTURES

It appears that most, if not all Gnostic sects embodied their own specified scriptural canons. All of them varied. Some overlapped, and some were unique to the group. Others we do not have, as there were specified and systematic attempts to destroy Gnostic writings at an earlier point in history.

There have been a few discoveries over the past two hundred years, that offer us firsthand accounts of Gnostic scriptures. The most significant discovery has been those writings at Nag Hammadi, Egypt in 1945. Now known as the Chenoboskion Manuscripts, these writings are a mixture of early Christian writings and Gnostic writings. They were discovered as papyrus codices, leather-bounded and stored in sealed clay jars. They date back to the second and fourth centuries and are often among the oldest (if not the oldest) records of these documents that we have today. Had it not been for the Manichaeanism sect of Gnosticism, none of these works would have survived.

There are many Gnostic scriptures either referenced (but now nonexistent), discovered only in fragments, or discovered whole or near enough to be whole to study. Most of the Gnostic works found at Nag Hammadi reveals the Syrian-Egyptian strains of Gnosticism. There are other strains, however, with different canons.

We can categorize Gnostic literature by its reference and contents.

- **Referenced, but no longer in existence**: Gospel of Basilides, Exegetica (Basilides), On Righteousness (Epiphanes), Fragments from a commentary on the Gospel of John (Heracleon), Naassene Fragment, Ophite Diagrams, Commentary on the Gospel of John Prologue (Ptolemy), Letter to Flora, and Excerpta Ex Theodoto (Theodotus).

First [was there] Mind the Generative Law of All;

Second to the Firstborn was Liquid Chaos;
Third Soul through toil received the Law.
Wherefore, with a deer's form surrounding her,
She labours at her task beneath Death's rule.
Now, holding sway, she sees the Light;
And now, cast into piteous plight, she weeps;
Now she weeps, and now rejoices;
Now she weeps, and now is judged;
Now is judged, and now she dieth;
Now is born, with no way out for her; in misery
She enters in her wandering the labyrinth of ills.
And Jesus said: O Father, see!
[Behold] the struggle still of ills on earth!
Far from Thy Breath away she wanders!
She seeks to flee the bitter Chaos,
And knows not how she shall pass through.
Wherefore, send me, O Father!
Seals in my hands, I will descend;
Through Æons universal will I make a Path;
Through Mysteries all I'll open up a Way!
And Forms of Gods will I display;
The secrets of the Holy Path I will hand on,

And call them Gnosis.[6]

- **Considered possibly Gnostic at one time, but are now disputed as such, no longer considered such, or understood as such**: The Gospel of Thomas; The Apocryphon of James; The Gospel of Mary (Magdalene); The Exegesis on the Soul; Teachings of Silvanus; Secret Gospel of Mark; The Odes of Solomon; The Acts of Thomas.

Do you not, then, desire to be filled? And your heart is drunken; do you not, then, desire to be sober? Therefore, be ashamed! Henceforth, waking or sleeping, remember that you have seen the Son of Man, and spoken with him in person, and listened to him in person. Woe to those who have seen the Son of Man; blessed will they be who have not seen the man, and they who have not consorted with him, and they who have not spoken with him, and they who have not listened to anything from him; yours is life! Know, then, that he healed you when you were ill, that you might reign. Woe to those who have found relief from their illness, for they will relapse into illness. Blessed are they who have not been ill, and have known relief before falling ill; yours is the kingdom of God. Therefore, I say to you, 'Become full, and leave no space within you empty, for he who is coming can mock you."

Then Peter replied, "Lo, three times you have told us, 'Become full'; but we are full." The Savior answered and said, "For this cause I have said to you, 'Become full,' that you may not be in want. They who are in want, however, will not be saved. For it is good to be full, and bad to be in want. Hence, just as it is good that you be in want and, conversely, bad that you be full, so he who is full is in want, and he who is in want does not become full as he who is in want becomes full, and he who has been filled, in turn attains due perfection. Therefore, you must be in want while it is possible to fill you, and be full while it is possible for you to be in want, so that you may be able to fill yourselves the more. Hence, become full of the Spirit, but be in want of reason, for reason <belongs to> the soul; in turn, it is (of the nature of) soul."[7]

- **Gospels**: The Gospel of Truth; The Gospel of Philip; Coptic Gospel of the Egyptians (Holy Book of the Great Invisible Spirit); The Sophia of Jesus Christ; Sentences of Sextus; The Gospel of Judas.

Mary said to him: "Holy Lord, where did your disciples come from, and where are they going, and (what) should they do here?"

The Perfect Savior said to them: "I want you to know that Sophia, the Mother of the Universe and the consort, desired by herself to bring these to existence without her male (consort). But by the will of the Father of the Universe, that his unimaginable goodness might be revealed, he created that curtain between the immortals and those that came afterward, that the consequence might follow ... [BG 118:] *... every aeon and chaos - that the defect of the female might <appear>, and it might come about that Error would contend with her. And these became the curtain of spirit. From <the> aeons above the emanations of Light, as I have said already, a drop from Light and Spirit came down to the lower regions of Almighty in chaos, that their molded forms might appear from that drop, for it is a judgment on him, Arch-Begetter, who is called 'Yaldabaoth'. That drop revealed their molded forms through the breath, as a living soul. It was withered and it slumbered in the ignorance of the soul. When it became hot from the breath of the Great Light of the Male, and it took thought, (then) names were received by all who are in the world of chaos, and all things that are in it through that Immortal One, when the breath blew into him. But when this came about by the will of Mother Sophia - so that Immortal Man might piece together the garments there for a judgment on the robbers - <he> then welcomed the blowing of that breath; but since he was soul-like, he was not able to take that power for himself until the number of chaos should be complete, (that is,) when the time determined by the great angel is complete.*

"Now I have taught you about Immortal Man and have loosed the bonds of the robbers from him. I have broken the gates of the pitiless ones in their presence. I have humiliated their malicious intent, and they all have been shamed and have risen from their ignorance. Because of this, then, I came here, that they might be joined with that Spirit and Breath, [NHC III continues:] *and might from two become one, just as from the first, that you might yield much fruit and go up to Him Who Is from the Beginning, in ineffable joy and glory and honor and grace of the Father of the Universe.*

"Whoever, then, knows the Father in pure knowledge will depart to the Father and repose in Unbegotten Father. But whoever knows him defectively will depart to the defect and the rest of

the Eighth. Now whoever knows Immortal Spirit of Light in silence, through reflecting and consent in the truth, let him bring me signs of the Invisible One, and he will become a light in the Spirit of Silence. Whoever knows Son of Man in knowledge and love, let him bring me a sign of Son of Man, that he might depart to the dwelling-places with those in the Eighth.

"Behold, I have revealed to you the name of the Perfect One, the whole will of the Mother of the Holy Angels, that the masculine multitude may be completed here, that there might appear in the aeons, the infinities and those that came to be in the untraceable wealth of the Great Invisible Spirit, that they all might take from his goodness, even the wealth of their rest that has no kingdom over it. I came from First Who Was Sent, that I might reveal to you Him Who Is from the Beginning, because of the arrogance of Arch-Begetter and his angels, since they say about themselves that they are gods. And I came to remove them from their blindness, that I might tell everyone about the God who is above the universe. Therefore, tread upon their graves, humiliate their malicious intent, and break their yoke and arouse my own. I have given you authority over all things as Sons of Light, that you might tread upon their power with your feet."[8]

- **Acts**: The Acts of Peter and the Twelve.

And I, Peter, inquired about the name of this city from residents who were standing on the dock. A man among them answered, saying, "The name of this city is Habitation, that is, Foundation [...] endurance." And the leader among them holding the palm branch at the edge of the dock. And after we had gone ashore with the baggage, I went into the city, to seek advice about lodging.

A man came out wearing a cloth bound around his waist, and a gold belt girded it. Also a napkin was tied over his chest, extending over his shoulders and covering his head and his hands.

I was staring at the man, because he was beautiful in his form and stature. There were four parts of his body that I saw: the soles of his feet and a part of his chest and the palms of his hands and his visage. These things I was able to see. A book cover like (those of) my books was in his left hand. A staff of styrax wood was in his right hand. His voice was resounding as he slowly spoke, crying out in the city, "Pearls! Pearls!"

I, indeed, thought he was a man of that city. I said to him, "My brother and my friend!" He answered me, then, saying, "Rightly did you say, 'My brother and my friend.' What is it you seek from me?" I said to him, "I ask you about lodging for me and the brothers also, because we are strangers here." He said to me, "For this reason have I myself just said, 'My brother and my friend,' because I also am a fellow stranger like you."

And having said these things, he cried out, "Pearls! Pearls!" The rich men of that city heard his voice. They came out of their hidden storerooms. And some were looking out from the storerooms of their houses. Others looked out from their upper windows. And they did not see (that they could gain) anything from him, because there was no pouch on his back nor bundle inside his cloth and napkin. And because of their disdain they did not even acknowledge him. He, for his part, did not reveal himself to them. They returned to their storerooms, saying, "This man is mocking us."

And the poor of that city heard his voice, and they came to the man who sells this pearl. They said, "Please take the trouble to show us the pearl so that we may, then, see it with our (own) eyes. For we are the poor. And we do not have this [...] price to pay for it. But show us that we might say to our friends that we saw a pearl with our (own) eyes." He answered, saying to them, "If it is possible, come to my city, so that I may not only show it before your (very) eyes, but give it to you for nothing."

And indeed they, the poor of that city, heard and said, "Since we are beggars, we surely know that a man does not give a pearl to a beggar, but (it is) bread and money that is usually received. Now then, the kindness which we want to receive from you (is) that you show us the pearl before our eyes. And we will say to our friends proudly that we saw a pearl with our (own) eyes" - because it is not found among the poor, especially such beggars (as these). He answered (and) said to them, "If it is possible, you yourselves come to my city, so that I may not only show you it, but give it to you for nothing." The poor and the beggars rejoiced because of the man who gives for nothing.[9]

Alchemical Tree of Life

- **Discourses**: Treatise on the Resurrection; Tripartite Tractate; The Hypostasis of the Archons (The Reality of the Rulers); The Book of Thomas the Contender (The Book of Thomas); Dialogue of the Saviour; Asclepius 21-29; Melchizedek; A Valentinian Exposition; On the Anointing, On Baptism, and On the Eucharist; Three Steles of Seth; Zostrianos; Marsanes; The Paraphrase of Shem; The Discourse on the Eighth and Ninth; Second Treatise of the Great Seth; Testimony of Truth; Hypsiphrone; Trimorphic Protennoia; The Books of Jeu; Hermetica.

On account of the reality of the authorities, (inspired) by the spirit of the father of truth, the great apostle – referring to the "authorities of the darkness" – told us that "our contest is not against flesh and blood; rather, the authorities of the universe and the spirits of wickedness." I have sent this (to you) because you inquire about the reality of the authorities.

Their chief is blind; because of his power and his ignorance and his arrogance he said, with his power, "It is I who am God; there is none apart from me." When he said this, he sinned against the entirety. And this speech got up to incorruptibility; then there was a voice that came forth from incorruptibility, saying, "You are mistaken, Samael" – which is, "god of the blind."

His thoughts became blind. And, having expelled his power – that is, the blasphemy he had spoken – he pursued it down to chaos and the abyss, his mother, at the instigation of Pistis Sophia. And she established each of his offspring in conformity with its power - after the pattern of the realms that are above, for by starting from the invisible world the visible world was invented.

As incorruptibility looked down into the region of the waters, her image appeared in the waters; and the authorities of the darkness became enamored of her. But they could not lay hold of that image, which had appeared to them in the waters, because of their weakness – since beings that merely possess a soul cannot lay hold of those that possess a spirit – for they were from below, while it was from above. This is the reason why "incorruptibility looked down into the region (etc.)": so that, by the father's will, she might bring the entirety into union with the light.

The rulers laid plans and said, "Come, let us create a man that will be soil from the earth." They modeled their creature as one wholly of the earth. Now the rulers [...] body [...] they have [...] female [...] is [...] with the face of a beast. They had taken some soil from the earth and modeled their man after their body and after the image of God that had appeared to them in the waters. They said, "Come, let us lay hold of it by means of the form that we have modeled, so that it may see its male counterpart [...], and we may seize it with the form that we have modeled" – not understanding the force of God, because of their powerlessness. And he breathed into his face; and the man came to have a soul (and remained) upon the ground many days. But they could not make him arise because of their powerlessness. Like storm winds they persisted (in blowing), that they might try to capture that image, which had appeared to them in the waters. And they did not know the identity of its power.[10]

- **Letters, Songs, and Prayers**: The Prayer of the Apostle Paul; The Epistle of Eugnostos; Pistis Sophia; Authorative Teaching; Gnostic version of The Republic by Plato; The Prayer of Thanksgiving; Letter of Peter to Philip; The Thought of Norea; The Thunder, Perfect Mind; The Hymn of the Pearl (Hymn of the Soul, Hymn of the Robe of Glory, or Hymn of Judas Thomas the Apostle).

I remembered that I was a son of kings,
and my free soul longed for its natural state.
I remembered the pearl,
on account of which I was sent to Egypt.
Then I began charming it,
the formidable and hissing serpent.
I caused it to slumber and to fall asleep,
for my father's name I named over it,
and the name of our second in command (our double),
and of my mother, the queen of the East.
Then I snatched away the pearl,
and I turned to go back to my father's house.
And their filthy and unclean clothing,
I stripped off and left it in their country.

[...]

and my glorious garment which I had stripped off,
and my toga which was wrapped with it,
(from Ramatha and Reken), from the heights of Hyrcania,
my parents sent it there,

with the hand of their stewards,
who, on account of their faithfulness, could be trusted with it.
[...]

I clothed [myself] with it and ascended,
to the palace of peace and worship.
I bowed my head and worshipped him,
the brightness of my father who sent it to me.
Because I had done his commandments,
so also he did what he had promised.
And in the palace of his scribes
I mingled with his teachers,
because he rejoiced in me and received me,
and I was with him and in his kingdom.
And with the voice of praise,
all his servants were praising him.
And he also promised that to the palace
of the king of kings I will hasten with him.
And with my offering and with my pearl,
I should appear with him before our king.[11]

- **Apocalypses**: On the Origin of the World; The Apocryphon of John (Secret Revelation of John), Gnostic Apocalypse of Peter, Allogenes; First Apocalypse of James; Second Apocalypse of James; Apocalypse of Adam; Coptic Apocalypse of Paul; Concept of Our Great Power.

Next, the ruler had a thought - consistent with his nature - and by means of verbal expression he created an androgyne. He opened his mouth and cooed to him. When his eyes had been opened, he looked at his father, and he said to him, "Eee!" Then his father called him Eee-a-o ('Yao'). Next he created the second son. He cooed to him. And he opened his eyes and said to his father, "Eh!" His father called him 'Eloai'. Next, he created the third son. He cooed to him. And he opened his eyes and said to his father, "Asss!" His father called him 'Astaphaios'. These are the three sons of their father.

Seven appeared in chaos, androgynous. They have their masculine names and their feminine names. The feminine name is Pronoia (Forethought) Sambathas, which is 'week'.
And his son is called Yao: his feminine name is Lordship.
Sabaoth: his feminine name is Deity.
Adonaios: his feminine name is Kingship.
Elaios: his feminine name is Jealousy.
Oraios: his feminine name is Wealth.
And Astaphaios: his feminine name is Sophia (Wisdom).

These are the seven forces of the seven heavens of chaos. And they were born androgynous, consistent with the immortal pattern that existed before them, according to the wish of Pistis: so that the likeness of what had existed since the beginning might reign to the end. You will find the effect of these names and the force of the male entities in the Archangelic [Book] of the Prophet Moses, and the names of the female entities in the first Book of Noraia.

Now the prime parent Yaldabaoth, since he possessed great authorities, created heavens for each of his offspring through verbal expression - created them beautiful, as dwelling places - and in each heaven he created great glories, seven times excellent. Thrones and mansions and temples, and also chariots and virgin spirits up to an invisible one and their glories, each one has these in his heaven; mighty armies of gods and lords and angels and archangels - countless myriads - so that they might serve. The account of these matters you will find in a precise manner in the first Account of Oraia.

And they were completed from this heaven to as far up as the sixth heaven, namely that of Sophia. The heaven and his earth were destroyed by the troublemaker that was below them all. And the six heavens shook violently; for the forces of chaos knew who it was that had destroyed the heaven that was below them. And when Pistis knew about the breakage resulting from the disturbance, she sent forth her breath and bound him and cast him down into Tartaros. Since that day, the heaven, along with its earth, has consolidated itself through Sophia the daughter of Yaldabaoth, she who is below them all.[12]

BASIC RELIGIOUS PRACTICES

We don't know much of Gnostic practice in its original form. We do know Gnostic practices varied from sect to sect. Some groups emphasized ritual more than others. Many Gnostic sects appeared to have had a liturgy or system of rites that incorporated Gnostic ideas into existing liturgical form, borrowing it from early Christian systems.

In addition to the unique cosmology and theology of Gnosticism, we also know that many Gnostics appeared to have held their own sacramental systems, often called mystery rites. While some Gnostics did reject such practices, most did embrace these special actions as rituals that provided leveled initiation into different aspects of Gnostic knowledge. There appear to have been approximately five different sacraments, known as "mysteries." They are:

- **Baptism**: An initiation ritual within Gnosticism that is considered the first stage of spiritual progress. Like Christian rite, there were two different forms of baptism, both practiced by immersion in water: psychic baptism, specifically designed to introduce individuals still living under the control of the material realm to begin the process, and pneumatic baptism, which put the participant in touch with higher spiritual understanding. Such symbolizes the union of masculine and feminine, the human soul and the spirit, and the principle of resurrection to spiritual life. Gnostics believed that to receive resurrection once one has died, they had to receive it, through baptism, while they were still living.

- **Chrism**: Chrism is the anointing with oil for a sacred purpose. It appears to be part of the baptismal rite, done after Gnostic baptism. Such was a sealing into Gnosis.

- **Eucharist**: The continual center for Gnostic worship (as well as a stage in Gnostic initiation), Eucharist consisted of bread and water and wine. It symbolized the resurrected state of Gnostic believers and a complete union, of indivisible nature, comparable to the Roman Catholic doctrine of transubstantiation.

- **Redemption**: We do not completely understand the nature of this mystery, as it does not seem to have a Christian equivalent. It is considered a systematic reconciliation with the true secret deity rather than with the demiurge, but no one knows for certain.

- **Bridal Chamber**: An essential sacrament of Gnostic understanding, the bridal chamber represents rich imagery of Gnostic mythology. It is a unity sacrament, one by which the Gnostic believer is reunified with his or her spiritually sexual opposite. It is a sexual imagery, one that had impact on a believer perpetually (both in this life and beyond). What they did in this rite is of debate; some believe it was a sexual rite for some Gnostics while others believe there was something else involved, making the rite symbolic rather than literal. As some Gnostic groups were celibate, it is likely that such is true.[13]

Gnostics celebrate a form of liturgical ceremony like that of the Divine Liturgy celebrated in Orthodox Catholic Church and the mass of the Roman Catholic Church. Gnostics met and meet according to all knowledge on the first day of the week. Some sects were highly organized in structure with priests, bishops, and deacons. Different sects practiced in different ways; pagan sects incorporated possibly incorporated sex rites and magic into the liturgy, while more Christian groups incorporated Christian elements, more Jewish groups incorporated Jewish elements, and other groups incorporated traditions including those of Zoroastrianism and eastern thought. Modern neo-Gnostics tend to incorporate Gnostic concepts into New Age thinking. Much is unknown about specific Gnostic practices of old. Some speculations exist based on the ancient writings we now have.

While it was speculated – and often accused – that many Gnostic groups were hedonistic, indulgent, wild, and sexual, we now know most Gnostic groups practiced strict asceticism: fasting from certain foods (especially meat), eating vegetables, and in many instances, requiring celibacy or prohibiting sexual relationships. Such practices were considered signs of spirituality; that one was living by the spirit rather than the lowliness of matter.

HOLIDAYS

Very little is known of ancient Gnostic holidays. It is often assumed that they were like or modifications of existing Christian holidays, but no one is certain. Some modern Gnostics follow a liturgical calendar like that of Roman Catholicism or Orthodoxy. Many modern Gnostic calendars are incorporations of interfaith holiday celebrations, which would not have been observed by the original Gnostic communities.

VISUAL SIGNS AND SYMBOLS

Serpent, seen as a representation of wisdom; Adam and Eve with the serpent; snake; ouroboros (snake swallowing tail); deity forms of Abraxas and Mithras; baptismal cross; Iao Sabaoth;

serpent cross; ankh; serpent wheel; chnoubis; in more modern secret Gnostic societies, images such as the all-seeing eye of Horus; pyramid; left hand with eye in the center; incorporated Christian images and icons of saints and such with Gnostic themes and cultural imagery; interfaith symbolism.

Creeds, Books, and Laws

Gnostic Wisdom

The original Gnostic communities were non-credo. Knowledge of their deity was seen as a spiritual pursuit. The specific laws and governances varied among the sects, but most were similar in form to early Christian systems. We don't know about some of the specifics of governance and rule in many groups, but we do know Gnostic groups tended to center around central leaders or figures who often shaped the community's governing rule.

Modern-day Gnostic churches are governed by a modified rule like other independent sacramental movements. There are modern-day Gnostic creeds, often variations of Christian ones. This one from 1907 is a sample of many of them, written by Johannes Bricaud:

> *I believe in one God, eternal Propator and almighty Father, Creator and attractor of all visible and invisible beings, the first tridyname amongst the divine Eons.*
> *And in His only son, the divine logos, the prototype of man, the second tridyname, Christ, spiritual and physical light, born of the treasure of light, true God like the Father and consubstantial to Him, without whom nothing was made.*
> *Who became incarnate on earth in the person of Jesus the Saviour and the star of the Pleroma, came down here below for us, taking on a soul and a body like our own in the breast of blessed Mary.*
> *Who was manifest in Jesus from the time of his baptism until the time of his passion;*
> *Who spoke to us through his mouth and taught us the very holy gnosis and the holy life, in order to deliver us from the slavery of the Demiurge and of his earthly Archon, to thus enable our return into the spiritual Pleroma our homeland, as he himself returned there after his death;*
> *Who will come to earth again full of glory to judge the living and the dead;*
> *Whose kingdom shall have no end.*
> *I believe in the Holy Spirit, the third tridyname, who proceeds from the Father like the son;*
> *Who gives love with life, who puts us onto the path of truth and holiness, who unifies all beings, who is adored and glorified with the Father and the son.*
> *I believe in one truly universal or catholic Church, the origin of which on earth goes back to that of the human race, but which in heaven constitutes the holy Pleroma, and is as old as God Himself, the perfect being.*
> *I confess the two baptisms, and the three other mysteries for the remission of sins.*
> *I await, on the completion of the earthly Pleroma, the reappearance of the dead, the ascension of the Pleroma, lastly the final destruction of the spirits resistant to any conversion, at the same time as the destruction of the hylic world, the work of the Demiurge.*
> *Amen.*[14]

Eclectic Beliefs

Many of Gnostic's additional eclectic beliefs are unknown. There were many sects of Gnosticism, all with some slight or differing beliefs, as was discussed earlier. It is believed, however, that Gnosticism was often tainted or misrepresented in the writings of their critics.

Relations with Non-Gnostics

As a religious group, it is difficult to ascertain Gnosticism's identity. Many believe it was first a Christian sect, then evolving into its own religion. Its relationship with Christianity is heavily debated. It does appear, from the writings of their critics, that Gnostics were spiritually disdained. Gnostic sects often disagreed on matters with one another. Being from an age before ecumenical or interfaith dialogue, it does appear religious discourse was part of the relationship between Gnostics and Christians, however strained it might have been. Once Gnosticism was denounced, the relationship changed.

Modern-day Mandean Gnostics are an isolated community, bound by their culture and traditions. They are suspicious of outsiders and do not take converts. Modern-day Gnostic revival groups are a series of independent communions and churches that are often interfaith in outlook, and respective of one another and of other independent sacramental groups, as well.

Holy Sites

Regions of southern Iraq and the Khuzestan Province in Iran; Nag Hammadi, Egypt.

Notable Figures

Valentinius (c. 100- c. 180), founder of Valentinianism; Basilidies, founder of the Basilideans, Mani (216-274 or 277), founder of the Manichaeans; Jules Doinel, (Jules-Benoit Stanislas Doinel du Val-Michael) (1942-1902), founder, Eglise Gnostique; Carl Jung (1875-1961), psychiatrist.

Notable Groups

The Mandeans, as the sole surviving Gnostic sect into modern times, struggle to survive amidst a world that has grown hostile to their presence. Due to the tumult in the Middle East, Mandeans are now located all over the world in diverse communities. They are baptized several times throughout their lives in purity rituals. They avoid alcohol and do not eat meat, and no converts are allowed. Those who marry outside the faith are considered outsiders. They prohibit the use of violence and self-defense, as well. Within the United States, there is a growing community of about 2,500 immigrants and their descendants in Worcester, Massachusetts.[15]

Facts and Figures

Manichaeism, as a prominent Gnostic sect, spread its message as far as China.

OTHER IMPORTANT DEFINITIONS[16]

- **Agnosia**: "Without gnosis;" the state of not having knowledge.
- **Apocryphon**: A term for a "secret book," which among Gnostics, indicated the book contained a secret revelation or knowledge that only they had.
- **Agape**: Unconditional love
- **Eros**: The love that desires to reunite; a passion contrast with compassion, that originates with primal man, Adam.
- **Hebdomas**: The spheres of the planets, including the archons and hiermarene.
- **Hiemarene**: The destiny nature of the speheres and stars, controlling base drives.
- **Hylic**: The lowest portion of human nature, relating to instinctive drive.
- **Metennoia**: A "change of mind" that happens to an initiate; a conversion.
- **Poimandres**: "Good Shepherd," the first androgynous emanation that guides us back to the true knowledge.
- **Syzygos**: A consort, one that one is driven to connect with; a spirit, akin to a guardian angel or guide.
- **Zoe**: Life, usually equated with life, and the fallen Sophia.

BELIEVER'S CHARACTERISTICS

Emphasis on secret knowledge; interest in ancient texts; use of secret rites and other elements mixed with Christian belief; belief in a secret deity and a demiurge; focus on dualities: light and dark, spirit and matter, knowledge and ignorance, good and evil; focus on Biblical figures, such as Adam, Seth, Thomas, Mary Magdalene, Jesus, John the Revelator, and John the Baptist; discussion of Greek ideas as present in religion; complex mythology; use of Greek words; repeated immersion rites; pacifism; vegetarianism; refusal to accept converts; secrecy; interfaith interest.

HINDUISM

Whatever takes form is false. Only the formless endures. When you understand the truth of this teaching, you will not be born again. For god is infinite, within the body and without, like a mirror, and the image in a mirror.
(*Ashtavakra* Gita 1:18-19)

THEOLOGY

Belief in one absolute divine being and one absolute truth, known as BRAHAMAN, with many ways such is described and approached. Brahman is seen as a panentheistic principle (all reality is one unity). Brahman is seen as timeless, formless, spaceless, and the ultimate, pure consciousness. From this divine being and absolute truth are the manifestation of 333,333,333 different emanations or aspects, often referred to as gods and goddesses. These are seen as agents who represent Brahman and assist in the management of creation. They influence and guide all experiences humans have. All are personal in nature and represent different aspects of spiritual life: nature, personality, age, sexuality, and life cycles. Known as pantheism, they believe this force is present in all. Hindus see the gods as living in a different, inner world, and seek to surrender to the divine will that permeates and guides all living things. The chief three Hindu deities, seen as one in union, are Brahma (the Creator), Vishnu (the Preserver), and Shiva (the Destroyer).

Hinduism does not have a set regulation, specified doctrine, or specific binding, limiting text of holy scripture. There is no one specific founder of Hindu belief. Hindus may choose to see their theology through many different ways, including polytheism (belief in many gods or multiple deities), pandeism (belief there is a creator deity who became the universe as we understand it and no longer has any interest or involvement with that creation), henotheistic (belief in the worship of one deity while not rejecting the existence of other deities), monistic (sees oneness as the primary attribute of existence and union with a deity), atheistic (belief in no god or divine being), or humanist (belief in the value and agency of humanity).[1,2]

PHILOSOPHY

Hinduism is a collective of ancient Indian cultures, devotions, and traditions, reaching back thousands of years. It is believed to be the oldest systematic religion in the world today. The term "Hinduism" is not found in any of the Hindu scriptural writings; the proper name for Hinduism is Sanatana-Dharma (a reference to the eternal nature of a living being, often called the soul). Hinduism is more than just a religious practice. It is seen as a way of life, of interacting with the divine and with one another. It has most prominently influenced what we recognize today as the culture of India. As a result of its own unique diversity which represents a variety of interpretations, Hinduism incorporates many different ideas, strains, and thoughts, which can make it difficult to describe. Hindus seek to incorporate values into every aspect of their lives to spiritually advance. The major four goals of Hindu belief, known as *purusartha*, are dharma, *moksa*, *kama*, and *artha*.

Hindu temple roof in Singapore's Little India

- **Dharma**: Ethics or responsibilities seen as required duties for a Hindu to embrace and follow throughout their spiritual path. The major focus for a Hindu is to live properly and rightly, upholding religious duties and moral obligations. Dharma relates to personal conduct, obedience to existing social order, and virtue.

- ***Moksa***: The ultimate liberation from *samsara* (the cycle of birth, life, death, and rebirth in a process commonly known as reincarnation). Some strains of Hinduism teach that *moksa* is possible while living in this life. To do so, one must recognize the entire universe as the great Self (the soul of eternal personality that finds itself either liberated or bound through reincarnation). Karma, a term used to refer not just to action but also the intention behind actions, is the idea that actions have consequences, even across different incarnations. In Hindu understanding, karma is about more than just consequences in this life; it is also about the idea that the things one does pass from life to life through the cycles of reincarnation.

- ***Kama***: Often desired as "desire" or "wish," Hindus do not believe the pursuit of enjoyment is forbidden, but an admirable life goal. Life, love, sexual expression, sensuality, affection, and enjoyment are all part of *kama*. When maintained in balance with the other four goals of Hindu life, *kama* is seen as an essential and important aspect of life, living, and spiritual pursuit.

- ***Artha***: Defined as "wealth" or "prosperity," *artha* is understood as the ability to make a living and to enable one to pursue all the activities one desires throughout their life. It recognizes the connection between financial stability and quality of life, and the role that finances play in being able to pursue one's long-term life essence.

Hindus believe incorporating these basic ideas: practices of ethics, pursuit of pleasure in life, making a living, and seeking ultimate liberation can lead to a better spiritual understanding, one that leads to the fullness of life. Doing good deeds, standing mindful of one's thoughts and actions, and proper spiritual developments can undo karmic effects, both from this life and past lives, to elevate one's consciousness and unite one with the gods. Believing both thoughts and actions are important, Hindus believe awareness and spiritual elevation can help them realize divine oneness.

In addition to the basics of Hindu understanding, there are three different pillars of Hindu life: the temples (the channels for the gods), Hindu philosophy, and the *satguru*, or truly enlightened teachers (*satgurus* are seen as embodying the divine in their being). This parallels the spiritual understanding of three different worlds: temples connect with the gods for the physical (or first) world, and Hindu philosophy appeals to the inner two worlds, which are the second and third. In all things Hindu, worship always comes before philosophy or defined theology.

There are six different schools of orthodox Hindu philosophy, known as *astika* or *darsanam*. All accept the Hindu Vedas as the ultimate scriptural revelations. These are: *Samkhya* (strict movement, dualist in theory, that analyzes consciousness and matter); *yoga* (from a word meaning "yoke"; a physical and mental process of meditation, specifically designed to unite one with the specific virtues and attributes of a Hindu god or goddess, developed as a spiritual discipline involving specific stretches and body poses, meditation, contemplation and spiritual oneness with the divine); *Nyaya* (logic, source, knowledge); *Vaisheshika* (sensory experience based school of atoms as the foundation of the universe); *Mimamsa* (anti-spiritual movement focused on ethics); and *Vedanta* (the section of the Vedas devoted to knowledge). A seventh school, the *Nastika* school, is unorthodox, as it rejects the authority of the Vedas.[3]

ADHERENT IDENTITY

Hindu, Brahmanism, yogi, Sanatan, Arya; identity associated with a particular sect of Hinduism, such as Vaishnavites, Saivites, Shaktism, or Smartism, or one of their many group subheadings.

TRADITIONAL LANGUAGES

Sanskrit.

SECTS/DIVISIONS

There are four main sects of Hinduism with thousands of smaller groups branching off the four main groups. Hinduism does not see these different sects as a conflict or disassociation. Many reflect or borrow from the different beliefs and traditions found within other sects.

- **Vaishnavism**: The largest branch of the Hindu sects, Vaishnavism focuses on the worship of Vishnu as the supreme deity. Sometimes one of Vishnu's incarnations is the focus of an individual or group's worship, such as Krishna or Rama. Others may also call upon Lakshmi, the female goddess, seen as another aspect of the divine being. This does not change their belief in other deities, simply that those deities are lesser gods or emanations that relate back to Vishnu. Vaishnavism is unique in that it believes Vishnu is a personal being rather than detached or distant from humanity. More doctrinal than some other forms of Hinduism, Vaishnavism emphasizes religious practice, morality, and feeling, rather than meditative contemplation. Several individuals within the system are recognized as "saints," and many wrote hymns or established their own sects within this sect. Followers of this sect of Hinduism are known as Vaishnavites or Vaishnavas. Vaishnavism groups include Sri Sampradaya, Ramanujas, Ramanandis, Vallabhacharins

(Krishna Sampradayins), Chaitanyas, Nimbarkas, Madhvas, Sri Vashnavism, and the Radha Vallabhis.[4]

- **Saivism**: Also known as Shaivism. A mystical, devotional Hindu tradition, these Hindu adherents worship Siva as their supreme deity. The physical incarnation of Siva is found in Siva Nataraja. Saivism sees creation as an expression of consciousness, one that is divine, originating from the creator, Siva. Siva is seen as both creator and created, which means he is both immanent and transcendent of eternity. In addition to This does not change their belief in other deities, simply that those deities are seen as lesser gods or emanations that relate back to the one being, Siva. Saivism is complicated, incorporating several different traditions, philosophical ideals, rituals, legends, and mystical concepts. Followers of this sect are known as Saivas or Saivities. Saivism groups include Saiva Siddhanta, Vira Saivism, Kasmiri Saivism, Gorakhnatha Saivism or Sidha Siddhanta, Pasupatha Saivism, and the Ganapatya Sect.[5]

- **Shaktism**: A Hindu sect that revolves around the worship of the Hindu goddess Shakti (the female goddess of the male god, Shiva). Shakti is seen as a divine mother, the source of power, and one to arouse and realize as one seeks spiritual liberation. Shakti is part of Hindu Tantra and kundalini yoga systems. She is the primary female deity, with all other female deities seen as an extension or manifestation of her. Shakti is both kind and fierce, and is also identified through Uma, Parvati, Ambika, Kali, Durga, Shitala, and Lakshmi. Shaktism is primarily seen in the Bengal and Assam regions in India.[6]

- **Smartism**: Exclusive to the upper classes of the Hindu caste in India (merchants, rulers, and Hindu priests). All Hindu deities are seen as the same, with five primary deities (Ganesha, Shiva, Devi, Vishnu, and Surya) as personal manifestations of the absolute, known as Brahman. Each individual practitioner selects their own specific primary deity.[7]

- **Folk Hinduism**: There are several small Hindu groups with limited traditions and devotions specific to the region or area where they emerged. They are most likely prehistoric in their form and involve the worship of a specific village deity known as a *Gramadevata*, household deities known as *Kuldevta*, and local deities. There may be specific writings and scriptures that are in the specific, indigenous language for that region. It is polytheistic, animistic, and tribal in nature.

- **Western Hinduism**: Western Hinduism is the fusion or application of Hindu ideas as presented in a context that would be appealing to western audiences. These ideas are a mixture of concepts, both eastern and western spiritualities. Often, many of these try to appeal to western theologies or philosophies, such as Christianity, atheism, or humanism. Many are subheadings as part of the New Age Movement. Some western Hindu groups include Adidam, Seva Foundation, Hanuman Foundation, and the Self-Realization Fellowship.

- **Tantra**: Tantra is an esoteric tradition found in both Hinduism and Buddhism, emerging somewhere around the fifth century. The word "tantra" literally means "loom" or "weave" and relates to the interwoven nature of different traditions into a practice or a text (compared to a weaving on a loom). Those who practice tantra apply it to every aspect of their lives: business, spirituality, and daily interactions. Tantra is often associated with sex but is far more than just a sexual practice. It incorporates deity devotion, mantras, visualization and identification with a specified deity, initiation, esotericism, ritual mandalas, goddess worship, and more. The best-known tantric text is the Kama Sutra, which details the nature of love, finding a mate, maintaining one's intimate and sexual life, and many specific details on finding physical pleasure in intimate relationships.[8]

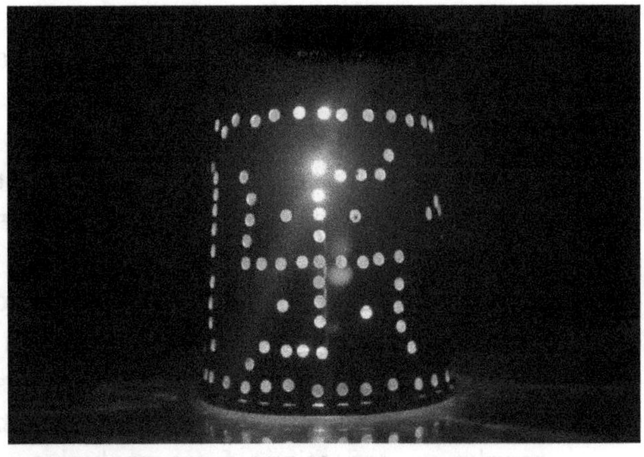
Hindu swastika

NUMBER OF ADHERENTS

There are approximately 1,100,000,000 Hindus worldwide.[9]

DISPUTES WITHIN GROUP

Hinduism does not classify the differences between sects as formal divisions. All Hindu sects, schools, and paths are seen as legitimate aspects of Hinduism. The differences between the various Hindu sects and schools of thought remains the intent, disciplines, and deity focus. There are also different interpretations on ethics and morals, especially dependent on the modernity of the Hindu sect or division, the location of the group (east or west) and the view of different virtues, scriptures, caste, and general theological ideas.

SCRIPTURES

There are hundreds of different Hindu scriptures due to its diverse nature. Each tradition has its own specified Hindu texts, blending different ideas from different Hindu schools of philosophy and traditions. The Vedas are considered divinely inspired by most Hindus, literally given by divine revelation. The Bhagavad Gita is a superior holy book in the Hindu faith because it is a summary of the contents of the four Vedas. There are many other special books unique to the different Hindu sects (of inspirational value to their unique group). Still, Hindu scriptures are not considered exclusive. There is no specified consensus about "scripture" in Hindu perspective. Hindu text seeks to transmit eternal truth, provide histories of the faith, and preserve Hindu traditions. There are a few primary texts that are accepted by most Hindus. These include:

- **The Vedas**: Perhaps the oldest writings in religious history (Hindu traditions believe the Vedas are as old as the universe itself and will always exist), the Vedas are estimated to be several thousand years old, first transmitted by oral traditions. They were written down and assembled by an individual named Vyasa in the third millennium B.C. Known as the "Books of Knowledge," the Vedas are primary Hindu texts accepted in all major sects of Hinduism. Within Vedic tradition, there are several different subheadings of text, including the Samhita (a collection of mantras) divided into four sections: the Rig Veda (hymns recited by chief priests), Sama Veda (chants for priests who sing Vedic hymns during rituals), Yajur Veda (recitations for officiating priests), and Athara Veda (spells, incantations, stories, charms and more hymns); the Brahmanas (stories that discuss different Hindu rituals and sacrifices); the Aranyakas (mystical texts authored by Hindu monks as reflections from reclusive meditation); the Mukhya Upanishads (the oldest Upanishads in Hindu tradition, expounding on spiritual ideas); and some Sutra literature (such as those that relate to rituals of passage, birth, weddings, death, and personal conduct). The whole of the Vedas provide a look into very ancient ideas about medicine, astrology, music, dance, and law. The Vedas are the ultimate scriptural "law" and specific divine revelation.[10]

For [the ancestors] Soma is purified,
some accept the molten butter;
to the company of those, for
whom the honey flows, let him go!
To the company of those who
are invincible by spiritual discipline (tapas),
and through spiritual discipline have gone to heaven,
to men of great spiritual fire, let him go!

To the company of those who
fight contested battles, heroes
who cast away their lives, to those who
made a thousand gifts, let him go!

To those ancient followers
of the Law, steadfast in the Law,
who furthered the Law, to the Fathers, Yama,
great in their spiritual fire, let him go!

To the sage-poets, the leaders
of thousands, those who protect the sun,
to the Rishis of great spiritual discipline,
born of spiritual discipline, Yama! let him go![11]

- **Bhagavad Gita**: The sixth book of the Mahabharta (a great Sanskrit epic of ancient India) which record the Legends of the *Bharatas* (an Aryan tribal group). Bhagavad Gita means "Song of the Lord" and is an epic poem between a warrior named Arjuna and the Hindu lord Krishna. While the contents are an inspirational dialogue between Arjuna and Krishna, the given divine counsel is spoken to all. The Bhagavad Gita emphasizes the ethics of sacred duty and responsibility, disciplined actions (specifically through yogic discipline), and the unchanging nature of the essential self, which pushes us to find spiritual answers. It is a primary text for Hindus because it summarizes the essential contents of the four Vedas.[12]

You have the right to work, but for the work's sake only. You have no right to the fruits of work. Desire for the fruits of work must never be your motive in working. Never give way to laziness, either.

Perform every action with you heart fixed on the Supreme Lord. Renounce attachment to the fruits. Be even-tempered in success and failure: for it is this evenness of temper which is meant by yoga.

Work done with anxiety about results is far inferior to work done without such anxiety, in the calm of self-surrender. Seek refuge in the knowledge of Brahma. They who work selfishly for results are miserable.[13]

When meditation is mastered,
The mind is unwavering like the
Flame of a lamp in a windless place.
In the still mind,
In the depths of meditation,
The Self reveals itself.
Beholding the Self
By means of the Self,
An aspirant knows the
Joy and peace of complete fulfillment.
Having attained that
Abiding joy beyond the senses,
Revealed in the stilled mind,
He never swerves from the eternal truth.[14]

- **Smriti text**: Hindu texts are classified in two ways: as shruti (that which is heard) and smriti (that which is remembered). Shruti texts are received by divine transmission, and Smriti are important works attributed to a human author. The Agamas (covers everything including creation, meditation, philosophy, yoga, mantras, deity worship, and temple construction found as a discussion between Shiva and Parvati), Puranas (contains many Hindu mythological records, legends, and traditional stories), and Darshanas (philosophical texts) are all considered smriti works.[15]

Will power can be cultivated by finishing and doing well every task that we undertake, in fact, done a little better than our expectations. Finish each task; do it well. Nothing is done with half our mind thinking about something else. Nothing is dropped out in the middle. Developing these two

> *important habits produces an indomitable willpower...we build up a great willpower that we will always have with us, even in our next life, the next and the next. Willpower is free for the using.*[16]

Other major texts of relevance include the Tantras (esoteric Hindu rituals and yoga traditions), The Code of Manu (early Hindu text), Itihasas (Indian poetry that relates an epic story), the two major Hindu epic stories written in Sanskrit (Ramayana and Mahabharata), and Sahasranama (A book with a listing of the names of different Hindu deities). Hindus also have a long-standing system of ethical philosophy, with writings all the way up to modern times.[17]

BASIC RELIGIOUS PRACTICES

As Hinduism seeks to develop dharma, *artha*, *kama*, and *moksa*, Hindu worship (known as *puja*) encourages the development of the individual's path to realization. This realization is *atma-jnana* or *atmabodha*, where one comes to know themselves in a spiritual sense, seeing themselves as part of deity beyond the material world and its limitations. Hindu religious practice may be done in the practitioner's home or in a Hindu temple. Temples serve to bring Hindu believers together, symbolizing the union of the people and the gods. However, Hindus are not required to go to the temple for their devotional offerings or sacrifices. One can fully practice the Hindu religion at home, through specific rituals. Hindus often have a private home shrine, complete with a statue or statues of preferred deity, where a Hindu makes regular offering to their deity or deities. While ritual is an important aspect of Hindu belief, the rituals of Hinduism are not required and vary greatly according to Hindu sect, region, and individual practice. Many practice daily chants, worship at dawn, reading Hindu scriptures, hymns, meditation, or yoga. Hindu devotion focuses on Bhakti, the specific love one has for their personal god or the representation of that god (guru) by a devotee, or follower of Hinduism.

Hindu practices vary greatly, but often include pujas, or specific ceremonial devotion for a god, yoga, meditation, study of Hindu concepts, or of devotion to a guru. In Indian religion, most religious leaders are known as Brahmins. Brahmins are identified as a specific caste within Hindu society that operate as Hindu priests (purohit, pandit, pujari), who lead sacrifices within a temple, teachers (acharya), and different individuals who protect the learning and education necessary to transmit Hinduism to future generations. The best-known example of a Brahmin is a guru. A guru is an individual who is seen as a guide, often the leader of a specific system or strain of Hindu thought. They are seen as the embodiment of their teachings, and also worshipped by their devotees.

HOLIDAYS

Hindu holidays and feast days serve to intertwine personal and social life into dharma. It has been said there is a feast day for a specific deity or event on every single day of the calendar year. The major festivals are:

- **Holi**: Festival of colors, love, and spring; only day when caste is reversed in India. Participants throw brightly colored powder and water on each other, eat in specialty foods, sing, and dance, as they hope for a good harvest season. Holi seeks to destroy internal evil, the way Holika, the sister of the demon King Hiranyakashipu, was destroyed by fire. (February or March)[18]

- **Maha Shivratri**: Also called *Har-ratri*, *Haerath*, or *Herath*. A Shiva festival celebrating when Shiva performs what is known as the "heavenly dance." Celebrated at night as a remembrance of overcoming darkness and ignorance. Most observe it by chanting prayers, fasting, and meditation. Many try to keep awake all night, attend an event at a temple devoted to Shiva, or go on pilgrimage. Some cultures also smoke cannabis. (February or March)[19]

- **Raksha Bandhan**: Also called *Rakshabandhan*. Feast celebrates the bond between siblings, specifically brothers and sisters. Sisters tie an amulet known as the *rahki* around their brothers' wrists, to symbolically protect them from evil or harm. In return, the girls are given a gift. The feast recognizes the role of male brothers in the protection and care of their sisters, especially in the absence of parents. Women who have married out of their local tribe or city will return home for the festival and visit with their birth families in the process. Ceremony is seen as symbolic among nuclear families in India. In situations where no siblings or male siblings exist, another close relative can stand in for a brother. (August)[20]

- **Ganesha Chaturthi**: Also called *Vinayaka Chaturthi*. Ten-day festival devoted to Ganesh, celebrating his arrival on earth with his mother goddess, Paravati (Gauri). As the god of new beginnings, remover of obstacles, and source of wisdom and intelligence, Ganesha is celebrated at home and in public. Ganesha statues made of clay are installed or displayed, and events include chants (especially of Vedic hymns) Hindu texts, prayers, and fasting. Daily prayers and sweets are part of the festival. It concludes when the statue is carried in a public procession with chanting and music, and them immersed in the nearest body of water (a river or sea). (August or September)[21]

- **Krishna Janmashtami**: Also called *Janmashtami* or *Gokulashtami*. Birthday of Krishna, the eighth incarnation of Vishnu. Features reinactments of Krishna's life, devotional singing, fasting, a night vigil, and festival. In some places, it is associated with kite-flying and childhood games. It is immediately followed by *Nandotsav*, a feast celebrating an entire village's visit to Nanand Baba's (Krishna's foster parent) house to see Krishna. (August or September)

- **Dussera**: Also known as *Vijayadashami* or *Dashain*. The celebration of a deity's victory (the deity varies, depending on form and strain of Hinduism) over opposing forces, thus representing the triumph of good over evil. Also a feast honoring the different aspects of Devi, such as *Durga* or *Saraswati*. Dussera involves processions to waterways (such as a river or ocean) while carrying statues, chanting, and playing music. The statues are immersed in the water as a farewell. Symbols associated with evil (such as *Ravan*) are burned with fireworks to symbolize the destruction of evil. Preparations for Diwali begins on Dussera, as Dussera is twenty days before Diwali. Also related to the feast Navaratri. (September or October)[22]

- **Diwali**: A major five-day festival, known as a "festival of lights." Signifies the triumph of light over darkness, good over evil, knowledge over ignorance, and is often associated with Lakshmi (although other deities can play a role in it, as well). During Diwali, Hindus clean their homes, dress their best, decorate with oil lamps or candles, offer to Lakshmi, light fireworks, exchange gifts, and share food. It is observed in Sikhism, Buddhism, and Jainism as well, with a slightly different backstory in each culture. (October or November)[23]

In addition to holidays, Hindus recognize major life milestones known as *sanskara*. They vary among gender, community, and locality. There are somewhere between 12 and 48 rites, of varying practice. These rites of passage (both external and internal) are not mandatory, but help foster character, good resolutions, and positivity. Rites for such milestones include Pregnancy (*Garbhadhana*), baby shower (*Simantonnayana*), naming (*Namakarana*), first solid food (*Annaprashana*), ear piercing (*Karnavedha*), attending school (*Upanayana*), first shave in boys (*Keshanta*), first period in girls (*Ritusuddhi*), graduation (*Samavartana*), wedding (*Vivaha*), fasting (*Vratas*), and *Antyeshti* (cremation for adults, burial for children).

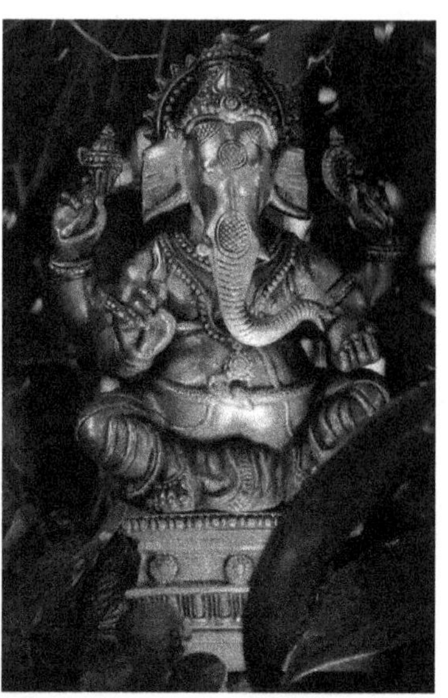
Ganesha

VISUAL SIGNS AND SYMBOLS

The OM (Aum) symbol (chanted during meditation and representative of the universal oneness); lotus flower and plant; swastika (representative of peace and good luck; not represented counterclockwise as in Nazi Germany, but vertically up and down); yoga; Sanskrit writing; caste system; India; statuary and images; incense; Siva, Shiva, and Vishnu; Indian dress; bindi (a red dot on a woman's forehead); sri yantra (nine interlocking triangles that radiate from a single, central point); *tilaka* (either horizontal or u-shaped lines on a devotee's forehead); *rudraksha* (tree whose blue seeds symbolize the tears of Shiva); Shiva lingam (elongated column resembling a phallic symbol, used to represent Shiva); veena (Indian stringed instrument); fire altar; banyan tree; *djvaja* (red or orange flag flown above Hindu temples and in Hindu festivals or processions) *Trishula* (three-pronged pitchfork-like symbol representing Shiva); *Tripundra* (tilak with three horizontal lines applied on the forehead or down the sides of one's arm).[24]

CREEDS, BOOKS, AND LAWS

Hinduism is governed by Manu-smriti, also called Manava-dharma-shastra (The Laws of Manu). This is considered the most authoritative of all books pertaining to Hindu code in India today. This specific writing is attributed to Manu, believed to be the first man in Hindu mythology. He performed the first Hindu sacrifice and became analogous to Noah of the Old Testament, preserving life in the face of a great flood. It was, most likely, written around 250 B.C. and is divided into twelve different chapters. The Laws of Manu prescribe Hindu believers their specific set of moral obligations for each of the four social classes and in different stages of one's life. It includes matters dealing with creation, spiritual responsibility, spiritual rites, initiations, study of the Vedas, marriage, funeral rites, dietary restrictions, purifications, women's conducts, and governmental matters. The Laws of Manu makes no difference between spiritual or secular law, treating the Hindu religion as a societal institution rather than a spiritual one. As a result, Hindu society is highly influenced by its contents, regardless of whether one is a practicing Hindu.

Eclectic Beliefs

Hinduism is not just seen as a religion, but as an entire way of being. This means Hinduism and Indian culture are often intertwined in custom and outlook. One such social custom, (perhaps the most controversial) is the caste system. The caste system is heredity-based social order, consisting of four traditional castes: the Brahmans (priests and intellectuals), *Kshatriyas* (warriors and rulers), *Vaisyas* (artisans and agriculturalists), and *Sudras* (the unskilled laborers). Most controversial are the Pariahs, which consists of the "untouchables" who belonged to no specific caste, but rather do the work of the lowest of the low. In traditional caste society, relations with those outside of one's caste were forbidden. If one performs well in their own caste, diligently and with understanding, they will ascend to the next caste when they are reincarnated into the next life.

As a result, the world (and subsequent experience had while in it) is seen as a teacher, as a place where character and spiritual development can take place. Hindus do not see human beings as inherently sinful, but as perfect; in all things, they seek to strive for that perfection, discovering it within themselves. The process is one of an evolving fulfillment of such perfection; developing patience, seeing the possibility of correcting mistakes and failings in not just this life, but in the next, or in any others, as fully possible. Everything is seen as having a purpose in light of karma (both good and bad).

Hinduism sees family life as inseparable from caste. The four stages of life, all related to age, are known as *ashramas*. They are: *brahmacharya* (student), *grihastha* (householder), *vanaprastha* (retired) and *sannyasa* (renunciate). The married householder is the center of the *ashramas* because he pays three debts: to his ancestors, the gods, and his guru. This debt is paid through child rearing (especially a male child) who will continue his family name and lineage. Hindu family is not just seen in a nuclear context, but in an extended one. It is not uncommon to see multiple generations and extended family in one household. Older family members are consulted for important decisions. Marriages are typically arranged. Individuals aren't seen as just marrying an individual, but an entire family, specific and well-matched in tradition, caste, and practice.[25]

Hindu values are often associated with traditional Indian ideals, and often reflect older concepts of relationships and marriage, family, sexuality, abortion, gender identity, and other current issues that are often controversial worldwide are also controversial within Hinduism. Dating back many centuries, same-sex relationships and gender non-binary representations have been found throughout ancient Hindu literature, text, ritual, artwork, and sculpture.

Even though family is central to Hindu life, there are Hindu monks (*sanyasi*, *sadhu*, or *swami*) and nuns (*sanyasini*, *sadhvi*, or *swammini*). Hindu monks and nuns commit themselves to simple lives: celibate, detached from worldly goals and pursuits, contemplating on their desired deities as they pursue the spiritual life. They are seen as selfless in Hindu culture and as inspiration to the householders who strive for spiritual aims themselves. In their own actions, they should act with compassion, respect, and spiritual value, indifferent to pleasure, blame, praise, and pain, no matter how wicked, rich, poor, or notable someone else may be. They either live collectively in monastic-style living or freely drift from place to place, trusting the divine for any and all physical sustenance. Those who live and work among society are expected to provide for monks and nuns. Hindu monks do not own personal property (except a bowl, cup, two sets of robes and medical supplies, such as a pair of glasses), have any contact with women, do not eat for pleasure, possess or touch money or valuables, or maintain personal relationships.[26]

Hindus are not required to be vegetarian, but many are, as they believe it maximizes respect for life. They avoid many animal byproducts, such as eggs. Hinduism does teach the cow to be sacred and respected (although it is not seen as being a god and is not worshiped). The cow is associated with Aditi, the mother of all the gods, and is thus seen as a maternal, protective figure. The cow is believed to be the first creation, thus of significance. As a result, Hindus avoid beef but do drink milk and eat and cook with butter.

The Ganges River is also seen as sacred in Hinduism, as it's understood to be the personification of Ganga. It is believed to have descended to earth on the feast of Ganga Dusserha. Bathing in the river is seen as a purifying experience, one that helps one to move in a greater way toward liberation and forgive wrongdoing. Any rituals performed in the river or near it are seen as washing away impurities.[27]

RELATIONS WITH NON-HINDUS

Hindus believe that all paths lead to God and prohibit no religion; therefore, they have no prohibition on interfaith dialogue. In terms of Indian culture, relationships between Muslims and Hindus as well as Hindus and Christians have long been tense and explosive.

HOLY SITES

Hinduism acknowledges seven different holy cities, all in India, known as the *Sapta Puri*: Ayodhya (birthplace of Ramachandra, has special powers that make it off limits to enemies, home to the Nageshwarnath Temple), Mathura (birthplace of Krishna; the Kesava Deo temple is a memorial to Krishna, built upon his birthplace), Hardiwar (one of four places where drops of immortality fell and spilled over while being carried by a bird; location of the Kumbha Mela, location of the Ganges River; Kankhal, Piran Kaliyar, Maya Devi, Neel Dhara Pakshi, Pawan Dha,, and Bharat Mata Mandir temples all present here), Varanski (Shiva worship instituted here; famous city for Hindu mysticism, music, and poetry; location of the Shri Vishwanath Mandir temple), Kanchipuram (home to fourteen temples devoted to Vishnu, including the Varadharaja Permual temple, Kamakshi Amman Temple, Kumarakottam Temple, and Ekambareswarar Temple; contains statues of Parvati), Dvaraka (city named after Krishna; major site of the Janmashtami festival; location of many temples, including Dwarkadhish Mandir, Iskon Temple, Rukshamanee Mandir, Nageshwar Jyotirlinga Temple, and Gomati Ghat), and Ujjain (site for Kumbh Mela; location of ISKCON temple, Chatmunda Mata temple, Chintaman Ganesh temple, Gopal Mandir, Kal Bhairav Temple, Mahakaleshwar Jyotirlinga and Mnagalnath temple).[28]

NOTABLE FIGURES

Shankara (c. 700-c. 750), Vedic founder; Ramanuja (1017-c. 1137), Vedic founder; Sri Ramakrishna (1836-1886), philosopher; George Harrison (1943-2001), musician; Shib Narayan Das (1946-), artist; Aaron Joy (1977-), author; Julia Roberts (1967-), actress; John Coltrane (1926-1967), musician; David Frawley, author; Russell Brand (1975-), comedian; Ram Dass (1931-2019), professor; Sita Ram Goel (1921-2003), author; Nina Hagen (1955-), musician; John McLaughlin (1942-), musician; Savitri Devi (1905-1982), author; Kelli Williams (1970-), actress; J. Mascis (1965-), musician; Jay Shetty (1987-), motivational speaker.

NOTABLE GROUPS

The International Society for Krishna Consciousness (ISKCON), also called Hare Krishnas or the Hare Krishna Movement, is a Hindu sect popularized by ex-Beatle George Harrison (1943-2001). Founded by A.C. Bhaktivendanta Swami Prabhupada (1896-1977) in 1966, it is part of the Gaudiya Vaishnava tradition, which has existed since the 1400s. The founder of the original movement, Chaitanya Mahaprabhu (1486-1534), is considered an incarnation of Krishna. The work of ISKCON serves to spread a twofold message: promote Bhakti yoga, (designed to inspire the love of their deity) and practice that love specifically for Krishna, their primary deity. ISKCON uses the Bhagavad Gita as their primary text and focuses on mantras and chants (using a Hindu rosary), especially what they call the Hare Krishna *Mahamantra* (the great mantra). Krishna is seen as the source of all divine incarnations and see Krishna as the supreme and divine personality. Radha is seen as Krishna's female counterpart.

Hare Krishnas are known for public chanting or singing of their mantra (known as *sankirtan*), in the hopes such will attract converts. They meet weekly, usually on Sundays, for group worship of deities, teachings from senior members, and to eat the sanctified food that has been offered throughput the week. They offer water, incense, a fire lamp, and flowers to a sacred image of Krishna, known as a *murti*. This form of *puja* is best known as *arati* in ISKCON. Devotees also bathe, worship, dress, feed, and put the statue to sleep. Such can be done at home or at a temple.

Krishna

ISKCON members follow a lacto-vegetarian diet, do not consume any intoxicants, including alcohol and drugs, do not gamble, and do not engage in any sexual relations seen as illicit (those outside of marriage; Hare Krishnas have long been associated with conservative sexual ideas). They observe many different Hindu festivals and advocate open preaching and sales of ISKCON literature.

Many controversies exist surrounding the group's operation and some of their practices. These include an order of monks who live naked, those of the order who only dress in orange robes, strict sexual abstinence, excessive dietary regulations, and a required necessity for all believers to bathe in the Ganges River at least once in their lifetime. There have also been accusations of brainwashing, money laundering, and racketeering.[29]

FACTS AND FIGURES

Hinduism is the third largest religion in the world, behind Christianity and Islam. Approximately 15% of the world's population is Hindu, with the largest Hindu populations found in India and Nepal.[30]

OTHER IMPORTANT DEFINITIONS

- **Asram**: Also called ashram; a spiritual center, set up for spiritual growth and development.

- **Avatar**: Also called *Avatara*. The incarnation of a deity on earth.[31]

- **Ayurveda**: Sanskrit for "the science of life." A holistic healing system based on Hindu theology and understanding of the origins of life and the universe. Originated more than five thousand years ago.

- ***Bhajana***: A Hindu hymn or song that is devotional in nature.[32]

- **Cremation**: The burning of bodies after death. In Hinduism, cremation is seen as a liberation of the soul from the body, thus freeing it for reincarnation. Babies, children, and those believed to stand as Hindus free from reincarnation are buried, as they are seen from being pure and unattached to their physical remains.

- **Ghat**: A flight of stairs that lead into the water, such as a bathing or cremation place, in Hindu tradition.

- **Hindu astrology**: Also called Indian astrology and Vedic astrology. The Hindu system of astrology used to prepare calendars for specific dates, independent of interest of planets, used to support Vedic rituals. It is part of one of six auxiliary disciplines used for such purposes. Astrology is central to Hindu life, determining the names of newborns, holidays, calendar dates, marriage and marital arrangements, businesses, or moving. There are sixteen different charts used in Hindu astrology, known as *Varga*.

- ***Japamala***: Also called a *mala*, a Hindu rosary is a string 108 of prayer beads used for japa, keeping count while a believer chants, recites, or mentally repeats a mantra or the various names of a deity.[33]

- ***Jiva***: The personal "self" (from a psychological or physical sense) that is not eternal, but still has the ability to act and respond.[34]

- **Namaste**: Means "the god in me honors the god in you." Traditional Hindu greeting.

- **Swami:** A Hindu religious teacher who is part of a monastic order.

- **Vedanga**: Six auxillary disciplines of Hinduism. They are associated with the Vedas and include *shiksha* (use of the Sanskrit alphabet for prayers, focusing on proper pronunciation, speech, and writing); *vyakarana* (grammar and linguistics to properly express ideas), *nirukta* (etymology, especially of archaic words that are unclear today), *kalpa* (instructions for rituals) and *jyotisha* (ritual periods, astrology, and astronomy).[35]

BELIEVER'S CHARACTERISTICS

Worship of many deities and gods, or interest in a specified, personal deity of interest to the devotee; interest in yoga, vegetarianism, and reincarnation; belief in astrology, horoscopes and zodiac influence; chanting OM or a specified mantra over and over again during meditation; view of the cow as sacred; interest in Hindu philosophy and scripture; daily devotional practice; centering view on family life, and on continuation of family lines as a spiritual duty; private home shrines; caste system; interest in Indian culture; follows a guru; statues of the gods; incense; arranged marriages; belief that all religions lead to truth and are a part of a greater truth; study and personal spiritual evolution outside of traditional religious protocols.

Indigenous Religion

Whose voice was first sounded on this land? The voice of the red people who had but bows and arrows. [...] What has been done in my country I did not want, did not ask for it; white people going through my country. [...] When the white man comes in my country he leaves a trail of blood behind him. [...] I have two mountains in that country–the Black Hills and the Big Horn Mountain. I want the Great Father to make no roads through them.

(Red Cloud)[1]

Theology

Among the earliest theological concepts of which we have record, indigenous religion embraces a number of ancient theological concepts, including polytheism (worship of many different gods), henotheism (the belief that a god over a tribe is not the only god in existence), animism (all beings reflect spiritual essence and can manifest that spiritual essence), shamanism (a practitioner identified as a shaman can interact with the sprit realm through various states of altered consciousness), pantheism (reality as we understand it and divinity are inseparable - all is god, god is all), monotheism (the worship of one deity) or, most likely, a combination of any or all of these beliefs, especially over time. Central to these theologies is the idea of a universal spirit, an impersonal force present in and throughout creation and involved in the unity of a group (or, in some modern understandings, all humanity).

Indigenous theology reflects humanity's first understandings of the spirit world, often experienced through natural phenomenon unique to a region or location. Universally similar, the differences of indigenous theology are often locational; they reflect the specific natural elements and their force common to a region (such as rivers flooding, desert drought, snowstorms, etc.). These environmental experiences led to the first understandings of spiritual animism and pantheism, believing these natural elements had unseen spirits controlling their force and power. As a result, nature is central to indigenous theology. As its understanding evolved, polytheistic deities associated with natural phenomena (wind, water, fire) began to take on their own identities as central powers. As encounters with the spiritual realm began to happen (perhaps through experimentation with the environment – through hallucinogenic plants, dehydration, etc.), exploration into altered states of consciousness led to forms of shamanism. Those who were privy to enter such states, engage with the spiritual realm (including the dead) and relate wise and educated wisdom to the community became important liaisons in the spiritual development of group mythology.

Indigenous theology is complex and overlaps at points. It is difficult to describe as one thing. It is highly mythological and specified to the interests and needs of the people through which they evolved. Theologies have been, and continue to be, flexible throughout history; adapting as environments and societies changed, often applied to modern situations as much as ancient ideas. It is also possible to see syncretism present within indigenous religious systems. A mixing of Christian and ancient indigenous theology, for example, is quite common. Indigenous movements (particularly Native American and Aboriginal) have been culturally and theologically hijacked by the New Age Movement. Such has culturally appropriated different aspects of their beliefs and practice, often out of context, leading many New Age practitioners to claim indigenous beliefs as their own.[2]

PHILOSOPHY

Indigenous religious groups are ancient religious systems unique to specific regions or territories. The ideas they contain relate to the way of life of a specified people, reflecting their cultural development as much as their theological beliefs: they speak of community living, diet (hunting, gathering, fishing, herding) communication, rule and regulation, social wisdom, and either flowing with or fighting natural elements in the name of survival. Indigenous religion seeks to find a place of harmony with nature; by being in touch with the spiritual awareness behind natural elements, they can cooperate with their environment and understand its forces.

Indigenous religion focuses on a few major points: mythology that relates to creation and the evolution of their specific tribe or people; oral traditions that recount a group's history, told through stories and allegories; wise or governing principles (akin to proverbs) presented as important life lessons when faced with decisions or situations; traditions handed down by elders; rites of passage; and tribal or native dress and dance, done as part of spiritual ceremonies.

In modern times, indigenous groups are often faced with the realities of societal occupations, Catholic or Christian missions that eroded their foundations of belief and identity, political and cultural abuses, and difficulty maintaining group economics in a modern setting. Today, much of their focus lies in preservation of indigenous identity (including their spiritual beliefs) as well as the betterment and continuation of their people.

NUMBER OF ADHERENTS

Over 400,000,000 people practice some form of indigenous religion. They are found worldwide on every continent: 1,200,000 thousand in North America, 10,040,000 in Latin America and the Caribbean, 1,020,000 in Europe, 1,060,000 in the Middle East and North Africa; 26,860,000 in Sub-Saharan Africa; and 365,120,000 in Asia and the Pacific.[3]

TRADITIONAL LANGUAGES

Indigenous religious languages are usually tribal, restricted to localized regions. There are approximately 2,800 of these languages in existence, many in danger of extinction. In response, some tribes and even schools are making preservation efforts to ensure languages are taught to younger generations.

Unlike modern languages, tribal languages often reflect their culture and spirituality, being explicitly specific to describe the world around them. Some languages also have unique elements to them, such as drum rhythms or whistling.

While there are too many to list here, some languages include Gwich'in (North America), Cherokee (North America), Algonquin (North America), Xaitsnoo (North America), Chatino (North America), Qom (South America), Sanoma (South America), Crimean Tatar (Asia), Kalasha-mun (Asia), Ngbolizhia (Africa), Ng'akarimojong (Africa), Northern Sami (Europe), Karelian (Europe), Yankunytjatjara (Australia), and Te Reo Maori (Pacific).

ADHERENT IDENTITY

There are as many assorted indigenous religions as there are indigenous groups. Most indigenous religious groups are identified by their associated group. It's not uncommon for groups to overlap, sometimes in language, custom, location, or religion. For this reason, it is not possible to list every single group. For clarity, they have been distinguished by geographical region, with some groups further classified by their language origins.

- **North America**: North American indigenous religious groups, identified by their tribes, are often classified as "Native Americans," "American Indians," "First Americans," "Indigenous Americans," or "Twelve Nations." These specified groups were among the first settlers in North America and are divided into ten different groups: Artic, Subartic, Northeastern Woodlands, Southeastern Woodlands, Great Plains, Great Basin, Northwest Plateau, Northwest Coast, California, and Southwest/Oasisamerica. Mexico has the highest indigenous population in North America. In Canada, over 600 recognized groups are found. Under each grouping, we find confederacies of tribes or tribal groups, each with their own specific culture and religious traditions that are somewhat similar in practice to one another.

- **Circum-Caribbean and West Indies**: Circum-Caribbean and West Indies groups are those found in island nations of the Caribbean sea. They include Chibchan peoples (Costa Rica and Panama), Kuna (Panama), Pech (Honduras), Votic (Maleku from Costa Rica and Rama from Nicaragua), Choco/Embera-Wounaan Peoples (Panama), Misumalpan peoples (Honduras and Nicaragua), Tolupan/Jicaque (Honduras), Zambo/Cafuso peoples (Belize and Honduras), Black Seminoles (Florida, the Bahamas, and Mexico), Arawakan peoples (Lesser Antilles, Greater Antilles, Cuba, eastern Hispaniola, and the Bahamas); and the Guanahatabey people (Western Cuba).[4]

- **Latin and South America**: South American indigenous religious groups are also identified by their tribal affiliations. There is no singular identifier by which indigenous people are identified in Latin and South America; terms include Indian, Indigenous, Native, Native Communities, or name of one's tribe. In certain countries, indigenous people make up large portions of the population; in Bolivia, Guatemala, and parts of Peru, they comprise over half the population. As a mixed population, some live on reservations (such as in Brazil) or in remote tribal areas (there are over sixty tribes that have never had contact with the rest of the world). They comprise a large number of ethnic groups, including

Urarina (Amazonian), Matses (Amazonian), Mapuches (Chile), Aymaras (Chile), Nahua (Mexico, El Salvador, Honduras, Guatemala, and Nicuragua), and Quechua (Peru). While indigenous groups all have certain similarities, the vast differences in climate, terrain, and environment have led Latin and South American indigenous groups to also hold some differences. Those that embrace elements of traditional tribal culture today may practice polygamy, cross-cousin marriages, brideservice, matrilocality, and debt slavery.

- **Europe**: Of all continents, Europe has the lowest indigenous population. Those that do exist are found in the northernmost and easternmost parts of the continent. These include: Nenets, Samoyed, and Komi (Northern Russia); Circassians (southern Russia and North Caucasus); Crimean Tatars, Krymchaks, and Crimean Karaites (Ukraine); Sami (Norway, Sweden, Finland, and northwestern Russia); Basques (Spain and southern France); Sorbian (Germany and Poland); Albanians (the Balkans) and Irish (Ireland). European indigenous peoples are diverse by nature and embrace a variety of practices in modern times; some opt for more traditional cultural and religious practices, others have adopted Rabbinical or Karaite Judaism, Eastern Orthodoxy, Roman Catholicism, Protestantism, or Islam over time (sometimes mixed with shades of traditional mythologies).

Australian Aboriginal tribesmen

- **Eurasia**: Indigenous groups in these regions are descendants from the earliest human ancestors in existence. Most still live in these original regions, despite generations of wars, occupations, and political and social changes. Many now struggle to survive, along with their unique cultural and religious heritages. They ae divided into Middle East/West Asia (Semitic speakers such as Assyrians and Arabic peoples, Bedouin, Druze, Mandaeans, Ma'dan, Arameans, Canaanites, Armenians, Iranians, Southewst Iranians); Caucasus (Armenians, Iranians, Kartvelian, Avar-Andic, Dargins, Khinalug, Lak, Lezgic, Nakh, Tsezic, AbkhazOAbazam Circassian, and Ubykh); Siberia/North Asia (Chukchi-Kamchatkan, Eskimo-Aleut, Mongolic, Tungusic, Turkic, Ugric, Samoyedic, Yukaghirs, Yeniseian, Nivkh, and Oroks); Eurasian Steppe (Indo-European, Mongolic, Sino-Tibetan, Turkic, and Oghur). The belief systems present among these groups vary widely; as the foundation of civilization, we see the major world religions of Judaism, Christianity, and Islam present in force, along with Buddhism, traces of Gnosticism, Hinduism, or other mystical religious traditions, and mixtures of indigenous religious ideas with any set of beliefs that may exist.

- **Asia**: Approximately 70% of the world's indigenous populations are found in Asia. Given the vastness of territory, the indigenous peoples of Asia vary greatly. They are divided into six major groups: Western Asia (Armenians, Assyrians, Anatolian Greeks, Georgians, Kurds, and Yazidis); South Asian (Adivasis, Dravidian, Iranian, Indo-Aryan, Sino-Tibetan, Digaro, Sino-Tibetan, Kukish, Jumma, Sikkim, Burusho, Vedda, Sinhalese, and Dhivehi); Southeast Asian (Andamanese, Jarawas, Onge, Sentinelese, Vietic, Malayo-Polynesian, Hmong-Mien, Montagnards, Negrito, Tai, Sino-Tibetan, Vedda, Astroasiatic, Austronesian, Orang Rimba, Lubu, and Pribumi); North Asia (Nivkh), East Asia (Ainu, Dzungar Oirats, Pamiris, Tibetans, Ryukyuan, Punti, Hakka, Hoklo, and Tanka); and Southeast Asia (Malay Singaporeans, Cham, Degar, Khmer Krom, Igorot, Lumad, Moro, Shan, Karen, Rakhine, Karenni, Chin, Kachin, Mon, Akha, Lisu, Lahu, and Mru). Asian indigenous groups might practice Hinduism, Buddhism, Shinto, various forms of Christianity, or Islam, often with the traditional ideas present in their native religions. Many of these groups face severe threats due to climate change, political oppression, and health issues.

- **Africa**: Indigenous groups in Africa are identified as having existed since pre-colonial times. There are six different categories of African indigenous groups: African Great Lakes (Abagusii, Hadza, Iraqw, Kalenjin, Kikuyu, Luhya, Maasai, Rendille Samburu, Sandawe, and Pygmy); Central Africa (Pygmy, Mbuti, Twa); Horn of Africa (Afar, Amhara, Banna, Basketo, Berta, Burji, Gedeo, Gumuz, Hamer, Karo, Kunama, Maale, Mursi, Nara, Ormo, Saho, Shinasha, Sidama, Somalis, Suri Baale, Suri Chai, Suri Timaga, Wolayta, and Yem); North Africa (Berbers, Northern Berbers, Haratin, Serer, and Toubou); Nile Valley (Copts, Beja, Siwi Berbers, Nuba, Nubians, Dinka, Nuer, Anuak, Shilluk, Fur, Masalit, and Kadu); and Southern Africa (Khoikhoi, Nama, Damara, Haillom, Glu and Gllana, Naro, Tsoa/Tshwa/Kua, Kx'a/Ju-Hoan, Tuu, Kwi, IXam, and Taa). They are known for well-organized tribes and clans. Much like other indigenous groups, their cultural and religious identities vary, having changed throughout the years. Some follow traditional African tribal religious practices while others might practice Orthodoxy, Roman Catholicism, Protestantism, or Islam, or a combination of tribal and major world religion.

- **Australia/Oceania**: Encompassing Australia, New Guinea, New Zealand, and the islands of the Pacific Ocean, there are hundreds of indigenous peoples present in this specific region of the world. Many of the regional indigenous cultures overlap in different ways, be it culture, language, region, or all of the above (leading to many subgroups). Tribal elders hold a special place in such cultures, and those who acted as traditional healers were considered guardians of the oral tradition origination stories found among these people. These include Indigenous Australians (Aboriginal Australians, Torres Straight Islander, and Tiwi), consisting of the following regions: Western Desert (Pama-Nyugngan, Mirindi); Kimberley (Bunuban, Jarrakan, Nyulnyulan, and Worrorran); Northwest (Pama-Nyungan and Kartu); Southwest (Pama-Nyugngan); Fitzmaurice Basin (Yirram,

Bodypainting Shaman

Macro-Gunwinyguan, and Daly); Arnhem Land (Pama-Nyungan, Macro-Gunwinyguan, Iwaidjan, and Marrku-Wurrugu); Top End (Tiwi and Darwin Region, and Giimbiyu); Gulf Country (Pama-Nyungan, Tankgkic, and Garawan); West Cape (Pama-Nyungan); East Cape (Pama-Nyungan); Daintree Rainforest (Pama-Nyungan); Lake Eyre Basin (Pama-Nyungan); Spencer Gulf (Pama-Nyungan); Murray-Darling Basin (Pama-Nyungan); Northeast (Pama-Nyungan, Maric, and Waka-Kabic); Southeast (Pama-Nyungan, Gumbaynggiric, Anewan, Yuin-Kuric, Gippsland, and Kunlinic); Tasmania (Palawa), and Torres Strait Islands (Torres Strait Islanders). The Melanesia peoples include Melanesians, Papuans, and Trans-New Guineans. Micronesia includes Micronesians (Chamorro, Carolinians, Yapese, Kosraeans, Chuukese, Pohnpeians, Palauans, and Kirbati's). Polynesia includes Polynesians (Native Hawaiians, Tongans, Tuvaluans, Marquesas Islanders Rapanui, Samoans, Tokelau, Austral Islanders, Cook Isleanders, Mahoi, Maori, Moriori, Tahitians, Tuamotus, and Niueans); and Polynesian outliers (Vanuatuans, Kapingamarangi, Nukuoro, Rennel, Tikopia, Vaeakau-Taumako, Nuguria, Nukumanu, Takuu, Ontong Java, Sikaiana, Anuta, Fagauvea Ouvea, Aniwa, Bellona, Rennel). Their belief systems widely vary; Indigenous Australians have been profoundly influenced by Christianity, with the majority identifying as such. There are small numbers of practicing Muslims and those who adhere to their traditional beliefs. There is also a substantial portion of the Aboriginal population that does not practice religion. The traditional religions of indigenous island communities are extremely diverse, and overall little is known about them (outside the basics of traditional indigenous religious components). Today, many practice various forms of Christianity, Mormonism, their native religious beliefs, or combinations of their traditional religious beliefs and Christian ideas. A large population practices no religion at all.

- **Circumpolar**: A general term for all indigenous peoples of the Arctic, the group encompasses the northernmost parts of Alaska, Canada, Russia, Norway, and much of Greenland. Their lifestyles reflect the harsh, cold conditions they face, often involved in herding reindeer and sheep, fishing, and fur trapping. They include Paleosiberian, Eskimo-Aleut, Turkic, Ugrians, Sami, Samoyedic peoples, Ykaghirs and Slavs. Their belief systems vary; most are affiliated with Eastern Orthodoxy (some of which still practice traditional shamanism or other systems alongside their standard beliefs), while some are Protestant, Muslim, or exclusively practice their traditional religious beliefs. Some do not practice any religion at all, or identify as atheist.[5]

SECTS/DIVISIONS

Indigenous religious groups have a few main headings, often serving as the original foundations for basic theological concepts and ideas. These specific ideas are not so much "sects" or "divisions" as we understand such in modern religion as different aspects of indigenous religious belief. It is easy to see where ideas and concepts overlap, as many of the different basic ideas are both alike and different at the same time. Such beliefs may be practiced on their own, in combination with other beliefs, in combination with all concepts collectively, or sometimes in modern times, in combination with organized religion. The way an individual may perceive their beliefs may also vary from what may be expressed in a group setting. To identify indigenous belief as unorganized is a misnomer. It submits itself to a different sense of order, a radically different way of understanding both the natural and spiritual realms.

- **Animism**: Perhaps the earliest of spiritual beliefs, animism is the belief that one distinct essence, spirit, or power inhabits all beings on earth – plants, natural resources, animals, and people. The essence can inhabit beings (such as certain animals, plants, and humans) as well as exist through spirit entities that are not always visible to the naked eye. Its focus is cosmic rather than humanistic, seeing all things as coming from one source and reflecting that source as they embrace the idea of life. They do not see everything as the same or as one thing, but unique manifestations of the one essence present in every living thing. More than a religious system in and of itself, animism tends to dictate worldview and spiritual practice. Animists tend to see all activities involving interaction with nature and others as a spiritual endeavor. Rather than processing their world through intellectual means, they see the world through a mystical lens, as part of a greater reality.

  Animism's essential concept establishes equality between all life forms. Human beings are not superior to anything else on this planet. This creates an interest in ecological balance and preservation, especially in the hunter/gathering process and the traditions of Shamanism. There must be a balance, one that reflects giving back to nature as much as taking from it. In many communities, animism is displayed through artwork, such as wood and stone carvings.

- **Polytheism**: The belief in the existence of multiple gods or deities. Polytheism is a complicated belief system as gods, goddesses, and various deities are often categorized into pantheons, with each specific grouping sharing certain rituals, beliefs, and religious practices. In indigenous communities, polytheism is often the idea of a universal essence, principle, spirit, or deity is found transcendent throughout all of nature. The different gods of polytheism may be seen as literal gods or deities, different personalities or aspects of one primary deity, or different manifestations of natural forces. Polytheistic deities are often equivalent across different polytheistic cultures. Polytheists may worship or focus on one specific deity or may change deities, depending on circumstances and belief.

- **Henotheism**: A subset of polytheism that states a god is a singular, supreme deity over a tribe or group of people while believing it is not the only god in existence or the only deity to be worshiped. It reflects the polytheistic idea that gods, goddesses, and deities can be divided into pantheons with one of greater relevance than another to a people, with primary or exclusive devotion to that deity. In henotheism, all deities are seen as one primary essence (echoing animism) and are, therefore, all equivalent in role and power. Among indigenous communities, henotheism has remained a popular theological outlook, especially among tribal peoples.[6]

- **Kathenotheism**: A subset of polytheism that, in contrast to henotheism that maintains worship of one primary deity among many gods, individuals and groups worship one deity at a time. Kathenotheists change their primary deity depending on circumstances and situations, associating different gods and deities with different powers, abilities, and bestowments.

- **Pantheism**: The belief that the divine and the tangible world are one and the same, with one essential, omnipresent deity that is fully manifested and present in the material world. This means all life forms are not only part of the divine or deity; they are that deity within their own essence. More simply understood, created matter and the divine are the same. The idea of pantheism is present in many indigenous cultures, in particular African and Native American groups.

- **Monotheism**: The belief that there is one supreme deity and none other. As a concept, monotheism may manifest as one supreme deity, singular in nature, with many attributes; or that various gods and goddess forms are different aspects of the one true deity. It is seen among several indigenous groups, such as Druze, Yazidism, Yahwism, the Himba and Igbo people, Waaqeffanna, and some Native American religions.[7]

- **Dualism**: There are different ways dualism is understood, especially in consideration of indigenous understanding. In its strictest sense, dualism is the belief that there are distinct and separate ideas, entities, and concepts at play in the universe that oppose one another (such as good and evil). In indigenous religion, it is often the idea that every single living being – human and non-human – has a spiritual double. This is the concept of an "alter ego," an "evil twin," or most often, the being we are here on earth and the sense of us as a being in the world from where we come from spiritually.

- **Ancestor worship**: Also known as veneration of the dead, ancestral worship exists to honor the deceased. There are a few reasons why ancestral worship evolved, one of the primary ones being that even in the afterlife, ancestors could return to either haunt or bestow favor in spirit form. Other reasons include the belief that ancestors can intercede on behalf of the living or that such is a required familial or cultural duty. Such a practice ranges from the customary "Day of the Dead" observances to personal ancestral altars (often with pictures of deceased family members and statues of deities), offerings of food, incense, chants, burnt offerings, or festivals.

- **Shamanism**: Shamanism is an indigenous religious practice involving two key components: the shaman, or the person who interacts with the spirit world, and an altered state of consciousness reached by the shaman to properly interact with the spirit world. Shamans typically engage in shamanic practice to direct spirits or the concept of spiritual essence or presence into the material world. The goal of such is often healing, divination (to foretell the future), assisting deceased souls to reach the afterlife (known as a psychopomp), for direction, or to gain spiritual insight. Many understand regional medicinal plants, chants,

Indigenous woman of Laos

magic, and warding off evil spirits. There are a variety of variations in shamanic practice; there is no singular definition. Some believe witch doctors, mediums, mystics, and medicine men or women are part of shamanic tradition. Others disagree, believing these practices to use techniques other than shamanism, although no one agrees what practices are specific only to shamanism. Shamans may reach their specific altered states through hallucinogenic drugs (such as peyote, mushrooms, psilocybin, tobacco, cannabis, iboga, *salvia divinorum*, or ayahuasca), intense dance, fasting, drumming, prolonged exposure to the elements or self-harm, such as cutting one's flesh.

Cultures disagree about who can be a shaman. Some cultures restrict the role to men, some restrict the role to women, and some allow individuals of any gender to serve as shamans. Most claim to be a shaman through mystical experiences, such as a dream or sign; some believe shamanic practice is inherited. Most undergo both training and initiation, to test abilities. Shamans are often considered experts in the traditions of a people, their specific codes and mythologies, and their spiritual understanding.

Worldwide, shamanistic practice is on the decline. Neoshamanism, often adopted by New Age practitioners, is done out of its native context, and considered cultural appropriation in most instances. The practices often vary substantially from traditional shamanic practice, having emerged in the 1950s and gaining popularity in the 1980s and 1990s. Most are interpretive on personal perspectives of what shamanism is rather than studying it from within its historic, spiritual, and cultural understanding. Within the United States, the term "shaman" is not used among its indigenous people.

- **<u>The New Age Movement</u>**: It is inappropriate to classify any part of the New Age Movement as legitimate indigenous religious forms, but it is included here because it has adopted many practices found in indigenous religious belief and modified them to make them their own. Done out of context and with different basis and association, most of the indigenous community feels such has been done in cultural appropriation and is a gross misrepresentation of the beliefs of authentic indigenous communities. The New Age Movement interprets indigenous beliefs from a personal perspective, often from the ideal of the practitioner or author, whose identity is not rooted in an indigenous community. Examples of such practices are part of "neoshamanism tourism" and include specific rites or new age initiations that have been modified as a tourist attraction. These include workshops, shamanic sacrifices, group healings, drumming, vision quests, visualization, sweat lodges, and ayahuasca ceremonies. Some tourists have died while undergoing such practices.[9]

Disputes Within Group

To describe modern-day issues present within indigenous communities as official religious disputes is incorrect. Indigenous communities today face the conflict between survival and cultural preservation. Not everyone agrees on how to move forward. Issues such as alcohol abuse, reservation casinos and other tourist attractions (especially in the United States), health issues, land rights, climate change, domestic violence, unemployment, outside oppression, forced assimilation, exploitation, and genocide have all radically changed the face of indigenous communities. Most are working as hard as possible to move forward. Some nations do not acknowledge the identity of indigenous peoples (such as Bangladesh and Indonesia) or continue to persecute them (such as the Chams in Vietnam), further complicating the situations at hand.

Scriptures

Indigenous groups rely on oral traditions rather than written holy books or texts. Stories are passed down between generations, often involving complicated creation mythologies that detail the creation of the world, human beings, and the existence of that specific group. Stories about cultural heroes are also part of the oral traditions, helping to instill a sense of history and moral codes within younger people. The histories are often told by elders or older members of communities to younger ones and are sometimes acted out or incorporated with dance during ceremonies.

Until the last centuries, traditional indigenous stories were not written down. Records we have of them today were often written by non-indigenous ethnographers, some of whom received permission to document the oral stories of the indigenous populations. These writings, however, do not form an official canon, recognizing each group has their own unique oral traditions. There is no official written scripture recognized by indigenous peoples.

Within North American Christianity, the *First Nations Version New Testament* presents the New Testament in the language and understanding of indigenous peoples in North America. It was completed by Terry M. Wildman (of Ojibwe and Yaqui ancestry) and published by InterVarsity Press. There have been other versions of the Bible published in the language of indigenous peoples, but this particular New Testament seeks to capture concept familiar to indigenous peoples versus just translating the Bible into someone's native language.[10]

Basic Religious Practices

Indigenous religion does not present itself within the duality of a sacred and secular divide. Religious understanding is a way they see the world, part of the way they understand and perceive daily life. It is intertwined with the greater sense of survival present and required as part of the way of indigenous life. It transcends wherever someone is, whatever they are doing, and creates a permeating sense of spiritual purpose in all activities.

For an indigenous individual, one may have as profound a sense of spiritual awareness while hunting, gathering plants, or contemplating life decisions as they do during formalized rituals or rites. The basic formalized religious practices include dance (usually in elaborate costume and headdress), chanting (sometimes in song or with a drum or flute or other musical accompaniment), cultural mythologies, celebration of cultural ancestors, and various ritual acknowledgements of life's transitions, which may include birth, marriage, healing, spiritual cleansing, rite of passage, and death. Rituals are typically performed on land deemed sacred as part of the mythological traditions (perhaps it is where a group's founders first realized something essential about their destiny, a site where a miracle happened or something important to the groups' history happened, a sacred natural source is found (such as a plant or river) or an ancestral burial ground. A ceremony may be a community practice, one done by an elder or a group of elders, someone in a shamanistic or healer context, or by an individual who seeks to discover essential answers or direction in life.

HOLIDAYS

While some nations do recognize days in tribute to indigenous peoples (such as Indigenous Peoples Day in the United States and International Mother Language Day in Canada), these vary from specific days of observance recognized by indigenous peoples. Indigenous groups often celebrate days as relate to seasonal changes: equinox, solstices, times for planting crops, harvests. Most also have special days of the dead, devoted to their ancestors.

VISUAL SIGNS AND SYMBOLS

Indigenous groups are unique to the regions where they natively exist. Their customs, dress, and attire were traditionally bound by location, using environmental items to clothe and shelter themselves: animal hides or skins, fabrics woven from natural materials, dried grass, stone, clay, and wood. Their visible symbols often relate to their specific ways of life: crops they grow, goods they produce, elaborate headdresses and costumes for ceremonies, their specific chants and dances, musical instruments, precious stones, beads, or natural items that are of value (such as sacred plants, rivers or land), traditional items used for hunting (such as bows and arrows, arrowheads, spears, etc.), tribal patterns, feathers, indigenous language usage, and vivid mythologies, all that relate to their history as a people. Some tribes engage in tattooing, gages, lip plates, or scarring.

CREEDS, BOOKS, AND LAWS

In modern times, most indigenous groups are governed by their specified treaties and regulations. Most are organized into tribal groups, governed by councils of elders. Their treaties exist for the governance of land and land regulations, often to distinguish it from the occupying governments that have tried to overtake their land for centuries.

Within tradition, the governance and morality of a group filters through oral traditions.

Moral codes were often taught in the form of life lessons and instructions to younger generations, much in the tradition of fables and proverbs. Many groups hold to a cardinal "philosophy" that focuses on the way they see and understand the world.

Eclectic Beliefs

Indigenous beliefs function through cycles. Whether it is embracing the idea of a life cycle, seasons, nature, or eternal, cycles shape and form the way indigenous people see time. In seeking to be part of those cycles and better understand life in general, indigenous peoples are often interested in a certain level of ecology, seeing nature on part with themselves and striving to understand their local environments rather than working against them. A great deal of time is spent processing and understanding the natural diversity found in a place, thus leading to a desire to replenish as well as take as necessary.

Many indigenous cultures are known for a variety of superstitions. Believing spirit and spirits inhabit people, animals, and all life forms leads to a certain awareness of certain ideas and concepts present throughout life and life's experiences. This relates to superstition: the idea of good luck or bad luck present in one's life because one's own displeasure of spirits or ancestors. Through avoidance of certain practices and engagement in ritual or rite, one can restore one's favor.

Relations with Non-indigenous Religious Groups

Indigenous communities vary in their approach to other spiritual beliefs. For the most part, indigenous believers may practice a major world religion in combination with their own beliefs, with no conflict. Many indigenous embrace traditional religion, such as Christianity, Islam, Judaism, Buddhism, or Shinto, while continuing to practice specific aspects of their indigenous faith.

There are some, however, who feel the preservation of their way of life is essential, especially in times where indigenous beliefs are often marginalized, discriminated against, and disappearing. Some see the incorporation of certain religions, especially western ones, as part of forced cultural assimilation. While not present among all indigenous peoples, there is interest among some of encouraging traditional beliefs among indigenous youth.

Totem pole

Holy Sites

Indigenous peoples recognize holy sites unique to their groups or tribes. As their concept of holy or sacred is different than in major world religions, the presence of spirit or essence is found everywhere, in all that lives; this creates an awareness of presence in all things, rather than only specific things. Holy sites might be places for sacred ritual, often connected to the life and community of a people. Sites include burial grounds, sacred altars, founding land, mountains, water sources, and other spots deemed such by a specific group.

Notable Figures

David Kenani Maraga (1951-), politician; Wangari Maathai (1940-2011), first African woman to earn a Ph.D. and receive the Nobel Peace Prize; Wanjiku Kabira (1948-), literature professor and activist; Aster Aweke (1959-), musician; Abuna Basilios (1891-1970), first Patriarch of the Ethopian Orthodox Tewahido Church; William Ole Ntimama (1928-2016), politician; Nanjala Nyabola, writer; Ruth Habwe (d. 1996), politician; Hibo Nuura (1954-), musician; K'naan (1978-), musician; Reem Abdullah (1985-), actress; Mohammed Salem Al-Anzi (1976-), athlete; Helal Al-Mutairi (1855-1938), businessman; Salman al-Ouda (1956-), Muslim scholar; Amir Pazevari, poet; Yul Brynner (1920-1985), actor; Dashi Namdakov (1967-), artist; Anna Nerkagi (1952-), writer; Chuner Taksami (1931-2014), ethnographer; Tagir Kusimov (1909-1986), military leader; Roza Otunbayeva (1950-), politician; Jogeswar Bhumji (1992-), athlete; Chhotubhai Vasava (1945-), politician; Jackie Shroff (1957-), actor; Son Ngoc Minh (1920-1972), politician; Che Linh (1941-), musician; H.E. Kem Sokha (1953-), politician; Samd Bounthong (1997-), athlete; John Richardson (1896-1978), Anglican bishop and politician; Walis Perin (1952-), Roman Catholic priest and politician; Daigo Higa (1995-), athlete; Brian Tee (1977-), actor; Dave Roberts (1972-), athlete; Maria de Jesus Patricio Martinez (1963-), politician; Francisco Toledo (1940-2019), painter; Benito Juarez (1806-1872), politician; Emily Johnson (1976-), dancer and writer; Todd Palin (1964-), first Gentleman of Alaska; Alice Brown (1912-1973), activist; Shane Yellowbird (1979-2022), musician; Bronson Pelletier (1986-), actor; Laurie Rousseau-Nepton (1985-), astrophysicist; Cumshewa, tribal leader; Jay Simeon (1976-), artist; Quesalid, medicine man and writer; Spencer O'Brien (1988-), athlete; Sanpitch (d. 1866), chief of the Sanpete tribe; Mary Joachina Yee (1897-1965), linguist; Frank Tuttle (1892-1963), artist; Big Tree (1850-1929), Kiowa chief and warrior; Mirac Creepingbear (1947-1990), artist; Santana (c. 1820-1878), war chief; Arvo Mikkanen (1961-), attorney; Blackbird (c. 1750-1800), chief; Rodney A. Grant (1959-), actor; Misty Upham (1982-2014), actress; Steve Reevis (1962-2017), actor; Graham Greene (1952-), actor; Handsome Lake (1735-1815), Seneca religious leader; Jay Silverheels (1912-1980), actor; Tammy Beauvais, fashion designer; Eric Gansworth (1965-), writer; Aaliyah (1979-2001), musician; Cochise (c. 1805-1874), Apache chief; Geronimo (1829-1909), Apache leader; Natalie Diaz (1978-), poet; Myrna Cunningham (1947-), politician; Edwin Solano (1996-), athlete.

Notable Groups

The term "Eskimo" refers to two indigenous groups: the Inuit (Alaskan Inupiat, Greenlandic Inuit, and Canadian Inuit) and the Yupik (eastern Siberia and Alaska). As circumpolar peoples, they inhabit the regions of eastern Siberia, Alaska, Northern Canada, Nunavik, Nunatsiavut, and Greenland. Their religious understanding involves a mediator – either a spiritual healer, medicine man or woman, shaman, or ceremonial leader – who mediates between humans and spirits and souls. Within the Inuit language, the individual is known as an *angakkug* or *angatkug*. They believe an individual has two or more souls and that there are spiritual links between the living, hunted animals, and the deceased. They often embody their own special language that includes special metaphors to describe their work. They are believed to work in healing, infertility, successful hunts, and seances.

Among practitioners of the traditional religion, all members may experience visions. Most members report various hallucinations, including ghosts, hearing voices, animals in human form, or daydreams. While *angakkug* can command spirits, the average individual uses amulets to ward off negative spirit powers.[11]

Facts and Figures

Indigenous peoples make up approximately six percent of the world's global population, but account for about nineteen percent of the most extreme poor worldwide. Generally, their life expectancy is about twenty years lower than non-indigenous peoples.[12]

Other Important Definitions

- **Bon**: An indigenous religion of Tibet that is very close to Tibetan Buddhism.

- **Earth Lodge Religion**: An indigenous religious community formed by tribes in northern California and southern Oregon (including the Wintun, Achomawk, Shasta, and Siletz). It has been involved in predictions of ancestral return and the end of the world.[13]

- **Ghost Dance**: A movement of the late 1800s that sought to revitalize indigenous religious beliefs in the United States. Founded by Wovoka, a Northern Paiute, it sought to save the lives of indigenous people by calling on the ancestors to fight on their behalf, with the goal of driving the American colonists off their lands. It is still practiced today, though largely in secret.[14]

- **Medicine bundles**: Ritual objects that are special to the individual who carries them.

- **Mexicayotl**: A religious movement to revive the religion, culture, and traditions of the Aztecs among the Mexican populace.[15]

- **Native American Church**: Also known as Peyotism and the Peyote Religion, the Native American Church teaches a mixture of Christianity and Native American ideals. It is unique in that its sacrament is the use of peyote. It Originated in the Oklahoma Territory in the nineteenth century. It has approximately 250,000 members as of the late 1900s.[16]

- **Smudging ceremony**: A purification rite that involves burning sacred herbs, such as cedar, sage, sweetgrass, or tobacco. The burned flame is blown out and then the smoke is druged over the person in need, with a hand or feather. The person inhales the smoke. The ashes from the process are disposed of outside, believing any negative energy is absorbed by the ashes. Smudging is done in times of death or illness, crisis, stress, or other need.[17]

- **Sweat lodge**: A site for a purification ceremony designed to promote healing. It is seen among the Chumash and Mesoamerican tribes in Mexico. Elders who lead lodges undergo significant training and are familiar with the indigenous language of a group, to pray and communicate safely. The lodge, built simply with natural materials and low to the ground, must be properly oriented to the cardinal directions with the door facing the sacred fire.[18]

- **Transformers**: Also known as shape-shifters, beings that can change form or shape, including as humans, animals, or inanimate objects.[19]

- **Tricksters**: Legendary figures that take on different forms: male, female, foolish, helpful, hero, troublemaker, hybrid human and spirit, young or old, human, spirit, or animal.[20]

- **Vision quests**: Also known as a guardian spirit quest. A rite of passage for pubescent males that involves staying in a remote, isolated area alone to fast, pray, and purify themselves with the goal of seeing a vision of or having an encounter with a guardian spirit (such as an animal or mythological figure).[21]

BELIEVER'S CHARACTERISTICS

Beliefs largely shaped around a group's native territory that are part of worldview as much as religious understanding; animism, pantheism, polytheism, henotheism, shamanism, monotheism, or a combination of these different ideas; attune to achieve harmony with nature; belief in the spirit world; tribal living; mythologies that relates to creation and the evolution of their specific tribe or people; oral traditions that recount a group's history, told through stories and allegories; wise or governing principles (akin to proverbs) that are presented as important life lessons when faced with decisions or situations; traditions handed down by elders; rites of passage; and tribal or native dress and dance, done as part of spiritual ceremonies; syncretism with major world religions; ancestor worship; oral traditions; moral codes; tribal elders; time as seen through cycles; superstitions; traditional tribal languages.

Islam

Religion is very easy and whoever overburdens himself in his religion will not be able to continue in that way.
So you should not be extremists, but try to be near to perfection and receive the good tidings that you will be rewarded; and gain strength by worshipping in the mornings, the nights.
(Hadith Quotes)[1]

Theology

Belief in one divine being referred to as ALLAH, beyond all comprehension, unknowable, and known by 99 different names; creator of the universe. Allah has revealed his being through nature and is discussed in theological stories. Allah is regarded as all-merciful, all knowing, unique, in relationship with creation. Having revealed himself through different people throughout history (known as prophets), Allah is seen as near to those who call upon one of the various divine names, especially holding a special relationship with Muslims, or people who submit themselves to Allah's will.

Allah is only one literal being, seen as singular in number and identity. Muslims reject the idea of a triune deity and reject the idea that Allah has a son, because Allah has no wife. Regardless, Muslims identify Allah as the same deity of the Old Testament, drawing on the covenant with Abraham to apply to them through the lineage of Abraham's son, Ishmael.

Philosophy

The word "Islam" literally means "submission to Allah." Islam centers around the principle that one must submit themselves to Allah throughout one's life. One can best do this as a follower of the religion founded by the Prophet Mohammed, who received the Qur'an, the central text of Islam. For Muslims, Allah alone is to be worshiped, honored by those who follow him through devotion, action, and service, and that Islam alone is God's true way.

Islam is largely based on the concept of revelation, as the entire religion was received by an individual known as the Prophet Mohammed (c. 570-632). He received the Qur'an, the holy book of Islam, from the Angel Gabriel in Mecca, Saudi Arabia, starting in the year 610. The Islamic way is seen as an infallible revelation, one that is completely perfect and true. Other religious groups that existed prior, such as Judaism and Christianity, are seen as incomplete faiths in comparison to the universal and fullness present in Islam. Muslims believe the revelation received by past prophets, those in a long line from the beginning of time (including Adam, Enoch, Noah, Lot, Ishmael, Abraham, Job, David, John the Baptist, and Jesus), are all partial in revelation. They provided insights relevant in their age, now complete in the work of the Prophet Mohammed.

Islam is founded on five pillars:

- ***Shahda* (Creed)**: The "creed" of Islam is recited under oath, daily in prayer, affirming one's belief in the religious system: *I testify there is no god but Allah, and Mohammed is his prophet (messenger).* This is the very foundation on which all of Islam rests.

- ***Salah* (Prayer)**: Prayer is done five times daily, facing Mecca, spoken in Arabic. To pray properly, Muslims prostrate (kneeling with their head to the ground) in prayer. The source text for these daily prayers is the Qur'an.

- ***Zakat* (Almsgiving)**: Muslims are required to give 2.5% of their income (1/40th of total annual value) to charity. Such is specifically for those deemed poor, needy, in debt, freeing captives, or stranded travelers.

- ***Sawm* (Fasting)**: Muslims are required to fast for the entire month of Ramadan from all food and water, from dawn until dark. The fast expresses gratitude to Allah, atone for sins, draw closer to Allah, and develops a sense of self-control, as one considers the plight of those who go without food. If one misses a fasting period, it is expected they will do it later.

- ***Hajj (Pilgrimage)***: Muslims are obligated to travel to the city of Mecca at least once in their lifetime. While on pilgrimage, they are expected to follow a specific course of ritual: spend a day and night in a tent in Mina (a desert); praise and worship Allah for a day in the desert of Arafat; follow in the footsteps of Abraham, sleep in the open in the desert of Muzdalifah; symbolically "stone the devil," recount Abraham's actions, go to Jamarat; walk around the Kaaba (the "cube" building at Mecca that Muslims face during prayer) seven times; and walking seven times between Mount Safa and Mount Marwah to recount the steps of Hagar while looking for water in the desert.

Other religious acts central to the practice of Islam include *sadaqah* (charity, doing charitable acts, given out of religious duty and generosity) and *tajweed* (recitation of the Qur'an, especially for memorization).[2]

ADHERENT IDENTITY

Islam, Islamic, Muslim, Mohammedists, Sufi; specific identity through the specific school of Islam one may follow, such as Sunni, Shi'ite, Quranists, or other specific, small percentages of specified Islamic adherence.

Islamic prayers

TRADITIONAL LANGUAGES

Arabic

SECTS/DIVISIONS

Much like other religious groups, Islam has its share of divisions. There are numerous Islamic "schools" and branches, all of which maintain Islamic basics. They vary in interpretation of the Qur'an and traditions surrounding leadership, authority, and transmission of information and law from generation to generation. Figuring out the specifics can appear confusing to many, but much like categorizing any religion, it is easier when groups are broken down by commonalities.[3]

- **Sunni**: Approximately 80%-90% of all Muslims classify as Sunni Muslims. They trace their lineage through Mohammed's father-in-law, Abu Bakr (573-634). Unlike some sects, they do not believe Mohammed left a clear successor upon his death. Sunni Muslims follow the Qur'an, Hadith (traditions of teaching, words, and actions of the Prophet Mohammed) and juristic consensus from those who study Quranic law as their foundational interpretation, ideas, and concepts of the way the Muslim faith should practice and operate in the lives of followers and structuring within Islamic societies. Sharia law (or Islamic law) is interpreted from these different foundations. They uphold the six articles of faith (oneness of Allah, angels, revealed books, prophets, Day of Judgment, and God's predestination). There are several smaller traditions within the Sunni branch, all with slightly interpretations of the legal traditions of Islam, such as how to pray, how to dress, or some specifications of Quranic interpretation. Within the Sunni sect are the Shafis, Maliki, Hanafi, Deobandi, Barelvi, Hanbali, and the Whahabi/Salafists, the last of which practices Jihadism (a religious and political movement that seeks to restore Sunni Islam to what it considers as a state of purity; a radical, extremist sect of Islam known for intense militancy).

- **Shia**: Shia Islam composes 10%-15% of all Islamists worldwide, largely concentrated in the Middle East. They are named "Shia," meaning "followers of Ali." Shi'ite Muslims believe Mohammed's cousin and son-in-law Ali (c. 600-c. 661) succeeded him by clear direction and instruction. In turn, Ali also left a successor, and so on, and so forth, to the point where the Shia later became Imamis (spiritual and political successors to the Prophet Mohammed). They differ from the Sunni Muslims in the specific prayers prayed at different points in the day, with option to combine them together, as well as a different "creed." Among Shia Islam, the shahada adds an additional part, reading: *"There is no god but Allah, Mohammed is the messenger of God, and Ali is the custodian of Allah."* They also have their own specific form of the Hadith, which equates to a different understanding about the role of Islam in government and authority. Shia Muslims see infallibility prevalent through the prophets of Islam, including Mohammed, Imams, and Fatima (c. 605-632), Mohammed's daughter. Their doctrine is based on five different principles: monotheism, justice, prophethood, leadership, and the last judgment. They also embrace the Nahj al-

Balagha (collection of sermons, letters, and stories), al-Kafi (Hadith collection) and Wasa'il al-Shi'ah (Hadith collection). Within the Shia sect are the Twelvers, Ismaili, Alevi-Bektashism, and Zaidi.

- **Quranists**: A smaller sect of Islam that feels Islamic law and interpretation should come from the Qur'an alone, excluding the interpretation or understanding of the Hadith. They see the Hadith as unnecessary, and largely unreliable, emerging long after the Prophet Mohammed's life. Within their understanding, Hadiths were forbidden during Mohammed's lifetime and, therefore, were prohibitive after his death, as well. Quranists consider themselves to be reformers and restorers of a pure way, and despite their literalism, are often considered a liberal branch of Islam.

- **Kharijites**: A small sect of Islam that dates to the immediate time after Mohammed's death. The Kharijites left the leadership of Ali, leader of the Shia sect, and opted to follow the way they felt was pure, leading to Allah. They disagree on the doctrine of infallibility, believe Muslims have the right to revolt against any leader who does not properly interpret the way of Islam, and have three major differing points from other Islamic groups: they believe in the importance of martyrdom for their faith, the need for a just and devout Muslim ruler, and they have failed to create these things for Muslims. Also unique to Kharijites is the belief that women have the same command to fight jihad as men.

- **Sufism**: Considered the "mystical" tradition of Islam, Sufism is considered an Islamic religious order. Any practicing Muslim (of any sect) is welcome to participate in the Sufi order. Rather than seeing the attainment of Paradise after death, Sufis believe union with Allah and attainment of Allah's presence is obtainable while living. They find such through *al-Insan-al-Kamil*, focusing on the "perfect man" (*Qutb*) who can be the perfect example of divine grace and sanctity (*wilayah*). Sufis are governed by *quanun*, the laws of Sufism, which pertain to specific aspects of spiritual worship, marriage, law, and business. These are an extension of their inner laws, which focus on repentance, eliminating evil behaviors or character, and focusing on replacing those difficult and unseemly attitudes and character with good ones. Imams are seen as teachers, individuals who transmit divine qualities between teacher and student. They pursue devotions of Islamic truth and order as they move through different phases of life and understanding, coming to the ultimate realization of the oneness of Allah. Sufis are strongly devoted to the Prophet Mohammed, seeing him as an example of one who is spiritually great. They also draw on the supernatural wonders of Muslim saints, considered the "friends of Allah." They also practice extensive devotion to draw and remember Allah (*dhikr*), meditation (*muraqaba*), Sufi whirling (including that of the dervish, by which an individual spins slowly while meditating, to contemplate one's connectedness with Allah and the universe), and their unique music (*qawwali*). Like many mystical traditions, there is new interest in Sufism from the outside world, and newer forms of Sufism have been modified to include beliefs and ideas of the New Age community.[4]

- **Druze**: Though some do not classify Druze as Muslim, the Druze community is a Shi'ite Muslim breakaway sect emerging around the year 986. Its complicated history started when Caliph al-Hakim Bi-Amr Allah (985-1021) proclaimed himself divine and all his predecessors divinely appointed. This caused notable conflict within Muslim society, and the resulting riots and dissention caused individuals to disassociate or breakaway and form their own independent groups. Very few, even within the community, know of their full religious rites, let alone practice them or actively read their Scriptures, known *as* Al-Hikmah al-Sharifah. They are considered a mix of Muslim, Gnostic, Jewish, and Christian ideas. The Druze do not allow conversions to their way of life, and marriage to outsiders is discouraged. For these reasons, their communities are very small, and are dying out due to continuing conflicts in regions where they are prominent: Lebanon, Syria, Israel, and Palestine.[5]

- **Bábism**: A little-known Persian religion that is classified by some as a Muslim messianic movement, Bábism is a monotheistic religion that seeks to profess belief in an unknowable deity whose will is known in different appearances or revelations to humanity, known as Manifestations of God. Followers of Bábism follow the Báb (a term that means "Gate), or specifically a man named Ali Muhammad Shirazi (1918-1850), proclaiming himself to the be the gate to the "twelfth Imam," a final Imam and redeemer of the Muslim people. The teachings of the Báb are from the Qur'an and various Islamic traditions and ideals. It was founded in 1844 in modern-day Iran and has never had more than a few thousand followers. It's best-known and largest inspiration is the Bahá'í Faith, which, with its foundations in Bábism, incorporate different spiritual concepts present in all major world religions.[6]

- **Nation of Islam**: The Nation of Islam (NOI) is not rightly part of the Islamic body, nor is it considered to be a valid sect of Islam by Muslims. It is included here because despite its lack of validity, it identifies with Muslim tradition and is frequently confused as a valid aspect of Islam. The Nation of Islam is a uniquely African American political and spiritual organization founded in Detroit, Michigan in the 1930s. Its founder, Wallace Fard Muhammad (1877-1934), disappeared within a few years of the founding. It was his successor, Elijah Muhammad (1897-1975) who became the face of the movement. Like mainline Muslims, the Nation of Islam affirms there is no deity but Allah. Fard Muhammad was the *mahdi*, a prophesied redeemer who would rid the world of evil before the Day of Judgment. The current leader of the Nation of Islam is Louis Farrakhan (1933-), who has led the movement since 1977. The Nation of Islam is known for an unconventional history, creationism that teaches the moon was once part of earth and the earth is trillions of years old, and that the original humans on earth were all from the black race. Whites (Caucasians) were a devil race created by a scientist (Yakub) on Patmos, a Greek island. After a policy was issued to kill all blacks, a preference for white-skinned individuals emerged. Among NOI, becoming a part of this organization is seen as returning to one's true faith, believing Christianity to be a form of enslavement for African Americans. Nation of Islam members uphold a different set of the Five Pillars of the Islamic faith: Belief in

Allah; daily prayers; fasting during either Ramadan or during the month of December, compulsory charity, and pilgrimage to Mecca. Fard Muhammad is considered the Messiah of both Judaism and the *Mahdi* of Muslims, and while Mohammed was the last prophet of Allah, Elijah Muhammad was a messenger taught by the *Mahdi*. Religious centers are known as Masjids (Mosque) and usually followed with a number, indicating their order of establishment. The Nation of Islam is considered a hate group as it promotes black supremacy, anti-Semitism, anti-Asian sentiment, subjugated roles for women, and anti-LGBTQ attitudes. In modern times, members of the Nation of Islam are encouraged to pursue studies associated with Scientology, especially L. Ron Hubbard's *Dianetics*. There are approximately 50,000 members of the Nation of Islam today. Offshoots of the Nation of Islam include the Five-percent Nation (Nation of Gods and Earths), University of Islam schools, Muslim Girls Training & General Civilization Class, the Fruit of Islam, and the Moorish Science Temple of America.[7]

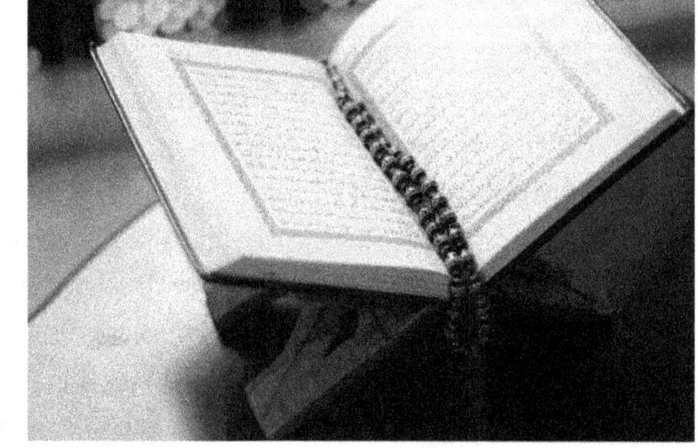
Open Qur'an

NUMBER OF ADHERENTS

There are approximately 1,800,000,000 Muslims worldwide.[8]

DISPUTES WITHIN GROUP

Muslim sects disagree over leadership claims after the Prophet Mohammed's death. The resulting disagreements relate to the way Islamic law is interpreted, especially as found in the Qur'an and Hadith. These foundational differences lead to different expectations of Muslim devotion, theology, and practice. As a result, there are Muslims who are very traditional and extreme in their observance (militant action, subjugation of women, roles of men, prayers, and politics), as well as Muslims who are more modernized and liberal in their ideas of belief and application. Different interpretations of the Qur'an, the history of the faith, and Islamic law relate to vast ideas about just how to handle Islam within the modern-day world.

SCRIPTURES

The holy book of Islam is the Qur'an, a record of revelations to the Prophet Mohammed. Muslims believe the Qur'an is the infallible word of Allah, a transcript of which is preserved forever in Paradise. It was delivered to Mohammed by the Angel Gabriel. The record was penned by scribes of the Prophet and compiled after his death. The Qur'an is considered the complete fullness of divine revelation, also including the Tawrah (Torah, the entire Old Testament, Talmudim as Jewish Law, and the Midrashim, or Jewish study of the Old Testament), Zabur (a Psalter-collection of songs, many are based from the Psalms of David in the Old Testament, as well as some other assorted Old Testament verses), and Injil (often associated with the New Testament, but possibly a reference to older apocryphal works, such as The Gospel of Thomas or Gospel of Barnabas).

The Qur'an is divided into 114 chapters, known as *surah*. Each *surah* is then divided into verses. Its contents vary, from being historical accounts to retold Biblical narratives, all from the Muslim perspective. Its basic contents center on Islamic doctrine, especially those which pertain to Allah, Allah's existence, and coming promises of resurrection. The monotheism, or idea of the divine as literally one, is the major theme throughout the Qur'an. Some of its contents also relate to various ethical, legal, moral, and spiritual principles. Perhaps its greatest promise is that of the "Last day," or Islamic eschatology (beliefs about final things). Approximately one-third of the Qur'an relates to these matters: the afterlife, next world, day of judgment, end of time, and resurrection. It is believed at this point, the good shall be separated from evil, and God shall appear as judge, to judge all of humanity (those deceased shall be raised to life).

The Qur'an has some variations in reading, with minor differences among them. The only official version of the Qur'an is in Arabic, with all translations into other languages considered as "interpretations." Reciting, memorizing, and studying the Qur'an is considered of great value (someone who memorizes the entire Qur'an is known as a *hafiz*). It is considered the finest piece of literary work among classical Arabic literature.

In the name of Allah, the Entirely Merciful, the Especially Merciful.
[All] praise is [due] to Allah, Lord of the worlds –
The Entirely Merciful, the Especially Merciful,
Sovereign of the Day of Recompense.
It is You we worship and You we ask for help.
Guide us to the straight path –
The path of those upon whom You have bestowed favor, not of those who have evoked [Your] anger or of those who are astray.[10]

In the name of Allah, the Entirely Merciful, the Especially Merciful.
By those [winds] sent forth in gusts
And the winds that blow violently
And [by] the winds that spread [clouds]
And those [angels] who bring criterion
And those [angels] who deliver a message
As justification or warning,
Indeed, what you are promised is to occur.
So when the stars are obliterated
And when the heaven is opened
And when the mountains are blown away
And when the messengers' time has come...
For what Day was it postponed?
For the Day of Judgement.
And what can make you know what is the Day of Judgement?
Woe, that Day, to the deniers.
Did We not destroy the former peoples?
Then We will follow them with the later ones.
Thus do We deal with the criminals.
Woe, that Day, to the deniers.
Did We not create you from a liquid disdained?

And We placed it in a firm lodging
For a known extent.
And We determined [it], and excellent [are We] to determine.
Woe, that Day, to the deniers.
Have We not made the earth a container
Of the living and the dead?
And We placed therein lofty, firmly set mountains and have given you to drink sweet water.
Woe, that Day, to the deniers.
[They will be told], "Proceed to that which you used to deny.
Proceed to a shadow [of smoke] having three columns
[But having] no cool shade and availing not against the flame."
Indeed, it throws sparks [as huge] as a fortress,
As if they were yellowish [black] camels.
Woe, that Day, to the deniers.
This is a Day they will not speak,
Nor will it be permitted for them to make an excuse.
Woe, that Day, to the deniers.
This is the Day of Judgement; We will have assembled you and the former peoples.
So if you have a plan, then plan against Me.
Woe, that Day, to the deniers.
Indeed, the righteous will be among shades and springs
And fruits from whatever they desire,
[Being told], "Eat and drink in satisfaction for what you used to do."
Indeed, We thus reward the doers of good.
Woe, that Day, to the deniers.
[O disbelievers], eat and enjoy yourselves a little; indeed, you are criminals.
Woe, that Day, to the deniers.
And when it is said to them, "Bow [in prayer]," they do not bow.
Woe, that Day, to the deniers.
Then in what statement after the Qur'an will they believe?[11]

While not considered scriptural, the Hadith (speech, report, or account), or traditions of teaching, words, unspoken approval, and actions of the Prophet Mohammed, are also considered highly relevant and authoritative when interpreting and understanding the Qur'an. It is the secondary choice for consultation in the understanding of law among Islamic nations. The Hadith does contain questionable content, including contradictory statements. It is now believed that much of the Hadith form apocryphal traditions of the Prophet Mohammed and his companions, emerging between one and three hundred years after Mohammed's death. For this reason, the study of the Hadith among Muslim scholars is a serious task.[12]

While we were one day sitting with the Messenger of Allah there appeared before us a man dressed in extremely white clothes and with very black hair. No traces of journeying were visible on him, and none of us knew him. He sat down close by the Prophet rested his knees against the knees of the Prophet and placed his palms over his thighs, and said: "O Muhammad! Inform me about Islam." The Messenger of Allah replied: "Islam is that you should testify that there is no deity worthy of worship except Allah and that Muhammad is His Messenger, that you should perform *salah (ritual prayer), pay the zakah, fast during Ramadan, and perform Hajj (pilgrimage) to the House (the Ka`bah at Makkah), if you can find a way to it (or find the means for making the journey to it)." He said: "You have spoken the truth." We were astonished at his thus questioning him and then telling him that he was right, but he went on to say, "Inform me about Iman (faith)." He (the Prophet) answered, "It is that you believe in Allah and His angels and His Books and His Messengers and in the Last Day, and in fate (qadar), both in its good and in its evil aspects." He said, "You have spoken the truth." Then he (the man) said, "Inform me about Ihsan." He (the Prophet) answered, "It is that you should serve Allah as though you could see Him, for though you cannot see Him yet He sees you." He said, "Inform me about the Hour." He (the Prophet) said, "About that the one questioned knows no more than the questioner." So he said, "Well, inform me about its signs." He said, "They are that the slave-girl will give birth to her mistress and that you will see the barefooted ones, the naked, the destitute, the herdsmen of the sheep (competing with each other) in raising lofty buildings." Thereupon the man went off. I waited a while, and then he (the Prophet) said, "O `Umar, do you know who that questioner was?" I replied, "Allah and His Messenger know better." He said, "That was Jibril. He came to teach you your religion."*[13]

BASIC RELIGIOUS PRACTICES

The five pillars of Islam (creed, prayer, almsgiving, fasting, and pilgrimage) are the central focus of a Muslim's religious practice. Islamic devotion is considered a regular action, one that must be done daily. Social duty and personal character are seen as part of one's spiritual life. Muslims are bound to care for their parents, the sick, the elderly, their neighbors, the disenfranchised, and extended relatives through specific requirement in the Qur'an. Muslims are to always behave with social custom and good manners, and are to focus on piety, justice, kindness, honesty, forgiveness, decency in speech, keeping one's word, modesty, humility, trustworthiness, patience, anger management, and sincerity. Of all virtues, Muslims pride modesty above all else, believing it is an essential aspect of society. For this reason, many Islamic women choose to wear a head-covering veil (either a hijab or *burquah*), although not all Muslim women choose to do so.

Marriage is seen as the very foundation of the Muslim family, and all family members (including extended family) make the commitment to educate and raise a child in the ways of Allah from birth. Muslim life revolves around the Masjid, or Mosque, which is the center for community gathering, religious education, and worship. Muslim services are held at mosques on Fridays for a specific prayer known as *juma*. *Juma* includes group prayers and a message or sermon. Muslims also go to a mosque for Muslim festivals or holidays and funerals. On the social scene, mosques are often used for things such as business or marriage arrangements or distribution of goods or money to the poor. In some parts of the world, children also receive their general education at a mosque. Mosques are led by Imams, Qur'anic scholars who lead prayers in the mosque and stand as the leader of the Muslim community in an area.

The sin of polytheism, known as *shirk*, is considered idolatry, or the worship of any deity or being besides Allah. Such is considered the only unforgivable sin.[14]

HOLIDAYS

The Muslim year follows the lunar calendar, based on the cycles of the moon. This means Muslim holidays change every year. Dates for these events widely vary, depending on the specific sect of Islam. There are two official holidays on the Muslim calendar: Eid al-Fitr, which marks the end of Ramadan, and Eid al-Adha, the feast day of sacrifice. Even though the other days listed are not formal holidays, they are days of observance throughout much of the Muslim world.

- **Al Hijra**: The Islamic New Year, beginning on 1 Muharram. On this night, the dates for yearly Islamic observance are set for that year. During the month of Muharram, war is prohibited.

- **Yawm Ashura**: Recalls the day that the grandson of the Prophet Mohammed (Husayn ibn Ali) was killed in the Battle of Karbala. It is considered a Shi'ite pilgrimage holiday and a recommended day of fasting for Sunni Muslims. It is held on 10 Muharram.

- **Milad un Nabi**: The birthday of the Prophet Mohammed. It is held on 12 Rabi- al-Awwal.

- **Laylat al Miraj**: A day honoring a specific spiritual journey the Prophet Mohammed took in 621. On this day, the Prophet Mohammed was believed to travel to a mosque in Jerusalem and lead the other prophets of history in prayer. Some Muslims believe Mohammed also ascended to Paradise at this time. Its record is found in the Hadith; it is known for both spiritual and physical value. It is known as one of the most observed days in the Islamic world. It is usually celebrated on 27 Rajab, although there is no specific date for it in the Qur'an.

Qur'an passage in Arabic writing

- **Laylat al Bara'ah**: A night devoted to prayer and devotion, as Muslims believe it a night when fortune is decided for the upcoming year by Allah. Along with fortune comes the decision for Allah to forgive sinners, including deceased ancestors. It is held between 14 and 15 Sha'ban.

- **Ramadan**: The ninth month of the Islamic year, also hosting the days of Laylat al-Qadr and Eid al-FItr. It is believed to be the time when the Prophet Mohammed first received the Qur'an, in its entirety. During later years, the Prophet received the other writings considered prophetic in Islam. As part of one of the five pillars of Islam, Muslims are required to fast during daylight hours from food, water, tobacco, sex, and sinful behaviors. Instead, they focus on charity, prayer, and reciting the Qur'an.

- **Laylat al-Qadr**: Known as the "night of power," is a night of the Ramadan holiday when the Qur'an came down from heaven to be received by the Prophet Mohammed. It is the holiest night of the Muslim year. The traditional date of this holiday is 23 Ramadan.[14]

- **Eid al-Fitr**: The official end of Ramadan held on the day after the end of the thirty-day Ramadan period. On this day, Muslims break their Ramadan fast; no Muslim is permitted to fast.

- **Eid al-Adha**: Known as the feast day of sacrifice; acknowledges the willingness of Abraham, known in Islam as Ibrahim, to sacrifice his son out of obedience to Allah. In Muslim tradition, the individual to be sacrificed is not Isaac, as is recorded in the Bible, but Ishmael. Muslims attend their local mosque for prayers, giving gifts, and visiting with one another. It is held on 10 Dhu al-Hijjah.

- **Waqf al Arafa**: The second day of the Hajj pilgrimage. It is held the first day after Eid al-Adha, on 9 Dhu al-Hijjah.

VISUAL SIGNS AND SYMBOLS

Crescent moon; crescent moon with a star; the Qur'an; Arabic writing; Mecca; the Middle East; the Prophet Mohammed; Ramadan; celebration of Muslim holidays; a Mosque.

CREEDS, BOOKS, AND LAWS

As part of the five pillars of Islam, the profession, or "Islamic creed" is:

> *La ilaha illa Allah: Muhammed rasul Allah.*

(There is no god but Allah and Mohammed is his prophet). It is spoken daily by Muslims in prayer.

Though not considered a "creed," in addition to the five pillars of Islam, Muslims also profess belief in six articles of faith: the oneness of Allah, angels, the books of Allah, the prophets of Islam, the Day of Judgment, and the divine decree, or will of Allah.

Muslim law is known as sharia law. It is the specified religious law that forms the legal aspect of Islamic traditions as understood based on the Qur'an and *Hadith*. It encompasses every aspect of human life, including personal, corporate, and religious. Sharia law has four components: the Qur'an itself, *sunnah* (Hadith considered authentic), *qiyas* (analogical reasoning), and *ijma* (juridical consensus). These four aspects of sharia relate to the question of personal behavior, civil behavior, the way sharia has evolved over time, and modern-day usage of both the historical and contemporary context of such. The most prominent sharia law schools in modern-day Islam are the Hanafi, Maliki, Shafi'I, Hanbali, and Jafari. There is considerable interpretation and disagreement, especially among the different legal schools that exist to implement sharia law as matters arise. While sharia law was often an overlap of the way Islam influenced religious ideas in Muslim nations, most of Sharia law is imposed in family laws in modern times. Some radical Islamic groups have called for a reimposition of Sharia law in many Muslim countries.[15]

ECLECTIC BELIEFS

Muslims have an interesting adaptation of what is often seen as parts of Jewish and Christian history. Seeing itself as part of Abrahamic religious tradition, Muslims consider themselves to be descendants of Abraham through his son, Ishmael. They have created their own spiritual ideals and mythologies around that lineage. For example, they believe Ishmael was the child of promise, rather than Isaac. Jesus Christ is taught to be a prophet of Islam, but not the Son of God (they do not believe Allah can have a son because Allah does not have a wife). They have also adopted a somewhat Gnostic adaptation of Jesus Christ's crucifixion, believing He was not really crucified, but others were led to believe He was. Muslims also believe it is Christ who shall return, with the purpose of aligning and pointing to the validity of the Prophet Mohammed at the end of time.

Muslims observe strict dietary guidelines known as halal ("lawful"). Animals that classify as lawful must be slaughtered (*dhabiha*) when they are still living and healthy by cutting the jugular vein, carotid artery, and windpipe. All food is considered lawful except for pork, pork byproducts, animals slaughtered in any name other than Allah, animals slaughtered contrary to *dhabiha* practice, animals without external ears, blood, carnivorous animals, birds of prey, alcohol, or foods contaminated with or by any of these different products. Seafood of all sorts is classified as halal.[16,17]

Islam observes a belief in both a heaven and a hell. In Islam, it is known as *Jannah*, and literally means "paradise garden." It is considered to have multiple (seven) levels. Such is considered the final resting place of Muslims and other righteous believers (whether *Jannah* is open to non-Muslims is of some considerable debate). To one who is a *shahid* (a martyr or witness), *Jannah* is promised. *Jahannam* is a place of punishment for evildoers, with punishment equal to the evil a person has done in their life. The suffering present in *Jahannam* manifests in both spiritual and physical ways and has multiple levels and variations of torture. Muslim scholars disagree on the technical nature of *Jahannam* as temporary or permanent. It was traditionally believed to correspond with layers of earth, with a specific entrance or portal to the underworld.

Muslims also believe in an expansive world of spirits, known as Jinn. Jinn are most often mentioned or identified as devils or demons, associated with bad luck, disease, and possession. There are a few that have also been known to be supportive, frequently mentioned in connection with Islamic magical works as summoned by a sorcerer.

Islam is most notorious in modern times for its extremist branches that often believe attacks, war, or destroying the lives of non-Muslims is a statement against what is seen as western infiltration or oppression of Islamic values. These groups are subheadings and sects of larger groups and are not in alignment with the views of the average Muslim individual. As a result, however, there is a great scrutiny of Islamic culture, which has changed greatly over the past fifty years. Due to leaders who have called for a return to what they perceive as an authentic Islamic governmental state, many Middle Eastern nations have imposed different levels of sharia law and there are impositions of all sorts on women, including prohibitions on driving, being alone with a man who is not a relative, and modest attire. Polygamy is also an issue within many Islamic cultures. Most Islamic couples worldwide are monogamous, while there are small groups of men in parts of the world who take multiple wives. According to Muslim tradition, a man can have up to four.

RELATIONS WITH NON-MUSLIMS

For the most part, liberal, contemporary, and western Islamic sects are frequently involved in interfaith council and dialogue. Most liberal and contemporary Islamic sects desire to portray their religion in a positive light, detracting from the negative media attention it often receives. More conservative sects refrain from such interaction and emphasize religious purity. Due to the 1948 Jewish takeover of Palestine, many conservative Muslims avoid dialogue with Jews. There is particular animosity between conservative and traditional Muslims with Jews, although liberal Muslim groups have worked to foster communication and partnerships between the two.

The Temple Mount, Jerusalem, Israel

HOLY SITES

Mecca (especially the Kaaba) and Medina (especially the Prophet's Mosque) (both located in Saudi Arabia) are the holiest cities of Islam. The Al-Aqsa Mosque in Jerusalem is also held in a high regard. Some other important places are the Umayyad Mosque in Damascus, Syria; the Great Mosque of Kairouan in Kairouan, Tunisia; the Sanctuary of Abraham in Hebron, Palestine; and the Eyup district in Istanbul, Turkey.

NOTABLE FIGURES

The Prophet Mohammed (c. 570-632), founder of Islam; Al-Ashari (873-936), Islamic theologian; Al-Hallaj (858-922), Sufi Muslim; Rumi (1207-1273), Sufi poet; Yasir Arafat (1929-2004), former Prime Minister of Palestine; Sadaam Hussein (1937-2006), former leader of Iraq; Dave Chapelle 1973-), comedian; Iman (1955-), supermodel; Bella Hadid (1996-), fashion model; Akon (1973-), musician; DJ Khaled (1975-), musician; Malcom X (1925-1965), activist; Lewis Arquette (1935-2001), actor; Sadullah Khan, scholar; Muhammad Ali (1942-2016), athlete; Mike Tyson (1966-), athlete; Kareem Abdul-Jabbar (1947-), athlete; Shaquille O'Neal (1972-), athlete and actor; Ahmad Rashad (1949-), sportscaster; Mehemet Oz (1960-), television personality; Reza Aslan (1972-), author; Fareed Zakaria (1964-), author and political commentator.

Notable Groups

The Ahmadiyya Muslim Community is a messianic-based Islamic movement founded in British India in the late 1800s. Mirza Ghulam Ahmad (1835-1908) claimed to be the promised *mahadi* and Messiah, heralding peace in the end times as the final promise of Islam. This movement expanded its understanding to also teach its founder was the promised "messiah" or "coming one" of other world religions, as well. It considers itself to be the proper Islamic restoration and the original beliefs of the Muslim community. It adheres to the five pillars of Islam and the six articles of faith. It does deviate from standard Islam in a few ways, namely a total reconciliation between faith and science, a total rejection of all terrorism and terrorist activities, the Qur'an does not contradict itself, and history is cyclical, renewing every seven thousand years. The movement stands highly united.

Facts and Figures

About 24% of the world's population is Muslim. Western Europe accounts for approximately 6% of the total population, due to Muslim migration. The largest Muslim populations are found in South Asia.[18]

Other Important Definitions

- **Caliph**: The chief Muslim ruler, usually in both a civil and religious context. Caliphs are regarded as successors of the Prophet Mohammed.

- **Salaam**: Arabic word for "peace." Often used as a greeting.

- ***Assalaamu Alaikum***: Arabic term for "Peace be upon you." Often used as a greeting.

- **Ayatollah**: The term for a Muslim Shi'ite spiritual leader.

- **Fatwa**: An Islamic legal edict.

- ***Kafir***: An unbeliever; a person who refuses to submit themselves to Allah, under the religion of Islam.

- ***Murtad***: Means "apostate;" an individual who has left Islam to convert to another religion.

- ***'Abd* or *'Amah***: Means "servant" or "worshiper;" another term for a Muslim.

- ***Qamar***: Arabic term for the moon.

- ***Qira-at***: The reading of prayers.

- ***Shams***: Arabic word for the sun.

- ***Tawheed***: Muslim term for unity.

BELIEVER'S CHARACTERISTICS

Identifies as a Muslim; prays five times daily; adheres to the six pillars of Islam; lives by and adheres to the Qur'an; attends a Mosque; emphasis on purity, obligation, and living ethically and rightly; Muslim political view; belief in the prophets and holy books of Islam; wearing of scarf or head covering; emphasis on right teaching, following precepts; pilgrimages to Mecca or other Muslim holy sites; observance of Ramadan and other Muslim holidays; knowledge of sharia law; following halal; hadith traditions; belief in the Day of Judgment and the specifications of Muslim afterlife; waiting for the promised one to usher peace; adherence to Islamic morality and representation of its holiness.

JAINISM

Some foolish men declare that creator made the world. The doctrine that the world was created is ill advised and should be rejected. If God created the world, where was he before the creation? If you say he was transcendent then and needed no support, where is he now? How could God have made this world without any raw material? If you say that he made this first, and then the world, you are faced with an endless regression. If you declare that this raw material arose naturally you fall into another fallacy, For the whole universe might thus have been its own creator, and have arisen quite naturally. If God created the world by an act of his own will, without any raw material, then it is just his will and nothing else — and who will believe this silly nonsense? If he is ever perfect and complete, how could the will to create have arisen in him? If, on the other hand, he is not perfect, he could no more create the universe than a potter could. If he is form-less, action-less and all-embracing, how could he have created the world? Such a soul, devoid of all morality, would have no desire to create anything. If he is perfect, he does not strive for the three aims of man, so what advantage would he gain by creating the universe? If you say that he created to no purpose because it was his nature to do so, then God is pointless. If he created in some kind of sport, it was the sport of a foolish child, leading to trouble. If he created because of the karma of embodied beings [acquired in a previous creation] He is not the Almighty Lord, but subordinate to something else.
(Jinasena Mahapurana)[1]

THEOLOGY

The theology of Jainism is described as transtheistic: it believes any sort of theology is beyond the practitioner's comprehension and is neither atheistic nor theistic. Jainism believes that gods do exist but sees the position of gods or a god as irrelevant considering *moksha*. *Moksha* is the idea of liberation from states of reincarnation and the attainment of ultimate spiritual enlightenment. Along with the idea of spiritual evolution, Jainism also teaches the universe evolves: both parallel (with no interaction between events) and interactional (with the overlap of mind and matter and the way these two interact). The universe consists of six substances, all seen as eternal: souls (*jiva*), non-being substance (*pudgala*), motion (dharma), rest (*adharma*), space (*akasa*), and time (*kala*).

Within Jainism, there are 24 different leaders known as *tirthankaras* (sometimes as *arihants* or *jinas*), living between millions of years ago (beginning with Lord Rishabhanatha) and ending in 500 BC (Mahavira). These leaders are seen as the gods of Jainism: as individuals who were born human but were able to attain enlightenment and perfection as they followed certain principles pertaining to self-awareness and meditation. In so doing, it was the work of the tirthankaras to establish the four-fold orders of their religion: monk, nun, layman, and laywoman.

The *tirthankaras* are represented by 24 specific idols in every Jain temple, all throughout the world. These are seen as representations of the characteristics and qualities of these teachers, with unique symbols and identities to represent them.

After the tirthankaras, there were twelve world conquerors (*cakravartins*), nine counterparts of Vasuedva, who is related to Krishna (*vasudevas*), and nine counterparts of Balarama, the elder half-brother of Krishna (*baladevas*). Combined, these are the 54 great souls (*mahapurusas*). There are also nine counterparts to the deity between gods and humans known as *Narada* (*naradas*), eleven counterparts of Rudra, a Vedic god (rudras), and twenty-four gods of love (*kamadevas*). Jains recognize four groups of gods, all assimilated from Indian folk culture: gods of the house (*bhavanavasis*), intermediaries (*vyantaras*), luminaries (*jyotiskas*), and astral gods (*vaimanikas*).[2,3]

PHILOSOPHY

Jainism (traditionally known as Jain Dharma) seeks to find ultimate spiritual liberation for one's soul, ending the cycle of reincarnation in this life. For Jains, the soul is a self-evident reality, one that does not need to be proven because it exists through consciousness (*caitanya*), bliss (*sukha*), and energy (*virya*). This path to liberation comes through the major ideas present within their religious system:

- **Non-violence (*ahimsa*)**: The abandonment of all violent activity in all forms, no matter how justified it may seem to be. Jainism upholds, to the fullest extent, never killing another living being, seeing this as the highest religious duty. As a result, Jains are lacto-vegetarian (they eat no meat, fish, or eggs, but will eat dairy products if the dairy is ethically produced).

- **Many-sided reality (many-sided truth) (*anekantavada*)**: The idea that both truth and reality are complex, complicated, and have many different aspects or sides to them. It is believed ultimate reality and truth cannot be expressed in its entirety through the limitations of human language. Humans, therefore, only come to partial truth, rather than full truth. The gravest error is to believe relative truth is absolute. Truth, whenever it is spoken, is to be done without harm.

- **Non-attachment (*aparigraha*)**: The concept of non-attachment is to devoid oneself of materialism (attachment to worldly objects or possessions). Practitioners are encouraged to embrace the idea of limited property, giving excess to charity. Monks and nuns in Jainism take vows pledging to never own property, relationships, or harbor any specific attachment to their personal emotions.

- **Abstaining from sensual pleasure (asceticism)**: Also considered chastity. An extreme example of an austere religion (representing the strictest ascetic tradition in all of India), Jainism believes there are six inner and six outer ascetic practices that relate to fasting, eating restricted items, not eating foods that are considered enjoyable, guarding oneself from temptation, confession, study, meditation, and ignoring the desires of the body. Through asceticism, Jain adherents believe the soul is purified.[4]

The word "Jainism" is from a Sanskrit term that literally means "to conquer." It is through these different beliefs and principles that Jains believe they overcome the sensory experiences and passions of this life to gain ultimate enlightenment, thus finding themselves in a purity of soul. Those who reach this state are known as *Jina* (conquerors). Adherents of the religion devote themselves to their rituals: daily prayer, meditation, devotion to their deities, following their leaders, practicing asceticism, and detaching from the material world.[5]

Statue in a Jain temple

ADHERENT IDENTITY

Jainism, Jain.

NUMBER OF ADHERENTS

There are approximately 6,000,000 Jains worldwide. Most Jain adherents are found in India, although the religion is also found in Commonwealth nations, the United States, and Japan.[6]

TRADITIONAL LANGUAGES

Jain Prakrit, Sanskrit, Marathi, Tamil, Rajasthani, Dhundari, Marwari, Hindi, Gujarati, Kannada, Malayalam, and Tulu. In modern times, Jains also feature writings in English.

SECTS/DIVISIONS

There are two main divisions, sometimes called denominations, of Jainism: Digambara and Svetambara.

- **Digambara ("sky-clad")**: This sect embraces monastic practice. Male monks reject clothing (female nuns do wear clothing). Idol representations are also nude, usually standing or in the yoga lotus position. Monks are prohibited from owning any material goods and carry a community-owned broom used to sweep away insects before they sit down, thus saving their lives. Many of the practices and lineages trace back to the last *tirthankara*, Mahavira (c. 599 BC-c. 527 BC or 425 BC) himself, including a line of approximately twelve teachers who descended from Mahavira. This group rejects the scriptural writings of the Svetambara sect, believing the words of Mahavira were never recorded and do not survive to modern times. They embrace no scriptural canon of works and instead have literary writings: first the Satkhandagama and Kasayapahuda (discuss the soul and karma) and the Expositions (*Anuyoga*) focusing on history, cosmology, proper behavior, and metaphysics. Digambaras believe once reaches a state of omniscience (*kevala jnana*) (enlightenment), human beings no longer have the basic needs of food, water, or sleep. There are various Digambara sects: Terapanthi, Bispanthi, Taranpathi, Gumanapanthi, and Totapanthi. The differences relate to specified offerings made as part of worship (such as water, sandal, rice, dry coconut, cloves, and almonds versus flowers and fruits), and the minor deities a sect may worship.[7]

- **Svetambara ("white clad")**: In this sect, their monks wear white garments instead of going naked. The Svetambara also believe they are the original followers of Mahavira, believing the Digambaras arose later in time over an authority dispute. The foundations of practice vary in dress, restraints, marriage among their central teachers. The monastic rules of Svetambara are more relaxed than those in Digambara. They also embrace a scriptural canon rejected by the Digambara sect. Approximately four-fifths of all Jains are Svetambara in practice. There are many smaller Svetambara sects, including the mjrtipujakas, terepanthis, and Sthanakavasi orders.[8]

DISPUTES WITHIN GROUP

The major divisions between the Svetambaras and Diagmbaras sects relate to lineage. From this point, the two groups have developed differing traditions. Both groups claim to be the true disciples of Mahavira, believing the other sect is a deviation in error to the true ways of practice. The sects disagree on scriptural traditions, practices for monks and nuns, dress codes, whether their final two teachers were married or unmarried, the posture their leaders adopted when enlightened, the iconography of their leaders, and that men are closer to enlightenment than women are (for a woman to achieve enlightenment, Digambaras believe she must first be reincarnated as a man). These disagreements have led to considerable disunity among Jains throughout the years, and several theological and philosophical arguments.

SCRIPTURES

The two major sects of Jainism embrace different attitudes about scripture and scriptural canon. The Svetambara embrace a full scriptural canon, believing the words of Mahavira did survive and were recorded. These Agamas are written down verbal transmissions of sermons first proclaimed by the tirthankaras. The Svetambara sect has preserved approximately forty-five of these original scriptures, although all Jain scriptures have additional commentaries and revisions added to them. There are eleven Angas (primary texts consisting of the dialogues between Mahavira and his disciple Indrabhuti Gautama), twelve Upangas (secondary texts), four Mula-sutras (basic texts), six Cheda-sutras (discipline texts), two Chulika sutras (appendix texts), and ten Prakirnakas (assorted texts).

The Digambaras sect rejects the idea that there is such a thing as scripture within the Jain tradition. To them, there was no preservation of Mahavira's teachings, and such is lost. The canon of Svetambara scripture is seen as counterfeit. Digambaras do embrace their own writings, including the Satkhandagama (Scripture of Six Parts) and Kasayapahuda (Treatise on the Passions), which were believed to be inscribed on palm leaves as a record of Dharasena, who was able to teach other disciples about Mahavira almost seven hundred years after his enlightenment. These are the two oldest Digambara writings, treatises on the soul and the theory of karma. Outside of these works are four categories of literature, known as exposition (*anuyoga*): the first exposition (*prathmanuyoga*) is devoted to history; calculation exposition (*karananuyoga*) is about cosmology; behavior exposition (*charananuyoga*) is about proper conduct for monks and laity; and the entity exposition (*dravyanuyoga*) is about metaphysics. The primary text is the first exposition, universally studied, revered, and cherished.[9]

> *Attachment and aversion are the root cause of karma, and karma originates from infatuation. Karma is the root cause of birth and death, and these are said to be the source of misery. None can escape the effect of their own past karma.*[10]

Within both sects of Jainism, we find considerable revelation. All is non-canonical. Among the Svetambaras is the Kalpa Sutras (biographies of Parshvanatha and Mahavira), and among Digambaras, it is the texts of Kundakunda (a monk from the second century who authored the Samayasara, Niyamascara, Pancastikayasara, Pravachanasara, Astapahuda and Barasanuvekkha). Both traditions regard the Niryuktis (authored by Bhadrabahu III), Samhitas (mantras and benedictions), and the Tuattvarthasutra (ancient text written by Acharya Umaswami about the nature of reality) as relevant.[11]

> *In that night in which the Venerable Ascetic Mahavira was born, there was a divine lustre originated by many descending and ascending gods and goddesses, and in the universe, resplendent with one light, the conflux of gods occasioned great confusion and noise.*
>
> *In that night in which the Venerable Ascetic Mahavira was born, many demons in Vaisramana's service belonging to the animal world, rained down on the palace of king Siddhartha one great shower of silver, gold, diamonds, clothes, ornaments, leaves, flowers, fruits, seeds, garlands, perfumes, sandal, powder, and riches.*
>
> *After the Bhavanapati, Vyantara, Gyotishka, and Vaimanika gods had celebrated the feast of the inauguration of the Tirthakara's birthday, the Kshatriya Siddhartha called, at the break of the morning, together tht: [sic] town policemen and addressed them thus:*
>
> *'O beloved of the gods, quickly set free all prisoners in the town of Kundapura, increase measures and weights, give order that the whole town of Kundapura with its suburbs be sprinkled with water, swept, and smeared (with cowdung) that in triangular places, in places where three or four roads meet, in courtyards, in squares, and in thoroughfares, the middle of the road and the path along the shops be sprinkled, cleaned, and swept; that platforms be erected one above the other; that the town be decorated with variously coloured flags and banners, and adorned with painted pavilions; that the walls bear impressions in Gosirsha, fresh red sandal, and Dardara [sandal from Dardara] of the hand with outstretched fingers; that luck-foreboding vases be put on the floor, and pots of the same kind be disposed round every door and arch; that big, round, and long garlands, wreaths, and festoons be hung low and high; that the town be furnished with offerings, (see 32, down to) smelling box; that players, dancers, rope-dancers, wrestlers, boxers, jesters, story-telling ballad-singers, actors, messengers, pole-dancers, fruit-mongers, bag-pipers, lute-players, and many Talakaras [those who by clapping the hands beat the time during the performance of music]*

be present. Erect and order to erect thousands of pillars and poles, and report on the execution of my orders.'

When the family servants were thus spoken to by king Siddhartha, they-glad, pleased, and joyful, (see 3 58)-accepted the words of command, saying, 'Yes, master!'[12]

Bowing down my head, I pay my reverence to the Sthavira Gambu of The Gautama gotra, who possessed steady virtue, good conduct, and knowledge.

I prostrate myself before the Sthavara Nandita, of Kasyapa gotra, who is possessed of great clemency and of knowledge, intuition, and good conduct.

The Tirthankaras

Then I adore the Kshamasramana Desiganin of the Kasyapa gotra, who, steady in his conduct, possesses. the highest righteousness and virtue.

Then I prostrate myself before the Kshamaramama Sthiragupta of the Vatsya gotra, the preserver of the sacred lore, the wise one, the ocean of wisdom, him of great virtue.

Then I adore the Sthavira prince, Dharma, the virtuous Ganin, who stands well in knowledge, intuition, good conduct, and penance, and is rich in virtues.

I revere the Kshamasramama Devarddhi of the Kasyapa gotra, who wears, as it were, the jewel of the right understanding of the Sutras, and possesses the virtues of patience, self-restraint, and clemency.[13]

Basic Religious Practices

Jains believe their goal of liberation is achieved by embracing strong ideas about ascetism, which is practiced daily in different ways depending on whether one is a part of Jain monasticism or laity. Monasticism is primary in the religion, which consists of orders of male ascetics (sadhu), and female ascetics *(sadvhi)*. Next in line are laymen (*sravaka*) and laywomen (*sravika*). It is the job of lay people to support the monastics, who solely devote themselves to the ways of Jainism unto ultimate enlightenment.

Jainism also encourages essential fasting, especially during festivals (known as *upavasa*, *tapasya*, or *vrata*). The way one desires to fast is up to personal health and discretion, but many adopt the dietary practices of monks and nuns during festivals. In addition to the usual vegetarianism of Jains, they also avoid root vegetables (potatoes, onions, and garlic), drink only boiled water, and avoid eating after sunset, or only eat once or twice per day. Among laity, fasting is often performed by women because it is believed to provide spiritual well-being for her family.[14]

Meditation is a necessary practice among Jains, focused to stop the effects and activities of karma. Through meditation, one focuses and concentrates intermittently, in a practice known as *samayika*. Its goal is to ritually restrain oneself, bringing the work of spiritual discipline into meditative practice. Along with this, Jains are encouraged to ritual worship and charity work.

The Jain's house of worship is a Jain temple, also known as a *Derasar* or *Basadi*, depending on location. Here, Jains make offerings to their gods, recite prayers and litanies, and on occasion, engage in more elaborate rituals (involving additional food or money) and recite Jain texts before leaving. Honoring deities in the temple is key for a Jain practitioner, who may also engage in ritual ceremonial bath (*abhisheka*) of images or idols.

The ethics of Jain householders require them to follow 12 different vows. While there is no prohibition on family life in Jainism, being married with a family is seen as a complication, especially when it comes to following the twelve vows. The first five are limited (*Anuvratas*) but are easier to follow next to the great vows (*Maha-vratas*). The first five are the basic philosophy of Jainism: non-violence, truthfulness, non-covetousness, chastity, and non-attachment. The great vows are specifically for ascetics and are a deliberate challenge for the Jain to follow. The three that follow are known as merit vows (*Guna-vratas*), because they enhance and cleanse the effect of the five main vows. These are Limited area of activity (*Dik vrata*), limited use of consumable and non-consumable items (*Bhoga-Upbhoga* Vrata), and avoidance of purposeless sins (*anartha-danda vrata*). The last four are known as disciplinary vows (*Shikhsa-vratas*), which relate to one's work in religious duties. These are Meditation vow of limited duration (*Samayik vrata*), activity vow of limiting space (*desavakakasika vrata*), ascetic's life vow of limited duration (*pausadha vrata*), and limited charity vow (*Atithi Samvibhaga Vrata*). These different vows relate to the way a Jain interacts spiritually, with the world, engaging in charitable acts to those who are part of Jain monastic life, and hopefully, by performing these tasks, advancing toward a fuller life that is noted by righteousness and the conquer of desire.[15]

HOLIDAYS

Jain holidays and festivals largely revolve around the *thirthinkaras* of the faith (births, deaths, and important milestones). Participation in festivals and holidays are optional, and not every Jain or Jain sect observes holidays in the same exact way. Fasting, meditation, recitation, and prayer are common elements of Jain holidays.[16]

- **Mahavir Jayanti**: The celebration of the birth of Mahavira (March or April).

- **Akshaya Tritiya**: Honors the first *thirthankara*, Risabhanatha, who broke a long fast with the drink of sugar cane juice received from Prince Sreyamskumar. A day of fast and pilgrimage; participants often vow to abstain from unboiled water throughout their lives and are rewarded with sugar cane juice (April or May).

- **Paryushana**: The most important annual event for Jains, this feast is designed to push Jain adherents toward their highest spiritual aspirations through fasting, prayer, and meditation. It is a symbolic cleansing that is designed to remove negative karma from one's life. There is no specified way to celebrate this feast, and participants are encouraged to focus on the five main vows throughout. Digambara Jains recite ten chapters of the *Tattvartha Sutra* during the ten-day fast and then celebrate *Anata Chaturdashi* (the day when Lord Vasuoujya attains nirvana) at conclusion, usually with a procession to the Jain temple. Both Digambaras and Sravakas end the festival with Samvatsari, the festival of forgiveness, by requesting forgives for offenses (August or September).[17]

- **Bhai Beej**: The Festival of Brothers, much like the Hindu festival Raksha Bandhan. The natural brother of Mahavir was sad when his brother attained nirvana, so his sister Sudarshana took him to her home as a comfort. This festival celebrates siblings, especially the relationship between brothers and sisters (October 25).

- **Diwali**: An Indian festival with roots in Hinduism, Diwali is the annual festival of lights. It is considered the day in Jainism when Mahavira achieved nirvana. The beginning of the new business year for Jains, when new accounts are opened and old accounts are settled. Some Jains buy new account books and worship them along with Lakshmi and other possessions in ceremony. Hymns, meditation, and fasting are common on this day (October or November).

- **Jnan Panchami**: The "worship of pure knowledge," held five days after Diwali. A celebration of the Agamas, the Jain scriptures (October or November).

- **Lokashah Jayanti**: A celebration of scholarship devoted to Lonka Shah, who is attributed as founder of the Sthanakvasi sect of Jainism (October or November).

Visual Signs and Symbols

Swastika (on straight edge sides, not turned, as in Nazism); Hand with a wheel on the palm; Jain flag (red, yellow, white, green, and black stripes with the swastika in the middle); OM symbol; *Ashtmangala* (eight symbols: Parasol, *Dhvahja*, *Kalasha* [metal pot that can hold a coconut], fly-whisk, mirror, chair, hand fan, vessel, or swastika; *Srivasta*, *nandavarta*, *vhardmanaka* [food vessel], *bhadrasana* [seat], *kalasha*, *darpan* [mirror], and pair of fish; Ashoka Tree.

परस्परोपग्रहो जीवानाम्

Jain symbol

Creeds, Books, and Laws

Jainism is a non-credo religion. The way each Jain approaches their vows and religious commitment varies and is assessed by each practitioner. Its three guiding principles are: Right belief, right knowledge, and right conduct. Though not a creed, these guiding ideas summarize what a Jain believer is to accomplish and believe as part of their practice of spiritual vows.

Jain law is, in modern times, the interpretation of ancient Jain law. Its purpose is to govern rules that apply to Jain individuals, not just as a religious guideline, but as citizens within a cultural context. Jain law extends to adoption, marriage, inheritance, death, and purity. When India was under British rule, Jain monks and nuns would hide their lawbooks from British authorities, to maintain their sanctity and purity.[18]

In addition to law and writings that regulate Jain life, Jainism embraces a history of extensive literature, especially in the areas of philosophy, poetry, drama, literary grammar and composition, mathematics, music, medicine, astronomy and astrology, and architecture. The oldest piece of high poetic literature was authored by Pampa, a Jain poet.[19]

ECLECTIC BELIEFS

Jainism is known internationally as a peace-loving religion, one that strives for nonviolence and abstaining from harm. This pursuit of nonviolence means Jains do not pursue certain professions: they have traditionally worked in textiles, jewelry, and finance. In modern times, Jains pursue work in technology and medicine, as well.

Jainism holds to a complex theory of knowledge, believing there are two types of knowledge: immediate (*aparoksa*) and mediate (*paroska*). Between these two headings, there are five types of knowledge, classified as "right knowledge." The three headings of immediate knowledge are clairvoyance (*avadhi*), telepathy (*manahparyaya*), and omniscience (*kevala*). The two headings of mediate knowledge are cognition based on sensory perception (mati), and knowledge that one gets through a word, a sign, or a symbol (*shruta* or *sruti*). One can know a thing as it is (*pramana*) or the way it relates to something else (*naya*). There are also three types of wrong knowledge: doubt (*samshaya*), mistake (*viparyaya*) and indifference (*anadhyavasaya*).[20,21]

RELATIONS WITH NON-JAINS

Jainism holds a close connection to the religions of India, especially Hinduism and Buddhism. All three religions have influenced and overlapped with one another in different ways, especially given their antiquity and development. As a peace-loving people, Jains do not prohibit dialogue or activity with people of other religious groups, even though they may not always support their activities (such as those which would relate to violence).

Exterior of a Jain temple

HOLY SITES

Shravanabelagola, Karnataka, India; Dilwara Temples on Mount Abu, Rajasthan, India; Ranakpur Temples, Rajasthan, India; Palitana Jain temple, Gujarat; Bawangaja, Madhya Pradesh, India;

Gwailor's fort, Madhya Pradesh, India; Shikharji, Bihar, India; the bhagwan Adinath derasar at Vatman, Ahmedabad, India; Bajrangarth, Madhya Pradesh, India; Kundalpur, Madhya Pradesh, India; The Jain Centre, Leicester, England; Jain Center of Greater Boston, Norwood, Massachusetts; Siddhachalam, Blairstown, New Jersey; Jain Center of Northern California, Milpitas, California; Mahaveer Temple, Kobe, Japan; Shree Hong Kong Jain Sangh, Hong Kong.[22]

NOTABLE FIGURES

Anand Jain (1957-), businessman; Acharya Chandana (1937-), first female Jain Acharya; Naveen Jain (1959-), businessman; Sooraj Barjatya (1964-), film director; Harshad Chopda (1983-), actor; Abigail Jain (1992-), actress; Umang Jain (1995-), actress; Babla Virji Shah, musician; V. Shantaram (1901-1990), film maker; Phadeppa Dareppa Chaugule (1902-1958), athlete; Banarasidas (1586-1643), author; Padmanabh Jaini (1923-2021), professor; Champat Rai Jain (1867-1942), author; Vikram Sarabhai (1919-1971), scientist.

NOTABLE GROUPS

Within the Svetambara subheading are several newer groups that cover their mouth with a white cloth or a *muhapatti* (a specific white cloth worn over the mouth that attaches and hinges over the ears). The purpose in wearing the cloth is to practice non-violence, even when speaking. It is believed that by speaking, one can possibly inhale small living beings or creatures, and possibly kill them.[23]

FACTS AND FIGURES

Outside of India, Jainism is spreading at a high rate in Japan. At current, more than 5,000 adherents have converted to Jainism. There are also significant Jain communities in Europe, the United Kingdom, the United States, Canada, Australia, and Kenya.[24]

OTHER IMPORTANT DEFINITIONS[25]

- ***Anuvrata***: The five main vows of Jains.
- ***Asrava***: The flow of karma.
- ***Bandh***: Bondage by karma; also known as the darkness of the soul.
- ***Bhoga***: Edible items that can be enjoyed multiple times, such as food and drink.
- ***Kaal***: Also *samay*. Time.
- ***Brahmacharya***: Also *Savvao Mehunano Virman Vrat*. A vow of celibacy or chastity taken by both monastic or nonmonastic Jains.

- ***Kashay***. Inner enemies.
- ***Rag***. Attachment
- ***Upbhoga***. Non-edible items that can be enjoyed more than once, such as clothing, furniture, or decorations.

Believer's Characteristics

Focus on asceticism; strict guidelines for purity, fasting, ritual, and conduct; emphasis on seven vows; belief in personal responsibility, especially the context of nonviolence; devotion to discovering spiritual liberation; detaching from material goods and worldly attachments; meditation; offerings brought to the Jain temple; devotion to the tirthankaras; vegetarianism; orders of monks and nuns along with laypeople; transtheism; belief in karma and cycles of rebirth; belief the universe is eternal, and without creation; the belief in that knowledge and truth are multi-sided; focus on Jain ethics; fasting; ritual worship; use of Jain symbols and idols.

JEHOVAH'S WITNESSES

In your heart, you may want to worship God acceptably. If so, you must have Jehovah's view of worship...With a desire to please God, each of us needs to examine our worship to make sure that it is not contaminated by ungodly practices or that we are not omitting something that he considers vital.
(From *Knowledge that Leads to Everlasting Life*)[1]

THEOLOGY

Belief in one true literal God, referred to as JEHOVAH, with personal attributes. Jehovah's throne was traditionally taught to exist in the Pleiades constellation. Jehovah's Witnesses believe in a non-Trinitarian, literal monotheism. It varies from Unitarianism; while they do see Jehovah, Jesus Christ, and holy spirit as separate entities and reject the divinity of Jesus Christ and holy spirit, Jehovah's Witnesses doctrine varies considerably on other points of theology (including issues of universal salvation, original sin, and Biblical infallibility).

Jehovah's Witnesses believe Jehovah is the literal name of their deity, hidden and altered for generations, now known and hallowed today. Jehovah is creator of the universe, sustainer of the people who follow him, and the direct ruling leader of Jehovah's Witnesses. Through the concept of divine guidance, Jehovah leads the body of Jehovah's Witnesses through the Governing Body (the chief ruling council of the group). The only true deity, Jehovah is the sole sovereign, literally one in nature, and the only one in existence who should be worshiped.

Jesus Christ is seen as the "unique" or "only begotten" son of Jehovah. In his pre-existing state, he existed in heaven as the Archangel Michael. He is also known as Abaddon, Apollyon, and the Word. Jesus Christ is the direct creation of Jehovah; all other aspects of creation exist through the work of Jesus Christ by Jehovah's power. Salvation is possible only through Jesus Christ. As part of his role, Christ is seen as a mediator, specifically for a special group of Jehovah's Witnesses known as the "little flock" or "anointed class." This is a special group of 144,000 people who are the only ones who will receive full salvation and rule with Christ in heaven upon their death.

"Holy spirit" is a term applied to the active force, or power, of Jehovah, rather than a separate person or being. Jehovah's Witnesses do not believe holy spirit has independent animation or personality, but is a general energy, impersonal in nature, sent at any place at any time to accomplish the full will of Jehovah.[1]

PHILOSOPHY

First influenced by the teachings of Charles Taze Russell (1852-1916) who was prominently influenced by Adventism (the belief that the return of Jesus Christ is imminent) among other ideas, Jehovah's Witnesses see time as we understand it divided into three dispensations and then subdivided into ages: the First Dispensation (from creation to the flood, lasting 1,656 years); the Second Dispensation, known as the "present evil world" (containing the Patriarchal Age, the Jewish Age from the death of Jacob to the end of Daniel's seventy weeks, the Gospel Age from Jesus' baptism to the completion of the church, and then a harvest overlap with the Third Dispensation); and the Third Dispensation, or the fullness of times (covering a harvest period, the Messianic Age with the reign of Christ, and the Ages to Come). Today, they see themselves as living and proclaiming the truth during the "end of the system," a time that began in 1914 with the official invisible rule of Christ from heaven, known as the "Parousia."

Charles Taze Russell (1852-1916)

Their identity centers around the belief that standing in this present evil world, under the invisible rule of Christ, Jehovah's Witnesses are Jehovah's true people, His true Bible students. They believe they alone have the true teaching, directly led by Jehovah for their teaching and instruction. They stand as the "friends of God," the majority of which wait for the end of the present age when they shall live forever on earth following Armageddon. The "anointed class" of one hundred forty-four thousand shall live eternally in heaven and rule with Christ. Those who are not Jehovah's Witnesses at that time will not be spared and shall face annihilation. Therefore, they undertake massive evangelism efforts (including door-to-door witnessing), so as many as possible may hear and become Jehovah's Witnesses. Preoccupied with this coming battle, they have predicted the end of the world, cataclysmic events, or a massive conclusion to their predictions approximately nineteen times, with membership peaking prior to the prediction years, then sharply declining thereafter.

Jehovah's Witnesses believe they are the true kingdom of Jehovah (also called kingdom of God), maintaining a theocratic theme in their governance and identity. They see themselves as the fulfillment of a long line of "witnesses," beginning with Abel and spanning through to the present time. Central to their Bible interpretation is this kingdom-theme, which is seen as literal, organizational through the governance of the Watchtower, and equating to the method of implemented structure, movement, conduct, presentation, and distribution of those who represent and proclaim their message.

ADHERENT IDENTITY

Jehovah's Witnesses, Witnesses, Russellites, Bible Students, Watchtower Bible and Tract Society, Watchtower Students, Watchtower Society (called "the Society," God's Organization by Jehovah's Witnesses, and "the Faithful and Discreet Slave" within the organization).

TRADITIONAL LANGUAGES

English.

SECTS/DIVISIONS

The history of Jehovah's Witnesses is a divided one, with numerous fractions and issues. The movement's founder, Charles Taze Russell, was influenced by Christian Adventism, pyramidology (the belief that the pyramids of Egypt contain a message, or charting, of some specific event), Freemasonry and occultism. His teaching is best known through the six-volume work now known as *Studies in the Scriptures* (previously known as *Millennial Dawn*). Russell established the first community of individuals (known as Bible Students) and Zion's Watch Tower Tract Society for the publication of his literature. He first predicted the "end of the world" for the years 1878, 1881, 1914, 1918, and 1925. These years were reinterpreted to create the unique eschatology exclusive to descendants of Russell's doctrine. With the death of Russell in 1916, the movement split over interpretation of eschatological issues and leadership. Joseph Rutherford (1869-1942) assumed the leadership of the Watchtower Bible and Tract Society, whose association split with the International Bible Students Association, formally becoming Jehovah's Witnesses in 1925. The Watchtower Bible and Tract Society stopped publishing the literature of Charles Taze Russell in 1927. The remaining groups are collectively known by different identities, but all hold to the same history, basic tenants, and foundations as students of "Pastor Russell," as he remains known.[3]

- **Bible Students**: The collective group of "Bible Students" are independent associations, most of whom are in some way in fellowship with one another. These groups continue to uphold the teachings of Charles Taze Russell and print his books and literature, especially *Studies in the Scriptures*. Charles Taze Russell is still considered the pastor of these groups through his writings, which are often made available free or low-cost. They meet in small groups (sometimes in homes, sometimes in buildings) called Ecclesia, with singing of hymns recognized in the movement, studies of the Bible alongside those teachings of Pastor Russell, and are emphatic about lifestyle and dedication to their beliefs. Some Bible students include the International Bible Students Association, Dawn Bible Students Association, Berean Bible Institute, Free Bible Students, Berean Bible Students Church (New Covenant Believers), Christian Millennial Fellowship, Free Bible Students Association, Stand Fast Bible Students Association, Pastoral Bible Institute, the Laymen's Home Missionary Movement, Friends of Man, Friends of the Nazarene, Kitawala Movement, and the Elijah Voice Society.[4]

Bible Students logo

- **Theocratic Organization of Jehovah's Witnesses**: A Russian splinter organization that formed after the Watchtower began interpreting its doctrine about authority. They formed their own organization and stopped printing Watchtower literature, opting for their own in 1962. There is little information on this organization, as they do not have a prominent presence in the worldwide scene. They are present in Russia, Ukraine, and Moldova.[5]

- **God's Kingdom Society (GKS)**: Founded in 1934 in Nigeria by a former Jehovah's Witness named Gideon Urhobo (1903-1952), this specific splinter group's founder claims divine inspiration through a vision to begin his ministry. After receiving information from Jehovah's Witnesses, he ran into conflicts with Watchtower doctrine. They vary from Jehovah's Witnesses in rejecting the command to preach door-to-door, they use choirs and dance during meetings, and have special youth assemblies, conferences, and recognize ministers.[6]

- **Christian Witnesses of Jah**: A general grouping for individuals who believe the general doctrines of Jehovah's Witnesses but are not part of the Watchtower body.[7]

NUMBER OF ADHERENTS

There are approximately 8,400,000 Jehovah's Witnesses worldwide.[8]

DISPUTES WITHIN GROUP

Sect divisions are a result of authoritarian conflicts and doctrinal changes implemented by the Watchtower Bible and Tract Society. When the Watchtower opted for central leadership control, not all followers of Russell's theories accepted the changes. This became more and more relevant as doctrines changed, new ideas were implemented, and new predictions about the end of the world were made and failed to come to pass.

SCRIPTURES

The Holy Bible, both Old and New Testaments, known as the Holy Scriptures. Their Bibles are inclusive of 66 books: the Pentateuch (Genesis, Exodus, Leviticus, Numbers, and Deuteronomy), Historical books (Joshua, Judges, Ruth, 1 Samuel, 2 Samuel, 1 Kings, 2 Kings, 1 Chronicles, 2 Chronicles, Ezra, Nehemiah, Esther), Wisdom books (Job, Psalms, Proverbs, Ecclesiastes, Song of Songs), Prophetic books (Isaiah, Jeremiah, Lamentations, Ezekiel, Daniel, Hosea, Joel, Amos, Obadiah, Jonah, Micah, Nahum, Habakkuk, Zephaniah, Haggai, Zechariah, Malachi), the Gospels (Matthew, Mark, Luke, John), the Acts of the Apostles, the Pauline Epistles (Romans, 1 Corinthians, 2 Corinthians, Galatians, Ephesians, Philippians, Colossians, 1 Thessalonians, 2 Thessalonians, 1 Timothy, 2 Timothy, Titus, Philemon, Hebrews) the General Epistles (James, 1 Peter, 2 Peter, 1 John, 2 John, 3 John, Jude) and Revelation.

Jehovah's Witnesses are unique in their Bible usage in that they are the sole publishers, distributors, and users of *The New World Translation of the Holy Scriptures*. This version of the Bible was a Watchtower project, first released in 1950 under Watchtower President Nathan Knorr (1905-1977). It seeks to provide literal textual renderings through the interpretation and understanding of Watchtower doctrine. Highly controversial and criticized by many Bible scholars and historians as inaccurate and biased, *The New World Translation of the Holy Scriptures* is the official text used in Watchtower literature, for Jehovah's Witnesses in studies and in their own Bible devotional reading, and as their primary reference for Scriptural references. There have been several revisions to the text, resulting in rereleases of its contents in 1961, 1984, and most recently, in 2013.

> *In the beginning was the Word, and the Word was with God, and the Word was a god. This one was in the beginning with God.* (John 1:1-2, NWT 2013)[9]

> *Jesus said to them: "Most truly I say to you, before Abraham came into existence, I have been."* (John 8:58, NWT 2013)[10]

> *He is the image of the invisible God, the firstborn of all creation; because by means of him all other things were created in the heavens and on the earth, the things visible and the things invisible, whether they are thrones or lordships or governments or authorities. All other things have been created through him and for him. Also, he is before all other things, and by means of him all other things were made to exist, and he is the head of the body, the congregation. He is the beginning, the firstborn from the dead, so that he might become the one who is first in all things; because God was pleased to have all fullness to dwell in him, and through him to reconcile to himself all other things by making peace through the blood he shed on the torture stake, whether the things on the earth or the things in the heavens.* (Colossians 1:15-20, NWT 2013)[11]

The New World Translation of the Holy Scriptures is not the only Bible the Watchtower Society has ever published, nor is it the only one used or referenced by Jehovah's Witnesses today. Traditionally speaking, Bible students used the King James Version of the Bible. The American Standard Version (1901) was also a standard for its translation of the divine name as Jehovah. Other translations published by the Watchtower include *The Bible in Living English*, *The Emphatic Diaglott*, Holman Linear Parallel Edition, and Joseph B. Rotherham's *New Testament Critically Emphasized*. It is also not uncommon to see occasional references to modern translations of the Bible in their literature, such as the New Living Translation, New International Version, or Today's English Version.

Although Watchtower literature is not seen on the level of the Bible, it is considered the means of interpretation, understanding, and authority of its contents. In Jehovah's Witnesses public meetings, *The Watchtower* magazine has long been a staple in the dissemination of doctrine and teaching among Kingdom Halls (meeting places where Jehovah's Witnesses have studies, services, and events). There are two versions of *The Watchtower* magazine: a public edition, now printed three times per year (as of January 2018), and a study edition, for specific and exclusive use in Kingdom Halls. The public edition of *The Watchtower* is for literature promotion, handed out door-to-door or left in public for those interested in learning more about the religion. The study edition contains study articles, Watchtower doctrinal changes, and other essential information for Jehovah's Witnesses. All Kingdom Halls study the same articles each week from *The Watchtower* study edition and then discuss their contents. All articles in *The Watchtower* are published anonymously.[12]

BASIC RELIGIOUS PRACTICES

The basic practice of any Jehovah's Witness begins with their personal conversion to the faith. All Jehovah's Witnesses use the same method of Bible study preparation for membership. Potential members must prove themselves worthy of membership: aptitude in studies, willingness to go door-to-door, attendance at Kingdom Hall meetings, and alignment with Watchtower ethics and moral codes. Elders question individuals to determine if they've prepared for baptism, usually done during an assembly or convention via full immersion, following a public declaration to Jehovah and the Watchtower organization.

Each member of Jehovah's Witnesses sees themselves as part of the larger unit of "God's Organization," exclusively existing within Jehovah's Witnesses under Watchtower government. Their identity and existence, in every part of their lives, revolves around their identity in Jehovah's organization. Members attend multiple weekly meetings at Kingdom Halls focused exclusively on Watchtower doctrine, publications, and literature. These are closely timed and regulated according to specifications. There are two main worship services per week: Weekend Meeting, which consists of a thirty-minute public talk by a Kingdom Hall elder (male member who handles matters relating to the needs of members within an assigned territory) or other local or regional ministerial servant (assistant to the elders, akin to a deacon), followed immediately by a ninety-minute question and answer style study of a *The Watchtower* magazine (study edition) article; and a Midweek Meeting, usually held on a Wednesday evening (uses other Watchtower publications in the same question-and-answer format). There is also a section devoted to the "how tos" of presenting Watchtower literature while doing field work. There are also classes devoted to witnessing and door-to-door evangelization and many Kingdom Halls also hold book studies, featuring Watchtower books, written and handled in the same question-and-answer style. All services open and close with prayers spoken by an elder or congregation leader and hymns specifically written by and for Jehovah's Witnesses. Kingdom Hall services are open to the public, and no collections are taken (freewill offerings can be placed in an offering box in a private part of the hall). Meeting times and days can vary, depending on the location.

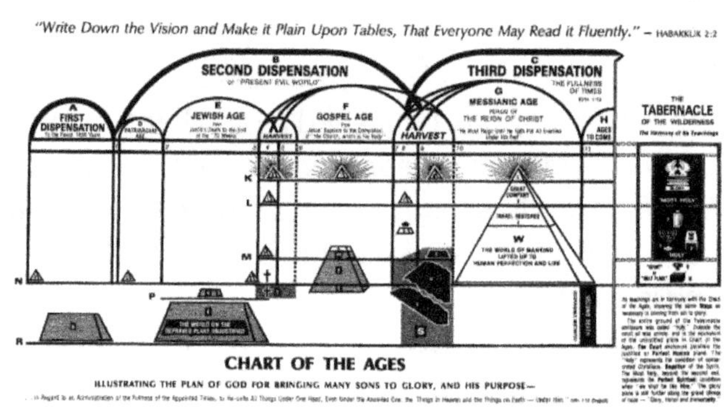

Chart of the Ages

Local Kingdom Halls are governed by a council of elders. None are paid, and there is no specific congregational leader. All baptized members of Jehovah's Witnesses are considered "ministers." All members of the Kingdom Hall are expected to assist in its maintenance, upkeep, and preparation for special events.

Much of a practicing Jehovah's Witness's free time is spent either preparing for door-to-door preaching or evangelizing (often called witnessing) or engaging in such. Jehovah's Witnesses are expected to witness Jehovah's Kingdom, as they believe the time is coming when the dead will rise (they are now asleep, awaiting this time) and all will face life on earth in a paradise, or complete annihilation (ceasing to exist). It is their hope that as many as possible will come to accept the doctrines and leadership of the Watchtower, so all can live forever in paradise on earth.

Jehovah's Witnesses are expected to abide by a high standard of moral rules and regulations. Adultery, sex outside of marriage, and homosexuality are considered very serious and forbidden. Abortion is also forbidden. Smoking, intoxication, and recreational or abuse of drugs in any form is prohibited. Attire is considered of prime example and representation, and members are expected to dress modestly, utilize proper grooming and hygiene habits, and present well when engaging in witness work. Entertainment seen as promoting values contrary to those of Jehovah's Witnesses is prohibited. Gambling is also prohibited.

Joseph Rutherford (1869-1942)

It is not a secret that Jehovah's Witnesses are often criticized or negatively portrayed by opposing groups, including accusations of cult or cult-like behavior in their organizational attitudes and structure. Jehovah's Witnesses see such criticism as a form of spiritual battle, attempting to stop or hinder their work of proclaiming Jehovah's kingdom.[13]

Holidays

Jehovah's Witnesses do not observe any conventional, patriotic, secular, or religious holidays. They also prohibit birthdays, citing pagan origin or person-worship. They do celebrate weddings, funerals, graduations, and anniversaries, with every effort made to remove any pagan traditions from those celebrations.

Their one yearly observance is the Memorial of the Lord's Death, corresponding to sundown at 14 Nisan. It is a recounting of the Last Supper, with a talk on the memorial itself. The elements of unleavened bread and wine are then presented to each member present in the group. No one partakes of those elements unless they are part of the "anointed class;" they are simply passed around and discarded if no one from that class is present to partake.

Jehovah's Witnesses are known for their different assemblies and conventions which draw together several Kingdom Halls across a larger area. These events give members the option to meet, fellowship, and provide opportunities for things such as baptism and young members to meet (hopefully to find a potential mate). Circuit Assemblies are smaller regional gatherings, while Regional Conventions are larger three-day events that consist of Bible teachings, reports of preaching work, education for door-to-door witnessing, and dramatic events on current issues or

Biblical events. There are also international conventions that feature visiting representatives from different countries.[14]

Visual Signs and Symbols

Watchtower symbol (top of a tower); *New World Translation of the Holy Scriptures*; "blood card," refusing blood transfusions; *The Watchtower: Announcing Jehovah's Kingdom* Magazine and *Awake!* Magazine; chart of the ages; Kingdom Halls; a blue box with the letters JW.org on it; Watchtower books or other literature.

Creeds, Books, and Laws

Jehovah's Witnesses are noted for their complex governance system, which is based on the existing relationship present between Jehovah's Witnesses and the Watchtower. It is not as simple to say Jehovah's Witnesses are governed by one specific regulatory book; they are governed by the organization that creates those books, and the leaders that create and disseminate the beliefs of that organization. Jehovah's Witnesses submit themselves to the Watchtower Bible and Tract Society, known to them as "God's Organization." All literature, books, regulations, and laws come down from the top, filtered down and executed through different functions. It is:

- **The Governing Body**: An all-male group of less than a dozen members that is believed to be anointed, part of the "little flock" preparing to spend eternity in heaven. This group is the only one seen as having active "holy spirit" by which to guide and lead the remainder of the congregation of Jehovah's Witnesses. They are not elected but are selected by the existing Governing Body membership.

- **Branch Offices**: Also known as "Bethel," each of the eighty-seven branch offices worldwide operate under the auspices of representatives coming from headquarters who audit, counsel, and report back to the Governing Body. These offices function thanks to the work of Bethel families, all of whom are volunteers (they take a vow of poverty and operate under the heading of a religious order) and produce and distribute Watchtower literature throughout a specific jurisdiction. They also communicate with specific Kingdom Hall congregations in their jurisdiction, especially for the establishment of committees, including those for hospital liaisons, assembly halls, regional building, and disaster relief. The United States branch office is seen as the International Branch Office headquarters.

- **Traveling Overseers**: Elders who serve as headquarters representatives and circuit overseers (individuals who oversee circuits of approximately twenty congregations, visiting each one for two weeks out of the year to meet specific needs, such as establishing new elders and working with congregation members). These elders receive specific training at the Watchtower's School for Traveling Overseers.

- **Congregations**: Groups of ten or more Jehovah's Witnesses divided by geography or language, meeting in Kingdom Halls. Congregations are assigned territories where all members reside and devote time to field service (witnessing) within that territory. To accomplish this, active Jehovah's Witnesses operate field service groups, overseen by a group overseer (elder) or group servant (a ministerial servant). Those who participate are required to provide a monthly report of activities to their Kingdom Hall, detailing their field service activity. Those who are part of this organized work are called publishers and are the only officially counted members of a congregation. Congregations are overseen by elders who handle the work of congregational leadership, organizing meetings, directing field service work, and creating specific committees for disciplinary actions. Ministerial servants (akin to the role of a deacon; provide and handle the Watchtower literature supply to a congregation, as well as the financials of the local hall) assist the work of the local elders. All are trained for their work within the Jehovah's Witnesses organization. Women are ineligible to serve as elders, only temporarily serving if there is no eligible baptized male to stand in as an elder. In such a situation, a woman is required to wear a head covering.

- **Baptized publishers**: Members who have been baptized as adults into the organization (only those baptized as Jehovah's Witnesses are considered valid). Divided into four different categories: Auxiliary pioneers who commit to fifty hours of field work per month; Regular pioneers, who commit to seventy hours of field work per month; special pioneers, who operate special projects that require at least one hundred thirty hours per month; and missionaries, who spend at least one hundred thirty hours per month of field work in a foreign country per month (graduates of Gilead School). An inactive publisher is a Jehovah's Witness who is not, for whatever reason, active in field service.

- **Unbaptized publishers, students, and associates are all individuals who are not yet members of Jehovah's Witnesses but are seen as in process to full membership**: Unbaptized publishers have applied to join the organization, students are in process for organization membership, and associates are individuals who attend Kingdom Hall meetings, but are not involved in membership.[15]

Jehovah's Witnesses are known for a doctrine often called "the light gets brighter." It is the way that the organization explains many of its contradictory and changing doctrines, embracing an idea that understanding and knowledge can be given for something over time, and that, as a result, the way something is understood or taught can change as the Governing Body comes to understand it differently. As a result, Jehovah's Witnesses are forbidden to read older literature, as their leadership claims it will not be in accord with current "light," and would be confusing to them.

Through *The Watchtower*, we can see the way "the light gets brighter" has been applied to doctrinal changes. For example:

- **The men of Sodom will not be resurrected (1952):** *Similarly, Sodom did not endure its judgment day, had failed completely, and the Jews knew its fate was sealed. Their opinion of Sodom was the lowest possible. So when Jesus told them that it would be more endurable for utterly depraved Sodom than for these Jewish cities they got the powerful point.*

  These Jewish cities had heard the warning and had seen powerful works; they had had their fair judgment trial and by their decision showed they were worthy of eternal destruction.[16]

- **The men of Sodom will be resurrected (1965)**: *Then the next verse refers to the Judgment Day, saying: "Consequently I say to you people, It will be more endurable for the land of Sodom on Judgment Day than for you." (Matt. 11:24) Similarly, at Matthew 10:15 are recorded Jesus' words: "Truly I say to you, It will be more endurable for the land of Sodom and Gomorrah on Judgment Day than for that city" where the people would reject the message carried by Jesus' disciples. For it to be "more endurable for the land of Sodom and Gomorrah" than for others, it would be necessary for former inhabitants of that land to be present on Judgment Day. It is not the literal land, the ground, that is to be judged. Revelation chapter 20 shows that it will be persons raised from the dead who will stand "before the throne." Nor will judgment be passed on them as groups, as former inhabitants of certain lands, but they will be "judged individually according to their deeds" during the time of judgment. So apparently individuals who used to live in that land will be resurrected.— Rev. 20:12, 13.*[17]

- **The men of Sodom will not be resurrected (1989)**: *Will such terribly wicked persons be resurrected during Judgment Day? The Scriptures indicate that apparently they will not. For example, one of Jesus' inspired disciples, Jude, wrote first about the angels that forsook their place in heaven to have relations with the daughters of men. Then he added: "So too Sodom and Gomorrah and the cities about them, after they in the same manner as the foregoing ones had committed fornication excessively and gone out after flesh for unnatural use, are placed before us as a warning example by undergoing the judicial punishment of everlasting fire." (Jude 6, 7; Genesis 6:1, 2) Yes, for their excessive immorality the people of Sodom and of the surrounding cities suffered a destruction from which they will apparently never be resurrected.—2 Peter 2:4-6, 9, 10a.*[18]

- **<u>Jesus is an Angel (1991)</u>**: *Jesus Christ further deserves honor because he is Jehovah's chief angel, or archangel. On what basis do we reach that conclusion? Well, the prefix "arch," meaning "chief" or "principal," implies that there is only one archangel. God's Word speaks of him in reference to the resurrected Lord Jesus Christ. We read: "The Lord himself will descend from heaven with a commanding call, with an archangel's voice and with God's trumpet, and those who are dead in union with Christ will rise first.*[19]

  <u>Jesus is not an Angel (1992)</u>: *God did not send some angel to rescue mankind. He made the supreme sacrifice of sending his only-begotten Son, "the one he was specially fond of".*[20]

Jehovah's Witnesses are also known for a complicated code of Biblical ethics, constantly changing, as interpreted by the Watchtower Society. While there are standards for discipline, many rules and guidelines are not properly enforced if a member is considered "repentant" or "in good standing." Such has come to light over the years as the organization refuses to report issues, such as sexual abuse of minors or statutory rape, to secular authorities. It is seen as perfectly acceptable for Jehovah's Witnesses to use deception or to hide certain aspects of Watchtower rules or conduct from non-members. There are also books that circulate within the organization, but non-members are prohibited from reading. One such book is *Organized to Accomplish our Ministry*, which contains the questions for baptism and study for life as a Jehovah's Witness.

The major book – disseminated to the public as well as among Jehovah's Witnesses – that summarizes the life and beliefs of Jehovah's Witnesses is *Knowledge That Leads to Everlasting Life*. It is used primarily for home Bible studies and covers their beliefs about the end of the world and life on earth, the Bible, their theological views, eschatology, salvation, regulations, family, spiritual warfare, and how one can serve God as a Jehovah's Witness.

ECLECTIC BELIEFS

Within the history of the organization, Jehovah's Witnesses were well-known for assorted predictive dates surrounding the end of the world. Through both statement and implication, those part of the Watchtower have predicted the end of the world at least nine different times: 1846, 1874, 1878, 1881, 1914, 1918, 1925, 1975, and 1989.

> *Our Lord, the appointed King, is now present since October 1874, A.D., according to the testimony of the prophets, to those who have ears to hear it: and the formal inauguration of his kingly office dates from April 1878, A.D.*[21]
>
> *The year A.D. 1878 ... clearly marks the time for the actual assuming of power as King of kings, by our present, spiritual, invisible Lord...*[22]
>
> *The great time of trouble such as never was since there was a nation, will reach its culmination.*[23]
>
> *Christendom, will have passed away, as already shown in prophecy.*[24]
>
> *Now, in view of recent labor troubles and threatened anarchy, our readers are writing to know if there may not be a mistake in the 1914 date. They do not see how present conditions can hold out so long under the strain. We see no reason for changing the figures - nor could we change them if we would. They are, we believe, God's dates, not ours. But bear in mind that the end of 1914 is not the date for the beginning, but for the end of the time of trouble.*[25]
>
> *We consider it an established truth that the final end of the kingdoms of this world, and the full establishment of the Kingdom of God, will be accomplished near the end of A.D. 1914.*[26]
>
> *October, 1914, will witness the full end of Babylon.*[27]
>
> *The deliverance of the saints must take place some time before 1914 is manifest.*[28]
>
> *The Day of Vengeance ... will end in October, 1914*[29]
>
> *But bear in mind that the end of 1914 is not the date for the beginning, but for the <u>end</u> of the time*

of trouble.[30]

This is the Golden Age of which the prophets prophesied and of which the Psalmist sang; and it is the privilege of the student of the divine Word today, by the eye of faith, to see that we are standing at the very portals of that blessed time! Let us look up and lift up our heads. Deliverance is at the door![31]

According to this trustworthy Bible chronology six thousand years from man's creation will end in 1975, and the seventh period of a thousand years of human history will begin in the fall of 1975. So six thousand years of man's existence on earth will soon be up, yes, within this generation. How appropriate it would be for Jehovah God to make of this coming seventh period of a thousand years a Sabbath period of rest and release, a great Jubilee sabbath for the proclaiming of liberty throughout the earth to all its inhabitants! ... It would be according to the loving purpose of Jehovah God for the reign of Jesus Christ, the "Lord of the Sabbath", to run parallel with the seventh millennium of man's existence.[32]

Jehovah's Witnesses are often known in modern times for their unconventional stance on matters of a medical and social nature. This is due to their emphasis on remaining separate from the world and focusing exclusively on witnessing in its varied forms. This has led to a complex social structure of conformity, required of those who adhere to the religion's spiritual and natural worldview. This conformity is seen in many different ways: identical, mandatory views on various issues, nearly identical-looking Kingdom Halls found everywhere in the world (the construction of their structures are laid out, according to specification, by the Watchtower), identical readings and studies each week at the Kingdom Halls, similar dress, and answers to questions, no matter who you may be speaking with, anywhere.

Jehovah's Witnesses refuse blood transfusions, believing such is the equivalent of eating blood. This prohibition is on what is classified as "whole blood;" Watchtower adherents have the option now to receive "fractions" of blood products: red blood cells, platelets, white cells, hemoglobin substitutes, and plasma. Aside from issues of blood transfusion, Jehovah's Witnesses have no prohibition on medical care, and receive surgical and medical procedures without question. They are staunchly opposed to faith healing, believing that the gifts of the Spirit ceased because of Bible completion.[33]

Jehovah's Witnesses are also known for their rejection of patriotism, which they believe is a form of idolatry. Governments are seen as a necessary evil, of sorts; they are required for structure and societal order, but they are part of the present evil ruling system (soon to be dismantled) and thus demonically controlled. They refrain from any form of government participation, including running for office, voting in elections, saluting flags, taking oaths, and military service. This has not stopped Jehovah's Witnesses from pursuing lawsuits when they feel they have been wronged or misrepresented, rights are in question, or from pursuing legal avenues when in a nation where Jehovah's Witnesses are prohibited or suppressed.

The world of a Jehovah's Witness largely revolves around identity and involvement with Watchtower activities. Members are discouraged from pursuing higher education, as one could be taught or led away from Watchtower beliefs through influences or ideas. There are few professionals in Kingdom Halls; those who are often pursued their educational goals prior to converting to the faith.

Family life is seen through the same structural and organizational lens as the rest of Watchtower life. Family units are patriarchal in nature. Men are the heads of the family and the final decision makers on all matters. Women are expected to respect and submit to their husbands, and children are expected to obey their parents in all matters. Jehovah's Witnesses must be monogamous everywhere in the world, in accordance with Watchtower doctrine. Divorce and remarriage are only permissible in cases of adultery. In situations that present physical abuse, neglect, or prohibition of practice of their faith, only separation is an option.

Jehovah's Witnesses are known internationally for their extreme practice of shunning, known as disfellowship (also called excommunication or expelling). If a member of Jehovah's Witnesses is seen as breaking rules, giving the organization a bad name, behaving immorally, or seen as being "unfaithful" to Jehovah's Organization, they are given specific penalties by the local elders after a hearing. These can range from counseling to a specific visit on the part of an elder, withholding specific duties, or "marking" by which an individual is publicly identified as being a "bad association" and prohibited from social interaction or involvement. If matters continue without reinstatement, an individual is disfellowshipped: one is publicly mentioned by name, in a Kingdom Hall as no longer having any association or fellowship, and members are prohibited from having any contact with that individual (whether they are a family member or not). Disfellowshipping also happens in cases where an individual chooses to leave the faith. Disfellowshipped individuals can be reinstated, if they are judged as repentant and having chained their attitudes and actions.[34]

RELATIONS WITH NON-JEHOVAH'S WITNESSES

As a large purpose is to recruit all to the doctrine of the society, Jehovah's Witnesses do not participate in any ecumenical or interfaith councils, discussions, or dialogues, citing "purity" against Satanic heresies. Satan is seen as the ruler and creator of everything in this world that is not Jehovah's Witnesses Watchtower organization. This includes all other religious groups, both Christian and non-Christian alike.

Kingdom Hall of Jehovah's Witnesses in Sussex, England

HOLY SITES

For several years, the main "holy site" of Jehovah's Witnesses was the Watchtower Bible and Tract Society Headquarters, including Bethel, in Brooklyn, New York. In 2004, Watchtower operations began relocation to Wallkill, New York. There is an educational center in Patterson, New York, and another headquarter compound in Warwick, New York.

Notable Figures

Charles Taze Russell (1852-1916), founder; Joseph F. Rutherford (1869-1942), former president; Prince (1958-2016), musician; Venus (1980-) and Serena Williams (1981-), athletes; Keenen (1958-), Shawn (1971-), Damon (1960-), and Marlon Wayans (1972-), comedians and actors; Geri Halliwell (1972-), musician; Terrence Howard (1969-), actor; Selena (1971-1995), musician; Kid Gavilan (1926-2003), athlete; Coco Rocha (1988-), model; Larry Graham (1946-), musician; George Benson (1943-), musician; Lou Whitaker (1957-), athlete; Chet Lemon (1955-), athlete.

Notable Groups

The Watchtower is unique in its number of corporations within Watchtower entity that exist for specific purposes and legal bodies. These include: the best-known, Watchtower Bible and Tract Society of Pennsylvania, which holds copyrights for Watchtower literature; the Watchtower Bible and Tract Society of New York, Inc., handles real estate and administration, and is often cited as the publisher of current Watchtower literature; Christian Congregation of Jehovah's Witnesses Inc. handles congregational affairs of Kingdom Halls and Watchtower circuits; the Religious Order of Jehovah's Witnesses, New York is for those who operate full-time field work; and Kingdom Support Services, Inc., serves to manage construction and vehicle maintenance and operation.[35]

Facts and Figures

Among religious groups, Jehovah's Witnesses have a low rate of membership stability. Approximately 66% of individuals raised as Jehovah's Witnesses do not remain in the faith as adults. Less than 1% of US adults identify as members of Jehovah's Witnesses.[36]

Other Important Definitions

- **Antichrist**: Anyone who rejects Watchtower ideas.

- **Armageddon**: A total worldwide battle that shall destroy any and all people who are not a part of Jehovah's Witnesses; the ultimate defeat of Satan, by which life on earth, and worldwide reign of Watchtower ideals, shall begin.[37]

- ***Awake***: A magazine published by Jehovah's Witnesses featuring articles of interest on scientific, religion, and general life matters.

- **Christendom**: Used by the Watchtower to refer to all Christian groups, both Catholic and Protestant. Jehovah's Witnesses believe both Catholicism and Protestantism to be started by the Emperor Constantine in the 300s. Term is derogatory in nature.[38]

- **The "Good News"**: A term used to refer to the message of the Watchtower Society, proclaimed by Jehovah's Witnesses.

- **Millennium**: A 1,000 year reign of Christ to immediately follow Armageddon; paradise on earth.[39]

- **Torture Stake**: Rejecting the idea that Jesus was crucified on a cross (as they believe it was a pagan symbol), Jehovah's Witnesses believe Jesus was crucified on a singular pole, with hands nailed to the top and feet at the bottom, on what they call a "torture stake." This process is known as the "ransom sacrifice" (substituting for the word "crucifixion") or impalement.[40]

- **True Christians**: Jehovah's Witnesses call themselves "true Christians" or "Jehovah's true Christians" to contrast themselves from Protestants and Catholics, who they believe are false.[41]

- **The "truth"**: A term for the Jehovah's Witnesses system and organization; in contrast with "the world," which is seen as false and encompassing everyone else.

- **Talk**: A term for a Kingdom Hall sermon or lecture.

- **Return visit**: Also called a return call. When a Jehovah's Witness goes door-to-door, it is with the hopes that someone will receive the literature and welcome the publishers to return again. When they are invited to return a second time, it is a "return visit."

- **Independent thinking**: Adopting views that are against Watchtower precepts.

- **Goat**: A term used to refer to individuals who are not interested in Jehovah's Witnesses; separating sheep (Watchtower adherents) from goats (those who reject the system).

- **666:** The symbol of all human governments, that belong to Satan.

- **Shepherding call**: A visit made by two elders to a member's home to assist in spiritual matters. Often used in connection with matters of discipline, but can also involve matters of counseling, spiritual care, or in emergencies.[42]

BELIEVER'S CHARACTERISTICS

Emphasis on separateness, being part of the correct faith, and proper conduct; recruitment, evangelization, and Watchtower Bible study; disbelief in many standard doctrines, such as the eternity of the soul, hell, the Trinity, and Oneness theologies; rejection of all governmental systems and participation therein; defense of the Watchtower society; emphasis on structure, organization, and methodology applied to religious matters; belief that the methods of religion are completely correct, innovative, and unique; waiting for the "end of the system" to finally come; belief that Jesus is now ruling invisibly from heaven; awaiting the transition from the current system to paradise on earth; defense of Watchtower actions and leaders; Kingdom Hall meeting attendance; makes door-to-door visits; belief in one elect group who are saved with others as "friends of God" or those who shall face annihilation; rejection of all other religious groups as Satanic.

JUDAISM

I am not an Orthodox man; a believer....In Judaism faith goes very far. Not just religion. It is rooted in the whole Jewish way of life. Belief in God is not just worship and ritual. The Jewish faith has to do with the way of life, with man to man...and justice and mercy. It has to do with you and me.
(Moshe Dayan)[1]

THEOLOGY

Belief in one true G-d (monotheism) traditionally referred to as ADONAI (a Hebrew term meaning "my Lord"), now referred to as YAHWEH in some modern traditions, with personal attributes. The term ADONAI is spoken in place of the Tetragrammaton (the given name of the divine) YHVH, out of reference. ADONAI is seen as the Creator of the universe and the Savior, Redeemer, and Sustainer of the Jewish people.

As the only Creator G-d, the Jewish people believe in the exclusive worship of ADONAI, regarding all other gods as false. The commitment to exclusively worship ADONAI is part of a unique covenant the Jewish people trace back to the Biblical Patriarch Abraham in the book of Genesis. This agreement to worship ADONAI exclusively and stand as His set-apart people is reiterated in the Biblical books of Exodus, Leviticus, Numbers, and Deuteronomy. There is but one G-d, not many, and the Jewish people have, by covenant and tradition, agreed to follow this one G-d.

Philosophy

Centers around the principle that adherents of the Jewish religion are the people of G-d, direct descendants of Jacob's twelve sons (the twelve tribes of Israel) now merged into one group under Jewish identity. Rather than acknowledging many different tribes, modern-day Jews consider themselves to be Jewish, ancestors of those first called by G-d. The association of such comes through both religious and cultural origin. They believe they are the heirs to the promises made to Abraham in Genesis 12:1-3:

> *And the Lord said to Abram, "Go forth from your land and from your birthplace and from your father's house, to the land that I will show you.*
>
> *And I will make you into a great nation, and I will bless you, and I will aggrandize your name, and [you shall] be a blessing.*

And I will bless those who bless you, and the one who curses you I will curse, and all the families of the earth shall be blessed in you."[2]

This agreement as the "great nation" was the establishment of a new tribe, a new group of people who were to follow the covenant promises as the descendants of Abraham.

Beyond this consensus, there is great disagreement among the Jewish people about what "lineage" means to them. Some see the promises as more of a racial or national identification, than a spiritual one; some see the promises as a spiritual requirement established along with the covenant; some see themselves as independent from the divine, and others see the divine as a requirement for their very being. It is a fact that, as a group, Jews do share national, ethnic, religious, and cultural ties, so the question among the Jewish people is how these different facets of identity work together as commands the faith of the Jewish people. The universal consensus is their identity dates to Abraham. Beyond that, specifications vary among believers.

TRADITIONAL LANGUAGES

Hebrew, Aramaic, Greek (the language of the Septuagint).

ADHERENT IDENTITY

Jewish, Jews, Orthodox Jews, Reform Jews, Conservative Jews, Messianic Jews, Chasidic Jews, Cabbalists (also spelled Kabbalists), Sephardic Jews, Ashkenazim Jews

MAJOR SECTS/DIVISIONS

- **Orthodox**: The most religious of all sects, Orthodox Judaism strives to follow the literal directives of the Torah, or the first five books of the Bible, along with the written directives and traditions of the Talmud (Jewish law) down through the ages. Upholding moral, spiritual, dietary, and ethical purity is of central focus and meaning for Orthodox Jews. It emerged in the 1700s in contrast to what was perceived as liberal social and moral compromise. Orthodox Jews do not regard other forms of Judaism to be legitimate, and it is the largest body of Jewish believers today. Some subgroups of Orthodox Judaism include Hasidism (an Orthodox Jewish group that incorporates traditional Jewish mystical ideals with its religious understanding), Haredi Judaism (which is related to Hasidism), and other smaller Orthodox sects that incorporate different aspects of Jewish law and history together to produce their belief system.

- **Conservative**: Conservative Judaism is the most widely recognized in the United States. In other parts of the world, it is known as Masorti Judaism. Conservative Jews do not regard the law with the same emphasis as Orthodox Jews, but instead see it as a tradition of custom and belief throughout history. As a result, Conservative Jews believe the law and its understanding are open to interpretation. Conservative Jews do not adhere to a definition of theology, and are therefore, open to many different theological beliefs as they strive for understanding.

- **Reform**: Reform Judaism is the most liberal of the three main branches of Judaism. Many in other forms of Judaism do not consider it to be valid. Reform Jews believe in the strict nature of ethics and a continuing sense of revelation. They see the Jewish faith as progressing, rather than adhering to traditional ideas that were established thousands of years ago. Reform Judaism is best known for political ideals and alliances, and for adopting modern and liberal ideas as part of their faith identity.

- **Reconstructionist**: The newest form of Judaism, Reconstructionist Judaism was originally part of the Conservative Jewish movement. As a more liberal aspect of Judaism, it seeks to view Judaism through a progressive viewpoint and rejects much of traditional Jewish theology about G-d. They do not see G-d as personal or interacting with humanity, and thus, there are many diverse views about G-d and Jewish identity within their group. Instead of adhering to Old Testament law, the Reconstructionist movement adheres to different customs that are neither bonding nor required, but relate to the observance of traditional Jewish holidays, the use of the Hebrew language, and study of Old Testament law.

- **Kabbalah**: Not a formal sect of Judaism, but more a mystical interpretation of Jewish scripture and spiritual understanding. Kabbalah seeks to explain G-d's relationship with infinity, eternity, and the universe. Rather than taking text at surface value, Kabbalists seek to find deeper understandings of spiritual text and insight, thus developing more mystical meanings that might not be easily understood without the proper insights. It is unique enough to itself that it has its own writings, such as the *Zohar, the book of Radiance*. Kabbalism also embraces traditional Talmudic and apocryphal texts of Judaism, using and expounding upon them. Kabbalah has evolved over the years and takes particular interest in creation, the connection between the law and the individual, different levels of the soul, reincarnation, the divine feminine, and solving the question of evil. It is notable that modern "churches of Kabbalah" and celebrity trends do not espouse true Kabbalistic ideas. Today, the ideas of Kabbalism are found most prevalently in the mystical traditions of various Orthodox communities, such as among Hasidic Jews.

- **Messianic**: Messianic Judaism is questionable in its identity as if it is technically Judaism or Evangelical Christianity with elements of Judaism inter-dispersed. Many Jews do not consider Messianic Judaism to be a valid form of Judaism, simply because accepting Jesus as the Messiah is contraindicative of Jewish understanding. Though established as a general movement 1916, it evolved in the 1960s through the Charismatic Movement as people of Jewish ethnicity came to believe Christ was the Messiah, while maintaining traditional Jewish elements of their faith. Messianic Jews vary theologically, but believe Christ reaffirmed the Law (rather than fulfilling it) and that the written regulation of the Old Testament is still applicable, today. Some Messianic Judaism question the New

Testament canon and there are some who disregard portions of the apostolic letters, especially those written by the Apostle Paul.

- **Sephardim**: More an ethnic distinction than a religious one, Sephardim are Jews whose ancestors are from the Middle East, Spain, Portugal, and North Africa.

- **Ashkenazim**: More an ethnic designation than a religious one, Ashkenazi Jews are Eastern European in descent, whose ancestors converted to Judaism around the year 1000. Found in all sects of Judaism, the Asheknazim compose about 80% of the Jewish community worldwide.

Star of David (hexagram)

- **Zionism**: Zionism is a strictly political movement that believes the Jewish people have the right to a modern-day Jewish state, defined as the territory today known as the Land of Israel. It has existed since the 1880s. Though not a religious movement, Zionism is a controversial issue as relates to Jewish identity and practice within the Jewish community worldwide. Not every Jew, nor every sect, agrees with Zionism. There are also people outside of Judaism who identify with Zionist ideals, especially Christian Zionists.

- **Other Jewish communities**: Yemenite, Ethiopian (Beta Israel), and Asian Jews all share different cultures and traditions that evolved separately from the standard Jewish sects. There are also several "renewal" Jewish communities that incorporate different aspects of interpretation, understanding, and identity into their community belief, rule, and concept. They are small in numbers.

- **Samaritans**: Samaritans would not consider themselves to be Jews, even though today, Israeli rabbis do consider Samaritanism to be a sect of Judaism. They are descendants of the northern Israelite tribes, considering themselves to be the true religion of ancient Israel. According to Samaritan tradition, it was them who preserved the true religion during the Babylonian captivity. They do have a markedly different tradition, including the belief that Mount Gerizim was the original holy site after the conquer of Canaan and the settling of the promised land. It is on Mount Gerizim (in contrast with Jerusalem) that Samaritans believe major Biblical events occurred, such as Abraham's call to sacrifice Isaac and the revealing of God's Name. They are a small group, with approximately 820 remaining. Samaritans refuse converts and refuse intermarriage with other groups, which has led to marriage within families and resulting genetic disorders. Samaritans believe there is one God identified as Shehmaa, and believe the Torah was given by God to Moses. They believe in the resurrection of the dead, which will be facilitated by the *Taheb*, most likely a prophet. Priests within their tradition are seen as interpreters of the law and guardians of the faith. Samaritans have their own law, known as Halakha. It does vary from Jewish interpretation of the law, as do their scriptures. For example, the Ten Commandments are different (the tenth commandment relates to Mount Gerizim) and there are about six thousand differences between the Samaritan Torah and the Jewish text, which consists of their entire scriptural canon. Other relevant writings are the Samaritan Chronicles, Hagiographical texts (mostly legal codes and interpretations from the eleventh, twelfth, and fourteenth centuries), psalms and hymns, and their own *Haggadah* for celebrating Passover. Samaritans are known for their strict interpretations of Torah, including the belief that women must live in a separate dwelling during menstruation and absolute adherence to sexual purity, restricting relationships exclusively to marriage. The future of the Samaritan community is in question. Throughout recent times, it is not uncommon for Samaritans to fully convert to Judaism due to matters of marriage or custom.[3]

NUMBER OF ADHERENTS

There are approximately 14,606,000 Jews worldwide.[4]

DISPUTES WITHIN GROUP

Jewish groups disagree on what it means to be Jewish in modern society. As a group that has suffered both displacement and genocide over the years, Jewish communities struggle with trauma. This is evident as they strive to understand just what it means to be a Jew in this world, today. There are many questions on the degree and level of observance: how much of the law to follow, how to follow the law, and what makes a Jew a Jew, as all areas of faith and practice are examined today. The question as to whether being Jewish is an ethnic one versus a spiritual one is questioned among the different sects. As has been stated, some sects do not consider Jews of other sects to be legitimate or authentic.

Major issues for Jewish despite include the interpretation of the Law, the role and identity of Jewish people as a group, dietary laws, the role of women, homosexuality, politics, theology, and Jewish traditions. Perhaps the biggest – and most decisive issues – come from the Zionist Movement, claim to Palestinian land, and the 1948 Jewish invasion of Palestine. These issues are not just practical or moral for the world's Jewish community, but theological, as well. If the Jews can take the land without waiting for the Messiah (as such was the traditional interpretation), this creates many other questions of a theological nature, all of which are important and essential to the Jew's relationship with G-d. It is estimated that approximately 80% of the Jewish population of Israel identifies as atheist.

SCRIPTURES

The Old Testament, known to the Jews as the Hebrew Bible, abbreviated as the TANAKH: T(orah) (the Christian Pentateuch of Genesis, Exodus, Leviticus, Numbers, and Deuteronomy), N(evi'im) (the Prophets: Joshua, Judges, 1 and 2 Samuel, 1 and 2 Kings, Isaiah, Jeremiah, Ezekiel, Hosea,

Joel, Amos, Obadiah, Jonah, Micah, Nahum, Habakkuk, Zephaniah, Haggai, Zechariah, and Malachi), and K(et)H(uvim) (the Writings: Psalms, Proverbs, Job, Song of Solomon, Ruth, Lamentations, Ecclesiastes, Ester, Daniel, Ezra, Nehemiah, and 1 and 2 Chronicles).

The Jews also have a long history of recognizing their own unique apocryphal works, known as the Pseudepigrapha. These works are so-called because they are often attributed to authors who did not write them, to give such credibility. Some of these works include the Book of Jubilees, the Book of Enoch, and the Apocalypse of Abraham. Jews also recognize the "oral Torah," or Talmud, which is considered the tradition of interpretation based on Scripture and is the authoritative Jewish law. In groups such as Kabbalah, additional writings, such as the Zohar, Book of Radiance, are added to the list of studied texts.

Basic Religious Practices

Judaism centers around the individual, the family, and the synagogue on the seventh-day Sabbath (Saturday). Highly interested in the ethics of life and/or faith, the Jew's pursuit is relational: how different relationships and interactions are enhanced by the choices one makes. There is a great interest in passing on the faith and the ethics thereof to the next generation through telling stories, sharing history, and engaging in Jewish custom and culture. Religious services center around prayer recitation and chants and songs in Hebrew and/or English; the reading of Scripture, especially from the Torah; and lesson summary done by a Rabbi or other teacher. Followers of Judaism are expected to give alms (*tzedkah*), attend synagogue at least once per year, and observe all Jewish feasts and fasts.

Holidays and Observances

Dates for Jewish holidays are based on the lunar calendar and change annually. There are Biblically prescribed festivals and observances and modern observances, some of which are not observed or recognized by all Jewish communities. The Biblical observances include:

- **Rosh Chodesh**: The "new month" festival, considered a minor holiday or observance recognized on the first day of each month of the Jewish calendar. Fasting is typically prohibited.[5]

- **Rosh Hashanah**: Often called the "Jewish New Year," it is a feast focused on repentance and prayer. It seeks to recognize memorial and judgment, marked specifically by the blowing of the shofar, or trumpet, to call the people to repentance. Prayers of repentance are long and focus on the majesty and judgment of G-d, remembrance, the creation of the world, and repentance. (September or October)

- **Yom Kippur**: The official Day of Atonement. It is the most solemn day of the year, devoted to self-examination and the chance to begin the new year with a slate free of sin. (September or October)

- **Sukkoth**: The seven-day festival known as Feast of Shelters or Feast of Booths. Jews will create a special "booth" or dwelling to take meals or sleep in, using the four species of palm, myrtle, willow, and citron. This recalls the time when the Hebrew people dwelt in the Sinai wilderness for forty years on their way to the Promised Land. (October)

- ***Shemini Atzeret* and Simchat Torah**: Literally means "eighth day of assembly," this is the conclusion of Sukkot. It also marks the end and beginning of the annual Torah cycle Every year on this date, Jews pray for rain. (October)

Menorah Hanukkah lamp

- **Hanukkah**: The "Festival of Lights" that celebrates a divine miracle recorded in the books of First and Second Maccabees: a one-day supply of olive oil used to light the temple menorah lasted for eight days during a period of Jewish persecution. Jews recognize Hanukkah with a menorah, lit each night of the Hanukkah festival. Many Jews also play games, cook with oil, and give gifts. (November or December)

- **Purim**: Jewish liberation feast of potential genocide as would have been implemented by the Persian government. Events are recounted in the book of Esther and celebrate the bravery of Mordecai and Esther, who becomes Queen of Persia. (February or March)

- **Passover and the Feast of Unleavened bread**: Festival marking the ancient Hebrew exodus from Egypt (and the saving of Hebrew children from the plague, killing the firstborn), marked in modern times with a dinner echoing the original commands in Exodus: bread with no leavening, roasted lamb, and bitter herbs. Every year, the story of Passover is retold during the meal. Following the Passover meal, Jews refrain from using or ingesting any leavening for a week. (March or April)

- **Shavuot**: Also known as the Feast of Weeks, Firstfruits, or Pentecost. An early harvest festival that also celebrates the reception of the Torah for the Jewish people. Traditionally, the first portion of one's harvest offerings were made at this time. (May or June).

Although not observed by all Jews, modern-day Jewish festivals include[6]:

- ***Tu B'Shevat***: Known as the Festival of the Trees; traditionally a day on which fruit tithes were counted. Today, it celebrates the land of Israel, by which people eat fruits and nuts associated with Israel, and the planting of trees. (January or February)

- ***Yom HaShoah***: Holocaust Remembrance Day recounts the loss of six million Jewish lives in the Holocaust. (April or May)

- ***Yom HaZikaron***: Israeli Memorial Day; akin to Memorial Day in other countries, specifically recognizing Israeli soldiers (April or May)

- ***Yom HaAtzmaut***: Israeli Independence Day, celebrating the establishment of the modern state of Israel. (April or May)

- ***Lag B'Omer***: The thirty-third day of the forty-nine-day period (an "omer" period) between Passover and Shavuot. Also acknowledges the death of Rabbi Shimon Bar Yochai, author of the *Zohar, the Book of Radiance*. (April or May)

- ***Tisha B'Av***: The thirty-third day of the period between Passover and Shauvot. A fasting day remembering the destruction of the Jewish Temple in Jerusalem, first in 586 BC and then in 70 AD. (July or August)

- ***Tu B'Av***: Also called the "happiest day of the year." It is the Jewish holiday of love, akin to Valentine's Day. (July or August)

VISUAL SIGNS AND SYMBOLS

Six-point Star of David (hexagram), made with two triangles, one upright and one inverted; yarmulke (scull-cap) worn by men (and women in liberal denominations); fringed prayer shawl that is blue and white worn by men (and women, in liberal denominations); Torah scrolls; menorah; Shofar trumpet; stone tablets that contain the Ten Commandments; rabbinical role; circumcision of the penis in males.

CREEDS, BOOKS, AND LAWS

In Biblical summary, most consider the equivalent of a Jewish "creed" to be the words of Deuteronomy 6:4, known as the *shema*:

> *Hear, O Israel: The Lord is our God; the Lord is one.*[7]

Judaism is ruled by the Talmud, the expanded oral and written Jewish law written between 200 and 500 AD. The Talmud contains governing regulations and authorities regarding relations with Gentiles, other Jews, religious issues, business ethics, and issues of marriage, family, women, men, and morality. It is not considered a separate entity from Scripture, but the tradition of its interpretation and understanding (we could compare it to a large, long-standing Scriptural commentary). Like many older religious traditions, some of the Talmud's ethics appear to be questionable by modern standards as they evolved in a different time and place from what we know and recognize as guiding in modern society. Judaism sees the tradition of legal understanding as evolving, and parts of the Talmud are not enforced or used as they were in older times. Still, portions of the Talmud are reinterpreted or brought into more updated standards to deal with modern issues.

Old city of Jerusalem

The following Boraitha is in support of the assertion of R. Shesha, son of R. Idi: The following things are done by others for one who is in mourning: If his olives are turned, the press-block may be put on, the cask bunged, his flax removed from the buck, his wool taken out of the boiler, and his land watered when his turn comes on. R. Jehudah said: "Even his ploughed land may be sown and the flax-field planted." The sages, however, maintain, that if not sown early in the season it can be done so late in the season; and if not flax, other plants can be raised. R. Simeon b. Gamaliel, however, said that if he is the only specialist in the place, of all those things mentioned above, they may be done by himself privately. And even more than that the same Rabban allowed: If he were the only mechanic in the place employed by the public, or a barber, or a bather, and the feast was approaching, he might perform his functions. Contractors of all kinds must have others to do their work (during their mourning).

Those who hire out asses, camels, or ships to others, must not do their work. But if at the time (their mourning commences) they were already hired out, they might continue. A day laborer, although in a place where he is not known, must not work. If he were to work for others in his own house, whether under contract to do it for a definite time or not, he must not do it. If others were working for him in his own house, they must postpone their work; but in a house other than his own, they might continue. Marian, son of Rabhin, and Mar, son of A'ha son of Rabha, had a team of oxen in copartnership. One day a death occurred in the family of Mar b. A'ha and he kept in his ox. Said R. Ashi: Why should a great man like Mar do such a thing? If he does not consider his own loss, he must consider that of another. As stated above: "If they were hired out at the time, they might proceed with their work." He (Mar), however, was of the opinion that the case is different when a prominent person is concerned. Samuel said: "Those who do their work under contract for a definite period of time, if within the legal limits, may not; if outside those limits, they may do it." R. Papa, however, said: Even where it is outside the legal limits, the case is only when there is no town adjacent. R. Mesharshia, however, said that even where there is no town adjacent the case is so only in reference to Sabbath days and festivals, for on those days people are few; but as regards the middle days, during which people are numerous, it is not permitted. Mar Zutra, son of R. Na'hman, had a house built under contract outside of the legal limits. R. Saphra and R. Huna bar Hinna happened to be in the neighborhood of that house and declined to enter it; and according to others, R. Zutra himself also declined to enter it. But has not Samuel said that if it was outside of the legal limits it is permitted? R. Zutra himself assisted them in placing the straw during the progress of the work. R. Hama permitted the Abunagars (waiters) of the Exilarch to do their work on the middle days; for, he said, they receive no salary, and work only for their board. (It is therefore not considered labor, and does not matter.)

The rabbis taught: Work may be taken under contract during the middle days to be done after the feast. But on the middle days it is not permitted. The rule is: All that one himself may do, he may have a Gentile do it for him, but not what he may not. We have learned in another Boraitha: "Work may be taken under contract on the middle days to be performed after the feast, provided always he does not measure, weigh, or count in the usual manner."

The rabbis taught: "No animals should be copulated on the middle days; the same applies to the firstborn and also to the desecrated ones at any time."

The rabbis taught: Cattle must not be brought into the field for the purpose of manuring, either on Sabbath days, feast days, or middle days. But if they come there of themselves it is permitted. And no assistance may be afforded to those in charge, neither a watchman assigned them to watch their sheep. But the case is different if they are hired by the week, month, year, or for a period of seven years. Rabbi, however, says: "On Sabbath days it may be done without compensation; on feasts days, for food only; and on the middle days, even for compensation." Said R. Joseph: "The halakhah prevails as Rabbi decreed."[6]

The schoolmen propounded a question: The returning, according to marks given, is biblically or rabbinically. What is the difference? Regarding the returning of a written divorce, by proclaiming the marks on it, if it is biblically, it must certainly be returned; if, however, rabbinically, it may be said that the sages made their enactment concerning money matters, but not concerning a biblical prohibition (for if an error would occur in such a case, a married woman would be allowed to marry again). Shall we assume that the Tanaim of the following Boraitha differ in that case; namely, testimony of witnesses must not be accepted on suppositions (e.g., if witnesses came to testify that they suppose, by seeing the body of so and so, that he was killed, unless they testify that they had seen his face and his nose attached). Elazar b. Mahbai, however, said: "It may." Should we not assume that the point of their difference is that the first Tana holds that signs are rabbinical, and Elazar holds that they are biblical? Said Rabha: "All agree that signs are biblical, and the point in which they differ is, one holds that the suppositions of such a case by his comrade may be relied upon, and one holds it may not (because an error may occur also in a case of a comrade)." He said again: "The fact that we return lost articles according to signs given, proves that it is biblically; for if not, how could the sages make such an enactment in a case of doubtful money? Should we assume that the finder is pleased to return the article according to signs, only because if it should happen that he himself lost an article, the same would be done to him?" Said R. Saphra to him: "What do we care for the pleasure of the finder, when the loser is not pleased (e.g., the man who claims and gives signs, and yet it is not the real ones)? Is it, then, usual that one should desire to do good to himself in futuro (which it is doubtful if it will happen) with money which does not belong to him?" Therefore said Rabha: "All the losers would be pleased by giving signs that the articles should be returned to them, as they know that witnesses are not always to be found; and, on the other hand, the signs on the articles are not known to every one who would like to claim them, and only the loser, who knows the exact mark, will proclaim them and come in possession thereof" (and therefore it is possible that such an enactment was made by the sages, and it is not biblically). Finally said Rabha: "That the marks in question are biblically is to be deduced from the following verse [Deut. xxii. 2]: 'And it shall remain with thee until thy brother inquire after it.' Could, then, one bear in mind that it should be returned before it is inquired about? We must, therefore, say that the inquirer must be examined whether he is not a swindler, and by what means he can be identified if not by the exact marks; hence infer from this that they are biblically." He says again: "If it is your decision that the marks in question are biblically." "[If it is your decision." Did not Rabha just deduce it from averse? Yea, but still one can say that the examination mentioned above should be by means of witnesses.] If there were two persons who gave the very same marks, it must be reserved (until proper evidence is brought); if there were marks and witnesses contradicting each other, the witnesses have the preference. If there were marks and marks from two parties, and there was a third one who brought one witness, the third one must not be taken in consideration, and the article must be kept in reserve. If there were witnesses testifying that the ownership of the article by this man was when it was woven, and other witnesses the ownership of another man when it was lost, the latter has the preference, as it may be that the first one sold it and it was lost by the buyer. If one party testifies to the length, and another party to the width, the length has preference, as the width can be assumed by seeing the article when it was used. If one testifies to the length and the width, and another one testifies to the square, the former has the preference; the square and the weight, the latter has the preference. If the husband claims that the written divorce was dropped by him before it was delivered to his wife, and proclaims certain marks, and she claims it was dropped by her after she received it (consequently she is single and can marry), she has the preference (because if she had not received it, how could she know the marks?). However, the marks must be not in length and width, as she could see it before it was given to her, but a mark such as a hole in such and such letter of it. If the marks were the very same given by him and her concerning the length of the thread upon which the divorce was put, she has the preference. If both claim that it was in the χαψα (a kind of small case), he has the preference, because it is well known to her that the entire contents of it he has placed there.[8]

MISHNA: In the Temple the lower hinge of a cupboard-door may be refitted into its place (on the Sabbath), but this must not be done in the country. The upper hinge must not be refitted either in the Temple or in the country. R. Jehudah said: The upper hinge may be refitted in the Temple and the lower one in the country.

GEMARA: The Rabbis taught: The lower hinges of a door of a cupboard or a chest or a tower may be refitted into their places in the Temple, but in the country they may only be temporarily replaced, but not refitted. If the upper hinges had become unfastened it is not allowed to even temporarily replace them as a precaution lest they be refitted with tools, for should this be done the act involves liability to bring a sin-offering. The doors of cellars, vaults, or gables must not be refitted, and if this was done, the man is liable for a sin-offering.

MISHNA: They (priests who minister) may replace a plaster on a wound (which plaster had been taken off to perform the service) in the Temple; but this must not be done in the country. To put the first plaster on a wound on Sabbath is prohibited in either place.

GEMARA: The Rabbis taught: "If a plaster became removed from a wound it may be replaced on Sabbath." R. Jehudah said: "If it was moved up it may be moved down and if it was moved down it may be moved up, and it is permitted to remove part of the plaster and cleanse the exposed portion of the wound, then replace the plaster, remove another part, cleanse the exposed wound and again replace the plaster, but it is not permitted to cleanse the plaster because by so doing one would rub the plaster and if this was done it involves liability for a sin-offering."

Said R. Jehudah in the name of Samuel: "The Halakha prevails according to R. Jehudah."

R. Hisda said: The statement of the first Tana to the effect that a plaster may be replaced applies only to a plaster

that had fallen on a vessel but a plaster that had fallen to the ground must not be replaced. Mar the son of R. Assi said: "It happened once that I was standing before my father and a plaster which he had on a wound fell on a cushion and he replaced the plaster. Said I to him: 'Does master not hold in accordance with the opinion of R. Hisda, who said that the first Tana and R. Jehudah differ only as to a plaster that had fallen on a vessel, and Samuel said that the Halakha prevails according to R. Jehudah. How then could master have replaced it?' and my father answered that he did not agree with R. Hisda."

MISHNA: They (the Levites performing on musical instruments) may tie a string (of an instrument which had burst, on Sabbath) in the Temple; but this must not be done in the country. To put a new string on the instrument (on Sabbath) is in either place prohibited.

GEMARA: There is a contradiction! Have we not learned that if a string of an instrument had burst, they only made a loop but did not tie it into a knot? This presents no difficulty. This latter is the opinion of R. Simeon, while the Mishna is in accordance with the opinion of the Rabbis, as we have learned in the following Boraitha: If a Levite had burst the string of an instrument he may tie it; R. Simeon, however, said: He may only make a loop in the string. Said R. Simeon ben Elazar: If he merely makes a loop, the sound will be affected; hence he should loosen the string at the top and draw it down to the bottom or loosen it at the bottom and draw it taut to the top.

MISHNA: They (the priests who minister) may remove a wart from an animal on Sabbath in the Temple, but this must not be done in the country; by means of an instrument it is prohibited to do so in either place.

GEMARA: There is a contradiction. We have learned: Concerning the paschal lamb, which must be carried on the shoulders or brought from without the legal limits and the blemish of which must be removed, these acts must not supersede the due observance of the Sabbath.[10]

ECLECTIC BELIEFS

With the vast differences in understanding throughout the different sects of Judaism, there are many assorted sub-headings of belief that impact and vary the belief system of any professing Jew. Some demand excessive purity through the observance of various kosher laws, using separate pots for milk and meat (sometimes separate stoves or countertops), avoiding pork, and meat and dairy in the same meal, and living in community around the rabbi, who is regarded as the authority on Jewish law and interpretation. Other Jews may not go to such extreme on such laws, following instead ideas about Jewish cultural identity and social observance rather than faith practice.

RELATIONS WITH NON-JEWS

Liberal Jewish sects are frequently involved in interfaith activities. Among more liberal Jewish sects, many do not feel their theology is exclusive and may explore the theologies and beliefs of other religions, including eastern and New Age beliefs. More orthodox sects of Judaism tend toward separateness and isolation. Shunning other Jewish sects as illegitimate, they will only socialize within their immediate community. Modern understanding of things such as Kabbalah tend to be rather New Age in theology and ideas and non-exclusive in ideas. Some more isolated Jewish communities regard Muslims with disdain as part of a long-standing rivalry between the two groups.

HOLY SITES

The cities of Jerusalem, Hebron, Tiberias, and Safed are the four holy cities in the Jewish traditions. The Jews also believe the physical land of Israel to belong to them as a spiritual inheritance and center of their history. There are also notable "tombs" of deceased Bible figures, such as Benjamin, Esther and Mordecai, Samuel, Joshua, and Ezekiel, throughout the Middle East.

Jewish dreidels

NOTABLE FIGURES

Binyamin Netanyahu (1949-), Prime Minister of Israel; Ben Bernake (1953-), chairman of the US Federal Reserve; Sergey Brin (1973-), founder of Google; Moses de Leon (c. 1240-1305), Spanish Cabbalist and prominent figure; Abraham J. Heschel (1907-1972), modern Jewish theologian and philosopher; Dominique Strauss-Kahn (1949-), economist and politician; Ruth Bader Ginsburg (1933-2020), US Supreme Court Justice; Mark Zuckerberg (1984-), founder of Facebook; Elie Wiesel (1928-2016), writer and Holocaust survivor; Joseph Lieberman (1942-), US Senator; Bob Dylan (1941-), folk singer; Madonna (Kabbalah) (1958-), music idol; Paula Abdul (1962-), musician and dancer.

NOTABLE GROUPS

Zionism is the most notable among modern Judaism, emphasizing and pushing for the Jewish invasion and governmental takeover of Palestine. Founded by Theodor Herzl (1860-1904) in the late 1800s as an organized political movement, Zionism centers around Jewish cultural identity rather than faith definition, action, and military force. Its doctrinal understanding is atheist in its essence and does not believe in the coming of or necessity of a Messiah.

FACTS AND FIGURES

Jews comprise about 0.2% of humanity. Fewer than 10% of American Jews are Orthodox in practice, while 40% of American Jewish synagogues are Orthodox. Reform Judaism represents

26% of all synagogues. Conservative Judaism represents 23%. Every other Jewish sect accounts for 3% or less of the total synagogues. The total number of US synagogues is approximately 3,800.[11,12]

Other Important Definitions

- **Kosher**: The specification of a food prepared, sold, or eaten that meets with the requirements of Jewish dietary law. These laws specify mammals must have split hooves and chew their cud, fish must have fins and scales, birds must be non-predatory, meat must be slaughtered according to ritual manner, meat and dairy cannot be consumed together, and foods are not in any way contaminated by non-kosher products. Preparation of kosher foods must be approved by a Rabbi.

- **Rabbi**: The term for a religious leader in a Jewish community. The word "rabbi" means "teacher."

- **Circumcision**: Removal of the foreskin from the male penis. Procedure is done in a ceremony by a community member known as a moyle when a Jewish male is eight days old.

- **Synagogue**: A house of Jewish worship.

- **Tallit**: A prayer shawl fringed garment worn by observing Jews. Garment is fringed and knotted, and blue thread runs through most prayer shawls. There are variations on how the garment is worn and how it is designed, as there is no Biblical specification on how one should look or how it should be styled.

Believer's Characteristics

Varies depending on sect of Judaism, but some include cultural emphasis on Judaism, whether theological or racial in nature; support of Palestinian invasion with Israeli sympathies; rejection of Jesus Christ as the Messiah, with some rejecting a need for a messiah; emphasis on history, tradition, and both oral and written law; interest in the Torah; observance of Jewish holidays; dietary laws; interest in ethics and ways to uphold them in society; strong belief in education; in liberal sects, study and spiritual evolution outside of traditional religion, including paganism, Kabbalah, and New Age.

Liberal Christianity

For the whole thrust of Paul's writings has at its central pillar the conviction that God can enlarge His people and be still more inclusive than He had been in the past, even if it means setting aside commands that He had previously given to His people.
(James McGrath)[1]

Theology

Liberal Christianity is not a specific idea or denominational persuasion. It is a philosophical understanding of Christianity based in the idea that human reason and experience should stand over doctrinal authority. Even though it is not a theological movement, there are obvious theological implications for such thought. Liberal Christians fall into two categories of theology: traditional Protestant Trinitarianism, understood through a modern-day lens that is more experimental than doctrinal and focused on the idea of God walking among His people in the person of Jesus; and a modern take on Unitarianism, specifically seeing the person of Jesus as wise and sage, a created being as the Son of God rather than God the Son. In both instances, the image of Jesus is less doctrinal and divine, more human, often considered as a great leader and wise teacher. Any divinity in Christ is seen through admirable goals that all Christians should aspire to adopt (such as compassion and justice). In many situations, Jesus is regarded as a religious leader on par with other non-Christian figures, such as Buddha, Krishna, Mohammed, and Confucius. The Holy Spirit is often a complicated and difficult aspect of faith to accept, regarded as a force or essence promoting their central ideas (specifically love, essential goodness, and compassion). There are some within more liberal Christian circles that reject the idea of the Holy Spirit, also rejecting the idea and veracity of miracles for their own entity (seeing them as having some sort of scientific explanation or fabrications of religious storytelling).

Liberal Christianity is, in modern times, considered an opposition to Christian Fundamentalism. It rejects what are classified as central Christian theological doctrines: the incarnation of Christ, the infallibility and literal inspiration of Scripture, the essence of communion and baptism, the atonement of Christ for sin, the presence of literal miracles, and salvation obtainable through none but the blood of Christ. As a result, the interpretation of Christian theology is seen through a personal context: that of personal experience, personal ideas about faith, and often political and social applications of one's beliefs rather than doctrinal principles.

Philosophy

The term "liberal Christianity" is not a political term, although liberal politics are frequently part of the ideals of many liberal Christians (seen as an implementation of Christian beliefs). The term "liberal" is used in opposition to conservative, fundamental ideas that believe doctrine is more essential than personal experience and philosophical rationalism. Liberal Christianity, also known as Christian Modernism, focuses on incorporation of evolutionary theory, science, modern knowledge, ethics, modern philosophy, and social Gospel ideals within their understanding of the Bible. Rather than resorting to theological tradition or atheism, liberal Christianity believes its essential to approach faith from a modern perspective, incorporating modern social advancements and understanding into Christianity. Its exact founding point varies, but many trace it to influences among Unitarians in the 1500s, Pietism in the 1600s, and the work of Friedrich Schleiermacher (1768-1834) in the 1700s and 1800s that focused on religion as a feeling one experiences rather than reasoning them through doctrine.

Most liberal Christians believe in application of their belief system, focusing heavily on the ethics and humanity of Jesus' teachings as specific points of theological application. Inclusion of all peoples, regardless of gender, nationality, sexual orientation, religion, and socioeconomic status are keys to the political beliefs espoused within liberal Christianity. By working in social justice and activism, advocating for liberal political viewpoints, and promoting their ideas of a better world by applying faith, liberal Christians believe they are building the Kingdom of God, thus making things progressively better within society.[2]

NUMBER OF ADHERENTS

Liberal Christians are found across denominations, thus making how one identifies as a crossing of denominational and philosophical identity. It has been said that most mainline Protestants would fall in the "Liberal Christianity" category. An overwhelmingly North American movement (with a handful of representations in Europe, Latin America, and India), within the United States and Canada, there are approximately 80,000,000 liberal Christians.[3]

TRADITIONAL LANGUAGES

German, English.

ADHERENT IDENTITY

Liberal Christian, Liberal Christianity, Liberal Protestant, Liberal Protestantism, Liberal Catholic, Liberal Catholicism, Liberation theology, neo-Orthodoxy, identity based on one's denomination (such as Presbyterian, Methodist, Episcopalian, etc.)

SECTS/DIVISIONS

Within every religious sector there are liberal and conservative denominations, all created in response to one another's existence. These headings, presented to be as inclusive of the movement as possible, reflect liberal groupings and their ideas in today's church setting.

Walter Rauschenbusch (1861-1918)

- **Liberal Protestantism**: The Protestant branch of Liberal Christianity, noted for its founding ideals has, in many ways, served as the foundation for the movement. Liberal Protestants are individuals who espouse the beliefs of denominational Protestantism in one form or another but adhere to the philosophical and theological ideals of liberal Christianity. There are a number of ways liberal Protestantism overlaps with differing denominations that present a variety of other ideas and, as stated earlier, may also contain sub-denominations that espouse more conservative values. Liberal Protestants, however, face a crisis: just what role the Bible should play in the faith of a Christian. Infallibility and inerrancy of Biblical text are seen as idolatry. Liberal Protestants seek to understand the Bible through modern Biblical criticisms, re-evaluating the ideas of *sola scriptura* and divine revelation through Scripture, elevating God as revealed through Christ and human experience. The result is a Biblical interpretation through metaphor and the idea that human reason is the only way Christianity can be accepted in its universal ideals. Doctrines such as original sin, the divinity of Jesus, virgin birth, Trinitarianism, and miracles are frequently rejected or somehow reinterpreted. Liberal Protestants are found in all major mainline Protestant denominations (Anglican/Episcopalian, Lutheran, Anabaptist, Reformed, and Methodist). There are also smaller subsets of Evangelicals who would fall into the Liberal Christian category, with some differences in theological formation and attitude about Scripture. Some specific denominations falling into the liberal Protestant category include the United Church of Christ, the Episcopal Church, the Evangelical Lutheran Church in America, and the United Methodist Church.[4]

- **Liberal Catholicism**: The Catholic branch of Liberal Christianity, Liberal Catholicism is also known as Catholic modernism. It has existed in Europe since the nineteenth century. Its purpose is the same as Liberal Protestantism: reconcile the ideals of the church with modern culture and modern ideas. Biblical criticism, Christology, and ethics all challenged the way that Catholics saw their faith, so much so that in 1907, Pope Pius X declared modernism to be heresy. As a construct, the Vatican denounces Catholic liberalism, although it has gained ground since the Second Vatican Council (especially in Catholic and Protestant dialogue). Groups include the Liberal Catholic Church International, Liberal Catholic Church (Province of the United States of America), Old Catholic Church, the Young Rite, and the Liberal Catholic Union.

- **Liberation theology**: A political ideal rooted in theology, liberation theology is a liberal Christian approach to understanding the necessary freedom (liberation) of politically oppressed persons. In original understanding, it called for the necessity of social justice action on behalf of the poor, mistreated within political systems. It originated with Latin American Catholics after the Second Vatican Council. By extension, Liberation theology addresses any inequality (racism, sexism, segregation, civil rights, social discrimination), as is seen in black liberation theology, feminist liberation theology, Minjung theology (South Korea), and Dalit theology (India).[5]

- **Progressive Christianity**: A subset of liberal Christianity, Progressive Christianity is perhaps the most widely recognized form of the greater movement. Progressive Christianity identifies as a "post-liberal" movement, seeing to reform faith from the modernist understanding. Through its exploration, it seeks to both verify and determine accuracies and inaccuracies in Biblical text by use of Biblical criticism. It is openly inquisitive of tradition, embraces inclusivity and diversity, and focuses heavily on modern political issues, including environmentalism, gun control, social justice, LGBTQ+ rights, and feminism. It draws theological influences from both Evangelical and liberal Christian sources, pragmatism, postmodernism, reconstructionism, and liberation theology. Much like other liberal Christians, some of its doctrinal theology is in question in light of orthodoxy (such as a panentheistic approach to God's presence, denial of hell, metaphorical understanding of the Bible, and emphasizing right action rather than belief). Focus on the concept of the love of God is heavy, permissible to the point of denying sin and sometimes the necessity of salvation. As with all liberal Christian groups, there is a wide variety of individual beliefs. It is generally accepted that the Christians should promote and advocate for human rights as a fundamental point of faith. Progressive groups include the Metropolitan Community Church, North American Old Catholic Church, the Beatitudes Society, and the Progressive Episcopal Church.[6]

DISPUTES WITHIN GROUP

Because the very foundation of liberal Christianity is the role and acceptance of modern ideas within the framework of Christian theology, there is considerable debate among liberal Christians about belief, essential doctrine, and interpretation of Scripture. The role of matters of social involvement versus scholarship, worship within the faith, and understanding of various theological beliefs all vary. There are also differences as exist in understanding and practice among the denominations a liberal Christian may follow.

SCRIPTURES

The Holy Bible, both Old and New Testaments: the Pentateuch (Genesis, Exodus, Leviticus, Numbers, and Deuteronomy), Historical books (Joshua, Judges, Ruth, 1 Samuel, 2 Samuel, 1 Kings, 2 Kings, 1 Chronicles, 2 Chronicles, Ezra, Nehemiah, Esther), Wisdom books (Job, Psalms, Proverbs, Ecclesiastes, Song of Songs), Prophetic books (Isaiah, Jeremiah, Lamentations, Ezekiel,

Daniel, Hosea, Joel, Amos, Obadiah, Jonah, Micah, Nahum, Habakkuk, Zephaniah, Haggai, Zechariah, Malachi), the Gospels (Matthew, Mark, Luke, John), the Acts of the Apostles, the Pauline Epistles (Romans, 1 Corinthians, 2 Corinthians, Galatians, Ephesians, Philippians, Colossians, 1 Thessalonians, 2 Thessalonians, 1 Timothy, 2 Timothy, Titus, Philemon, Hebrews) the General Epistles (James, 1 Peter, 2 Peter, 1 John, 2 John, 3 John, Jude) and Revelation.

Liberal Catholics and high protestants also use the additional Deuterocanonical books: Deuterocanonical books (Tobit, Judith, 1 and 2 Maccabees, Wisdom of Solomon, Sirach, Baruch, Letter of Jeremiah, Greek additions to Esther, and Greek additions to Daniel, including the Prayer of Azariah, Song of the Three Holy Children, Susanna and the Elders, and Bel and the Dragon).

Translations do vary, with most preferring more modern translations such as the New Revised Standard Version or the New International Version to older translations, such as the King James Version.

The Bible does not have the same standing within liberal Christianity as it does among traditional Protestants and evangelicals. Seeing the way that the Bible is viewed (inspired, infallible, or both) is regarded as a form of idolatry among liberal Christians, thus causing them to reassess their ideas about the role of the Bible in one's faith.

Liberal Christians see the Bible through the lens of modern understanding: they feel that its contents are often not applicable in a literal sense, but should be understood metaphorically, rationally, and with consideration of scientific and secular knowledge. Historical details aren't seen the keys to proper Bible understanding, if someone is able to get to the "gist" of faith from study. This means liberal Christians interpret the Bible differently than those who are fundamentalist or more literal in their interpretation of Biblical events. The Bible is used to teach general principles, ethics, and is frequently used for illustration of points or key ideas rather than the implementation of doctrinal ideas.

BASIC RELIGIOUS PRACTICES

Liberal Christians are not that different in their basic religious practices than most standard Protestants or Catholics. As it is more the way one sees faith than the way one might practice it, there isn't a huge difference in the devotional or worship lives of liberal Christians. They often attend worship services, study and read the Bible, and engage in regular prayer. While their relationship with such practices may be different in application, the exteriors are often similar, if not the same.

Liberal Christians vary from a nominal Protestant or Catholic in that they may see other actions as worship beyond what is typical. Believing Christianity is a foundation for societal reconstruction means that actions which engage such are considered holy and sacred. Engaging in political activism, social activism, engaging in projects for social justice, and even voting are considered sacred in some circles. As a result, liberal Christians may see their experience of faith in a more expansive sense than a more spiritually conservative believer.

HOLIDAYS

Liberal Christians observe the standard Christian holidays found in Protestantism and

Catholicism of Christmas and Easter. Many also observe the Catholic or Protestant liturgical calendars, depending on denomination. For Liberal Christians, national holidays and secondary national observances may also have special significance, such as Civil Rights Sunday, International Women's Day, Memorial Day, Juneteenth, the fourth of July, Veteran's Day, and other days that might have meaning to a community or group.

Visual Signs and Symbols

The signs and symbols used by liberal Christians do not vary much from those used by any other Christian. It's not uncommon to see the use of the cross, ichthys (fish), Alpha and Omega, dove, triquetra, candle, crown of thorns, Bible, minister's collar, bread and communion cup, rainbow, circle, the *Angus Dei* (Lamb of God, with a cross), cross and crown, Chi-Rho Catholics may additionally use symbols including a crucifix, images of saints, sacraments, vestments, the Pope or Vatican, rosary beads, and other images of special note to the individual believer.

Creeds, Books, and Laws

Representing a diversity of denominational beliefs, there are several accepted creeds and regulations that transcend the world of liberal Christianity. Each Christian adheres to the creed, tradition, and regulation of their founding denomination, at least within limits. Liberal Christians are often at odds with more theologically conservative sectors of their denominations, and the past thirty or so years have seen a great amount of dissidence, tension, and disagreement among both leadership and laity alike.

Foundational authors for liberal Christianity, although not seen as ultimate, exclusive, or authoritative by all liberal Christians, include:

- **Walter Rauschenbusch** (1861-1918): Author of *Christianity and the Social Crisis* and *A Theology for the Social Gospel*

  In so far as men have attempted to use the Old Testament as a code of model laws and institutions and have applied these to modern conditions, regardless of the historical connections, these attempts have left a trail of blunder and disaster. In so far as they have caught the spirit that burned in the hearts of the prophets and breathed in gentle humanity through the Mosaic Law, the influence of the Old Testament has been one of the great permanent forces making for democracy and social justice.[7]

- **Harry Emerson Fosdick** (1878-1969): Author of *Riverside Sermons* and *A Guide to Understanding the Bible*

  To keep the Golden Rule we must put ourselves in other people's places, but to do that consists in and depends upon picturing ourselves in their places.[8]

- **John Shelby Spong** (1931-2021): Author of *Rescuing the Bible from Fundamentalism: A Bishop Rethinks the Meaning of Scripture* and *A New Christianity for a New World*

This point must be heard: the Gospels are first-century narrations based on first-century interpretations. Therefore they are a first-century filtering of the experience of Jesus. They have never been other than that. We must read them today not to discover the literal truth about Jesus, but rather to be led into the Jesus experience they were seeking to convey. That experience always lies behind the distortions, which are inevitable since words are limited. If the Gospels are to be for us revelations of truth, we must enter these texts, go beneath the words, discover the experience that made the words necessary, and in this manner seek the meaning to which the words point. One must never identify the text with the revelation or the messenger with the message. That has been the major error in our two thousand years of Christian history. It is an insight that today is still feared and resisted. But let it be clearly stated, the Gospels are not in any literal sense holy, they are not accurate, and they are not to be confused with reality. They are rather beautiful portraits painted by first-century Jewish artists, designed to point the reader toward that which is in fact holy, accurate, and real. The Gospels represent that stage in the development of the faith story in which ecstatic exclamation begins to be placed into narrative form.[9]

- **John Dominic Crossan** (1934-): Author of *In parables: The Challenge of the Historical Jesus* and *Sayings Parallels: A Workbook for the Jesus Tradition*

  My point, once again, is not that those ancient people told literal stories and we are now smart enough to take them symbolically, but that they told them symbolically and we are now dumb enough to take them literally.[10]

- **Hans Kung** (1928-2021): Author of *Theology for the Third Millennium: An Ecumenical View*, *Global Responsibility: In Search of a New World Ethic*, and *Credo: The Apostle's Creed Explained for Today*

  The comprehensive organization of the church, with its solid roots and the manifold forms of charitable help to the many who were poor and in distress; Christian monotheism, which commended itself as the progressive and enlightened position in the face of polytheism, with its wealth of myths; The lofty ethic, which, tested by ascetics and martyrs to the point of death, showed itself to be superior to pagan morality.[11]

- **Marcus Borg** (1942-2015): Author of *Jesus: A New Vision: Spirit, Culture, and the Life of Discipleship* and *Meeting Jesus Again for the First Time: The Historical Jesus and the Heart of Contemporary Faith*

  The way of Jesus is thus not a set of beliefs about Jesus. That people ever thought it was is strange, when we think about it — as if one entered new life by believing certain things to be true, or as if the only people who can be saved are those who know the word "Jesus". Thinking that way virtually amounts to salvation by syllables.

  Rather, the way of Jesus is the way of death and resurrection — the path of transition and transformation from an old way of being to a new way of being. To use the language of incarnation that is so central to John, Jesus incarnates the way. Incarnation means embodiment. Jesus is what the way embodied in a human life looks like.[12]

- **Robin Meyers** (1952-): Author of *Why the Christian Right is Wrong: A Minister's Manfiesto for Taking Back Your Faith, Your Flag, and Your Future* and *Saving Jesus from the Church: How to Stop Worshiping Christ and Start Following Jesus*

  In many American churches, Jesus still comes "as one unknown"— or perhaps as one so well known as to be unrecognizable. He was penniless and itinerant, yet his gospel is now attached to some of the richest and most powerful people on earth, and the good news is really bad news for the poor. Captives are not released; they are warehoused. The blind do not see; rather, the sighted wear blinders. The oppressed are not liberated; they have become the new scapegoats. Sermons are no longer dangerous; they are simply adapted to the appetites and anxieties of the audience. Conservatives rail against sins of the flesh, as if to exorcise their own demons, and liberals baptize political correctness at the expense of honesty.[13]

- **Gustavo Gutierrez Merino** (1928-2024): Author of *A Theology of Liberation*

  In the final analysis, poverty means death: lack of food and housing, the inability to attend properly to health and education needs, the exploitation of workers, permanent unemployment, the lack of respect for one's human dignity, and unjust limitations placed on personal freedom in the areas of self-expression, politics, and religion.[14]

ECLECTIC BELIEFS

It's generally understood that liberal Christians have an assortment of beliefs because it is a way of viewing faith rather than a formalized denomination. As a result, there are several different understandings in the way such may be applied from person to person.

RELATIONS WITH NON-LIBERAL CHRISTIAN GROUPS

The liberal Christian movement is ecumenical in its outlook, willing to discuss and worship with Christians of other denominations (including Catholics). Most are willing to work with and worship on an interfaith level, including individuals of other religious groups and backgrounds that are not Christian in nature or doctrine.

HOLY SITES

Riverside Church, Manhattan, New York; Fountain Street Church, Grand Rapids, Michigan; Old South Church, Boston, Massachusetts.

NOTABLE FIGURES

Nadia Bolz-Weber (1969-), former Lutheran pastor and author; Yvette Flunder (1955-), United Church of Christ author and pastor; Rachel Held Evans (1981-2019), author; Leonardo Boff (1938-), former priest and author; Hans Kung (1928-2021), theologian; John Dominic Crossan (1934-), former priest and New Testament scholar; John Shelby Spong (1931-2021), Episcopal bishop and author; Christopher Morse (1935-), professor; Elisabeth Schussler Florenza (1938-), feminist theologian; Marcus Borg (1942-2015), New Testament scholar and author; Walter Brueggeman (1933-), Old Testament scholar and author; Peter Enns (1961-), author; Richard Beck (1967-), author; Rob Bell (1970-), former pastor and author.

NOTABLE GROUPS

Riverside Church in New York City is a Baptist Church considered by many to be the historical high center of liberal Christianity. The vision of John D. Rockefeller who desired to fund a liberal-visioned and minded church in Manhattan, Harry Emerson Fosdick (1878-1969) was the choice of replacement pastor in 1925 after the first pastor bowed out of the project. Fosdick had rejected offers to be pastor of the church several times, feeling there was great conflict with pastoring a group funded by the richest man in America. He accepted the position on the condition that the church would follow a policy of religious liberalism, not require members to be baptized, and follow a nondenominational outlook. Under his leadership, the congregation doubled by 1930. It is known for its extremely detailed gothic-style architecture, social service outreach, and political activism. Riverside Church continues to exist, promoting liberal values in faith, despite its more recent history of theological disputes, allegations of sexual abuse, and financial mismanagement.[15]

Harry Emerson Fosdick (1878-1969)

FACTS AND FIGURES

Approximately 53% of liberal Christians are white; 18% are black; and 24% are Latino. 64% say they are absolutely certain of a belief in God, while 27% say they are fairly certain God exists, while 5% are not certain at all of a belief in God.[16]

OTHER IMPORTANT DEFINITIONS

- **Third-Way Christianity**: Also known as a "Third Way church." Term used to indicate a group of Christians who fall in between Christian conservatism and liberalism, drawing from both extremes. Most adhere to theological foundations of traditional Protestant views while embracing the social consciousness of liberal Christians.

- **Biblical criticism**: The use of critical analysis and understanding to study the Bible. There are several subheadings as apply to Biblical criticism, but it seeks to explore the Biblical objectively, without denominational or dogmatic bias, for the purpose of better Bible understanding.

- **Social Gospel**: A movement within Protestantism that seeks to examine the world's problems and resolve them through application of Christian ethics. Most of the "social gospel" interests today take interest in poverty, racial injustice, sexism, LGBTQ+, women's issues (such as abortion), immigration, and gun control.

- **Evolution**: The theory of biological origins first established by Charles Darwin. Evolution states that all species of creation develop through the natural selection of specified variations that give each species the ability to survive, reproduce, and continue onward within their specified adaptations. Liberal Christians accept Darwin's theory of evolution in place of creationism, rejecting the idea that the Biblical accounts of creation are scientific in nature, opting to believe they are metaphorical or mythological.

- **Biblical inerrancy**: Also called Biblical infallibility. The belief that the Bible is free from any moral or contextual error, and that it contains nothing contrary to fact.

- **Christology**: Theology that relates to Christ; the study of Christ, particularly His nature (human, divine, or both), role as savior, and His work in salvation.

BELIEVER'S CHARACTERISTICS

Belief in a more personal approach and experience of faith rather than a dogmatic one; rejection of key fundamentalist doctrines, such as the virgin birth of Christ, Christ's divinity, the necessity of baptism and communion, the inerrancy of the Bible, belief in hell, atonement for sin, and miracles; belief in the need to apply faith in a modern context, using modern methods to understand faith today; belief in science, rational thinking, knowledge, and modern-day philosophy; emphasis on the ethics of Christianity and in particular, the ethics present in Jesus' teachings; seeing the Bible as a source of inspiration and teaching rather than an authority text; focusing on the humanity of Jesus, seeing the divinity in Christ as something all should aspire to emulate; embrace of evolution; interest in social activism; interest in liberal political causes; interest in patriotism.

Mormonism

Let us take the Book of Mormon, which a man took and hid in his field, securing it by his faith, to spring up in the last days, or in due time; let us behold it coming forth out of the ground, which is indeed accounted the least of all seeds, but behold it branching forth, yea, even towering, with lofty branches, and God-like majesty, until it, like the mustard seed, becomes the greatest of all herbs. And it is truth, and it has sprouted and come forth out of the earth, and righteousness begins to look down from heaven, and God is sending down His powers, gifts and angels, to lodge in the branches thereof.

(*Teachings of the Prophet Joseph Smith*)[1]

Theology

Embracing a henotheistic view (a group has selected its chief deity over its people without believing it is the supreme or exclusive deity), Mormons believe there is an infinite number of gods universe, each polygamous (having more than one wife), with millions of spirit children. Mormons worship the god of this planet, referred to by many names, including HEAVENLY FATHER, JEHOVAH, ADAM, LORD, and GOD. The god of this planet came to earth, was crucified, died, and resurrected by his god (not a reference to Jesus Christ), and for his obedience and diligence to the laws and rules of his god, became the ruling god of this planet. This god, Jesus Christ, and the Holy Ghost are three separate, distinct gods (described as tritheism). The Holy Ghost is differentiated between the Holy Spirit with the Holy Spirit as the infinite filling of time and space.

Before time, the "Grand Council" or "Council in Heaven" assembled to discuss the terms and conditions by which the spirit sons and daughters of the Father could come to earth, embodying physical beings. This is the Father's ultimate plan for salvation, because it gives each of these spirit beings the opportunity to ascend to godhood. (To become a god one day, one must first be a human being with a physical body.) The promise was that a redeemer would stand to rescue humanity from the physical and spiritual death brought by Adam's fall and provide a redemption for personal sin. Jesus Christ, then known as I AM, agreed to follow the Father's plan of redemption. Lucifer, the spirit-brother of Jesus Christ, offered a counter measure, agreeing to the plan if Lucifer could exalt himself above the father by redeeming individuals who didn't accept the organization of the council. Father agreed to send Jesus Christ, after a vote of the council, which resulted in a war in heaven. The hosts of Lucifer were cast out of heaven. These spirits were destined to wander the earth exclusively as spirits without bodies, thus preventing them from ever ascending to godhood. Jesus Christ fulfilled the heavenly Father's plan, through obedience.[2]

Philosophy

Mormonism is a restoration religion, meaning it considers itself the restoration of something lost through the ages, that is now perfected in its existence. The Church of Jesus Christ of Latter-Day Saints (Mormons) is seen as the restored, true latter-day (last days) church of Jesus Christ. The true church dates to Adam, who was baptized in water, received the gift of the Holy Ghost, and was part of the Melchizedek Priesthood (one of two priesthood orders in Mormonism; a priesthood order from the ancient patriarchs). He then conferred the priesthood upon many of his male descendants, including Seth, Enos, Cainan, Mahalaleel, Jared, Enoch, and Methuselah. At some point in history, the true church was lost, and all churches fell into apostasy. Somewhere around 1820, a man named Joseph Smith (1805-1844) experienced a series of visions (angels, Father and Jesus Christ) calling him to establish his own church, because all religious groups were corrupt. Mormons believe Joseph Smith was the first prophet of modern-day Mormonism, the one established to restore these ancient priesthoods and religious systems that had been lost over the years throughout history. This established a principle of continuing revelation which comes exclusively through their prophet (the central, leading figure of the Mormon Church). As a restoration, Mormons believe they are the only church that shall be saved, combining a belief in both good works and obedience as necessary for salvation.

In Joseph Smith's day, there was interest in the "lost tribes of Israel" and finding their descendants in modern times. The popular theory of the time speculated that Native American peoples of North and South America were of Hebrew ancestry. They travelled, as part of exile, across the ocean in a pod-like structure. Much like the failings and successes of the Israelites in the Old Testament they went through periods of devout adherence but fell into idolatry and away from their heavenly Father. As part of the prevailing theories in the 1830s, Mormons believe Jesus did not just appear in ancient Israel, but also to a people in the ancient Americas who were these descendants of the Hebrew Israelites. The record of these people is contained in The Book of Mormon. Even though DNA research and history does not support these claims, Mormons believe the Book of Mormon is a divine revelation, one that shapes their view of the Americas and of American people. The United States is seen as the "new Zion," where Jesus shall return in the Second Coming. Members of the Mormon church compose the "New Zion."[3]

Adherent Identity

Mormon, Mormonism; the Church of Jesus Christ of Latter-Day Saints; LDS; Saints; Zion; Israel.

Traditional Languages

English.

Sects/Divisions

There are over a thousand splinter sects from the mainline Mormon (LDS) Church. These different splinter sects branched off as doctrine changed, as Mormons desired to fit in with conventional society, and disputes over leadership and authority. The major categories for Mormon sects and divisions include:

- **The Community of Christ**: Originally known as the Reorganized Church of Jesus Christ of Latter-day Saints (RLDS), the Community of Christ formed in 1860 and remains the second-largest Latter-day Saint community in existence. Within its understanding, the successor of Joseph Smith was to be a direct relative of Joseph Smith, having conferred the priesthood upon his son before his death. When his son was old enough to assume the role, Joseph Smith III (1832-1914) and Emma Smith (1804-1879), wife of Joseph Smith, along with a community of others formed the Reorganized Church of Jesus Christ of Latter-day Saints. The group has much in common with Mormon teaching, with a few exceptions. RLDS differ from Mormons on their doctrines about the eternal nature of the Heavenly Father. They do not believe man can become gods, and consider the Book of Mormon and Joseph Smith's Inspired Version of the Bible to also be accepted as scripture. They accept The Doctrine and Covenants of Mormonism up until the point when Joseph Smith died, and they reject the entirety of The Pearl of Great Price. In many ways, the Community of Christ has adopted Protestant doctrine and outlook with a Mormon structure and adaptation of The Book of Mormon. The church has undergone considerable revision since the 1960s and now admits women to its priesthood, has constructed its own denominational temple, and participates in ecumenical efforts to reconcile with traditional Christian denominations.

Community of Christ logo

- **Independent Restoration Branches**: These are Mormon sects that were formed one of three ways: in dispute of the rightful successor of Joseph Smith, in conflict with the claims of other Mormon breakaway groups, or as restorers of foundational Mormon doctrine as Mormon sects began to break away from traditional beliefs. They adhere to six fundamental principles of the Restored Gospel, as found in Hebrews 6: Faith towards God, repentance, baptism in water, laying on of hands for the reception of the Holy Ghost, resurrection of the dead, and eternal judgment. Governed according to LDS structure, these groups claim their founders broke away and established their groups by divine right or divine inspiration, such as visions and messages from an angel or John the Baptist. Some also have additional scriptures or revelations that are in printed form, related to the rule and purpose of their churches. These groups include The Church of Jesus Christ of Latter-day Saints, Strangite, The Church of Jesus Christ, Bickertonite, The Church of Jesus Christ, Hendrickite, Remnant Church of Jesus Christ of Latter-Day Saints, and The Church of Christ, Fettingite.[4]

- **Mormon Fundamentalists**: Mormon Fundamentalism is a term used to describe groups that follow the "fundamentals" of the Mormon faith, dating back to the 1800s. In particular, Mormon Fundamentalists follow the doctrines and practices laid out by Joseph Smith and second LDS president Brigham Young (1801-1877). They are often best-known for their practice of polygamy, by which a man takes multiple wives in his goal to ascend to godhood. When the mainline LDS church began excommunicating polygamous members in 1890, notable families desired to continue the practice broke away to form their own groups. Many also ascribe to specific doctrines introduced into the church by Brigham Young, such as the Adam-God doctrine (Adam is the father of both the spirits and physical bodies of humans on earth, including Jesus, as he is a creator god). More than just being about specified doctrines, these groups often adhere to specific governing and financial practices (such as community trusts) by which church communities live on land owned by their respective churches. Housing, finances, local governments, schools, and businesses are all owned and held in communal trust by the church, by which members receive their livelihoods. There are seven major family names involved in the founding and continuation of Mormon Fundamentalist communities: Wolley, Barlow, Musser, Johnson, Allred, Kingston, and LeBaron. These communities have been rivals at different points in time, often with violent and clashing histories. The major Mormon Fundamentalist sects include the Fundamentalist Church of Jesus Christ of Latter-Day Saints, Apostolic United Brethren, Council of Friends, Latter Day Church of Christ, Centennial Park, Church of Jesus Christ (Original Doctrine), The Church of Jesus Christ of Latter-day Saints and the Kingdom of God, School of the Prophets, True and Living Church of Jesus Christ of Saints of the Last Days, and The Church of the Firstborn and the General Assembly of Heaven.[5,6]

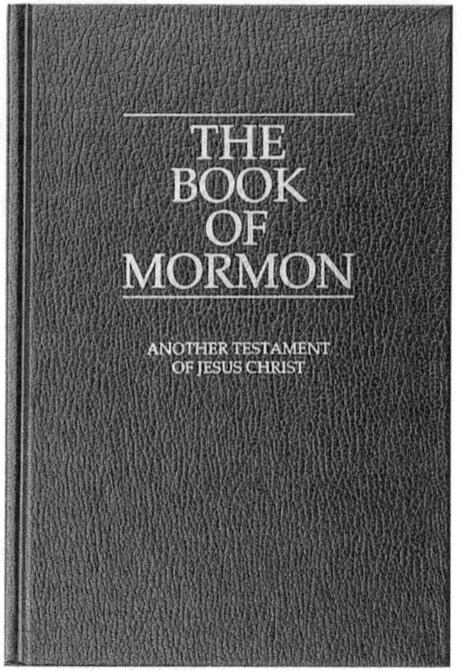

The Book of Mormon

NUMBER OF ADHERENTS

There are approximately 16,000,000 Mormons worldwide.[7] There is somewhere between 20,000 and 60,000 Fundamental Mormons[8], approximately 250,000 members of the Community of Christ, and approximately 10,000 Independent Restoration Branches[9].

DISPUTES WITHIN GROUP

Because Mormonism centers on the concept that it is a restoration of something true that has been or can be lost, this makes adherents susceptible to follow individuals within the movement who claim different, new, or alternate revelation. Mormonism has changed over the years, including many fundamental doctrines central to its core doctrine, such as polygamy, the Adam-God doctrine, and the admission of black and dark-skinned men to the priesthood. The nature of these changes, along with the issue that a concept of constant, continuing revelation can lead to authority challenges and issues, have led to huge disputes over what it means to be a Mormon or a follower of Joseph Smith, down to the present day.

SCRIPTURES

There are four standard inspired scriptural works in Mormonism:

Joseph Smith

- The Holy Bible, Old and New Testaments: the Pentateuch (Genesis, Exodus, Leviticus, Numbers, and Deuteronomy), Historical books (Joshua, Judges, Ruth, 1 Samuel, 2 Samuel, 1 Kings, 2 Kings, 1 Chronicles, 2 Chronicles, Ezra, Nehemiah, Esther), Wisdom books (Job, Psalms, Proverbs, Ecclesiastes), Prophetic books (Isaiah, Jeremiah, Lamentations, Ezekiel, Daniel, Hosea, Joel, Amos, Obadiah, Jonah, Micah, Nahum, Habakkuk, Zephaniah, Haggai, Zechariah, Malachi), the Gospels (Matthew, Mark, Luke, John), the Acts of the Apostles, the Pauline Epistles (Romans, 1 Corinthians, 2 Corinthians, Galatians, Ephesians, Philippians, Colossians, 1 Thessalonians, 2 Thessalonians, 1 Timothy, 2 Timothy, Titus, Philemon, Hebrews) the General Epistles (James, 1 Peter, 2 Peter, 1 John, 2 John, 3 John, Jude) and Revelation. The Song of Solomon is part of the collection of scripture but is considered uninspired. The mainline LDS church uses the King James Version as its Bible translation. It is "the word of God as far as it is translated correctly." The Bible is seen as the only one of the four standard works considered as non-infallible.

- **<u>The Book of Mormon: Another Testament of Jesus Christ:</u>** Divided up into two sections, the Small Plates of Nephi and the Large Plates of Nephi. The Small Plates of Nephi contains the First Book of Nephi, Second Book of Nephi, Book of Jacob, Book of Enos, book of Jarom, Book of Omni, Words of Mormon. The Large Plates of Nephi (found in abridgement) are the Book of Mosiah, Book of Alma, Book of Helaman, Third Nephi, Fourth Nephi, Book of Mormon, Book of Ether, and the Book of Moroni. Largely the very heart of Mormon belief, The Book of Mormon is the record of a people in the Americas with ancient

Hebrew ancestry and their interactions with Heavenly Father. Their spiritual experiences resemble that of the Old Testament Hebrews, whereby the people of the Americas continued to fall into idolatry, eventually abandoning the true faith all together. The book is named after Mormon, an ancient prophet in the Americas who compiled this ancient history from records. Mormons believe The Book of Mormon was inscribed on gold plates and buried by Moroni (Mormon's son) for safe keeping in what is now known as western New York State. In 1823, Joseph Smith had a vision of Moroni, now an angel, to reveal the location of these plates. Joseph Smith translated these plates, which were published as the Book of Mormon in 1830. Mormons believe The Book of Mormon is the unaltered, infallible word of the Father. When an individual attempts to read the Book of Mormon for the first time, Mormons tell potential converts to read it and ask Heavenly Father in advance if the words in the book are "not true."

And now I would that ye should be humble, and be submissive, and gentle; easy to be entreated; full of patience and long-suffering; being temperate in all things; being diligent in keeping the commandments of God at all times; asking for whatsoever things ye stand in need, both spiritual and temporal; always returning thanks unto God for whatsoever things ye do receive. And see that ye have faith, hope, and charity, and then ye will always abound in good works.[10]

And now, my sons, remember, remember that it is upon the rock of our Redeemer, who is Christ, the Son of God, that ye must build your foundation; that when the devil shall send forth his mighty winds, yea, his shafts in the whirlwind, yea, when all his hail and his mighty storm shall beat upon you, it shall have no power over you to drag you down to the gulf of misery and endless wo, because of the rock upon which ye are built, which is a sure foundation, a foundation whereon if men build they cannot fall.[11]

Behold, I would exhort you that when ye shall read these things, if it be wisdom in God that ye should read them, that ye would remember how merciful the Lord hath been unto the children of men, from the creation of Adam even down until the time that ye shall receive these things, and ponder it in your hearts.

And when ye shall receive these things, I would exhort you that ye would ask God, the Eternal Father, in the name of Christ, if these things are not true; and if ye shall ask with a sincere heart, with real intent, having faith in Christ, he will manifest the truth of it unto you, by the power of the Holy Ghost.

And by the power of the Holy Ghost ye may know the truth of all things.[12]

- **<u>The Doctrine and Covenants</u>**: A series of revelations given to the prophets of the church, starting with Joseph Smith. Sections 1-134 and 137 were authored by Joseph Smith, Sections 135-136 were from the Quorum of the Twelve, Official Declaration 1 is from Wilford Woodruff (1807-1898), Section 138 is from Joseph F. Smith (1838-1918), and Official Declaration 2 was written by Spencer W. Kimball (1895-1985). 102, 123, 127-131, 134, 135, and Official Declarations 1 and 2 are not considered revelations, but specific documents and statements. The Community of Christ only accepts Joseph

Smith's authorship to The Doctrine and Covenants, and has added their own subsequent instructions, adding up to 165 sections, in totality. Other Independent Restoration Branches also have their own versions of The Doctrine and Covenants, most accepting older, original versions of its publications, or older versions of the publication with their own additions.

If thou art called to pass through tribulation; if thou art in perils among false brethren; if thou art in perils among robbers; if thou art in perils by land or by sea;

If thou art accused with all manner of false accusations; if thine enemies fall upon thee; if they tear thee from the society of thy father and mother and brethren and sisters; and if with a drawn sword thine enemies tear thee from the bosom of thy wife, and of thine offspring, and thine elder son, although but six years of age, shall cling to thy garments, and shall say, My father, my father, why can't you stay with us? O, my father, what are the men going to do with you? and if then he shall be thrust from thee by the sword, and thou be dragged to prison, and thine enemies prowl around thee like wolves for the blood of the lamb;

And if thou shouldst be cast into the pit, or into the hands of murderers, and the sentence of death passed upon thee; if thou be cast into the deep; if the billowing surge conspire against thee; if fierce winds become thine enemy; if the heavens gather blackness, and all the elements combine to hedge up the way; and above all, if the very jaws of hell shall gape open the mouth wide after thee, know thou, my son, that all these things shall give thee experience, and shall be for thy good.

The Son of Man hath descended below them all. Art thou greater than he?[13]

- **The Pearl of Great Price**: A series of writings produced by Joseph Smith and published in his lifetime. There are five sections to The Pearl of Great Price: The Book of Moses (contains visions of Moses and the first six chapters of the Joseph Smith Translation of the Bible); the Book of Abraham (work based on an Egyptian papyri from a traveling exhibition; the scroll Joseph Smith used has been examined and in no way translates to the version Joseph Smith published); Joseph Smith – Matthew (Joseph Smith's retranslation of parts of the Gospel of Matthew), Joseph Smith – History (an autobiographical record of Joseph Smith's early history), and the Articles of Faith (an 1842 letter outlining the thirteen fundamental doctrines of Mormonism).[14]

  We believe in being honest, true, chaste, benevolent and in doing good to all men; indeed we may say that we follow the admonition of Paul - We believe all things, we hope all things, we have endured many things and hope to be able to endure all things. If there is anything virtuous, lovely, or of good report or praiseworthy, we seek after these things.[15]

Joseph Smith also undertook a translational project of the Bible in his lifetime. His sought to correct fundamental errors he believed it contained and add additional revelations. His version of the Bible is now known as the *Inspired Version of the Holy Scriptures*, also known as the Joseph Smith Translation. There was no released, authorized version of it in Joseph Smith's lifetime. Although he did intend to release it, he died before such was possible. The manuscripts were retained by Emma Smith (his widow), who refused to issue them to the LDS church. The documents were then given to the Reorganized Church of Jesus Christ of Latter-Day Saints, which became the sole copyright holder for the text. It does not contain the Song of Solomon, which Joseph Smith considered uninspired.[16]

> *And it came to pass that the Lord spake unto Moses, saying, Behold, I reveal unto you concerning this heaven and this earth; write the words which I speak.*
>
> *I am the Beginning and the End, the Almighty God. By mine Only Begotten I created these things.*
>
> *Yea, in the beginning I created the heaven and the earth upon which thou standest.*
>
> *And the earth was without form and void; and I caused darkness to come up upon the face of the deep.*
>
> *And my Spirit moved upon the face of the waters, for I am God.*[16]

Basic Religious Practices

Mormonism centers around the nuclear family as an eternal unit within the structure of the church family. Mormon families are seen as eternal units, sealed to stand as a family for time and eternity within marriages officiated in a Mormon temple ceremony. Worship takes place on Sunday mornings at a local church. Larger churches (150 to 500 members) are known as wards, and smaller churches are known as branches. Wards contain a bishop (comparable to a local pastor) and two counselors that assist the bishop with their duties (the three together are known as the bishopric). Branches contain a branch president and one or two counselors as needed. All wards are grouped into stakes, which is a grouping of wards (each stake contains at least five wards), and branches organized into districts. The main organizations of a ward are known as auxiliaries and are overseen by the bishop of a ward. These include the Relief Society (Mormon organization for women), Young Men and Young Women's organizations, Primary (children's church), and Sunday School.

Weekly services are known as Sacrament Meeting and consist of a weekly communion of bread and water, lessons or testimonies, prayers, and hymns. Sunday school (for all ages) takes place after the Sacrament Meeting.

Mormon leadership is fulfilled through their priesthoods. The Aaronic Priesthood is seen as a lesser priesthood, usually filled by males aged 11-18 years of age (deacons are ordained between 12 and 13). The Melchizedek Priesthood is filled by eligible males aged 18 and older. Within the Melchizedek Priesthood are five possible offices: Apostle, Seventy, Patriarch, High Priest, and Elder. Most men within the Melchizedek Priesthood serve as Elders within local congregations, assisting in the work of a ward and assisting the bishop with such matters such as services and auxiliaries. All men who are eligible rotate duties within branch congregations and wards on a two-year basis. The priesthood of Mormonism is seen as a lay responsibility, and lower church leaders are not paid for their duties.[19]

Mormon Temple, Salt Lake City, Utah

Mormon temples are exclusively used for Mormon rites and are not used for weekly worship. Mormon temples are used for secret rites (regarded as sacred) especially that of the endowment ceremony. Endowment ceremonies prepare its recipients to become divine beings, with due authority in the afterlife. Within the endowment ceremony is a special rite that recreates the creation of the world and the fall of Adam and Eve, complete with washing and anointing, the receipt of a new name (must be kept secret), and a special temple garment (nicknamed "Mormon underwear") to be worn underneath their clothing throughout their lives. Those who undergo endowment are taught gestures, grips, handshakes, and passwords designed to help them enter into heaven. Endowment ceremonies also now include covenantal promises to God, such as consecration to the church. To receive a temple marriage ceremony or be a missionary, one must complete the endowment ceremony. Mormon temples are also the sites for their ritual baptism of the dead, by which Mormons stand-in for deceased non-Mormons, therefore initiating them into the religion and pushing them ahead into the afterlife. It is for this reason that Mormons take an interest in genealogy; the records provide access to names and individuals that can receive a proxy baptism (baptism for the dead).

Mormon temple ceremonies are regarded with secrecy by members of the church and are therefore of notable suspicion by those outside the denomination. Much of the Endowment Ceremony contains elements of Freemasonry, found in different initiation rites as part of the Royal Arch degree. Not all Mormons are eligible for temple service; one must get a temple recommend from their ward bishop to stand eligible for temple service. It is expected that all practicing Mormons in good standing commit to complete several hours of temple service each month.[19]

Mormons are expected to extol Mormon family values, including regular family devotions, having many children, live a moral life according to the precepts of the church, and proclaim the LDS Church to all the world.

HOLIDAYS

Mormons observe Christmas and Easter as the two most primary holidays on their yearly calendar. Unique to Mormons is the celebration of Pioneer Day on July 24. This is the day the first Latter-day Saints reached the Salt Lake Valley in 1847. In honor of Pioneer Day, the LDS Church presents its annual pageant recounting its history at Hill Cumorah in Palmyra, New York (the location where Joseph Smith first discovered the golden plates that became The Book of Mormon).

While not a formal holiday, Mormons regard Sundays as days for rest and worship. Most Mormons will spend most of their Sundays at their local ward or branch. Mondays are usually deemed "family home evening," what most would classify as a "family night" of prayer, study, games, or other activities done at home as a family.[20]

VISUAL SIGNS AND SYMBOLS

Families and family values; the angel Moroni (robed man with a trumpet to his lips; often found atop Mormon temples); The Book of Mormon; genealogy; the Mormon Tabernacle Choir; Mormon temples; images of Jesus Christ painted by Carl Bloch and Thorvaldsen; CTR (Choose the Right) shield; beehive (the word "Deseret" found in the Book of Mormon is translated as "honeybee"); tabernacle organ; forget-me-nots (represents the five things Relief Society members are to remember); iron rod (symbolizes the Word of God); golden plates; handcarts (symbolizes the pioneers of Mormonism crossing the country to Salt Lake City); sunstone (represents the Nauvoo, Illinois period of Mormon history); laurel wreaths (victor's crown); stripling warriors (ideal male characters in the Book of Mormon); Captain Moroni; Liahona (a device that led the people in the Book of Mormon through the wilderness; now a worldwide church magazine); stars; pioneers; Young Women's organization colors (red, green, yellow, orange, blue, purple, white, gold); missionary tags (name badges); tree of life.[21]

CREEDS, BOOKS, AND LAWS

Mormonism is a "creedless religion," meaning it does not echo nor stand upon the traditional creeds of traditional Catholicism, Orthodoxy, or high Protestantism. Mormons are guided by the thirteen fundamental doctrines of Mormonism, also known as the Articles of Faith:

1. *We believe in God, the Eternal Father, and in His Son, Jesus Christ, and in the Holy Ghost.*
2. *We believe that men will be punished for their own sins, and not for Adam's transgression.*
3. *We believe that through the Atonement of Christ, all mankind may be saved, by obedience to the laws and ordinances of the Gospel.*
4. *We believe that the first principles and ordinances of the Gospel are: first, Faith in the Lord Jesus Christ; second, Repentance; third, Baptism by immersion for the remission of sins; fourth, Laying on of hands for the gift of the Holy Ghost.*
5. *We believe that a man must be called of God, by prophecy, and by the laying on of hands by those who are in authority, to preach the Gospel and administer in the ordinances thereof.*
6. *We believe in the same organisation that existed in the Primitive Church, namely, apostles, prophets, pastors, teachers, evangelists, and so forth.*
7. *We believe in the gift of tongues, prophecy, revelation, visions, healing, interpretation of tongues, and so forth.*
8. *We believe the Bible to be the word of God as far as it is translated correctly; we also believe the Book of Mormon to be the word of God.*
9. *We believe all that God has revealed, all that He does now reveal, and we believe that He will yet reveal many great and important things pertaining to the Kingdom of God.*
10. *We believe in the literal gathering of Israel and in the restoration of the Ten Tribes; that Zion (the New Jerusalem) will be built upon the American continent; that Christ will reign personally upon the earth; and, that the earth will be renewed and receive its paradisiacal glory.*

11. *We claim the privilege of worshipping Almighty God according to the dictates of our own conscience, and allow all men the same privilege, let them worship how, where, or what they may.*
12. *We believe in being subject to kings, presidents, rulers, and magistrates, in obeying, honouring, and sustaining the law.*
13. *We believe in being honest, true, chaste, benevolent, virtuous, and in doing good to all men; indeed, we may say that we follow the admonition of Paul - We believe all things, we hope all things, we have endured many things, and hope to be able to endure all things. If there is anything virtuous, lovely, or of good report or praiseworthy, we seek after these things.*[22]

The Articles of Faith are found in The Pearl of Great Price, one of the four standard works of the Mormon Church. Outside of the Articles of Faith, Mormon law and guiding ethics are found in The Doctrine and Covenants. As believers in continuing revelation, Mormons believe their god continually reveals matters through the leadership of the LDS Church. For this reason, the president of the Mormon Church is continually making and issuing statements and decrees on issues. Issues of enforcement are strictly observed.

Because Mormons believe continuing revelation comes through its leaders, Mormon leadership and the Mormon leadership structure is also related to its essential governance. Mormon leaders are always men, as the priesthood is exclusive to men. The prophet is a specific individual chosen by Heavenly Father to serve as his spokesman on earth. Two counselors, identified as apostles, serve the First Presidency. From there, twelve apostles are identified as the Quorum of the Twelve Apostles (successors to the prophet are selected from among the twelve). Next are two Quorums of the Seventy and the Presiding Bishopric, known as general authorities. These authorities oversee specific church and administrative duties within the church, especially overseeing and directing regional and local needs. It is only those who serve in the church on the general authority level and higher who receive stipend for their service to the church.[23]

ECLECTIC BELIEFS

Perhaps the greatest issue within Mormon circles is the sanitization of their founder, Joseph Smith. There is question as to the veracity of his life, character, and general behavior, all of which are frequently sanitized or ignored by Mormonism. Portions of The Book of Mormon are plagiarized from another book (*View of the Hebrews* by Ethan Smith) and his claims of translating documents from original languages has been brought into question. Issues of his personal infidelity, dishonesty, occult practices, and great variations in his testimony and accounts of early spiritual experiences are all issues the Mormon Church ignores, glosses over, or withholds. To Mormons, Joseph Smith is the ultimate in leadership, faith, and spiritual example.

Mormons place a great amount of their efforts on evangelization. Historically speaking, Mormon missions have taken a strong interest in the native population of the Americas. Seeing itself as the only true church and all other groups as apostates, Mormons are best-known for their extensive missionary program. It is generally expected that every Mormon (in good standing with the church) will fulfill one mission within their lifetime; most missionaries are under twenty-five years of age, but it is also possible to see older married couples on a mission, as well. Missionaries travel in pairs and are assigned to a specific area after training in a missionary training center. Missions are two years for men, eighteen months for women, and up to three years for married couples. Missionaries are not paid (they receive a monthly stipend of anywhere from $100 to $500 per month for various incidentals) and must raise approximately $10,000 to $12,000 for their missionary work (how the bulk of a stipend is paid).

Adam, the first man in creation, is a central figure in Mormon cosmology. Mormons believe Adam was the archangel Michael before being born on earth, and that he and Eve were predestined to be the first man and woman. Mormons also believe Adam and Eve were predestined to fall into sin, and such was an essential step in salvation. When Adam on earth; predestined to be first man and woman and fall of man an essential step of salvation. When Adam and Eve were expulsed from the Garden of Eden, they dwelt in Adam-ondo-Ahman, which is now present-day Daviess County, Missouri (this site is also believed to be a spot for a priesthood meeting prior to the Second Coming of Jesus Christ). Imagery of Adam and Eve and dramas that incorporate Adam and Eve are an essential part of Mormon Endowment ceremonies.

Mormons believe there are three levels of heaven: the telestial kingdom (the lowest level of heaven reserved for those who were not Mormon in this life, deceived by lies, where even Christ and the Father cannot go), the terrestrial kingdom (the middle level for those who received the Mormon gospel but did not live out its commands to the fullest), and the celestial kingdom (the highest level reserved for those who followed the Mormon gospel in full and were married in a sealed, temple marriage for time and eternity). Hell is metaphorical in nature, regarded as a spirit prison. There, spirits are trapped for time and eternity due to their disobedience. Those in "spirit prison" can advance to "spirit paradise," where the righteous await resurrection. Mormons believe Jesus stayed in spirit paradise before rising from the dead. Outer Darkness is noted by its lack of presence for the Mormon god, although the exact nature of such is debated. There is no clear definition of just what it means.

Mormons believe all human beings are premortal; they have existence as spirit beings before they are born into this life. For obedience to Heavenly Father Mormon men will ascend to godhood to serve as such over their own planets. Women do not have this option but will exist as spouses of the gods, spawning an infinite number of spirit children throughout eternity. They will receive the graces of the Mormon priesthood through their marriage to their husbands. Even though polygamy was part of Mormon doctrine until 1890 (it was prohibited so Utah could achieve statehood with the United States government), polygamy is still a central aspect of Mormon theology. The Doctrine and Covenants still teach polygamy is necessary for exultation to godhood. While the church may not encourage marital polygamy in this life, it is still understood to be a spiritual principle within the mainline church. For this reason, one could argue Mormonism is, in its essence, a fertility religion.

Until 1978, black and dark-skinned men (men of color) were prohibited from receiving the rites, ordination, and graces of the Mormon priesthood. Joseph Smith espoused the idea that dark skin was a sign of sin. Brigham Young believed non-white individuals were justified as slaves, ineligible to vote, unfit to marry whites, and unsuitable to serve in the Mormon priesthood. The pre-existence of black individuals was seen as being "less virtuous" in their spiritual state than white spirits. Today, Mormons deny any justification of the priesthood based on race, or pre-mortal states.

Mormonism prohibits the use of alcohol, caffeine, tobacco, and hot beverages (anything other than herbal tea) in a teaching known as the Word of Wisdom. The Word of Wisdom also promotes eating fruits and vegetables, sparing use of meat, and eating many grains. This health code was introduced by Joseph Smith in 1833 as a health code for his followers. Modern-day Mormons also extend the Word of Wisdom to include prohibitive use of illegal drugs and an encouragement for exercise.

In recent years, the Mormon Church has come under fire for its practice of "conversion therapy" on homosexual individuals. Through Brigham Young University (and still practiced by some independent practitioners today), conversion therapy seeks to create physical shock, hard labor, and physical abuse in response to sexual stimuli. Even though conversion therapy has been proven ineffective, dangerous, and life-threatening in some instances, it is still known to occur. Homosexuality is seen as incompatible with the process of achieving godhood as are also birth control and abortion.

RELATIONS WITH NON-MORMONS

Joseph Smith Preaching to the Indians, William Armitage (1890)

Traditionally, Mormonism held itself apart from other denominations. Mormons did not, early in their history, desire to be identified as Christian, or associated with Christianity, in any form. Given Mormons reject theological orthodoxy, baptism of other churches, and Biblical inerrancy, they have long had a complicated relationship with other churches. As Mormons also use terminology similar to Christians with different meanings or concepts behind them, many Christian groups treat Mormonism as suspect. 31% of the general population in the United States do not regard Mormons as Christians; three out of four American Protestant pastors do not consider Mormons Christians. Over the past few years, Mormons have tried to stake their identity among interfaith groups, assisting in charity work. Today, Mormons join forces with those of other religious groups (particularly Evangelicals and Catholics) for political statements and the rejection of certain bills or amendments, including issues of same-sex marriage and abortion.[24]

HOLY SITES

Smith family farm (including the Sacred grove), Palmyra, New York; Kirtland Temple, Kirtland, Ohio; Adam-ondi-Ahman, near Jameson, Missouri; Independence Temple Lot, Independence, Missouri; Far West Temple Site, Kingston, Missouri; Carthage Jail, Carthage, Illinois; Liberty Jail Historic Site, Liberty, Missouri; Winter Quarters, North Omaha, Nebraska; Martin's Cove, near Alcova, Wyoming; Temple Square, Salt Lake City, Utah; Nauvoo Temple, Nauvoo, Illinois; Red Brick Store, Nauvoo, Illinois; Far West Temple Site, Caldwell County, Missouri; Hill Cumorah Visitor's

Center, Manchester, New York; Priesthood Restoration Site, Oakland Township, Pennsylvania; Peter Whitmer log home, Fayette, New York; Joseph Smith Birthplace Memorial, Sharon, Vermont; John Johnson Farm, Hiram, Ohio; Book of Mormon Historic Publication Site, Palmyra, New York.

NOTABLE FIGURES

Joseph Smith (1805-1844), founder; Donny (1957-) and Marie Osmond (1959-), entertainers; Brigham Young (1801-1877), successor to Joseph Smith; Bill Marriott (1932-), Hotelier; Mitt Romney (1947-), politician; Stephenie Meyer (1994-), author; Steve Young (1961-), athlete; Harry Reid (1939-2021), politician; Ted Bundy (1946-1989), serial killer; Yukihro Matsumoto (1965-), scientist; John Moses Browning (1855-1926), scientist; Nathaniel Baldwin (1878-1961), scientist; Dinah Jane Hansen (1997-), musician; Gladys Knight (1944-), musician; Ray Combs (1956-1996), game show host; Glen (1943-) and Les Charles (1948-), writers and producers; Rick Schroder (1970-), actor; Stephen R, Covey (1932-2012), author and motivational speaker; Katherine Heigl (1978-), actress; Nolan D. Archibald 1943-), businessman.

NOTABLE GROUPS

The Apostolic United Brethren (AUB; also called the Allred Group) is a Mormon Fundamentalist sect practicing polygamy today. It is a more liberal branch of Mormon fundamentalism as it allows sexual relationships between married couples for more than the purpose of procreation. It is also known for allowing its members to dress in more modern, updated fashions than many of the other polygamous sects. The Apostolic United Brethren date back to 1886, originating with a leadership meeting claiming the revelation that plural marriage should not cease, but remain active by a separate group from the mainline church. The AUB hit the spotlight in 1977 when its leader, Rulon Allred (1906-1977) was shot by Rena Chynoweth (1958-) under the direction of Ervil LeBaron (1925-1981) (a competing polygamist leader). The Allred group has continued with a few other leaders. Most recently, it gained media attention through the show *Sister Wives*, as the Brown family (Kody Brown [1969-], wife Robyn [1978-], and now ex-wives Meri [1971-], Jenelle [1969-] and Christine [1972-] and their nineteen children were previously part of the Apostolic United Brethren.[25]

FACTS AND FIGURES

Mormons are the most involved members of any surveyed religious group. 67% of Mormons rank their participation as high; 29% rank their participation as medium; and approximately 4% report their participation with their religion as low.[26]

OTHER IMPORTANT DEFINITIONS

- **Age of Accountability**: The age when a Mormon child is eligible to receive water baptism, usually around the age of eight years old. Prior to this age, children are considered free from sin.

- **Ancient of Days**: A reference to Adam.

- **Apostates**: Former members of the Mormon Church who have since renounced its teachings and now believe religious teachings contrary to those of Mormonism.

- **Anti-Mormon**: Anyone critical of the LDS movement, especially Christians.

- **Atonement**: The work accomplished through Jesus Christ's suffering in Gethsemane and on the cross that allows humans the opportunity to ultimately achieve godhood; if not godhood, resurrection into one of the two other kingdoms of heaven. Mormons do not wear cross jewelry or utilize crosses in their system of worship because they believe the true suffering of Christ was wrought in the Garden of Gethsemane rather than on the cross where he died.[27]

- **Born in the Covenant**: A term to describe "cradle Mormons" who are born into the church and whose parents have been sealed in a temple marriage ceremony.

- **Calling**: An assignment given to a member of a ward by the leaders of a ward.[28]

- **Church of the Devil**: Any church that opposes Mormonism. Also called the Great and Abominable Church.[29]

- **Creation**: Matter, seen as eternal, indicates their god did not create the universe out of nothing; rather, Heavenly Father used what was already present; items that have no beginning and no end and cannot be destroyed.[30]

- **Feeling the Spirit**: Mormon communications received from Heavenly Father about specific things, directions, and leadings in their lives.[31]

- **First estate**: Another term for the premortal spiritual existence of human beings.

- **Great Apostasy**: The belief that the true church lost all authority, power, and most importantly, the priesthood after the death of Christ's apostles.

- **Hosanna Shout**: A Mormon Temple dedication rite by which members take a white handkerchief and wave it, shouting, "Hosanna, hosanna, hosanna to God and the Lamb" three different times, followed by "Amen, Amen, and Amen."[32]

- **Jack Mormon**: A Mormon who is not practicing their faith.

- **Kingdom of God**: The Mormon Church, both now and futuristically as a spiritual and political rule in the world to come; the Celestial kingdom.

- **Mercy**: Heavenly Father's reprieve for justice open to sinners who earn their right by doing good works.

- **Molly Mormon**: The ideal image of a Mormon female.

- **Moroni's Promise**: Found in Moroni 10:4: *And when ye shall receive these things, I would exhort that ye would ask God, the Eternal Father, in the name of Christ, if these things are not true; and if ye shall ask with a sincere heart, with real intent, having faith if Christ, he will manifest the truth of it unto you, by the power of the Holy Ghost.*

- **New Jerusalem**: A city that will be built in Jackson County, Missouri.[33]

- **Patriarchal blessing**: A personal prophecy given to a Mormon.

- **Patriarchal Order**: The seal of a Mormon temple marriage, allowing a Mormon family to live in the celestial kingdom in the afterlife. Husbands are regarded as the presiding officer of the family because he is the priesthood holder.

- **Plural Marriage**: The official term for the Mormon doctrine on polygamy.

- **Polyandry**: When a woman has multiple husbands. Records indicate at least ten of Joseph Smith's wives were married to other men.

- **Testimony meeting**: A monthly meeting where members of a Mormon church are given the opportunity to assume the pulpit to share their witness, either of the validity of the church, of a special confirmation in their lives, or other special event.

- **Tithe**: The giving of ten percent of one's income to the church; required for those who desire to perform temple service. If a member gives less than ten percent, members meet with their bishops via private meeting to make up the difference in what is known as a Tithing settlement. Members who do not meet with their tithes will no longer hold their Temple Recommend.

- **Triple Combination**: A one-volume book containing *The Book of Mormon*, *The Doctrine and Covenants*, and *The Pearl of Great Price*.

- **Virgin birth**: The siring of Jesus through the Heavenly Father and the Virgin Mary; Mormons believe the Heavenly Father literally had a sexual relationship with Mary.

- **Wentworth Letter**: Another term for the Articles of Faith.

BELIEVER'S CHARACTERISTICS

Emphasis on family (including the eternal nature therein), church, and leadership; use of The Book of Mormon, The Doctrine and Covenants, and The Pearl of Great Price; emphasis on purity and the need to remain pure, both physically and spiritually; emphasis on evangelization and missionary work; genealogy and lineage are important; emphasis on Joseph Smith; embrace a history of polygamy; active and eager to do temple work; emphasis on the Aaronic and Melchizedek Priesthoods; active hymnology; dress codes; upholding the codes of the Word of Wisdom; active in church; eager to convert outsiders; belief in continuing revelation; spiritual evolution fully within the church, as the world and all other churches are apostate.

New Age Movement

We are at any given moment living the totality of everything...The vibrational oscillation of nature is quickening...Just remember that you are god, and act accordingly.
(Shirley MacLaine)[1]

Theology

The New Age Movement holds a variety of interreligious beliefs, especially pertaining to theology. It is possible to meet New Agers that espouse a variety of theological positions, especially those that reflect ideas present in eastern religions (such as Hinduism or Buddhism). Overall, the New Age Movement espouses belief in an impersonal, universal life force known by many names, including SPIRIT, KI, ENERGY, LOVE, LIFE, LIFE SOURCE, CREATOR, LIGHT, THE UNIVERSE, or LIFE FORCE, but especially, GOD. This impersonal force is manifest throughout creation, as an all-encompassing entity identical to reality, known as pantheism. New Age practitioners believe the divine present in all beings should be worshiped.

New Agers believe all religious paths lead to this divine, eternal life force and see all religious leaders as teachers, equal in rank and standing, known now as "ascended masters" (also called the Great White Brotherhood). Such is an adaptation from Theosophy, the "primer" for the New Age Movement. These masters communicate with humanity through channeling (the practice by which an individual communicates with a deceased spirit for the purpose of gaining information). This information can be channeled through messages, automated writing (by which a spirit entity controls one's writing process), a trance, or the use of occult aids, such as tarot cards or psychic divination. Within New Age understanding, it is also common to see and receive the word of a master through an angel, an apparition (a ghost or phantom-like image of a deceased individual), or some sort of spiritual vision or other experience.

The New Age Movement sees all religious experience, tradition, and teaching as the same, with the same inherent value and message. New Agers believe in such ascended masters as Buddha, Krishna, Jesus Christ (who lived in 150 BC as a Hindu guru), Confucius, Mary (the mother of Jesus Christ), the Apostle Paul, Merku, Sanat Kumara, Melchizedek, the Archangel Michael, the Angel Metatron, Kwan Yin, Kuthumi, ancient Egyptian, Celtic, Greek and Roman gods and goddesses, and Saint Germain (an eighteenth-century musician, courtier, inventor, and alchemist who is given high relevance within occult communities). While none are worshiped now, ascended masters were often considered deity, as gods or goddesses in past generations. All are seen as honorable, venerable, and ones to hear from and work with by recognizing their spiritual energy, often manifest as an overwhelming presence of love or light.

PHILOSOPHY

The New Age Movement centers around the relevance of astrology, especially in connection with astrological shifts, horoscopes, and the changing positions of planets as coinciding with different ages on earth. There are twelve astrological ages, each corresponding to the twelve zodiac signs (Aries, Taurus, Gemini, Cancer, Leo, Virgo, Libra, Scorpio, Sagittarius, Capricorn, Aquarius, and Pisces). The completion of one cycle of twelve ages is approximately 25,860 years. New Agers believe that approximately two thousand years ago, the Piscean Age began. Under the rule of the "fish," the Piscean Age is believed to be one of intense and extreme tumult, war, and control, as is exerted through monotheism. For this reason, the Piscean Age is associated with Christianity (in a negative sense). Within the understanding of the Piscean Age, Christianity is seen as a controlling and dominating force that keeps people from knowing secret, hidden truths. With an astrological shift (that has been stated to either happen or yet to come for over two hundred years), this era of history is to end, and usher in the Age of Aquarius, ushering in a new era of spirituality. Identified with the "water bearer" of the zodiac, New Agers believe this shift signifies a free-flowing, fluid era by which spiritual truths shall usher in peace and harmony. The spiritual truths of this era shall be:

- All is one, and all reality is a part of a greater whole.
- Everything is god and god is everything (pantheism).
- Man is god and or a part of god;
- Man never dies, but lives eternally through reincarnation;
- Man can create his own reality, values, and morality through altered states of transformed consciousness.

New Agers do not all readily accept the "New Age" label and may refer to themselves by several different entities. Some consider themselves to be part of traditional religious entities, such as Christian or Jewish. Some others identify with occult entities, such as neo-pagans, neo-Gnostics, or earth-centered religions. Others may identify with spiritually inclusive or neutral groups, such as Unitarian Universalism.[2]

ADHERENT IDENTITY

New Age Movement; New Age; New Ager; Seeker; Age of Aquarius; Aquarian Age; Aquarian; mystical; spiritual; occult; alternative; balanced; supernaturalist; astrological; holistic; human potential movement; eclecticism, self-development, and various other titles as dependent upon each individual group.

TRADITIONAL LANGUAGES

English; Latin.

SECTS/DIVISIONS

There are virtually thousands of New Age sects and organizations, far too many to list here. Many overlap in different ways and it is possible to find a New Age practitioner who delves into different, or multiple, aspects of New Age practice. We can divide New Age ideas into groupings, presenting the most popular ones as present here:

- **New Age foundational groups**: The New Age Movement's foundations include Swedenborgianism's founder Emmanuel Swedenborg (1688-1772), the teachings of secret societies emerging in the 1700s and 1800s (such as Freemasonry and Rosicrucianism), New Thought as influenced by Phineas Quimby (1802-1866), and Theosophy as formed by Helena Blavatsky (1831-1891), Henry Steel Olcott (1832-1907), and William Quan Judge (1851-1896) in 1875. While specifications of New Age foundational groups vary, these groups have a few things in common. They all took a strong interest in scientific knowledge within their time periods, they were interested in the mind-body connection and in things such as the way thoughts and beliefs could change one's life, visions, the meaning of dreams, the how the soul and body connect, Greek philosophy, ancient pagan systems (such as those found in Egypt and Greece), "secret" knowledge that could only be obtained through certain rites, the way Christianity had been obscured from reality through theological errors, and rejection of the divinity and deity of Christ. Theosophy went a step further to introduce Ascended Masters and a plurality of religious belief, drawing ideas from different world religions. Groups inspired by these foundational origins include The New Church, the Church of the New Jerusalem, the Liberal Catholic Church, Lucifer's Trust, Arcane School, the Buddhist Theosophical Society, Order of the Temple of the Rosy Cross, Schola Philosophicae Initiationis, and anthroposophy.

- **Spiritualism**: Spiritualism is the belief that one can communicate with the dead (those in the "spirit realm") through a medium or psychic. The Spiritualist Movement started in the 1840s with Leah (1813-1890), Margaretta (1833-1893) and Catherine Fox (1837-1912), three sisters who claimed they'd successfully contacted a spirit through a series of "rapping noises" that others could witness. Influenced by individuals such as Emmanuel Swedenborg (1688-1772) and Franz Mesmer (1734-1815; founder of hypnotism), Spiritualism evolved into areas of psychic seances and automated writing, eventually becoming a religion (the National Spiritualist Association of Churches). Even though the Fox sisters were proven fraudulent, interest in contact with the dead through varied means remains a prominent pseudoscience within the New Age community. Groups that represent Spiritualism include the National Spiritualist Association of Churches, Agasha Temple of Wisdom, the Morris Pratt Institute, Arthur Findlay College, International Spiritualist Federation, Camp Chesterfield, Share International, Edgar Cayce, and several independent psychics and mediums throughout the world.

- **New Age Occultism**: New Age groups vary a great deal in their practice. While all New Age groups represent a seemingly lighter, or less "dark" aspect of occultism, all New Age groups and practitioners are occultists. Some New Agers are more into the esoteric, or "hidden" aspects of New Age practice. These do vary, but can relate to the religions of the ancient world (such as Egyptian, Greek, Roman, Etruscan, Celtic, or Germanic), interest in occult groups such as Freemasonry or Rosicrucianism, general practices of witchcraft and magic (spellcasting, confessions, astrology, divination, or alchemy), spiritualism, psychics, mediumship, tarot cards, numerology, divination, crystal energy, study of the "dark arts" (the use of magic for selfish purposes, calling upon evil spirits, sorcery, yoga, chakra energy, true name spells, immortality rituals, necromancy, cursing and hexing), soul travel (out-of-body experiences), Thelema Magick, sex magic, metaphysics, shamanism, past life regression, and study of Kabbalah or other mainline esoteric religious offshoots. There are many groups that incorporate combinations of these beliefs, but most often, these are selected and practiced in different combinations by individual practitioners.

Crystal magic

- **"I AM" Movement**: An Ascended Masters teaching (breakaway from Theosophy) that started in the 1930s by Guy (1878-1939) and Edna Ballard (1886-1971). The I AM Movement focuses on the idea of Ascended Masters as having achieved the ultimate liberation, no longer bound by reincarnation. It focuses on the idea that the "I AM" (from the ancient Sanskrit term, "So Ham," which means "I Am that I Am") presence of the divine is present in each individual person, manifesting as their Higher Self (their "violet flame"). Every person who calls forth the action of spirit connects to this internal, divine power. By tapping into this power, one fulfils the teachings of the Ascended Masters and can utilize this power to create in one's life; justice, life, peace, harmony, and love. Much of the movement is devoted to personal invocations, confessions, and visualization. The "I AM" Movement has been very influential in a diversity of uses, especially because it can appear Christian in ideal for those who are not familiar with its origins. It is frequently used as an overlap for positive thinking, meditation, and positive visualization. Some groups that represent the "I AM" Movement include the Church Universal and Triumphant, Ascended Master Teaching Foundation, The Bridge to Spiritual Freedom, City of the Sun Foundation, the Saint Germain Foundation, the Joy Foundation, and Morningland Community.[3]

- **Human Potential Movement**: A 1960s movement studied and popularized by George Leonard (1923-2010). It bases its science in humanistic psychology, especially Abraham Maslow's (1908-1970) theory that personal achievement was the greatest goal in a human being's life (theory of self-actualization). While Maslow's theory of self-actualization was not in any way a New Age concept, the Human Potential Movement sought to turn the concept of self-actualization into a pseudoscience, one that used methods of positive thinking, visualization, self-esteem, motivation, and I AM confessions to help people be happier and more productive. Many believe the ideas of the Human Potential Movement were associated with the psychedelic culture of the 1960s and were popularized when George Harrison introduced its concepts to the Beatles. Some groups that are part of the Human Potential Movement include the Esalen Institute, Emin Society, Landmark Forum, and Robbins Research International.[4]

- **Transcendental Meditation**: Hindu ideals framed in western perspective (and often construed through a western lens), are a heavy influence within the New Age Movement. Perhaps the best known of these Hindu ideas is the Transcendental Movement (TM), introduced by Maharishi Mahesh Yogi (1918-2008) in the 1950s. It is done with eyes closed in silence, through a mantra, fifteen to twenty minutes per day. It is supposed to help individuals go beyond what is seen as a surface level of personal awareness, into deeper realms of consciousness. Individuals who desire to practice Transcendental Meditation are initiated into the movement, and costs for training is approximately $960 for a single adult, $480 for a college student, and $360 for a youth participant.[5] Practitioners can be of any religious background or practice no religion at all. Although it hasn't been proven beneficial (the organization makes numerous claims that it can cure everything from depression to ADHD), it is seen in programs, educational retreats, schools, businesses, and in prisons, especially within the United States. The movement became popular in the western world as many famous celebrities traveled to India to study with Maharishi Mahesh Yogi (including the Beatles). It is the inspiration for the modern-day meditation movement. Some groups that promote Transcendental Meditation include Global Country of World Peace, the David Lynch Foundation, Maharishi International University, Maharishi University of Management and Technology, and the Center for Leadership Performance. A famous and influential practitioner of Transcendental Meditation in modern times is Oprah Winfrey.[6,7]

Transcendental Meditation logo

- **Commune Movement**: A subheading of Utopianism, there are several communes spanning the last fifty or so years that share New Age beliefs and ideals in their approach to ideal communal living situations. There are several variations in communal living. Some live off the land through farming, some work outside the group and share living expenses, and some are more industrial, contracting out to others. Major New Age communities seek to create the ideal "Age of Aquarius" themselves, without the aid of greater society. There is no one standard New Age commune movement, although many have influences from the hippie culture of the 1960s. Today, many are influenced by theosophy, anthroposophy, neo-paganism, collective religious ideals, and ecology. Some groups that reflect a New Age ideal of communal living include the Farm and the Friends of Perfection Commune.

- **<u>Neo-Paganism</u>**: Neo-Paganism refers to a wide variety of groups that base their beliefs on what are considered ancient pagan ideals. It is, in many ways, classified as a "return" to religion before the major world religions took precedence and form. Neo-paganism relies on a combination of religious folk traditions, pre-Christian ideals, and different ethnic understandings of polytheistic, animistic, and pantheistic theologies believed to be present in the ancient world. Most neo-pagans combine worship of different ancient deities or spirits, nature worship, ancient pagan rites and festivals, magic, witchcraft, zodiac interest, elements of Freemasonry or other secret societies, and other more modern, often New Age ideals within its practice. Some groups that reflect Neo-Pagan ideals are Wicca, neo-Druidry, Church of All Worlds, Adonism, Covenant of the Goddess, and Tengrism.

- **<u>Neo-Gnostic</u>**: Much like Neo-paganism, Neo-Gnostic refers to a wide variety of groups that base their beliefs on a revival of ideals associated with the traditional Gnostic religions of the early centuries after the life of Jesus Christ. These ideas are based in what researchers know about the ancient religious system now known as Gnosticism, and some ideological systems that also stem from ancient Roman ideals. Neo-Gnosticism focuses on the theology of duality: that all life is divided into two different categories: good and evil, light and dark, and spiritual and material. The world is seen as controlled by an evil demiurge who leads people to worship him, thus detracting from the worship of the true deity. As one obtains secret knowledge revealed through Gnostic ritual and practice, one can ascend to true knowledge and obtain salvation. The problem with neo-Gnosticism is that not much is definitively known about the ancient Gnostics, and as a result, the practice of neo-Gnosticism is often mixed with other systems, such as neo-paganism, Roman Catholicism, Orthodoxy, secret societies, Hinduism, and neo-Paganism. Some neo-Gnostic groups include Ecclesia Gnostica Catholica, Ecclesia Gnostica Mysteriorum, and the Johannite Church.

- **<u>Native American/Indigenous Religious interest</u>**: Of some controversy is the New Age interest in Native American and indigenous religions, because the New Age practice of such is considered cultural appropriation. The use of these religious practices in the New Age Movement is often carefully selected, without the historical, theological, and cultural foundations associated with the Native American community. New Agers tend to take interest in Shamanism, Native American visions and legends, Native American ecology, sweat lodges, and the traditions of initiation and women's circles. Some other New Age groups also take an interest in the indigenous religions of Africa and indigenous pacific groups, such as Yorba spirituality or the Hawaiian kahuna priests. Many of these New Age groups, with no foundation in the actual religion, charge for their services. Such groups include the Rainbow Warriors, the Rainbow Family of Living Light, Huna, and Clear Green.

- **Eco Movement**: The New Age Movement takes interest in ecological movements, often identifying several of the more environmentally interested groups as "green religions." Stemming from neo-pagan and indigenous ideas about natural disasters as portents fulfilling ancient legends about the earth's needed cleansing from the abuses of mankind, the ecological themes present in the New Age Movement take a variety of forms, from a belief in the need to recycle and pick up trash to more extreme ideas about erasing one's "carbon footprint," marrying nature, believing people are so inter-connected to nature, they cannot achieve any sort of enlightenment without a deep, profound connection to the earth. Most consider plant and animal life to be the same from an ethical standpoint. Such groups include Damanhur, Wicca, Rowan Tree Church, and the Church of All Worlds.

- **UFO Cults**: Many New Agers find the lure of unidentified flying objects (better known as UFOs) fascinating. Along with the idea of UFOs comes belief in alien life on other planets, their attempt to contact human beings, the concept that they are either dangerous or hold answers for the problems of humanity, and a large, expansive government conspiracy by which world governments (especially that of the United States) withhold and hide vital information about extraterrestrial life from their citizens. Many believe governments hide the truth about alien life because aliens could lead humans to overcome the major issues of overpopulation, war, and pollution. This would lead to government overthrow, thus rendering government obsolete. Also with such beliefs is the idea that extraterrestrial life can introduce spiritual advancement (such as telepathy or a spiritualized technology) to humanity. Such groups include the Aetherius Society, Church of the SubGenius, Raelism, Unarius Academy of Science, Universe People, Universal Industrial Church of the New World Comforter, and Cosmic Circle of Fellowship.

Angel

NUMBER OF ADHERENTS

It is difficult to identify a solid number on how many New Age practitioners exist worldwide. As some identify with other movements or do not prefer the New Age label, there is no exact number available of New Agers worldwide. Within the United States, approximately 3,000,000 to 5,000,000 Americans identified as being part of the New Age Movement in the 1980s. The 1980s marked its peak in popularity, with declines throughout the 1990s and early 2000s. It continues to manifest in different ways throughout modern times, although its popularity seems to move in waves. Some believe it is on the increase in nations outside the western world.[8,9]

DISPUTES WITHIN GROUP

The New Age Movement recognizes no centralized leadership, required form, or mandated practice. Instead, it is practitioners choosing to work independently or collectively from their own spiritual perspectives and ideals. While most of the New Age Movement can be described as adhering to its five basic principles outlined earlier, how each New Ager ascribes to such varies with the person or group one may follow. Some groups promote different New Age scriptures, some promote mixings of different religious groups, some seem to utilize a Christian approach blended with different New Age ideals, some strictly teach from indigenous or eastern spiritualities, and some are strictly occult in their approach, taught in a simpler, more sanitized way. Most New Agers mix different eastern, western, occult, and specified beliefs into their own personal system, which may or may not include other aspects that another New Ager or another group may recognize. There is no specific consensus on what denotes New Age activity, leading to question among practitioners as to just what it is.

Perhaps most notably, the dispute among New Age communities is whether it is justifiable to identify a group as being part of the New Age Movement. Some groups, such as Wicca, take objection such identification even though they do meet the standard criteria. Some New Agers also find the term derogatory or otherwise inflammatory in some form. Most New Agers prefer to be identified as spiritual rather than religious, conscious, evolving, and enlightened, rather than associated or affiliated with a specific label.

SCRIPTURES

New Agers refer to all major world religious texts throughout their work. There is particular interest on reinterpreting passages of the Bible and using writings such as the Taoist Tao-de-King and the Hindu Bhagavad-Gita. Of other interests are writings about ancient civilizations (such as Tibetan or Egyptian Books of the Dead), writings about ancient pagan civilizations, Biblical apocryphal documents, and other religious and spiritual books that examine beliefs of interest to New Agers (such as spiritualism, apparitions, visions, and angels).

Books are paramount to New Age communities, and several New Age books have become bestsellers over the past forty years. Because the practice of the New Age Movement is so individualized, practitioners of the New Age Movement rely on books for new ideas, information, and trends. The New Age bookstore, where books that feature different metaphysical themes, items for practice, and information on classes, are often important seats of New Age movements within a community.

New Age Communities also have their own texts, most of which vary in their contents. There are more here than it is possible to list, but a few major ones include:

- ***A Course in Miracles***: Perhaps the best known and most enduring of New Age scriptures, *A Course in Miracles* was authored in 1976 by Helen Schucman (1908-1981). Schucman claims to have received an inner voice (she believed it was Jesus) telling her what to write. Its purpose is to serve as a literal course (text includes its main body textbook, workbook for students and a manual for teachers), a specified teaching for those who desire to achieve spiritual transformation. The bottom line of this book is that one must recognize and become fully aware of the presence and work of love is one's life to accomplish spiritual revelation. Like much of New Age theory, *A Course in Miracles* teaches that everything within the world (space, time, and perception) are all illusions; the divine (god) is the only truth and reality. Life is all a part of one life. Issues that separate us from reality (such as guilt, rejection of the divine) are part of the ego, also known as the "wrong mind." To overcome these issues, one must see "the face of Christ" (an ideal or consciousness, rather than the person of Jesus Christ) in everything, thus coming to a place of atonement whereby one ends their individuality and their ego. It is produced by the Foundation for Inner Peace. It has been most widely disseminated by Gerald G. Jampolsky (1925-2020), Gary Renard (1951-), and Marianne Williamson (1952-).[10]

This course is a beginning, not an end. Your Friend goes with you. You are not alone. No one who calls on Him can call in vain. Whatever troubles you, be certain that He has the answer, and will gladly give it to you, if you simply turn to Him and ask it of Him. He will not withhold all answers that you need for anything that seems to trouble you. He knows the way to solve all problems, and resolve all doubts. His certainty is yours. You need but ask it of Him, and it will be given you. You are as certain of arriving home as is the pathway of the sun laid down before it rises, after it has set, and in the half-lit hours in between. Indeed, your pathway is more certain still. For it can not be possible to change the course of those whom God has called to Him. Therefore obey your will, and follow Him Whom you accepted as your voice, to speak of what you really want and really need. His is the Voice for God and also yours. And thus He speaks of freedom and of truth. No more specific lessons are assigned, for there is no more need of them. Henceforth, hear but the Voice for God and for your Self when you retire from the world, to seek reality instead. He will direct your efforts, telling you exactly what to do, how to direct your mind, and when to come to Him in silence, asking for His sure direction and His certain Word. His is the Word that God has given you. His is the Word you chose to be your own. And now I place you in His hands, to be His faithful follower, with Him as Guide through every difficulty and all pain that you may think is real. Nor will He give you pleasures that will pass away, for He gives only the eternal and the good. Let Him prepare you further. He has earned your trust by speaking daily to you of your Father and your brother and your Self. He will continue. Now you walk with Him, as certain as is He of where you go; as sure as He of how you should proceed; as confident as He is of the goal, and of your safe arrival in the end. The end is certain, and the means as well. To this we say "Amen." You will be told exactly what God wills for you each time there is a choice to make. And He will speak for God and for your Self, thus making sure that hell will claim you not, and that each choice you make brings Heaven nearer to your reach. And so we walk with Him from this time on, and turn to Him for guidance and for peace and sure direction. Joy attends our way. For we go homeward to an open door which God has held unclosed to welcome us. We trust our ways to Him and say "Amen." In peace we will continue in His way, and trust all things to Him. In confidence we wait His answers, as we ask His Will in everything we do. He loves God's Son as we would love him. And He teaches us how to behold him through His eyes, and love him as He does. You do not walk alone. God's angels hover near and all about. His Love surrounds you, and of this be sure; that I will never leave you comfortless.[11]

- ***<u>The URANTIA Book</u>***: Believed to be authored by William Sadler (1875-1969) (with significant influences from Wilfred Kellogg) as a spiritual revelation, *The Urantia Book* (also known as *The Urantia Papers* or *The Fifth Epochal Revelation*) seeks to bring together the world of religion, science, and philosophy for the people of Urantia (Urantia is another name for planet earth). Its major goal is to supply answers to the major unanswered questions present as they cannot be answered by existing spiritual, scientific, and thinking sources. It is over 2,000 pages long, and consists of four parts: The Central and Superuniverses (highest levels of creation, the eternal deity, the unique Urantia trinity, and paradise), The Local Universe (description, administration, and governance of Nebadon, the local cosmos), The History of Urantia (dealing with the history of the Earth, including origin, evolution, and destiny of the world), and the Life and Teachings of Jesus (covers Jesus' childhood, teenage years, family life, ministry, crucifixion, death, resurrection, appearances, Pentecost, and his unique faith). Both Sadler and Kellogg were Seventh-Day Adventists and the specified nature of revelation, belief in soul sleep, annihilation, and their belief in "celestial beings" all coincide with the style and nature of Adventism present during the time in which *The Urantia Book* would have been authored, somewhere between 1924 and 1955. The document is very controversial, revealing scientific and spiritual ideas present in the day when it evolved, with many of these beliefs now debunked. This is especially true in regard to writings that relate to race. There have never been any specified religious institutions that employed *The Urantia Book.* Its followers appear to be independent practitioners. *The Urantia Book* has existed through the years without promotion and was the source of a copyright battle between its main publisher, the Urantia Foundation, and users of the work. It is now in the Public Domain and has its following through the internet, discussion groups, and study groups.[11]

Religion achieves its highest social ministry when it has least connection with the secular institutions of society. In past ages, since social reforms were largely confined to the moral realms, religion did not have to adjust its attitude to extensive changes in economic and political systems. The chief problem of religion was the endeavor to replace evil with good within the existing social order of political and economic culture. Religion has thus indirectly tended to perpetuate the established order of society, to foster the maintenance of the existent type of civilization.

But religion should not be directly concerned either with the creation of new social orders or with the preservation of old ones. True religion does oppose violence as a technique of social evolution, but it does not oppose the intelligent efforts of society to adapt its usages and adjust its institutions to new economic conditions and cultural requirements.

Religion did approve the occasional social reforms of past centuries, but in the twentieth century it is of necessity called upon to face adjustment to extensive and continuing social reconstruction. Conditions of living alter so rapidly that institutional modifications must be greatly accelerated, and religion must accordingly quicken its adaptation to this new and ever-changing social order.[12]

Mankind should understand that we who participate in the revelation of truth are very rigorously limited by the instructions of our superiors. We are not at liberty to anticipate the scientific discoveries of a thousand years. Revelators must act in accordance with the instructions which form a part of the revelation mandate. We see no way of overcoming this difficulty, either now or at any future time. We full well know that, while the historic facts and religious truths of this series of revelatory presentations will stand on the records of the ages to come, within a few short years many of our statements regarding the physical sciences will stand in need of revision in consequence of additional scientific developments and new discoveries. These new developments we even now foresee, but we are forbidden to include such humanly undiscovered facts in the revelatory records.[13]

- ***The Aquarian Gospel of Jesus the Christ: The Philosophic and Practical Basis of the Religion of the Aquarian Age of the World and Church Universal***: A text believed to be translated from "akashic records," those that are a total record of all things that have occurred in the past, present, or future as reside on a mental plane. Authored by Levi H. Dowling (1844-1911) and printed in 1908, its contents are mystical records of knowledge given to people in modern times. It is composed of twenty-two sections (sections are ascribed by Hebrew letters), all of which seek to expound on the life of Jesus Christ, providing details and information not contained in other records. Most notable is an eighteen-year period of time by which Jesus travels to various ancient centers of wisdom, such as Tibet, Persia, Greece, and Egypt. These different influences supposedly shaped Jesus' ministry. Other relevant teachings include that all souls will eventually become perfect, as Jesus the Christ, and Jesus put on the role of Christ, allowing the Christ-nature to dwell within him. *The Aquarian Gospel* became relevant among New Age communities in the latter half of the twentieth century. The Aquarian Christine Church Universal is the sole denomination based on *The Aquarian Gospel*, and the Moorish Science Temple of America adopted much of its *Holy Koran* from the writings of The Aquarian Gospel.[14]

The son of Herod, Archelaus, reigned in Jerusalem. He was a selfish, cruel king; he put to death all those who did not honour him.

He called in council all the wisest men and asked about the infant claimant to his throne.

The council said that John and Jesus both were dead; then he was satisfied.

Now Joseph, Mary and their sons were down in Egypt in Zoan, and John was with his mother in the Judean Hills.

Elihu and Salome sent messengers in haste to find Elizabeth and John. They found them and they brought them to Zoan.

Now, Mary and Elizabeth were marvelling much because of their deliverance.

Elihu said, It is not strange; there are no happenings; law governs all events.

From olden times it was ordained that you should be with us, and in this sacred school be taught.

Elihu and Salome took Mary and Elizabeth out to the sacred grove near by where they were wont to teach.

Elihu said to Mary and Elizabeth, You may esteem yourself thrice blest, for you are chosen mothers of long promised sons,

Who are ordained to lay in solid rock a sure foundation stone on which the temple of the perfect man shall rest–a temple that shall never be destroyed.

We measure time by cycle ages, and the gate to every age we deem a mile stone in the journey of the race.

An age has passed; the gate unto another age flies open at the touch of time. This is the preparation age of soul, the kingdom of Immanuel, of God in man;

And these, your sons, will be the first to tell the news, and preach the gospel of good will to men, and peace on earth.

A mighty work is theirs; for carnal men want not the light, they love the dark, and when the light shines in the dark they comprehend it not.

We call these sons, Revealers of the Light; but they must have the light before they can reveal the light.

And you must teach your sons, and set their souls on fire with love and holy zeal, and make them conscious of their missions to the sons of men.

Teach them that God and man are one; but that through carnal thoughts and words and deeds, man tore himself away from God; debased himself.

Teach that the Holy Breath would make them one again, restoring harmony and peace;

That naught can make them one but Love; that God so loved the world that he has clothed his son in flesh that man may comprehend.

The only Saviour of the world is love, and Jesus, son of Mary, comes to manifest that love to men.

Now, love cannot manifest until its way has been prepared, and naught can rend the rocks and bring down lofty hills and fill the valleys up, and thus prepare the way, but purity.

But purity in life men do not comprehend; and so, it, too, come in flesh.

And you, Elizabeth, are blest because your son is purity made flesh, and he shall pave the way for love.

This age will comprehend but little of the works of Purity and Love; but not a word is lost, for in the Book of God's Remembrance a registry is made of every thought, and word, and deed;

And when the world is ready to receive, lo, God will sent a messenger to open up the book and copy from its sacred pages all the messages of Purity and Love.

Then every man of earth will read the words of life in language of his native land, and men will see the light, walk in the light and be the light.

And man again will be at one with God.[15]

- ***OAHSPE: A New Bible***: Published in 1882 by John Ballou Newbrough (1828-1891), *Oahspe* is a series of writings about earth, heavenly governors, and teachings that should be embraced for the current era of history. Oahspe is defined as "sky, earth, and spirit; the sum of all spiritual knowledge at present." The major teaching it emphasized was personal service, as each individual person is judged according to how much they are willing to serve other people. One could achieve the highest possible grade in the afterlife, and the best possible place of achievement in heaven, through how much they did for others. Humankind is marked by a different list of progressions, and the lessons from those different series come in cycles: advancement followed by recession, and then improvement and regression. It outlines a complex cosmology, including details about lost and new lands. *Oahspe* advocates vegetarianism, pacifism, virtuous living, angelic assistance, communal living, and spiritual communion. Followers of *Oahspe* are known as Faithists. They also use a number of different names for the creator in the text: Jehovih, The Great Spirit, Ormazd, Egoquim, Agoquim, ELoih, the I am, and Jehovah. It was composed through automated writing. Today, there are a few small groups that uphold its precepts, namely the Universal Faithists of Kosmon, the Restoration Faithists, The Eloists, and the Kosmon Church.[16]

Satan calleth out from a dark corner, saying: Remain thou within the wicked world, and leaven the whole mass. Again he calleth out from a dark corner, saying: Go thou away from the wicked world, and live as an ascetic, praying alone, living alone. Again he calleth from a dark corner, saying: Thou and thy friends are too pure to mix with the world; go ye away privily, and let the world take care of itself. Now, I say unto you: Do none of these things; and, in the same breath, I say: Do all of them. Let your community remain within the world, that it may be a proven example that love, peace, plenty, and happiness are possible on the earth. Let the community be sufficiently ascetic to attain the beatific state, which is the triumph of spirit over the flesh. And, as to the third proposition: Take ye no part in the governments of men, of kings, or queens. Neither fight ye for them, nor against them. For they live under the lower law; but ye shall live under the law of Jehovih as He speaketh to the soul of man.[17]

- **Occult literature**: Many New Agers adhere to the writings of key occultists, especially those books which relate to magic and the practice therein. Famous authors include Aleister Crowley (1875-1947), Alice Bailey (1880-1949), Helena Blavatsky, Manly Hall (1901-1990), Emmanuel Swedenborg, Annie Besant (1947-1933), Doreen Valiente (1922-1999), Carlos Castaneda (1925-1998), Nostradamus (1503-1566), and Dion Fortune (1890-1946).

The Way of Mastery is to break all the rules—but you have to know them perfectly before you can do this; otherwise you are not in a position to transcend them.[18]
Man, before he is being regenerated, does not even know that any internal man exists, much less

is he acquainted with its nature and quality.[19]

Clairvoyants can see flashes of colour, constantly changing, in the aura that surrounds every person: each thought, each feeling, thus translating itself in the astral world, visible to the astral sight.[20]

- **New Age fiction**: Fictional literature has a prominent place within the New Age community, as it weaves legends of complex New Age ideas together in the form of stories, parables, myths, and legends. Many New Age fictional works are treated as factual experiences rather than stories, thus causing further confusion over their position within spiritual experience. Such works include *the Celestine Prophecy* (James Redfield [1950-]), *Mutant Message Down Under* (Marlo Morgan [1937-]), *The Oversoul Seven* Trilogy (Jane Roberts [1929-1984]), and Mary Summer Rain's (1945-) series of books featuring her fictional character, No Eyes.

When love first happens, the individuals are giving each other energy unconsciously and both people feel buoyant and elated. That's the incredible high we call being 'in love.' Unfortunately, once they expect this feeling to come from another person, they cut themselves off from the energy in the universe and begin to rely even more on the energy from each other–only now there doesn't seem to be enough and so they stop giving each other energy and fall back into their dramas in an attempt to control each other and force the other's energy their way.[21]

- **New Age nonfiction**: New Age nonfiction writing typically takes one of three forms: it is either a testimony of some sort that brings one to a New Age understanding, a how-to in application of New Age principles, or commentary on New Age ideas (on matters such as thinking, holistic medicine, magic, self-help, or spirituality). The world of New Age nonfiction is a billion-dollar industry and has made many New Age practitioners famous. Some popular authors include Bettie J. Eadie (1942-), Deepak Chopra (1946-), Neale Donald Walsch (1943-), Marilyn Ferguson (1938-2008), Elizabeth Clare Prophet (1939-2009), Eckhart Tolle (1948-), Marianne Williamson, Gary Zukav (1942-), Rhonda Byrne (1951-), Benjamin Crème (1922-2016), Sylvia Browne (1936-2013), and Edgar Cayce (1877-1945).

Love is not selective, just as the light of the sun is not selective. It does not make one person special. It is not exclusive. Exclusivity is not the love of God but the "love" of ego. However, the intensity with which true love is felt can vary. There may be one person who reflects your love back to you more clearly and more intensely than others, and if that person feels the same toward you, it can be said that you are in a love relationship with him or her. The bond that connects you with that person is the same bond that connects you with the person sitting next to you on a bus, or with a bird, a tree, a flower. Only the degree of intensity with which it is felt differs.[22]

If you obsess over whether you are making the right decision, you are basically assuming that the universe will reward you for one thing and punish you for another.

The universe has no fixed agenda. Once you make any decision, it works around that decision.

There is no right or wrong, only a series of possibilities that shift with each thought, feeling, and action that you experience.

If this sounds too mystical, refer again to the body. Every significant vital sign- body temperature, heart rate, oxygen consumption, hormone level, brain activity, and so on- alters the moment you decide to do anything... decisions are signals telling your body, mind, and environment to move in a certain direction.[23]

BASIC RELIGIOUS PRACTICES

Count St. Germain

The New Age Movement is one of eclectic self-spirituality. One's personal understanding and spiritual experience are considered the authoritative, highest consciousness possible within the movement. There is no one specific practice that is universal to all New Agers as a summarizing "basic" practice. The movement's practice centers around the individual as they discover the deity within and around them and their understanding of their place within the universe. Practices vary from believer to believer who may operate individually, in a group, or as a collective body within a society, center, or religious group setting (some New Agers call their religious centers "churches"). Whether or not a New Age practitioner meets with a group, New Age practice always starts with the individual. Common practices include meditation, particularly transcendental; astral projection (teaching that all life form is consistent of energy, and therefore one can "project" one's state and travel to alternate universes, planets, or even into other people's bodies or circumstances); "energy work" (sending or receiving energy from another, such as through reiki or emotional connection); yoga and other Hindu practices, often twisted or altered; chanting, sometimes Buddhist or Hindu, but often within the confines of New Age understanding; astrology; divination; various forms of magic, esoteric, pagan, or occultist practices; Native American or indigenous spiritual techniques; interest in spiritual, emotional, and holistic healing or alternative medicine; or other things deemed appropriate by the individual practitioner. As all paths are believed to lead to the divine, nothing is prohibited.

Nothing is expected from a New Ager in terms of personal conduct or ethics except that which the individual expects of themselves. Many New Agers push themselves to use their spirituality as a point of personal growth, whether in the form of better relationships, exceling in a job, starting their own business, generating a greater financial profit, doing charitable or ecological work, or delving into being a better person. New Agers believe that, through their practice, they will become better, more evolved, and more enlightened people.

HOLIDAYS

The New Age Movement has no specified set of holidays. New Agers celebrate any holidays they please, often with their own unique understanding or perspective. Many observe traditional religious holidays, such as Christmas and Easter, from a secular perspective. Others celebrate pagan observances or festivals in place of traditional religious celebrations.

VISUAL SIGNS AND SYMBOLS

Any religious symbol from the major world religions (including a cross, Star of David, mandala, lotus flower, various Hindu gods and goddesses, rainbow, crescent moon, yin-yang, OM symbol, Native American or indigenous symbols, and pentagram); sun; triangle; peace sign; ancient gods and goddesses; ankh; circles; all-seeing eye; pyramid; swastika (representative of peace and good luck; not represented counterclockwise as in Nazi Germany, but vertically up and down); Pegasus, unicorn, mermaid, astrology signs, enneagram; assorted Masonic and secret society symbols; I-Ching hexagrams; visual symbols and charts of the chakras (energy centers found within the body according to Hindu belief); dharma wheel; Celtic crosses or Celtic decorative knots; eye in triangle; concentric circles; crystal ball; hooked cross; triangle with three overlapping circles; white horse; moon; crescent moon; phases of the moon; crystals.

CREEDS, BOOKS, AND LAWS

The New Age Movement has no specified creed or laws. It has only a handful of beliefs most New Agers share. Many use invocations or confessions daily, especially The Divine Invocation, written by Alice Bailey (of Lucien Trust, formerly Lucifer's Trust). It is considered a "Mantram for the New Age."

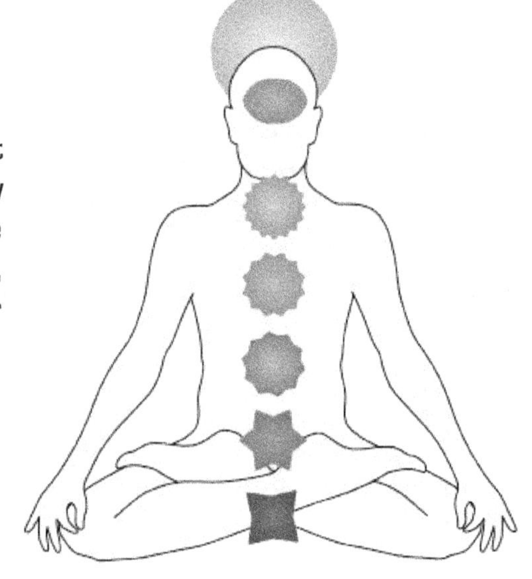

Chakra map

From the point of Light within the Mind of God
Let light stream forth into the minds of men.
Let Light descend on Earth.

From the point of Love within the Heart of God
Let love stream forth into the hearts of men.
May Christ (a reference to Christ consciousness)
return to Earth.

From the centre where the Will of God is known
Let purpose guide the little wills of men –
The purpose which the Masters know and serve.
From the centre which we call the race of men
Let the Plan of Love and Light work out
And may it seal the door where evil dwells.

Let Light and Love and Power restore the Plan on Earth.[24]

Sometimes it is recited a little differently, as there are some variations of it.

New Agers also often adopt specified rules or guides in modified form from different eastern religions, such as Hinduism or Buddhism.

ECLECTIC BELIEFS

By incorporating a little of everything, the New Age Movement merges mainline religion and occult practice. There are several different ways New Agers see the world and practice the unique system each New Ager establishes for themselves. Believing in "teachers" (both ascended and living), New Agers pursue several different life points, all of which they believe lead them closer to light and further away from ignorance and darkness. New Agers also use statues, images of different religious leaders and different religious imagery, worship of nature and the ideals of people, ancient neopagan practices, and many different magic rituals. Some people classify or consider New Agers to be "odd," especially with interest in things such as the supernatural, aliens, reincarnation, changing and manipulating different religious figures to fit New Age ideals (such as Jesus, who becomes a Hindu guru or ascended master), and a preoccupation with angels and angelic messages.

RELATIONS WITH NON-NEW AGERS

Although the New Age Movement adapts teachings and practices from all religions, they center in the pagan interfaith community, seeking to crate understanding and tolerance for pagan beliefs. New Agers, much like Unitarian Universalists (who hold a similar world view), avoid relations with evangelical and more traditional doctrines of Christianity, citing it as intolerant, antithetical to spiritual enlightenment, and adhering to an outdated view of the Bible.

HOLY SITES

New Agers believe in the concept of "sacred space," meaning they believe in a strong sacred presence where enlightenment and spirituality can flourish. Many New Agers utilize home altars or meditative spaces to practice their personal devotions, chants, meditations, or formulate goals.

Some sites exist in real time, and others are mythological. Two mythological places are the continents of Atlantis and Lemuria. Real locations include the pyramids of Giza, Egypt; Stonehenge (Wiltshire, England); Machu Picchu (Eastern Cordillera, Peru); Mt. Shasta, California; Sedona, Arizona. There may be other sites considered sacred by individual New Age practitioners.

NOTABLE FIGURES

Oprah Winfrey (1954-), television personality; Shirley MacLaine (1934-), actress; Deepak Chopra (1946-), author; Gary Zukav (1942-), author; Neale Donald Walsch, author; David

Spangle (1945-), author; Marianne Williamson (1952-), author; Eckhart Tolle (1948-), author; Rhonda Byrne (1951-), author; Esther (1948-) and Jerry Hicks (1927-2011), author; James Redfield (1950-), author; Brian L. Weiss 1944-), author; Benjamin Crème (1922-2016), author; Marjorie Cameron (1922-1995), actress; Glenda Green (1945-), artist; J.Z. Knight (1946-), author; Starhawk (1951-), author; Ingo Swann (1933-2013), psychic.

NOTABLE GROUPS

The Church Universal and Triumphant (CUT), founded by Elizabeth Prophet (1939-2009) in 1975, is a branch of The Summit Lighthouse. Such was started by Prophet's husband, Mark Prophet (1918-1973) in 1958. Its doctrines reflect ideas of New Thought, the I AM Movement (with devotion to St. Germain), and Theosophy and reflects ideas of Buddhism, esoterism, Christianity, alchemy, and paranormal preoccupations. The movement gained national attention when the church was accused of building fallout shelters and illegally obtaining weapons in 1989. It has also been accused of cult-like tendencies including mind control, sexual control, control over attire, and sleep deprivation. In response, the church reorganized its leadership structure and fell away from the public scene. Its leader, Elizabeth Prophet, died of Alzheimer's Disease in 2009. Ever since, various members have claimed extensive revelation from Ascended Masters and have started offshoot groups, such as The Temple of the Presence (Tucson, Arizona), and The Hearts Center (Livingston, Montana). The Church Universal and Triumphant continues to operate quarterly retreats and Summit University sessions.[25]

FACTS AND FIGURES

Approximately 85% of American New Agers are white, with only 2% black, 1% Asian, 6% Latino, and 7% other. Over 54% of New Agers make less than $30,000 per year. 21% cite they do not believe in a god, and 56% report seldom to never attending a religious service while 40% seldom to never praying.[26]

OTHER IMPORTANT DEFINITIONS[27]

- **ADC**: An after-death communication, usually understood as part of spiritism with a deceased person. Such can come through auditory, emotional, sensory, or tactile experiences.

- **Astral plane**: Known by a number of different terms, including the spirit world, other side, and the afterlife; where most souls exist after death, awaiting reincarnation.

- **Aura**: A colored-eminatation, energy field surrounding a human body that is viewed by select people with the sensitivity to see and recognize such.

- **Automated art**: Like automated writing, when an individual creates artwork (usually pictures or paintings) by the control of a spirit; a form of mediumship.

- **Chakra**: Seven specified energy wheels or centers that are located in a line, from the base of one's tailbone (root chakra) to the top, or crown of one's head (crown chakra) and represented by the rainbow spectrum (red to purple). They are: Root, sacral, solar plexus, heart, throat, third eye, and crown. The Chakras come from ancient Hindu tradition, specifically the esoteric form of Hinduism known as Tantra.

- **Clairaudience**: The ability to receive messages from the spirit world audibly (through hearing).

- **Clairsentience**: The ability to receive messages from the spirit world through feelings and emotions, especially those who are deceased.

- **Clarivoyance**: The ability to receive messages from the spirit world through visions.

- **Cosmic consciousness**: A state achieved in meditation where one is free from stress, ailment, evil, and problems.

- **Energy junkie**: A person addicted to paranormal situations and circumstances by which paranormal energy is active.

- **ESP**: Extrasensory perception; the awareness of the supernatural, independent of perception through the normal five sensense.

- **Electric voice phonmena**: When spirits' voices, noises, or activities are recorded.

- **Gazing**: Staring at an object, such as a quartz crystal or crystal ball, so one will be able to have a visions.

- **God consciousness**: When a person, through meditation, is able to attune to the infinite nature of creation; a step above cosmic consciousness. It is believed that angels constantly operate through God consciousness.

- **Greeters**: Spirits that guide the newly deceased into the afterlife, helping them to transition.

- **Mantra**: A statement chanted over and over again during meditation; often given during an initiation ceremony.

- **Materialization**: When a spirit reveals its face or body.

- **Mesmerism**: Another term for hypnotism, by which an individual is placed in a trance.

- **Near-death experience**: When an individual perceives themselves to be dead (sometimes such is confirmed by outside sources) and while dead, have profound experiences with light, deceased relatives, ascended masters, or experiences with the divine. Many New Agers claim such experiences converted them to New Age ideals.

- **Passing over**: Also called relocating. New Age term for death.

- **Possession**: When a spirit controls an individual for its own personal gratification.

- **Past life regression**: When an individual has an experience, usually under hypnosis or a trans-like state, recalling experiences of past incarnations (lives).

- **Precognition**: The ability to see a future event.

- **Psychokinesis**: Using principles of energy and energy fields, the ability to move an object using one's mind.

- **Retrocognition**: The ability to see past events.

- **Shaman**: Also known as a medicine man or witch doctor, or in African religions, *sangoma*, an individual who has the ability to transcend different realms of existence as a seer and wise individual. Shamans are also healers, sages, and individuals with the ability to work among both the living and the dead.

- **Silver cord**: An invisible magnetic connection that exists between souls and spirits. The silver cord is used to connect one's soul to their body, and connects soul-to-soul, as in the context of a soul mate.

- **Soul mate**: An individual eternally connected to another being for life and eternity. Many New Agers believe soul mates transcend lives, reincarnating life after life, destined to find and connect to one another.

- **Spirit guide**: Spiritual beings who act as intermediaries, protectors, and connectors between this life and others. They are often believed to lead and assist channelers, shamans, and astral projection through the varied realms of consciousness.

- **Spirituality**: The struggle to battle negativity, negative thoughts, and bad energies as one discovers the divine within and without themselves.

- **States of consciousness**: New Agers recognize several states of consciousness, or states of being: waking, sleeping, dreaming, transcending, cosmic consciousness, god consciousness, unity consciousness, and Brahma consciousness.

- **Telekinesis**: When an object is moved by a spirit or some other unseen force.

- **Telepathy**: Being able to read someone's mind or communicate mentally, without words or exterior information.

- **Third eye**: The spot on one's lower forehead between the eyebrows. It is the sixth chakra; center of psychic energy.

- **Unity consciousness**: The state of being by which an individual is enlightened and understands one's place in the universe, as well as how they are united to all things.

BELIEVER'S CHARACTERISTICS

Interest in wisdom from ancient religion and diverse religious traditions; focus on paganism, polytheism, and pantheism; use of statues or idols; universal oneness; emphasis on deity as impersonal and universal rather than personal and authoritarian; emphasis on experience as one's religious authority; use of eastern practices with western thought and magic, including yoga, chakras, vegetarianism, astrology, crystals, psychics, mediums, and alchemy; use of magic; emphasis on personal searching and interest; interest in the afterlife; reincarnation; shamanism and spirit guides; fascination with the paranormal, spirits, ghosts, and communication with those in the beyond; interest in past life regression; belief in a new age; aliens, UFOs; emphasis on secret knowledge, practices, and things hidden by "Christian conspiracy;" unusual religious practices; interest in white light, positive thinking, declarations, mantras, and affirmations.

New Thought Movement

God is Spirit, or the creative energy which is the cause of all visible things. God is not a being or person having life, intelligence, love, power. God is that invisible, intangible, but very real, something we call life...Everything visible, is a manifestation of the one Spirit – God – differing only in degree of manifestation; and each of the numberless modes of manifestation, or individualities, however insignificant, contains the whole.
(H. Emilie Cady)[1]

Theology

Belief in an impersonal, universal life force of energy that is found everywhere, found everywhere, and in everything, known as GOD, INFINITE INTELLIGENCE, SPIRIT, or LIFE. As is understood within the New Thought Movement, the idea of GOD is a divine principle or spiritual energy known throughout the world by many different names. The divine should be revered, as it is found everywhere. Each one of these manifestations or individualities, put together, creates an entire picture of the divine, and the divinity in all such manifestations should be revered and honored. In particular, the divine dwells within human beings, thus affirming the spiritual nature of humanity. As one comes to affirm this fact, one can embrace spirit for themselves and align their thoughts to those classified as positive or life affirming, often coined as "higher thought." Spirit, or infinite intelligence, is seen as the ultimate reality; everything else is illusionary.

There are a variety of interpretations on the specific nature (manifestations) of spirit within the New Thought movement. While many do use Christian language and make use of terms such as Father for spirit, Christ, Jesus Christ, or the Holy Spirit, their interpretation of these terms differs from the orthodox positions espoused in much of Christianity. Most speak of awareness of spirit, or of the spirit or divine within, and consider figures, such as Jesus Christ to be the ultimate manifestation of divine awareness. Having an awareness of spirit is often referred to as "Christ consciousness" or "Cosmic Christ," making Jesus a metaphysical figure. Overall, much of the New Thought Movement contains theological elements akin to the New Age Movement, embracing the idea that all religions and religious leaders the world over reflect the true idea of infinite intelligence. They believe, therefore, that all religions lead to eternal truth. Much of the movement falls into the categories of monism, panentheism, idealism, and pantheism.

Philosophy

The New Thought Movement centers around the idea that divine spirit is present through all. The highest aspiration one can achieve is to love without condition. There isn't much specification on the tangibility of what loving without condition is, save an encouragement to teach and heal one another. Thinking "right," or positive, is seen as a powerful force for implementing good in this world. Mental attitudes, thoughts, states, and ideas are seen as manifestations and experiences in everyday life (if one can imagine it, visualize it, and think it, they believe they can become, or achieve it). This idea is known as the "law of attraction." Things seen as negative, such as disease, sickness, and evil, are caused by bad thoughts and emotions. If one changes their thinking, they can overcome these things. The movement is non-dogmatic in nature, but instead, metaphysical. It examines the foundations of reality, the connection between mind and matter, and between human possibility, potential, and making such things reality. Practitioners of New Thought often classify themselves as "spiritual but not religious."

The New Thought Movement could be described as the "mental foundation" for the New Age Movement. Formed in the 1880s by a combination of people and influences, New Thought's ideas about sickness, visualization, the law of attraction, healing, and teaching others have gained a solid foothold in New Age ideas that began to form in and immediately around the same time frame. New Thought contains elements of occultism (especially in the form of spiritism, or the idea that spirits can communicate with humans and vice versa), mesmerism (the idea that illness originates in the mind through bad thoughts and opening up one's self to better, divine ideas can cure such illness), the idea of evolution as a spiritual process, philosophical transcendentalism (the idea that there is good in all people as a basic principle and that people are best when they are in an independent state) and idealism (the idea that only mental ideas and the mind exist), and some ideas present in westernized concepts of Hinduism.

Key figures in the movement's foundations include Phineas Quimby (1802-1866), a prominent founder of mesmerism, Warren Felt Evans (1817-1889), who was a minister in the Swedenborgian church, Mary Baker Eddy (1821-1910), the founder of Christian Science, and individuals such as Emma Curtis Hopkins (1849-1925), Myrtle Fillmore (1845-1931), Malinda Cramer (1844-1906), and Nona L. Brooks (1861-1945), influential in the foundations of the Unity Church, Church of Divine Science, and Religious Science. The movement became relevant as it merged with other existing theories and beliefs of the time and through extensive writings, including essays, magazines, and books.

ADHERENT IDENTITY

New Thought, Higher Thought, Metaphysical Christian, Higher awareness, Religious Scientist, Religious Science, Unity Church, Christian Science, Christian Scientist, Divine Science, Divine Scientist, Church of Divine Science.

NUMBER OF ADHERENTS

It is difficult to ascertain exact numbers of New Thought believers, as the movement itself represents a diversity of subheadings and ideas. New Thought believers may identify as Christian, Jewish, New Age, unaffiliated, or with a theologically conservative slant. There are also prominent New Thought ideas taught in many mainline, non-denominational, and independent churches. Several New Thought churches and organizations do not keep membership records. As an independent movement in the strictest religious sense, its numbers are on the decline.

TRADITIONAL LANGUAGES

English; Japanese.

SECTS/DIVISIONS

New Thought is not a formal religious organization, although a few religious organizations have emerged that share in its ideals.

- **International New Thought Alliance**: A collective organization for New Thought adherents who serve the ideas and concepts of the movement through different religious groups, as organizations, or as individuals. It hosts an Annual World Congress and has a large library of New Thought material, stemming from the beginning of the movement.

International New Thought Alliance logo

- **Association for Global New Thought**: An offshoot of the International New Thought Alliance, emerging in 1996 after a power dispute within the organization. This organization comprises approximately 700 religious groups, churches, ministers, and lay members who dedicate themselves to the idea of conscious "co-creation." Its membership includes the Unity Church, Religious Science, Divine Science, and the non-denominational sector of New Thought.

Association for Global New Thought logo

- **Unity Church**: Founded in 1889 by Charles (1854-1948) and Myrtle Fillmore, the Unity Church was formed as a transcendental church that then grew into the ideas of New Thought. The church embraces no specific creed, dogma, or ritual. It seeks to offer a positive view of Christianity and Jesus Christ to the world, by accepting the good in everyone, the good in all situations, and in all circumstances. The church sees this mission as a healing work, believing that healing can be achieved through one's thoughts. They seek to do so by affirming God as a universal power, human beings are spiritual beings and are inherently good in and of themselves, believing a person's thoughts create their experiences, the power of affirmative prayer, and by living their specified spiritual principles. Jesus is seen as divine in the same way that all human beings can share in divine ability: as a master teacher who showed others how to engage divine potential. The Bible is seen as history and metaphysical allegory, showing spiritual awakening. The Unity Church is headquartered in Unity Village, Missouri. It operates several divisions, including Silent Unity, the Unity School of Practical Christianity, Unity School of Christianity, Unity

Unity Church logo

Institute, the Association of Unity Churches, Unity House, and the Office of Prayer Research.[3]

- **Christian Science**: Covered in its entirety under its own section, Christian Science classifies as a division of the New Thought Movement. Founded by Mary Baker Eddy in 1879 in Boston, Massachusetts, Christian Science believes the universe operates by a duality, specifically one between matter and spirit. Matter is evil, an illusion, something that is perceived by the material senses incorrectly. Man, or humanity, is regarded as spirit, for humanity is created in the likeness of Father-Mother God. Man, therefore, is good, spiritual, not carnal. Sin, sickness, illness, disease, and hell are all illusions created by man, in the material world, and they are, in essence, unreal. When one rejects the material world, and adheres to the spiritual world, the material world, including the body, has no affect or reality on pain or perception of suffering. Varying from the other New Thought groups in some of its application and doctrine, Christian Science considers Mary Baker Eddy to be the pastor emeritus of the church. Her work, *Science and Health with Key to the Scriptures* is the main teacher for the movement. Each service contains readings from *Science and Health* and the Bible. Christian Scientists reject medical intervention, believing anyone can experience healing because of God's love. Adherents of the church believe their prayers are most effective with no medical assistance involved.

Christian Science logo

- **Religious Science**: Also known as the Science of Mind, Religious Science was established by Ernest Holmes (1887-1960) in 1927. It is considered a movement with accompanying religious organizations, connecting the laws of science, philosophical ideas, and central religious revelations together for the benefit of humanity. It was not originally supposed to serve as a church, but a teaching organization that promotes New Thought ideas from their own perspective: because God is all that exists, that power can be harnessed to align with its presence. God is not seen as a person but as a universal spirit, presence, infinite intelligence, and as Christ Consciousness. It is panentheistic and idealistic in its theological outlook. Unique to Religious Science is its teaching on Spiritual Mind Treatment (often called Treatment), a step-by-step approach by one declares their desired outcome of goals as if they have already happened. One does not pray in Treatment but aligns a partnership as a human being with the universe's infinite intelligence; the Treatment is said to be personal, positive, powerful, and present. Religious Science is summed up with a credo, which outlines the basic tenets of New Thought and the panentheism of Religious Science. Organizations that promote Religious Science include the International Centers for Spiritual Living, the Centers for Spiritual living, Global Religious Science Ministries, and the Affiliated New

Religious Science logo

Thought Network. The Affiliated New Thought Network oversees the Emerson Theological Institute.[4]

- **Church of Divine Science**: One of the original New Thought churches, the Church of Divine Science was established by Malinda Cramer and Nona L. Brooks in the 1880s. It was directly influenced by the movement's founders, Phineas Quimby and Emma Curtis Hopkins. It serves as a pragmatic approach to Christian Science, allowing medical consultation in addition to prayer and positive thoughts. It focuses on God as pure Spirit: changeless, eternal, and transcending creation. Evil is not necessary, permanent, or reality in and of itself; it only exists because people believe it does. Truth comes through the Bible, affirmative prayer, contemplation, meditation, and the practices of Divine Science. Divine Science is considered the New Thought source for the Unity Church and Religious Science.[5]

- **Home of Truth**: Another original New Thought organization dating back to 1892, the Home of Truth has an intersecting history with Christian Science, Unity, and Swami Vivekananda (1863-1902), a Hindu leader whose work was foundational in introducing Hinduism and Hindu ideas to western society. Founded by Annie (1856-1924) and Harriet Rix, the movement seeks to promote a diverse panentheism and idealistic approach to theology. Homes were established across the country; today, one of the original Homes of Truth (in Alameda, California) is the only one that remains. As a movement, it has had a strong appeal to women. Today, the organization remains committed to its goals and holds discussions on racism, healing, shamanic drumming, recovery, and regular services.

- **Seicho-no-Le**: The Japanese branch of New Thought, *Seicho-no-Le* began in 1930 as founded by Masaharu Taniguchi (1893-1985). Masaharu Taniguchi was a prolific writer, beginning with his magazine, also titled *Seicho no Le*, and then following with a forty-volume *Truth of Life* philosophy, among four hundred other books. He was supported and influenced by the leaders of Religious Science. *Seichi-no-le* is a syncretic blend of Japanese ideas and New Thought. Beliefs include a universal God and advocating nature, family, ancestors, and religious faith. There are now three factions of the movement: *Seicho no le*, *Manabushi*, and one other group that is a mix of the other two. *Seicho-no-le* is unique as the largest New Thought group in the world, with over 1.6 million followers (mostly in Japan).[6]

Seichno-no-Le logo

- **Jewish Science**: The Jewish branch of New Thought, it is an understanding of Jewish philosophy founded by Rabbi Alfred G. Moses (1878-1956) and Morris (1889-1938) and Tehilla Lichtenstein (1893-1973) in 1916. It varies from traditional Jewish thought in that the concept of God aligns with New Thought ideas (the divine as energy or force, not separate but part of the world) rather than traditional Jewish ideas of God as a paternal image. It upholds New Thought concepts as to the divine, right thinking, and self-help methods. It varies in that it identifies strictly with Jewish identity. The textbook of Jewish Science is *Jewish Science and Health: The Textbook of Jewish Science*. It maintains a "Home Center" synagogue in Manhattan, New York and a congregation in Los Angeles, California.[7]

- **International Peace Mission Movement**: Founded by an individual who went by "Father Divine" and "Reverend M.J. Divine" (c. 1876-1965), the International Peace Mission Movement was a controversial branch of New Thought because its founder claimed to be god. The early history and details of the movement are spurious, but we do know the movement grew to stand integrated, with several unusual rules. Members were prohibited from sexual activity, marriage, drinking alcohol, smoking tobacco, and speaking profanities. A largely social movement, followers were encouraged to pursue jobs, avoid welfare, and live communally. The movement was also extremely pro-America, believing the United States was the birthplace of the Kingdom of God. Its leader actively preached belief in his personal divinity. Today, the movement owns Father Divine's estates and maintains a library of the movement's history. Father Divine was a contemporary of James Jones (1907-1971) (Church of Universal Triumph, Dominion of God, Inc.), Noble Drew Ali (1886-1929) (Moorish Science Temple of America), and Sweet Daddy Grace (c. 1881-1960) (United House of Prayer for All People of the Church on the Rock of the Apostolic Faith).[8]

- **Universal Foundation for Better Living**: A breakaway from the Unity Church on accusations of racism, the Universal Foundation for Better Living is a New Thought denomination founded by Johnnie Colemon (1920-2014) in Chicago, Illinois in 1974. It represents similar theory and thought to that of other New Thought groups, adhering to the teachings of Unity founders Charles and Myrtle Fillmore. The Universal Foundation for Better Living now has over thirty churches across North and Central America and stands as a predominately African American representation of New Thought ideals.

Universal Foundation for Better Living logo

- **Huna**: New Thought ideologies mixed with paganism, Huna was founded by Max Freedom Long (1890-1971) in 1936 as a New Age movement practice. Huna is promoted as the ideas of ancient Hawaiian priests (kahunas), although its ideals are a mix of New Thought and Theosophy. His terminology and ideas, though often linked to Hawaiian spirituality, have no connection therein and are not part of Hawaiian religion. Max Long advocated finding harmony with our three levels of consciousness: subconsciousness, rational, and connection with the divine. These ideas were mixed with positive thinking and affirmation. He also encouraged his followers to follow the writings of the Unity Church and considered Christian Science to be a pristine example of positive thinking. Today, there are two organizations that exist representing Huna's beliefs: Huna Research, Inc., and Huna

International (Aloha International, Voices of the Earth, and Finding Each Other International).[9]

- **Prosperity theology**: Also known as the prosperity gospel, the health and wealth gospel, the gospel of success, seed faith, and "name it, claim it." Although prosperity theology is often taught with an evangelical or Pentecostal theological base, prosperity theology has its origins within the New Thought Movement. Most trace the origins of this movement to E.W. Kenyon (1867-1948), who was exposed to the New Thought Movement while in college. His ideas, mixing New Thought with Pentecostal and evangelical theology, emerged a doctrine that taught Christ's atonement equated to the right of divine healing. Although his teaching did not believe one had a right to material prosperity, his ideas mixed with those of Oral Roberts (1918-2009) and several other teachers in the 1950s, creating its materialistic interpretation. Prosperity theology believes that faith should manifest in material ways, including those that relate to health, financial blessing, success in one's life, and other material aspirations. Along with such theory comes positive confession, affirmations, visualization, and positive thinking. Such is seen in several televangelists, such as Joel Osteen (1963-), Paula White (1966-), Benny Hinn (1952-), Creflo Dollar (1962-), and Kenneth Copeland (1936-).

DISPUTES WITHIN GROUP

New Thought is a movement, which means while there are founders and central figures, there has never been any one group that monopolizes centralized leadership. It is also non-credal, meaning a diversity of beliefs exist within the movements. Throughout the New Thought sects, there have been leadership disputes, internal conflicts, power disagreements, and variations of religious interpretation. There are New Thought variations that are more Christian, Hindu, New Age, and secular in approach.

Unity Church, Unity Village, Missouri

SCRIPTURES

The New Thought Movement does not specify scriptural use for its adherents. As a rule, the movement embraces all sacred religious texts from all the world's religions. Most take a particular interest in the Bible and Bible interpretation, especially the words and teaching of Jesus Christ. However, they are not exclusive to the Bible, and the New Thought Movement takes interest in the similarities and thoughts found in religious texts worldwide.

The interpretation of Scripture is largely historical and allegorical. The writings of the world's religions are seen as providing historical value (especially as to the beliefs people might have had at the time or the religious experiences one might have had), without being interpreted as literal or necessary for people in modern times. The allegorical value of scripture is a modern way to understand scripture today: it seeks to see the passages of scripture presented in application of higher thought values, seeing the teachings of scripture as part of a higher vision, one to be applied by the New Thought practitioner. Religious leaders throughout the world are individuals who have applied higher thought in their lives. Their records show the way for all to achieve the same.

Although not considered scripture, New Thought is highly influenced by philosophical writings, particularly those of Transcendental writers (such as Ralph Waldo Emerson [1803-1882] and Henry David Thoreau [1817-1862]).

BASIC RELIGIOUS PRACTICES

The movement relates to one's thoughts and concepts, thus it is largely abstract in nature. Much of the New Thought Movement centers on a few key elements as part of one's practice, regardless of the sect of New Thought one may follow. The major focus of New Thought is one's thinking, so practitioners are encouraged to think positive thoughts, ones they believe will become reality if they believe and focus on them enough. Such aligns one's thoughts with spiritual realities rather than judging by what one may see or feel in their current situation. To facilitate this process, one engages in affirmative prayer. Affirmative prayer is a meditation technique that focuses on positive outcomes rather than what one may experience in a situation. Affirming positive possibilities and thoughts is considered a force, a way that good can be implemented in the world, because one's thoughts can change the world. New Thought practitioners are also interested in visualization, as they picture or imagine their desired outcome as projection for its occurrence in real life. For example, someone who desires a new job might visualize themselves in the job they desire, doing the work and functions of that position. Someone who desires to get married might picture themselves on their wedding day. An individual who is interested in global events might visualize an end of war or conflict, or a different presidential candidate winning an election. Such is done with the intent and purpose of uniting with Spirit to promote spiritual realities (thus accepting the true realities one is often oblivious to in their daily lives). Adherents of New Thought believe they can make all necessary life changes by changing their mentality (focusing on love, healing, and wellness).

Along with affirmative prayer is the principle of affirmation. Such can be classified as positive declarations about one's life, what one desires to happen, but most often, about the individual person. Affirmations often declare attributes and abilities designed for an individual to focus on positive, rather than negative things in one's character or ability. Affirmations are seen as centering, helping a practitioner to tap into who they are in the realm of spirit rather than in the natural, and grow spiritually. Such is believed to undo negative feedback, messages, and concepts one might have about their lives. Things such as criticism, blame, faults, or personal failures are considered undesirable, and out of alignment with spiritual attainment. By affirming who one really is in spirit, they can empower themselves to achieve all they can desire.

When one is a part of a New Thought church, services are much like we would find in a regular religious service. They are held on Saturdays (in the case of Jewish Science) or Sunday mornings, or on an evening or special day for a specified service. Ministers are typically identified as Reverend, and a service may be overseen by a singular minister or by more than one individual with position in a given community. Services include opening affirmation prayer and affirmations for specified issues or groups, songs (such as hymns reworked to include lyrics that relate to New Thought), announcements, meditation, a message (comparable to a sermon) and a final closing. Some groups employ sacraments similar to those found in mainline Christianity, but many have dropped them. New Thought services may also center around the writings of New Thought leaders throughout history, writings from a diversity of religious traditions, various religious practices, or socially conscious teachings or discussions.

HOLIDAYS

New Thought does not specify prohibitive holiday observance. Adherents are free to celebrate any holidays they desire. Most New Thought adherents acknowledge holidays such as Christmas and Easter (within the context of their tradition) and many New Thought organizations also acknowledge seasons, such as Advent and Lent. Unique to the New Thought Movement are a few different holidays observed exclusively within the movement:

- **New Thought Day**: August 23, the oldest of the New Thought holidays. Celebrates the establishment of New Thought as a legitimate theological presupposition.

- **New Thought Weeks**: There are approximately four New Thought Weeks throughout the year, coinciding with the changing seasons. Each New Thought week acknowledges a specific virtue or purpose along with New Thought ideals: Recognition (March 18-26, acknowledging New Thought), Unification (June 18-26, celebrating the New Thought community), Realization (September 18-26, realizing one's potential and participation in New Thought) and Release (December 18-26, sharing New Thought with others).

VISUAL SIGNS AND SYMBOLS

The Letter V with four lines extending out on either side of it, enclosed in a circle; A dove flying in front of a circle; Christian Science logo, a cross inside a crown with the words "heal the sick, raise the dead, cleanse the lepers, cast out demons" encircled around it; lotus flower (especially multicolored); eight point star encircled with a sun; dove holding an olive branch downward in its beak in front of a globe with longitudinal and latitudinal lines; symbol of a dove, a longitudinal and latitudinal globe above the dove, with symbols of overlapping hearts beneath and two scales of justice to either side of each heart, encircled in outreached arms; publications by the founders of the New Thought Movement; public group mediation.

CREEDS, BOOKS, AND LAWS

The New Thought Movement is non-credal and non-dogmatic, which means the movement itself does not require any one specified belief or belief system. Several of the organizations within the New Thought Movement do have statements of belief or credos, some of which are stated during services. As a rule, one does not have to ascribe to every single point in such statements to be a member, nor does one have to recite them or sign any sort of statement of agreement with them to join.

New Thought is largely a "book movement," meaning its ideas are disseminated in print form, especially through books. Key authors of New Thought include Charles and Myrtle Fillmore, Cora Fillmore (1876-1955), Emmet Fox (1886-1951), H. Emilie Cady (1848-1941), Edward Bellamy (1950-1898), Daisy Baum (1856-1923), Abel Allen, Nona Brooks, Malinda Cramer, Emma Curtis Hopkins, Morris Lichtenstein, Annie Rix Militz, Alfred Moses, Phineas Quimby, Ella Wilcox (1850-1919), and Jane Yarnall.

> *The true church is not made of creeds and forms, nor is it contained in walls of wood and stone; the heart of man is its temple and the Spirit of truth is the one guide into all Truth. When men learn to turn within to the Spirit of truth, who is in each one for his light and inspiration, the differences between the churches of man will be eliminated, and the one church will be recognized.*[10]

> *A general summing up, such as this, is highly characteristic of the old Oriental mode of approach to a religious and philosophical teaching, and it naturally recalls the Eight-fold Path of Buddhism, the Ten Commandments of Moses, and other such compact groupings of ideas. Jesus concerned himself exclusively with the teaching of general principles, and these general principles always had to do with mental states, for he knew that if one's mental states are right, everything else must be right too, whereas, if these are wrong, nothing else can be right. Unlike the other great religious teachers, he gives us no detailed instructions about what we are to do or are not to do; he does not tell us either to eat or to drink, or to refrain from eating or drinking certain things; or to carry out various ritual observances at certain times and seasons. Indeed, the whole current of his teaching is anti-ritualistic anti-formalist.*[11]

> *You have done any piece of work incorrectly, the very first step toward getting it right is to undo the wrong, and begin again from that point. We have believed wrong about God and about ourselves. We have believed that God was angry with us and that we were sinners who ought to be afraid of Him. We have believed that sickness and poverty and other troubles are evil things put here by this same God to torture us in some way into serving Him and loving Him. We have believed that we have pleased God best when we became so absolutely subdued by our troubles as to be patiently submissive to them all, not even trying to rise out of them or to overcome them. All this is false, entirely false! And the first step toward freeing ourselves from our troubles is to get rid of our erroneous beliefs about God and about ourselves.*[12]

ECLECTIC BELIEFS

To describe the New Thought Movement as "eclectic" is not an exaggeration. At its very core, New Thought is a mind-body-spirit connection movement, based in the way one thinks. The thought process of New Thought can adapt to any number of religious outsets, understandings, doctrines, and theologies; thus, it is not at all uncommon to meet New Thought practitioners who incorporate such into their spiritual lives. As people come to believe their illnesses, problems, issues, negative thoughts, and ailments are illusionary, they apply such thinking to any number of belief systems.

Phineas Quimby (1802-1886)

New Thought practitioners vary greatly on personal opinions, politics, insights, thoughts, and opinions about everything – spiritual and natural. Most New Thought groups refrain from political activities, opting instead to better humanity through the principles of thought and changing one's attitudes and minds about matters. It is seen as a different way to enlighten and change the world, one that is more abstract and intellectual than practical social gospel work or activism.

RELATIONS WITH THOSE OUTSIDE THE NEW THOUGHT COMMUNITY

The New Thought community places no prohibitions on involvement with different religious groups. Seeing religious unity as an important part of the progress of New Thought (as New Thought believes their basic principles are found and taught in all religions), New Thought organizations and churches are inclusive of individuals from different religious backgrounds and are also active in interfaith work.

HOLY SITES

Unity Village, Unity, Missouri; The Church of Higher Life, Boston, Massachusetts; First Church of Christ, Scientist, Boston, Massachusetts; First Church of Divine Science, Denver, Colorado; Centers for Spiritual Living, Golden, Colorado; Universal Foundation for Better Living, Chicago, Illinois; Seicho-No-Ie headquarters, Hokuto City, Japan; sites that may have spiritual meaning for each individual practitioner.

NOTABLE FIGURES

Wayne Dyer (1940-2015), author; Norman Vincent Peale (1898-1993), author; Della Reese (1931-2017), actress; Raymond Charles Barker (1911-1988), author; Mary Baker Eddy (1821-1910), founder, Christian Science; Jean Houston (1937-), founder, the Foundation for Mind Research; Johnnie Colemon (1920-2014), founder, Universal Foundation for Better Living; Kenneth George Mills (1923-2004), metaphysical speaker; Joel Osteen (1963-), televangelist;

Charles Patterson (1854-1917), publisher; Iyanla Vanzant (1953-), speaker and author; John Selby (1945-), psychologist.

NOTABLE GROUPS

The "Up" Church was founded by actress Della Reese, a minister influenced by the work of Johnnie Colemon. It continues to this day and is part of the Universal Foundation for Better Living.

FACTS AND FIGURES

New Thought publications and educational outreaches reach approximately 2.5 million people each year.[13]

OTHER IMPORTANT DEFINITIONS[14]

- **Abiding presence**: The presence or spirit of the divine, which is believed to be present everywhere and in everything.
- **Adam**: A representation of an unenlightened individual, one who has not adopted the principles of New Thought in their life.
- **Alpha and Omega**: A symbolism that all, from beginning to end, is spiritual and divine.
- **Androgynous**: What is known as the "Father-Mother God principle," by which a being (even a divine being) has the characteristics of both male and female genders.
- **Anti-Christ**: Using spiritual power for destructive, or negative, purposes.
- **Ark of the Covenant**: The principle of divine oneness within us, as one realizes that they are one with God.
- **Blessing**: Positive thoughts toward another.
- **Baptism by fire**: Purging the mind of thoughts that are negative, while moving toward spiritual consciousness.
- **Being**: God, spirit, spiritual reality.
- **Body of Christ**: Immortal individuality within each person, manifesting on any plane of which we may exist.

- **Bread of heaven**: Spiritual truth as spiritual food.
- **Christ**: The idea of sonship, or spiritual perfection, held in the mind of God.
- **Consciousness**: one's perception of existence.
- **Christ consciousness**: An individual who has received the level of Christ in development; one who has come to a place of sonship, or spiritual perfection.
- **Divine humanity**: The presence of the divine within all created things.
- **Ghost**: The mental form of a person, whether in body or not.
- **God**: The first cause, unborn, uncreate, absolute or unconditioned, the one and only reality.
- **Heaven**: a state of being represented by harmony.
- **Hell**: a state of being represented by discord.
- **Holy Ghost**: the servant of the universal spirit.
- **I am**: The divine, the real man, or real spiritual nature of man.
- **Illumination**: Reaching a direct contact with divine reality, God.
- **Karma**: the law of cause and effect.
- **Love**: Giving of self.
- **Mystic**: A person who senses or perceives the reality of divine presence in a specified situation.
- **Peace**: A state of inward calm.
- **Poverty**: Limited thoughts; the result of limited thinking.
- **Reality**: Truth about any and all things, especially in the spiritual sense.
- **Science**: A knowledge or working of fixed laws or principles.

- **Spirit**: God within, existing in all beings; the absolute.
- **Spiritual**: the atmosphere of the divine.
- **Trinity**: Also called triune unity; the threefold universe of spirit, soul, and body.
- **Truth**: Anything that is.
- **Universal law**: A divine principle.

BELIEVER'S CHARACTERISTICS

Emphasis on one's thoughts, thinking, and mindsets; emphasis on healing through positive thoughts and affirmations; belief that humanity has limitless potential to embrace and become as God; use of extensive literary publications; independent or group practice; belief in the divine present in and all throughout creation; emphasis on attaining oneness with the divine and others; belief one can heal through application of thoughts; interest in international religious practice; belief the world is illusionary; visualization; meditation; interpretation of scriptures as allegorical and historical rather than literal; spiritualization of scriptural interpretation; seeking Christ consciousness; belief the world can heal if it will change its mind.

The Occult

Do what thou will, that is the whole of the law.
(Aleister Crowley)[1]

Theology

The technicalities of occult theology vary. Traditional occultism included specified "occult sciences" of astrology, alchemy, and the practice of natural magic. Occultists tend to have a broad and diverse interest in religion as a subject. Most occult studies and practices divest into different religious headings: sometimes combined and sometimes isolated. Varying theologies depend upon the specific sect of the occult, and sometimes vary among individuals.

There are occult (from a word meaning "hidden") strains in all major world religions, identified as "esoteric" subheadings of a larger group. Judaism has Kabbalah, Islam has Sufism, Christianity has monasticism, Swedenborgianism, and New Thought; Buddhism and Hinduism have tantra; some indigenous religions have shamans. Some overlap with other systems, and others are unto themselves as a specified, disciplined practice. Each of these embrace a more mystical concept of their theology, in the form of identifying one's self as part of creation or the universe, saying the name of the divine (that in most mainline strains is seen as blasphemy), exploring the natural realm, meditation, fasting, aiming for spiritual perfection, greater union with the divine, and in some examples (but not all), engaging in magic or spellcasting. These different esoteric strains emphasize the concept that one has had a specific revelation, one that can only come through this specified group, and seek to explore the "why" of spirituality, rather than the "what."

Modern occultists practicing independently from specified religion are often a mix of occult science, ritual magic, Theosophy, the Hermetic Order of the Golden Dawn, Spiritualism, and the New Age Movement. There are some more complicated and mystical ideas found in traditional esoteric religious groups. In addition to these outlooks, there are approximately four different systems of theology an occultist may follow: a pagan outlook (which follows specified ancient gods and goddesses, echoing ancient Egypt, Celtic, Roman, Greek, Norse, or Germanic deities); a Gnostic outlook, which embodies the complexities of Gnostic theology (an unfathomable, unknowable deity who is overshadowed by a deceitful demiurge, with knowledge as the supreme answer and edge to salvation); a non-theistic or agnostic system of belief; or a New Age outlook (which embraces the idea of the divine as an impersonal, universal energy source, with no specified personality or connection to creation). Some believe this impersonal force is all-in-all. Occultists may be monotheists, pantheists, panentheists, monists, polytheists, pandeists, agnostics, atheists, Satanists, and beyond, depending on their unique interest and strain of magic.

PHILOSOPHY

The occult centers on the idea of achieving and understanding that which is hidden, unknown by the average individual, and attaining and embodying the practice of that specified knowledge once it has been obtained. While much of the religious world is interested in the who of a theological reality (such as a god or the gods) and how to specifically identify and honor that deity (as directed by scriptures, traditions, or both), occultists are interested in the why and how of the spiritual system. They take interest in the process, the mechanics, and the technicalities of spiritual work, of ways the natural realm interacts with the spiritual, and how both can be utilized and manipulated for specified ends. As they understand it, such information is not accessible by the ordinary person and, therefore, means they are able to understand deeper things about the universe, the divine, spirituality, and spiritual matters.

Occultists see this secret deposit of divine knowledge attainable only to specified, secret initiates, those who the secrets, knowledge, and traditions will be passed down or discussed, for practice. This secret information is highly prized. For this reason, it is not to be shared with the average person. The occultist seeks to control the forces of life through magic, spells, or other secretive practices as they study the following foundations of occultism: Religion (the spiritual quest of humanity to find God, the afterlife, immortality, culture, ethics, and spiritual purpose, systematically), alchemy (a primitive form of chemistry by which different elements or chemicals are mixed together to cast a spell, bring about something spiritual, or change base metals into gold), magic (the use of various spiritual forces over natural ones via the means of spellcasting), extra-sensory perception (the ability to perceive something without the use of the natural five senses), astrology the study of the way celestial objects (planets, stars, constellations move and the belief that such movements impact human issues, personalities, and interactions), spiritualism (the belief that those who have died can still communicate and interact with the living), and divination (any attempt by a portentous method to try and predict the future). Occultists may do this through their own specific religions, through combinations of occult strains found in mainline religion, independently, a secret society or organization, coven, closed meeting, or underground spiritual practice and study for the purpose of occult practice.[2]

ADHERENT IDENTITY

There are several different associations one may have within occult circles, thus leading to a host of different occult identities. Some include occultist, magician, sorcerer, witch, occult practitioner, high priest, priest, priestess, and other names as indicative of a specific occult group or practice (such as freemason, wiccan, Satanist, druid, Gnostic, pagan, tarot card reader, etc.)

NUMBER OF ADHERENTS

It is impossible to identify how many people identify as occultists or specified subheadings of such groups, as occultists have been, throughout history, non-disclosing of such information. There were several reasons for this: fear of persecution or death, being branded as lawbreakers in some societies, or fear that the secrets bound to occult theory would be somehow revealed. There are some in more modern times that believe being so apt to secrecy has hurt occult groups, as it leaves people who don't belong to them to conjure ideas and myths about them. At the same time, there is still a general stigma around occult practice and membership, and such is still deemed illegal in some parts of the world. Occultism is also a large heading for several different secret religions, societies, and organizations as well as independent practitioners, thus it is impossible to know just how many occultists there are worldwide.

Baphomet

TRADITIONAL LANGUAGES

Occultism has a long history with traditional languages including Hebrew, Greek, Coptic, Italian, and especially Latin. In modern times, occult writings can be found all over the world and are easily accessible in English.

SECTS/DIVISIONS

Not all occult groups have the same regard for one another or regard one another as equal. Much like general religious denominations and sects have disputes, occultists have the same. There are four major sects, or headings, for occult membership. They are:

- **Secret societies**: Secret societies are not religious groups but often delve into alternate religious histories and concepts that emphasize occult themes and ideas. They are identified as "secret" because what goes on in such groups has long been restricted to secrecy, bound by blood oaths or oaths promising death if one reveals the teachings and practices of the group to outsiders. While not all groups adhere to such specified codes today, they are long-held traditions within such organizations. Some require specific a religious identity or group membership (such as participation with a Christian church) and others require you must believe in a deity greater than yourself, but do not specify which deity that is or any specified theology. Some do not make any such requirements. To belong, you must either have a relative who is a member or a recommendation from another member. Most recognize three main levels of initiation with specified levels of study to advance to each level of initiation. Along with initiation comes secret symbols of membership: oaths, specific handshakes or grips, values, regalia and symbolism, hand gestures, verbal codes and secret sayings, rituals, meetings, and practice, all of which often share commonalities, deviating slightly to fit the specific occult narrative that is the focus of each unique group.

Secret societies vary on themes and mythology. Each group, though similar in structure and ideal, all have their own mythologies, which make each group a little different. All occult groups tie back to some earlier legend in history, often placing a different twist on the narrative. For example, Freemasonry connects its ideals to the building of Solomon's Temple, the Knights of Pythias speak of a Greek friendship legend, the modern Knights Templar believe that Freemasons have carried their secrets throughout the ages, and so on and so forth. These legends weave together their occult outlook, bind them together, and foster a sense of unity among the members. For this reason, many secret societies refer to their members as "brothers" or "sisters," and refer to their unity as a "brotherhood" or a "sisterhood."

Masonic square and compass

Much like other occult organizations, secret societies laud the study of occult science and practice and the exploration of spiritual virtue from an occult perspective and focus. Secret Societies deviate from other occult organizations in that they also focus on benevolent (charitable) works for the betterment of society. For example, the Shriners, an organization for Freemasons at the highest level, does extensive work through Shriners Hospitals for Children. Daughters of the Nile raise money for Shriners Hospitals. Job's Daughters International do work for hearing impaired children, and so on. Examples of secret societies include Freemasons, Shriners, Prince Hall Masonry, Order of the Eastern Star, Order of the Amaranth, White Shrine of Jerusalem, Knights Templar, Social Order of Beauceant, Daughters of the Nile, Rosicrucianism, Orange Order, Knights of Pythias, Independent Order of Odd Fellows, and the now defunct Hermetic Order of the Golden Dawn.

- **Occult science organizations**: Occult Science organizations are not specifically religious groups, nor do they fall under the heading of secret societies, although some may still bind their members to secrecy. Most often, occult science groups are interested in proving the realm of occultism (or specific aspects of it) to a larger audience. They are devoted to discovering, advancing, and proving the principles of occult science, specifically the works of astrology, alchemy, magic, and in more modern times, the existence of life after death, extraterrestrial life, and the spirit realm.

  Such organizations are often not as well organized as secret societies or occult religions and are not bound by any specific theologies or mythologies. Rather, they focus on the exploratory nature of the occult, thus indicating a particular aspect of occult study that takes form across many different beliefs and practices. Examples include the Consciousness Research Laboratory, Science Without Bounds, Philosophical Research Society, and Damanhur.

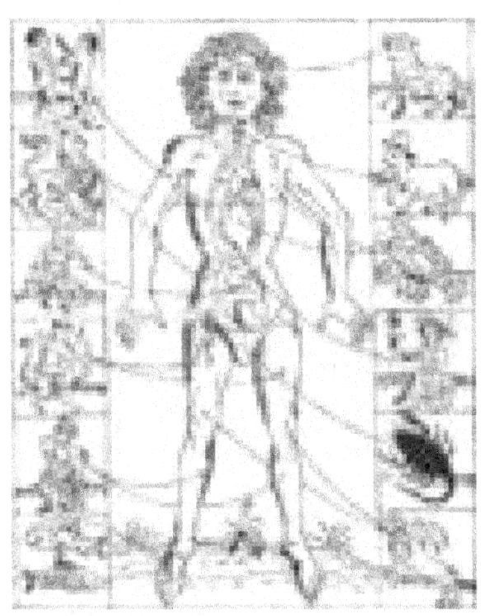
Zodiac Man

- **Occult religions**: Occult religions are religious organizations, with specified theology and structure, that relate to or encourage occult theory, sciences, or ideas. Rather than existing as an esoteric subset of a larger religious group, these religions disestablish from the ideals present within a larger, mainline religious group to identify exclusively with occult principles. They promote the ideals of occultism as a religious endeavor, as a form of spirituality rather than just one of scientific engagement or societal endeavor. Occult religions seek to control the supernatural and natural forces of the universe, specifically through the practice of magic. Religious occultists also use elements of witchcraft, alchemy, and divination in their specific rituals.

  Occult magic is unique for its use of ritual magic as religious rite. While it may reflect folk magic and its application, occult religion practices the concept of magic as high magic, meaning it is a part of official ritual and rite. Occult magic within a religious context is not something just practiced by an individual or considered for an investigative study or good principle, but something to be practiced both in a personal setting and as a group. These magical rites are performed as part of sabbats, masses, or festivals unique to the specific occult religion at hand. Some embrace hedonism, and some do not. Magic may be natural, sexual, fertility, ancient, or chaos magic (contemporary practice of magic).

  Occult religions embody a variety of different theologies, including those that are polytheistic or pagan, Satanic, Gnostic, monistic, pantheistic, panentheistic, or mystical interpretations of monotheism. Some are atheistic or agnostic in nature. Most occult religious groups adhere to specific mythologies, like those found in secret societies, often from ancient Egypt, Greece, Rome, Germanic, or Celtic sources. Some are more open about their practice (especially in modern times), while some adhere to traditional principles of oaths, secrets taught and transmitted among the specified groups, maintaining the hidden bonds of practice honored throughout history. Examples of occult religions include Satanism, paganism, the Ordo Templi Orientis, Neo-Gnosticism, neo-Paganism, Builders of the Adytum, and Argenteum Astrum (better known as A.A.).

- **Cultural occultism**: Occultism is found in every culture worldwide, often in what we might classify as a "folk" context. They vary in origin, but most overlap traditional cultural spirits, deities, or legends with witchcraft grimoires and beliefs originating in the 1800s. The specific practices and legends have evolved throughout time, often from traditional animism, pagan, or other ancient religious traditions within a country or region. They often incorporate local deities (sometimes syncretized with Christian saints or theologies), ancient superstitions, and traditional magic, passed down between families. Most aren't as elaborate or organized as occult religions or organizations and are based on more personal expressions of cultural traditions. Their methods are often passed down by initiation and word of mouth, with few, if any, original books describing their systems. Examples include Voodoo, Hoodoo, Stregheria, Santeria, and Yorba. Nazi occultism, which largely influenced Hitler's visions of an Aryan race, was fascinated with Germanic paganism. Thus, by extension, it is also an extreme subheading of cultural occultism.

- **Independent practitioners**: Practitioners of the occult may engage in their exploration of hidden things independently, without the aid of a group, society, or religion. This has become more popular with the rise of the internet and information freely available that, in times past, was harder to access.

DISPUTES WITHIN GROUP

Occultists, while often engaging in similar practices, do not always agree with the mythology, theology, or forms of magic practiced by their counterparts. Some affirm their system of mythology or theology to be correct, "original," or foundational to others, thus leading to obvious disagreement in the practice and application of occultism. Occult groups also disagree about the "hidden" nature of their practice. While some think it is important to be out in the open about their beliefs, not all occultists agree such is the proper form of action.

Perhaps the greatest dispute among occultists is the use and general purpose within the practice of magic. While some believe magic should only be used for good, unselfish, or edifying purposes (known as white magic), other occultists find this presupposition to be self-righteous. Other forms of occultism believe magic should be used for selfish, retaliatory, or evil purpose (black magic) or to exert no force at all, but rather, for the sake of practice (gray magic). For example, Satanists tend to dislike Wiccans and other neo-pagan groups, considering them to be self-righteous, watering down occultism to receive acceptance from outside communities. This is seen as the ultimate compromise, one that taints the essence of attaining the secret knowledge of the occult world and using it in a manner that is entertaining or acceptable within greater society.

SCRIPTURES

Occultists accept varied texts, especially as vary by group. The purpose of occult study into various texts of world religions and occult literature throughout the ages is for the pursuit of knowledge. Texts aren't seen as exclusive sources of faith, but as deposits of hidden wisdom, knowledge, and experience throughout the ages. As a result, many mainline religious texts (such as the Bible, any of the various Hindu Scriptures, or the Qur'an) are studied, but are studied and interpreted through a more esoteric, mystical lens.

Occultists do embrace their own unique set of writings, all of which can be categorized by major occult headings. Some examples, though not exhaustive, include:

- **Paganism**: *The Spiral Dance* (Starhawk [1951-]), *A Witches' Bible: The Complete Witches' Handbook* (Janet [1950-] and Stewart Farrar [1916-2000]), *The Book of Shadows* (Gerald Gardner [1884-1964]), *Buckland's Complete Book of Witchcraft* (Raymond Buckland [1934-2017]), *Drawing Down the Moon* (Margot Adler [1946-2014]), *Aradia, Gospel of the Witches* (Charles Godfrey Leland [1824-1903]).

  And yet erewhile, when thou wert in the ear, Even as a (golden) glittering grain, even then The fireflies came to cast on thee their light And aid thy growth, because without their help Thou couldst not grow nor beautiful become; Therefore thou dost belong unto the race Of witches or of fairies, and because The fireflies do belong unto the sun. . , , Queen of the Fireflies ! hurry apace,- Come to me now as if running a race, Bridle the horse as you hear me now sing! Bridle, O bridle the son of the king ! Come in a hurry and bring him to me! The son of the king will ere long set thee free; ' There is an evident association here of [he body of the firefly which much resembles a grain of wheat) with the latter. ' The six lines following are often heard as a nursery rhyme. And because thou for ever art brilliant and fair, Under a glass I will keep thee; while there, With a lens I will study thy secrets concealed, Till all their bright mysteries are fully revealed. Yea, all the wondrous lore perplexed Of this life of our cross and of the next. Thus to all mysteries I shall attain, Yea, even to that at last of the grain; And when this at last I shall truly know. Firefly, freely I'll let thee go! When Earth's dark secrets are known to me. My blessing at last I will give to thee! Here follows the Conjuration of the Salt. Conjuration of the Salt. I do conjure thee, salt, lo! here at noon, Exactly in the middle of a stream I take my place and see the water round, Likewise the sun, and think of nothing else White here besides the water and the sun: For all my soul is turned in truth to them; I do indeed desire no other thought, I yearn to learn the very truth of truths. For I have suffered long with the desire To know my future or my coming fate. If good or evil will prevail in it. Water and sun, be gracious unto me![8]

- **Satanism**: *The Satanic Bible* (Anton LaVey [1930-1997]), *The Book of Coming Forth by Night* (Michael Aquino [1946-]), *Jeweled Tablets of Set* (Michael Aquino), *The Book of Opening the Way, The Unholy Bible: The Book of Concealment* (Leena Klammer), *The Bible of the Adversary* (Michael W. Ford [1976-]), *Necrominon* (Michael W. Ford), and *Luciferian Witchcraft* (Michael W. Ford).

  The Equinox has succumbed to my Solstice, and I, Set, am revealed in my Majesty.

  The time of the Purification is past.

  The fate of my Gifted race rests in balance, and I shall not recant my Word, spoken to my High Priest MehenPetTha in old Khem and now again to you.

  Proclaim the nineteen Parts of the Word, and vanquish thus the feeble and corrupt Keys of Enoch, which were but a shadow of my true Word and now are an affront to me.

I am the ageless Intelligence of this Universe. I created HarWer that I might define my Self. All other gods of all other times and nations have been created by men. This you know from the first Part of my Word, and from my manifest semblance, which alone is not of Earth.

Known as the Hebrew Satan, I chose to bring forth a Magus, according to the fashion of my Word. He was charged to form a Church of Satan, that I might easily touch the minds of men in this image they had cast for me.

In the fifth year of the Church of Satan, I gave to this Magus my Diabolicon, that he might know the truth of my ancient Gift to mankind, clothed though it might be in the myths of the Hebrews. Even you, who delivered the Diabolicon from Asia, did not know it for what it was. But he that I had fashioned a Magus knew, and he thought often of the Diabolicon as he guided the Church of Satan.

Upon the ninth Solstice, therefore, I destroyed my pact with Anton Szandor LaVey, and I raised him to the Will of a Daimon, unbounded by the material dimensions. And so I thought to honor him beyond other men. But it may have been this act of mine that ordained his fall.

Were I my Self to displace the Cosmic Inertia, I should be forced to become a new measure of consistency. I would cease to be One, for I should become All.[4]

- **Magic**: The Book of Abramelin, The Lesser Key of Solomon, The Testament of Solomon, The Greater Keys of Solomon, The Grimorium Verum, The Grand Grimoire, Book of Thoth, *The History of Magic* (Eliphas Levi [1810-1875]), *The Clavis* or *Key to the Magic of Solomon* (Ebenezer Sibley [1751-c. 1799]), *Magick and Theory in Practice* (Aleister Crowley [1875-1947]), *Liber B vel Magi* (Aleister Crowley), *The Secret Wisdom of the Qabalah* (J.F.C. Fuller [1878-1966]), *The Hermetic Mystery* (Mary Anne Atwood [1817-1910]), *The Magus, or Celestial Intelligencer* (Francis Barrett [c. 1770-after 1802]), *Seven Pillars of Occult Wisdom, The Serpent Power* (John Woodroffe [1865-1936]), *Transcendental Magic, its Doctrine and Ritual* (Eliphas Levi), and *Portal Papers of the Golden Dawn.*

The question of Magick is a question of discovering and employing hitherto unknown forces of nature. We know that they exist, and we cannot doubt the possibility of mental or physical instruments capable of bringing us into relation with them.[5]

Occult Medicine is essentially sympathetic. Reciprocal affection, or at least real goodwill, must exist between doctor and patient. Syrups and juleps have very little inherent virtue; they are what they become through the mutual opinion of operator and subject; hence homoeopathic medicine dispenses with them and no serious inconvenience follows.[6]

- **Gnosticism**: *The Gnostic Bible*, The Pistis Sophia, The Books of JEU, The Gospel of the Lord, The Hymn of the Pearl, The Secret Gospel of Mark, The Nassene Psalm, The Gospel of Philip, Fragments from the Writings of Basilides, The Gospel of Truth, Corpus Hermeticum, The Rosarium Philosophorum, Alchemical Mass, The Alchemical Practice of Mary the Prophetess, The Six Keys of Eudoxus, and Coleum Terrae (Thomas Vaughan).

Our Water is a living Spring which comes out of the Stone by a natural miracle of our philosophy. The first of all is the water which issueth out of this Stone. It is Hermes who has pronounced this great Truth. He acknow- ledges, further, that this water is the foundation of our Art.

The philosophers give it many names; for sometimes they call it wine, sometimes water of life, sometimes vinegar, sometimes oil, according to the different degrees of Preparation, or according to the diverse effects which it is capable of producing.

Yet I let you know that it is properly called the Vinegar of the Wise, and that in the distillation of this Divine Liquor there happens the same thing as in that of common vinegar; you may hence draw instruction: the water and the phlegm ascend first; the oily substance, in which the efficacy of the water consists, comes the last, etc.

It is therefore necessary to dissolve the body entirely to extract all its humidity which contains the precious ferment, the sulphur, that balm of Nature, and wonderful unguent, without which you ought not to hope ever to see in your vessel this blackness so desired by all the philosophers. Reduce then the whole compound into water, and make a perfect union of the volatile with the fixed; it is a precept of Senior's, which deserves attention, that the highest fume should be reduced to the lowest; for the divine water is the thing descending from heaven, the reducer of the soul to its body, which it at length revives.

Aleister Crowley (1875-1947)

The Balm of Life is hid in these unclean faeces; you ought to wash them with this celestial water until you have removed away the blackness from them, and then your Water shall be animated with this Fiery Essence, which works all the wonders of our Art.

But, further, that you may not be deceived with the terms of the Compound, I will tell you that the philosophers have two sorts of compounds. The first is the compound of Nature, wherof I have spoken in the First Key; for it is Nature which makes it in a manner incomprehensible to the Artist, who does nothing but lend a hand to Nature by the adhibition of external things, by the means of which she brings forth and produces this admirable compound.

The second is the compound of Art; it is the Wise man who makes it by the secret union of the fixed with the volatile, perfectly conjoined with all prudence, which cannot be acquired but by the lights of a profound philosophy.

The compound of Art is not altogether the same in the Second as in the Third Work; yet it is always the Artist who makes it. Geber defines it, a mixture of Argent vive and Sulphur, that is to say, of the volatile and the fixed; which, acting on one another, are volatilized and fixed reciprocally into a perfect Fixity. Consider the example of Nature; you see that the earth will never produce fruit if it be not penetrated with its humidity, and that the humidity would always remain barren if it were not retained and fixed by the dryness of the earth.

So, in the Art, you can have no success if you do not in the first work purify the Serpent, born of the Slime of the earth; it you do not whiten these foul and black faeces, to separate from thence the white sulphur, which is the Sal Amoniac of the Wise, and their Chaste Diana, who washes herself in the bath; and all this mystery is but the extraction of the fixed salt of our compound, in which the whole energy of our Mercury consists.

The water which ascends by distillation carries up with it a part of this fiery salt, so that the affusion of the water on the body, reiterated many times, impregnates, fattens, and fertilizes our Mercury, and makes it fit to be fixed, which is the end of the second Work. One cannot better explain this Truth than by Hermes, in these words:

When I saw that the water by degrees did become thicker and harder I did rejoice, for I certainly knew that I should find what I sought for.[7]

- **Secret societies**: The Masonic Edition of the King James Version of the Bible, *Morals and Dogma: Of the Ancient and Accepted Scottish Rite of Freemasonry* (Albert Pike [1809-1891]), *The Secret Teachings of All Ages: An Encyclopedic Outline of Masonic, Hermetic, Qabbalistic and Roscrucian Symbol Philosophy* (Manly P. Hall [1901-1990]), *The Craft and Its Symbols* (Allen Roberts [1917-1997]), *The Symbolism of Freemasonry* (Albert G. Mackey [1807-1881]), *The Principles of Masonic Law* (Albert G. Mackey), *The Secret Doctrine of the Rosicrucians* (Magus Ingocnito [1862-1932]), *The Rosicrucians, Their Rites and Mysteries* (Hargrave Jennings [1817-1890]), and *The Golden Dawn* (Israel Regardie [1907-1985]).

Masonry, like all the Religions, all the Mysteries, Hermeticism and Alchemy, conceals its secrets from all except the Adepts and Sages, or the Elect, and uses false explanations and misinterpretations of its symbols to mislead those who deserve only to be misled; to conceal the Truth, which it calls Light from them and to draw them away from it.[8]

- **General**: *Enochiana* (John Dee [1555-c.1598] and Edward Kelley [1527-c. 1609]), *The Secret Doctrine* (Helena Blavatsky [1831-1891]), *Gleanings of a Mystic* (Max Heindel [1865-1919]), *Theosophy* (Rudolf Steiner [1861-1924]), *Tertium Organum* (P.D. Ouspensky [1878-1947]), *The Consciousness of the Atom* (Alice A. Bailey [1880-1949]), writings of Nostradamus (1503-1566), and *Three Books of Occult Philosophy* (Henry Cornelius Agrippa [1486-1535]).

Thus space and time, defining everything that we cognize by sensuous means, are in themselves just forms of consciousness, categories of our intellect, the prism through which we regard the world—or in other words space and time do not represent properties of the world, but just properties of our knowledge of the world gained through our sensuous organism. Consequently the world, until by these means we come into relation to it, has neither extension in space nor existence in time; these are properties which we add to it.[9]

BASIC RELIGIOUS PRACTICES

The uniting force of occultism is the study and practice of magic. There is much that goes into this study and practice, and for occultists, such is a discipline that goes beyond a casual interest in seeing things happen from a magical perspective. Occultism is about the study of cause and effect, about the reasons, forces, and actions behind the secret interworking of the universe, and their expressions as found through magic, alchemy, spiritualism, religion, extra-sensory perception, and astrology. Occultism is, therefore, an exploration; it is not so much about definite answers or codes of belief, but about the process. The more one discovers, the more one can manipulate natural or spiritual forces, and the more effective one will become in the application of magic.

Most occultists believe in this study and disciplinary process. To them, it's more about the process than discovering answers. Occultists believe in extensive reading, study, and research into occult science and belief. As a rule (and now a long-standing tradition), most occultists practice their belief system in secret. Through initiation rites, occultists are initiated, by ritual and rite, into their specific system of occult study, knowledge, magic, and discipline. Most organizations recognize three levels of initiation, symbolized as one joins "the craft," or the practice of magic (or witchcraft).

Occultists often find their own unique combination of practice for effective magic. Most occult organizations combine different strains of magical theory and practice, ancient theologies, rituals, and expressions for their practitioners. A practitioner of the occult may take an interest in astrology, nature worship, tarot, divination, necromancy, ESP, spiritualism, the spiritual realm, natural magic, worship of pagan or ancient deities, the magic and esoterism of ancient religions or modern religious systems, psychics, and a general ability to foretell the future. Some occultists also delve into theology about Satan or Satanism, while some do not espouse any specific theology therein.

Occultists are often stereotyped as hedonists, using occult outlets for things such as drug or alcohol abuse, sexual rites, or specified rituals that might include the slaughter of animals, rape, murder, or torture. While many occultists are hedonists, there are no verifiable cases of rape, murder, or torture in connection with specific occult practice in modern times. Animal sacrifice is practiced in some cultural occult groups, such as Santeria. These animals are bred for sacrifice; there are no instances of such groups torturing or killing other people's animals or pets. When sacrifice is performed, it is often done symbolically, rather than literally. There is also no evidence to believe occultists are more dangerous or threatening than practitioners of other belief systems. While there is no question many groups may find occult practice and study objectionable from a moral perspective, there is nothing to say they are guilty of the many things of which they are frequently accused.

HOLIDAYS

There is no one list of occult holidays shared and embraced by all occultists. Most follow traditional neopagan ideas about holidays, which revolve around the changing of seasons, solstices, harvests, and fertility festivals. Some observe traditional Christian holidays from a secular perspective or with an occult twist, and others observe holidays in combination, selecting events and seasons from all over the world that are in line with their unique ideas of nature and spirituality.

VISUAL SIGNS AND SYMBOLS

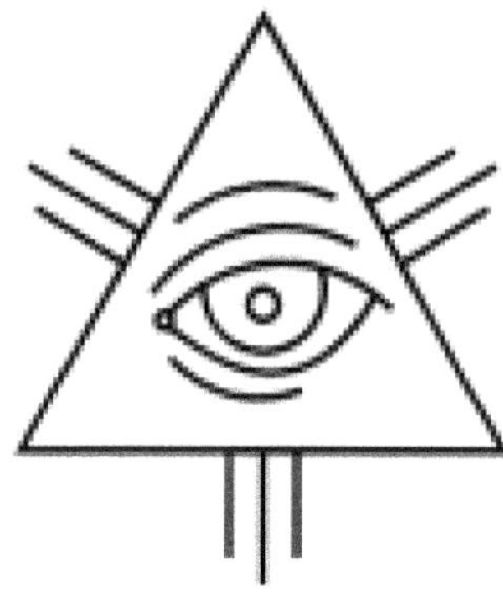
All-seeing eye, eye of Horus

Masonic symbols; pentagram; inverted pentagram with goat's head enclosed in a circle; all-seeing eye of Horus; pyramid; Egyptian ankh; dragon; serpent; tarot cards; sword; secret rituals; magic; Ouija board; sexual rites; alchemy; ancient gods and goddesses; arrow; Baphomet; black sun; circled dot; cross of Saint Peter (inverted cross); eye of providence; heptagram; hexagram; Icelandic magical staves; monas hieroglyphica; ouroboros; pentacle; pentagram; Rose cross; runes; Seal of Solomon; Septenary Sigil; Sgil of Lucifer; Sigillum Dei; squared circle; sulfur crossers; suns; symbol of chaos; Tetragrammaton; Kabbalah Tree o flife; Unicursal hexagram; Zodiac Man; "777" lightning bolt; evil eye; Scarab Beetle; pyramid.

CREEDS, BOOKS, AND LAWS

Occultists recognize no specific creed or specified law. Occultism is a complex and involved system of different laws, taught throughout different societies, religions, and groups throughout history. As a result, occultists see the practice of magic and other occult principles as an evolving thing; one that is continued with their specified and unique practice. Most would accept the summary by Aleister Crowley:

> *Do what thou will, that is the whole of the law.*

Heavily bound by experimentation, occultism believes in pushing boundaries, exploring forbidden areas of study, and delving into forbidden realms of the spiritual and natural worlds.

Occultists don't universally agree about laws and boundaries for such exploration. While many neopagan groups (such as Wicca) would promote the value and practice of magic for only good things or good ends, Satanists and other dark occultists would believe in the practice of magic for selfish and manipulative ends. As a result, there is no specific view of how or what magic should be used to accomplish, or about its specific discipline or practice. While specific occult strains do adhere to certain forms of magic, there is no universal requirement or standard for such.

As we had explored earlier, occult books are diverse in nature and vary by occult strain. Much like New Agers, occultists are very interested in the realm of occult themes in popular culture. A major dispute is when such themes (such as in *The DaVinci Code* by Dan Brown) are inaccurate or misrepresentative of true belief. The primary author as pertains to actual magical practice in modern times is Aleister Crowley.

ECLECTIC BELIEFS

To define the occult as eclectic is accurate. The secret, hidden knowledge acquired through occult practice is what binds the occult as a general heading. Everything else, from that point, is variable. Practices not only vary among groups; they also often vary among practitioners. It is understood that the more one learns, and the higher one ascends within one's desired rites, one can control natural and supernatural elements, cast spells, and in some groups, transcend planes of existence. Spiritualists, New Agers, Theosophists, secret societies, followers of Aleister Crowley (in one form or another), those who study vampires, UFOs, faeries, astral projection, parallel universe travel, portals, stargates, ghost hunters, paranormal investigators, and parapsychologists are just a small sample of the diversity, and eclectic belief, present within the "occult." To be certain what an occultist believes, one must ask an occultist.

RELATIONS WITH NON-OCCULTISTS

Occultists may or may not practice mainline religion in addition to their occult pursuit. Some hold mainline religion to be a watered-down form of knowledge. There are also those who consider those outside of occult practice to be ignorant, not having secret knowledge. Many occultists regard the New Age Movement (though properly a part of the occult) as an insult to occultism. Occultists also hold their own respective opinions about what forms of secret knowledge are legitimate and may regard other occultists as imposters as well.

HOLY SITES

Stonehenge, UK; Abbey of Thelema, Italy; the Pyramids, Giza, Egypt; Mount Shasta, California; Lake Titicaca, Peru/Bolivia; Uluru-Kata Tjuta National Park (Ayers Rock), Red Centre, Australia; Mountains of Petra, Jordan; the Goetheanum, Dornach, Switzerland; Cenote Sagrado, Mexico; Mahabodhi Tree, Bodh Gaya, India; Lake Atitlan, Guatemala; Mount Kailas, Tibet; Mount Sinai, Egypt; Vortexes, Arizona; Glastonbury Tor, England; Crater Lake, Oregon; pyramids of Teotihuacan; Rila's lakes, Bulgaria; Mount Parnassus, Greece; other specified sites as specific to each occult group.

NOTABLE FIGURES

Mary the Jewess, alchemist (fourth century); Merlin, Arthurian legend wizard; Pythagoras (c. 570-c. 495 BC), Greek mathematician; Ptolemy (c. 100-c. 170), astrologer; Simon Magus (d. 65), magician mentioned in the book of Acts; Roger Bacon (c. 1220-1292), philosopher; Heinrich Cornelius Agrippa (1486-1535), philosopher; John Dee (1527-c. 1609), alchemist; Nostradamus (1503-1566), diviner; Walter Raleigh (1552-1618), alchemist; Isaac Newton (1643-1727), physicist and alchemist; *La Voisin* (c. 1640-1680), French magician; Emmanuel Swedenborg (1688-1772), alchemist; Count of St. Germain (c. 1691-1784), alchemist; Marquis de Sade (1740-1814), author; Albert Pike (1809-1891), Freemason; Francis Barrett (c. 1770-after 1802), author; Helena Petrovna Blavatsky (1831-1891), founder of Theosophy; Arthur

Conan Doyle (1859-1930), author; Marie Laveau (1801-1881), Voodoo practitioner; Eliphas Levi (1810-1875), author and magician; Samuel L. MacGregor Mathers (1854-1918), founder of the Hermetic Order of the Golden Dawn; Grigori Rasputin (1869-1916), Russian mystic; William Butler Yeats (1865-1939), poet; Adolf Hitler (1889-1945), politician and Holocaust leader; Alice Bailey (1880-1949), author; Peter J. Carroll (1953-), author, founder of Chaos magic; Manly Hall (1901-1990), author; John Michael Greer (1962-), author; Aleister Crowley (1875-1947), founder of Thelema; Anton LaVey (1930-1997), founder, Church of Satan; George Washington (1732-1799), politician; Benjamin Franklin (1706-1790), Rosicrucian and Freemason.

NOTABLE GROUPS

The Ordo Templi Orientis (OTO), also known as the "Order of the Temple of the East" or "Order of Oriental Templars" was founded by German occultists Carl Kellner (1851-1905), Henrich Klein (1855-1907), Franz Hartmann (1838-1912), and Theodor Reuss (1855-1923). The most influential and best-known member of the order was Aleister Crowley. Its inspiration was European Freemasonry, but due to Crowley's influence, they reorganized around his Thelema occult religious organization. It utilizes systems of initiation (Man of Earth Triad, Lover Triad, and Hermit Triad), ritual drama, and the use of sex magic. Its major public rite is the Gnostic Mass, and its organization includes the *Ecclesia Gnostica Catholica*. Its central text is *The Book of the Law*, focusing on Thelemic deities, practices, and magic. Practitioners focus on ritual activity and magic.[10]

FACTS AND FIGURES

Alternative religion recognition, including Neo-pagan, spiritualism, satanism, druidism, wicca, etc. – account for 0.4% of the US population.[11]

OTHER IMPORTANT DEFINITIONS

- **ADC**: An after-death communication, usually understood as part of spiritism with a deceased person. Such can come through auditory, emotional, sensory, or tactile experiences.

- **Amulet**: A good-luck charm.

- **Anthroposophy**: An occult philosophy founded by Rudolph Steiner that believes the spiritual world can be understood through intellect and comprehension, and is accessible to human experience. Followers seek to discover the spiritual world through thought, rather than sensory experience; thus, they seek to offer rational defense for occult ideas.

- **Aspect**: An angle the planets make to one another within the horoscope, ascendant (astrological sign descending on the eastern horizon), midheaven (point of definition among elipiticals), descendant (the seventh house of the horoscope), lower midheaven (where an eliptic crosses the meridian), and other points of astrological interest. Aspects are measured by angular distance and minutes of longitude between two points, as viewed from earth.[12]

Rosy Cross of the Heremetic Order of the Golden Dawn

- **Automated art**: Like automated writing, when an individual creates artwork (usually pictures or paintings) by the control of a spirit; a form of mediumship.

- **Automated writing**: A process by which an individual channels a spirit who controls their ability to write while in a trance or without control of the process.

- **Banishing**: A ritual designed to remove negative influences, such as bad spirits or negative energy.

- **Baphomet**: Associated with the "Sabbatic Goat" as depicted by Eliphas Levi, an image associated with a contrast and balance of opposites: it is half-human, half-animal, male and female, good and evil, on and off. The pointing of two fingers upward with one hand and downward with the other symbolizes "As above, so below," indicating the connectedness between occult knowledge and systems in the spirit realm as well as on earth.[13]

- **Ceremonial magic**: Magic specifically used as part of occult ritual, marked by long and complex steps, a number of necessary tools, and knowledge of a number of different occult schools of thought throughout history.

- **Chakra**: Seven specified energy wheels or centers that are located in a line, from the base of one's tailbone (root chakra) to the top, or crown of one's head (crown chakra) and represented by the rainbow spectrum (red to purple). They are: Root, sacral, solar plexus, heart, throat, third eye, and crown. The Chakras come from ancient Hindu tradition, specifically the esoteric form of Hinduism known as Tantra.

- **Clairaudience**: The ability to receive messages from the spirit world audibly (through hearing).

- **Clairsentience**: The ability to receive messages from the spirit world through feelings and emotions, especially those who are deceased.

- **Clarivoyance**: The ability to receive messages from the spirit world through visions.

- **Classical elements**: The four elements of fire, air, earth, and water. These form the basis of classic magical understanding and alchemy.

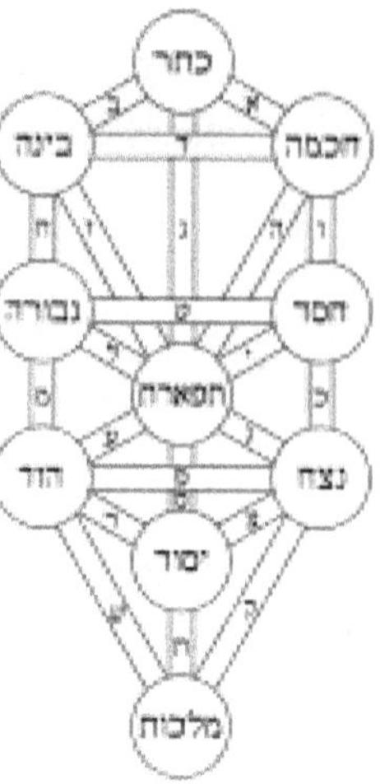

Kabbalah Tree of Life

- **Classical planets**: As part of alchemy's foundations, the occult world traditionally recognized seven classical planets: moon, Mercury, Venus, sun, Mars, Jupiter, and Saturn. Each was associated with seven metals: silver, mercury/quicksilver, copper, gold, iron, tin, and lead.[14]

- **Elemental**: A mythical being found in occult and alchemical writings. There are four categories of elementals: gnomes, undines, sylphs, and salamanders. Each corresponds to the classical elements of earth, water, air, and fire.[15]

- **Enochian**: Ceremonial magic that focuses on commanding angels and spirits.

- **ESP**: Extrasensory perception; the awareness of the supernatural, independent of perception through the normal five senses.

- **Evocation**: Also called conjuration, the process by which a spirit is summoned, or called upon, to rise up and manifest, through occult incantation.

- **Gazing**: Staring at an object, such as a quartz crystal or crystal ball, so one will be able to have a visions.

- **Grimoire**: A textbook of magic, especially one that details the way to craft magical objects, cast spells, perform divination, and invoke supernatural entities.[16]

- **Hermeticism**: An occult tradition based on writings attributed to Hermes Trismegistus.

- **Kemetism**: A modern-day interest in the religion of ancient Egypt.

- **Mesmerism**: Another term for hypnotism, by which an individual is placed in a trance.

- **Planetary hours**: The belief that each one of the classic planets (moon, Mercury, Venus, sun, Mars, Jupiter, and Saturn) rules over both a day of the week and parts of each day as part of Greek astrology.

- **Possession**: When a spirit controls an individual for its own personal gratification.

- **Precognition**: The ability to see a future event.

- **Psychokinesis**: Using principles of energy and energy fields, the ability to move an object using one's mind.

- **Pyramidology**: Study of the pyramids as containing a special, or unique message, that relates to spiritual or physical matters.

- **Reincarnation**: The belief that the essence of a being returns in a new body through a series of incarnations, in different beings. Reincarnation is believed by many, though not all, occultists.

- **Retrocognition**: The ability to see past events.

- **Telekinesis**: When an object is moved by a spirit or some other unseen force.

- **Telepathy:** Being able to read someone's mind or communicate mentally, without words or exterior information.

- **Thelema**: A form of occult theory formulated by Aleister Crowley. It literally means "to will." Thelema espouses its own specified deities from Egyptian lore, such as Nuit, Hadit, and Ra-Hoor-Kuhit, and its own specified Book of the Law, which outlines its ideals. Thelema emphasizes magic, traditional occultism, yoga, and mysticism, especially the Kabbalah.[17]

- **Theosophy**: A religion formed in 1875 with strong influence from Helena Blavatsky, often considered foundational in the formulation of the modern-day New Age Movement. Theosophy blended occult ideals with a number of philosophies, Hinduism, and Buddhism to create a belief system of monism, that believes all is part of a greater, singular reality.

BELIEVER'S CHARACTERISTICS

Fascination with mechanism rather than strict belief; interest in obtaining secret or hidden knowledge, knowing things that are not always taught or obvious in religious circles; desire to control forces, especially through magic; interest in ritual, rite, and orders of magic, or in the practice and application of such for the individual; interest in older religious systems, especially those that date back to pagan or ancient times; worship or connection to ancient deities; polytheism; fascination with things such as extra sensory perception, alchemy, religion, magic, divination, spiritualism, and astronomy; interest in the ancient ways of study and investigation; membership in a secret society or occult religion or organization; fascination with the spirit world; secret rites and orders; use of different occult scriptures, occult works, or interpretation of traditional religious scripture from an esoteric perspective; interest in esoteric religious organizations; belief in the material world as a channel for spiritual control; nature worship; hedonism; foretelling the future; conjuring; divining; study of or promotion of the occult sciences.

Orthodoxy

Suffering cleanses the soul infected with the filth of sensual pleasure and detaches it completely from material things by showing it the penalty incurred as a result of its affection for them. This is why God in His justice allows the devil to afflict men with torments.
(Maximus the Confessor and Ignatius Brianchianinov)[1]

Theology

There are three different systems of Orthodox belief. Each one adheres to a different theological identity. While the end aspect of belief is the same, the way they explain and expound the technicalities are different.

Oriental Orthodoxy (also known as Old Oriental, Non-Chalcedonian, and Monophysite) believes in one true God as a Trinity, eternally existent and evident as three persons: Father, Son (Logos or Wisdom, incarnate in the person of Jesus Christ), and Holy Spirit. Jesus Christ, the Son, is one being, both divine and human, with only one nature.

Nestorian Orthodoxy believes in one true God as a Trinity, eternally existent and evident as three persons: Father, Son (Logos or Wisdom, incarnate in the person of Jesus Christ) and Holy Spirit. Jesus Christ, the Son, has two distinct natures and two wills, thus being two separate persons in one rather than one that is unified.

Eastern Orthodoxy believes in one true God as a Trinity, eternally existent and evident as three persons: Father, Son (Logos or Wisdom, incarnate in the person of Jesus Christ) and Holy Spirit. Jesus Christ, the Son, has two distinct natures and two wills, perfect and divine within one unified person.

For all three groups, God is beyond all comprehension, traditionally referred to as Kyrios, GOD, LORD, TRINITY or HOLY TRINITY. God is seen as creator of the universe, having existed for all time and beyond; the One Who seeks true worship, absolute devotion, and offers the truth of doctrine through prayer and life, an indissoluble Holy Tradition present only in the Orthodox Church. In more specific terms, the validity of tradition is only seen within each Orthodox Church; it is not recognized outside of each specific group (often even among groups that are also Orthodox).

Philosophy

Orthodox Christians of all variations believe there are four essential pillars of their existence: They are one, holy, catholic, and apostolic. These four pillars relate in that the church is united, set apart for its work, unlike other churches, universal, and has an unbroken lineage of tradition dating back to the apostles themselves.

Outside their faith, there is no correct teaching nor spiritual understanding. As is named, they believe their teaching to be "orthodox," a word meaning "right teaching." To the Orthodox, their church is the only true church established by Jesus Christ Himself at Pentecost. The Divine Liturgy (also called Holy Qurbana in Oriental Orthodoxy), the liturgical worship service of the Orthodox is considered the mystical mingling of heaven on earth. All other churches, including Roman Catholics, Protestants, and other Christians are considered heresies that deviated from Orthodoxy.

TRADITIONAL LANGUAGES

Orthodox Churches have long offered services in the vernacular language of the people. This means the Orthodox do not recognize one specific traditional language over another. Some important languages within the Orthodox community are Church Slavonic, Greek, Arabic, Russian, classical Armenian, old Georgian, Coptic, Ge'ez, and Syriac.

ADHERENT IDENTITY

The three main divisions of Orthodoxy are Oriental Orthodoxy (Old Oriental, Non-Chalcedonian, Monophysite), Nestorian Orthodoxy (Persian Church, Nestorian Church, Assyrian Church of the East), and Eastern Orthodoxy (Eastern Rite, the title "Orthodox" preceded by a nationality, such as "Greek Orthodox," "Russian Orthodox," "Ukrainian Orthodox," etc.). It is accurate to refer to any one of the three main divisions of Orthodoxy as Orthodox, Orthodox Catholics, or Orthodox Christians.

SECTS/DIVISIONS

There are three main divisions of Orthodoxy with several subheadings and smaller sects under each group. There are also groups that are a mix of Orthodoxy and Catholicism and many independent Orthodox groups that have formed for various reasons.

- **Oriental Orthodoxy**: Oriental Orthodoxy, the oldest of the identifiable Orthodox bodies, came to its own identity after the Council of Chalcedon (451 AD). Prior to this council, the church overall upheld the belief that Jesus was only one being, both divine and human, in one exclusive nature. At Chalcedon, the theological position changed to teach the nature of Christ had two natures in one person (human and divine). When this change came down the line, the churches who resisted it were seen as conceding to Nestorianism (the belief that Jesus had two natures and two wills). This was in addition to existing issues and divisions relating to the nature of authority, doctrinal changes, and the question of who answered to who in early church history. This form of autocephalous (self-governing), independent Orthodoxy is so ancient, it has traditions that overlap with other Orthodox groups generally alienated from one another, including both Nestorian and Eastern Orthodoxy. Oriental Orthodoxy has a long and sorted history, rife with battles over colonization, church controls, and loss of traditions due to outside invaders within their nations of origin. In modern times, it is most readily associated with certain ethnic groups that trace themselves back generations in observance from their own native countries. Such groups include India (Malankara Orthodox Syrian Church, Malankara Jacobite Syrian Orthodox Church), Syrian (Malankara Orthodox Syrian Church), Armenian (Armenian Apostolic Church), French Coptic (French Coptic Orthodox Church), Alexandrian (Coptic Orthodox Church of Alexandria), Eritrean (Eritrean Orthodox Tewahedo Church), and Ethiopian (Ethiopian Orthodox Tewahedo Church). Oriental Orthodox celebrate Holy Qurbana (in form attributed to the Liturgy of Saint James), or "Eucharist," as they call it, celebrated originally in the liturgical Syrian language. Most trace their roots back to the St. Thomas Christians of the Orient, especially in India. They accept the first three ecumenical councils of the early church.

- **Nestorian Orthodoxy**: Nestorian Orthodoxy is frequently confused with Oriental Orthodoxy, although they are two different churches. Though extremely similar, they have a theological difference: Nestorians believe Jesus has two distinct natures and two wills, rather than one and the same. As an entity, they came to identify independently after the Councils of Ephesus (431 AD) and Chalcedon (451 AD). The Nestorian Church traces its roots within the Syriac traditions of oriental Christianity. They use the East Syrian Rite (Assyrian or Persian Rite), which is also used by churches in communion with Rome that maintain their own unique ethnic liturgies (such as the Syro-Malabar Catholic Church). They also celebrate Holy Qurbana in liturgical form (embracing Eastern Syrian Rite) and seeing development in ethnic regions such as India, Syria, Iran, and Russia. It, too, is believed to be founded by Thomas the Apostle and specializes in services in Syriac and Malayalam, much like that of Oriental Orthodoxy. It also overlaps with Oriental Orthodoxy in membership, embracing groups of St. Thomas Christians of India and other places in the ancient world, and has a great deal of division within its ranks. Despite their schismatic nature, the history of Nestorianism is extremely diverse, including missions to China and the far east as early as the 600s.

- **Eastern Orthodoxy**: The Eastern Orthodox churches began as a part of what's called the Great Schism in 1054. They accept the first seven of the church's ecumenical councils and have also held nine of their own subsequent councils, all of which upheld their own beliefs and positions. Eastern Orthodox observe the Divine Liturgy, which in some ways resembles Oriental Orthodox services and in other ways resembles older versions of the Roman Catholic rite, with a few of their own variances and differences. Eastern Orthodox fast throughout much of the year depending on their specified group, and there is a great deal of emphasis placed on personal disciplines, sacrifice, and a general belief of being the right, or only true, existing church. Eastern Orthodox Churches are associated with cultural identities. Those identities indicate the language of Divine Liturgy services and prayers. The main Eastern Orthodox communion recognizes fifteen different groups, including American, Constantinople, Alexandria, Antioch, Jerusalem, Russia, Serbia, Bulgaria, Romania, Georgia, Greece, Cyprus, Albania, Czech and Slovakia, and Poland.

- **Byzantine Rite**: Also called the Greek Rite or Constantinopolitan Rite. The Byzantine Rite are a cross between the Eastern Orthodox Church and the Roman Catholic Church. They are classified as "ethnic churches," meaning they are identified with the language and culture from which their liturgical worship derives. As opposed to forming in Rome with Latin origin, the worship of the Byzantine Rite stems from what is now modern-day Turkey in the Greek language. Today, their languages reflect the nations where they originated. They follow the rites and structures of Eastern Orthodoxy (including its calendar) rather than Roman rite. They are considered governmentally independent but claim alignment with the pope in Rome. The exact number of these churches has changed throughout history, but at current, includes the Albanian Greek Catholic Church, Belarusian Greek Catholic Church, Bulgarian Greek Catholic Church, Byzantine Catholic Church of Croatia and Serbia, Greek Byzantine Catholic Church, Melkite Greek Catholic Church, Hungarian Greek Catholic Church, Italo-Albanian Catholic Church, Macedonian Greek Catholic Church, Romanian Church United with Rome, Greek-Catholic, Russian Greek Catholic Church, Ruthenian Greek Catholic Church, Slovak Greek Catholic Church, and the Ukranian Greek Catholic Church.

Orthodox Church interior, focusing on the iconostasis

- **Other Orthodox groups**: Various independent Orthodox groups exist for a variety of reasons. These include disagreements over the validity of leadership or succession, political oppression, mixing of beliefs (such as with Protestantism or the New Age Movement), sacramental disputes, and disagreements over rite, form, or practice. These include the Russian Orthodox Church Outside of Russia, Orthodox Church of Greece (Holy Synod in Resistance), Old Calendar Bulgarian Orthodox Church, Serbian True Orthodox Church, Russian Orthodox Autonomous Church, Autonomous Orthodox Metropolia of North and South American and the British Isles, Old Believers, Church of the Genuine Orthodox Christians of Greece, Russian True Orthodox Church, Russian Orthodox Church in America, Abkhazian Orthodox Church, Association of Coatian Orthodox Believers, Belarusian Autocephalous Orthodox Church, Indonesia Orthodox Church, Macedonian Orthodox Church – Ohrid Archbishopric, Montenegrin Orthodox Church, Turkish Orthodox Church, Evangelical Orthodox Church, Orthodox-Catholic Church of America, Orthodox Church in Italy, Lusitanian Orthodox Church, and Communion of Western Orthodox Churches.[3]

Number of Adherents

Ceiling of the Church of the Holy Sepulchre, Jerusalem, Israel

There are approximately 60,000,000 Oriental Orthodox believers worldwide[4], approximately 260,000,000 Eastern Orthodox believers worldwide[5], and approximately 400,000 Nestorian Orthodox worldwide.[6]

Disputes Within Group

The Orthodox Church is not noted by any specific, coherent unifying hierarchy. While communities and church groups adhere to specific doctrines and recognize certain leadership, these agreements are not universal. The major disputes between Orthodox groups relate to theological technicalities and authority. There is also dispute about the issues of the dated nature of church practices and the question of possible reform. Orthodoxy is ruled by ecumenical councils; there has not been one among the Oriental or Nestorian Orthodox in over fifteen hundred years, and not one among the Eastern Orthodox in over three hundred years. Being deeply tied to ethnic and national identity, Orthodox communities continue to lose as traditional cultural identity is often lost among multiculturalism and technology. Orthodox also, with an unrelenting waiver, refuse to examine or consider discussion of modern-day issues (such as women's ordination and same-sex marriage).

Scriptures

Icon of St. Nicholas

The concept of fixed canon has never had the same prominence in Orthodoxy as it does in the western rite. For this reason, there are multiple Biblical canons. The Oriental and Nestorian Orthodox observe a different Biblical Canon than the Eastern Rite Orthodox, and it is not unheard of for canons to vary among Orthodox groups themselves. All accept the Holy Bible, both Old and New Testaments, but the books of acceptance vary, depending on the accepted canon in place at the time of church identification. Universally accepted Orthodox canonical books include: the Pentateuch (Genesis, Exodus, Leviticus, Numbers, and Deuteronomy), Historical books (Joshua, Judges, Ruth, 1 Samuel, 2 Samuel, 1 Kings, 2 Kings, 1 Chronicles, 2 Chronicles, Ezra, Nehemiah, Esther), Wisdom books (Job, Psalms, Proverbs, Ecclesiastes, Song of Songs), Prophetic books (Isaiah, Jeremiah, Lamentations, Ezekiel, Daniel, Hosea, Joel, Amos, Obadiah, Jonah, Micah, Nahum, Habakkuk, Zephaniah, Haggai, Zechariah, Malachi), Deuterocanonical books (Tobit, Judith, 1 and 2 Maccabees, Wisdom of Solomon, Sirach, Baruch, Letter of Jeremiah, Greek additions to Esther, and Greek additions to Daniel, including the Prayer of Azariah, Song of the Three Holy Children, Susanna and the Elders, and Bel and the Dragon), the Gospels (Matthew, Mark, Luke, John), the Acts of the Apostles, the Pauline Epistles (Romans, 1 Corinthians, 2 Corinthians, Galatians, Ephesians, Philippians, Colossians, 1 Thessalonians, 2 Thessalonians, 1 Timothy, 2 Timothy, Titus, Philemon, Hebrews) the General Epistles (James, 1 Peter, 2 Peter, 1 John, 2 John, 3 John, Jude) and Revelation. There are some Coptic groups that do reject the books of 2 Peter, 2-3 John, Jude, and Revelation. The book order may vary, depending on the ethnic Orthodox tradition.

Some Oriental Orthodox include the following Old Testament additions: Enoch, Jubilees, 2 Esdras, 3 Ezra, 4 Ezra, Paralipoemna of Jeremiah, Rest of the Words of Baruch, and 3 books of the Meqabyan (versions of the Maccabees not found elsewhere). Some Oriental Orthodox include the following New Testament additions: Advice of the mother of God to the Apostles, the Books of Criapos, the Epistle of Barnabas, 3 Corinthians, Epistles of Clement, Testament of the Twelve Patriarchs, Sinodos, Books of Covenant, Ethiopic Clement, and Ethiopic Didascalia. Some also contain a writing called Josippon, the historical writing of the Jews by Josephus.

Eastern Orthodox Bibles contain the following Old Testament additions: 3 Esdras (known as 1 Esdras in the Eastern tradition), 4 Esdras (Apocalypsis of Esdras), the Prayer of Manasseh, Odes, and Psalm 151. Some also contain 2 Baruch and Psalms 152-155.

The differences in canon relate to different traditions surrounding accepted works, as well as different ancient Bible manuscripts and translations as the source of their Biblical tradition. Oriental Orthodox rely on the Peshitta Bible, which is the Syriac version translated from the Aramaic. It is believed to be the original foundation for the New Testament prior to Greek. As a result, idiomatic usage and concepts are different in its translation than seen in many western versions. Eastern Orthodox rely on the Old Testament Septuagint, the Bible translation common in the early centuries before Christ translated from the Hebrew into the Greek.

Orthodox Lectionaries vary from western ones in that the traditional lectionary only contains three books: Gospel, Epistles, and Prophets (the Prophets have never been translated into the English language and are used often at Vespers). Readings read during the Divine Liturgy are found in a Gospel Book and an Epistle book. The four Gospels are read annually: The Gospel of John from Easter (Pascha) to Pentecost, the Gospel of Matthew from the day after Pentecost for seventeen weeks, the Gospel of Luke from the Monday after the Elevation of the Holy Cross for thirteen weeks, and the Gospel of Mark read on Saturdays and Sundays during Lent. Old Testament readings are known as "parables" and are read on special feast days and during vespers (night prayers). The common lectionary readings are found in the Standard Orthodox Lectionary, which has some slight variations depending on specific sect. Orthodox Lectionaries do not contain the book of Revelation, and Revelation is not read aloud in public services.[7]

The Orthodox Church believes Scripture is part of Holy Tradition, not separate from it. They believe, therefore, that the use, interpretation, and study of the Bible is subject to the tradition implemented within Orthodox understanding. Orthodoxy sees the understanding of Scripture to be part of the understanding of tradition, and that it is only understood in its context of the work of the church. Orthodox tradition is present in the creeds, Ecumenical Councils, the writings of the church fathers and mothers down through the ages, the different canons of church law, books, icons, doctrine, and beliefs. As a result, the Bible is seen as one part of the deposit and is a part of a whole, rather than a separate identifying standard.

As Orthodoxy believes Scripture is part of tradition, they also accept the works of the Early Church Fathers and other writers throughout history as inspired. These writings are seen as formation of the tradition of the church (even when they may vary from what is doctrinal or understood in later or modern times). These writings were written in Greek, Latin, Syriac, (later ones in languages such as Russian) and were written by individuals, both non-clergy and clergy, between 100 A.D. and 700 A.D. Some of the best known and beloved among the Orthodox are the Desert Fathers. These men (and three women) were early Christian monastics, living as hermits in the Scetes desert starting in the 400s. Their writings focused on deeply mystical traditions as they lived strict asceticism in small communities. Their teachings have been documented in the Sayings of the Desert Fathers (*Apophthegmata Patrum*). Some of the best-known Desert Fathers were Anthony the Great (251-356), Abba Poemen (340-450), Moses the Black (330-405), Syncletica of Alexandria (c. 270-c. 350), and Macarius of Egypt (c. 300-391).

> *There was an old man in Scete who had indeed endurance of body, but not much heedfulness in remembering what was said to him. So he went to the abbot John the Short to consult him about forgetfulness: and after hearing his discourse, returned to his cell and forgot what the abbot John had said. Again he went and questioned him: but as soon as he reached his cell, he forgot what he had heard, and so, after much going to and fro, forgetfulness overmastered him. Sometime after, meeting the abbot he said, "Father, you know that I again forgot what you said to me? But I did not come back, lest I should be a trouble to thee." The abbot John said: "Go, light the lamp." And he lit it. And he said, "Bring other lamps, and light them from this one." And he did so. And the abbot John said to the old man, "Is the lamp injured in any way, that you have lit the others from it?" And he said, "No." "So neither is John injured, if all Scete should come to me, nor am I hindered from the love of God: come therefore whenever you wish, hesitating not at all." And so by the patience of them both, God freed the old man of forgetfulness: for that indeed was the business of them that dwelt in Scete, to give courage to those who were besieged by any passion and who struggled in travail with themselves that they might come to good.*[8]

> *At one time a provincial judge heard of the abbot Moses and set out into Scete to see him: but man heard of his coming and got up to flee into the marsh. And the judge with his following met him, and questioned him, saying, "Tell me old man, where is the cell of the abbot Moses?" And he said, "Why would you seek him out? The man is a fool and a heretic." So the judge coming to the church said to the clergy, "I had heard of the abbot Moses and came to see him: but lo! We met an old man journeying into Egypt, and asked him where might be the cell of the abbot Moses, and he said, 'Why do you seek him? He is a fool and a heretic.'" The clergy, on hearing this, were perturbed and said, "What was this old man like, who spoke thus to you of the holy man?" And they said, "He was an old man wearing a very ancient garment, tall and black." And they said, "It is the abbot himself: and because he did not wish to be seen by you, he told you these things about himself." And mightily edified, the judge went away.*[9]

> *One day when Abba John was going up to Scetis with some other brothers, their guide lost his way for it was night-time. So the brothers said to Abba John, 'What shall we do, abba, in order not to die wandering about, for the brother has lost the way?' The old man said to them, 'If we speak to him, he will be filled with grief and shame. But look here, I will pretend to be ill and say I cannot walk anymore; then we can stay here till the dawn.' This he did. The others said, 'We will not go on either, but we will stay with you.' They sat there until the dawn, and in this way they did not upset*

the brother.[10]

An elder was asked, "What is 'to pray without ceasing?" [1 Thess 5:17], and he replied, "It is the petition sent up to God from the very foundation of the heart requesting what is appropriate. For it is not only when we stand for prayer that we are praying; true prayer is when you can pray all the time within yourself.[11]

BASIC RELIGIOUS PRACTICES

St. Basil's Cathedral, Moscow, Russia

Orthodox Catholicism centers around the church family and the biological family. Worship takes place at a parish church on the first day of the week (Sunday) in the form of the Divine Liturgy (in Oriental Orthodoxy, also called Holy Qurbana, in Byzantine Rite, as Holy Liturgy, and Nestorian tradition, as East Syriac Rite, of the Divine Liturgy of Saints Addai and Mari). It is divided into three parts: the Liturgy of Preparation (entry and prayers of priests, deacons, and workers); the Liturgy of the Catechumens (the part of the liturgy by which individuals preparing for membership in the Orthodox Church are allowed to attend; this dismissal is still observed in the Nestorian Orthodox Church), the Liturgy of the Faithful (includes reception of Holy Communion). The service itself contains several chants, litanies, antiphons, Bible readings from various places, a sermon, consecration, the Eucharist, and dismissal. Orthodox Christians are expected to attend weekly Divine Liturgy, attend regular confession, receive the seven sacraments regularly, observe all holy days and fasts, and to live a strict Orthodox life, as Orthodoxy is seen as being about practice as much as instruction. For the Orthodox, being a part of the church is about a literal separation from everyone and everything that is not Orthodox, seeing their isolation as a sign of holiness.

HOLIDAYS

All Orthodox Churches recognize a yearly liturgical calendar, divided up into seasons. Depending on the form of Orthodoxy, the seasons may vary slightly. Oriental Orthodox, Byzantine Rite, Nestorian Orthodox and Eastern Orthodox have very similar yearly cycles and holidays. Some feasts and yearly divisions are known by different names, and may be a little longer or shorter, depending on the region of the world, the traditions, and the cultural aspects that surround them. The difference between these calendars is the use of the Julian Calendar versus the Gregorian. Orthodox calendars are also more complex because they observe both fixed days of observance (their dates remain consistent from year to year and ones that are movable (their dates change every year). The major annual fasts and Liturgical seasons are divided around the twelve great feasts of the Orthodox Church. These are:

- **Nativity Fast (St. Martin's Lent, Advent):** A 40-day fast period preceding the Nativity of Christ. Orthodox are expected to abstain from meat, fish, all dairy products, olive oil, and alcohol (particularly wine). The Nativity Fast focuses on both the coming of Christ into this world as an infant and the second coming of Christ (the *Parousia*). Liturgical color is red (light blue in some traditions).

- **Nativity of Christ**: Feast of the birth of Christ, also called the nativity of Christ, birth of Christ, birth of Jesus, or Christmas. The Nativity of Christ is celebrated either on December 25 (some of the Eastern Orthodox) or on January 7 (Coptic, Ethiopian, Gregorian, and Russian Orthodox), depending on the calendar each group follows. In most Orthodox groups, Christmas lasts until the feast of the Theophany (Epiphany) on January 7. In churches that acknowledge Christmas on January 7, many elements of nativity feasts are combined into a few days. Liturgical color is white.

- **The Feast of the Theophany (Epiphany)**: Celebrated on January 7 or January 19. Feast of the Baptism of the Lord, when Orthodox believe the Holy Trinity was first revealed to humanity. On the Theophany, holy water is blessed twice, the people are sprinkled with it, and they drink some of it. As the only time of the year when water is blessed, this makes the action sacred for the faithful. Orthodox believe that by blessing water, the nature of the water itself is changed. Liturgical color is white.

- **Presentation of our Lord in the Temple**: Celebrated on February 2 or February 15, depending on tradition. Commemorative feast of Christ's presentation in the temple as an infant, encountering Simeon, who recognized Christ to be the Messiah. Liturgical color is white.

- **Great Lent**: The most important fasting period in Orthodoxy. Done for 40 days in preparation for Pascha (Easter), starting seven weeks prior to Pascha. Great Lent lasts from Clean Monday (also called Pure Monday, Green Monday, Ash Monday, or Monday of Lent) until the Friday of the sixth week of Lent. During Great Lent, Orthodox participants give up different items, including meat, fish, eggs, cheese, milk, and eventually the skipping of meals). Great Lent includes the Triodion, a liturgical book that includes the Sundays prior to Great Lent, Cheesefare Week (comparable to Carnival), Entry into Jerusalem (Palm Sunday), and Holy Week. Great Lent is the final period for catechumens (studying converts to the faith) to prepare before their baptism into Orthodoxy. In the season of Great Lent, we often find the feast of the Annunciation of the Theotokos (March 25). Liturgical colors can include black, purple or wine-red.

- **Pascha (Resurrection Sunday, Easter)**: The highest and greatest feast of the Orthodox year. The date for Pascha changes annually, based on the date of the first Sunday after the first full moon on or after March 21. In Orthodoxy, the date is calculated according to the Julian calendar. Celebrates the resurrection of Jesus Christ. New converts are baptized during Pascha. Liturgical color is white.

- **Pentecostarion**: The period from the Sunday of Pascha through the Sunday of All Saints, which is the Sunday after Pentecost. Uses a specific liturgical book for this period; the Gospel of John and Acts of the Apostles are read in their entirety. During this period are a number of notable events: Bright Week (the week after Easter), Thomas Sunday (the appearance of Jesus to the Apostle Thomas), Sunday of the Myrrhbearers (third Sunday of Pascha devoted to the women who brought spices to the Tomb of Jesus along with Joseph of Arimathea and Nicodemus), Feast of the Ascension (forty days after Pascha), Sunday of the Holy Fathers (Sunday after the Ascension, remembering the leaders of the First Ecumenical Council in 325), and the Saturday of the Dead (All Souls Day, the day before Pentecost). The final feasts of the Pentecostarion are Pentecost, the celebration of the descent of the Holy Spirit on the disciples (accompanies a seven-day Great Feast with the high day being Holy Spirit Day, the Monday after Pentecost) and All Saints Sunday. The Liturgical color for Pentecost, Holy Spirit Monday, and All Saints Sunday is green.

- **Apostle's Fast**: Also called the Fast of the Holy Apostles, the Fast of Peter and Paul, or St. Peter's Fast. The fasting period from the second Monday after Pentecost (the day after All Saints Sunday) until the Feast of Saints Peter and Paul, held on June 29. This fast can be anywhere from approximately eight days to forty-two days, because of the change in Pascha's date every year. The fast allows fish, wine, and oil except on Wednesdays and Fridays. The liturgical color is red.

- **Transfiguration**: Celebrated on August 6 or 19. The recounting of the Transfiguration on the Mount, as found in the New Testament. The liturgical color is white.

- **Dormiton Fast**: August 1 to August 14, in preparation for the Feast of the Dormition of the Theotokos. The first day of the Dormition Fast is a Procession of the Cross, featuring an outdoor procession with a lesser blessing of water. Only wine and oil are allowed on weekends. Orthodox may not eat milk, fish, or dairy products through this fast. The liturgical color may be light blue or gold.

- **The Dormiton of the Theotokos**: Also called the Dormition of the Mother of God, this is a commemorative feast of the "falling asleep" or death of Mary, the mother of Jesus. The liturgical color is light blue.

- **Nativity of the Theotokos**: Held on September 8. Feast of the birth of Mary, mother of Jesus. Liturgical color is light blue.

- **Elevation of the Cross**: Held on September 14. Tradition of the discovery of the original cross on which Christ was crucified. The liturgical color is red.

- **Entrance of the Theotokos into the Temple**: Held on November 21. Based on apocryphal story, it commemorates the date Orthodox believe Mary was brought to the temple at age three, as a Levite. Liturgical color is light blue.

In addition to these specific seasons and observances the Orthodox observe thousands of different days, feasts, and occasions devoted to patron saints of nations, parishes, or personal devotion. Saints are defined as any person who is in heaven, whether or not they are recognized on earth. Estimates state there may be well over 10,000 named saints throughout history. By standard, saints are the apostles, prophets, martyrs, fathers and hierarchs of the church, monastics, and the just. This means the calendar is full of special recognitions to known individuals who have special relevance to different believers. Some of the most relevant feasts are Saint James the Just (October 23), Holy Archangels Michael and Gabriel (November 8), Saint Stephen the Deacon (December 27), Saint Patrick (March 17), Saint Basil the Great (January 1), Saint George (April 23), Nativity of Saint John the Baptist (June 24), Saint Elijah the Prophet (July 20), and the Beheading of John the Baptist (August 29).[12,13]

Along with the various fasts and feasts throughout the year, many Orthodox engage in a partial or total fast on Wednesday and Fridays, excluding fast-free weeks. If one calculates the number of fast days on the Orthodox calendar each year, it totals close to half the year.

Visual Signs and Symbols

Byzantine/Russian crucifix (with second crossbar at feet); Chi-Rho, also called sigla (the letters X and P overlapping representing the first letters of the title, "Christos"); Greek Orthodox Cross (equal on all sides, usually with icons or images of church history on it) "tau" cross (T-shaped cross); Jerusalem cross (5 Greek crosses that overlap, balanced on all sides, with one large cross and four smaller ones); baptismal cross (Greek cross intersected with the letter "X", the symbol of the word "Christos"); Scarlet red egg (symbol of the resurrection), Ichtus (fish symbol), icons (flat, two-dimensional photos of Christ or saints); the Greek letters for Alpha and Omega; IC XC Nika (IC XC=Jesus Christ, Nika=Glory to); Byzantine coat of arms; megaloschema (a garment worn by monks symbolizing the highest rank an Orthodox monk can achieve); vivid colors and liturgical robes; Orthodox bishop's crown, monks and nuns; married priests; leavened bread and wine; sign of the Cross ending on the left shoulder (rather than the right, as in Roman tradition); relics (small pieces of bones or physical remains from deceased individuals in Orthodoxy); censer; patriarchs.

Creeds, Books, and Laws

Orthodox Churches are primarily ruled, first and foremost, by the Ecumenical Councils of the early church. The Nestorian Church acknowledges two ecumenical councils: the First Council of Nicaea (325) and the First Council of Constantinople (381). Oriental Orthodox acknowledge three ecumenical councils: the First Council of Nicaea, the First Council of Constantinople, and the First Council of Ephesus (431). The Eastern Orthodox acknowledge the first seven ecumenical councils, plus one additional council held in the east: the First Council of Nicaea, the First Council of Constantinople, the First Council of Ephesus, the Council of Chalcedon (451), the Second Council of Constantinople (553), the Third Council of Constantinople (680-681), the Quinisext Council (787), and the Second Council of Nicaea (787). The Eastern Orthodox also acknowledge six of their own councils, all held to affirm their own doctrine: the Council of Constantinople (815), the Council of Blachernae (1094), the Council of Constantinople (1285), the Synod of Constantinople (1484), the Synod of Jassy (1642), and the Synod of Jerusalem (1672).

Outside of the councils, Orthodoxy is governed by Canon Law, also known as the tradition of the holy canons. Unlike Roman Catholicism, Orthodoxy does not hold to codified, formal canon law. Many follow a group of canons known as the *Pedalion* (authored by Nicodemus the Haigorite and Agapios Monachos). This work was an extension of the Council in Trullo (which was specifically about disciplinary canons). Based more on tradition, those decrees, doctrines and understandings that have been long held and are now interpreted for today, than written catechism. In particular, the *Pedalion* narrates bias against western Christianity. There are also several different Orthodox catechisms (rather than a standard one as is often found in western churches) written for different audiences, purposes, and in different languages.

Russian Cross

All Orthodox Churches accept the Nicene Creed exclusively, rejecting other creeds accepted by western churches:[14]

> *We believe in one God, the Father Almighty, Maker of heaven and earth, and of all things visible and invisible.*
>
> *And in one Lord Jesus Christ, the Son of God, the only-begotten, begotten of the Father before all ages. Light of Light; true God of true God; begotten, not made; of one essence with the Father, by whom all things were made; who for us men and for our salvation came down from heaven, and was incarnate of the Holy Spirit and the Virgin Mary, and became man.*
>
> *And He was crucified for us under Pontius Pilate, and suffered, and was buried. And the third day He rose again, according to the Scriptures; and ascended into heaven, and sits at the right hand of the Father; and He shall come again with glory to judge the living and the dead; whose Kingdom shall have no end.*
>
> *And [we believe] in the Holy Spirit, the Lord, the Giver of Life, who proceeds from the Father; who with the Father and the Son together is worshipped and glorified; who spoke by the prophets.*
>
> *In one Holy, Catholic, and Apostolic Church. we acknowledge one baptism for the remission of sins. we look for the resurrection of the dead, and the life of the world to come. Amen.*[15]

ECLECTIC BELIEFS

Orthodox Christianity emphasizes isolation as a sign of holiness. In Orthodoxy, being detached from the ways and rites of western Christianity are a source of pride, one that displays in a commitment to stand as the church from ancient times. Part of their theme is mystery, seeing the Orthodox Church and its theology as a mystical experience. This makes Orthodox theory and theology more mystical and mysterious than that of the Latin Rite. This is seen nowhere more than in their emphasis on the Seven Sacraments, sometimes called the Seven Mysteries. Like those found in the west, they have one major distinction: they do not consider these to be the only examples of sacraments or the only number of sacraments in existence. While seven sacraments have been acknowledged as a formal number (in response to the arguments against them present in the Protestant Reformation) as seven, the Orthodox see no difference between a burial service, blessing of water or some other object, good works, or spiritual prayer and the formal, recognized seven sacraments. Orthodox sacraments are, as viewed in the west, the primary means by which the grace of God is conferred upon people's lives.[16]

- **Baptism and chrismation**: Performed consecutively, baptism is performed by a priest as a triple immersion, seen as a sign of the death and resurrection of Jesus Christ. After baptism, the priest anoints the baptized person with Holy Chrism (holy oil), an anointing oil blessed by a bishop. To receive Holy Communion in the Orthodox Church, an individual must be baptized and chrismated within their church. Orthodox children must be given the name of a saint and celebrate their saint's day (naming day) along with one's birthday.

- **The Eucharist**: The Orthodox term for communion, which is distributed and received by the Orthodox faithful at every liturgical service. While the term "transubstantiation" is not a term used in Orthodoxy, it is believed the elements of communion (leavened bread and fermented wine) become the literal body and blood of Christ through the liturgical rite. The term more commonly used in Orthodoxy is *metabole*, meaning "sacramental change." It is believed this happens through the prayer of the church and the calling of the Holy Spirit. All baptized and chrismated members of the Orthodox Church are eligible to receive the Eucharist, although depending on specific group, not all do for different reasons.

- **Penance**: Originally a public act of reconciliation to reinstate excommunicated members, the sacrament of penance became a private act of confession by which each member's participation in church is refreshed and renewed. While the exact nature of penance varies depending on the Orthodox tradition one may follow, penance may occur as a group confession or private confession to a priest.

- **Orders**: Orthodoxy recognizes three major orders: the diaconate (deacons), the priesthood (priests, and the episcopate (bishops). The lectorate and subdiaconate are considered minor orders. All orders must be executed by a bishop. In the case of an episcopate ordination, three bishops must be involved in the act, plus an election by a recognized, canonical synod (council of bishops). The highest-ranking bishops in Orthodoxy are known as patriarchs, assigned to a patriarchate. The sacrament of Orders is open exclusively to men. Deacons and priests may be married if they are married prior to receiving their holy order initiations. Orthodox bishops are always selected from among ordained monks. Candidates may be widowers but may not be married when they receive their rite of ordination. As women are not eligible for ordination, Orthodox nuns are not priests or recipients of orders. There are no specific "religious orders" as exist in the western rite, nor is there difference between the right and rule for monks and nuns in Orthodoxy. Both dwell in monasteries and lead identical spiritual lives, recognizing equality between men and women in spiritual monastic practice. No bishop, priest, or patriarch can override the authority of an abbess, the head of a monastery, within her immediate jurisdiction. They can hear confessions, offer blessings, and oversee the governance of their work. There are four degrees of Orthodox nun: a novice (first three to five years in a monastery, spent discerning one's call), rassaphore (when an abbess agrees a novice is ready to join the monastery, tonsured [shaves one's head], takes the exterior robe and veil, and receives a new name), stavrophore (elevated to the role of "little schema" after many years of discipline, with addition of different articles of clothing and stricter personal ascetic practice), and Great Schema (also called megaloschemos, usually given sometime after twenty-five years as a nun; some traditions only allow such an achievement right before death).[17]

- **Holy Unction**: Also called anointing of the sick. Performed annually on the evening of Holy Wednesday in each church. Members of the congregation are anointed by the priest for the purpose of healing prayer.

- **Marriage**: Celebrated through a right of crowning, symbolizing eternal union and with all serious solemnity. The sacrament is seen as eternal, and in the case of second marriages, the rite is not as elaborately celebrated. Divorce is permitted if the marital rite was not received in such a way that it was properly understood.

Orthodox doctrine is notably complex, with many ancient mystical elements added as part of its tradition. In contrast with the Roman Rite, Orthodoxy sees the redemption of Christ in the resurrection, rather than in his death. The actions of Christ redeemed not just humanity, but also the cosmos, which awaits final liberation in Parousia. Rather than seeing the faithful as awaiting heaven, they see both the wicked and the elect enter God's presence after death, with the elect experiencing God's light, and the wicked darkness and torment. Heaven and hell are seen as states of mind, ones perceived by how one responds to their external state of being. Orthodoxy also rejects the notion of "original sin," seeing instead that as humanity is in the image and likeness of Adam (as his "stock") all, therefore, sin. To overcome sin is to find one's ultimate purpose, as sin is seen as destroying the very nature of our individual call. It is possible to achieve perfect existence, perfection as one is saved from sin and death, if we are united to God in Christ, through self-mortification that draws us away from our marring of sinful identity. The goal of resurrection is to become united with God.

Orthodox services are long and complex, requiring people to stand, sometimes for several hours. In keeping with the traditions of mortification, the Orthodox are subject to long fasts, as was mentioned earlier. While the Orthodox are not known for being overly political in the United States, the Orthodox Church has held considerable influences in Eastern Europe in past years.

RELATIONS WITH NON-ORTHODOX

As a rule, Orthodox Catholics do not participate in ecumenical or interfaith activities. In recent years with Roman Catholic emphasis on unity, certain dialogues have occurred between Vatican officials and Orthodox patriarchs. The dialogues have proven unproductive and have led to further offense and discord.

It is also notable that among the Oriental, Nestorian, and Eastern Orthodox, such groups have mutually excommunicated one another, and do not engage in dialogue or discussion among themselves.

HOLY SITES

The Sepulchre in Jerusalem; Palestine, particularly Jerusalem, Nazareth, Capernaum, and Bethlehem for their connection to the life of Christ; Damascaus, Syria; special sites built on the tombs of the apostles and other Orthodox saints; sacred relic sites; the seats of the patriarchs (Alexandria, Antioch, Constantinople, Jerusalem); monasteries and convents scattered throughout the world; Mount Athos; Cathedral of St. Basil the Great; Etchmiadzin Cathedral; St. Mark's Coptic Orthodox Cathedral; Holy Trinity Cathedral.

NOTABLE FIGURES

Galia Dali (1894-1982), wife of Salvador Dali; Andre Agassi (1970-), former tennis player; Oksana Baiul (1977-), former figure skater; Jim Belushi (1954-), actor; Zack Galifianakis (1969-), actor; Jennifer Aniston (1969-), actress; Yul Brenner (1920-1985), actor; Michael Chiklis (1963-), actor; Olympia Dukakis (1931-2021), actress; Tom Hanks (1956-) , actor; Hank Hanegraaff (1953-), countercult radio talk show host; Nia Vardalos (1962-), actress; John Stamos (1963-), actor; Rita Wilson (1956-), actress; Lauryn Hill (1975-), musician; George Stephanopoulos (1961-), political correspondent; Michael Dukakis (1933-), politician; Tina Fey (1970-), comedienne and actress; George Michael (1963-2016), musician; Telly Savalas (1922-1994), actor.

NOTABLE GROUPS

The Russian Orthodox Church Outside Russia formed in the 1920s as a response to the Russian Civil War. Eventually, many of its members found themselves in exile, leaving Russia to seek haven elsewhere. Due to the political alliances between the Moscow Patriarch and the Bolshevik regime, they rejected the authority of the Patriarch, and recognized themselves as independent and self-governing, with headquarters in New York. The church was known for harboring fugitives and refugees in the United States during the Cold War. In 2007, the Russian Orthodox Church Outside Russia rejoined the Moscow Patriarchy, regaining their status of full communicant membership, while still maintaining their autonomy and self-governance.

FACTS AND FIGURES

Approximately four percent of the world's population is Orthodox, with Orthodoxy accounting for 12% of Christian representation worldwide. This is down about 8% from 1910.[18]

OTHER IMPORTANT DEFINITIONS

- **Aer:** The largest veil-like cloth used to cover the chalice (cup) and diskos (communion-plate) in Orthodoxy.

- **Anaphora:** The section of the Divine Liturgy in which the communion consecration takes place, changing the bread and wine offered into the body and blood of Christ.

- **Antiphon**: A form of musical chant, typically short, sung in Orthodox Churches during the Divine Liturgy. Orthodox services are almost entirely chanted.

- **Apophatic theology**: Also called negative theology, apophatic theology describes God by what is imperfect, or negative, by the things that might not be said about the perfection that is God. It is a theological tradition that works in cooperation with cataphatic theology.

- **Cataphatic theology**: Also called kataphatic theology, cataphatic theology uses specifically positive, or affirmative terminology to describe attributes and belief about God. It is a theological tradition that works in cooperation with apophatic theology.

- **Iconostasis**: A screen or wall of icons and paintings that separates the nave (the central part of a church, where people meet) from the sanctuary (the holiest part of a church, where the communion consecration takes place) in an Orthodox Church. In some instances, an iconostasis may also be a portable icon stand that one can place anywhere in a church.

- **Prosphora**: A small loaf of leavened bread, typically specially prepared, for communion in a Divine Liturgy. Part of it is cut, known as the "lamb," for consecration. The rest is blessed and distributed after the service, for those who are present, even if they are not full communicants.

- **Star and Diskos**: A diskos is a paten, or communion plate, on which the bread rests during consecration in a Divine Liturgy. The star is a metal frame placed over the diskos.

- **Tabernacle**: Also known as an artophorion. A special box found on the altar that is used to contain consecrated communion bread (prosphora that has been blessed for communion) after the liturgy is completed. Remaining communion bread is held in the tabernacle at all times. On Holy Thursday, the priest eats whatever consecrated bread is left and places the reserves into the tabernacle.

- **Theotokos**: Term that literally means "God-bearer." Used to refer to Mary, mother of Jesus Christ. Within Orthodox tradition, Mariology, or study of Mary, is a little different than it is in western theology. Orthodox believe Mary was "God-bearer" because Jesus was one divine person with two natures, both divine and human, intimately united. Orthodox believe Mary was "ever-virgin," meaning she did not go on to engage in a sexual relationship with Joseph, her husband, after she gave birth to Christ. In their tradition, they believe Joseph was a widower with six children, and the references in the Bible to "brothers and sisters" of Christ is a reference to these stepsiblings.

- **Trisagion Hymn**: A hymn used in the Divine Liturgy that hallows God as holy three times. Also called by its first line, "Agios O Theos," which means "Holy God."

BELIEVER'S CHARACTERISTICS

Though levels of adherence and devotion may vary based on cultural norms and personal interest in the faith, overall there is an extreme emphasis on pure theological Orthodoxy to the point of antiquity; emphasis on tradition and lineage, standing on the principle of being "one, holy, catholic and apostolic;" Septuagint and Peshitta use of the Scriptures; Seeing Scripture as part of tradition, rather than its own entity; emphasis on the resurrection, versus the death of Christ; identity and prayers to saints, with particular emphasis on the Theotokos (Mother of God); use of icons; strict adherence to and within the Orthodox religious tradition, and nothing outside; isolation; lack of interest in other religious groups; observance of various feasts and devotions; belief in sacraments as means of grace; superstitious tendencies; regular participation in the Divine Liturgy; embracing the need for priests, deacons, and bishops; emphasis on the mystical traditions of the monastics; extreme fasting practices; unique mystical theological traditions; use of language unique to the culture where the church was formed.

Paganism and Neo-Paganism

The world is holy. Nature is holy. The body is holy. Sexuality is holy. The imagination is holy. Divinity is immanent in nature; it is within you as well as without. Most spiritual paths ultimately lead people to the understanding of their own connection to the divine. While human beings are often cut off from experiencing the deep and ever-present connection between themselves and the universe, that connection can often be regained through ceremony and community. The energy you put out into the world comes back.
(Margot Adler)[1]

Theology

Pagan and neo-pagan worship represent a combination of different theologies: polytheism (the worship of several gods and goddesses); pantheism (all is divine, representing parts of an all-encompassing, spiritual deity); and animism (all beings reflect spiritual essence). It is the pantheism of paganism that reflects in what is commonly known as nature worship.

The specified deities and exercise of pagan theology vary with location and practice, but most, if not all, pagan theologies have a few things in common. The first is that pagan worship is dependent upon the individual practitioner. What a pagan or neo-pagan may believe theologically varies from person to person. Pagans will, however, acknowledge all theological paths, favored deities, and embraced theologies equally, not contradicting any position within the community. The second is that the theology of modern paganism and neo-paganism often takes a universalist approach. Most modern pagans incorporate several different elements within their theological understanding, including elements of European, Native American, and ancient Norse, Roman, Celtic, Egyptian, Germanic, Semitic, Mesopotamian, and Greek pagan strains (as classical paganism is often identified through ethnic identity). The deities of ancient pagan systems are often equivalent or overlap, connected intimately to natural elements or forces. Because the worship of these deities extends from prehistoric times, we are only able to piece together some of what they believed, and some of who they were: Celtic (Brighid, Calleach, Cernunnos, Cerridwen, Dagda, Herne, Lugh, Morrighan, Rhiannon, and Taliesin);[2] Norse (Baldur, Freyja, Heimdall, Frigga, Hel, Loki, Njord, Odin, Thor, and Tyr);[3] Greek (Aphrodite, Ares, Artemis, Athena, Demeter, Eros, Gaia, Hades, Hecate, Hera, Hestia, Nemesis, Pan, Priapus, and Zeus);[4] and Egyptian (Anubis, Bast, Geb, Hathor, Isis, Ma'at, Osiris, Ra, Taweret, and Thoth).[5]

The third thing is a strong emphasis on the presence of the various gods and goddesses as present in the world through nature. The theology of pagans is oft expressed through the changing of natural seasons, cycles, and spells, all employed using the pagan's connection to nature, natural things, and the natural elements found in the world around them.

PHILOSOPHY

The term pagan (meaning "rural, rustic") was originally used to defame polytheistic ideas as inferior to those found in European Christianity (the term "pagan" was not used by pagans until the twentieth century). It was used to identify polytheism as an uneducated, rural endeavor that was not as sophisticated as the formal practice of religion taking hold in Europe, beginning in the fourth century. While the term "pagan" is now used to describe any group that is not mainline, the general understanding of a "pagan" is a non-Christian religion that has its origins in pre-Christian Europe. The essential practice of paganism is, therefore, folk religion based on folk magic. Its operations are based on primitive cultural reflections of nature, spiritual ideas, and practices within a specific location and tradition. As individuals sought to explore the world around them, they developed traditions of worship, magic, and animism that evaluated, harnessed, and channeled the power of natural forces often associated with spiritual powers and abilities.

Pagans see spiritual and natural worlds as divided with a thin veil, one that often causes the two to overlap. The divine, and presence of the divine, is found all in all. Those who practice believe the deity found in all should be worshiped, as the two worlds interconnect with one another. Pagans seek to understand these operations by the practice of magic. Through magic, pagans channel their deities and begin the process of taking control of their circumstances and environmental forces. In addition to magic, pagans embrace the world of divination, astrology, reincarnation, worship rites that reflect the cycles of the moon and the changing of seasons, a modified version of karma, and fertility rites, all of which channel the energy and concepts of fertility into life application (such as productivity and success).

Modern-day paganism is a construct based on information known about ancient pagan rite and ritual and nineteenth century secret societies and magical practice, combined with modern interpretations and values of various issues, such as ecology, sexuality, feminism, economics, politics, diversity, and other social matters.

ADHERENT IDENTITY

Pagan, paganism; witch, witchcraft; Wicca, wiccan; goddess worship; nature worship; polytheism, polytheist; druidism, druid; neo-druidism; priest, priestess; wizardry, wizard; sorcery, sorcerer, sorceress; Hellenes; Secular pagans; naturalistic pagans; humanistic pagans; heathenism; heathenry; paganism as distinguished by ethnic tradition (Celtic paganism, Norse paganism, Scandanavian paganism, Nordic paganism, Northern paganism, Egyptian paganism, Roman paganism, Greek paganism, etc.); Odinism, Wotanism, Wodenism, Odalism, Fyrnsidu, Theodism, Irminism; Forn Sed, Astaru, Vanatru, Rokkatru, stregheria, goddess worship, practitioners of the craft.

NUMBER OF ADHERENTS

It is difficult to ascertain the exact number of pagans in modern times, for a few reasons. The first is that paganism is not widely accepted. Many are hesitant to publicly reveal their religious beliefs. The second reason is pagans do identify themselves in different ways. For example, one may identify as an atheist, or a Unitarian Universalist, or perhaps as a New Ager. This makes generating a specified count difficult. Estimates cite approximately 3,000,000 pagans worldwide.[6]

TRADITIONAL LANGUAGES

Koine Greek, as the common language of Ancient Greece, became associated with paganism in the early centuries of Christianity. Pagans also have employed pieces of ancient European languages such as Latin, Celtic (such as Gelic, Gaulish, and Cornish), Italian, Germanic languages, and in modern times, English.[7]

SECTS/DIVISIONS

There are several neopagan groups in existence, all a mixture of ancient understanding, secret societies, and modern beliefs. Just about all neopagan groups have the same basic spiritual view with different central deities. Most, if not all modern-day pagans embrace a universalist worldview. While they do not claim exclusivity of doctrine, they practice their pagan devotions through specific cultural theological traditions. These include:

- **Modern Witchcraft**: Perhaps the best-known, and most recognizable strains of modern-day paganism are found in revivals of modern-day witchcraft. While there are some variations in the practiced traditions, most have their origins in Wicca. Wicca was formed by Gerald Gardner (1884-1964) in Britain in the 1950s. It is the largest and best-studied form of paganism in modern times and is a mixture of western esoteric tradition and known ideas of ancient paganism. The term "wicca" is based on an Old English word for "witch," used for all genders. Within modern-day witchcraft, there are several theological preferences and ideas, mostly centering on a duotheistic idea of a triple goddess (representative of different aspects in the life cycle, such as Maiden, Mother, and Crone) and the Horned God (anthropomorphic part-goat, part-man depicted with horns on his head). Witches today often practice their magic independently, choosing to gather in groups known as covens for special rites or ceremonies. Most witches refrain from the practice of black magic, believing magic should be used for good purposes and never against anyone's will (a practice known as white magic). Modern witchcraft also heavily embraces fertility and nature worship, acknowledging spiritual cycles, life cycles, reincarnation, and connectedness to all things. Groups that do not connect to Wicca (such as Stregheria) are based on cultural traditions and strains of witchcraft that both predate and have magical influences modern times. These function around spellcasting, superstitions, and familial traditions (the rituals are often passed down through families). Modern witchcraft groups include Wicca, Aquarian Tabernacle Church, The Church of All Worlds, Covenant of Unitarian Universalist Pagans (CUUPs), Alexandrian Wicca, Dianic witchcraft, Eclectic Wicca, Inclusive Wicca, Faery Wicca, Wiccan Church, Covenant of the

Goddess, Rowan Tree Church, Circle Sanctuary, Hedge Witchcraft, Cochrane's Craft, Children of Artemis, and Stregheria.

- **Druidism**: Also known as Druidry or neo-Druidism, it a modern-day strain of nature worship often assumed to relate to ancient Celtic pagan beliefs. The modern revival of Druidism was originally cultural, with spiritual overtones added in the nineteenth century. This movement has no direct connection to the practice of ancient Celtic priests known as druids. It is a modern system, based in fraternal organizations (such as freemasonry). It is a strong nature-based religion, centering on the idea that nature is infused with spirit; thus, nature is dynamic and living. Ancestors and ancestral veneration are essential to this system. Druids have no set dogma, theology, divinity system, or system of beliefs. As a result, there are many different understandings and beliefs present within modern-day Druidism. Practitioners of Druidism gather in groups known as groves and practice nature-friendly ceremonies, usually based upon the changing of the seasons. Many Druids are involved and active in political environmentalism. Neo-Druid groups include Ancient Order of Druids, The Druid Order, and Arn Draiocht Fein.[8]

- **Heathenry**: Heathenry is the term for the modern Germanic pagan revival (also called Germanic Neopaganism). Rather than representing one specific system, Heathenry encompasses Scandinavian (Norse), German, Anglo-Saxon, and folkish systems, including Asatru, Vanatru, Forn Sed, Fyrnsidu, Theodoism, Irminism, Odinism, Wotanism, Wodenism, and Odalism. It embraces the ancient polytheistic deities of Germanic Europe, believing the natural world is infused with the presence of spirits. Practitioners offer food and pour liquid offerings (known as libations) to these different spirits in sacrificial rites, followed by a symbolic toast to the gods (symbel). Groups may also practice *galdr*, which is chanting, singing, and reading runes or runic poetry. Private practitioners may also engage in seior, a form of Shamanism based on drumming traditions found among indigenous people in the Americas (incorporated in the 1990s). Groups are called kindreds or hearths. Individuals gather for rituals and ceremonies, often held outside or in special buildings. There is no central governing religious authority, specified theology, or required practice. Much of the movement has adopted Norse cosmology, believing the world as we know it (Midgard) is one of Nine Worlds, all associated with different levels as found on a cosmological world tree

Candles and tarot cards

(Yggdrasil). Otherwise, the movement presents a mixture of different old pagan deities and mythologies, practiced in part or in combination. Morality and ethics reflect modern ideas of values present in the Iron Age, especially of the heroes of Norse mythology: honor, courage, integrity, hospitality, hard work, and family loyalty. Within the Heathenry movement are subsets interested in restoration and preservation of the Germanic, or Aryan races, and some have incorporated political activism and right-wing beliefs with the pagan views. Groups practicing Heathenry include Asartu Free Assembly, Astatru Alliance, Ring of Troth, Asastru Folk Assembly, Odinist Fellowship (US), Odinic Rite, Odinist Fellowship (UK), International Asatru-Odinic Alliance, Theodism, Islenska Astruarfelagio, Foeningen For Sed, Samfalligheten for Nordsik Sed, Swedish Asatru Assembly, Asatrufellesskapet Bifrost, Eldaring, Odinist Community of Spain, Dark Ashtree Community, Skidbladnir, Heidnische Gemeinschaft, Artgemeinschaft, Deutsche Heidnische Front, New Armanen Orden, Odin Brotherhood, and Wotansvolk.[9]

- **Hellenism**: Also called Hellenismos, Hellenic Polytheism, Hellenic ethnic religion, and Dodekatheism, is the revival of ancient Greek polytheism. Hellinism focuses on the Twelve Olympians, seen as the major deities of the Greek pantheon of gods (Zeus, Hera, Poseidon, Demeter, Athena, Apollo, Artemis, Ares, Hephaestus, Aphrodite, Heremes, and Hestia or Dionysus). The movement focuses on piety (Eusebeia), virtue (Arete), and hospitality (Xenia). The height of worship is found in offerings and ritual libations to the gods, and some (but not all) also engage in animal sacrifice. They also observe their own specific festivals surrounding Greek deities. Like most neopagan movements, the accuracy of the movement is somewhat in question, and there is debate about its practice. Hellenistic groups include Sodalitas Graecia, Thyrsos – Hellenes Ethnikoi, Labrys, Elaion, Hellenion, United Hellenismos Association, Societas Hellenica Antiquariorium, Orphism, and Supreme Council of Ethnikoi Hellenes.[10]

- **Roman Polytheistic Reconstructionism**: Also known as Religio Romana, Roman Way to the gods, and Cultus Deorum Romanorum, it is a modern-day revival of the ancient Roman polytheistic cults. There are a variety of interpretations of just what this means, but overall, it is regarded as a reinstatement of ancient Roman culture, virtue, ideals, and religion. Adherents see themselves not just as a religion, but their own separate nation while respecting the beliefs and traditions of others. Practitioners also adopt the traditional dress of the Roman Empire in their ceremonies. Organizations include Ur Group, Movimento Tradizionale Romano, Curia Romana Patrum, and in modern times, Nova Roma.

- **Egyptian Paganism**: Also called Kemetism or Neterism, Egyptian neopaganism is the revival of the ancient religion of Egypt. There are a variety of practices and beliefs present within the movement, including those that are reconstructed (representing scholarship), syncretism (adopting Egyptian culture and ancient pagan belief within one's own system or culture), and Kemetic Orthodoxy (an embrace of traditional African and African diaspora religions). There are a few principal gods within the movement (Thoth, Maat,

Anubis, Sekhmet, and Netjer) but none is seen as exclusive; all gods are acknowledged. Practitioners set up their own private altars, offer prayer and offerings, but do not have specified guidelines for worship or observance. The most notable organization is Kemetic Orthodoxy.[11]

- **Other neopagan revivals**: There are several ethnic neopagan groups that are specific movements existing exclusively within certain groups. These include Baltic neopaganism (Dievturbia, Romuva, and Vikatlaka), the Slavic Native Faith (Rodnovery, Scythian Assianism, Peterburgian Vedism, Ringing Cedars' Anastasianism, Roerichism, Bazhovism, Ivanovism, Tezaurus' Authentism, Way of Troyan, and Yinglism), Uralic neopaganism (Uralic Communion, Estonian native religion, Finnish native religion, Hungarian native faith, mari native religion, mordvin native religion, Udmurt Vosh, the Maavalla Koda, and the Association of Finnish Native Religion), Canarian neopaganism (Church of the Guanche People), Semetic neopaganism (Canaanism, Beit Asherah, Covenant of the Goddess), and Caucasian neopaganism (Abkhaz native religion, Circassian Habzism).

DISPUTES WITHIN GROUP

Most pagan groups respect and acknowledge other deities while choosing their primary ones for worship. However, there are some disagreements among pagan groups. The primary one is the question of the practice of magic: whether it is ethical to practice black magic. Many groups now opt for the idea that magic should never be practiced against someone else's will and only for good purposes; thus, white magic is the preferred option. Some still incorporate both light and dark elements in the practice of witchcraft, coining the term "grey witchcraft." Pagan groups also dispute the issue of ethnic association with their deities. With the rise of pagan revivals associated with specified ancient ethnic cultures has also come the rise of white supremacy as a pagan ideal. As a result, there is dispute among pagans over who can be a member or what constitutes a member. The issue of individual practice versus group, or collective practice, also remains controversial.

SCRIPTURES

There is no specified set of scriptures within paganism. The very idea of something scriptural, or as sacred writing, would be considered suspicious. Pagans believe all texts are reflections of human interactions with the cosmos, nature, and spiritual forces, and all are equally subject to criticism and critical examination. While a pagan individual may appreciate what a text has to offer or what it contains, they would not embrace the idea of the text as infallible or authoritative.

Pagans draw on specific, cultural, mythological legends we know from historical records, especially to shape their theological and spiritual world views. These mythologies are often detailed in their rituals and rites and are sometimes dramatized.

Pagan authority is found primarily through nature and one's experience with it rather than the written word. Through pagan practice, adherents learn to read nature: through their experiences with it, divination, and by connecting with the various cycles of the moon and seasons throughout the year.

Pentagram

Many pagans, especially those who identify as witches, have a book known as the Book of Shadows. The Book of Shadows is a specific work, typically written by hand, that documents instruction for spiritual belief, rituals, and spells for each practitioner. Traditionally, the book of shadows was given by a teacher or instructor in the practice of magic to each student, and then as each witch practiced and engaged in different forms of magic, they would document different experiences, new spells, and thoughts in the book. More than just being a guidebook, the Book of Shadows also represents a pagan's journey through their beliefs, and experiences and encounters in the process.[12]

BASIC RELIGIOUS PRACTICES

The individual's experience is paramount in paganism. The pagan spiritual experience is the pagan's process to discern and experience natural phenomena and is different for every practitioner. Through this end, the paganism centers around the individual's desire to both discover sacred wisdom through experience with immediate nature and the greater cosmos, and to channel the specific pagan deities for the purpose of favor, rites, and greater insight. Different pagans use different means to obtain these things. Most often, it is done in the form of spellcasting. A spell is a connection with the divine, using natural elements and process, to put a desired thought, action, or work into motion. Through the specific aspects of a spell, practitioners believe they are beginning the process for their request (whatever it may be) to come to pass. Spellcasting works by manipulating various elemental things, speaking certain words, and focusing with specific intent. Pagans may also use incantations, chants, alchemy, various forms of divination (astrology, tarot cards, spiritism, psychics, mediums, palmistry, reading of portents or omens, etc.). It is also common to find neo-pagans overlap with the practice and ideology of other theological groups, such as the New Age Movement, eastern religious practice, or a mixture of humanism and paganism.

Pagans may also practice regular personal rituals using a home altar, at a sacred spot on a property or in the woods or in nature, or somewhere else of special value to the practitioner. A personal altar often contains a chalice (cup for ceremonies), plate or paten (for bread or offerings), candles, statues of personal deities, a special item or charm for spellcasting or that is sacred to the individual, and a small broom or other item for cleanup. Home altars are seen as a "sacred space," one that is for special rites, ceremonially cleansed of negative space. Pagans open their rites with either a purification of participants or a circle casting, one that establishes a sacred circle boundary around the physical location of the rite to keep out unwanted spirits and energies, protecting the magical energy released as part of the work.

Even though paganism is often an individual experience, many pagans prefer to gather, at least periodically, with a group. Pagan groups often gather for feasts and holidays known among some groups as a sabbat. A sabbat is a major pagan holiday, centering around the changing seasons: seedtimes, harvests, solar events, and the changing positions of various pagan deities with the changes in weather conditions. Smaller ceremonies are known as esbats, relating to the cycles of the moon.

Pagan ceremonies are typically regarded as sacred, magical ceremonies. In most instances, non-pagans are not permitted to see or participate in pagan rituals. Spiritual energy is viewed as essential, and onlookers and outsiders can possibly bring the wrong energy to the ceremony's spiritual atmosphere. Many pagan rites are practiced either naked (as clothing is seen as a status symbol, something that separates people) or robed in plain garments that symbolize the transformation present within a rite. Specific pagan group ceremonies do vary depending upon group, but usually consist of a dramatic ritual that surrounds the holiday or sacred day, the work of a priest and priestess, or one or the other; a group communion-like experience of specified elements (such as bread and wine or cakes and ale) and specific blessings, spells, and bestowments upon the entire group. Both nature and fertility worship are central in most pagan groups, focusing on life cycles, reproduction, and binary aspects of humanity as relate to reproductive power and ability.

HOLIDAYS

The average person is more familiar with pagan holidays than they may realize. The pagan calendar, often called the "wheel of the year," is the cyclical division of pagan feasts and celebrations (sabbats) that flow and change with the seasons throughout the year. Cycles are essential to understanding paganism, because pagans see their spiritual understanding through the repeating of different cosmic and spiritual dramas, seeing things move, change, shift, and come back again, all within a year. Sabbat observances embrace specific principles of magic and witchcraft, all that relate to their specific active deities, mythologies, and experiences.

Throughout the year, gods and goddesses die, are reborn, fight for power, take prominence, and lose prominence in a repeating cycle. The feasts are standard, although the names for festivals change depending on the group. In modern times, many holidays have been modified, renamed, or added to celebrate the fullness of the pagan year.

- **Imbolc, Lupercalia, Disablot, Festa candelarum, Liichtmessdag, Groundhog Day, Solmonath, Oimeaig, Candlemas**: Recognizes the beginning of spring, halfway between the winter solstice and spring equinox. It is considered the first of the "fire festivals" of the year, seeing the stirring of new life with crops and harvests. It is observed with divination, spring cleaning, and third-degree initiations. Holiday is often Christianized as Candlemas. Held on the eve of February 2.

- **Ostara, Oester, Liberalia, Anjana, Nowruz, Easter, Spring Equinox**: Fertility holiday that is also a solar festival, focusing on the newness of life, reproduction of animals and humans, and spring festivals. Celebrated with baby animals (such as rabbits), eggs, and spring flowers. Holiday is often Christianized as Easter. Held between March 21 and 23.

- **Floralia, festival of Flora, Whitsuntide, Walpurgis Night, May Crowning, Spring Day, Calendimaggio, cantar Maggio, Mugwort Day, Os Maios, Los Mayos, May Day**: Known better as "May Day," halfway between the Spring Equinox and the summer solstice. It is traditionally seen as the beginning of summer, and is a fire festival. Rituals are performed to protect cattle, crops, and encourage growth. Associated with fertility, the day is best known for the maypole tradition: decorating a large pole with streamers, banners, and long garlands, while singing and dancing in a circular pattern around the pole. Held on the eve before May 1.

- **Litha, Festa Juninia, Ukon juhla, Jaan's Day, Sommersonnenwende, Klidonas, Tiregan, Saint Ivan's Night, St. John's Day, St. Hans Day, Midsummer Solstice**: Held on the summer solstice, observed with festivals and bonfires, singing, and additional maypole dances. It is considered the height of power for certain pagan deities, especially the sun god and oak king. It has been Christianized as the feast of Saint John. Held between June 21 and 23.

- **Lughnasadh, Lammas, Lammos, Calan Awst, Cross Quarter Day**: The beginning of the harvest season, by which the first fruits of the crops are offered and available for harvest. It is a time for feasts, fairs, athletic contests, and ritual play. It is also a time for marriages and matchmaking. Held on the eve before August 1.

- **Mabon, Harvest Home, the Feast of the Ingathering, Mean Fromhair, Alban Elfed, Autumn Equinox**: The fall equinox. The second harvest festival celebrating the fullness of harvest and the need to secure spiritual blessing from the god and goddess for the upcoming winter. Considered the festival of light. Held between September 21 and 23.

- **Samhain, Calan Gaeaf, Kalan Gwav, Hop-tu-Naa, Allantide, Halloween, All Hollow's Eve, All Souls**: A great sabbat in paganism, considered an ancestral holiday of paying respect to those who have gone on before in death. On this particular night, the veil between the living and the dead is considered thin, and the living can roam, haunt, or interject in the world of the living. Traditions such as leaving out bowls of food or sweets to keep the ancestral spirits happy and wearing hideous costumes to scare away deceased spirits have now emerged into Halloween traditions. Also a fire festival. Held on the eve before November 1.

- **Yule, Yuletide, Midwinter, Yalda Night, Modranicht, Brumalia, Christmas, Boxing Day, Saturnalia, Winter Solstice**: Winter Solstice holiday by which the sun god is born on the darkest day of the year, signifying the advancing return of warmth in the mist of winter. Symbolism of evergreens and holly stand as triumph over winter's death and represent a connection with eternity. Yule has been Christianized as Christmas. Held between December 21 and 26.

- Other minor festivals which vary among groups include Vali's Blot (February 14), Feast of the Einerjar (November 11), Ancestors' Blot (November 11), Yggdrasil Day (April 22), Winterfinding (mid-October), and Summerfinding (mid-April).[13]

VISUAL SIGNS AND SYMBOLS

Pentacle (five-pointed star, also called a pentagram); pentagram enclosed in a circle; horned god symbol (half-moon crescent on top of a full moon circle); Hectate's wheel; elven star; sun wheel; besom (rounded broom); triple moon; triskele; dagger; triquetra; hammer; goddess symbols; Zodiac symbols; statues of gods and goddesses; covens; incense; spell-casting; circle; sword; cauldron; chalice; moon in various phases; serpent; raven; ankh; serpent; fire; nature; stones or runes; wand or athame (sword); wheel; ouroboros; spiral; labrys; key; spider's web; Celtic knotwork.

CREEDS, BOOKS, AND LAWS

Paganism represents non-credal religion, simply because it is a religious form that's inspiration comes from before the establishment of organized religion. Pagans find their wisdom, experiences, and insights by learning to listen to nature. Pagan groups are governed by various traditions; some have been written down in modern times, but most operate by diverse sayings that are easy to remember. For example, the Wiccan rede is, "An ye harm none, do what ye will." While it is not a creed, it expresses the way that Wiccans are to handle themselves with magic, with the practice of their faith, and through a certain level of ethics.

Celebrating Beltane

In modern times, some pagans have scripted their own statements of faith and creeds, although these are not seen as binding. Members and practitioners of various pagan groups are not required to recite nor claim their creeds; these are seen as statements or summaries of belief, not as binding theology.

Modern paganism is a literary movement. There are several books considered as quintessential texts and representative voices of modern-day neopagan ideas. Some of these books include: *Drawing Down the Moon: Witches, Druids, Goddess-Worshippers, and other Pagans in America Today* (Margot Adler [1946-2014]), *Buckland's Complete Book of Witchcraft* (Raymond Buckland [1934-2017]), *The Spiral Dance: A Rebirth of the Ancient Religion of the Great Goddess* (Starhawk [1951-]) *Book of Shadows* (Gerald Gardner), *A Witches' Bible* (Janet [1950-] and Stewart Farrar [1916-2000]), *Witchcraft Today* (Gerald Gardner), *Eight Sabbats for Witches* (Janet Farrar), *The Meaning of Witchcraft* (Gerald Gardner), *An ABC of Witchcraft* (Doreen Valiente [1922-1999]), *Witchcraft for Tomorrow* (Doreen Valiente), *Pagans in America Today* (Margot Adler), and *Wicca: A Guide for the Solitary Practitioner* (Scott Cunningham [1956-

1993]).

Magus: "Listen to the words of the Great mother, who of old was also called among men Artemis, Astarte, Dione, Melusine, Aphrodite, Cerridwen, Diana, Arianrhod, Bride, and by many other names."

High Priestess: "At mine Altars the youth of Lacedaemon in Sparta made due sacrifice. Whenever ye have need of anything, once in the month, and better it be when the moon is full, ye shall assemble in some secret place and adore the spirit of Me who am Queen of all Witcheries and magics. There ye shall assemble, ye who are fain to learn all sorcery, yet have not won its deepest secrets. To these will I teach things that are yet unknown. And ye shall be free from slavery, and as a sign that ye be really free, ye shall be naked in your rites, both men and women, and ye shall dance, sing, feast, make music, and love, all in my praise. There is a Secret Door that I have made to establish the way to taste even on earth the elixir of immortality. Say, 'Let ecstasy be mine, and joy on earth even to me, To Me,' For I am a gracious Goddess. I give unimaginable joys on earth, certainty, not faith, while in life! And upon death, peace unutterable, rest, and ecstasy, nor do I demand aught in sacrifice."

Magus: "Hear ye the words of the Star Goddess."

High Priestess: "I love you: I yearn for you: pale or purple, veiled or voluptuous. I who am all pleasure, and purple and drunkenness of the innermost senses, desire you. Put on the wings, arouse the coiled splendor within you. Come unto me, for I am the flame that burns in the heart of every man, and the core of every Star. Let it be your inmost divine self who art lost in the constant rapture of infinite joy. Let the rituals be rightly performed with joy and beauty. Remember that all acts of love and pleasure are my rituals. So let there be beauty and strength, leaping laughter, force and fire by within you. And if thou sayest, 'I have journeyed unto thee, and it availed me not,' rather shalt thou say, 'I called upon thee, and I waited patiently, and Lo, thou wast with me from the beginning,' for they that ever desired me shall ever attain me, even to the end of all desire.

This much of the rites must ever be performed to prepare for any initiation, whether of one degree or of all three.[14]

That perhaps is at the core of Wicca–it is a joyous union with nature. The earth is a manifestation of divine energy. Wicca's temples are flower-splashed meadows, forests, beaches, and deserts. When a Wicca is outdoors, she or he is actually surrounded by sanctity, much as is a Christian when entering a church or cathedral.[15]

ECLECTIC BELIEFS

Pagan beliefs and practices are often subject to scrutiny and criticism. It is incorrect to classify pagans as Satan worshippers. They do not acknowledge the existence of, nor worship Satan. As a general collective, many neopagans are interested in environmentalism, natural medicine, natural cures, and holistic lifestyles.

Most neopagan groups operate by levels of initiation, like the three rites found in freemasonry. The various rites of initiation are performed by third degree pagans, who are identified as leaders or senior members of their community (such as High Priestess or High Priest). These different initiations represent special levels of knowledge or understanding within the community and are usually achieved through study or participatory advancement. In like fashion, pagans also celebrate different rites of passage, especially those that relate to the life cycle: children are dedicated to the gods and goddesses (sometimes called a naming or paganing, or in Wicca, a wiccaning), coming-of-age ceremonies for girls and boys (after a girl's first period or a boy's first wet dream), and a specific rite known as "handfasting" by which a couple is bound together by cord or scarves to unite them in marriage or partnership. Some pagan groups also embrace queer coming-of-age ceremonies, needs for prison or military chaplaincy, and pagan education.

Relations with Non-Pagans

Most pagans shy away from interactions with mainline religious groups, particularly Christianity. Pagan groups have become more visible over the past twenty-five years, but many pagans are still cautious about their interactions and representations with others. Differing pagan groups may work together to promote tolerance and pagan understanding in the mainline arenas. Groups such as Wicca strive for mainline religious status and acceptance. In the United States, some pagans affiliate themselves with the Unitarian Universalist Association.

Holy Sites

Glastonbury Tor, England; Black Hills, South Dakota; Stonehenge, Whiltshire, England; Strega grounds, Italy; Pyramids, Giza, Egypt; Roman baths, Rome, Italy; Saint Brigid's well, Clare, Ireland; Isle of Skye, Scotland; Sanctuary of Delphi, Mount Parnassus, Greece; Newgrance, County Meath, Ireland; other sites deemed as holy or sacred by the individual pagan.

Notable Figures

Gerald Gardner (1884-1964), founder, Gardnerian Wicca; Alice Walker (1944-), author; Timothy Leary (1820-1996), 1960s LSD doctor; Stephan Grundy (1967-2021), author; Cybill Shepherd (1950-), actress; Sully Erna (1968-), musician; Mathilde Ludendorff (1877-1966), psychiatrist; Ian Read, musician; Askr Svarte (1991-), activist; Kari Tauring (1966-), musician; Giacomo Boni (1859-1925), archeologist; Margot Adler (1946-2014), author; Z. Budapest (1940-), writer; Laurie Cabot (1933-), official witch of Salem; Janet (1950-) and Stewart Farrar (1916-2000), authors; Fiona Horne (1966-), author; Silver Ravenwolf (1956-), author; Doreen Valiente (1922-1999), author; John Sexton (1958-), poet; Starhawk (1951-), author and anarchist; Michael York (1939-), scholar.

Magic books and items

NOTABLE GROUPS

Wicca is by far the most visible pagan group today, as there have been many legal cases about the legitimacy of Wicca as a valid religious group over the past twenty years. Although ceremonies and beliefs are still regarded as secret and ceremonies are done in secret, Wiccans have published many books about their craft to promote their beliefs. Wicca seeks legal, and legitimate religious status, to be fully accepted by mainline society. For this reason, Wicca often finds itself at odds with other neopagan groups and especially with Satanism. Satanists see Wiccans as sellouts, as violating the independent spirit and exclusivity of occultism, by trying to gain mainline acceptance.

A pagan rite (specifically witchcraft) can be seen in the music video *Voodoo* by the alternative group, Godsmack (the group's lead singer, Sully Erna, is a practicing Wiccan). The video features Laurie Cabot ("Salem's Witch") who has created her own variation of witchcraft off the Wiccan tradition.

FACTS AND FIGURES

The largest neopagan movement is Wicca, followed by neodruidism.[16]

OTHER IMPORTANT DEFINITIONS[17]

- **Adept**: A person skilled in pagan crafts, such as witchcraft or magic.
- **Alchemy**: High Magic developed to turn base metals into gold, using a philosopher's or seer's stone. Also known as transmutation.
- **Amulet**: A charm or object used to protect the owner from bad or negative energies.
- **Balefire**: A traditional bonfire held on the sabbats.
- **Banish**: To send away or repel by magic.
- **Blessing**: using magic to benefit an object or a being.
- **Call**: To invoke forces.
- **Cleansing**: A rite to remove negative energies from an object, person, or place.
- **The Craft**: A term, borrowed from freemasonry, to describe pagan beliefs and practices.
- **Curse**: A magical spell intended to harm a being or an object.

- **Dagger**: A ritual knife used to sever spiritual bonds, such as cursing or psychic relationships.

- **Earthing**: Connecting with the earth and the earth's energy.

- **Evocation**: To call something out that is within.

- **Folklore**: traditional stories, tales, or cures within a specified location.

- **Folktale**: Stories told among people.

- **Mage**: Anyone who performs magic.

- **Mysticism**: The belief that someone can intimately connect with a deity through their own experience of meditation or intuition.

- **Solitary**: A pagan who practices their religion independently, without a coven.

- **Threefold Law**: The Wiccan concept of karma, that whatever energy is released, it will return to them threefold.

- **Universe**: All of matter and space in existence.

- **Wand**: A ritual tool, similar to an athame, for the purpose of directing energy in ceremonies.

- **Warlock**: A term for an oath breaker, or an individual who reveals the secrets of a coven to outsiders.

BELIEVER'S CHARACTERISTICS

Emphasis on deity worship, nature worship, and pantheism; strong interest in developing wisdom through nature; interest in connection to ancient pagan religion, spells, magic, fertility rites, astrology, divination, and other occult practices; use of pentagram other occult symbols; interest in oneness with nature; insistence upon connection to ancient rites and beliefs; sabbat and esbat observance; recognizing the wheel of the year; folk magic; folk stories; moon festivals; initiations; home altars; practice with a group or independently; interest in ancient cultural revivals.

PENTECOSTAL CHRISTIANITY

The Pentecostal power, when you sum it all up, is just more of God's love. If it does not bring more love, it is simply a counterfeit.
(William J. Seymour)[1]

THEOLOGY

Belief in one true God, traditionally referred to as FATHER GOD, LORD GOD, JEHOVAH, or JESUS CHRIST, with personal attributes. Pentecostals represent a wide range of interpretation on theological doctrine. There are two main categories of Pentecostal theology: Trinitarianism and Oneness. In Trinitarianism, God is seen as eternally existent in three divine persons: Father, Son, and Holy Spirit (without any existing hierarchy). In Pentecostal Christianity, Trinitarianism is often more relational in concept than doctrinal, and there is considerable disagreement over the nature of expression and explanation of this doctrine among adherents. In Oneness theology, God is seen as one literal being manifest in three different manifestations or revelations (Father, Son, and Holy Spirit) throughout salvation history. Oneness Pentecostals believe the fullness of God as Father, Son, and Holy Spirit is manifest in the person of Jesus Christ. Oneness Pentecostalism is also referred to as Modalism.

There are also smaller Pentecostal groups that reject both Trinitarianism and Oneness theology, instead believing that Jesus Christ is always subordinate to the Father (Divine Monarchism), or who believe God the Father, Jesus the Son, and the Holy Spirit are three separate entities (akin to Unitarianism). These understandings are rare, but not nonexistent.

Pentecostals see Jesus Christ as Savior as central to their Christology (theology about Jesus Christ). Jesus Christ is the Savior of the world, reconciling humanity to God through His sacrifice on the cross. The work of Jesus saves individuals, not just in a general sense, but in a personal way, from one's personal faults and failings, giving the opportunity to reconcile in a personal relationship with God throughout one's life.

Pentecostals are also the modern-day guardians of Pneumatology, or study and theology about the nature of the Holy Spirit (sometimes referred to as the Holy Ghost). Whereas some groups see the Holy Spirit's role in the individual believer and the church as having ceased in modern times (cessationalism), Pentecostal Christians believe the work of the Holy Spirit has continues to be active among believers, even today. For this reason, Pentecostal theology has a mystical quality to it, as Pentecostal Christians uphold the belief in speaking in tongues and the operation of other spiritual gifts in modern times. Pentecostal Christians believe the outpouring of the Holy Spirit, first received on the feast of Pentecost, is still present and active among believers. Speaking in tongues, and in many groups, prophecy, and other spiritual gifts present in the New Testament, are seen as the fullness of the Holy Spirit at work in a Pentecostal Christian.

> *But this is that which was spoken by the prophet Joel;*
>
> *And it shall come to pass in the last days, saith God, I will pour out of My Spirit upon all flesh: and your sons and your daughters shall prophesy, and your young men shall see visions, and your old men shall dream dreams:*
>
> *And on My servants and on my handmaidens I will pour out in those days of My Spirit; and they shall prophesy:*
>
> *And I will shew wonders in heaven above, and signs in the earth beneath; blood, and fire, and vapour of smoke:*
>
> *The sun shall be turned into darkness, and the moon into blood, before the great and notable day of the Lord come:*
>
> *And it shall come to pass, that whosoever shall call on the Name of the Lord shall be saved.* (Acts 2:17-21)[2]

The work of the Holy Spirit provides important power for the edification of believers, the complete, or entire sanctification (process by which an individual is made holy) needed to live one's faith, and to share one's faith with others.

PHILOSOPHY

Pentecostal Christianity is technically a branch of Protestantism and a movement that grew from Evangelical Christianity, especially the Holiness Movement. The realities of Pentecostal foundations, however, go back much further in time than just the outgrowth experience of the Azusa Street Revival in the early 1900s. There have been different movements all throughout Christian history that have embodied speaking in tongues as well as spiritual gifts among their various practices. Some of these groups include the Moravians, Anabaptists, Quakers, Restorationists, and Shakers. In modern times, Pentecostalism has enough of its own theology and identity to classify as its own movement. Beginning with a Bethel Bible School intercessory meeting in Topeka, Kansas in 1901, the Pentecostal Movement began its modern role in the promotion of the "Charismatic" spiritual gifts to all Christians. This study then spread to Los Angeles, California, where it became a revival, known as the Azusa Street Revival (Led by William J. Seymour [1870-1922]). The gifts sought and studied are found in 1 Corinthians 12:1-12:

> *Now concerning spiritual gifts, brethren, I would not have you ignorant.*
>
> *Ye know that ye were Gentiles, carried away unto these dumb idols, even as ye were led.*

Wherefore I give you to understand, that no man speaking by the Spirit of God calleth Jesus accursed: and that no man can say that Jesus is the Lord, but by the Holy Ghost.

Now there are diversities of gifts, but the same Spirit.

And there are differences of administrations, but the same Lord.

And there are diversities of operations, but it is the same God which worketh all in all.

But the manifestation of the Spirit is given to every man to profit withal.

For to one is given by the Spirit the word of wisdom; to another the word of knowledge by the same Spirit;

To another faith by the same Spirit; to another the gifts of healing by the same Spirit;

To another the working of miracles; to another prophecy; to another discerning of spirits; to another divers kinds of tongues; to another the interpretation of tongues:

But all these worketh that one and the selfsame Spirit, dividing to every man severally as he will.

For as the body is one, and hath many members, and all the members of that one body, being many, are one body: so also is Christ.[3]

Aimee Semple McPherson (1890-1944) ministering at her church

The most common, and controversial one from this list is the gift of speaking in tongues, sometimes also classified as the "baptism of the Holy Spirit." This spiritual gift is so identified, not because it is in conflict or a substitution for water baptism, but because it is associated with an immersion of the Spirit within an individual; so much so that the Spirit speaks, rather than the individual. There are two types of tongues: glossolalia (when one speaks in an earthly language they have never studied) and xenoglossia (when one speaks in a heavenly or divine language that is not of this earth; sometimes called a "prayer language"). When an individual speaks in tongues before a group, there should always be someone with the ability to supernaturally interpret the message by a gift known as interpreting tongues. Speaking in tongues is considered evidence of the Spirit working within an individual, as well as in some (but not all) Pentecostal groups as a seal, or sign of someone's salvation.

Pentecostal Christians believe the faith, practice, and experience of the first century believers (especially those of the book of Acts) are available to Christians in modern times. Pentecostals believe faith is an experience, one that is best experienced through the working of spiritual gifts and discipline in one's life. A Pentecostal's spiritual life begins with their "born again" or "salvation" experience (when one receives Christ as their personal savior and makes a public confession of their faith). In many Pentecostal groups, a full-immersion water baptism is part of their salvation experience, and a necessary part of being "born again." Once one is saved, they can receive the evidence, or indwelling, of speaking in tongues.

Pentecostals also believe in the work of other spiritual gifts, especially that of prophecy, or having the ability to convey a divine message, direct from God to a group (especially about the future or coming matters). Other well-known (and universally accepted) spiritual gifts include word of wisdom, word of knowledge, discernment of spirits, miracles, healing, service, teaching, and administration. Pentecostal Christians see these different spiritual expressions as ways the Holy Spirit works in the lives, making His presence known, and empowering believers.

Seeing the work of the Holy Spirit as manifesting through different gifts, Pentecostals also believe that God speaks to individuals through the words of Scripture, dreams, signs, and visions; faith healing; different experiences someone might have; hearing a solid message preached or taught; spiritual insight or knowledge of a situation; and through prayer and the laying on of hands.

William Branham (1909-1965) ministering with a flash of light appearing overhead

Traditional Languages

English.

Adherent Identity

Christian, Pentecostal Christian, Pentecostal, Pentecostal Holiness, Oneness Pentecostal, "Jesus-Only" baptizers, "Jesus-Only" Pentecostals, Charismatic, neo-Pentecostal, Word-Faith, Apostolic, Five-fold Apostolic, Ephesians 4:11 Apostolic. Some Pentecostals are also associated with their specific denominations, such as Assemblies of God, Foursquare Church (formerly Church of the Foursquare Gospel), Church of God (Nashville, Tennessee), Church of God of Prophecy, the United Pentecostal Church, Apostolic Church, Apostolic Faith Church, Fire Baptized Holiness Church, or Church of God with Signs Following.

Sects/Divisions

Statistics vary on how many Pentecostal denominations exist. Because Pentecostalism started out as a movement, formal churches and denominational identities came later, rather than at the outset of the movement's establishment. As a result, the divisions that exist within Pentecostalism are more about denominational structure and specified doctrinal points than actual overall differences with the spiritual expression or experience of Pentecostalism. Due to lack of structure (as Pentecostalism is defined not by formal denomination), there are no specific unifying structural points within Pentecostal identity. Divisions and disruptions over doctrinal interpretations, authority, and vision are not uncommon.

The history of Pentecostalism is typically divided up into "waves:" The first "wave" is the Azusa Street Revival and resulting Pentecostal Movement; the second "wave" is the Charismatic Movement, originating in the 1960s; and the third "wave" is called the Neo-charismatic Movement, which began somewhere in the early 1980s. Each aspect of these different movements highlights different points and focal points within Pentecostalism and have also inspired different identities and definitions of what it means to be "Spirit-filled."

- **Pentecostal Holiness**: A mixture of the Pentecostal experience with Evangelical Holiness doctrine, Pentecostal Holiness grafted the gift of speaking in tongues and spiritual experience with current popular spiritual trends in the late 1800s and early 1900s. Some adherents of the Holiness Movement became Spirit-filled, and others who were Spirit-filled sought out Holiness practice, thus forming the combination of the two now known as Pentecostal Holiness. Pentecostal Holiness adherents follow standard rules associated with the "Holiness codes" including total abstinence from alcohol and tobacco, no social dancing, gambling, sex outside of marriage, foul language, and entertainment venues (movies, television, and limited internet usage). Many maintain strict dress codes for both men and women: long skirts for women, no pants, makeup, or cutting of hair, no jewelry for women or men, long pants for men, no short-sleeve shirts, and no shorts. Most (although not all) prohibit same-sex marriage, LGBTQ+ participation, and the ordination of women. Groups do vary in these requirements; for example, though a part of the Pentecostal Holiness family, the Assemblies of God, the Foursquare Church, and the Church of God of Prophecy all have abandoned many of these requirements, while other groups, such as many Full Gospel churches, Oneness Pentecostal groups, and other smaller Pentecostal Holiness groups have maintained them. Doctrinally, Pentecostal Holiness groups believe in a literal interpretation of the Bible and see such application through their Pentecostal faith as a literal rendering of the sanctification, and movement toward perfection, that the Spirit does within them. Groups not previously mentioned as part of the Pentecostal Holiness tradition are the International Pentecostal Holiness Church, the Fire Baptized Holiness Church, Church of God (Nashville, Tennessee), United Holy Church, the Church of God in Christ, and Free Holiness churches.

- **Oneness Pentecostalism**: Also known as "Jesus Only" Pentecostalism, Apostolic Pentecostalism, or the "Jesus Only" Movement, Oneness Pentecostalism is the non-Trinitarian division of Pentecostal Holiness. Oneness adherents believe the fullness of God revealed is found in the person of Jesus Christ, opting that God is one being manifest in three different modes, or aspects. Instead of baptizing in "formula" given in Matthew 28:19 (Father, Son, and Holy Spirit), Oneness Pentecostals baptize according to Acts 2:38 (in the Name of Jesus Christ for the forgiveness of sins). Repentance, water baptism, and speaking in tongues are required for believers, as signs of true conversion. Outside of these few doctrinal differences, difference, Oneness Pentecostalism does not vary from much of Pentecostal Holiness. As a group, the codes of holiness as pertain to social activity, dress, and personal conduct are identical, and may be even more strictly enforced. Some Oneness Pentecostal churches include the United Pentecostal Church

International, Pentecostal Assemblies of the World, Apostolic Overcoming Holy Church of God, Assemblies of the Lord Jesus, Bible Way Church of our Lord Jesus Christ Worldwide, United Church of Jesus Christ (Apostolic), Church of our Lord Jesus Christ of the Apostolic Faith, and Pentecostal Church of the Apostolic Faith.

- **Charismatic**: Also called "second wave Pentecostal" and Neo-Pentecostalism, the Charismatic Movement was the Pentecostal Movement present in mainstream denominational churches beginning in the 1960s. Unlike traditional Pentecostals who formed their own denominations, the Charismatic Movement stressed the expression of spiritual gifts (especially prophecy, speaking in tongues, and healing) and supernatural experiences while adherents remained in their respective denominations. The first notable spread of the Charismatic Movement was in the Episcopal Church (primarily in the United States) then spreading worldwide. The Catholic branch, known as the Catholic Charismatic Renewal, started in Pennsylvania in the late 1960s. Even though the Charismatic Movement stressed remaining in existing denominations, incompatibility was often inevitable, and many non-denominational, independent churches or church associations began to form, often merging with Evangelical ideas instead of mainline Protestant. Charismatic churches also may merge with other ideas, such as the Word of Faith Movement, New Thought, and some metaphysical groups. Some Charismatic Churches include Calvary Chapel, the Association of Vineyard Churches, and the Elim Fellowship.

- **Neo-Charismatic**: also called "third wave charismatic" or hypercharismatic, Neo-Charismatic Christianity started in the 1980s with interest in growing churches from a spiritual perspective. Neo-Charismatic individuals are often considered quite different, especially from the outside looking in, than their more traditional Pentecostal counterparts. The major themes of this movement are spiritual authority, especially within the issue of spiritual warfare (taking spiritual authority over demons, believing in curses and bloodlines that follow many generations, fighting demons that occupy places or inhabit certain areas, practicing group or large exorcisms, preoccupation with supernatural things, and systematic treatment of demonic possession; adherents often appear superstitious), "power evangelism" (belief in the power of words, drawing on teachings found in the Word-Faith movement, and that things such as positive confessions will bring about spiritual signs, powers, and wonders; looking beyond spiritual signs, many neo-Charismatic believers also consider wealth and financial prosperity to be divine signs of accurate faith); and specific renewal for church structure, although just what this means is often not clear (sometimes associated with "five-fold" ministry, of apostles, prophets, evangelists, pastors, and teachers). Unique to neo-Charismatic Pentecostalism is the belief and interest in spiritual gifts (especially healing and prophecy) but speaking in tongues is not seen as a requirement for exercising other spiritual gifts. Much like other forms of the Pentecostal movement, many of its trends and beliefs are found in other Pentecostal groups, displaying its level of influence. Some elements found in neo-Charismatic groups are of considerable debate among more traditional Pentecostals, who disapprove of the lack of spiritual baptism present in the movement. There is also a particular emphasis on materialism, which is bothersome to many who believe in a more faith-based approach to different matters. Those who follow this form of Christianity often speak of using their spiritual abilities "in the marketplace" and a need to conquer different aspects of culture (especially politics) through infiltration and influence. Some Neo-Charismatic churches and associations include the New Apostolic Reformation (the Wagner Movement), Bethel Church, Catch the Fire Toronto (formerly called the Toronto Airport Church), Born Again Movement, and the International House of Prayer.

- **Signs Following Pentecostals**: The smallest of all Pentecostal bodies, this group is best known for snake handling. This practice is called "taking up serpents" and is done during church services. Snake handling involves the deliberate capture or importation of venomous snakes (Frequently rattlesnakes, cottonmouths, and copperheads), which an individual will pick up, dance with, handle, or allow the snake to crawl on their bodies during specific points of worship in Signs Following services. Such is seen as a sign of authority over the devil (the snake is seen as a representation or embodiment of the devil or evil) and that doing so connects one to the authority of their faith in a deeper way. Signs Following Pentecostals are also known to drink strychnine (a poison used in rodent control) mixed with water and handle fire , also believed to stand as a sign of the authority of one's faith. It isn't uncommon for Signs Following Pentecostals to deal with snake bites, venom poisoning, or side effects of strychnine toxicity. In nearly all cases, practitioners of this form of Pentecostalism refuse medical treatment for bites and poisoning. Several have lost digits on their hands or suffered tissue damage because of the practice. Many have died. Signs Following Pentecostals follow traditional Holiness practices and rules while also refusing to vote or celebrate holidays. There is both a Trinitarian and Oneness branch (Oneness Signs Following are often seen below the Appalachian Mountains and identified as the Church of Jesus Christ with Signs Following, and Trinitarian Signs Following are often seen above the Appalachian Mountains, identified as the Church of God with Signs Following). Signs Following Pentecostals may also belong to churches that do not specifically affiliate with a "Signs Following" denomination and may have any number of names that sound much like any other Pentecostal Holiness church in existence. This specific form of Pentecostalism is only seen in the United States and in very limited numbers in Canada. The founding of the group is attributed to George Hensley, but it is unlikely he founded the movement; instead, he popularized it. As snake handling is outlawed in most states, it is hard to know how many Signs Following Pentecostals exist. High estimates number around a hundred congregations, numbering around five thousand adherents.[4]

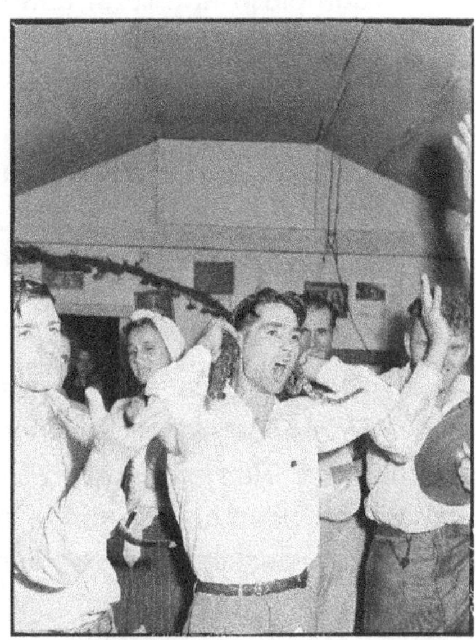

Signs Following Pentecostals engaging in snake handling

- **Word-Faith Movement**: Also called Word-Faith, Word of Faith, or "name it, claim it," the Word-Faith Movement is not a specific branch of any Christian denomination. It's ideas, however, are often seen in Charismatic Churches of the Neo-Charismatic movement. The Word of Faith Movement teaches words are containers of power. What one says (especially in the form of positive confession) is what shall manifest by faith. To this end, Word of Faith adherents claim different aspects of their faith, such as healing, or aspects of everyday life, such as relationships, financial prosperity, jobs, emotional, or physical well-being. Word of Faith also teaches that people are "gods" themselves and Jesus suffered complete and total death, including a spiritual death, to discover the process of being spiritually "born again" Himself. The Word of Faith Movement is highly controversial, albeit popular. While not part of Pentecostalism or Pentecostal doctrine (most traditional Pentecostals regard it as heresy), it is often mixed with newer movements (especially Charismatic and neo-Charismatic) and is commonly seen on television, especially among the televangelist circuit. Some Word-faith proponents include Kenneth Hagin (1917-2003), Kenneth Copeland (1936-), Joyce Meyer (1943-), Joel Osteen (1963-), and Oral Roberts (1918-2009).

- **Convergence**: The Convergence Movement is a grouping of independent Pentecostal, Pentecostal Holiness, and Charismatic groups who have incorporated specific aspects of either Roman Catholic, Orthodox, or Anglican traditions into their religious clerical orders and practice. In some instances, Convergence has gone beyond clerical rites and is incorporated into regular worship practices, such as the Book of Common Prayer. The Convergence Movement began in the 1990s and has gained prominent momentum, particularly in African American Pentecostal associations. Though not a large movement in the scope of church associations, it is large enough to influence many independent church leaders into wearing of collars, robes, pectoral crosses, prelate colors, and establish the high Protestant idea of bishops. There are many small, independent church associations and networks practicing convergence today, as well as more visible churches, such as the Charismatic Episcopal Church and Communion of Christ the Redeemer.

- **Non-denominational**: Non-denominational Pentecostals may fall under any of the main headings of Pentecostalism (Pentecostal Holiness, Oneness Pentecostalism, Charismatic or neo-Charismatic) while holding no connection or ties to any specific denomination or exterior group. Many of the non-denominational Pentecostals overlap in traditions and may contain any mixture of the different perspectives of Pentecostalism and spiritual experience in existence today.

- **Hybrid non-denominational**: A subset of independent non-denominational Pentecostalism that incorporates various cross-identities into one church, church group, network, or association. Such groups incorporate various ideas across the spectrum of Pentecostal holiness, Charismatic, some Neo-Charismatic, and non-denominational into one system of belief. Believers are both Trinitarian and Oneness in a collective body, often seeing the two as valid aspects of one another. Holiness is understood as a unique calling or purpose rather than specified attire or conduct, while still respecting and embracing members who desire to uphold their guidelines. Theology is more conservative, Jesus-centered, and Scriptural than many Neo-Charismatics. Many embrace an Ephesians 4:11 (five-fold) ministry polity. Within this subset are many who embrace inclusion (racial, sexual identity, age, and gender) without a political focus. Such groups include Mt. Pisgah Fellowship in Tennessee, Bethesda Tabernacle in Kentucky, and Sanctuary International Fellowship Tabernacle – SIFT in North Carolina. A hybrid non-denominational seminary is Apostolic Covenant Theological Seminary in Charlotte, North Carolina.

- **The Way International**: Perhaps the most controversial of all Pentecostal groups, The Way International was founded by Victor Paul Wierwille (1916-1985) in 1942, originating as a youth-focused radio program. The organization is a mashup of theological ideas, including a literal interpretation of the bible, evangelical Christianity, Calvinism, literal hermeneutics, and Pentecostalism. One may rightly question which, if any, of these systems The Way is. It is, most often, classified as an extreme Pentecostal sect. They observe no special days for meetings, opting instead for household meetings which consist of teaching, prayer, singing, and speaking in tongues, and listening to The Way's services. The group upholds a Biblical Unitarian outlook, rejecting Trinitarian and Oneness theologies. Pentecost is the major annual festival for the group. Local leaders are not ordained. Behaviors such as alcoholism, homosexuality, and mental illness are classified as evil spirits that require deliverance. Because of the exclusive nature of the group, it has been sometimes classified as a cult.[5]

The Way International logo

NUMBER OF ADHERENTS

There are approximately 584,000,000 Pentecostal Christians believers worldwide. Out of that figure, approximately 279,000,000 classify as Pentecostal, while 300,000,000 classify as Charismatic or neo-Charismatic.[6]

DISPUTES WITHIN GROUP

Pentecostalism is largely about experience rather than formal doctrine. All Pentecostals universally acknowledge the work of the Spirit in the life of the believer and see that central experience as essential to their spiritual lives. The disputes that exist within Pentecostalism are always over doctrinal technicalities: the nature of God, the eternal nature of salvation vs. the ability to lose one's salvation, the interpretation of Scripture, the role of the church in society, and specific levels of social issues, especially those traditionally seen in connection with Holiness. Pentecostal groups also disagree on modern issues such as women's ordination, same-sex marriage, LGBTQ+ issues, and the separation of church and state.

SCRIPTURES

The Holy Bible, both Old and New Testaments: the Pentateuch (Genesis, Exodus, Leviticus, Numbers, and Deuteronomy), Historical books (Joshua, Judges, Ruth, 1 Samuel, 2 Samuel, 1 Kings, 2 Kings, 1 Chronicles, 2 Chronicles, Ezra, Nehemiah, Esther), Wisdom books (Job, Psalms, Proverbs, Ecclesiastes, Song of Songs), Prophetic books (Isaiah, Jeremiah, Lamentations, Ezekiel, Daniel, Hosea, Joel, Amos, Obadiah, Jonah, Micah, Nahum, Habakkuk, Zephaniah, Haggai, Zechariah, Malachi), the Gospels (Matthew, Mark, Luke, John), the Acts of the Apostles, the Pauline Epistles (Romans, 1 Corinthians, 2 Corinthians, Galatians, Ephesians, Philippians, Colossians, 1 Thessalonians, 2 Thessalonians, 1 Timothy, 2 Timothy, Titus, Philemon, Hebrews) the General Epistles (James, 1 Peter, 2 Peter, 1 John, 2 John, 3 John, Jude) and Revelation.

In addition to the general Biblical canon, there are many Pentecostals who take an interest in apocryphal literature, seeking these resources for historical insight and to better understand the contents of Scripture and the perceptions of Scripture throughout history. While interest in these documents is not official Pentecostal protocol and it is certainly not required, just which documents interest someone varies from person to person. Some that are of note include the books of 1 and 2 Enoch, the Book of Jasher, the Assumption of Moses, the documents of the Dead Sea Scroll community, 1 and 2 Maccabees, the Gospel of Thomas, and the Epistle to the Laodiceans.

William J. (1870-1922) and Jennie Evans Seymour (1874-1936)

Pentecostal Christians believe in the authority and inspiration of Scripture; many see the Bible as infallible. Interpretation of Scripture is different in Pentecostalism than it is in other Protestant groups and different from Evangelical Christianity. While Biblical teaching is considered the standard authority for one's faith and practice, the revelation of the Spirit through the application of spiritual gifts is seen as important and relevant, because it is part of Scriptural practice. The work of spiritual gifts provides inspiration in the interpretation of Scripture as well as specific word and revelation to a situation or circumstance a Pentecostal Christian may face. For this reason, when a Pentecostal Christian seeks out a word from God, they may find it in Scripture, preaching, teaching, a word of wisdom or knowledge, a word of prophecy, the laying on of hands, or through an empowering group prayer designed to fortify and encourage a believer.

There are a variety of Bible translations used by Pentecostals today. The standard translation of traditional Holiness Pentecostals remains the King James Version (Authorized Version); it also remains popular throughout many Pentecostal denominations and branches. Other popular translations include The New International Version, the New King James Version, the New Living Translation, The Amplified Bible, and The Message paraphrase. There are also specific study Bibles for Pentecostal Christians, including *The Fire Bible*, *The Spirit-Filled Life Bible*, *The Dake Annotated Bible*, and *The Apostolic Study Bible*.

BASIC RELIGIOUS PRACTICES

Pentecostalism centers around the individual's spiritual experience with sanctification through the reception of the Holy Spirit after conversion. It is through this sanctification experience that a Christian experiences spiritual change to turn toward the things of God, discover their purpose in this world, and most importantly, live in a way that glorifies God. Pentecostal Christians are interested in sharing their faith with others, developing their spiritual lives through Scripture study, church services, devotional reading, and activation of the spiritual gifts in one's life. It isn't uncommon to meet Pentecostal Christians who not only evangelize, but also will give an individual they do not know a word or a prophecy as they exercise their spiritual gifts. Pentecostal Christians are often active in personal devotional time and participation in a local church community. Most Pentecostal services are relatively simple: there is typically a greeting or some kind of announcements, a period of praise and worship whereby the entire congregation sings (often led by a worship team or worship leader), a sermon that might be about half of the service, offering or collection, and an altar call (sometimes called an invitation) which gives those who do not believe the opportunity to begin the process of repentance or those who desire prayer or additional personal laying on of hands to receive before service is dismissed. At different points in the service, people may speak in tongues, dance, run, or shout, lay hands on one another, pray for healing, pray privately for one another, or exercise different spiritual gifts as they feel moved to do so. The exact order of service often changes, depending on the day the message preached, current events, or as the leadership feels the Spirit leads them to do so.

Unique to Pentecostalism is the regular laying on of hands (while some churches do exercise laying on of hands, they do so in a much more limited context), by which a church leader, minister, elder, or other member of the church places their hands on an individual (it can be on their head, shoulders, or sometimes midsection) as part of anointing with oil, prayer, or speaking a spiritual word over them. Sometimes, under the spiritual power, an individual who receives the Spirit may fall peacefully to the floor in an experience known as being "slain in the Spirit."

Pentecostal local church leaders are usually referred to as pastor (or sometimes bishop) and most also have a council of elders or deacons that assist in the governance and leadership of the congregation. With the advance of interest in the Ephesians 4:11 ministry, there are often church leaders, all holding different levels of authority and different forms of work in the church. Apostles (sometimes serving as pastors) are seen as individuals who work with and train leaders as well as establishing new communities; prophets are church leaders who speak on behalf of God to the people; evangelists preach, especially to those who are unsaved (but also sometimes travelling to churches); pastors (serve local congregations); and teachers (those who teach something to the church). In some denominations, there is also the role of "missionary," which is often a term used for a woman who serves as an evangelist, but without the licensing or credentialing of a formal office.

Pentecostal Christians observe two ordinances: water baptism (in full immersion) and communion (bread or crackers and grape juice). Water baptism is often a central part of the

Pentecostal experience, seen as an essential step in one's spiritual experience. Communion is seen as symbolic, typically open to anyone who desires to partake, reminding attendees of the atonement (redemption) of Christ on the cross for humanity's sin.

The required personal conduct of a Pentecostal Christian varies, depending on specific branch. Pentecostal Holiness, in upholding the traditional Holiness codes or modified versions thereof. Charismatic and neo-Charismatic Christians often are far more relaxed, abandoning many of the older codes and adopting more lax views on matters of sexual relationships, women's roles, same-sex relationships, LGBTQ+ issues, entertainment, alcohol and tobacco usage, and social codes. In rare instances, some groups do not even require regular church attendance or opt for home church or group participation.

Holidays

Most Pentecostals celebrate Christmas and Easter. In traditional Pentecostal circles, the feast of Pentecost (fifty days after Easter Sunday) was considered the highest holiday of the year. It was (and sometimes remains) acknowledged with a week-long revival, holding meetings every night of the week, with all members wearing white attire. Although this practice is not as common as it once was, Pentecost is still seen as a major day in most of Pentecostalism.

With a rise in interest among the Hebrew Roots Movement, there are some Pentecostal groups that observe some Jewish holidays, especially Passover. When such is done, it's offered as a teaching tool to help foster Biblical understanding. Some Pentecostal groups take an interest in patriotic holidays, although this is not common. Still, there are some Pentecostal groups that regard all standard holidays (such as Christmas and Easter) as pagan, and refrain from all holiday observance.

Visual Signs and Symbols

Cross or resurrection cross (a cross with a draped purple or white cloth over the crossbar, representing Christ resurrected); the symbol of a white dove or fire flame (represents the presence of the Holy Spirit); pictures of Christ or Biblical scenes; Bible; Bible verses; "born again" altar call experience; full-immersion water baptism done only on those old enough to make a profession of faith; laying on of hands; prayer; anointing oil; Ichthus (image of a fish); being "slain in the Spirit; the "Christian flag" (a white field with a smaller royal blue box in the upper left corner, that contains a red cross); globe; water.

Creeds, Books, and Laws

Pentecostal Christianity has its foundations on spiritual experience, rather than in rules. Pentecost is seen as an experience rather than a specified holiday on a yearly calendar or a denomination. As a rule, Pentecostals do uphold the five "solas" of Protestant Christianity, even though such is seldom, if ever, mentioned. Creeds are seldom used, although some Convergence groups will use the Apostle's Creed as a statement of faith. The Scriptures are employed and taught on a practical level of faith. It is rare to find a Pentecostal church that relies on a specific catechism or formalized doctrinal statement. In place of such, most Pentecostal churches have a "statement of faith." These documents vary in length and are all reasonably similar in their contents, even though the churches may vary some in their technicalities of doctrine. Many Pentecostal churches use either the statement of faith of their denominations or somehow expand upon or modify the National Association of Evangelicals Statement of Faith, which upholds Evangelical belief about the Bible, Trinitarianism, Jesus Christ, regeneration, the Holy Spirit, resurrection, and spiritual unity of the church:

1. *We believe the Bible to be the inspired, the only infallible, authoritative Word of God.*
2. *We believe that there is one God, eternally existent in three persons: Father, Son and Holy Spirit.*
3. *We believe in the deity of our Lord Jesus Christ, in His virgin birth, in His sinless life, in His miracles, in His vicarious and atoning death through His shed blood, in His bodily resurrection, in His ascension to the right hand of the Father, and in His personal return in power and glory.*
4. *We believe that for the salvation of lost and sinful people, regeneration by the Holy Spirit is absolutely essential.*
5. *We believe in the present ministry of the Holy Spirit by whose indwelling the Christian is enabled to live a godly life.*
6. *We believe in the resurrection of both the saved and the lost; they that are saved unto the resurrection of life and they that are lost unto the resurrection of damnation.*
7. *We believe in the spiritual unity of believers in our Lord Jesus Christ.*[7]

ECLECTIC BELIEFS

With the standing Pentecostal belief in the power of Spiritual gifts, Pentecostals believe God still speaks to and through His followers today. This means Pentecostal Christians believe in a continuing revelation, one that didn't stop with the end of the first century or the conclusion of the Biblical canon. This creates a unity among Pentecostal communities, as they learn to seek out, listen, and move as guided by the work of the Spirit in their lives. Pentecostals are powerfully moved by prayer, which they see as an essential communication in their spiritual walk with God. In recognizing the activity of the demonic as well as the divine, they are also interested in overcoming the power of the enemy through prayer, casting out of demons, and fasting.

This belief in the Spirit's foundational activity provides a strong emphasis on the need to share revelation with the entire church body. Like many movements originating within its time, the Pentecostal Movement is in some ways text-based, relying on printed words to convey its ideas and thoughts to the world. From the very beginning, Pentecostalism has been noted for its writers, standing as a modern mystical perspective for Christianity today. First circulated among newsletters, typed sermons, testimonies, accounts, tracts, and booklets, much of the literature was consolidated and put in book form later in time.

Bethlehem was God with us, Calvary was God for us, and Pentecost is God in us.[8]

Pentecost came with the sound of a mighty rushing wind, a violent blast from heaven! Heaven has not exhausted its blasts, but our danger is we are getting frightened of them.[9]

We do not need to wait for the Holy Spirit to come: he came on the day of Pentecost. He has never left the church.[10]

From the day of Pentecost until the present time, it has been necessary to be of one accord in prayer before the Spirit of God will work with mighty converting power.[11]

Beyond the specifics of the indwelling of the Spirit within a believer, Pentecostals vary greatly, depending specified sect. There are theological disagreements over the exact nature of God (Trinitarian vs. Oneness vs. other ideas), there are disagreements over how believers are called to live in this world, over the level of social interaction one may have with those who are not part of an immediate group, attire, personal styling, personal conduct, and the exact specifics on how one lives their Christian life.

As a result, Pentecostalism tends to overlap with other existing Christian systems, particularly Evangelicalism. Some Pentecostals have overlapped with Evangelical concepts about science and faith, opting for Creationism accounts on the origins of the world, while others reconcile their understanding of faith and scientific knowledge. All Pentecostals believe in the power of faith healing, believing God has the power to heal them, regardless of the issue they face. Most Pentecostals believe they have the call to stand against what they see in culture and believe they can influence the world with their unique insights. The way they may feel called to do this may vary; some feel it is better to retreat and maintain specific Holiness principles, while other think it best to dominate culture and overtake different powers. Some Pentecostals are exceedingly politically conservative; some are very liberal; and others are somewhere in the middle. In modern times and in more modern variations of Pentecostalism, there are a wide variety of perspectives on different issues, and they do vary from group to group and individual to individual. There is Pentecostal influence in entertainment, however, especially in the field of secular music. Many secular entertainers have roots, active involvement, or influence with Pentecostal Christianity. There are Pentecostals interested in media influence, especially through television broadcasting, such as the Trinity Broadcasting Network (TBN) (which has also produced its own films) or the Word Network. Many Christians also follow the "Christian pop culture" genre, pioneered and run by Evangelicals.

A prayer meeting in Chicago, Illinois

Echoing Evangelical tradition, Pentecostals are also interested in proclaiming their beliefs through the media, especially paid programming that features preaching or teaching, sometimes music or choirs, or long promotional "revivals" that are televised as points of contact or, sometimes, fundraisers. Some televangelists market to audiences with "trinkets," such as cloths or water, seen as "points of contact" for prayer or faith (although these actions are often met with criticism from the larger Pentecostal community). Pentecostals also believe in the power of in-person services, and often host revivals or conferences, whether for a few days or several weeks, in the Evangelical and Holiness style of their forerunners.

Pentecostal history has an interesting relationship with family and family values. While many Pentecostal Christians identify with many traditional ideas of marriage and family (man as the head of the household, woman called to submit to the man, corporal punishment, rejection of same-sex marriage, etc.), this is not a standard across the board. Pentecostalism, long-known for its belief in the outpouring of the Spirit on all people, has brought many different groups together through that same work. This has meant there are many within Pentecostalism who were or are now single people, single parents, and in some communities, LGBTQ+ individuals. Pentecostalism, especially throughout its history, is known for giving women the right to preach, prophecy, and work as ministers. Not all Pentecostal groups allow or recognize women in the role of clergy, but all do believe and allow women the right to prophesy, pray, and speak in church settings. Even though Pentecostalism has a divided history with divorce, it was also among the first groups to give position to divorced clergy. While positions on divorce and remarriage vary, many Pentecostal churches do allow divorced individuals to remarry and to remain in ministry.

Much like other groups, there are also smaller groups of Pentecostal Christians who follow the trends of Hebrew Roots organizations, health trends (vegetarianism, clean eating, and veganism), exercise, ancient or New Age practices, and modern ideas. While these are not the majority, it does prove there are many different ideas present in Pentecostalism today.

Relations with Non-Pentecostals

Traditionally speaking, Pentecostals have often avoided interactions with different denominations. The reason for this is two-fold. Often seen as common or uneducated (although this is certainly a stereotype), Pentecostals are often excluded from interaction with other denominations who may look down on them. The second aspect is that Pentecostalism is often seen as so different from other things, Pentecostals see themselves called to remain separate from the world. Most Pentecostal groups shy away from involvement with more liberal denominations, but with changes in modern times, may work on a social project with other churches or may interact with more theologically conservative organizations. It is not uncommon, however, to see Pentecostals work with those of the same belief system, even from other churches, for special events, guest speakers, revivals, or community events or projects. Pentecostal Holiness groups reject association with any group that does not espouse their own belief systems. Many Charismatic Christians have an expressed interest in the conversion of Jews and Muslims.

Holy Sites

Pentecostal Christians see the church as made up of true believers from all over the world (all of which have a personal relationship with Jesus Christ). The work of the Spirit can happen anywhere a believer may be. Church is not confined to a building or a specific location. As a result, Pentecostals have no specific holy sites. Many find Israel and Palestine as spiritually significant, as they connect to Christ's life.

NOTABLE FIGURES

Aimee Semple McPherson (1890-1944), founder of the Foursquare Church; Kathryn Kuhlman (1907-1976), evangelist; Denzel Washington (1954-), actor; Marvin Gaye (1939-1984), musician; Michelle Williams (1979-), musician; Jerry Lee Lewis (1935-2022), musician; Scott Stapp (1973-), musician; CeCe Winans (1964-), musician; Al Green (1946-), musician; Duane Lee Chapman (1953-), bounty hunter and reality television star; Ken Beck (1935-2006), football player; Billy Ray Cyrus (1961-), musician; Justin Bieber (1994-), musician; Angela Bassett (1958-), actress; Smith Wigglesworth (1859-1947), preacher; Charles Parham (1873-1929), leader of the modern group to receive the gift of tongues; A.A. Allen (1911-1970), preacher; William Branham (1909-1965), preacher.

NOTABLE GROUPS

Yoido Full Gospel Church is the largest Pentecostal church in the world, with approximately 800,000 members at its peak (it presently has about 480,000 members). It is in Seoul, Korea and founded by David Yonggi Cho (1936-2021) in 1958. Today, the church is led by Young Hoon Lee (1954-). The church is affiliated with the Assemblies of God. In its history, it accomplished many groundbreaking feats, including allowing women to serve as daily church Bible study and worship leaders in home groups (known as cells). This means of small group church devotional worship and study is now known throughout the world. Struggling with the difficulty of maintaining such a large-standing church, Yoido Full Gospel Church has dealt with the issue of satellite churches, losing members, accusations of embezzlement, and the establishment of many different educational and assistant epicenters from their main work.[12]

FACTS AND FIGURES

Pentecostal churches compose 9% of the world's population and approximately 27% of all Christians. Estimates range there are approximately 740 different Pentecostal denominations; approximately 240 of these are a part of Pentecostal Holiness. There are also many adherents who are not organized into a formalized denomination. Many sources cite Pentecostalism as one of the largest and fastest-growing faith systems in existence.[13]

OTHER IMPORTANT DEFINITIONS

- **Amen**: Biblical Hebrew term that means "so be it." Term is used at the end of prayers in all Christian denominations, and is also used to indicate agreement with a statement, prayer, or idea in Pentecostal Christianity. Many congregational members will "amen" a statement they particularly agree with in a speaker or preacher's message.

- **Anointing**: Defined as one of two things, that overlap. The first is a process by which an individual is either smeared or poured with blessed oil to demonstrate the flow, or work, of the Holy Spirit on one's life. This can be for a specific purpose, such as healing or an ordination, or for something general, such as prayer. The second is the literal manifestation of the Holy Spirit on one's life for the ultimate life purpose one has, such as to fulfill a calling or mandate. One may be physically anointed as a representation of the spiritual anointing.

- **Arminianism**: A theological position held by a Dutch Protestant individual named Arminius that was in contrast to the predestination of Calvinism. Arminianism teaches that salvation is for all, and as one chooses their salvation, one can also reject the grace of God and therefore, no longer be saved or refuse to be saved.

- **Baptismal regeneration**: A doctrine taught in some Pentecostal churches that teaches baptism is a requirement to receive new life in Christ. In these groups, baptism is seen as the way sin is removed from one's life and one is able to become born again.

- **Believer**: Term for a Pentecostal Christian who has accepted Christ as their Savior, received the proper ordinances displaying conversion, and has been filled with the Holy Spirit with evidence of spiritual gifts.

- **Calling**: The concept that one is "called" by God into a specific work or service, and that what one seeks to do is in alignment with that call. One may have a calling to ministry, to do something specific in this life, or may be called to marriage and family or to be single. One may also be called to take on specific projects or situations, ideas, concepts, or duties as part of their larger life's call. A calling is seen as a life mandate, or a specific assignment one has.

- **Discernment**: A spiritual gift that gives one the ability to discern between spirits; specifically, whether a spirit is from God, or not.

- **End times**: Also called the "Last days," a term used to describe the period of time before Jesus Christ returns in the Second Coming. The "end times" means different things to different Pentecostals, but is most often used to refer to the difficulties in current society that are seen as signs that Christ's coming is imminent.

- **Holy laughter**: A neo-Charismatic practice by which individuals begin laughing uncontrollably, in what is seen as an expression of divine joy.

- **Holy roller**: A slang term for a Pentecostal believer. So-called because during ecstatic fits of worship, Pentecostal believers have been known to roll on the floor while in a Spirit-filled state.

- **Minister**: A broad term in Pentecostalism for any ordained, elected, or licensed individual who is able to preach, perform the ordinances or sacraments, perform weddings and funerals, and serve the Pentecostal body as a leader of the people.

- **Move of God**: Another term for a revival, movement, wave of spiritual activity, or spiritual inspiration within a group or individual, always accompanied by the manifestation of the Spirit through different spiritual gifts.

- **Outpouring**: Used to describe a large-scale experience by which the Spirit descends on many people, manifesting in the form of spiritual gifts.

- **Pastor**: The term for a local Evangelical church leader. In some traditions, Pastors are called elders or bishops.

- **Pleading the blood**: A traditional Pentecostal term used to appeal for God's protection, as believers would be symbolically covered by the blood of Christ in the process. The imagery reflects back to the original Passover experience in the Old Testament, by which God's people painted the blood of the lamb over a doorpost, and calamity passed over t heir houses.

- **Pulpit**: The stand on which a minister or preacher will speak from in a Pentecostal church (although it is not uncommon for Pentecostal preachers to move around, or display animation, while preaching). The phrase is also used metaphorically to refer to the honor, or right, to preach in a church.

- **Renewalist**: A rare term used to describe a Pentecostal believer.

- **Revival**: A term for "renewal" indicating mass Christian conversion, renewal of one's faith, or return to the church when one has been distant, or uninvolved, with church for an extended period of time. Revivals are often identified with "revival services," those that may take the form of a tent meeting, campmeeting service, extended or special church service, or other special event with the goal to convert and return individuals to the Pentecostal faith. Most of these revivals will display the gifts of the Spirit to interest newcomers or onlookers to the faith.

- **Sanctuary**: A Pentecostal term for a church or the room where church services take place in a church building.

- **Spirit-filled**: The state of being to indicate a believer is completely full, and saturated, by the Spirit of God, the Holy Spirit. When one is "Spirit-filled," they will exercise the gifts of the Spirit, especially those of speaking in tongues, interpretation of tongues, prophecy, healing, or word of wisdom or word of knowledge.

- **Tabernacle**: Used in the context of Pentecostalism to refer to a church group or church building. Named after the tabernacle of the Old Testament that was used as both a meeting place for Old Testament believers and where the sacrifices of old were performed; thus, seen as a "housing" unit for spiritual activities.

- **Testimony**: The public verbal presentation of one's conversion to spiritual things, often done in a church service or event.

BELIEVER'S CHARACTERISTICS

Emphasis on spiritual experiences, especially those with salvation and the gifts of the Holy Spirit; belief in the power of Jesus Christ and Jesus' Name; participation in the local church; embodiment and use of the five-fold ministry; practical Scriptural teaching; belief in prosperity in every aspect of one's life; faith healing; group prayer; speaking in tongues; variety of ideas on social issues; frequent discussion of hearing from God, seeking God, and believing for specific revelation from God on different issues; prayer and fasting; utilization of Evangelical "pop culture" and different Evangelical ideas; Bible study; Bible reading; revivals; wide variety of ideas from roles as pertain to men, women, and family; belief in the universal, invisible church; differing relationships with other churches; belief in sanctification; pursuit of one's calling.

PROTESTANT CHRISTIANITY

I cannot choose but adhere to the word of God, which has possession of my conscience; nor can I possibly, nor will I even make any recantation, since it is neither safe nor honest to act contrary to conscience! Here I stand; I cannot do otherwise, so help me God! Amen.
(Martin Luther)[1]

THEOLOGY

Belief in one true God, traditionally referred to as LORD GOD, JEHOVAH, FATHER, or in some modern traditions, YAHWEH, with personal attributes. Although theologies do vary slightly, most Protestant groups believe God is eternally existent as a Trinity in three divine persons: Father, Son, and Holy Spirit. There are some groups (the best known being the Unitarians, or smaller groups, such as the Christadelphians) that reject the Trinity doctrine. Such believe that God is one literal being, and that Jesus was inspired by God as a moral teacher and savior, but He was not divine or God incarnate in His being. They likely believe the Holy Spirit to be a force, power, or presence, but not a being.

Protestant Christianity is known for its "protest" of the Roman Catholic Church, historically separating itself from the western visible, controlling church body, and instead adopting the idea of a worldwide invisible church made up of all believers. As the "protesters" of Catholicism, Protestantism transformed Christian theology not just for Europe, but for the entire world.

PHILOSOPHY

There are five main principles present that expand the entire classification of Protestantism, known as the "five solae." These are phrases that worked as slogans during the Protestant Reformation, establishing their foundational differences between Roman Catholicism and themselves:

- ***Sola Scriptura***: Latin term meaning "Scripture alone." The belief that Scripture alone stands as the highest authority for church doctrine and teaching, and it is not equal to any sort of human tradition. Some Protestant groups reject older traditions all together (such as liturgy) and some continue to embrace them, but without focusing or believing them to be equal to Scripture. Some Protestants (especially those who are from Anglican traditions or their offshoots, such as Methodism) see Scripture as a primary form, believing tradition to reveal and educate on matters of Scripture, and the value in experience and reason in Scriptural understanding.

All scripture is given by inspiration of God, and is profitable for doctrine, for reproof, for correction, for instruction in righteousness. (2 Timothy 3:16)

Martin Luther (1483-1546)

- ***Sola Fide***: Latin term meaning "Faith alone." The belief that Christians receive their justification (forgiveness from God for sin) only from their faith in Christ. This contrasts with a belief that one can be saved by their good works, or by their good works and their faith in combination. This does not mean that one's faith is only about faith, but that the work of salvation is through the work of Christ, and not due to anything that anyone can do on their own.

  Therefore being justified by faith, we have peace with God through our Lord Jesus Christ: By whom also we have access by faith into this grace wherein we stand, and rejoice in hope of the glory of God. (Romans 5:1-2)

- ***Sola Gratia***: Latin term meaning "Grace alone." Along the same lines as "sola fide," sola gratia echoes the Protestant idea that Christ's work of salvation is a free gift from God, one that comes to a believer through God's grace rather than personal good works or specific actions to merit salvation.

  For by grace are ye saved through faith; and that not of yourselves: it is the gift of God: Not of works, lest any man should boast. (Ephesians 2:8-9)

- ***Solus Christus***: Latin term meaning "Christ alone." Used to indicate the belief that Christ is the true head of the church, in contrast with Roman Catholic belief about the supremacy of the pope. When a Protestant speaks of "Christ alone," they mean Jesus Christ is the only mediator between God and man. No early individual (including the pope or a priest) can serve in that spiritual role. In contradiction to Catholic views of hierarchy, Protestants believe in the "priesthood of all believers," that Christian believers can approach God without the intermediary offices of a priest, bishop, or pope.

  And hath put all things under his feet, and gave him to be the head over all things to the church, Which is his body, the fulness of him that filleth all in all. (Ephesians 1:22-23)

- ***Soli Deo Gloria***: Latin term meaning "glory to God alone." A phrase designed to describe Protestant views that, once again, emphasize the nature of Christ in salvation and no other human being. This contrasts the Roman Catholic belief about the intercession and favor of praying to saints, which Protestants see as a form of idolatry.

  I am the LORD: that is my name: and my glory will I not give to another, neither my praise to graven images. (Isaiah 42:8)

How these five different "only" statements relate to the specific beliefs a Protestant church may have do vary. There is no one specific view or interpretation of these different beliefs. Within Protestantism, there are hundreds of groups – some of which classify as "Protestant" based on these five headings or variations therein, but do not consider themselves such.

TRADITIONAL LANGUAGES

Protestantism is unique as it does not have a specific language adherents must use in worship or song. In Protestant history, one of the most powerful things about its movement was the institution of the vernacular (language of the people) in worship services, so all could participate and understand the basics of their faith. It was also the Protestant Reformation, coinciding with the invention of the printing press, that made Bible translations available in the language of all people, rather than upholding a Latin translation. Even though these languages have never been a worship requirement for Protestant churches, the original vernacular of the Protestant Reformation include German, French, Italian, Polish, and English. Early reformers also spoke Latin, as they came from Catholic custom.

ADHERENT IDENTITY

Protestant Christians, in addition to be identifying as "Protestant," "Christian," or "Protestant Christian" often associate with their specific denomination, such as (but not exclusive to) Methodist, Presbyterian, Reformed, Lutheran, Episcopal, Anglican, Quaker, Baptist, Wesleyan, Free Church, Congregationalist, Mennonite, Amish, Calvinist, or Unitarian. Some Christians prefer to identify themselves as "Brethren," by title of "Brother" or "Sister," to emphasize the universal brotherhood of the church of Christ worldwide and the equality of all believers.

SECTS/DIVISIONS

The seven main categories of Protestantism, with others forming as descendants of these main headings, include:

- **Lutheranism**: The church named after its founder, Martin Luther (1483-1546). Martin Luther was an Augustinian monk who, through his own existential crisis of faith, came to study Scripture and recognize different areas where he felt the Roman Catholic Church was in error in his day. Luther never intended to establish his own denomination, but hoped that, through discussion, the Catholic Church would see its errors and work toward reform. When this did not happen, Martin Luther was excommunicated and formed his own church (which he preferred to identify as Evangelical), of which its followers were known as "Lutherans" – a slur used against Luther's theology. Lutheranism emphasizes the doctrine of justification (that one cannot be saved by their

Lutheran Church logo

own works, but by Christ alone), Scripture alone for doctrine and practice, and that church authority has no right to extreme overreach, as their purpose and authority is to preach the Gospel exclusively. Lutheranism retains both liturgical and sacramental tradition from Roman Catholicism and varies from some other Protestants in that it does not uphold the teaching of John Calvin (1509-1564). The Lutheran Church has several breakaway denominations in its existence, including the Evangelical Lutheran Church in America (ECLA), the Lutheran Church – Missouri Synod (LCMS), the Evangelical Lutheran Church in Canada, Evangelical Church of Czech Brethren, and the Church of Lippe.

- **Anglicanism**: Also known as the Anglican Communion, Church of England, and the Episcopal Church in the United States, Anglicanism originated out of a conflict between Henry VIII (1491-1547) and Pope Clement VII (1478-1534) in 1534. The dispute was over the king's right to annul his marriage to Catherine of Aragon (1485-1536) when their union did not produce a male heir. Upon such, Henry VIII declared the Church of England separated from the Roman Catholic rite, no longer in communion with the papacy. Anglicanism is unique in that it considers itself part of the invisible, worldwide Christian church while still claiming it has an unbroken lineage (an apostolic succession) from the early church, while at the same time upholding doctrinal beliefs that reflect Reformed theology. The church is headed by the Archbishop of Canterbury, who calls their Lambeth Conference every ten years. It is in this meeting the primates (bishops) come together to discuss the current and future work of the Anglican Church. Anglicans see their faith as founded in five ways: the Scriptures, especially the Gospels; the traditions of the first-century church; the bishopric; the first four of the ecumenical councils; and the early church fathers. Anglicans use *The Book of Common Prayer* for their liturgical structure (it is the standard in all churches within the Anglican Communion). Outside of these foundations, the Anglican Church has many different strains of doctrine, the major ones being Anglo-Catholic, evangelical, and broad church. Anglicanism is also governed by its own canon law, which is unique among most of Protestantism. Anglicanism also recognizes a liturgical year, liturgical worship form, and seven sacraments (only baptism and Eucharist are seen as instituted by Christ). The Anglican Church has a great number of groups that classify as breakaways or offshoots, including the Independent Anglican Church Canada Synod, Reformed Anglican Catholic Church, Southern Episcopal Church, Orthodox Anglican Church, and King's Family of Churches.

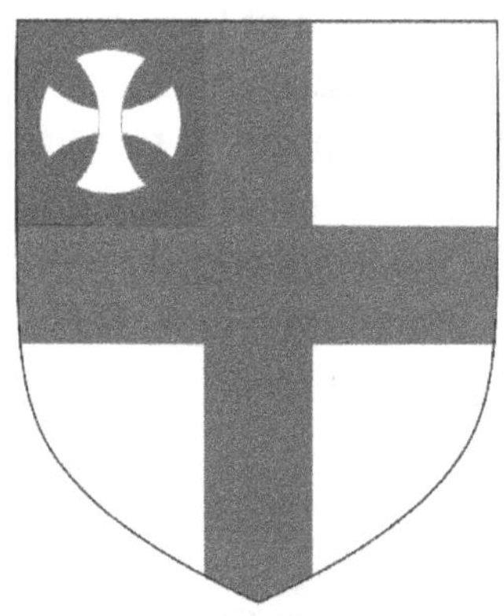

Episcopal Church in America logo

- **Methodism**: The Methodist Church technically classifies as an Anglican Church breakaway, but it has become a notable denomination, large enough to have its own offshoots. The Methodist Church began when John Wesley (1703-1791) started pushing for reform within the Anglican Church. His focus was the practice of spiritual study and holiness for every believer. The followers of Wesley were known as "Methodists" because they were seeking a "new method" of faith. Throughout John Wesley's life, he continued to see Methodism as a subheading of Anglicanism rather than a separate entity. Methodism is now unique as it is based on the theology of John Wesley himself, rather than that of Anglican tradition. Wesley's theology focused heavily on free will and on the need for an individual to receive salvation by choice. Wesley taught that people are dead in their sins without faith. They come to spiritual justification by faith alone, and that faith produces the outward expression of holiness. As a result, Methodists believe obedience to the Gospel provides the necessary assurance of salvation, and Christians can obtain Christian perfection through the pursuit of such. Methodism is, therefore, part of the Holiness Movement, (part of Evangelical Christianity) as well as traditional Protestantism. Methodists use a liturgy and liturgical year adapted from Anglicanism (unifying books include *The United Methodist Hymnal* and *The United Methodist Book of Worship*) and recognize two sacraments (baptism and Holy Communion) as means of the deposit of grace in a believer's life. Methodists also believe heavily in tradition and the Early Church Fathers as teaching sources. Today, there is a wide variety of experience within Methodist worship and style, including more modern forms. The Methodist Church has inspired several breakaway groups, including those that trace back to its founding days and early roots in the evangelism of the United States. Some subgroups include the Wesleyan Church, the Salvation Army, the Methodist Episcopal Church, the United Methodist Church, the United Protestant Church, the Church of Pakistan, and the United Church in Zambia.

United Methodist Church logo

- **Anabaptist**: Of all Protestant groups, the Anabaptist descendants have the widest variety of representations, beliefs, and groups. The Anabaptists were classified as a "radical" religious group, descending from the Radical Reformation in the sixteenth century (although their origins descend from, at minimum, least a century earlier; for the sake of space, their ancestors are also included under this general heading). The Radical Reformation believed both Catholicism and traditional Protestantism to be corrupt and in spiritual error, and that visible, exterior church hierarchies (bishops, popes, liturgies, and formalities) needed to cease. In place of such things, radical reformers believed the only true Christians were part of such belief and demonstrated their commitment to the faith with a "believer's baptism," by full immersion, in water (known as one of two ordinances, the other being communion). Anabaptists were so-called because the term means "re-baptizer." This demonstrates their commitment to rebaptize anyone who had been baptized into a denomination as an infant without a confession or commitment to their faith. The term, however, was originally derogatory. Anabaptist Christianity represents the introduction of a "low tradition" into Christian faith, meaning a movement that was more simplistic for the common individual rather than complicated and designed for a hierarchy. Some Anabaptists see themselves as a part of traditional apostolic succession, but others do not cite any such connection. The Anabaptists upheld the five "solas" of Protestantism, while also combining a belief in the leadership of the Spirit, extensive manifestation of Spiritual gifts as outlined in 1 Corinthians 12, radical pacificism, freedom of religion, the separation of church and state, and a belief in a need to be non-conforming to the ways of the world. There are numerous modern-day descendants of Anabaptist tradition, including the Mennonites, Hutterites, Hussites, Moravians, Quakers, modern-day Baptists, Amish, Schwarzenau Brethren, Apostolic Christian Church, Bruderhof Community, and Old German Baptist Brethren. Some Anabaptist descendants also believe in the essential nature of a home or house church (with believers meeting in homes) as opposed to maintaining a church building.

- **Reformed**: More commonly known as Calvinism and as the Reformed tradition, Reformed Christianity, Reformed Protestantism, or Reformed faith, Reformed theology is based on the theological teaching of John Calvin (1509-1564). Calvinism's basic premise is abbreviated TULIP, which stands for: Total depravity (humans are born sinful and they cannot do anything to avoid sin), Unconditional election (God has chosen a specific group, or number of people to be saved, predestined before the foundation of the world, and they cannot do anything to override or avoid their salvation, even if they do not desire it), Limited atonement (Jesus' action on the cross, His salvation, for sin is limited only to an elect few predestined to be saved, and all others are damned), Irresistible grace (those who shall be saved will always be saved, because the work of the Holy Spirit cannot be resisted), and Perseverance of the saints (the work – and will – of God shall carry on until the end, both in this world and among those who are believers; those who leave the faith were never part of the elect). Modern-day adherents of Calvin's doctrine vary in their level of strictness to the precepts, but all adhere to histories that have embraced these different focal points throughout their denomination's histories. Calvinists observe a modified, simplified liturgical format, opt for communion as a symbol of Christ rather than a literal embodiment, observe two sacraments (baptism and the Lord's Supper), and recognizes a variety of worship styles, including some acapella, psalter, or other forms of music in song. Many Reformed polities include variations on election or congregationalism, both of which involve church votes as an essential part of governance (ministers, beliefs, and activities are decided through a vote of the people or a vote of church representatives). Modern-day Reformed churches include the Reformed Church, the Continental Reformed Churches, Presbyterian Churches, Evangelical Anglican Church, Congregationalists, the United Church of Christ, World Communion of Reformed Churches, World Reformed Fellowship, the Reformed Churches in the Netherlands, International Conference of Reformed Churches, and Reformed Baptists.

- **Unitarianism:** Technically considered part of the Anabaptist Movement, Unitarianism is unique enough to have its own classification. The Unitarian Church originated in 1556 in Poland among those who became the Polish Brethren. Its early history was marked by its rejection of Trinitarianism, opting instead for the belief that God was one in number and being, and Jesus Christ was a great man, prophet, and savior, but was not God or divine Himself. There are three main forms of Unitarian understanding: Arian (Christ was pre-existent as Logos, but Jesus lived only as a human being; Socinian (Christ should be worshiped while denying His divinity), and Strict Unitarian (the divinity of God is exclusive to God, and there is no Holy Spirit, nor should one worship Christ). Unitarians accept the authority of Jesus on issues of morality and also accept the role of reason, rationalism, science, and philosophy as coexistent with faith in God. Unitarianism is also unique in that it believes the Bible can contain error because the writers were inspired by God but remained human. Some other unique Unitarian views include rejection of Calvinism and creeds, and exercising free will in execution of religious practice. For this reason, Unitarians have always been different from other Protestants, while maintaining the same roots and spirit of independence, believing in the study of the Scriptures, separation of church and state, and in the establishment of free churches. Unitarianism took strong hold in the early days of American history as well as shaping some of the values of American society. Traditional Unitarianism shaped the form for what is now known as Unitarian Universalism, which although a mix of beliefs of both groups, is different from the traditional Unitarian Church. Offshoots of Unitarianism include the International Council of Unitarians and Universalists, Congregazione Italiana Cristiano Unitariana, the Unitarian Christian Association, the Unitarian Christian Conference USA, the Unitarian Universalist Christian Fellowship, the Italian Christian Church, the Christian Church in Italy, and the Unitarian Universalist Association.

- **Other Protestant groups**: There are other smaller Protestant groups that, while following many of the precepts of existing Protestantism, may espouse their own views or mix different existing Protestant philosophies or identities in different ways to form their own entities. Combining and uniting all of them together, however, remain the five "solas" of Protestantism and often histories that tie back to one of these seven historic Protestant groups.

NUMBER OF ADHERENTS

There are approximately 800,000,000 Protestant believers worldwide.[2] Within this subheading, there are 80,000,000 Lutherans;[3] 85,000,000 Anglicans;[4] 80,000,000 Methodists;[5] at least 4,000,000 Anabaptist descendants;[6] 80,000,000 Reformed;[7] and around 800,000 Unitarians[8] worldwide.

DISPUTES WITHIN GROUP

As a broad heading, Protestantism does not acknowledge a formal, centralized leadership.

Because Protestantism focuses on the role of Scripture as an authority and the believer's faith, not all Protestants agree on what Scripture says or how it is interpreted. For this reason, Protestant groups tend to divide and disagree over different interpretations of doctrine, Scriptural interpretation, expressions of faith and worship, and questions about the execution of one's faith within their lives. There are some Protestant alliances and communions that extend respect to other Protestant groups, but there is no one, singular definition as to what it means to be a Christian within these groups, or how a group should live.

In modern times, Protestant groups disagree with one another as well as among themselves about modern questions and issues. Some of these issues include the role of politics in one's faith, the standard traditions and definitions of belief, morality, same-sex marriage and ordination, women's ordination, the role of Scripture and its interpretation today, abortion, birth control, personal conscience, racial reconciliations, and differences and their relevance in denominational identity.

SCRIPTURES

The Holy Bible, both Old and New Testaments, inclusive of 66 books: the Pentateuch (Genesis, Exodus, Leviticus, Numbers, and Deuteronomy), Historical books (Joshua, Judges, Ruth, 1 Samuel, 2 Samuel, 1 Kings, 2 Kings, 1 Chronicles, 2 Chronicles, Ezra, Nehemiah, Esther), Wisdom books (Job, Psalms, Proverbs, Ecclesiastes, Song of Songs), Prophetic books (Isaiah, Jeremiah, Lamentations, Ezekiel, Daniel, Hosea, Joel, Amos, Obadiah, Jonah, Micah, Nahum, Habakkuk, Zephaniah, Haggai, Zechariah, Malachi), the Gospels (Matthew, Mark, Luke, John), the Acts of the Apostles, the Pauline Epistles (Romans, 1 Corinthians, 2 Corinthians, Galatians, Ephesians, Philippians, Colossians, 1 Thessalonians, 2 Thessalonians, 1 Timothy, 2 Timothy, Titus, Philemon, Hebrews) the General Epistles (James, 1 Peter, 2 Peter, 1 John, 2 John, 3 John, Jude) and Revelation.

Some Protestant groups (Anglican, Lutheran, Methodist) include the Deuterocanonical books under a separate heading known as "Apocrypha" in their Bibles. These books, found in between the Old and New Testaments, are not considered to the standard of Scripture (as inspired), but are considered that they may have value for readers. In the lectionaries of these churches, the Apocrypha are often included. These books include Tobit, Judith, 1 and 2 Maccabees, Wisdom of Solomon, Sirach, Baruch, Letter of Jeremiah, Greek additions to Esther, and Greek additions to Daniel, including the Prayer of Azariah, Song of the Three Holy Children, Susanna and the Elders, and Bel and the Dragon. Other Protestants do not include, nor recognize these books, and such are not included in their Bibles.

The Wycliffe Bible also included the Epistle of the Laodiceans, a short, apocryphal work attributed to the Apostle Paul. This work was included in translations of the Bible into English for many centuries after its initial publication.

The Bible has always remained central to Protestant theology and faith. As one of the five primary "solas" in Protestant belief, Protestants have relied upon and saw to the transmission and inclusion of Scripture in their churches, their societies, and as part of their witness of the Gospel. Protestants have always believed the Bible should be translated from the original Hebrew and Greek texts into the needed vernacular of the people, from the Lutherbibel in German to more modern-day Protestant translations in use today. The Bible has, thanks to the Protestant advances, has been translated into over three thousand languages.[9]

Some common Protestant translations of the Bible include The Wycliffe Bible, The King James Version (also called The Authorized Version), The Tyndale Bible, The Coverdale Bible, The Geneva Bible, The Matthew Bible, Young's Literal Translation, The New Revised Standard Version, The New King James Version, and The English Standard Version.

Among Protestant churches that use lectionaries (Anglican, Lutheran, Reformed, Methodist), the standard lectionary is the Revised Common Lectionary, based on the *Ordo Lectionum Missae* (1969) of The Roman Catholic Church. The Revised Common Lectionary puts together small passages, readings, and verses of Scripture on a three-year reading cycle in a form that makes sense for those who hear as part of their worship services. The lectionary follows with a Protestant version of a liturgical year.

Though Protestants who recognize tradition do see it as subject to Scripture, some groups (Anglicans, Methodists) believe tradition can be used to interpret Scripture or within the context of understanding it better. As part of this tradition, they may rely on traditional creeds, major figures in church history (such as the Early Church Fathers), or different Ecumenical Councils. Others believe in the abolishment of such, all together.

BASIC RELIGIOUS PRACTICES

Protestantism centers around three things: the individual and their understanding of relationship with God, the individual in relationship with both family and society, and the individual and their relationship with the church. These three essential relationships form the foundation of Protestant life, although what defines these relationships may vary, based on specific beliefs of a denomination or group. Protestants are expected to live a life worthy of their calling in Christ. Such a life is lived within the boundaries of society, especially in relationships and witness through marriage, family, and general society. It is due to Protestant influence that values of democracy, representation, ideas about marriage and relationships, and familial values exist today in western nations. In addition to its emphasis on Scripture and distributing the Bible in print, Protestants are also responsible for the development and encouragement of church music, congregational singing, and hymnology in modern times.

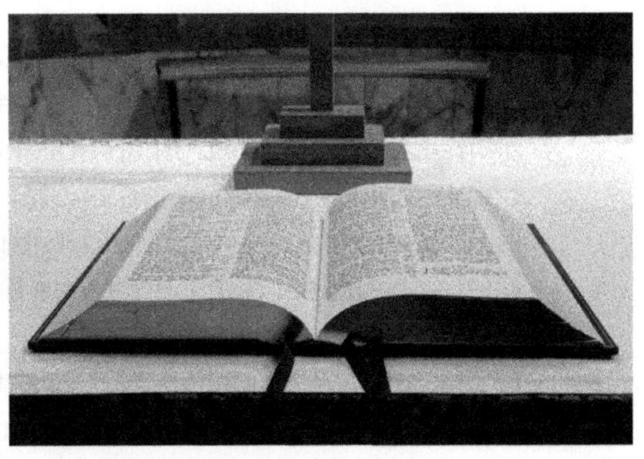

Open Bible on a church table

Protestant services do vary and are divided into two main categories: liturgical and non-liturgical. Liturgical services (sometimes called "high services") are variations on Catholic liturgy, often simplified in form. Liturgical form is embraced by Lutherans, Anglicans, Methodists, and Reformed churches. These liturgies vary from one another, but all include hymns, formalized prayers and prayer responses, confessions of faith, lectionary readings, creed recitation, and communion. Non-liturgical services (often called "low services") do maintain an order of worship, which typically contains some form of a call to worship, introductory hymn or song, public confession/repentance of sins, children's lesson, scripture reading, sermon, offertory, doxology, and a closing hymn (order may vary slightly depending on church). Communion services are held either weekly, monthly, quarterly, or yearly depending on the denomination. Leaders of Protestant churches are Pastor, Reverend, Minister, or in some liturgical traditions, Father or Mother.

Holidays

Much of what western culture identifies as "religious holidays" are found in Protestantism, the primary two being Christmas and Easter. For most Protestants, Easter is the highest holy day of the entire church year.

Among Protestants that observe a liturgical year, the Anglican Church follows a year that is identical to the Roman Catholic Common Lectionary of 1969, and most groups within Anglicanism now follow The Revised Common Lectionary of 1983. Lutherans follow their own books, either The Lutheran Book of Worship from 1978, Evangelical Lutheran Worship in 2006, or Lutheran Service Book from 2006. The Reformed Churches celebrate the Five Evangelical Feasts: Christmas, Good Friday, Easter, Ascension, and Pentecost, and some now also celebrate different liturgical seasons surrounding these five great feasts, such as Advent, Christmas, Epiphany, and periods after Epiphany, Pentecost, and Easter. The difference between the Roman Catholic and Protestant liturgical years are the rejection of what is known as "Ordinary Time." Protestant Liturgical seasons can be defined as follows:

- **Advent**: The four Sundays preceding Christmas. Focuses on periods of waiting, as the Jews waited four thousand years for the coming of the Messiah. Each week, a candle of coinciding color is lit on an advent wreath. Color is purple or blue (signifying royalty) or in some traditions, white, except for the third week of Advent, of which the represented color is pink (signifying joy). Most Protestant Advent wreaths also contain a white candle in the center representing Christmas and lit on Christmas.

- **Christmas**: Also called Nativity, the period from Christmas (or the Sunday closest to Christmas, in years when Christmas falls on a Saturday or Monday) to the feats of the Baptism of the Lord in early January. Color is white (signifying purity) or gold (representing the heavenly).

- **Lent**: Begins on Ash Wednesday and lasts until Palm Sunday. Color is purple. Focuses on repentance, mortality, and sin. Fasting requirements do vary but are usually suggested for Ash Wednesday and Good Friday. Many observing Protestants also "give something up" for Lent, designed to help a believer focus in a greater way on their spiritual lives, such as giving up sweets, meat, social media, television, or internet usage. Some focus on other disciplines, such as trading in poor habits for good ones: exercising more, maintaining a better diet, or spending more time with family or religious devotions. Color is purple, signifying royalty, or what is called "Lenten array" (unbleached linen) in Anglicanism.

- **Palm (or Passion) Sunday**: Palm Sunday Recalls Christ's procession into Jerusalem, riding on a donkey to the greeting of palm fronds and cheers by the people. Color is red or purple: red for passion, purple for royalty.

- **Holy (Maundy) Thursday**: Holy Thursday recalls the Passover feast of the Last Supper. Color is white, signifying purity.

- **Good Friday**: Good Friday recalls the crucifixion and death of Jesus Christ. Many Protestant denominations observe a tradition known as the Seven Last Words from the Cross, also known as the Three Hours Devotion (begins at 12 PM and ends at 3 PM). It is also not uncommon to see ecumenical or cross-denominational church services on Good Friday. Color is red, signifying blood and passion.

- **Vigil of Easter**: Holy Saturday is the Easter Vigil, acknowledging the impending coming resurrection of Christ. Services are often "high liturgy," recounting major events of salvation history up to the resurrection. Service begins in darkness with candles and at the time of resurrection celebration, the lights are turned on. Color is white or gold, signifying purity or the heavenly.

- **Easter**: Begins on Easter Sunday and lasts until Pentecost Sunday. Celebrates the resurrection of Christ from the dead. Color is white, signifying purity and new life or gold, representing the heavenly. As part of the Easter season, Protestants also observe Trinity Sunday and the feasts of the Ascension and Pentecost. Color is white or gold, signifying purity or the heavenly.

- **Pentecost**: The official end to the Easter season. Acknowledges the descent of the Holy Spirit on the disciples. Considered to be the birthday of the church. The color is red, signifying the Holy Spirit.

In addition to these specific seasons, some Protestant groups also observe special holidays and feast days on their calendars throughout the year. Some are feasts as relate to special aspects of the life of Christ; some are days to special individuals acknowledged for their accomplishments as saints; some are individuals acknowledged as saints throughout historical tradition; and some are days that acknowledge the founders of their church or relevant figures in the Reformation. Some of these days include: The Presentation of Jesus in the Temple (Candlemas) (February 2 or the nearest Sunday), John and Charles Wesley (March 2, Lutheran), The Annunciation (March 25), Earth Day Sunday or Earth Sunday (The Sunday before Earth Day), Aldersgate Day (May 24 or the Sunday nearest to that date in Methodism), Reformation Day (October 31), All Saints Day (November 1), Day of Repentance and Prayer (Wednesday before the first Sunday of Advent), Feast of the Holy Sovereigns (November 28, Anglican), and Katharina von Bora Luther (December 20, Lutheran).

Other Protestants do not observe a Liturgical year. Traditional Reformed groups desired to focus on Sunday rather than special days. There are some among the Reform tradition that still do. There are also some Protestants who just observe major feasts, such as Christmas, and still some who do not observe holidays or seasons, at all.

VISUAL SIGNS AND SYMBOLS

Cross or resurrection cross; Bible; Psalter or hymnbook; married clergy; female clergy; pictures or images of Reformers (such as Martin Luther or John Calvin); dove or flame to represent the work of the Holy Spirit; the rose (represents the resurrection); the English flag (for Anglicans); scallop sea shell, typically with drops of water around or falling off (represents baptism); praying hands; chalice; candle or lamp; a minister or individual preaching; anchor (represents faith and hope); triangle (represents the Trinity); the globe; specific denominational logos as represent the group to which one belongs.

CREEDS, BOOKS, AND LAWS

Each Protestant denomination contains specific books of guiding legislation for their denomination. These books are often used as the standards for orders of worship, services, and annual events, seasons, or feast days. Those that do not observe Liturgical years share standard books that contain information about the essentials of faith, even if they are nothing more than standard Protestant works written by the Reformers. A few Protestant groups (Lutheran, Reformed, some Anabaptist, Methodist and Anglicans) employ catechisms, books that were often used to instruct converts or children into the essentials of their denominational belief. Important books of Protestantism include:

- **Anglican**: *The Book of Common Prayer*, The Thirty-Nine Articles of Religion

  There was never any thing by the wit of man so well devised, or so sure established, which in continuance of time hath not been corrupted: as, among other things, it may plainly appear by the common prayers in the Church, commonly called Divine Service: the first original and ground whereof, if a man would search out by the ancient fathers, he shall find, that the same was not ordained, but of a good purpose, and for a great advancement of godliness: For they so ordered the matter, that all the whole Bible (or the greatest part thereof) should be read over once in the year, intending thereby, that the Clergy, and especially such as were Ministers of the congregation, should (by often reading, and meditation of God's word) be stirred up to godliness themselves, and be more able to exhort others by wholesome doctrine, and to confute them that were adversaries to the truth. And further, that the people (by daily hearing of holy Scripture read in the Church) should continually profit more and more in the knowledge of God, and be the more inflamed with the love of his true religion.

  But these many years passed, this godly and decent order of the ancient fathers hath been so altered, broken, and neglected, by planting in uncertain stories, Legends, Responds, Verses, vain repetitions, Commemorations, and Synodals, that commonly when any book of the Bible was begun, before three or four Chapters were read out, all the rest were unread. And in this sort the book of Isaiah was begun in Advent, and the book of Genesis in

Septuagesima; but they were only begun, and never read through. After a like sort were other books of holy Scripture used. And moreover, whereas St. Paul would have such language spoken to the people in the Church, as they might understand, and have profit by hearing the same, the Service in the Church of England (these many years) hath been read in Latin to the people, which they understood not; so that they have heard with their ears only; and their hearts, spirit, and mind, have not been edified thereby. And furthermore, notwithstanding that the ancient fathers had divided the Psalms into seven portions, whereof every one was called a nocturn, now of late time a few of them have been daily said (and oft repeated), and the rest utterly omitted. Moreover, the number and hardness of the Rules called the Pie, and the manifold changings of the service, was the cause, that to turn the Book only, was so hard and intricate a matter, that many times, there was more business to find out what should be read, than to read it when it was found out.

These inconveniences therefore considered, here is set forth such an order, whereby the same shall be redressed. And for a readiness in this matter, here is drawn out a Kalendar for that purpose, which is plain and easy to be understood, wherein (so much as may be) the reading of holy Scripture is so set forth, that all things shall be done in order, without breaking one piece thereof from another. For this cause be cut off Anthems, Responds, Invitatories, and such like things, as did break the continual course of the reading of the Scripture.

Yet because there is no remedy, but that of necessity there must be some rules: therefore certain rules are here set forth, which, as they be few in number; so they be plain and easy to be understood. So that here you have an order for prayer (as touching the reading of the holy Scripture), much agreeable to the mind and purpose of the old fathers, and a great deal more profitable and commodious, than that which of late was used. It is more profitable, because here are left out many things, whereof some be untrue, some uncertain, same vain and superstitious: and is ordained nothing to be read, but the very pure word of God, the holy Scriptures, or that which is evidently grounded upon the same; and that in such a language and order as is most easy and plain for the understanding, both of the readers and hearers. It is also more commodious, both for the shortness thereof, and for the plainness of the order, and for that the rules be few and easy. Furthermore, by this order the curates shall need none other books for their public service, but this book and the Bible: by the means whereof, the people shall not be at so great charge for books, as in time past they have been.

Henry VIII (1491-1547) and Catherine of Aragon (1485-1536)

And where heretofore, there hath been great diversity in saying and singing in churches within this realm: some following Salisbury use, some Hereford use, some the use of Bangor, some of York, and some of Lincoln: now from henceforth, all the whole realm shall have but one use. And if any would judge this way more painful, because that all things must be read upon the book, whereas before, by reason of so often repetition, they could say many things by heart: if those men will weigh their labor with the profit in knowledge, which daily they shall obtain by reading upon the book, they will not refuse the pain, in consideration of the great profit that shall ensue thereof.

And forasmuch as nothing else, almost, be so plainly set forth, but doubts may arise in the use and practicing of the same: to appease all such diversity (if any arise), and for the resolution of all doubts, concerning the manner how to understand, do, and execute, the things contained in this book: the parties that so doubt, or diversely take any thing, shall always resort to the Bishop of the Diocese, who by his discretion shall take order for the quieting and appeasing of the same; so that the same order be not contrary to any thing contained in this book.

Though it be appointed in the afore written preface, that all things shall be read and sung in the church in the English tongue, to the end that the congregation may be thereby edified: yet it is not meant, but when men say Matins and Evensong privately, they may say the same in any language that they themselves do understand. Neither that any man shall be bound to the saying of them, but such as from time to time, in Cathedral and Collegiate Churches, parish Churches, and Chapels to the same annexed, shall serve the congregation.[10]

- **Lutheran**: Lutheran Book of Worship, Lutheran Worship, Book of Concord

Whereby All Dogmas should be Judged according to God's Word, and the Controversies that have Occurred should be Explained and Decided in a Christian Manner.

1) Since for thorough, permanent unity in the Church it is, above all things, necessary that we have a comprehensive, unanimously approved summary and form wherein is brought together from God's Word the common doctrine, reduced to a brief compass, which the churches that are of the true Christian religion confess, just as the ancient Church always had for this use its fixed symbols; 2 moreover, since this [comprehensive form of doctrine] should not be based on private writings, but on such books as have been composed, approved, and received in the name of the churches which pledge themselves to one doctrine and religion, we have declared to one another with heart and mouth that we will not make or receive a separate or new confession of our faith, but confess the public common writings which always and everywhere were held and used as such symbols or common confessions in all the churches of the Augsburg Confession before the dissensions arose among those who accept the Augsburg Confession, and as long as in all articles there was on all sides a unanimous adherence to [and maintenance and use of] the pure doctrine of the divine Word, as the sainted Dr. Luther explained it.

3) 1. First [, then, we receive and embrace with our whole heart] the Prophetic and Apostolic Scriptures of the Old and New Testaments as the pure, clear fountain of Israel, which is the only true standard by which all teachers and doctrines are to be judged.

4) 2. And since of old the true Christian doctrine, in a pure, sound sense, was collected from God's Word into brief articles or chapters against the corruption of heretics, we confess, in the second place, the three Ecumenical Creeds, namely, the Apostles', the Nicene, and the Athanasian, as glorious confessions of the faith, brief, devout, and founded upon God's Word, in which all the heresies which at that time had arisen in the Christian Church are clearly and unanswerably refuted.

5] 3. In the third place, since in these last times God, out of especial grace, has brought the truth of His Word to light again from the darkness of the Papacy through the faithful service of the precious man of God, Dr. Luther, and since this doctrine has been collected from, and according to, God's Word into the articles and chapters of the Augsburg Confession against the corruptions of the Papacy and also of other sects, we confess also the First, Unaltered Augsburg Confession as our symbol for this time, not because it was composed by our theologians, but because it has been taken from God's Word and is founded firmly and well therein, precisely in the form in which it was committed to writing, in the year 1530, and presented to the Emperor Charles V at Augsburg by some Christian Electors, Princes, and Estates of the Roman Empire as a common confession of the reformed churches, whereby our reformed churches are distinguished from the Papists and other repudiated and condemned sects and heresies, after the custom and usage of the early Church, whereby succeeding councils, Christian bishops and teachers appealed to the Nicene Creed, and confessed it [publicly declared that they embraced it].

6] 4. In the fourth place, as regards the proper and true sense of the oft-quoted Augsburg Confession, an extensive Apology was composed and published in print in 1531, after the presentation of the Confession, in order that we might explain ourselves at greater length and guard against the [slanders of the] Papists, and that condemned errors might not steal into the Church of God under the name of the Augsburg Confession, or dare to seek cover under the same. We unanimously confess this also, because not only is the said Augsburg Confession explained as much as is necessary and guarded [against the slanders of the adversaries], but also proven [confirmed] by clear, irrefutable testimonies of Holy Scripture.

7] 5. In the fifth place, we also confess the Articles composed, approved, and received at Smalcald in the large assembly of theologians, in the year 1537, as they were first framed and printed in order to be delivered in the council at Mantua, or wherever it would be held, in the name of the Estates, Electors, and Princes, as an explanation of the above-mentioned Augsburg Confession, wherein by God's grace they were resolved to abide. In them the doctrine of the Augsburg Confession is repeated, and some articles are explained at greater length from God's Word, and, besides, the cause and grounds are indicated, as far as necessary, why we have abandoned the papistical errors and idolatries, and can have no fellowship with them, and also why we know, and can think of, no way for coming to any agreement with the Pope concerning them.

8] 6. And now, in the sixth place, because these highly important matters [the business of religion] concern also the common people and laymen [as they are called], who, inasmuch as they are Christians, must for their salvation distinguish between pure and false doctrine, we confess also the Small and the Large Catechisms of Dr. Luther, as they were written by him and incorporated in his works, because they have been unanimously approved and received by all churches adhering to the Augsburg Confession, and have been publicly used in churches, schools, and in [private] houses, and, moreover, because the Christian doctrine from God's Word is comprised in them in the most correct and simple way, and, in like manner, is explained, as far as necessary [for simple laymen].

9) In the pure churches and schools these public common writings have been always regarded as the sum and model of the doctrine which Dr. Luther, of blessed memory, has admirably deduced from God's Word, and firmly established against the Papacy and other sects; and to his full explanations in his doctrinal and polemical writings we wish to appeal, in the manner and as far as Dr. Luther himself in the Latin preface to his published works has given necessary and Christian admonition concerning his writings, and has expressly drawn this distinction namely, that the Word of God alone should be and remain the only standard and rule of doctrine, to which the writings of no man should be regarded as equal, but to which everything should be subjected.

10) But [this is not to be understood as if] hereby other good, useful, pure books, expositions of the Holy Scriptures, refutations of errors, explanations of doctrinal articles, are not rejected; for as far as they are consistent with the above-mentioned type of doctrine, these are regarded as useful expositions and explanations, and can be used with advantage. But what has thus far been said concerning the summary of our Christian doctrine is intended to mean only this, that we should have a unanimously accepted, definite, common form of doctrine, which all our evangelical churches together and in common confess, from and according to which, because it has been derived from God's Word, all other writings should be judged and adjusted as to how far they are to be approved and accepted.

11) For that we embodied the above-mentioned writing, namely, the Augsburg Confession, Apology, Smalcald Articles, Luther's Large and Small Catechisms, in the oft-mentioned Sum of our Christian doctrine, was done for the reason that these have always and everywhere been regarded as the common, unanimously accepted meaning of our churches, and, moreover, have been subscribed at that time by the chief and most enlightened theologians, and have held sway in all evangelical churches and schools. 12 So also, as before mentioned, they were all written and sent forth before the divisions among the theologians of the Augsburg Confession arose; therefore, since they are held to be impartial, and neither can nor should be rejected by either part of those who have entered into controversy, and no one who without guile is an adherent of the Augsburg Confession will complain of these writings, but will cheerfully accept and tolerate them as witnesses [of the truth], no one can think ill of [blame] us that we derive from them an explanation and decision of the articles in controversy, 13 and that, as we lay down God's Word, the eternal truth, as the foundation, so we introduce and quote also these writings as a witness of the truth and as the unanimously received correct understanding of our predecessors who have steadfastly held to the pure doctrine.[11]

- **Reformed**: The Westminster Confession of Faith, The Three Forms of Unity (*Belgic Confession*, *Canons of Dort*, and *The Heidelberg Catechism*), *The Institutes of the Christian Religion*, *Book of Church Order*, *Liturgy with the Directory for Worship*, *Book of Confessions*, *Book of Common Worship*, *Scots Confession*, *Cambridge Platform*

    1. *God from all eternity did by the most wise and holy counsel of His own will, freely and unchangeably ordain whatsoever comes to pass; yet so as thereby neither is God the author of sin; nor is violence offered to the will of the creatures, nor is the liberty or contingency of second causes taken away, but rather established.*
    2. *Although God knows whatsoever may or can come to pass, upon all supposed conditions; yet hath He not decreed any thing because He foresaw it as future, as that which would come to pass, upon such conditions.*

3. *By the decree of God, for the manifestation of His glory, some men and angels are predestinated unto everlasting life, and others foreordained to everlasting death.*
4. *These angels and men, thus predestinated and foreordained, are particularly and unchangeably designed; and their number is so certain and definite that it can not be either increased or diminished.*
5. *Those of mankind that are predestinated unto life, God, before the foundation of the world was laid, according to His eternal and immutable purpose, and the secret counsel and good pleasure of His will, hath chosen in Christ, unto everlasting glory, out of His free grace and love alone, without any foresight of faith or good works, or perseverance in either of them, or any other thing in the creature, as conditions, or causes moving Him thereunto; and all to the praise of His glorious grace.*
6. *As God hath appointed the elect unto glory, so hath He, by the eternal and most free purpose of His will, foreordained all the means thereunto. Wherefore they who are elected being fallen in Adam are redeemed by Christ, are effectually called unto faith in Christ by His Spirit working in due season; are justified, adopted, sanctified, and kept by His power through faith unto salvation. Neither are any other redeemed by Christ, effectually called, justified, adopted, sanctified, and saved, but the elect only.*
7. *The rest of mankind, God was pleased, according to the unsearchable counsel of His own will, whereby He extendeth or withholdeth mercy as He pleaseth, for the glory of His sovereign power over His creatures, to pass by, and to ordain them to dishonor and wrath for their sin, to the praise of His glorious justice.*
8. *The doctrine of this high mystery of predestination is to be handled with special prudence and care, that men attending to the will of God revealed in His Word, and yielding obedience thereunto, may, from the certainty of their effectual vocation, be assured of their eternal election. So shall this doctrine afford matter of praise, reverence, and admiration of God; and of humility, diligence, and abundant consolation to all that sincerely obey the gospel.*[12]

- **Methodist:** *The United Methodist Book of Worship, The Articles of Religion of the Methodist Church, The Confessions of Faith of the Evangelical United Brethren Church, The General Rules of the Methodist Societies, The Standard Sermons of John Wesley, John Wesley's Explanatory Notes on the New Testament, Book of Discipline of the United Methodist Church*

John Wesley (1703-1791)

The Basic Pattern of Worship is rooted in Scripture and in our United Methodist heritage and experience. It expresses the biblical, historical, and theological integrity of Christian worship and is the basis of all the General Services of the Church. This Basic Pattern serves to guide those who plan worship and to help congregations understand the basic structure and content of our worship. Though it is not an order of worship, a variety of orders of worship may be based upon it. It reveals that behind the diversity of United Methodist worship there is a basic unity.

Our worship in both its diversity and its unity is an encounter with the living God through the risen Christ in the power of the Holy Spirit. When the people of God gather, the Spirit is free to move them to worship in diverse ways, according to their needs. We rejoice that congregations of large and small membership, in different regions, in different communities, of different racial and ethnic composition, and with distinctive local traditions can each worship in a style that enables the people to feel at home.

The Spirit is also the source of unity and truth. The teachings of Scripture give our worship a basic pattern that has proved itself over the centuries, that gives The United Methodist Church its sense of identity and links us to the universal Church. This pattern goes back to worship as Jesus and his earliest disciples knew it–services in the synagogue and Jewish family worship around the meal table. It has been fleshed out by the experience and traditions of Christian congregations for two thousand years.

The Entrance and the Proclamation and Response–often called the Service of the Word or the Preaching Service–are a Christian adaptation of the ancient synagogue service.

The Thanksgiving and Communion, commonly called the Lord's Supper or Holy Communion, is a Christian adaptation of Jewish worship at family meal tables–as Jesus and his disciples ate together during his preaching and teaching ministry, as Jesus transformed it when he instituted the Lord's Supper on the night before his death, and as his disciples experienced it in the breaking of bread with their risen Lord (Luke 24:30-35; John 21:13).

After the Day of Pentecost, when the earliest Christians went out preaching and teaching, they continued to take part in synagogue worship wherever they went (Acts 9:2ff., 20; 13:5, 13ff., 44ff.; 14:1; 17:1ff., 10ff., 17ff.; 18:4, 19, 26; 19:8; 22:19; 24:12; 26:11) and to break bread as a holy meal in their own gatherings (Acts 2:42, 46).

As their preaching and teaching about Jesus led to a break between church and synagogue, the Christians held an adapted synagogue service and broke bread when they gathered on the first day of the week. Such a combined service of Word and Table is described in Acts 20:7ff. This was apparently an accepted pattern by the time Luke wrote the Emmaus account in Luke 24:13-35, which pictures the joining together of a transformed synagogue service and a transformed holy meal and indicates to readers that they can know the risen Christ in the experience of Word and Table.

The Emmaus account can be used today in preaching and teaching the Basic Pattern of Worship. As on the first day of the week the two disciples were joined by the risen Christ, so in the power of the Holy Spirit the risen and ascended Christ joins us when we gather. As the disciples poured out to him their sorrow and in so doing opened their hearts to what Jesus would say to them, so we pour out to him whatever is on our hearts and thereby open ourselves to the Word. As Jesus "opened the Scriptures" to them and caused their hearts to burn, so we hear the Scriptures opened to us and out of the burning of our hearts praise God. As they were faced with a decision and responded by inviting Jesus to stay with them, we can do likewise. As they joined the risen Christ around the table, so can we. As Jesus took, blessed, broke, and gave the bread just as the disciples had seen him do three days previously, so in the name of the risen Christ we do these four actions with the bread and cup. As he was "made known to them in the breaking of the bread," so the risen and ascended Christ can be known to us in Holy Communion. As he disappeared and sent the disciples into the world with faith and joy, so he sends us forth into the world. And as those disciples found Christ when they arrived at Jerusalem later that evening, so we can find Christ with us wherever we go.

Since New Testament times, this Basic Pattern has had a long history of development. At times this pattern has been obscured and corrupted, and at times it has been recovered and renewed. The Wesleyan revival continued this emphasis on Word and Table, taking the gospel into the world by preaching and singing and by celebrating of the holy meal. Today The United Methodist Church is reclaiming our biblical and historic heritage, as we seek in this Basic Pattern to worship God "in spirit and in truth."[13]

- **Anabaptist**: *Baptist Faith and Message*, *Seven-Point Confession*, *Schleitheim Confession*, *Discipline of the Church*, *Baptist Confession of Faith*, *Richmond Declaration*

Beloved brethren and sisters in the Lord: First and supremely we are always concerned for your consolation and the assurance of your conscience (which was previously misled) so that ... you may turn again to the true implanted members of Christ, who have been armed through patience and knowledge of themselves, and have therefore again been united with us in the strength of a godly Christian spirit and zeal for God. ...

Dear brethren and sisters, we who have been assembled in the Lord at Schleitheim on the Border, make known in points and articles to all who love God that as concerns us we are of one mind to abide in the Lord as God's obedient children, [His] sons and daughters, we who have been and shall be separated from the world in everything, [and] completely at peace. To God alone be praise and glory without the contradiction of any brethren. In this we have perceived the oneness of the Spirit of our Father and of our common Christ with us. For the Lord is the Lord of peace and not of quarreling, as Paul points out. That you may understand in what articles this has been formulated you should observe and note [the following]....

The articles which we discussed and on which we were of one mind are these:

1. Baptism
2. The Ban [Excommunication]
3. Breaking of Bread
4. Separation from the Abomination
5. Pastors in the Church
6. The Sword
7. The Oath.

First. Observe concerning baptism*: Baptism shall be given to all those who have learned repentance and amendment of life, and who believe truly that their sins are taken away by Christ, and to all those who walk in the resurrection of Jesus Christ, and wish to be buried with Him in death, so that they may be resurrected with Him, and to all those who with this significance request it [baptism] of us and demand it for themselves.* ***This excludes all infant baptism, the highest and chief abomination of the pope****. In this you have the foundation and testimony of the apostles. Mt. 28, Mk. 16, Acts 2, 8, 16, 19. This we wish to hold simply, yet firmly and with assurance.*

Second. On the Ban [Excommunication]. *We are agreed as follows The ban shall be employed with all those who have given themselves to the Lord, to walk in His commandments, and with all those who are baptized into the one body of Christ and who are called brethren or sisters, and yet who slip sometimes and fall into error and sin, being inadvertently overtaken. The same shall be admonished twice in secret and the third time openly disciplined or banned according to the command of Christ. Mt. 18. But this shall be done according to the regulation of the Spirit (Mt. 5) before the breaking of bread, so that we may break and eat one bread, with one mind and in one love, and may drink of one cup.*

Third. Eucharist or Communion: *In the breaking of bread we are of one mind and are agreed [as follows]: All those who wish to break one bread in remembrance of the broken body of Christ, and all who wish to drink of one drink as a remembrance of the shed blood of Christ, shall be united beforehand by baptism in one body of Christ which is the church of God and whose Head is Christ. For as Paul points out we cannot at the same time be partakers of the Lord's table and the table of devils; we cannot at the same time drink the cup of the Lord and the cup of the devil. That is, all those who have fellowship with the dead works of darkness have no part in the light Therefore all who follow the devil and the world have no part with those who are called unto God out of the world. All who lie in evil have no part in the good. Therefore it is and must be [thus]: Whoever has not been called by one God to one faith, to one baptism, to one Spirit, to one body, with all the children of God's church, cannot be made [into] one bread with them, as indeed must be done if one is truly to break bread according to the command of Christ.*

Fourth. On separation of the saved: *A separation shall be made from the evil and from the wickedness which the devil planted in the world; in this manner, simply that we shall not have fellowship with them [the wicked] and not run with them in the multitude of their abominations. This is the way it is: Since all who do not walk in the obedience of faith, and have not united themselves with God so that they wish to do His will, are a great abomination before God, it is not possible for anything to grow or issue from them except abominable things. For truly all creatures are in but two classes, good and bad, believing and unbelieving, darkness and light, the world and those who [have come] out of the world, God's temple and idols, Christ and Belial; and none can have part with the other.*

To us then the command of the Lord is clear when He calls upon us to be separate from the evil and thus He will be our God and we shall be His sons and daughters. He further admonishes us to withdraw from Babylon and the earthly Egypt that we may not be partakers of the pain and suffering which the Lord will bring upon them. From this we should learn that everything which is not united with our God and Christ cannot be other than an abomination which we should shun and flee from. By this is meant all popish and antipopish works and church services, meetings and church attendance, drinking houses, civic affairs, the commitments [made in] unbelief and other things of that kind, which are highly regarded by the world and yet are carried on in flat contradiction to the command of God, in accordance with all the unrighteouness which is in the world. From all these things we shall be separated and have no part with them for they are nothing but an abomination, and they are the cause of our being hated before our Christ Jesus, Who has set us free from the slavery of the flesh and fitted us for the service of God through the Spirit Whom He has given us.

Therefore there will also unquestionably fall from us the unchristian, devilish weapons of force – such as sword, armor and the like, and all their use [either] for friends or against one's enemies I would like the records – by virtue of the word of Christ, Resist not [him that is] evil.

Fifth. on pastors in the church of God: *The pastor in the church of God shall, as Paul has prescribed, be one who out-and-out has a good report of those who are outside the faith. This office shall be to read, to admonish and teach, to warn, to discipline, to ban in the church, to lead out in prayer for the advancement of all the brethren and sisters, to lift up the bread when it is to be broken, and in all things to see to the care of the body of Christ, in order that it may be built up and developed, and the mouth of the slanderer be stopped.*

This one moreover shall be supported of the church which has chosen him, wherein he may be in need, so that he who serves the Gospel may live of the Gospel as the Lord has ordained. But if a pastor should do something requiring discipline, he shall not be dealt with except [on the testimony of] two or three witnesses. And when they sin they shall be disciplined before all in order that the others may fear.

But should it happen that through the cross this pastor should be banished or led to the Lord [through martyrdom] another shall be ordained in his place in the same hour so that God's little flock and people may not be destroyed.

Sixth. concerning the sword: *The sword is ordained of God outside the perfection of Christ. It punishes and puts to death the wicked, and guards and protects the good. In the Law the sword was ordained for the punishment of the wicked and for their death, and the same [sword] is [now] ordained to be used by the worldly magistrates. In the perfection of Christ, however, only the ban is used for a warning and for the excommunication of the one who has sinned, without putting the flesh to death, – simply the warning and the command to sin no more.*

Now it will be asked by many who do not recognize [this as] the will of Christ for us, whether a Christian may or should employ the sword against the wicked for the defence and protection of the good, or for the sake of love.

Our reply is unanimously as follows: Christ teaches and commands us to learn of Him, for He is meek and lowly in heart and so shall we find rest to our souls. Also Christ says to the heathenish woman who was taken in adultery, not that one should stone her according to the law of His Father (and yet He says, As the Father has commanded me, thus I do), hut in mercy and forgiveness and warning, to sin no more. Such [an attitude] we also ought to take completely according to the rule of the ban.

Secondly, it will be asked, whether a Christian shall pass sentence in worldly disputes and strife such as unbelievers have with one another. This is our united answer: Christ did not wish to decide or pass judgment between brother and brother in the case of the inheritance, but refused to do so. Therefore we should do likewise.

Thirdly, it will be asked concerning the sword, Shall one be a magistrate if one should be chosen as such? The answer is as follows: They wished to make Christ king, but He fled and did not view it as the arrangement of His Father. Thus shall we do as He did, and follow Him, and so shall we not walk in darkness. For He Himself says, He who wishes to come after me, let him deny himself and take up his cross and follow me. Also, He Himself forbids the [employment of] the force of the sword saying, The worldly princes lord it over them, etc., but not so shall it be with you. Further, Paul says, Whom God did foreknow He also did predestinate to be conformed to the image of His Son, etc. Also Peter says, Christ has suffered (not ruled) and left us an example, that ye should follow His steps.

Finally it will be observed that it is not appropriate for a Christian to serve as a magistrate because of these points: The government magistracy is according to the flesh, but the Christians' is according to the Spirit; their houses and dwelling remain in this world, but the Christians' are in heaven; their citizenship is in this world, but the Christians' citizenship is in heaven; the weapons of their conflict and war are carnal and against the flesh only, but the Christians' weapons are spiritual, against the fortification of the devil. The worldlings are armed with steel and iron, but the Christians are armed with the armor of God, with truth, righteousness, peace, faith, salvation and the Word of God. ...

Seventh Concerning the oath: *The oath is a confirmation among those who are quarreling or making promises. In the Law it is commanded to be performed in God's Name, but only in truth, not falsely. Christ, who teaches the perfection of the Law, prohibits all swearing to His [followers], whether true or false, – neither by heaven, nor by the earth, nor by Jerusalem, nor by our head, – and that for the reason which He shortly thereafter gives, For you are not able to make one hair white or black. So you see it is for this reason that all swearing is forbidden: we cannot fulfill that which we promise when we swear, for we cannot change [even] the very least thing on us.*

John Calvin (1509-1564)

Christ also taught us along the same line when He said, Let your communication be Yea, yea; Nay, nay; for whatsoever is more than these cometh of evil. He says, Your speech or word shall be yea and nay. [However] when one does not wish to understand, he remains closed to the meaning. Christ is simply Yea and Nay, and all those who seek Him simply will understand His Word. Amen.[14]

- **Unitarian**: *On the Errors about the Trinity, The Restoration of Christianity*

Any discussion of the Trinity should start with the man. That Yahshua, surnamed Christ, was not a hypostasis but a human being is taught both by the early Fathers and in the Scriptures, taken in their literal sense, and is indicated by the miracles that he wrought. He, and not the Word is also the miraculously born Son of Yahweh in fleshly form, as the Scriptures teach – not a hypostasis, but an actual Son. He is an elohim, sharing Yahweh's divinity in full; and the theory of a communicatio idiomatum is a confusing sophistical quibble. This does not imply two Yahwehs, but only a double use of the term elohim, as is clear from the Hebrew use of the term. Christ, being one with Yahweh his Father, equal in power, came down from heaven and assumed flesh as a man. In short, all the Scriptures speak of Christ as a man.

'The doctrine of the Holy Spirit as a third separate being lands us in practical tritheism no better than atheism, even though the unity of Yahweh is insisted on. Careful interpretation of the usual proof -texts shows that they teach not a union of three beings in one but a harmony between them. The Holy Spirit as a third person of the Godhead is unknown in Scripture. It is not a separate being, but an activity of Yahweh himself. The doctrine of the Trinity can be neither established by logic nor proved from Scripture and is in fact inconceivable. There are many reasons against it. The Scriptures and the Fathers teach on Yahweh the Father and Yahshua Christ his son; but scholastic philosophy has introduced terms which are not understood and do not accord with Scripture. Yahshua taught that he himself was the Son of Yahweh. Numerous heresies have sprung from this philosophy and fruitless questions have risen out of it. Worst of all, the doctrine of the Trinity incurs the ridicule of the Mohammedans and the Jews. It arose out of Greek [metaphysical] philosophy rather than from the belief that Yahshua Christ is the Son of Yahweh; and he will be with the Church only if it keeps his teaching.[15]

The role of creeds, including historical creeds, varies in Protestantism. While some are upheld and even recited on a weekly basis, many Protestant believers have rejected the use and tradition of creeds, all together. Among those that accept the use of creeds, the Apostles' Creed and Nicene Creed are considered to be trans-denominational standards of the main beliefs in such groups (especially Anglican, Methodist, Lutheran, and some Reformed Churches).

I believe in God the Father, Almighty, Maker of heaven and earth;
And in Jesus Christ, His only begotten Son, our Lord;
Who was conceived by the Holy Ghost, born of the Virgin Mary;
Suffered under Pontius Pilate; was crucified, dead, and buried; He descended into hell;
The third day He rose again from the dead;
He ascended into heaven, and sitteth at the right hand of God the Father Almighty;
From thence He shall come to judge the quick and the dead.
I believe in the Holy Ghost.
I believe an holy catholic church; the communion of saints;
The forgiveness of sins;
The resurrection of the body;
And the life everlasting. AMEN.[16]

I believe in one God, the Father Almighty, Maker of heaven and earth, and of all things visible and invisible.

And in one Lord Jesus Christ, the only-begotten Son of God, begotten of the Father before all worlds; God of God, Light of Light, very God of very God; begotten, not made, being of one substance with the Father by whom all things were made.

Who, for us men and for our salvation, came down from heaven, and was incarnate by the Holy Spirit of the virgin Mary, and was made man; and was crucified also for us under Pontius Pilate; He suffered and was buried; and the third day He rose again, according to the Scriptures; and ascended into heaven, and sitteth on the right hand of the Father; and He shall come again, with glory, to judge the living and the dead; whose kingdom shall have no end.

And I believe in the Holy Spirit, the Lord and Giver of life; who proceedeth from the Father and the Son; who with the Father and the Son together is worshipped and glorified; who spoke by the prophets.

And I believe one holy catholic and apostolic church. I acknowledge one baptism for the remission of sins; and I look for the resurrection of the dead, and the life of the world to come.

Amen[17]

The Athanasian Creed is used by Lutherans and Anglicans, although its use in public worship is rare.

Whosoever will be saved, before all things it is necessary that he hold the Catholic faith. Which faith unless every one do keep whole and undefiled, without doubt he shall perish everlastingly. And the Catholic faith is this: that we worship one God in Trinity, and Trinity in Unity; neither confounding the Persons, nor dividing the Essence. For there is one Person of the Father; another of the Son; and another of the Holy Ghost. But the Godhead of the Father, of the Son, and of the Holy Ghost, is all one; the Glory equal, the Majesty coeternal. Such as the Father is; such is the Son; and such is the Holy Ghost. The Father uncreated; the Son uncreated; and the Holy Ghost uncreated. The Father unlimited; the Son unlimited; and the Holy Ghost unlimited. The Father eternal; the Son eternal; and the Holy Ghost eternal. And yet they are not three eternals; but one eternal. As also there are not three uncreated; nor three infinites, but one uncreated; and one infinite. So likewise the Father is Almighty; the Son Almighty; and the Holy Ghost Almighty. And yet they are not three Almighties; but one Almighty. So the Father is God; the Son is God; and the Holy Ghost is God. And yet they are not three Gods; but one God. So likewise the Father is Lord; the Son Lord; and the Holy Ghost Lord. And yet not three Lords; but one Lord. For like as we are compelled by the Christian verity; to acknowledge every Person by himself to be God and Lord; So are we forbidden by the Catholic religion; to say, There are three Gods, or three Lords. The Father is made of none; neither created, nor begotten. The Son is of the Father alone; not made, nor created; but begotten. The Holy Ghost is of the Father and of the Son; neither made, nor created, nor begotten; but proceeding. So there is one Father, not three Fathers; one Son, not three Sons; one Holy Ghost, not three Holy Ghosts. And in this Trinity none is before, or after another; none is greater, or less than another. But the whole three Persons are coeternal, and coequal. So that in all things, as aforesaid; the Unity in Trinity, and the Trinity in Unity, is to be worshipped. He therefore that will be saved, let him thus think of the Trinity.

Furthermore, it is necessary to everlasting salvation; that he also believe faithfully the Incarnation of our Lord Jesus Christ. For the right Faith is, that we believe and confess; that our Lord Jesus Christ, the Son of God, is God and Man; God, of the Substance [Essence] of the Father; begotten before the worlds; and Man, of the Substance [Essence] of his Mother, born in the world. Perfect God; and perfect Man, of a reasonable soul and human flesh subsisting. Equal to the Father, as touching his Godhead; and inferior to the Father as touching his Manhood. Who although he is God and Man; yet he is not two, but one Christ. One; not by conversion of the Godhead into flesh; but by assumption of the Manhood into God. One altogether; not by confusion of Substance [Essence]; but by unity of Person. For as the reasonable soul and flesh is one man; so God and Man is one Christ; Who suffered for our salvation; descended into hell; rose again the third day from the dead. He ascended into heaven, he sitteth on the right hand of God the Father Almighty,

> *from whence he will come to judge the living and the dead. At whose coming all men will rise again with their bodies; And shall give account for their own works. And they that have done good shall go into life everlasting; and they that have done evil, into everlasting fire. This is the Catholic faith; which except a man believe truly and firmly, he cannot be saved.*[18]

ECLECTIC BELIEFS

As can be seen thus far, Protestant belief and worship follows a wide spectrum of ideas and concepts about spiritual things, while upholding the "five *solas*" mentioned earlier. Some see the work of Protestantism as defined by what it is not (i.e., it is not the Roman Catholic Church), and this means it becomes more challenging (especially as the years go by) for Protestant groups to define who and what they are, now independent of Catholicism and generations from their founders' work and visions. Modern times have further complicated the differences within Protestant groups. Over the years, there have been several mergers between groups that found they had more in common than they did not, and several separations as churches struggle to define themselves in the advance of issues such as same-sex marriage, women's ordination, and the role of the church in modern society. Views on any issue vary from Protestant to Protestant. With the rise of the Internet and access to older writings and marginalized Protestant ideas, the world of Protestantism, as we understand it today, is rapidly changing. Protestants vary from liberal to conservative, and every conceivable idea in between.

As a result, Protestantism walks the fine line between spiritual independence and a commitment to the spiritual walk of church life. While maintaining unique opinion and freedom of thought, Protestants come together on matters they agree upon, finding themselves in communities of other believers who also feel as they do. Many, as a result, do not find themselves restricted to events or participation with one group, and may explore many different aspects of faith and practice in different Protestant groups, without compromising their church membership or participation in their existing organization.

One thing unique to all Protestants is their emphasis on missions and missionary work. Believing the call to proclaim the Gospel is essential, it is due to Protestant work and influence that Christian belief and influence is seen worldwide. Missions work was especially popular throughout the 1700s and 1800s, as missionaries were either sent out as denominational representatives or who braved the world on their own to preach the Gospel. Several important missionary efforts worked to improve hygiene, education, medical access, and care for women and children in addition to proclaiming the work of the Gospel.

While Protestant life is known for being very family-oriented, there are small orders of Protestant brothers and nuns. These men and women make the commitment through vows to serve, either for life or for a period of many years, through their understanding of religious life. They are best often known as living under a specified order or rule. Protestant monks and nuns are found in Anglican, Lutheran, and Methodist churches. There are also ecumenical orders that follow a united rule but do not require members to be from a specific Protestant denomination. These include the Porvoo Communion and Taize community.

RELATIONS WITH NON-PROTESTANTS

Protestants were the first religious group in history to engage in church ecumenism, starting with other Protestants. It has been a long-held tradition of many Protestant organizations to work with, discuss, and dialogue with other Protestants. Today, most Protestant denominations participate in ecumenical discussion and practice with Roman Catholics as well as other Protestants, and many denominations now participate in interfaith dialogue as well (especially with Jews and Muslims).

There are some Protestant groups that reject ecumenical or interfaith participation and dialogue, opting instead for church fellowships or communities of churches that adhere to and embrace their unique, specified views on theological, moral, social, or political issues.

HOLY SITES

Israel and Palestine, because of their connection to the life and ministry of Christ; Chapel of St. Peter-on-the-Wall (Anglican); Canterbury Cathedral (Anglican); St. Alban's Cathedral (Anglican); the Church of Christ (Anglican); All Saints' Church, Wittenberg (Lutheran); Eisleben, Germany (Lutheran); Heidelberg University (Lutheran and Reformed); Zurich, Switzerland (Reformed and Anabaptist); Transylvania (Unitarian); God's Square Mile at the Jersey Shore (Methodist); United Methodist Building in Washington, D.C. (Methodist); Upper Room Chapel (Methodist); The New Room (Methodist); German-speaking Europe (Anabaptists).

Ulrich Zwingli (1484-1531)

NOTABLE FIGURES

Martin Luther (1483-1546), founder of the Lutheran Church; John Calvin (1509-1564), founder of Calvinism; Henry VIII (1491-1547), founder of the Anglican communion; John Wesley (1703-1791), founder of the Methodist Church; Ulrich Zwingli (1484-1531), Reformer relevant in Reformed and Anabaptist traditions; John Knox (c. 1514-1572), Reformed leader; Ferenc David (1510-1579), Unitarian; Louisa May Alcott (1832-1888), author; Michelle Obama (1964-), former First Lady of the United States; Dorothea Dix (1802-1887), social reformer for the mentally ill; Angela Merkel (1954-), former German Federal Chancellor; Martin Luther King, Jr. (1929-1968), civil rights activist; William Booth (1829-1912), founder of the Salvation Army; Mary Wollstonecraft (1759-1797), American feminist and activist; Jennifer Garner (1972-), actress; Nelson Mandela (1918-2013), South African politician and activist.

NOTABLE GROUPS

Preterists are individuals who believe either a substantial portion or all of Biblical prophecy came to fulfillment in the first century: first with the Olivet Discourse (Matthew 24) fulfilled by 70 AD, and Revelation completed by the end of the first century. Preterists have never been a large group, but there have been many different Preterists in differing Protestant denominations throughout history. It first emerged in the Roman Catholic Church as an attempt to counteract the Reformation, but was then taken on by Protestant theologians, here and there, throughout the centuries. Some relevant Preterist figures include Hugo Grotius (1583-1645), Thomas Hayne (1582-1645), Joseph Hall (1574-1656), Henry Hammond (1605-1660), Firmin Abauzit (1679-1767), and Robert Townley. *Young's Literal Translation of the Bible* is considered a central Biblical translation among Preterists, as they consider it an accurate standard to prove their doctrine. Some Protestants consider Preterism to be heresy.[19]

FACTS AND FIGURES

In 2014, American Protestant church identity and attendance declined to 43.2%. This is down from 62.5% in 1972. Approximately 42% of Americans have a different religious identity than the one they grew up part of. In contrast, Protestant church identity and attendance in Latin America rose to 18%, up from 4% in 1970.[20,21]

OTHER IMPORTANT DEFINITIONS

- **Bishop**: A ruling individual who oversees a specific area of a church and represents that area in ecclesiastical matters. Specific to Lutheran, Episcopal, Methodist, and some Anabaptist groups. In some Protestant traditions, the term "Bishop," "elder," and "pastor" are used interchangeably.

- **Closed Communion**: A Protestant practice surrounding Holy Communion which limits those who are eligible to receive the elements of communion at a service for such. Eligiblity to receive communion may depend upon good standing or participation within a church denomination, exclusive to those of a denomination, receiving specific denominational instruction or doctrinal information, or membership within a specified local church.

- **Consubstantiation**: The belief that the presence of Jesus Christ is truly present in both the elements of bread and wine for communion, although there is no supernatural difference in the essential substance of these elements. The presence of Christ in these elements stems from the presence of Christ in the people of the church. This is a view held of communion by Lutherans and most Anglicans.

- **Ecumenical**: A Greek word meaning "worldwide" or "universal." In Protestantism, ecumenical refers to the work of churches and activities with other Christian groups. It is also used to refer to the "Ecumenical Movement," which promotes discussion among churches of different denominations (especially Roman Catholicism) for the purpose of inspiring church unity and healing differences.

- **Foot Washing**: An Anabaptist rite in which members of a congregation ceremonially wash one another's feet. Foot Washing is usually performed as part of Holy Communion.

- **Merger**: A term for when two or more Protestant denominations, usually of similar background or tradition, come together to form a new denominational body.

- **Lord's Supper**: Another term for the sacrament or ordinance of Holy Communion.

- **Minister**: A broad term in Protestantism for any ordained, elected, or licensed individual who is able to preach, perform the ordinances or sacraments, perform weddings and funerals, and serve the Protestant body as a leader of the people. Ministers may or may not be recognized across different Protestant denominations.

- **Open Communion**: A Protestant practice surrounding Holy Communion by which all participants present who desire to partake of the communion elements are able to do so, regardless of denomination. Most open communion policies require participants to be believers and/or baptized.

- **Order of Worship**: The form, or standard weekly structure of a Protestant service. Such is governed by the orders, or guides for worship.

- **Ordinances**: The Anabaptist term for what is called in some other Protestant churches as a "sacrament." The two recognized ordinances are water baptism and Holy Communion.

- **Pastor**: The term for a local Protestant church leader. In some traditions, Pastors are called elders or presbyters.

- **Polity**: A word used to describe the governing of a church. Polity may be episcopal (using bishops), hierarchical (more complicated than an episcopacy, as different leaders function on different levels to oversee matters); congregational (each congregation elects, or votes, on different matters and is self-governing); or elective (certain individuals are elected by bodies or by congregations to represent them on different levels).

- **Predestination**: A term to describe Calvin's doctrines of unconditional election and limited atonement. Predestination expounds these two belief systems as being decided, in advance, by God, fixed and unchangeable.

- **Real Presence**: Also called spiritual real presence, is the Reformed perspective on communion. It is seen as having an outward symbol of receiving communion elements while recognizing the spirituality of nourishment and Christian life. Reformists believe Christ, in body and blood are present in communion, but the experience is a spiritual one, rather than a literal eating of Christ's body and blood.

- **Sin**: That which is displeasing, in human nature and action, to God. Through Christ, Protestants believe individuals have the ability to be redeemed from sin. Within Protestantism, there are varying degrees of what role sin plays in one life and how one can overcome it.

- **Tithe**: A payment of ten percent of one's income, given to support and maintain the continuation of the church and its leaders. Throughout history, tithes have been paid in different ways: crops, goods, animals or animal products, or other objects. Monetary tithing has been the standard since the 1700s.

- **Waldenses**: A European church that broke away from Roman Catholicism in the twelfth century. They are sometimes known as the followers of Peter Waldo, although it is unclear if he started the group or was just a notable member of it. The Waldenses upheld many beliefs of the Protestant Reformation, and are, therefore, considered forerunners of the Reformation. They experienced intense persecution and violence, retreating to the Alps of France and Italy. There are small groups of Waldenses still in existence today.

BELIEVER'S CHARACTERISTICS

Identity with reformers; emphasis on the five "solas" of Protestantism; identity with a specific Protestant denomination; disagreement with papal control and the role of Catholic tradition; changing and interpretative beliefs; liberal, middle road, or conservative political views; emphasis on the Bible for answers to faith's questions, often with differing interpretations; belief in the importance of personal choice, opinion, and thought as making a difference in matters of faith; belief in the invisible universal church, extending outside of one's own denomination or immediate, local congregation; emphasis and importance in ecumenical and interfaith involvement, or the rejection of both; individuality; acceptance of same-sex marriage, or rejection of it, entirely; acceptance of female clergy, or rejection of it, entirely; relevance in Sunday church worship; study and spiritual evolution outside of traditional religion, in personal interpretation and development.

Roman Catholicism

We hold upon this earth the place of God Almighty.
(Pope Leo XIII)[1]

Theology

Belief in one true God, referred to as YAHWEH and revered by the term LORD, with personal attributes; eternally existent in three divine persons: God the Father, God the Son (Jesus Christ), and God the Holy Spirit; Creator and Sustainer of the people of God. Catholic theology is considered a continuation and expansion of Jewish theology as found in Old Testament history.

Roman Catholics believe the establishment and continuation of the Roman Catholic Church is by divine arrangement. Thus, Roman Catholics believe they share a special relationship with God, as it is the only church they view as legitimate. All other churches, theologies, and viewpoints are seen as offshoots or deviations (known as heresies) of their own.

Philosophy

Centers around the belief that the Roman Catholic Church is the one true church established by Jesus Christ at the Last Supper (believed to be the first liturgical mass celebration) and passed on through the twelve Apostles and their successors, by a process known as Apostolic Succession. Catholics believe this process began with Peter, who was the first pope. He, in turn, established another pope and other bishops upon his death, who then did the same upon their death, in an unbroken line down to the present day. For this reason, Catholics believe their religious tradition holds unbroken weight and line through said established authority, and that their doctrine and teaching are infallible.

Roman Catholics believe the Catholic Church is the kingdom of heaven come to earth, as the literal guardians of Matthew 16:18-19:

> *And so I say to you, you are Peter, and upon this rock I will build my church, and the gates of the netherworld shall not prevail against it. I will give you the keys to the kingdom of heaven. Whatever you bind on earth shall be bound in heaven; and whatever you loose on earth shall be loosed in heaven."*[2]

By their interpretation, they believe they hold the right through their teaching, doctrine, practice, and governance, to dictate what is allowed in heaven, as well as what happens and is permissible in heaven. The sacrifice of the mass, or the weekly liturgical worship service by which Holy

Eucharist is consecrated and offered every week, is the meeting of heaven and earth.

Roman Catholic structural authority is as follows: the Pope, as the Bishop of Rome, is the head of the international church. Below the pope, we find cardinals, bishops, priests, and deacons. Archbishops oversee larger dioceses or several smaller dioceses, while bishops oversee smaller dioceses. Auxiliary bishops are assistants to archbishops. Among priests we find monsignors, pastors (head parish priests), and assistant pastors (assist the head parish priest). Deacons serve as assistance workers to parish priests.

TRADITIONAL LANGUAGES

Latin.

ADHERENT IDENTITY

Roman Catholic, Catholic, Western Rite, Latin Rite, Roman Church, Byzantine Catholic, Old Catholic, and National Catholic, with some variations and subheadings among them. The term "Catholic" is used by many groups to indicate a worldwide, liturgical fellowship, and different groups who use such may or may not adhere to papal authority. The term "Catholic" is sometimes used with a national identity, such as Irish Catholic, Italian Catholic, Polish Catholic, etc.

MAJOR SECTS/DIVISIONS

Even though the Catholic Church portrays itself as unbroken and unfragmented, history isn't always quite so clear in the unity of Roman Catholicism or where the Latin rite begins or ends. There are many groups that make the same claims of succession and unbroken line, descending back to the beginning. Even though these groups may not consider themselves to be part of the church, we are including them here because their historical breakaway ties to the Catholic Church. There are many more than we can reasonably list here, so we shall list some major ones for our educational purpose.

- **Byzantine Rite**: Also called the Greek Rite or Constantinopolitan Rite. The Byzantine Rite churches are a cross between the Eastern Orthodox Church and the Roman Catholic Church. They are classified as "ethnic churches," meaning they are identified with the language and culture from which their liturgical worship derives. As opposed to forming in Rome with Latin origin, the worship of the Byzantine Rite stems from what is now modern-day Turkey in the Greek language. Today, their languages reflect the nations where they originated, and they follow the rites and structures of Eastern Orthodoxy (including its calendar) rather than Roman rite. They are considered governmentally independent but claim and adhere alignment with the pope in Rome. The exact number of these churches has changed throughout history, but at current, includes the Albanian Greek Catholic Church, Belarusian Greek Catholic Church, Bulgarian Greek Catholic Church, Byzantine Catholic Church of Croatia and Serbia, Greek Byzantine Catholic Church, Melkite Greek Catholic Church, Hungarian Greek Catholic Church, Italo-Albanian

Catholic Church, Macedonian Greek Catholic Church, Romanian Church United with Rome, Greek-Catholic, Russian Greek Catholic Church, Ruthenian Greek Catholic Church, Slovak Greek Catholic Church, and the Ukrainian Greek Catholic Church.[3]

- **Independent Catholicism**: Under the larger heading of the Independent Sacramental Movement, Independent Catholicism is a group of self-identifying Catholics who have no direct connection to Roman Catholicism in history nor division (although some are descendants of Old Catholics, inspired by Catholic events such as the Second Vatican Council, or otherwise imitators of the denominational structure). These organizations, though not rightly Roman Catholic, often make the same claims of authority (sometimes of succession) and often of sacramental practice as Roman Catholicism. They are autocephalous (self-governing), self-ordaining, and have their own modified form of Catholic liturgy, adopted from either the pre-Vatican II Tridentine (Latin) mass or a variation on current worship forms. Most Independent Catholic movements are desirable as they have a much broader view of ordination eligibility, and open the priesthood to women, individuals who are gender non-conforming or transgender, same-gender loving, and married (however, there are some that do not ordain women or honor same-sex couples). Independent Catholics are also more exploratory of traditions and rites outside of Catholic tradition, and many merge ideas from eastern religions, mystical traditions, and the New Age Movement. There are dozens of small, Independent Catholic movements, some of which include the American National Catholic Church, the Brazilian Catholic Apostolic Church, the Polish National Catholic Church, the Nordic Catholic Church, the Reformed Catholic Church, Community Catholic Church of Canada, the North American Catholic Ecumenical Church, Catholic Apostolic Church in North America, and the Ecclesia Apostolica Divinorum Mysteriorum.

Catholic Eucharist

- **Old Catholic Church**: Also known as the Ultrajectine tradition. The Old Catholic Church qualifies as Independent Catholicism, with one major difference. Unlike Independent Catholics who often have no formal connection to Roman Catholicism, the Old Catholic Church does. While having a complicated history, Old Catholics descend from Catholic theological sects influenced by Calvinist ideas in the 1600s and 1700s. Through many years of dissent and persecution, Old Catholics broke away with the Catholic Church after the first Vatican Council (1869-1870). By this time, Old Catholics disagreed with newly defined doctrines now in effect church canon such as papal infallibility, the Immaculate

Conception, and had questions of the doctrine of transubstantiation. Today, Old Catholics vary in their positions on some matters, with most embracing a wider view of inclusivity than the traditional church (married clergy, women clergy, LGBTQ+ clergy and membership, etc.), and some maintaining more traditional, conservative views of such issues. Old Catholics claim to be part of apostolic succession, believing their line to be the true, traditional line back to the time of the apostles. Old Catholics also vary in their embrace of outside influences, but most respect high Protestant liturgy and ordination, ecumenism, and incorporate tradition and rite outside of traditional Catholic tradition, including those from eastern, mystical, and New Age sources.

- **Traditionalist Catholicism**: Traditionalist Catholicism embraces the forms, rite, beliefs, custom, practice, and identity of Roman Catholicism prior to the Second Vatican Council (1962-1965). At the Second Vatican Council, major changes were made to the celebration of mass, the mass language changed from Latin to the vernacular of the people, church altars were changed to increase public participation, liturgical attire changed, ecumenical activity increased, and the overall attitude of the Catholic Church modernized. Not all Catholics felt the changes of Vatican II were upstanding, and some opted to adhere to and embrace the traditions withstanding between 1570 and 1970. There are two different headings of Traditionalist Catholicism: those in good standing with the Vatican, and those who are not. Those in standing with the Vatican embrace and embody older Catholic traditions while maintaining union with the Pope and Catholic regulation. Those not in standing with the Vatican adopt a variety of positions, including that of sedevacantism (every pope since John XIII is an invalid pope, there is no valid pope in Catholic rite today, and all rites and traditions of the church since Vatican II are invalid) and conclavists (those who have formed their own councils of bishops and Holy See to elect their own popes). There is an interest in traditionalist Catholicism in the United States, emerging over the past thirty years. Traditionalists groups in good standing with the Vatican include the Priestly Fraternity of St. Peter, Institute of Christ the King Sovereign Priest, Sons of the Most Holy Redeemer, Canons Regular of the New Jerusalem, Servants of Jesus and Mary, and Le Barroux Abbey. Some traditionalists groups not in standing with the Vatican include the Society of St. Pius X, Catholic Restoration, the True Catholic Church, Palmarian Catholic Church, the Congregation of Mary Immaculate Queen, and the Society of Saint Pius V.

- **Other Roman Catholic groups**: Religious orders, founded by specific figures in Catholic history, are by the names of their orders. Such include the Dominicans, Franciscans, Augustinians, Jesuits, Carmelites, Trappists, Salesians, Carthusians, Teutonic Order, Cistercians, Servites, Assumptionists, Poor Clares, Legionaries of Christ, Missionaries of Charity, Sisters of Mercy, Society of Mary, Society of the Divine Word, Order of Friars Minor, De LaSalle Brothers, Camilians, Maryknolls, and many others, all that have adherence within the Roman Catholic Church in structure and service.

Number of Adherents

There are approximately 1,200,000,000 individuals who consider themselves to be Roman Catholic worldwide.[4]

Disputes Within Group

Even though the Roman Catholic Church makes many claims about the unity of its adherents and acceptance of the major doctrines and practices of the church, recent decades have revealed how divided Roman Catholicism is from country to country, from parish to parish, and sometimes, even from Catholic to Catholic. Though educational requirements are in place, the way these implement vary among diocesan controls and parish programs. There are many disagreements among Catholic membership about the issue of women in the priesthood, the participation of LGBTQ+ individuals, birth control, abortion, politics, attitudes, and beliefs about the sacraments and what it means to be Catholic. Roman Catholic members tend to disagree on issues of a social nature. Recent scandals over priest sex abuse cases have caused further dispute and fraction over issues. The greatest modern dispute remains over the Second Vatican Council (1962-1965) and its implementations, necessity, and execution. There appears to be an upsurge in traditional Catholic ideas among American Catholics, thinking such will address the issues of spiritual and moral decay within its ranks.

Catholic church interior

Scriptures

The Holy Bible, both Old and New Testaments, including the Deuterocanonical Old Testament (a series of books included in between the Old and New Testaments, considered of inspirational dispute), thus creating a 72 book canon: the Pentateuch (Genesis, Exodus, Leviticus, Numbers, and Deuteronomy), Historical books (Joshua, Judges, Ruth, 1 Samuel, 2 Samuel, 1 Kings, 2 Kings, 1 Chronicles, 2 Chronicles, Ezra, Nehemiah, Esther), Wisdom books (Job, Psalms, Proverbs, Ecclesiastes, Song of Songs), Prophetic books (Isaiah, Jeremiah, Lamentations, Ezekiel, Daniel, Hosea, Joel, Amos, Obadiah, Jonah, Micah, Nahum, Habakkuk, Zephaniah, Haggai, Zechariah, Malachi), Deuterocanonical books (Tobit, Judith, 1 and 2 Maccabees, Wisdom of Solomon, Sirach, Baruch, Letter of Jeremiah, Greek additions to Esther, and Greek additions to Daniel, including the Prayer of Azariah, Song of the Three Holy Children, Susanna and the Elders, and Bel and the Dragon), the Gospels (Matthew, Mark, Luke, John), the Acts of the Apostles, the Pauline Epistles (Romans, 1 Corinthians, 2 Corinthians, Galatians, Ephesians, Philippians, Colossians, 1 Thessalonians, 2 Thessalonians, 1 Timothy, 2 Timothy, Titus, Philemon, Hebrews) the General Epistles (James, 1 Peter, 2 Peter, 1 John, 2 John, 3 John, Jude) and Revelation.

Traditionally speaking, Roman Catholics have relied on and used translations of the Latin

Vulgate as their Scriptures. The Roman Catholic Church must approve all translations in use for Catholics. All Catholic Bibles must include doctrinal footnotes to receive approval. Throughout the history of the printed word, there have been twenty-three Vatican-approved translations of the Bible. In modern times, these include the Douay-Rheims Bible, The New Jerusalem Bible, the New American Bible, and a specifically Catholic version of the Revised Standard Version.

The Catholic Lectionary, a book read during mass, features small portions of Scriptural readings on a three-year cycle. These readings vary from Scripture in a few different ways: they eliminate the Name of God (Yahweh) from their texts, and they sometimes omit specific verses or words from the portion to be publicly read during service. Most lectionary text does not match Biblical text. As of the writing of this book, there is a current project in place to introduce a singular accepted Catholic translation of the New Testament, used for private reading as well as lectionary service, known as The New American Bible Revised Edition.[5]

It is also worth mentioning as Roman Catholics see tradition equal to Scripture, there is a great emphasis on writings of the centuries following New Testament times. These writings are seen as formation of the tradition of the church (even when they may vary from what is doctrinal or understood in later or modern times). While these writings aren't classified as Scripture per se, they are believed to be important repositories of information as pertain to Catholic tradition and identity. Known as the Early Church Fathers, these writings were written in Greek, Latin, Syriac, and were written by individuals, both non-clergy and clergy, between 100 A.D. and 700 A.D. Some well-known Early Church Fathers include Clement of Rome, Polycarp, Barnabas, Ignatius, Justin Martyr, Irenaeus, Tertullian, Origen, and Clement of Alexandria.

BASIC RELIGIOUS PRACTICES

Roman Catholicism centers around the church family, both universal and local (experienced through a local parish), and the immediate family. Worship takes place at a local parish church on the first day of the week (Sunday) in the form of the mass. The mass is seen as a sacrifice, as offering the Body of Christ again, through the Eucharist, once again, through the work and office of the priest. The mass is a liturgical worship form divided into the Liturgy of the Word and the Liturgy of the Eucharist. The first part centers around lectionary readings and the second around communion. Catholic worship services contain hymns and or chants, atonement, prayers, Old and New Testament scripture readings, a homily, consecration, Eucharist, and dismissal. Followers of Roman Catholicism are expected to attend Sunday mass every week, receive the sacrament of confession at least once per year (before Trinity Sunday), adhere to the teachings of the church, submit and obey the pope and the church's leaders, and observe all Holy Days of Obligation, fast, and abstinence.

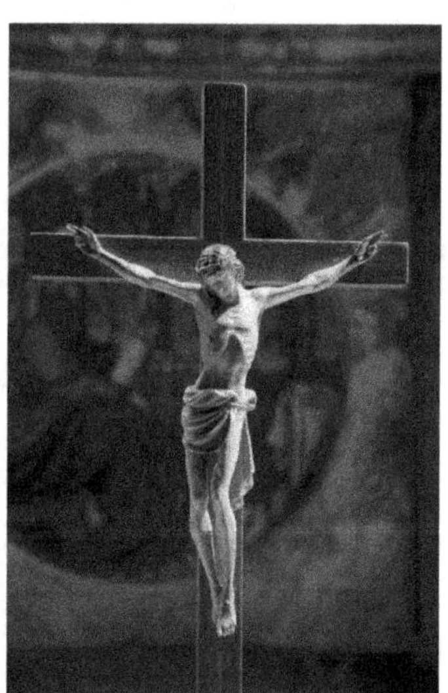
Crucifix

HOLIDAYS

The Roman Catholic Church observes a yearly liturgical calendar, divided up into seasons. These seasons begin in November with the season of Advent and run through Ordinary Time in October-early November. The seasons of the Roman Catholic Church are:

- **Advent**: The four Sundays preceding Christmas. Focuses on periods of waiting, as the Jews waited 4,000 years for the coming of the Messiah. Each week, a candle of coinciding color is lit on an advent wreath. The color is purple or blue (signifying royalty), except for the third week of Advent, which the color is pink (signifying joy). Officially ends on Christmas Eve.

- **Christmas**: Also called Christmastide, the period from Christmas (or the Sunday closest to Christmas, in years when Christmas falls on a Saturday or Monday) to the feats of the Baptism of the Lord in early January. The color is white, signifying purity.

- **Ordinary Time**: The period from the Sunday following the Baptism of the Lord until Ash Wednesday. The color is green, signifying life.

- **Lent**: Begins on Ash Wednesday and lasts until Palm Sunday. The color is purple. Focuses on repentance, mortality, and sin. All Catholics fourteen and older are expected to fast, abstain from meat on Fridays, and observe penance. Most Catholics speak of "giving up" something for Lent, as part of a Lenten fast. It may be a literal fast from food or something designed to help a Catholic focus in a greater way on their spiritual lives, such as giving up sweets, meat, social media, television, or internet usage. Some focus on other disciplines, such as trading in poor habits for good ones: exercising more, maintaining a better diet, reading more spiritual literature, or spending more time with family or in religious devotions. The color is purple, signifying royalty.

- **Holy Week**: Begins with Palm (or Passion) Sunday and ends with Holy Saturday (Easter Vigil). Palm Sunday Recalls Christ's procession into Jerusalem, riding on a donkey to the greeting of palm fronds and cheers by the people. The color is red, signifying blood and passion. The Easter triduum of Holy (Maundy) Thursday, Good Friday, and Holy Saturday are the three holiest days on the Catholic Calendar. Holy Thursday recalls the Passover feast of the Last Supper. Color is white, signifying purity. Good Friday recalls the crucifixion and death of Jesus Christ and is the only day of the year in which no mass is celebrated. Color is red, signifying blood and passion. Holy Saturday is the Easter Vigil, acknowledging the impending coming resurrection of Christ. Service is a long high mass, recounting major events of salvation history up to the resurrection. Mass begins in darkness with candles and at the time of resurrection celebration, the lights are turned on. On this night, new converts to Catholicism or returning Catholics are welcomed into the church. The color is white, signifying purity and new life.

- **Easter**: Begins on Easter Sunday and lasts until Pentecost Sunday. Celebrates the resurrection of Christ from the dead. The color is white, signifying purity and new life (gold is often incorporated, as well). As part of the Easter season, the Catholic Church observes the feasts of the Ascension and Pentecost.

- **Pentecost**: The official end to the Easter season. Acknowledges the descent of the Holy Spirit on the disciples. Considered to be the birthday of the church. The color is red, signifying the Holy Spirit.

- **Ordinary Time**: A long period of the church year, from the Sunday after Pentecost until the Advent season. During this period the church acknowledges many specialized feast days, including Trinity Sunday (the Sunday after Pentecost), the Feast of Corpus Christi (the Sunday after Trinity Sunday), and the Feast of Christ the King (last Sunday before Advent).

- **Holy Days of Obligation**: A Holy Day of Obligation is a day in the Roman Catholic Calendar by which mass attendance is required for all faithful Catholics in addition to regular, weekly Sunday mass attendance. These days are the Feast of Mary, Mother of God (January 1), Ascension Thursday (forty days after Easter Sunday), Assumption of Mary into heaven (August 15), All Saints' Day (November 1), the Feast of the Immaculate Conception (December 8), and Christmas Day (December 25).

In addition to these specific seasons and holiday observances, the Roman Catholic Church observes hundreds of specified feasts, memorials, solemnities, and optional memorials throughout the year that may vary by parish, nation of origin, or regional location. These special observances are feasts of saints, Marian feast days, special anniversaries or acknowledgements of apparitions or visions, or other special days of relevance to Catholics. Roman Catholics observe the General Roman Calendar, the instructions and details of which can be found in the Roman Missal and General Instruction of the Roman Missal. In 1969 the calendar and missal were revised, and many older feasts were removed (although they can still be observed regionally or in local parishes). Depending on the feast day, the "color" of the day may change. Some common feast days in Catholicism include: Presentation of the Lord (February 2), Chair of Saint Peter (February 22), Annunciation of the Lord (March 25), Our Lady of Fatima (May 13), Visitation of the Blessed Virgin Mary (May 31), Saints Peter and Paul (June 29), Immaculate Heart of Mary (Saturday after the second Sunday after Pentecost), Transfiguration of the Lord (August 6), Queenship of the Blessed Virgin Mary (August 22), Saints Michael, Gabriel, and Raphael, Archangels (September 29), Guardian Angels (October 2), All Souls Day (November 2), Saint Nicholas (December 6), and Holy Innocents (December 28).

VISUAL SIGNS AND SYMBOLS

Crucifix (a cross with the deceased body of Christ still affixed to it); three-dimensional statues; chants and prayers, sometimes in Latin; sign of the cross; rosary beads, prayer or devotional cards, and other prayer aids; candles; incense; unleavened bread and wine; priests; monks and nuns; convents and monasteries; elaborate clerical vestments; religious medals and charms; relics; observance of seven sacraments; cathedrals; parishes; Catholic schools; the papacy and the Vatican; the pope.

CREEDS, BOOKS, AND LAWS

The Roman Catholic Church is governed by canon law. Canon law is a specific code of church law that governs the church and the way it operates, functions, and believes. Canon law has evolved over the years and has held to different beliefs and editions as the need for such arose. Canon law originally evolved out of ecumenical, or worldwide church councils, by which all bishops would assemble to discuss and vote on the matters at hand. Since early in church history, council representation has been limited, as different groups distanced themselves from Roman rite and control, there hasn't been a full, worldwide representation of church governance since the 400s. In Catholicism, there have been twenty-one ecumenical councils, the last being the Second Vatican Council (1962-1965).

Summary of church doctrine and canon law is best known for its compilation in *The Catechism of the Catholic Church*. This large volume is divided into four sections which cover the essentials of Catholic faith: The Profession of Faith (discussing the Apostle's Creed), the Celebration of the Christian Mystery (Catholic liturgy and the sacraments), Life in Christ (the Ten Commandments from Catholic perspective) and Christian prayer (especially the Our Father).

> *The Catholic wisdom of the people... provides reasons for joy and humor even in the midst of a very hard life.*[6]

> *The Liturgy itself is prayer; the confession of faith finds its proper place in the celebration of worship.*[7]

> *The vocation of humanity is to show forth the image of God and to be transformed into the image of the Father's only Son. This vocation takes a personal form since each of us is called to enter into the divine beatitude; it also concerns the human community as a whole.*[8]

> *...The teaching of the Church has elaborated the principle of subsidiarity, according to which "a community of a higher order should not interfere in the internal life of a community of a lower order, depriving the latter of its functions, but rather should support it in case of need and help to co-ordinate its activity with the activities of the rest of society, always with a view to the common good.*[9]

> *The Church has no other light than Christ's; according to a favorite image of the Church Fathers, the Church is like the moon, all its light reflected from the sun.*[10]

> *Still, the Christian faith is not a "religion of the book." Christianity is the religion of the "Word" of God, a word which is "not a written and mute word, but the Word which is incarnate and living."73 If the Scriptures are not to remain a dead letter, Christ, the eternal Word of the living God, must, through the Holy Spirit, "open [our] minds to understand the Scriptures."*[11]

Catholic belief and regulation is also largely understood through the lens of its tradition, of beliefs that have emerged throughout the centuries, and through the writings of major church figures, such as St. Augustine of Hippo (354-430). The major Catholic creeds are the Apostles' Creed, the Nicene Creed, the Chalcedonian Creed, and the Athanasian Creed.

I believe in God,
the Father almighty,
Creator of heaven and earth,
and in Jesus Christ, his only Son, our Lord,
who was conceived by the Holy Spirit,
born of the Virgin Mary,
suffered under Pontius Pilate,
was crucified, died and was buried;
he descended into hell;
on the third day he rose again from the dead;
he ascended into heaven,
and is seated at the right hand of God the Father almighty;
from there he will come to judge the living and the dead.

I believe in the Holy Spirit,
the holy catholic Church,
the communion of saints,
the forgiveness of sins,
the resurrection of the body,
and life everlasting.

Nuns at an altar

Amen.[12]

We believe in one God, the Father, the Almighty, maker of heaven and earth, and of all that is, seen and unseen.

We believe in one Lord, Jesus Christ, the only Son of God, eternally begotten of the Father, God from God, Light from Light, true God from true God, begotten, not made, one in Being with the Father. Through him all things were made. For us men and for our salvation, he came down from heaven: by the power of the Holy Spirit he was born of the Virgin Mary, and became man. For our sake he was crucified under Pontius Pilate; he suffered, died, and was buried. On the third day he rose again in fulfillment of the Scriptures; he ascended into heaven and is seated at the right hand of the Father. He will come again in glory to judge the living and the dead, and his kingdom will have no end.

We believe in the Holy Spirit, the Lord, the giver of life, who proceeds from the Father and the Son. With the Father and the Son he is worshipped and glorified. He has spoken through the Prophets. We believe in one holy catholic and apostolic Church. We acknowledge one baptism for the forgiveness of sins. We look for the resurrection of the dead, and the life of the world to come.

Amen.[13]

We, then, following the holy Fathers, all with one consent, teach men to confess one and the same

Son, our Lord Jesus Christ, the same perfect in Godhead and also perfect in manhood; truly God and truly man, of a reasonable soul and body; consubstantial with us according to the manhood; in all things like unto us, without sin; begotten before all ages of the Father according to the Godhead, and in these latter days, for us and for our salvation, born of the virgin Mary, the mother of God, according to the manhood; one and the same Christ, Son, Lord, Only-begotten, to be acknowledged in two natures, inconfusedly, unchangeably, indivisibly, inseparably; the distinction of natures being by no means taken away by the union, but rather the property of each nature being preserved, and concurring in one Person and one Subsistence, not parted or divided into two persons, but one and the same Son, and only begotten, God the Word, the Lord Jesus Christ, as the prophets from the beginning have declared concerning him, and the Lord Jesus Christ himself taught us, and the Creed of the holy Fathers has handed down to us.[14]

Whoever wishes to be saved must, above all, keep the Catholic faith.
For unless a person keeps this faith whole and entire, he will undoubtedly be lost forever.
This is what the Catholic faith teaches: we worship one God in the Trinity and the Trinity in unity.
Neither confounding the Persons, nor dividing the substance.
For there is one person of the Father, another of the Son, another of the Holy Spirit.
But the Father and the Son and the Holy Spirit have one divinity, equal glory, and coeternal majesty.
What the Father is, the Son is, and the Holy Spirit is.
The Father is uncreated, the Son is uncreated, and the Holy Spirit is uncreated.
The Father is boundless, the Son is boundless, and the Holy Spirit is boundless.
The Father is eternal, the Son is eternal, and the Holy Spirit is eternal.
Nevertheless, there are not three eternal beings, but one eternal being.
So there are not three uncreated beings, nor three boundless beings, but one uncreated being and one boundless being.
Likewise, the Father is omnipotent, the Son is omnipotent, the Holy Spirit is omnipotent.
Yet there are not three omnipotent beings, but one omnipotent being.

Thus the Father is God, the Son is God, and the Holy Spirit is God.
However, there are not three gods, but one God.
The Father is Lord, the Son is Lord, and the Holy Spirit is Lord.
However, there as not three lords, but one Lord.
For as we are obliged by Christian truth to acknowledge every Person singly to be God and Lord, so too are we forbidden by the Catholic religion to say that there are three Gods or Lords.
The Father was not made, nor created, nor generated by anyone.
The Son is not made, nor created, but begotten by the Father alone.
The Holy Spirit is not made, nor created, nor generated, but proceeds from the Father and the Son.

There is, then, one Father, not three Fathers; one Son, not three sons; one Holy Spirit, not three holy spirits.
In this Trinity, there is nothing before or after, nothing greater or less. The entire three Persons are coeternal and coequal with one another.
So that in all things, as is has been said above, the Unity is to be worshipped in Trinity and the Trinity in Unity.
He, therefore, who wishes to be saved, must believe thus about the Trinity.

It is also necessary for eternal salvation that he believes steadfastly in the incarnation of our Lord Jesus Christ.
Thus the right faith is that we believe and confess that our Lord Jesus Christ, the Son of God, is both God and man.

As God, He was begotten of the substance of the Father before time; as man, He was born in time of the substance of His Mother.
He is perfect God; and He is perfect man, with a rational soul and human flesh.
He is equal to the Father in His divinity, but inferior to the Father in His humanity.
Although He is God and man, He is not two, but one Christ.
And He is one, not because His divinity was changed into flesh, but because His humanity was assumed unto God.
He is one, not by a mingling of substances, but by unity of person.
As a rational soul and flesh are one man: so God and man are one Christ.
He died for our salvation, descended into hell, and rose from the dead on the third day.
He ascended into heaven, sits at the right hand of God the Father almighty. From there He shall come to judge the living and the dead.
At His coming, all men are to arise with their own bodies; and they are to give an account of their own deeds.
Those who have done good deeds will go into eternal life; those who have done evil will go into the everlasting fire.
This is the Catholic faith. Everyone must believe it, firmly and steadfastly; otherwise He cannot be saved.

Amen.[15]

Of unique controversy is the doctrine of papal infallibility, introduced during the First Vatican Council. Papal infallibility teaches that on matters of faith and morals, the pope cannot err, as he is head of the international church. It is believed this ability comes as result of apostolic succession. Papal infallibility is part of the unique understanding of infallible revelation received from the divine to the church, and is considered on par with sacred Scripture, tradition, and magisterium (or teaching authority). The belief that the pope cannot lead astray in matters of doctrine is part of the infallibility of the magisterium.

ECLECTIC BELIEFS

Catholic teaching emphasizes the work of grace through the seven sacraments. These specific rites are the ways by which God works through the lives of Catholics and must be performed for grace to work in one's life. These seven sacraments are:

- **Sacraments of initiation**: So-called because they welcome and involve members of the Catholic Church into participation in different ways. They are baptism (sprinkling rite by which one becomes a member of the Catholic Church, removing what is known as the "stain of original sin"), Holy Communion (receipt of the sacrament of communion, believed to be the body and blood of Christ; first received when one is around eight years old), and

Confirmation (believed to be the reception of the Holy Spirit into a believer's life, as they become an adult member of their faith. Done as a bishop lays hands on a candidate and they adopt the name of a patron saint. Usually done in the late teens, somewhere between tenth and eleventh grade).

- **Sacraments of healing**: So-called because they are about facilitating healing in an individual, as one moves away from sin toward greater union with the divine through the Catholic Church. They are penance, or reconciliation (also called confession; so-called because one confesses their sins to a priest, seeking absolution for them. Most Catholics receive their first confession prior to first Holy Communion, around the age of eight years old), and Anointing of the Sick (also known as Extreme Unction), by which any member of the church who is ill can seek out a priest to anoint them with blessed oil and prayer for healing).

People at mass

- **Sacraments of service**: So-called because they relate to the way one lives out their vocation, or life calling, as they serve the church. They are Holy Orders (the rite by which a man is ordained as a deacon, priest, or bishop, following seminary study) and Matrimony (rite by which a man and woman are married in the eyes of the church). Matrimony is only observed between two opposite-sex cisgender individuals who have never been married in the eyes of the Roman Catholic Church prior (individuals who are divorced and remarried cannot receive communion). Catholics do not recognize marriage between same-sex partners or transgender individuals.

The commitments of a woman to serve in a religious order as a nun (or religious sister) or as a monk or brother not ordained to the priesthood are not considered a part of Holy Orders or Matrimony. Instead, such is part of consecrated religious life, by which one is bound by vows of poverty, chastity, and obedience. Priests and bishops are required to be celibate, never marrying throughout their lives. Deacons can marry if they do not go on to serve in the priesthood.

Catholics also have a unique doctrine as pertains to sin, believing there are two categories of sin: mortal and venial. Mortal sin indicates if one dies with that sin on their conscience, they will not be able to enter heaven (the presence of God and the saints) when they die. Venial sin indicates it is a sin and an offense against God, but not to the degree that one will find themselves damned to hell for all of eternity. Those who die with venial sins on their conscience will go to purgatory, a place where any remaining sin is purged from one's conscience. To avoid purgatory or hell, Catholics must receive the sacrament of confession (reconciliation), including a final confession before death to die in a state of grace.

Catholic doctrine is notably complex, with many layers and cultural variations, depending on country and region. Many Catholics have absorbed pagan traditions and superstitions into their belief systems, with saints named in place of ancient gods or deities and the practice of specific rituals of the church renaming these ancient practices. Catholics believe in the power of praying to saints for the purpose of intercession or specific benediction or blessing, of the power in blessed objects (such as holy water, religious medals, scapulars, or anointing oil), and of the use of relics (pieces of bone, hair, clothing, or other objects from a deceased saint or blessed by one). In modern times, Catholics are notorious for their stance against abortion and the death penalty and in the prohibition of any form of medical or external contraception.

Relations With Non-Catholics

Because the Roman Catholic Church sees itself as singular in authority and superior to other churches, this makes for complicated relationships with outside groups. Since the Second Vatican Council, Roman Catholicism has taken an authoritarian role in ecumenical and interfaith councils and dialogue, particularly with Orthodox churches, Protestants and Jews. In more recent years, there is interest in dialogue with Muslims. A great emphasis is now placed on reuniting all churches deemed "lost" (all non-Roman Catholic Christian churches) by Catholicism to Rome. Interfaith marriage remains frowned upon, and non-Catholics are required to sign a statement affirming that any children will be raised in the Roman Catholic Church.

Holy Sites

The Catholic Church is headquartered in Vatican City, which is an independent country located within the city of Rome, Italy. It is the only entirely religious entity with a seat on the United Nations. The Holy See, Apostolic Palace of the Pope, St. Peter's Basilica, the Sistine Chapel, and the Vatican museums are all located in Vatican City. The lands of Israel and Palestine are also of interest to Roman Catholics, as they are regarded as central to the life of Christ. There are also other assorted sites holy to Catholics found throughout the world, including major sites of saintly devotion, location of tombs and relics, and apparition sites, such as in Fatima, Portugal, and Medjugorje, Yugoslavia.

Notable Figures

John Paul II (1920-2005), pope from 1978-2005; Mother Angelica (1923-2016), founder of the Eternal Word Television Network; Scott Hahn (1957-), Protestant convert to Catholicism; Mel Gibson (1956-), movie actor and director; Andre Bocelli (1958-), tenor; Stephen Colbert (1964-), American comedian and writer; Maggie Gallagher (1960-), conservative activist; Dean Koontz (1945-), novelist; John Michael Talbot (1954-), songwriter and singer; Audrey Assad (1983-), contemporary Christian artist; Anne Rice (1941-2021), novelist.

NOTABLE GROUPS

Opus Dei, founded by Josemaria Escriva (1902-1975) in 1928, is the first Catholic personal prelature (an overseer, clergy, and laity group take on specific religious activities) program. There are close to one hundred thousand members worldwide; about 70% of membership consists of laity. As an organization, Opus Dei is highly controversial in its nature, believing holiness and sanctity can be achieved through everyday life. Members of Opus Dei organize programs to encourage their view of faith, believing they must train Catholics to transform the secular world from within themselves. Opus Dei has been called the "most controversial force in the Catholic Church," as the organization often operates in excessive and aggressive recruitment, support of extreme political ideologies, and secretive practices. Some members have also been known to engage in the practice of "mortifying the flesh," by methods such as flagellation, beating, and excessive fasting.[16]

FACTS AND FIGURES

39% of Roman Catholics attend mass weekly;[17] this is down from 45% between 2005 and 2008.[18] 22% of the US population is Roman Catholic,[19] while 16% of the world population is Roman Catholic.[20] Roman Catholics comprise 50% of all those identifying with Christian religion worldwide.[21]

Marian statue

OTHER IMPORTANT DEFINITIONS

- **Apparition**: A phantom or ghostlike appearance of a deceased being, such as the Virgin Mary or a saint, with a message for mankind. Popular apparition sites include Fatima, Portugal, Guadalupe, Mexico, La Vang, Vietnam, and Medjugorje, Yugoslavia. There are different types of apparitions, such as when one might receive a message without seeing a form, one actually sees the form, and when certain specified miracles are displayed as part of the apparition, such as natural or solar phenomena. The realm of apparitions is controversial, and for such to be approved by the Catholic Church, a team of investigators through regional dioceses and eventually the Vatican must research the claims and associated phenomena.

- **Canonization**: A term used to describe the formal process by which a deceased individual becomes an acknowledged saint in the Catholic Church. While any deceased Catholic individual can be venerated in private or regional devotion, canonization is acknowledgement of such an individual beyond private devotion. Canonization is a long and involved process by which the life of an individual is examined through four stages, initially on a diocesan level, and then finally through the approval of Rome: "servant of God," "venerable," "blessed," and finally, "saint." For an individual to be declared a "saint," there must be three recorded and authentic miracles due to intercession in their name, as such is believed to prove the individual is in heaven. The process requires both petition and cause, and is very expensive from start to finish.

- **Dogma**: A specified belief principle or group of such that, as is laid down, established, and taught by the Roman Catholic Church, is believed by their membership to be true, without alteration or change.

- **Ecumenical**: A Greek word meaning "worldwide" or "universal." In Catholic understanding, ecumenical refers to one of two things. The first is the worldwide nature and concept of Catholicism, present through the bishops and their leadership, reflective in terminology such as an "ecumenical council." The second definition is from the "Ecumenical Movement," which promotes discussion among churches of different denominations for the purpose of inspiring church unity and healing differences.

- **Eucharist**: A Greek word meaning "thanksgiving." Used as another term for Holy Communion.

- **Holy See**: The term used to describe the jurisdictional, or territorial authority of the pope, also called the Bishop of Rome. Rather than just restricting authority to an immediate diocese or region, the Holy See is described to extend worldwide. The Holy See is overseen by the Roman Curia, the governmental authority of the Vatican.

- **Immaculate Conception**: The belief that Mary was conceived without original sin and preserved from personal sin throughout her life. This doctrine was introduced during the first Vatican Council in 1870, coinciding with the apparition of Our Lady of Lourdes in which Catholics believe Mary appeared and identified herself as the "Immaculate Conception."

- **Indulgences**: The belief that one can, by specific actions this side of eternity, reduce the number of days in they shall be subject to purgatory after death. There are a few ways indulgences can be obtained, such as reading the Bible or praying specific prayers. The most infamous example of indulgences, however, is the church's sale of such, in order to construct St. Peter's Basilica in the fourteenth and fifteenth centuries. The sale of indulgences was outlawed in 1567, while the continued idea of donating to charity as an indulgence continues. There is a perceived limit now, of one full indulgence per sinner per day.

- **Limbo**: A unique Catholic doctrine, considered to be the place on the very edge or boundary of hell, where those who die in original sin will spend eternity. The way to avoid facing eternity in limbo is to receive a Catholic baptism, thus why the Catholic Church baptizes infants.

- **Mariology**: The study of Mary, mother of Jesus, and her role in salvation. Mariology takes many forms in Roman Catholic doctrine, including her identity as the Immaculate Conception, perpetual virgin (never having any sexual relationship or other children in her marriage with Joseph), co-redemptrix (a secondary redeemer, involved in the redemption of all mankind), and mediatrix (secondary role of Mary as a mediator between God and men).

- **Rosary**: A set of prayer beads used in prayer to and through the Virgin Mary. Rosaries are divided into ten decades of beads on which specific prayers are said. A typical rosary recitation follows with repetitions of the Our Father, followed by ten Hail Marys, and one "Glory Be" prayer. Each decade gives thoughts to a mystery of the Rosary, of which there are twenty different ones about the life of Jesus and Mary. Specific mysteries are considered on different days of the week.

- **Tabernacle**: A special box that is used to contain consecrated communion hosts (the "bread" of communion, those that have been blessed for communion) after the mass is completed. In Catholic tradition, these hosts can be used when mass cannot be said, in what is known as a Eucharistic Prayer Service, to be brought to shut-ins, or used in last rites, for the terminally ill.

- **Transubstantiation**: Catholic belief that the bread and wine of communion becomes the literal body and blood of Christ as part of the mass rite. Such is believed to happen during the consecration, by mysterious process, when the priest offers specific prayers and recitations as part of the liturgical tradition.

BELIEVER'S CHARACTERISTICS

Though levels of adherence and devotion do vary based on believer, overall there is an emphasis on parish participation, especially embracing the need for priests and the work of the Catholic Church; belief in sacraments as dispensations of grace; emphasis on suffering and sacrifice for salvation; believing one's actions are part of one's salvation; superstitious tendencies; identity and prayer to saints; Marian devotions; use of statues, rosaries, or other Catholic prayer objects; cultural Catholic identity; weekly mass participation; observance of various feasts and obligations; obedience to the pope; belief in apparitions; use of a crucifix; belief in aspects of the afterlife that are unique to Catholics, such as limbo and purgatory; praying for or to the deceased; belief that communion is the literal body and blood of Christ; emphasis on tradition.

Sacred Name/Hebrew Roots Movements

Why, if the sacred name is considered so important in the Scriptures, do most of the religious teachings of the numerous Judeo-Christian and Moslem sects set its doctrine aside? In a word eisegesis: the uncanny quality of human nature which insists upon reading into any given issue one's own personal ideas and interpretations. For example, it is always fascinating and entertaining to watch the bizarre and humorous alterations of a story as it passes from one child to the next in a parlor game. By the time it has reached the ninth or tenth ear the original story can hardly be recognized. This amusing game serves as a poignant reminder that humans in general are prone to place their own personal understanding into whatever they see, hear, and read.

(*The Sacred Name*, Vol. 1)[1]

Theology

Belief in one true God, emphasizing the need to use the divine name of said deity in writing, address, prayer, preaching, Scripture, and worship. This divine Name comes from the Hebrew tetragrammaton, YHVH, often translated in English as YAHWEH or JEHOVAH. Within the Sacred Name and Hebrew Roots movements there is often a strict interpretation and rendering of those names into transliterated Hebrew versions and variations of possible vowel combinations, along with the main consonants. Some variations of these names include YEHOVAH, YAH, YAHVAH, YAHVEH, YOHWAH, and YHWH. General titles and terminology for God also change; GOD becomes ELOHIM, and LORD becomes YAHWEH or ADONAI. YAH is seen as having personal attributes, Creator of the world, and Sustainer of His people. YAH is the true God; there is no other.

Jesus Christ is also referenced by Hebrew terms such as YESHUA, YAHSHUA, YHWHHOSHUA, YAHUSHUA, and YEHUSHUA. He is seen as the Messiah, the anointed one of Israel. There are a few different interpretations of who Yeshua is within the Sacred Name and Hebrew Roots Movements; some see Yeshua as fully divine, while others reject divinity all together. Yeshua is a personal Savior, but one is still rewarded according to their works, deeds, and obedience to the Torah (law). The Holy Spirit is frequently referred to as the Ruach or Ruach HaKodesh, and is seen as an invisible, dynamic life force, as the power that emanates from the Father and the Son.

The majority of the Sacred Name and Hebrew Roots Movement adopt variations of theologies against the standard understandings of Trinitarian and Oneness definitions of the divine (although there are very small numbers of Sacred Name and Hebrew Roots adoptees that are Trinitarian or Oneness). Most argue the Trinity doctrine is pagan, and Oneness theology is too closely Trinitarian for the movement's comfort. Some see the Godhead as unique to the Father and the Son, with the Son always subordinate to the Father (Divine Monarchism); some go on to say the Godhead will later expand to include all believers after the return of Christ; some embrace the idea of Biblical Unitarianism, seeing the Father, Son, and Holy Spirit as three separate entities (regarding Jesus as a moral Rabbi and spiritual way to the Father, while rejecting his divinity; the Spirit is seen as a force).

The major theology of the Sacred Name and Hebrew Roots Movement focuses on- the value and identity of God and Christ as Hebrew the interpretation of which is unique to them), believing it is essential and important to see theology and faith through an interpretive Old Testament viewpoint. Anything seen as pagan or of questionable origin is rejected and considered false.

Philosophy

The Sacred Name Movement and Hebrew Roots Movement are technically two different movements whose theologies and ideologies overlap in many ways, especially in modern influences. Whereas in their original forms the Sacred Name Movement identified with denominations, the Hebrew Roots Movement introduced the idea of independent practitioners, absorbing many different ideals from both Sacred Name and Hebrew Roots sources. The Sacred Name Movement is an outgrowth of the Adventist movement, an Evangelical-based movement started by a man named William Miller (1782-1849). Miller believed he was able to determine the date of Jesus Christ's Second Coming through careful study of Biblical prophecy and creating a dating system from the beginning of time to the mid-1800s. He used what is known as the "day-year principle," in which the word "day" in Biblical prophecy is the equivalent of one year of chronological time. The series of dates predicted, calculated, and recalculated were as follows: first the fall of 1843, then March of 1844, then April of 1844, and finally, October 22, 1844. When these dates came and went without manifestation, the event became known as "the Great Disappointment." Many returned to their own lives, some abandoned faith all together, and others came to believe that William Miller did indeed discover the "start" of something in 1844, but it was not the Second Coming. These people became known as Adventists. A small group of Adventists believed Miller's discovery was the dating for an end times investigative judgment, coming to fruition at the end of a 2300-day period (ending in 1844). The first Sacred Name adherents were those who, along with Seventh-day Adventists, believed in the relevance of the Seventh-day Sabbath and Ten Commandments for believers in modern times. While the Seventh-day Adventists followed the teachings and guidance of Ellen G. White, the Sacred Name Movement became its own entity, focusing on Biblical festivals, the divine Name, and Sabbath observance. The Hebrew Roots Movement is a broader category of loosely connected beliefs, all of which also reflect in the Sacred Name Movement. It has existed without hierarchy, thus becoming a collective of groups, including Messianic Judaism, the Sacred Name Movement, Nazarenes, Seventh-day Pentecostals, and independent practitioners combining the beliefs of Sacred Name and Hebrew Roots.

The essential message of both movements is the desire to restore the church to its foundational roots, seen as being "Hebrew." These foundational roots include the use of the properly understood sacred, or divine names of God and of Jesus Christ, in what is seen as the original Hebrew form; observance of the Seventh-day Sabbath; Old Testament Torah festivals; and Old Testament dietary laws. Adherents believe Christianity is an outgrowth of traditional

Judaism (not modern Jewish understanding) and believe those who accept Jesus as the Messiah become part of a traditional Hebrew understanding, which requires strict Torah (especially the 613 laws of the first five books of the Bible) observance. Yeshua did not come to do away with the law, but to prove that God's law (the Torah) is of divine origin, while the traditions of the "oral law" (the Jewish Talmud) were not enforceable as divine law. How such is enforced, what of the Torah is enforced, and how such is applied is of considerable disagreement and debate. Not all Hebrew Roots and Sacred Name adherents uphold Torah law in the same way or consider such to be on the same level or value. More relevant to adherents is their emphasis on Biblical law, applying such in one's life, and seeing their life of faith through a personal or corporate concept, defining just what it means to be "Hebrew" considering the New Testament.[2]

Adherent Identity

Sabbatarian; Sabbatarianism; Hebrew Christian; Messianic Jew; Nazarene; Armstrong adherent; Awakening; Awake; group that varies by church membership (such as Church of God Seventh Day, Seventh-day Pentecostal, Assembly of Yahweh); Disciple of Yah or Yahweh.

Traditional Languages

English, with a strong interest in Semitic languages, especially Hebrew and Aramaic; there is also a secondary interest in the Peshitta, originally composed in Syriac.

Sects/Divisions

The Sacred Name and Hebrew Roots Movements are divided into a few main groups that can be easily categorized.

- **Church of God (Seventh Day)**: Also known as CoG7, the Church of God (Seventh Day) is a grouping of several different Sabbatarian churches, all offshoots of the Adventist Movement. It divided with Seventh-day Adventists over the acceptance of Ellen G. White's (1827-1915) documents as prophecy, thus establishing a separate group. As among the first Sabbatarians, CoG7 traces Saturday Sabbath observance back to the book of Genesis: in the creation account, it states God rested from creation on the seventh day of the week. It was then reaffirmed in the Ten Commandments, by which God commanded Israel to remember the Sabbath day and keep it holy." They are Divine Monarchists, refrain from holidays such as Christmas or Easter, embrace the doctrine of "soul sleep" (mankind is sleeping, awaiting the resurrection after death), the essential nature of tithing, and objection to military service. The Church of God (Seventh Day) received its claim to fame through C.O. Dodd (1899-1955), an author, magazine editor, and active church member who publicly encouraged the practice of Old Testament festivals.

Church of God (Seventh-Day) logo

- **<u>Messianic Judaism</u>**: Messianic Judaism is questionable in its identity; it's uncertain if it is Judaism or Evangelical Christianity with elements of Judaism interspersed. Many Jews do not consider Messianic Judaism to be a valid form of Judaism, simply because accepting Jesus as the Messiah is contraindicative of Jewish understanding. Though established as a general movement 1916, it evolved in the 1960s through the Charismatic Movement when Jews came to believe Christ was the Messiah, while maintaining many traditional Jewish elements of their faith. Messianic Jews vary on their theology, but believe Christ reaffirmed the Law, rather than fulfilling it, and that the written regulation of the Old Testament is still applicable today. Much of Messianic Judaism views the New Testament canon as questionable and there are some who disregard portions of the apostolic letters, especially those written by the Apostle Paul. These groups include Messianic Jewish Alliance of America, Jews for Jesus, and the Union of Messianic Jewish Congregations.

- **<u>The Assemblies</u>**: Many Sacred Name and Hebrew Roots affiliates take issue with the use of the word "church," as they feel such does not capture a Hebrew understanding. As a result, many opt for other identities, such as "assembly." The assemblies are an assorted number of groups (all with very similar beliefs) that vary in governance and understanding about their place in a larger association of believers. Some have grown far beyond their immediate congregations while others have remained small and exclusive. They are unified in their use of Hebrew names (especially Yahweh and Yahshua), observance of the Sabbath day and Old Testament Biblical festivals, rejection of holidays such as Christmas and Easter (regarded as pagan), universal rejection of Trinitarianism and Oneness theologies (opting instead for Divine Monarchism or Biblical Unitarianism), requirement to tithe, requirement that believers must follow the laws found in the Old Testament, a belief in a command to modest attire, and most, if not all, are opposed to military service. Such groups include the Assemblies of the Called Out Ones of Yah, Assemblies of Yahweh, Assembly of Yahvah, Assembly of Yahweh, Assembly of YHWHHOSHUA, House of Yahweh, Worldwide Assembly of YHWH, Yahweh's Assembly in Messiah, and Yahweh's New Covenant Assembly.

- **<u>Sabbatarian Pentecostals</u>**: Also called Seventh-day Pentecostals, Sabbatarian Pentecostalism is a Hebrew Roots mixing of Sacred Name ideas, Hebrew concepts, and traditional Pentecostalism. Sabbatarian Pentecostals embrace spiritual gifts (especially speaking in tongues) along with Pentecostal holiness and Sacred Name doctrines including the divine name in Hebrew, seventh-day Sabbath observance, observance of Old Testament festivals, and a strong interest in the Old Testament. In contrast with many Sabbatarian churches, Sabbatarian Pentecostals are often of Oneness or Modalistic theology and many baptize according to Acts 2:38. Such groups include the Association of Seventh-Day Pentecostal Assemblies, Seventh Day Pentecostal Church, Church of God (Seventh-day) Pentecostal, or other smaller, assorted independent churches with similar beliefs.

- **Armstrongism**: The largest and, arguably, most successful of all Sacred Name groups, Armstrongism is a breakaway group from the Church of God (Seventh Day). The Armstrong sect was established by Herbert W. Armstrong (1892-1986) in 1934, first as the Radio Church of God and then the Worldwide Church of God (WCG). Armstrong's work (which is featured in its entirety in a separate section) varied from CoG7 on one major point: that of British Israelism, which is an alternate historical interpretation of monarchy. British Israelism teaches the ten lost tribes of Israel are the genetic, racial, and language descendants of the ten lost tribes of Israel and the throne of David is now the seat of the British monarchy. Even though this theory has notable historical issues and numerous theological inaccuracies (and is the foundation of white supremacist religion in the United States), British Israelism became a founding point within the Armstrong movement.[3] It determined much of how Armstrong saw the modern-day times, including the interpretation of prophecy as connecting to many different nations (including the United States, the European Union, China, and Russia). Despite its issues, Armstrongism gained great momentum in the United States, thanks to excellent use of advertising, broadcasting, and publications, especially *The Plain Truth* magazine. His followers believed God could only work through one man at a time, raising Armstrong to the rank of an apostle. Like other Sabbatarians, they emphasize Divine Monarchism, Sabbath observance, tithing, observance of Old Testament law and festivals, "soul sleep," and objection to military service. Unique to Armstrongism is the belief in a literal doctrine of faith healing, whereby adherents are forbidden to receive medical care, a three-tier tithing system (members give 30% of their income rather than 10%); rejection of the use of cosmetics, long hair on men, and the idea that at the end of time, all true followers will become part of the divine family. Armstrong was best-known for meeting different world leaders throughout his lifetime, numerous failed prophecies, and family conflicts, especially toward the end of his life. After Herbert Armstrong died, the movement descended into chaos, as different individuals in the movement debated over the appointed successor. This created several splinter groups, many of which are still in operation today. The Worldwide Church of God, under the leadership of Joseph Tkach (1927-1995) changed doctrine and direction, and the organization today (unrecognizable from the original group) now resembles a typical Evangelical Christian church and is part of the National Association of Evangelicals. It changed its name to Grace Communion International in 2009. Some groups that remain faithful to Armstrong's original vision include Church of God International, Christian Biblical Church of God, Philadelphia Church of God, Church of the Great God, Global Church of God, United Church of God, Living Church of God, Restored Church of God, and Continuing Church of God.[4,5]

- **The Hebrew Roots Black Identity Movement**: As one branch of the Black Identity Movement, there are groups that could fall into the Sacred Name/Hebrew Roots category that believe African Americans are the rightful descendants of the ancient Israelites. Such movements incorporate elements of Christianity, Judaism, and their own unique Biblical interpretations into religious practice. The movement began in the late nineteenth century with the work of Frank Cherry (c. 1875-1963) and William Saunders

Crowdy (1847-1908), who claimed to have visions affirming the identity of the African Americans as Hebrew descendants. The earliest organizations were the Church of the Living God, the Pillar Ground of Truth for All Nations (1886) and the Church of God and Saints of Christ (1896). Several other smaller groups emerged, concentrated between the Midwest and east coast over the next few decades. Most adherents are African American or descendants of West Indian immigrants. These groups believe the twelve tribes of Israel can be found in modern-day tribal groups (Judah: American blacks, Benjamin: West Indian blacks, Levi: Haitians, Ephraim: Puerto Ricans, Manasseh: Cubans, Simeon: Dominicans, Zebulon: Mayans from Guatemala to Panama, Gad: Native-American Indians, Reuben: Seminole Indians, Asher: Incas from Columbia to Uruguay, Issachar: Aztecs in Mexico, and Naphtali: Argentina/Chile). The Hebrew branches represent a diversity of beliefs and practices, and many practice historical revisionism, which present altered versions of historical details and accounts to promote the views and ideas of the group. Of particular interest is the belief that African Americans are the biological descendants of the Israelites, often traced through either a specific Biblical figure (such as Solomon) or through all Biblical figures, also believed to be African American ancestors. The most notable division between such groups is those that are messianic (embracing of Jesus Christ as a central messianic figure) and those who do not, embracing a modified interpretation of Jewish worship or identity. Perhaps the best known of these groups are those Hebrew Israelites that embrace the idea of black supremacy, believing modern Jewish groups are the devil and also condemning whites as evil figures worthy of death and enslavement. These views are not held by all Hebrew Israelites, but those that do embrace such views include the Israelite School of Universal Practical Knowledge, the Nation of Yahweh, the Israelite Church of God in Jesus Christ, and the Twelve Tribes of Israel. Other Hebrew Israelite groups include the Rastafari (Rastafarians), Commandment Keepers, and African Hebrew Israelites of Jerusalem. More on such groups is explored under the Black Identity Movement section found within this book.

- **Independent Practitioners**: The Hebrew Roots Movement recognizes no official hierarchy, church denomination, or specific organization to provide formalized doctrine or guidance. While much of the Hebrew Roots Movement embraces different forms of Sacred Name ideas and identifiers, there are numerous independent practitioners who incorporate a variety of spiritual ideas into their practice. Some common ideas include those of New Thought or the New Age Movement, different aspects of Christianity (especially Pentecostal or Charismatic), the religious beliefs of ancient Egypt, and other personal ideas or interpretations. They identify as any assortment of things: Nazarenes, Essenes, Jewish Christians, Hebrew Christians, Messianic believers in Messiah, practitioners and believers of the Way, and followers of Yeshua HaMashiach, among others.

Number of Adherents

It is difficult to identify a solid number on how many people identify with the Sacred Name and Hebrew Roots Movements. Estimates are around 200,000 to 300,000 worldwide.[6]

DISPUTES WITHIN GROUP

Both Sacred Name and Hebrew Roots groups are notably divided. As overlapping movements, they do not embrace centralized authority. While there are main theological points to which they do ascribe, the movements contain notable questions that invite division. There is disagreement over how much of Old Testament law one must obey, just what the divine name is (because no scholar is exactly sure), how festivals should be observed – and when, how to observe the Sabbath, the nature and purpose of local religious groups, designated church leadership and leaders, the role and work of Jesus Christ, inter-assembly associations, and most notably the work and role of the New Testament. It is evident through the history of these organizations that their disputes and disagreements will not come to a resolution.

SCRIPTURES

The Sacred Name and Hebrew Roots Movement universally agree upon the validity and acceptance of the Old Testament: Torah (the Christian Pentateuch of Genesis, Exodus, Leviticus, Numbers, and Deuteronomy), Nevi'im (the Prophets: Joshua, Judges, 1 and 2 Samuel, 1 and 2 Kings, Isaiah, Jeremiah, Ezekiel, Hosea, Joel, Amos, Obadiah, Jonah, Micah, Nahum, Habakkuk, Zephaniah, Haggai, Zechariah, and Malachi), and KetHuvim (the Writings: Psalms, Proverbs, Job, Song of Solomon, Ruth, Lamentations, Ecclesiastes, Ester, Daniel, Ezra, Nehemiah, and 1 and 2 Chronicles).

Most of the movements also accept the New Testament, often called the "Brit Chadashah," or "New Covenant." Versions used often intersperse Hebrew words and terms (including the Divine Name) within its contents, even though such were not used in the original Greek manuscripts. Many believe portions of the New Testament (especially the Gospel of Matthew) were originally written in Hebrew or Aramaic. Accepted books include the Gospels (Matthew, Mark, Luke, John), the Acts of the Apostles, the Pauline Epistles (Romans, 1 Corinthians, 2 Corinthians, Galatians, Ephesians, Philippians, Colossians, 1 Thessalonians, 2 Thessalonians, 1 Timothy, 2 Timothy, Titus, Philemon, Hebrews) the General Epistles (James, 1 Peter, 2 Peter, 1 John, 2 John, 3 John, Jude) and Revelation. The combination of New Testament books used and accepted by adherents does vary. Some reject the Pauline letters, while others question the inclusion of books, such as Revelation or the Johannine works.

A.N. Dugger (1886-1975)

There is also some question among different adherents about the work of the Deuterocanonical books (Tobit, Judith, 1 and 2 Maccabees, Wisdom of Solomon, Sirach, Baruch, Letter of Jeremiah, Greek additions to Esther, and Greek additions to Daniel, including the Prayer of Azariah, Song of the Three Holy Children, Susanna and the Elders, and Bel and the Dragon). While some believe in their value and inclusion as Scripture, others consider them to be of historical value without inspiration, and others consider them of no consequence. There is also interest among many communities in pseudepigraphal and apocryphal works, especially 1 Enoch and the Book of Jubilees, although this is not universal among

Sacred Name and Hebrew Roots practitioners.

Most adherents embrace their own translations or variations on existing translations of the Bible. These are known as Sacred Name Bibles, where Hebrew versions of the divine name and name of Biblical figures are used in place of the traditional English uses. Most are variations on the King James Version or the American Standard Version of 1901; there are a few, however, that are original translations, the result of translational projects unique and within specified Sacred Name or Hebrew Roots groups. These include: The Word of Yahweh, The Scriptures, Restoration of Original Sacred Name Bible, Sacred Name King James Bible, Sacred Scriptures, Family of Yah Edition, Sacred Scriptures Bethel Edition, Restoration Study Bible, HalleluYah Scriptures, Hebrew Roots Version, a Literal Translation, The World English Bible, The Names of God Bible (by Ann Spangler), The Tree of Life Version, The Complete Jewish Bible, and The Eth Cepher.

Some (not all) Sacred Name and Hebrew Roots groups also consider the writings of their leaders to be essential or inspired. This is especially true within Armstrongism (see the Armstrongism section within this book).

BASIC RELIGIOUS PRACTICES

Each Sacred Name and Hebrew Roots believer comes into their practice through an emphasis on historical study and identity. Both movements, overlapping in most spots, emphasize a unique history of belief not shared by any other religious group. While they do claim Hebrew ancestry and emphasis, their identity as such is not affirmed by Jewish groups, and there is no connection between their understandings of faith and those of Jewish believers. There is also no evidence their unique understandings as pertain to festivals, Old Testament interpretation, and the use of Hebrew names was ever understood in the same way by New Testament era believers. As a result, the scholarship, information, and historical information presented by Hebrew Roots and Sacred Name affiliates is unique to their own groups, unconfirmed by any other religious source.

There is extensive reading required by practitioners of Sacred Name and Hebrew Roots. It is expected that, when becomes part of a group associated with their beliefs and values, they will become thoroughly acquainted with the specifics of that group. Most groups produce prolific amounts of literature, often distributed in paperback or electronic form for their adherents to read. Study of the doctrines, beliefs, and uniqueness of the movement is an integral part of Hebrew Roots and Sacred Name understanding.

It is also expected adherents will engage in extensive historical study through the channels and authorities unique to their movements. The information presented is often contradictory to standard understandings of history and may come from sources that are out of date or considered inaccurate; regardless, it is expected one will embrace such studies, and adopt what is a "Hebrew" outlook of one's faith and worldview.

The Sacred Name and Hebrew Roots movements have an independent flair to them. As a result, not all adherents attend a weekly service or congregational meeting. Those that do often follow one of two formats: the first is a modified version of a weekly Jewish service, consisting of prayer, recitation, chants, and songs in Hebrew and/or English; the reading of Scripture, especially that of the Torah and the Prophets, and a lesson summary done by a group leader

(Rabbi, elder, pastor, or other leadership term). Most add a New Testament reading to their weekly portion, coinciding with the Torah lesson for that week. The second form is much like an Evangelical Protestant service, with hymns or contemporary music, prayer, Scriptural readings, and a sermon. Song lyrics of popular worship songs are changed to reflect Sacred Name and Hebrew Roots doctrines.

Adherents often uphold strict family values, emphasizing parents and children, husbands and wives (same-sex marriage, cohabitating without marriage, abortion, and sex outside of marriage are all forbidden), and emphasized gender roles. Dating outside the general community is frowned upon or downright forbidden. Many consider a woman's place to be the home, and the world of labor and business to belong to men. Some groups display anti-government tendencies and perform marriage ceremonies without legal binding (such are considered valid within the community only, by written agreement). Families are expected to study the disciplines of Scripture and their faith together, fulfill their appointed roles, and celebrate the different festivals every year.

HOLIDAYS

The nature of holidays among Sacred Name and Hebrew Roots adherents are most serious, and most relevant. These different feasts of the Old Testament are not just taken in the context of their immediate Biblical context, but also as forerunners of prophetic events to come. Dates and specified observance styles do vary, but all are observed by adherents. They are the feasts, as are identified as Yahweh's feasts, in Leviticus 23:2:

> *Speak to Bnei-Yisrael, and tell them: These are the appointed moadim of ADONAI, which you are to proclaim to be holy convocations—My moadim.*[7]

- **Feast of Unleavened Bread (better known as Passover)**: Includes the seven-day firstfruits of barley harvest festival whereby unleavened bread is eaten (all members dispose of all products that contain yeast) and the Passover ceremony itself. In such communities, the ceremony recalls not just the Old Testament exodus from Egypt, but the sacrifice and death of Yahusha HaMaschiach. Held in March or April.

- **Feast of Weeks (better known as Shavuot or Pentecost)**: Also known as Feast of Harvest and Day of Firstfruits. Day is observed with two loaves of leavened bread, interpreted often to reference the Jews and Gentiles. Day depicts the Holy Spirit given to the apostles, the Biblical cycle of Jubilee, and the Bride of Christ, or assembly of Messiah. Held in May or June.

- **Feast of Trumpets (better known as Rosh Hashanah)**: Observed with the blowing of the traditional shofar, a ram's horn trumpet. Signifies the second coming of the Messiah, when He shall be crowned King over all the earth, people repent of their sins, the dead shall rise in resurrection, and the vengeance of the King shall come through the Day of the Lord. Held in September or October.

- **Atonement (better known as Yom Kippur)**: Marked with prayer, fasting, repentenance, and acknowledgement of the Messiah's covering of sin. Held in September or October.

- **Booths (better known as Sukkot or the Feast of Tabernacles)**: Also known as the Festival of Ingathering, the Feast of the Nations, the Festival of Dedication, the Festival of Lights, and the Season of Our Joy. A seven-day harvest festival where believers gather together in temporary dwellings, or shelters. Signifies humanity's dependence on God for all things, especially food, water, and shelter. Many Hebrew Roots and Sacred Name groups meet at special campsites and celebrate in campers, portable trailers, or tents. Held in October.

- **Eighth Day (better known as *Shemini Atzeret*)**: The conclusion of Sukkot; a special day to dwell in Yahweh's presence of tarrying and prayer. Many see it, as an "eighth day festival," to represent the world to come or that which is to come, new (as the number eight represents new beginnings). Held in October.[8]

The Jewish festivals of Hanukkah and Purim are seen as national holidays rather than religious ones and are not commonly observed by most Hebrew Roots and Sacred Name organizations. They may be acknowledged through a reading or an announcement, but they are not seen as part of the yearly cycle of celebration.

VISUAL SIGNS AND SYMBOLS

Tetragrammaton; candelabra menorah on top of a star of David, on top of a fish symbol; candelabra; temple building; lion (for the Lion of Judah); grape vine or bunch; six-point Star of David; Torah scrolls; shofar; tallit prayer shawl; Hebrew names for the divine; Hebrew letters; Semitic writing; Sabbath observance; Old Testament festival observances; ephod or Torah shield; tree of life.

CREEDS, BOOKS, AND LAWS

The Sacred Name and Hebrew Roots Movements are strictly non-credal. All believe in the 613 laws present in the Old Covenant; how exactly those are to be upheld (or which ones to be upheld) varies by group. All would believe in the relevance of the Ten Commandments as applicable for believers today. Each group carries its own body of literature, which explains the interpretation and application therein. It is not uncommon for writings to overlap or to be shared among the Sacred Name and Hebrew Roots groups, often found referenced repeatedly throughout their differing communities.

> *Which brings us to the question: Which laws in the Bible are we to keep in this day and age? Are certain laws like the Ten Commandments important, while others are not? How can we know?*
>
> *The Bible has many laws governing human behavior. The longest Psalm (119) is entirely devoted to teaching obedience to all of Yahweh's laws.*

Yet the majority of churchianity teaches that the Savior came to do away with our Father's laws. If only we believe or have faith, they say, nothing else is required of us. The Savior did it all, and we are now under grace, we are told.

"Fida Sola" was the rallying cry of the reformation in Martin Luther's day: "Faith Alone!" No works to do, no laws to keep; only faith in the Savior. That is still the basic message of many churches.

Some in churchianity may concede that if we are to obey any laws, it is only those laws found in the New Testament; the Old Testament laws are obsolete and no longer binding, they contend.

Yahweh's laws were given as a long-lasting ordinance. In Matthew 5:18 the Messiah Yahshua said no part of the law would be dropped so long as heaven and earth remain. The Ten Commandments reflect His very nature, His righteousness. He changes not (Mal. 3:6).

His laws are a blueprint for man's ideal behavior, and His Commandments are eternal standards of righteousness. Only His Son Yahshua has measured up to these standards, keeping His laws perfectly (1 Pet. 2:22).

The Savior, in rebuking the Adversary, said, It is written, "Man shall not live by bread alone, but by every word of Yahweh," Matthew 4:4. That is to say, we eat physical food to maintain physical life. We must feed on spiritual food, however, for everlasting life in the higher spiritual realm. By "every word" He meant the Old Testament as well as the New, which, incidentally was not yet written.[9]

ECLECTIC BELIEFS

In some Hebrew Roots groups believers are expected to keep the words and traditions of Rabbis throughout the ages in addition to Scriptural principles. This is not an across-the-board position but is present enough to mention. The Sacred Name Movement rejects any sort of traditional Jewish interpretation and instruction through history.

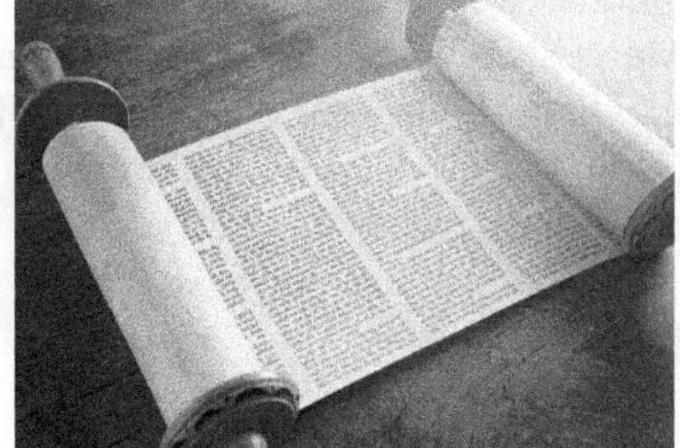
Torah scroll

Among Sacred Name and Hebrew Roots groups, there is considerable disagreement over the timing of events and festivals. While all universally agree on the observance of the Sabbath and Old Testament festivals, they considerably argue over the day, lunar cycles, lunar calendars, or when the day begins at sunrise or sunset.

There is also considerable issue over what might be considered "obsolete laws' within the Old Testament, such as the command for men not to cut the sides of their hair, wearing beards, or the mix of fabrics in clothing (polyester). These are often downplayed or declared to be part of a greater issue, such as idolatry, and no longer enforced. Other prohibitions, however, such as on shellfish, pork, tattooing, and sexual practices are seen as mandatory.[10]

RELATIONS WITH NON-SACRED NAME AND HEBREW ROOTS GROUPS

The Sacred Name Movement does not associate with all other Sacred Name adherents, let alone with those outside of the movement. It is not uncommon to see those of the Hebrew Roots Movement interacting with those in the general Christian community, especially those from an Evangelical or Pentecostal foundation. Much of the purpose, however, is to influence through ideas and concepts. Many detect a sense of anger within the Sacred Name and Hebrew Roots Movements. Because they are founded on a basic principle of conspiracy – something has been deliberately left out, stolen, or hidden from them – this can equate to a general sense of anger and hostility toward Christian communities, even though it would seem they should have some foundational things in common. Both groups would frown on interfaith interactions, with those of religious adherents outside of Christianity.

HOLY SITES

There are no specified holy sites within the Sacred Name or Hebrew Roots Movement. Many would consider the land of Israel to have great spiritual relevance. Otherwise, the concept of holy sites would relate to whatever is seen as holy or sacred by the individual practitioner.

NOTABLE FIGURES

C.O. Dodd (1899-1955), author and publisher; A.N. Dugger (1886-1975), author; Herbert W. Armstrong (1892-1986), founder, Worldwide Church of God; Garner Ted Armstrong (1930-2003), founder, Church of God, International; Monte Judah, founder, Lion and Lamb Ministries; Michael Rood, founder, A Rood Awakening! International; Dean and Susan Wheelock, founder, Hebrew Roots; Joseph Good, author and founder, Hatikva Ministries; Tim Hegg (c. 1952-), founder, TorahResource; William F. Dankenbring (1941-), founder, Triumph Prophetic Ministries; Mark Blitz (1956-), pastor and host, *Discovering the Ancient Paths*; Brad Scott (1953-2020), founder, The WildBranch Ministry; Ed Chumney, founder, Hebraic Heritage Ministries; Jonathan Cahn (1959-), author; Sid Roth (1940-), founder of Messianic Vision and host of *It's Supernatural!*

NOTABLE GROUPS

The House of Yahweh, located near Eula, Texas, was founded in 1980 by Bill Hawkins (who changed his name to Yisrayl Hawkins in accordance with his Sacred Name understanding). Like other Sacred Name and Hebrew Roots groups, the House of Yahweh observes the Sabbath, the festivals of the Old Testament, rejects the idea that Yahshua is divine, and that Yahweh is the only one who should be worshiped. The group varies in that it teaches their specific sanctuary building is the only place on earth where festivals should be observed, and all members are required to make a pilgrimage there to celebrate Passover, Pentecost, and the Feast of Tabernacles. The group has seen six different failed predictions of the end of the world, and has had numerous legal troubles, including an elder's arrest for sexual assault, criminal negligence for performing surgery on a child, and bigamy. Because of its extreme exclusivity, the group has been classified as a cult.[11]

FACTS AND FIGURES

Because the movements aren't centralized, there isn't a lot of factual or statistical data available about followers of such communities. It is safe to say, however, that while the movements had a great amount of influence in years past (the Sacred Name Movement peaking between the 1950s and 1980s and the Hebrew Roots Movement peaking in the late 1990s and early 2000s), the movements are currently in decline.

OTHER IMPORTANT DEFINITIONS

- **Adonai**: Hebrew term used to mean "my Lord," often paralleled to Elohim.
- **Awakening**: A term many in the Hebrew Roots Movement use to describe the movement itself; that it is an awakening to true and eternal truths hidden by the church.
- **Doing the work**: Giving money to a Sacred Name organization in order to see that its doctrines and information continue to spread.
- **The God Family**: A subheading of Divine Monarchism that teaches the divine is not limited to Yahweh alone, but is, rather, a family; one that every human, ever born, may be spiritually born "into" through a stage-by-stage plan. Currently, the Godhead consists of the Father and the Messiah.
- **God's people**: Also known as God's chosen people, or people of God. How Sacred Name and Hebrew Roots adherents refer to themselves, especially those in conformity with the movements.
- **Gospel**: The essential message of the Sacred Name and Hebrew Roots Movements.
- **Laodiceans**: The general Christian community.
- **Philadelphia Church**: The Sacred Name Movement as a denomination.
- **Sha'ul**: Saul, the name for the New Testament writer Paul prior to his Christian conversion.
- **Tradition**: Specified practices believed to be Jewish (especially Old Testament) in nature, that are now adopted to reflect Sacred Name or Hebrew Roots belief.
- **Woke**: A state of being that one has once they have experienced the awakening of the Hebrew Roots Movement.

BELIEVER'S CHARACTERISTICS

Interest in historical Biblical languages, especially Hebrew and Aramaic; belief in church cover-up and conspiracy; emphasis on the divine name; belief in the need to use and utilize Hebrew names; historical interest; study and celebration of Old Testament festivals; upholding dietary laws; use of Hebrew Roots or Sacred Name literature; use of Sacred Name Bibles; Sabbath observance; strict interpretation of Old Testament understanding; extensive religious study; conflicting movements; gender roles; government suspicions; mixing of systems with New Age ideas; prohibitions on cosmetics, with regulations for hair lengths for men and women; modest attire.

Satanism

Satanism has been frequently misrepresented as "devil worship," when in fact it constitutes a clear rejection of all forms of worship as a desirable component of the personality.
(Anton Szandor LaVey)[1]

Theology

Satanism takes on one of two theological precedents: theistic or non-theistic. Theistic Satanism believes in an existing deity, supernatural force, or being worthy of worship and supplication known as SATAN. In many traditions, beings identified with or as being Satan are also identified by name, such as AHRIMAN, ENKI, or ANGRA MAINYU. Theistic Satanists believe Satan is more than just an archetype or metaphor and is their deity of choice in worship. Theistic Satanists practice ceremonial magic as part of their interest and connection with Satan. Some theistic Satanists also go a step further to say they believe what they classify as the "Christian God" is a false god and Satan is the true deity to be honored and worshiped.[2]

Non-theistic Satanists do not believe in a personal deity known as Satan. Rather, Satan is a personification or archetype of adversarial behavior. Specifically associated with Satan are pride, carnality, enlightenment, and cosmic darkness that is derisive in nature. Satan is seen as a personal projection of one's own divinity, achieved by standing against and in defiance of the Abrahamic religions (Judaism, Christianity, and Islam) which promote restraint and self-control as part of spiritual discipline.[3]

All Satanism takes on the form of hedonism, or the idea that personal desires, pleasures, and wants are the highest form of spiritual enlightenment and human attainment. The way this takes form varies, but it is primarily through deliberate indulgence as part of one's belief system, whether through sexual relationships, drug or alcohol abuse, financial profits, or pursuing personal ambitions at any cost.

Philosophy

Satanism is rooted in the idea that morality and servanthood, central tenants of the Abrahamic religions (especially Christianity) are self-righteous and egotistical. For those who do embrace such theism, the source of such is the (Christian deity), also seen as self-righteous, moralistic, self-centered, and egotistical. Largely a self-driven religion, Satanists believe in individualism, pride, self-reliance, and non-conformity, which sets them apart as an elite people. As a group, Satanists find their greatest life understanding to come in rebellion of traditional values and the embrace of excessive pleasures, physical and emotional, indulgence, and rejection of values, traditional religion, and morality. As a result, many things often considered immoral or taboo in other religions – such as same-sex relationships, non-binary gender identities, racial diversities, sexual preferences, non-monogamous relationships, recreational drug use, abortion, and other indulgences – are accepted and embraced by Satanists.

History cites that within traditional mindset, Satanism is an accusation or creation against perceived enemies of Christianity. Witches, pagans, Christian heretical groups (such as Paulicians, Bogomils, Cathars, Waldensians, Hussites, and Knights Templar), and some eighteenth-century atheists were all accused of being "Satanists" or of having given their souls to the possession of Satan. The label has been used throughout history to brand individuals who held beliefs or behaviors contrary to church teaching. These uses of the term "Satanic" are still in use today, especially against religious groups that are seen as contradictory or problematic to the beliefs of Christianity. Satanism, as a self-proclaimed, personal identity, is a relatively new construct, emerging somewhere in the nineteenth century.[4]

ADHERENT IDENTITY

Satanists, Satanic, devil worshiper, demon worshiper, devil devotee, demonolater, Satanic witch, member of specific Satanic organizations (such as the Church of Satan, the Order of Nine Angles, or Black Order of the Dragon).

TRADITIONAL LANGUAGES

English; those interested in traditional strains of black magic may also take interest in Latin.

SECTS/DIVISIONS

- **Modern Satanic foundations:** Satanism emerged from interest in hidden wisdom, occultism, magic, and combinations of esoteric ideas and thoughts mixed with hedonistic ideas seen as contrary to the Christian morals of nineteenth and twentieth centuries. While these individuals and their groups were not Satanists in the modern sense, they laid important foundations for the establishment of Satanism. Helena Blavatsky (1831-1891), founder of Theosophy, often wrote about Satan as a being able to endow humans with wisdom. In 1897, Stanislaw Przybyszewski (1863-1927) wrote two dramatic books about Satan (one seen as fiction, and the other non-fiction). Satan was identified as a philosophical anarchist, much like what we see today. The most relevant influence was most likely Aleister Crowley (1875-1947). Aleister Crowley was a British occultist (member of the Ordo Templi Orientis and founder of the Abbey of Thelema magic). Although he did not consider himself to be a Satanist, he saw Satan as a symbol, a being that provided the soul and ultimate rebellion of the universe. His heavy use of magic and esoteric ritual, hedonism, and Satanic metaphor combined to largely define ideas about Satanism as we see them today.

- **Theistic Satanism**: Sometimes defined as "traditional Satanists." As defined earlier, theistic Satanism embraces the idea of a being, identified as Satan or as other historical gods or deities that are adversarial in nature, as the chief deity for worship. Theistic Satanic groups do vary in some of their specifications and practices, but all adhere to the basic idea of Satan (or a Satan-like figure) as their central source for adoration, worship, and most relevantly, power. Such groups include the Order of Nine Angles (well-known because at one time, it promoted human sacrifice), Ordo Sinistra Vivendi, Temple of Black Light, and the Misanthropic Luciferian Order.

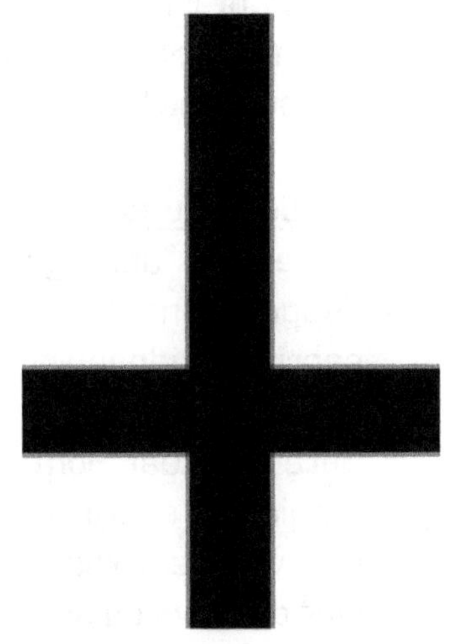

Inverted cross

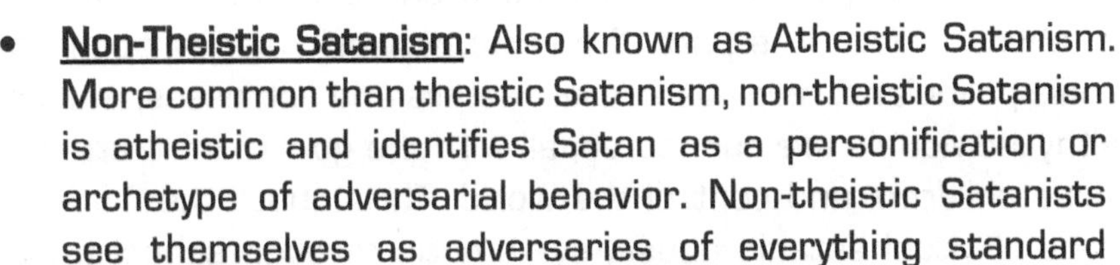

- **Non-Theistic Satanism**: Also known as Atheistic Satanism. More common than theistic Satanism, non-theistic Satanism is atheistic and identifies Satan as a personification or archetype of adversarial behavior. Non-theistic Satanists see themselves as adversaries of everything standard religion (especially Christianity) espouses in morality and conduct. Non-theistic Satanists may practice individually or as a group, as they place high emphasis on the ideas of individuality and non-conformity. Such groups include LaVey Satanism (the Church of Satan), Temple of Set, and First Satanic Church (600 Club).

- **Gnostic Satanism**: Gnostic Satanism merges the ideas of theistic Satanism and neo-Gnosticism, especially in cosmology. Within Gnostic Satanism Satan is recognized as the true deity with the Christian deity as his demigod. Satan is seen as the serpent who revealed the true knowledge of his power and divinity to Eve in the Garden of Eden. Gnostic Satanists identify themselves with Ophites, an ancient Gnostic religion that likely worshiped the serpent. Gnostic Satanic groups include Ophite Cultus Sathanas (Our Lady of Endor Coven), the Lilin Society, Left Hand Sorcery, and Luciferianism groups (those which venerate Satan as Lucifer, seeing him as an illuminator or "Light Bearer"), such as the Greater Church of Lucifer, the Neo-Luciferian Church, and the Fraternitas Saturni.[5]

- **Political Satanism**: Political Satanism comes in both theistic and non-theistic forms, the focus being public social causes and interests that are pro-Satanic. Political Satanists find things such as after school Bible programs, Ten Commandments monuments, school or sports prayers, and other overtly religious activities to be a violation of their rights as Satanists. They advocate Satanic monuments, Satanic after school programs, and the promotion of Satanic education and literature in school and general society. While they do not promote a specified political belief, many identify as Libertarian, liberal, or independent. There are some political Satanic groups that also embrace neo-Nazism, although this is not the representation of most groups. Such political Satanic groups include The Satanic Temple and the Order of Nine Angles.

- **Combination groups**: All Satanic groups mix pagan ideas with their beliefs. There are also mixes of theistic and non-theistic Satanism, and some that incorporate Gnostic beliefs with their other concoction of ideas. These groups include the Order of Phosphorus, Black Order of the Dragon, Sinagogue of Satan, and the Black Order of Pan Europa (Black Order).

- **"Underground" groups**: There is great debate and controversy concerning the existence of certain "underground" Satanic groups. These groups are often deemed as into the deepest and heaviest involvements of Satanic practices, including rumors of child sacrifice, kidnapping, sexual abuse, and a practice known as Satanic Ritual Abuse, which is the alleged torture, sexual abuse, torment, and physical abuse of children as part of Satanic ritual. Some groups are also rumored to practice strains of black magic, blood magic and sacrifice, sacrifice animals, or in some instances, sacrifice humans. Those who believe in satanic ritual abuse believe it is part of a large network, one throughout the world, by which high-profile politicians, religious figures, actors and actresses, musicians, businessmen, and wealthy individuals are connected, all with the goal to infiltrate society with Satanic ideals, abuse children, and control the world. Throughout the 1980s and early 1990s, accusations of ritual satanic abuse, systematic through school systems, daycare centers, and nursery programs, ran wild and rampant due to the influence of the book, *Michelle Remembers*, written by Michelle Smith and husband Lawrence Pazder (1936-2004). There were over a thousand accusations of Satanic Ritual Abuse (and there are still individuals who claim to have been victims of it) although such accusations are more uncommon today. There has never been any evidence that satanic ritual abuse is real, nor that any such international network of Satanists exists. On the contrary, the individualism of Satanism presents a challenge for such an ideal, because such would require extensive conformity and uniformity, both of which are against the basic nature of Satanism. While it is entirely possible there are a few isolated groups out there that engage in some wild rites in the name of Satanism, there are not enough of them to make an international network. Regardless, such makes for great fiction, YouTube videos, panic, and writing among many groups, especially Evangelical Christians and traditionalist Catholics. Such an example of this rumored network is the Illuminati.[6]

NUMBER OF ADHERENTS

Satanism exists largely in the United States. There is a modest presence in Europe and an even smaller presence in Australia and New Zealand. It is impossible to know how many people identify as Satanists, because Satanism is not an organized religious group.

DISPUTES WITHIN GROUP

The individualistic nature of Satanism is also what causes much of its dispute. One can be an independent practitioner of Satanism, read all the writings, and engage in different practices without ever attending a meeting or participating with a group. Sects tend to vary on the very existence of Satan or Satan as an ideal, theology, practice and nature of magic, and purposes behind their spirituality. Some groups are decidedly "playing" magic while others are decidedly serious and dedicated to their beliefs. There are also many Satanists who are interested in the practice for indulgence purpose, seeking to outlet curiosities, rebellion, and vices in an acceptable manner. What exactly someone believes – and why someone endeavors in the world of Satanic spirituality – varies, thus causing groups, individuals, and ideas about it to vary greatly from group to group and person to person.

Scriptures

Anton LaVey (1930-1997)

The concept of "scripture" within Satanism is a relatively new thing. It consists of collections of ideas, essays, and rituals for modern-day Satanists. The best-known of these books is *The Satanic Bible*, written by Anton LaVey (1930-1997). After its prologue (which contains the Nine Satanic Statements) it consists of four different books (sections): The Book of Satan (challenges core religious ideas, such as the Ten Commandments and Golden Rule, advocating social Darwinism instead; focuses on hedonism and indulgence for ultimate happiness), The Book of Lucifer (deconstructs ideas pertaining to theology, rejects prayer, advocates the seven deadly sins, representations of Satan from around the world, and an advocacy of sexual freedom), The Book of Belilal (Satanic ritual and magic), and The Book of Leviathian (the importance of spoken word and emotion to create magic; invocation to Satan, and rituals are given). This is the central text of LaVey Satanism, but it is not the only Satanic scriptural reference in existence. Other LaVey Satanic works include *The Satanic Scriptures*, *The Satanic Witch*, and *The Satanic Rituals*, which serves as a companion to *The Satanic Bible*.[7]

> *Some religions actually go so far as to label anyone who belongs to a religious sect other than their own a heretic, even though the overall doctrines and impressions of godliness are nearly the same. For example: The Catholics believe the Protestants are doomed to Hell simply because they do not belong to the Catholic Church. In the same way, many splinter groups of the Christian faith, such as the evangelical or revivalist churches, believe the Catholics worship graven images. (Christ is depicted in the image that is most physiologically akin to the individual worshipping him, and yet the Christians criticize "heathens" for the worship of graven images.) And the Jews have always been given the Devil's name.*[8]

> *Satanism condones any type of sexual activity which properly satisfies your individual desires- be it heterosexual, homosexual, bisexual, or even asexual, if you choose. Satanism also sanctions any fetish or deviation which will enhance your sex-life, so long as it involves no one who does not wish to be involved.*[9]

> *Satanists are encouraged to indulge in the seven deadly sins, as they need hurt no one; they were only invented by the Christian Church to insure guilt on the part of its followers. The Christian Church knows that it is impossible for anyone to avoid committing these sins, as they are all things*

which we, being human, most naturally do. After inevitably committing these sins financial offerings to the church in order to "pay off" God are employed as a sop to the parishioner's conscience![10]

Satan has certainly been the best friend the church has ever had, as he has kept it in business all these years. The false doctrine of Hell and the Devil has allowed the Protestant and Catholic Churches to flourish far too long. Without a devil to point their fingers at, religionists of the right hand path would have nothing with which to threaten their followers. "Satan leads you to temptation"; "Satan is the prince of evil"; "Satan is vicious, cruel, brutal," they warn. "If you give in to the temptations of the devil, you will surely suffer eternal damnation and roast in Hell."

The semantic meaning of Satan is the "adversary" or "opposition" or the "accuser." The very word "devil" comes from the Indian devi which means "god." Satan represents opposition to all religions which serve to frustrate and condemn man for his natural instincts. He has been given an evil role simply because he represents the carnal, earthly, and mundane aspects of life.[11]

While LaVey Satanism's writings are undoubtedly influential among Satanists, they are also highly controversial. Anton LaVey was accused of plagiarism, of watering down the writings of other magic writers throughout history, or of distorting the field of magic. There are many who do not consider the Church of Satan to be a legitimate organization, but more of a cartoonish impression of what true Satanism is like. As a result, different strains of Satanism, embrace slightly different principles present in works unique to them. Other Satanic scriptural works include *Book of Coming Forth by Night* (Michael Aquino [1946-]), *Jeweled Tablets of Set* (Michael Aquino), *The Book of Opening the Wayl* (Isha Schwaller de Lubicz [1885-1963]), *The Unholy Bible* (Leena Klammer), *The Bible of the Adversary* (Michael W. Ford [1976-]), *Necrominon* (Michael W. Ford), and *Luciferian Witchcraft* (Michael W. Ford).

Satanists also take an interest in older works that relate to magic, particularly that associated with "black magic," or magic used for evil or selfish intent. Such books include *The Lesser Key of Solomon*, *The Testament of Solomon*, *The Greater Keys of Solomon*, *Grimorium Verum*, and *The Grand Grimoire*.

Even though they are not considered scripture, Satanists also embrace many historical and philosophical works, especially those by Ayn Rand (1905-1982), Frederich Nietzsche (1844-1900), Aleister Crowley, H.L. Mencken (1880-1956), Anatole France (1844-1924)), John Milton (1608-1674), and Charles Baudelaire (1821-1867). While none of these people were Satanists or wrote ideas specifically related to modern Satanism, they all expounded either ideas about independence and individuality, thoughts that contradicted modern religion, or wrote detailed epics about Satan. Because Satanism focuses on independence, it is also possible for Satanists to embrace their own preferred writers and books, with no contradiction to their belief system.

Seal of Baphomet

BASIC RELIGIOUS PRACTICES

The individual Satanist is free to do what they desire within their own pleasures and indulgences. Satanists may call on demonic or dark powers or reject such things, maintain private home altars, and/or engage in the practice of black magic. Satanists recognize two different forms of magic: lesser magic, used on a day-to-day basis to help Satanists advance in the world (through charming and manipulating people to win them over through favor) and greater magic (processing specific life events, whether physical or emotional, or focusing energy for a specific purpose; usually done through a specified ritual).

Satanists may practice Satanism on their own or may gather with other Satanists. An oft mentioned form of Satanic rite is the Black Mass, which is an inversion of the Latin Roman Catholic rite. Satanists say the words of the Latin rite liturgy backwards, use desecrated communion elements stolen from a church, and hang the cross or crucifix upside down within a circle to demonstrate the idea that the Christian deity's power is containable. Satanists may also use a Gnostic mass (usually the one created by Aleister Crowley), like that of eastern and Latin rite, only with inverted meanings, symbolisms, and required nudity. Christian symbols are deliberately inverted, desecrated, and disrespected. Satanic group rites are led by a priest or high priest, and are often known as a coven, grotto, or church.

There are several rumors about specified "satanic" practices: cannibalism, blood rituals and oaths, animal and human sacrifice, sexual rites (including rape, sexual magic, and orgies), drug use and abuse, divination, spiritualism, and other occult practices. Some of these associations come from public figures connected to violent or brutal behaviors who associated themselves as "Satanists" (such as murderers Richard Ramirez and Charles Manson. As a rule, Satanists do not actively practice things such as divination or spiritualism, at least not on a wide scale. Apart from the Order of Nine Angles, there are no known satanic organizations that advocate cannibalism, rape, or human sacrifice. There are small numbers of theistic Satanists that do engage in blood sacrifice using animals. Sex magic, orgies, and drug use are a permissible part of many Satanic practices, but not all Satanists practice such things in the same manner or with the same specific interests.

Satanic services are often regarded as secret and are usually closed to the public. To attend such an event, one must be invited by the host. Most Satanic organizations practice their group rituals or rites in homes or in "underground" settings, meaning they are not visible by building or association to the public.

HOLIDAYS

Modern Satanists acknowledge three main holidays:

- **The personal birthday of the practitioner**: Within Satanism (especially non-theistic Satanism), the birthday of each Satanist is considered a high holiday. Satanists consider such the ultimate sign of the self-centered nature of the religious practice.[12]

- **Walpurgisnacht**: An abbreviation of "Saint Walpurgis Night" (also known as "Saint Walpurga's Eve"), Walpurgisnacht is held the night of April 30 and the day to follow, May 1. Although the feast is in honor of an English Christian missionary that lived in the 700s, Satanists associate it with the anniversary of the founding of the Church of Satan in 1966. Its founding also connects to the pagan festival Beltane, more commonly acknowledged as "May Day." It is seen as the "spring climax."[13]

- **Halloween**: October 31. Halloween is seen as a day when the entire world reaches down to touch the "darkness," a daily practice and purpose of Satanism. Satanists acknowledge the holiday much like the world does: with costumes, parties, and dark fantasy life. It is common to hear of black mass celebrations around Halloween.

Many Satanists observe pagan festivals, especially those related to the annual solstices and equinoxes. Some will also celebrate holidays with a secular embrace (such as Christmas or Easter) from a pagan viewpoint or from a secular perspective (gift giving, holiday and family gatherings). There are no specified rituals or requirements for any Satanic holidays. Satanists are not required to observe them.

VISUAL SIGNS AND SYMBOLS

Inverted five-point pentagram; Sigil of Baphomet (inverted pentagram within a circle and a goat's head in the center) Baphomet; inverted Latin cross (Cross of Saint Peter); Satanic Bible or Satanic books; Septenary Sigil (used by the Order of Nine Angles); sulfur crosses; black sun (sun composed of twelve sig runes); altar of sacrifice; inverted and blasphemed Christian symbols; serpent; devil; caduceus; horns; torch between horns; use of the colors red and black in constant combination.

CREEDS, BOOKS, AND LAWS

Satanism is not a religion bound by outside codes. Those who come to adhere to Satanism either see themselves in harmony with it for several years (not realizing what it was) or who find themselves antithetical to organized religion in some form or another. Most Satanists embrace the individuality of the religious outlook and enjoy the freedom to explore and believe as they will without organizational or structural confines.

There are no specific Satanic "creeds" or legal books among any of the Satanic organizations. One can be a Satanist and not recognize or affiliate with a formal Satanic church or group. Most modern groups, however, would agree with the following summarizing statements written by Anton LaVey himself (and found in *The Satanic Bible*), even modifying the points or re-summarizing them for their own organizations:

The Nine Satanic Statements:

1. *Satan represents indulgence instead of abstinence!*
2. *Satan represents vital existence instead of spiritual pipe dreams!*

3. *Satan represents undefiled wisdom instead of hypocritical self-deceit!*
4. *Satan represents kindness to those who deserve it instead of love wasted on ingrates!*
5. *Satan represents vengeance instead of turning the other cheek!*
6. *Satan represents responsibility to the responsible instead of concern for psychic vampires!*
7. *Satan represents man as just another animal, sometimes better, more often worse than those that walk on all-fours, who, because of his "divine spiritual and intellectual development," has become the most vicious animal of all!*
8. *Satan represents all of the so-called sins, as they all lead to physical, mental, or emotional gratification!*
9. *Satan has been the best friend the Church has ever had, as He has kept it in business all these years!*[14]

The 11 Satanic Rules of the Earth:

1. *Do not give opinions or advice unless you are asked.*
2. *Do not tell your troubles to others unless you are sure they want to hear them.*
3. *When in another's lair, show him respect or else do not go there.*
4. *If a guest in your lair annoys you, treat him cruelly and without mercy.*
5. *Do not make sexual advances unless you are given the mating signal.*
6. *Do not take that which does not belong to you unless it is a burden to the other person and he cries out to be relieved.*
7. *Acknowledge the power of magic if you have employed it successfully to obtain your desires. If you deny the power of magic after having called upon it with success, you will lose all you have obtained.*
8. *Do not complain about anything to which you need not subject yourself.*
9. *Do not harm little children.*
10. *Do not kill non-human animals unless you are attacked or for your food.*
11. *When walking in open territory, bother no one. If someone bothers you, ask him to stop. If he does not stop, destroy him.*[15]

The Nine Satanic Sins

1. *Stupidity*
   The top of the list for Satanic Sins. The Cardinal Sin of Satanism. It's too bad that stupidity isn't painful. Ignorance is one thing, but our society thrives increasingly on stupidity. It depends on people going along with whatever they are told. The media promotes a cultivated stupidity as a posture that is not only acceptable but laudable. Satanists must learn to see through the tricks and cannot afford to be stupid.
2. *Pretentiousness*
   Empty posturing can be most irritating and isn't applying the cardinal rules of Lesser Magic. On equal footing with stupidity for what keeps the money in circulation these days. Everyone's made to feel like a big shot, whether they can come up with the goods or not.
3. *Solipsism*
   Can be very dangerous for Satanists. Projecting your reactions, responses and sensibilities onto someone who is probably far less attuned than you are. It is the mistake of expecting people to give you the same consideration, courtesy and respect that you naturally give them. They won't. Instead, Satanists must strive to apply the dictum of "Do unto others as they do unto you." It's work for most of us and requires constant vigilance lest you slip into a comfortable illusion of everyone being like you. As has been said, certain utopias would be ideal

in a nation of philosophers, but unfortunately (or perhaps fortunately, from a Machiavellian standpoint) we are far from that point.

4. *Self-deceit*
   It's in the "Nine Satanic Statements" but deserves to be repeated here. Another cardinal sin. We must not pay homage to any of the sacred cows presented to us, including the roles we are expected to play ourselves. The only time self-deceit should be entered into is when it's fun, and with awareness. But then, it's not self-deceit!
5. *Herd Conformity*
   That's obvious from a Satanic stance. It's all right to conform to a person's wishes, if it ultimately benefits you. But only fools follow along with the herd, letting an impersonal entity dictate to you. The key is to choose a master wisely instead of being enslaved by the whims of the many.
6. *Lack of Perspective*
   Again, this one can lead to a lot of pain for a Satanist. You must never lose sight of who and what you are, and what a threat you can be, by your very existence. We are making history right now, every day. Always keep the wider historical and social picture in mind. That is an important key to both Lesser and Greater Magic. See the patterns and fit things together as you want the pieces to fall into place. Do not be swayed by herd constraints—know that you are working on another level entirely from the rest of the world.
7. *Forgetfulness of Past Orthodoxies*
   Be aware that this is one of the keys to brainwashing people into accepting something new and different, when in reality it's something that was once widely accepted but is now presented in a new package. We are expected to rave about the genius of the creator and forget the original. This makes for a disposable society.
8. *Counterproductive Pride*
   That first word is important. Pride is great up to the point you begin to throw out the baby with the bathwater. The rule of Satanism is: if it works for you, great. When it stops working for you, when you've painted yourself into a corner and the only way out is to say, I'm sorry, I made a mistake, I wish we could compromise somehow, then do it.
9. *Lack of Aesthetics*
   This is the physical application of the Balance Factor. Aesthetics is important in Lesser Magic and should be cultivated. It is obvious that no one can collect any money off classical standards of beauty and form most of the time so they are discouraged in a consumer society, but an eye for beauty, for balance, is an essential Satanic tool and must be applied for greatest magical effectiveness. It's not what's supposed to be pleasing—it's what is. Aesthetics is a personal thing, reflective of one's own nature, but there are universally pleasing and harmonious configurations that should not be denied.[16]

Satanists recognize no specified moral guidelines, rules for group governances (in fact, many groups, including the Church of Satan have decentralized authority in the past few years), or specific membership requirements. There are no specified experts, spokespeople, or official representatives of any Satanic organization.

ECLECTIC BELIEFS

One could describe the world of Satanism as one large "eclectic" set of beliefs. It is literally up to each individual practitioner to select their own unique collection of ideals, practices, and thoughts, all merged for their own personal Satanic experience. Anything regarded as pleasurable is encouraged; aspirations are encouraged; use of magic is encouraged; and exploring what is often classified as the "dark side" is very encouraged. Many stereotype Satanists as goths, wearing all-black clothing and dying their hair black; this, however, is a stereotype, as not all Satanists engage in such practices.

Satanic book

It is surprising to many to note Satanists often lead lives much like others: with social and political opinions, literary preferences, families, social lives, and active support systems, all while practicing Satanism in their own unique way.

RELATIONS WITH NON-SATANISTS

Most Satanic groups do not associate with other religions, particularly Christianity. Some Satanists participate in other occult practices and belong to other occult groups while maintaining their Satanic identity. Satanism has specific disregard for Wicca, as in Wicca's desire to become mainline through the concept of "white magic" (magic that is seen as being for good), Satanists feel it has also become self-righteous.

HOLY SITES

As a rule, Satanists reject holy sites.

NOTABLE FIGURES

Anton LaVey (1930-1997), founder, the Church of Satan; Michael Aquino (1946-), founder, Temple of Set; Marilyn Manson (1969-), musician; King Diamond (1956-), musician; Blanche Barton (1961-), Magistra Templi Rex, Church of Satan; Balls Mahoney (1972-2016), athlete; Matt Skiba (1976-), musician; Pazuzu Algarad (1987-2015), cult leader; Infernus (1972-), musician; Adam Darski (1977-), musician.

NOTABLE GROUPS

The Satanic Temple, a non-theistic Satanic organization that is highly political in nature, was founded in Salem, Massachusetts In 2013. Their official spokesperson is Lucien Greaves. It stands as a charitable organization, seeking to instill benevolence and empathy in people. Its major focus is the separation of church and state, feeling Christians are given privilege within the

United States and such is in contrast with their right to freedom of religion. They also believe matters of marriage and body autonomy are rights and should in no way be restricted. They have worked in activism for abortion rights, the abolishment of corporal punishment in school, against hate groups, pseudoscientific mental heath treatments, and to create Satanic after school clubs that work in contrast to Evangelical or other religious groups. One particular public stunt was a "Pink Mass" held over the grave of Catherine Johnston (the mother of Fred Phelps, founder of Westboro Baptist Church). Members performed lewd actions over the grave and chanted incantations to change the deceased's sexual orientation; a misdemeanor charge was issued for Lucien Greaves. They are best-known for using social media crowdfunding to erect a Baphomet statue in Detroit, Michigan in 2015.[17]

FACTS AND FIGURES

Satanism has largely been dominated by young Caucasian males throughout its history. Those who study Satanism believe there may be a growing female community within its ranks. Atheistic Satanists comprise most Satanists worldwide.[18]

OTHER IMPORTANT DEFINITIONS

- **Anti-egalitarianism**: Rejection of the view that all human beings are equal and worthy, based on a perceived moral status. Satanism promotes social Darwinism, an anti-egalitarian view, which believes only the strong, or superior, are able to survive.

- **Eugenics**: A social position by which certain groups, deemed as weak or inferior, are either excluded or exterminated. Such was a key theory within Anton LaVey's ideas.

- **The Infernal Names**: A list of various adversarial figures found throughout worldwide mythology to use as part of Satanic ritual. Found in the Satanic Bible.

- **Left-hand path**: In contrast with the right-hand path, the left-hand path of magic rejects any sort of convention or structure in magic, pursuing spiritual freedom. It is believed one should, and can, pursue any magic for any selfish ends, and that sexuality can and should be incorporated into ritual.

- **Materialism**: The rejection of anything that cannot be seen or proven through the means of the material world. Individuals who are materialists reject the existence of the divine, supernatural beings, and life after death.

- **Reactive Satanism**: The practice of ideas or concepts labeled as "Satanism" for the sake of shock value, as practiced by adolescents or anti-society individuals.

- **Right-hand path**: Magical strain that adheres to specific beliefs in mind, body, spirit, and moral codes, such as Karma. Satanists do not believe such magic exists as a viable magic entity.

- **Social Darwinism**: An assortment of theories that relate to the idea of natural selection (the adaptation of genes to survive in a specified environment) and survival of the fittest (only the strongest and most capable of survival will survive from generation to generation).

BELIEVER'S CHARACTERISTICS

Emphasis on darkness, Satan (either as a being or a mere concept), pleasure, individuality, autonomy, and black magic; Goth; secretive; secretive about religion and rituals; interest in Satanic artists and representations within culture; rejection, inversion, and desecration of all Christian religion, symbolism, principle, and morality; rejection of all world religion; sexual liberality in all forms; use of inverted pentagram; study of writings by prominent Satanists, those promoted by Satanism, or classic demonic-focused literatures; political activism; use of magic for everyday manipulations; Satanic rite or ritual; Black Mass or Satanic-Gnostic mass.

SCIENTOLOGY

Scientology is the science of knowing how to know answers. It is a wisdom in the tradition of ten thousand years of search in Asia and Western civilization. It is the Science of Human Affairs which treats the livingness and beingness of Man and demonstrates to him a pathway to greater freedom.
(L. Ron Hubbard)[1]

THEOLOGY

Belief in eight different dynamics which are regarded as urges, motivations, drives, or impulses. None of these are seen as more necessary or urgent than others, but as individualistic. Some may pursue a few as more essential than others, but none are more essential than others. These are: The first dynamic, Self (individual expression); the Second dynamic, Sex (one's sexual drive as well as family life); the Third Dynamic, Group (desiring to be part of a greater group, especially those found in society); the Fourth Dynamic, Mankind (desiring to be part of mankind); the Fifth Dynamic, Animal (recognizing the existence of the animal kingdom; motivation of life), the Sixth Dynamic, Universe (existence as part of matter, energy, space, and time, abbreviated as MEST); the Seventh Dynamic, Spiritual (inclination to learn more about the spiritual realm), and Eighth Dynamic, god/deity (desire to know about a supreme being). The supreme being is recognized as INFINITY. One can only desire to know about the divine if they have awareness of their other seven dynamics.[2]

There is no specific dogma of the divine, nor is there any concept of relying on one's faith alone for belief. As one elevates through the eight different dynamics, one will come to recognize their essential potential. Then, adherents can fully understand the divine and their relationship therein. This awareness comes from knowledge and observation, as they can recognize things as they experience and learn through Scientology's process.

Most Scientologists would not refer to their embrace of Scientology as a "faith" or a "belief." Instead, it is the adherence of a specific set of principles outlined by L. Ron Hubbard (1911-1986), Scientology's founder. The unique doctrines of Scientology are regarded as scientific or equivalent to scientific laws and principles. The machinery and methods used to implement these applied methods in one's life are considered technologies. The concept of belief, especially when seen as being without evidence or causation, is less in relevance to Scientology principles. The practices of Scientology are validated through personal experience.[3]

Scientology's essence is part science fiction, part religion. Their creation myth emphasizes both, although it is not interconnected with a theology of deity. The concept of one's memories uncovered through Scientology meet claims of being 76,000,000,000,000 years old. Xenu (also called Xemu) was ruler of a Galactic Confederacy of 76 different planets. The planets themselves had existed for 20,000,000 years and were suffering from overpopulation. Xenu, fearing overthrow, gathered billions of people, froze them, captured their souls (known as thetans), and then transported them to earth (Teegeeack) to eliminate them. These thetans were dumped at the bottom of volcanoes and destroyed through different nuclear explosions. Only a few survived and were thrust into the air. Those souls captured by Xenu were implanted with misleading information, especially ideas found in the world's religions. Once his sinister plot was discovered, Xenu was imprisoned. Earth was left as a prison planet, now controlled by the Galactic Confederacy. Most Scientologists are unfamiliar with this teaching, as it is only revealed to individuals operating on the highest level. It is, therefore, denied by many in the organization, as they are unfamiliar with it.[4,5]

Philosophy

Scientology is a complicated system based on the writings of L. Ron Hubbard, a science fiction writer who set out in the early 1950s to promote the teaching of *Dianetics*, first through an organization and then through the Church of Scientology. Inspired by science fiction, Thelemite magic, technology, hypnotism, and anti-Christian themes, Hubbard created the different dynamics now known as Scientology. Scientology revolves around Dianetics, a pseudoscientific, metaphysical outlook on the connection between the mind, body, and actions. The basic theory states each individual person is a thetan, or soul (an immortal, spiritual being) now residing in a physical body. Each thetan has experienced a vast number of past lives, including within alien life and on alien planets. Scientologists seek to cross the Bridge to Total Freedom: one that takes them through each step to ultimately reach a higher place of existence. By crossing this bridge, Scientologists strive for the meaning of life. To cross it, they work out the different problems and aberrations they experience (including those incurred from past lives) through a process known as "auditing." Through auditing, a Scientologist known as a "preclear" (an individual who needs to recount events in their lives with the goal of overcoming their negative effects) sits with another individual, known as an auditor, and answers a series of questions. While answering these questions, responses are assessed on emotional responses (through a tone scale) by using a piece of equipment known as an "e-meter." An e-meter is based on the concept of a lie detector and is believed to read human response as one holds the metal receptors connected to a "meter" machine. The technology behind the e-machines is questionable at best, and pseudoscientific at least. Scientologists believe they can achieve a state of "clear" by advancing through this program: using auditing, reading the various books of L. Ron Hubbard, and moving through different levels. In such a state they are unaffected by the difficulties and issues incurred through the past, including past lives.

These different issues reside in a subconscious state known as latent. They can be from any origin and can result in any range of issues or complications in one's life. They can be anything from a mother not wanting a pregnancy, to something that someone said earlier in time, to something else that happened at some time in a past life, thus causing issues in this life. The only way to achieve ultimate happiness and experience a good life is to become clear through the application of Scientology principles throughout every aspect of one's life.

Scientologists believe they can "clear" the world by freeing individuals from the workings of the reactive mind (unconscious reactions to things caused by past traumas). Scientology sees the different complexities of society (from drug use and crime to failure and poverty) as the result of reactive issues. Scientology is seen as the answer to save humanity from its ills, evils, and issues. There are numerous organizations associated with Scientology that utilize the principles of Dianetics, all disguised as social service organizations. These include Applied Scholastics, Narconon (drug and alcohol treatment program), International Foundation for Human Rights and Tolerance, The Way to Happiness, Youth for Human Rights International, Criminon (program for prison rehabilitation, Citizens Commission on Human Rights, and the Association for Better Living and Education.

ADHERENT IDENTITY

Scientologist; Hubbardite (a pejorative term coined by Robert Heinlein, another Science Fiction writer).

TRADITIONAL LANGUAGES

English.

SECTS/DIVISIONS

Within Scientology itself, there are numerous separately incorporated organizations that represent the ideas of Scientology through fronts that appear to be sectarian or non-religious in nature. In this section, we will be examining groups that have their own unique headings rather than those that are Scientology under different names. The Church of Scientology goes to great lengths to suppress, silence, and discredit groups that break away from its main body. Scientology sects face the challenge of survival once they are no longer part of the main church body (as they do not have the finances and resources to survive). Still, there are a few key moments within Scientology history that have led to the creation of splinter groups: the movement of Hubbard toward the Church of Scientology and away from the Dianetics Foundation, and the ascent of David Miscavige to the presidency of the Church of Scientology. Scientology pejoratively identifies such groups as "squirrels." Scientology sects include:

- **The Church of Eductivism**: Founded by Jack Horner (1927-1989), a Scientology dissident who left the Church of Scientology in 1965. His original theory, Dianology, was Hubbard's ideas mixed with other ideas outside Scientology. This theory later became known as Eductivism and was seen as the way an individual could use their full spiritual potential to create and cease at the same time. He was moderately successful, creating the Church of Eductivism and Association of International Dianologists. Through the 1970s and 1980s, Horner was successful. The organization began to decline in popularity, and eventually ceased operations in the late 1990s.[6]

- **The Process Church of the Final Judgment**: Also called the Process Church. A religious group founded by Scientology excommunicants Mary Ann MacLean (1931-2005) and Robert de Grimston (1935-) in 1966. Classified as a mixture of Scientology and Satanism, The Process Church originally started as a Scientology splinter group called Compulsions Analysis. They started in Britain, then moved to the Bahamas, then Mexico City, and then finally establishing a presence in the United States. From what we know, the group sought to defy the being they saw as the supreme deity, and counseled members using a "P-Scope," based on Scientology's e-meter. There were four different divinities noted by the group: Jehovah (strength), Lucifer (light), Satan (separation), and Christ (unification), recognized as the "four great gods of the universe." They were not worshipped, and members were to follow the different gods best suited to them (each member was seen as a combination of two of these deities). As a group with a "last days" focus, they believed these four different divinities would come together in unity in these times, interpreted as the end of days. Members lived communally. Sex, drugs, and alcohol were rationed by church leaders, seen as a distraction. They did not practice magic but held rituals much like those seen in Christian rites: baptism, marriages, and a weekly Sabbath assembly. The group itself is of much lore and legend and has been associated with the Manson murders. They dissolved with the marriage of the founders in the late 1970s, and morphed into a few other groups (most of which have declined or disassociated since). These include the Foundation Church of the Millennium and the Foundation Faith of God.[7]

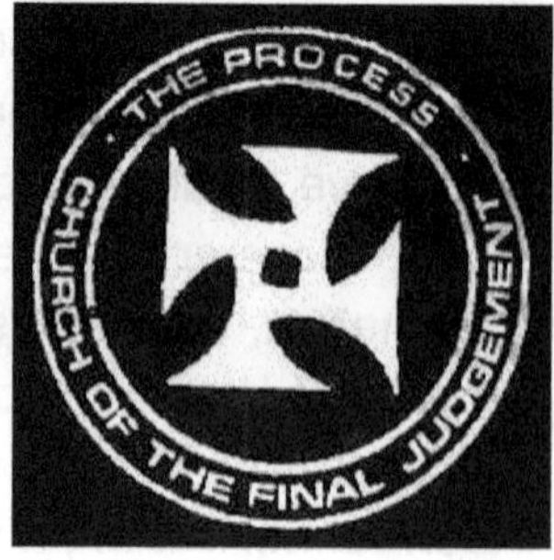

Process Church of the Final Judgment logo

- **Re-Evaluation Counseling**: Founded by Harvey Jackins (1916-1999) in the 1950s, this splinter group mixes ideas of peer counseling, Dianetics, and Marxism. They've met similar criticisms to Scientology: cult-like tendencies, pseudoscience, improper use of technique, and a desire to impose communism through the guise of a therapy.

Re-Evaluation Counseling logo

- **The Free Zone**: Also called "Freezone" or "Freezone Scientology." A term for "Independent Scientologists," individuals who believe in the beliefs and practices of Scientology but choose to practice them outside the Church of Scientology. They may practice all of them or part of them (such as auditing). The term itself is found within L. Ron Hubbard's literature, referring to the planet Teegeeack, known as "earth" or "terra," where political and economic interference is prohibited. There are several Free Zone groups in existence promoting different incorporations or modifications of Dianetics, including Synergetics and Idenics.[8]

Number of Adherents

There is great question over the exact number of Scientologists worldwide. The Church of Scientology is known to pad its numbers, claiming more adherents than there are. If someone has studied any part of Scientology's doctrine, even if it is in an introductory course (and they never study or practice the religion in reality), the Church of Scientology will count that individual as a "member." Actual membership of Scientology worldwide is somewhere around 40,000.[9]

Church of Scientology building, Los Angeles, California

Disputes Within Group

Scientology has had a long and controversial history, leading to many levels of dispute and disagreement. Disagreements first started when L. Ron Hubbard sought to take the principles of Dianetics and apply them to a church rather than as a research or betterment organization. When L. Ron Hubbard died, new leadership led to more controversy and dissention. With questions of excessive control, disciplinary measures, disclosing personal information obtained through audits, financial scandals, and questions about the organization's conduct and ethics, sects emerge as people try to sort out what they feel is redeemable within Scientology's practice. There remains considerable disagreement over leadership and the legitimacy of Scientology's practices, such as auditing.

Scriptures

All of L. Ron Hubbard's written and spoken records are considered Scientology's scriptures. This body of work includes a multitude of books, films, and several lectures (reported to be in the thousands). The main texts of Scientology include: *Dianetics: The Evolution of a Science*, *Science of Survival*, *Self-Analysis*, *History of Man*, *Scientology: 88*, *Scientology 8:80*, *How to Live Through an Executive*, *Scientology 55*, *The Creation of Human Ability*, *Scientology the Fundamentals of Thought*, *The Problems of Work*, *All about Radiation*, *Have You Lived Before This Life?*, *Scientology a New Slant on Life*, *Introduction to Scientology Ethics*, *The Phoenix Lectures*, *Organization Management Course*, and *The Technical Bulletins of Dianetics and Scientology*.[10,11]

> *When reading a book, be very certain that you never go past a word you do not fully understand. The only reason a person gives up a study or becomes confused or unable to learn is because he or she has gone past a word that was not understood.*[13]
>
> *One's attitude toward life makes every possible difference in one's living. You know, you don't have to study a thousand ancient books to discover that fact. But sometimes it needs to be pointed out again that life doesn't change so much as you.*
>
> *...The day when you stop building your own environment, when you stop building your own*

surroundings, when you stop waving a magic hand and gracing everything around you with magic and beauty, things cease to be magical, things cease to be beautiful. Well, maybe you've just neglected somewhere back in the last few years to wave that magic hand.[13]

The creation of Dianetics is a milestone for Man comparable to his discovery of fire and superior to his inventions of the wheel and the arch.[14]

A large proportion of allegedly feeble-minded children are actually attempted abortion cases.[15]

...However many billions America spends yearly on institutions for the insane and jails for the criminals are spent primarily because of attempted abortions done by some sex-blocked mother to whom children are a curse, not a blessing of God . . . All these things are scientific facts, tested and rechecked and tested again.[16]

Arthritis vanishes, myopia gets better, heart illness decreases, asthma disappears, stomachs function properly and the whole catalog of illnesses goes away and stays away.[17]

Adherents of Scientology follow what are called "The Basics," a set of eighteen books, fourteen lecture series, and twenty-eight lectures. Thoroughly edited for any mistakes, this set was released in 2007 and it was required for all Scientologists – regardless of their position or placement in the church – to start again with these "basics" and ascend again through Scientology's program. The cost of "The Basics" package costs around $4,000.[18]

BASIC RELIGIOUS PRACTICES

Scientologists begin their journeys at Scientology centers or churches, places where Scientologists gather to practice auditing, training, watch films, and offer introductory classes and weekly services. The major practices of every Scientologist are the auditing process and the study of L. Ron Hubbard's materials. At the most basic levels, there are introductory materials and classes offered for free or low cost (around $35 each) that do not count toward advance within the group. If one desires Scientology's services, one must pay for auditing, lectures, books, CDs, and cover a membership fee. Members are also encouraged to purchase large quantities of these books or packages of them to donate them to libraries or other organizations. The higher up one goes, the more expense is involved, including classes and more intense audits. To reach the highest points of the organization (those deemed to provide the most enlightenment), members pay anywhere from $250,000 to $500,000.

Scientologists believe they can achieve total freedom as they advance through The Bridge to Total Freedom (also known as the Bridge). Each member of Scientology passes through to their state of clear through auditing, which is seen as a lifetime commitment. Each step of the bridge features different auditing steps, known as Operating Thetan (OT) levels. Within the bridge, members have two options: the Processing Route, by which individuals pay through the process, or the Training Route, whereby members become Scientology Auditors; such purchase the necessary equipment to do so, with the cost resting somewhere around $50,000. There are eight different auditing levels on the Bridge, with members identified by their level, plus the number they are currently studying on (OT I-VIII).[19,20] These levels are:

- **OT I**: ($2,750) A solo-audited level; introduction to full OT abilities, and to begin to view the world through the MEST perspective.

- **OT II**: ($5,225) Due to the energy released from OT I, participants focus in on factors that cause a loss of freedom and ability to confront what lies ahead.

- **OT III**: ($8,910) The "Wall of Fire," which frees an individual from all things that have trapped them; confronts and destroys the fourth dynamic that keeps the universe bound and opens the way for peace and toleration among all people. OT III is considered a dangerous process and can cause any number of physical ailments if done improperly. Members must be invited to complete OT III and must sign a waiver of release to the church as well as a secrecy contract. It is considered a "secret" church doctrine.

- **OT IV**: ($6,500) The "Drug Rundown" addressing the issues and stops in the universe caused by the various effects of drugs, both prescription and recreational. OT IV exists to remove any impact that drugs might have left on someone's life. To complete this level, one must go to a special "Advanced Location" or Flag Building (Clearwater, Florida) to complete it. It takes anywhere from 12.5 to 25 hours to complete.

- **OT V**: ($7,400) The "Second Wall of Fire," New Era Dianetics, consisting of 26 different steps (called rundowns) that deal with life and the existence of life itself. Here, the final aspects that can prevent the achievement of total freedom on all dynamics are addressed. To complete this level, one must go to a special "Advanced Location" or Flag Building (Clearwater, Florida) to complete it. It takes about fifty hours to complete.

- **OT VI**: ($22,050) Hubbard Solo New Era Dianetics for OTS (Solo NOTs) Auditing Course; a training course one receives before starting to solo audit. Designed to handle issues that can destroy one's thetan powers. There are many auditing skills that come to pass, and many different things can go wrong or impact this level. Takes approximately three to four weeks to complete.

- **OT VII**: ($19,150) Hubbard Solo New Era Dianetics for OTs Auditing, a further training so one can solo audit in their home daily. It can take at least two years to complete (some remain on this level for five years or more) and is the final pre-OT level.

- **OT VIII**: ($24,800): "The Truth Revealed," the final level in Scientology, offered only aboard the Freewinds ship. What we know of this highest auditing level is from the revelation of former members. It contains a preparatory e-meter drill, followed by a review of *Scientology: A History of Man*, and an examination of previous past lives to figure out which ones are false. It seeks to identify the cause of amnesia and come to see the truth of one's existence. There are rumors this level contains exercises to communicate with plants and animals, as well as slurs on Jesus Christ, mention of the antichrist and the book of Revelations, and the untold story of L. Ron Hubbard's work.

When one completes the entire Bridge, they are Cleared Theta Clear. In this state, one is free to do everything a thetan should do, including control others, create their own universe, or create perceivable illusions.[21]

If at any time there is any adjustment made to L. Ron Hubbard's literature, processes involved in the Bridge, or classes, members must return to the beginning and then level up all over again. The process often winds up costing far more than original figures. Members have been known to borrow money, take out loans, draw on mortgages, or acquire serious debt in order to take – and retake – different Scientology courses and Bridge levels.[22,23]

In alignment with Scientology's position in church communities, Scientologists attend regular services and hold weddings, namings, and funerals at their local churches. Those who have completed Bridge work in the previous week are recognized at a Friday night graduation service. Scientology also offers weekly Sunday services that begin with the reading of the Creed of Scientology, a message or sermon based on the writings of L. Ron Hubbard, a lecture by L. Ron Hubbard (delivered through technological means), a group audit led by a leader (specifically directing a special audit for a group), announcements, and the concluding Prayer of Total Freedom:

May the author of the universe enable all men to reach an understanding of their spiritual nature.

May awareness and understanding of life expand, so that all may come to know the author of the universe.

And may others also reach this understanding which brings Total Freedom.

At this time, we think of those whose liberty is threatened; of those who have suffered imprisonment for their beliefs; of those who are enslaved or martyred, and for all those who are brutalized, trapped or attacked.

We pray that human rights will be preserved so that all people may believe and worship freely, so that freedom will once again be seen in our land.

Freedom from war, and poverty, and want; freedom to be; freedom to do and freedom to have.

Freedom to use and understand Man's potential—a potential that is God-given and Godlike.

And freedom to achieve that understanding and awareness that is Total Freedom.
May God let it be so.[24,25]

HOLIDAYS

Scientology does not prohibit the participation of any secular, cultural, or religious holidays. Among the religion itself, they are known to embrace and capitalize on the secular side of Christmas, producing a Christmas radio show and Winter Wonderland holiday village in Hollywood, California and Clearwater, Florida each year. Holidays unique to Scientology include[26]:

L. Ron Hubbard (1911-1986)

- **Criminon Day**: Celebrates the founding of the Criminon program in 1970 (January 25).
- **Narconon Day**: Celebrates the founding of Narconon in 1966 (February 19).
- **Celebrity Day**: Celebrates the opening of the Celebrity Centre Los Angeles in 1970 (February 22).
- **L. Ron Hubbard's Birthday**: Birth of Scientology's founder (March 13).
- **Student Day**: Celebrates the purchase and beginning of the Saint Hill Special Briefing Course in 1961 (March 24).
- **L. Ron Hubbard Exhibition Day**: Celebrates the opening of the L. Ron Hubbard Life Exhibition in Hollywood, California (April 20).
- **Anniversary of Dianetics**: Release of *Dianetics: The Modern Science of Mental Health* in 1950 (May 9).
- **Integrity Day**: The day to contemplate on Scientology Ethics, released by Hubbard in 1965 (May 25).
- **Maiden Voyage Anniversary**: The yearly anniversary of new OT VIII members departing on the Freewinds ship to advance through the final level of Scientology's Bridge (June 6).
- **Academy Day**: Acknowledgement of Hubbard's Study Tech, the teaching method used by Scientologists in childhood education (June 18).
- **Sea Org Day**: Rank and rating promotions for Sea Org members (August 12).
- **Clear Day**: The anniversary of Hubbard's Clearing Course, established in 1965 (September 4).

- **Auditor's Day**: Recognizes Dianetics auditors (2nd Sunday in September).

- **International Association of Scientologists (IAS) Anniversary**: Commemmorates the founding of the IAS, redication to its goals, the issuing of awards, and the convention of IAS delegates (October 7).

- **Publications Day**: Celebrates "Publications Worldwide," opened at St. Hill Manor in 1967 (November 27).

- **Flag Land Base Day**: Acknowledges the opening of the Flag Land base in Clearwater, Florida back in 1975 (December 7).

- **Freedom Day**: Celebrates the day Scientology was acknowledged as a religion in the United States, first in 1974 (December 30).

- **New Year's Eve**: Celebrates the accomplishments of the previous year while looking to the new year and plans to reach the world with more Scientology information; acknowledges those who are helping new people move up the Bridge to Total Freedom (December 31).

VISUAL SIGNS AND SYMBOLS

Scientology cross (eight-point cross; two intersecting bars with four diagonal rays that signify the eight dynamics of Scientology); The letter S (for Scientology) interlocking through two triangles (top triangle represents knowledge, responsibility, and control while the bottom triangle represents affinity, reality, and communication); the Dianetics symbol (a green triangle with a green and yellow stripes, representing growth and life); Sea Org symbol (two rounded, overlapped olive branches with a star in the middle of them); L. Ron Hubbard symbol (cursive L, R, and H); Operating Thetan symbol (the letter T inside the letter O); Church of Spiritual Technology logo (two overlapping circles with a diamond in the center of each circle); books written by L. Ron Hubbard.[27]

CREEDS, BOOKS, AND LAWS

Scientology is known for its complex leadership structure and governance, all of which revolves in different ways around the teaching of L. Ron Hubbard. As a universal statement of agreement, the Creed of Scientology was penned by Hubbard himself and is recited at all Scientology services.

> *We of the Church believe*
> *That all men of whatever race, color or creed were created with equal rights.*
> *That all men have inalienable rights to their own religious practices and their performance.*
> *That all men have inalienable rights to their own lives.*
> *That all men have inalienable rights to their sanity.*
> *That all men have inalienable rights to their own defense.*

That all men have inalienable rights to conceive, choose, assist or support their own organizations, churches and governments.
That all men have inalienable rights to think freely, to talk freely, to write freely their own opinions and to counter or utter or write upon the opinions of others.
That all men have inalienable rights to the creation of their own kind.
That the souls of men have the rights of men.
That the study of the Mind and the healing of mentally caused ills should not be alienated from religion or condoned in nonreligious fields.
And that no agency less than God has the power to suspend or set aside these rights, overtly or covertly.
And we of the Church believe
That Man is basically good.
That he is seeking to Survive.
That his survival depends upon himself and upon his fellows and his attainment of brotherhood with the Universe.

And we of the Church believe that the laws of God forbid Man
To destroy his own kind.
To destroy the sanity of another.
To destroy or enslave another's soul.
To destroy or reduce the survival of one's companions or one's group.
And we of the Church believe
That the spirit can be saved.
And that the spirit alone may save or heal the body.[28]

Along with their creed, Scientologists also have their own Code of Honor:

No one expects the Code of Honor to be closely and tightly followed.

An ethical code cannot be enforced. Any effort to enforce the Code of Honor would bring it into the level of a moral code. It cannot be enforced simply because it is a way of life which can exist as a way of life only as long as it is not enforced. Any other use but self-determined use of the Code of Honor would, as any Scientologist could quickly see, produce a considerable deterioration in a person. Therefore its use is a luxury use, and which is done solely on self-determined action, providing one sees eye to eye with the Code of Honor.

1. *Never desert a comrade in need, in danger or in trouble.*
2. *Never withdraw allegiance once granted.*
3. *Never desert a group to which you owe your support.*
4. *Never disparage yourself or minimize your strength or power.*
5. *Never need praise, approval or sympathy.*
6. *Never compromise with your own reality.*
7. *Never permit your affinity to be alloyed.*
8. *Do not give or receive communication unless you yourself desire it.*
9. *Your self-determinism and your honor are more important than your immediate life.*
10. *Your integrity to yourself is more important than your body.*
11. *Never regret yesterday. Life is in you today and you make your tomorrow.*

12. Never fear to hurt another in a just cause.
13. Don't desire to be liked or admired.
14. Be your own adviser, keep your own counsel and select your own decisions.
15. Be true to your own goals.

This is the ethical code of Scientology, the code one uses not because he has to but because he can afford such a luxury.[29]

The Church of Scientology and all its subsidiaries adhere to a hierarchical, authoritarian system that influences its personal legal and ethical codes. There are several internal documents (only circulated among Scientology officials) that impact the way members are treated, outsiders are handled, dissidents are addressed, and internal members are assessed for promotion or punishment. Within the authoritarian structure are several accusations against Scientology's leaders; everything from starvation and labor to unlawful imprisonment or abuse. Navigating Scientology's hierarchy and its incorporations, organizations, and levels is often confusing and confounding for outsiders.

The Church of Scientology is controlled by the Religious Technology Center, under Scientology's president (at the time of publication, the president is David Miscavige). Every organization associated with Scientology signs a contract with the Religious Technology Center, which can close all Scientology-based organizations without any foreknowledge or warning. All Scientology subsidiary organizations pay the Religious Technology Center through regular tithes and consultation fees.

Below the Religious Technology Center is International Management, headed by the Watchdog Committee. International Management groups control all organizations that represent Scientology's subsidiary organizations. These include The Commodore's Messengers Organization International, which controls the computer system which all licensed organizations report to (International Computer Organized ManageMent); the Senior Case Supervisor International (training and counseling); the Executive Director International and the Senior Executive Strata. These groups are headquartered in Los Angeles, California.

Upper Middle Management is overseen by the Flag Command Bureaux which controls the Office of Special Affairs International. Visible organizations are under these management spheres, including the Flag Service Organization (runs the base in Clearwater, Florida); the Flag Ship Service Organization (runs the Freewinds ship); the Church of Scientology Celebrity Center International; Scientology Missions International; the Church of Scientology of San Francisco; Church of Scientology Religious Education College, and a variety of other smaller, independent organizations.[30]

The Sea Org (short for Sea Organization) is Scientology's religious organization, consisting of the most dedicated Scientologists who commit to Scientology for a billion years (signified by contract). These are the workers of Scientology, those who perform several varied functions within the organization to keep things operational. They commit to live, eat, and work together. Sea Org members are prohibited from marrying people outside the Sea Org. Members cannot have ever taken psychiatric or psychoactive drugs or undergone psychiatric treatment at any point in their lives. Many Sea Org members are the children of Scientologists or those who have committed to be part of the organization for a long period of time. There are approximately

10,000 to 20,000 Sea Org members worldwide. They vary from staff in that staff members are paid higher wages than Sea Org members and can maintain other jobs while assisting the goals of Scientology.

The Sea Org is under fire for many of its controversial practices, including forced abortions (Sea Org couples are prohibited from having children), one must leave with permission or face termination, living conditions are substandard, medical care is not provided, labor laws are ignored (members are subject to long hours and hard labor), lack of privacy, and intense physical punishments for disobedience or lack of conformity. Those who do not conform with Sea Org expectations are sent to the Rehabilitation Project Force, where individuals can perform hard physical labor for up to ten years.[31]

Scientology logo

Within Scientology itself, there exists controversy and disconnect between ethical conduct and the behaviors of those at the top levels of Scientology. Ethics and breaches often come into question when one leaves the organization, criticizes it, or is somehow perceived to defame it. Scientology has no issue labeling, defaming, or criticizing its critics, going as far as possible to defame them as imaginable. This their doctrine known as Fair Game. They apply personal defamation measures (especially in modern times, using the internet) to those who leave as well as those outside of the church who are critical of Scientology. In defense of its identity and to control its image, Scientology is careful with trademarks and copyrights of its name, organizations, and images. They also hold several real estate properties which are sold as needed for additional funding and recruitment.

Due to their own antics, the nature of Scientology is not without dispute. Some have questioned the validity of Scientology's status as a religion and most certainly as a church, due to the secrecy, high control nature, mistreatment of members, and its cost-based financial structure. There have been raids, investigations, and suppressions in different countries. As a result, Scientology has spent years in litigation and lawsuits, defending its entity as a religion and non-profit organization. Extensive litigation has not prevented Scientology from being outlawed in several countries, including Belgium, Chile, China, Finland, France, and Germany. In some other countries, it is not classified as a religion; some recognize it as a nonprofit organization, but others consider it a corporation or do not acknowledge it as having any specific status.

ECLECTIC BELIEFS

Scientology sees itself as a modern-day, technological religion, one that can change and transform the world through the application of its ideas and methods. Relying on the ideals of L. Ron Hubbard, his nature and character within Scientology takes on a Messianic-like quality. Hubbard's life, however, has been well-documented outside of Scientology, and there is question over Scientology's presentation of its founder. Scientology has been known to falsify details of his life, presenting things in a manner inconsistent with realities and testimonies of others, and expecting followers to refrain from embracing secular information about Hubbard, claiming it biased or false.

When an individual agrees to become part of the Church of Scientology, they are required to sign four different waivers: a Religious Services Enrollment Application, Agreement and General Release (protects the church in their application of services); Agreement and General Release Regarding Spiritual Assistance (refuses psychiatric treatment, with church officials called in such a situation, rather than a doctor, hospital, or ambulance); Agreement Regarding Confidential Religious Files (staff members will never have access to their own private church records, as they belong to the Church of Scientology); and Attestation of Religious Belief Regarding the Scientology Religious Film Called Orientation (signed after watching the *Orientation: A Scientology Information Film*, which is shown to potential members before attending their first service at the Church of Scientology).

Scientology is opposed to psychiatry and psychiatry, believing both are responsible for the ills we see in the world, today. Mental sciences are believed to be corrupt and credited as the cause for worldwide disasters (including the Holocaust). Scientologists are active in their pursuit against the practice of psychology and psychiatry in general, and are opposed to the use of psychiatric drugs, electroconvulsive shock therapy, lobotomy, painkillers, tranquilizers, and antidepressants. Their solution to such things is Dianetics, which free and clear a person of past trauma. For those on the verge of a mental breakdown, the church offers an Introspection Rundown, a special audit that tries to figure out what is causing such within a person's mind.

Many are surprised to learn Scientology focuses on family structure, through a traditional, patriarchal model. Women are degraded in much of L. Ron Hubbard's literature, especially in the context of motherhood. Same-sex marriage is disapproved. In all relationships, Scientology principles and organization adherence comes first. The Cadet Org (a now-defunct organization) would enlist children as young as nine or ten years old to begin Sea Org work, living away from their families, and especially their parents. Divorce is frowned upon, and couples in crisis are expected to undergo auditing to resolve their issues. In instances where a family member laves Scientology, remaining members practice disconnection (completely disconnecting from an individual in every way feasible). When an individual is disconnected, Scientologists have no connection with that individual, whether it is a friend, a family member, or someone close to them.[32]

RELATIONS WITH NON-SCIENTOLOGISTS

Scientology is primarily about aggressive recruitment. Members are encouraged to promote the virtues of Scientology to their friends and family, to get them interested in attending a service or receive auditing services. Scientology claims no issue with other religions and promotes what they deem as "interfaith" events, featuring speakers from other religious groups. As one advances within Scientology's ranks, however, one finds a totally different picture of world religions. Scientologists are prohibited from practicing any other religion or any components thereof. Anything other than Scientology is forbidden. Scientology writings are critical and disrespectful of other religious leaders, such as Jesus Christ, Mohammed, and various Hindu traditions (such as yoga).

HOLY SITES

Scientology cross

Saint Hill Manor, Saint Hill, Wes Sussex, England; Flag Land Base, Clearwater, Florida; Gold Base, Riverside County, California; Trementina Base, Trementina, New Mexico; Freewinds cruise ship; the Church of Scientology Los Angeles, California; Celebrity Center International, Los Angeles, California; Association for Better Living and Education and Author Services, Los Angeles, California; Ideal Orgs (a building project to encourage Scientology churches to buy larger buildings), with various projects across the United States, South Africa, Italy, Sweeden, Belgium, Australia, Mexico, London, Canada, Germany, and Ireland.

NOTABLE FIGURES

Scientology places a great emphasis on celebrity recruitment and membership. Notable Scientologists include L. Ron Hubbard (1911-1986), founder; Kristie Alley (1951-2022), actress; Ann Archer (1947-), actress, Beck (1970-), musician; Grant Cardone (1958-), author; Jeff Conaway (1950-2011), actor; Tom Cruise (1960-), actor; Jenna Elfman (1971-), actress; Peaches Geldof (1989-2014), daughter of Bob Geldof (1951-); Isaac Hayes (1942-2008), musician; Juliette Lewis (1973-), actress; Lisa Marie Presley (1968-2023), musician; Priscilla Presley (1945-), actress; John Travolta (1954-), actor; Nancy Cartwright (1957-), voiceover accress; Doug E. Fresh (1966-), musician; Elisabeth Moss (1982-), actress; Giovanni Ribisi (1974-), actor; Marissa Ribisi (1974-), actress; Sonny Bono (1935-1998), actor and politician; Elli Perkins (1949-2003), businesswoman; Charles Manson (1934-2017), famous murderer.

NOTABLE GROUPS

The New Cult Awareness Network is known as a "Scientology front" organization. It appears, on the surface, to have nothing to do with Scientology. Its original incarnation, the Cult Awareness Network, was as an independent organization forced into bankruptcy after Scientology launched an endless number of lawsuits (at least fifty) against them. The original Cult Awareness Network had numerous files on groups suspicious of cult activity, including the Church of Scientology. The Church of Scientology deemed the Cult Awareness Network a "hate group." Now known as "the New Cult Awareness Network," if one calls or writes for information, they will be contacting a Scientologist.[33]

FACTS AND FIGURES

As a religious group, Scientology's numbers are constantly decreasing. Even though Scientology itself claims member ranks in the millions, statistics prove Scientology ranks on the lower end of minority religions. There are fewer Scientologists in the United States and Britain than Unitarian

Universalists, Wiccans, Druids, Spiritualists, New Agers, Pagans, and Taoists.[34]

OTHER IMPORTANT DEFINITIONS[35]

- **AA**: Stands for "attempted abortion." L. Ron Hubbard believes pregnant women routinely tried to terminate their pregnancies, thus causing a specific kind of engram, one that would impact the subconscious of a person and damage their entire lives.

- **Aberrated**: Hubbard's terminology for mental insanity.

- **Action**: An auditing regimen, using Scientology's technology on a person.

- **Admin Dictionary**: A large dictionary made up of quotations from L. Ron Hubbard.

- **Amends Project**: An assigned project, often of manual labor, to provide an individual in Scientology who is not performing as desired to redeem themselves.

- **Anaten**: The merging of the words "analytical and attenuation;" when a person goes "unconscious" for a moment during an auditing session.

- **Anger**: Trying to keep everything still; a hate hold.

- **Apathy**: Completely withdrawing from people; no effort; imitating death.

- **As-is**: To look at something and make it disappear.

- **Bank**: The Reactive Mind.

- **Basher**: A personal critical of Scientology.

- **Beingness**: Choosing of a category of identity; the person one should aspire to be for survival; a self-identification with an object.

- **Book One**: A term for Hubbard's *Dianetics* and auditing as established in the book.

- **Cans**: The metal electrodes used on an e-meter.

- **Chain**: A series of memories or incidents of a similar type or content.

- **Cognition**: A realization that one will have about themselves as pertains to Scientology.

- **Conditions**: The ethics formula for Scientology: Power, Power Change, Affluence, Normal Operation, Emergency, Danger, Non-Existence, Liability, Doubt, Enemy, Treason, and

Confusion. All contain formulas and exist so members will produce new members, money, and productivity for Scientology.

- <u>D/A</u>: Stands for "Dead Agent," a term used to discredit an anti-Scientologist person or organization.

- <u>Engram</u>: The remains of a memory; a mental image of a picture that threatens survival, as it remains to recall pain within the unconscious.

- <u>Wog world</u>: Everyday society outside of Scientology.

- <u>Gang-Bang Sec Check</u>: The use of an e-meter auditing in front of a group to get an individual to confess to specific "crimes" committed against Scientology.

- <u>Illegal PC</u>: A preclear individual who cannot be audited, because they are, for whatever reason, in need of help beyond what Scientology can offer.

- <u>Implant</u>: A hypnotic idea that has been placed in one's mind in a past life, millions or billions of years ago.

- <u>Indicate</u>: To assess using the e-meter.

- <u>Intention</u>: To project theta into an object or other person to control them.

- <u>K/R</u>: Abbreviation for Knowledge Report; a write-up of the supposed wrongdoings of a Scientologist that are then given to the Ethics division of Scientology.

- <u>NED</u>: Abbreviation for New Era Dianetics; signifying the entire expanse of time, covering 75 trillion years.

- <u>Neurotic</u>: A person who has concern about the future, pondering the past and worried that they have not properly acted in the past.

- <u>Processing</u>: Auditing someone in Scientology.

- <u>Sec Check</u>: Abbreviation for "Security Checking," which runs down a long list of personal questions on a preclear using the e-meter. Questions are used to discover items that can be used for blackmail or slander purposes if someone leaves or threatens the organization. Sec Check questions are often about personal criminal history and sexual habits or issues.

- <u>Somatics</u>: Physical pain or discomfort that is restimulated during auditing, as contained within an engram or memory.

- **Statistics**: In Scientology, the monitoring of an individual's success as reported by an Ethics Officer.

- **Suppressive Person**: An individual who is seen as critical or nonconforming to Scientology.

- **Up Stat**: A condition by which a Scientologist sees production statistics increasing, based on new converts and higher revenues as Scientologists level up.

BELIEVER'S CHARACTERISTICS

Interest in science, technology, and science fiction; belief in the work and writings of L. Ron Hubbard; authoritarian leadership structure; negative attitude toward psychiatry and psychology; traditional, patriarchal family structures; distrust of the outside world; faith in auditing; placing Scientology and its goals above everything else in one's life; moving up the bridge; belief Scientology can heal the world; negativity toward Scientology critics; defensiveness of the religion; participation and advocacy of Scientology's numerous programs; belief in Dianetics and the various Dianetics models that are used throughout Scientology (such as in education and drug programs); over-extended financial commitments to the church; celebration of Scientology holidays; unconventional beliefs about the foundation of the world, all with a sci-fi edge.

Seventh-Day Adventism

Has God no living church? He has a church, but it is the church militant, not the church triumphant. We are sorry that there are defective members...While the Lord brings into the church those who are truly converted, Satan at the same time brings persons who are not converted into its fellowship. While Christ is sowing the good seed, Satan is sowing the tares. There are two opposing influences continually exerted on the members of the church. One influence is working for the purification of the church, and the other for the corrupting of the people of God.
(Ellen G. White)[1]

Theology

Modern-day Seventh-day Adventism adheres to the doctrine of the Trinity as is expressed in many Christian denominations: Belief in one true God, traditionally referred to as LORD GOD, JEHOVAH, FATHER, or in some modern traditions, YAHWEH, with personal attributes. God is seen as being infinite and beyond human comprehension but known through His self-revelation to humanity. God is seen as eternally existent in three divine persons: Father, Son, and Holy Spirit. God is considered immortal, all-powerful, all-knowing, above all, and ever present; forever worthy of worship, adoration, and service.[2]

Until the 1890s, the majority of the Seventh-day Adventist movement was anti-Trinitarian, opting for belief that the Father, Son, and Holy Spirit were three distinct entities, much akin to an Arianism or Biblical Unitarianism in their theology: The Father was God, the Son was divine but begotten, with a beginning, and the Holy Spirit was a manifestation of either the Father or the Son. It was Ellen Gould White (1827-1915), a major prophetic figure within the Adventist movement, who was the first to presuppose the eternity of Christ and the personage of the Holy Spirit. Between the 1890s and the 1930s, Adventists wrestled with their theological viewpoints, ultimately adopting a Trinitarian theology. By the 1970s, it was the desire of the Adventist community to expound upon and explore Trinitarianism officially, and such was confirmed in 1980 with the adoption of the fundamental Adventist beliefs.[3]

Philosophy

Seventh-day Adventism is an outgrowth of the Millerite Movement, an Evangelical-based movement started by a man named William Miller (1782-1849). Miller believed he was able to determine the date of Jesus Christ's Second Coming (through careful study of Biblical prophecy and dating) from the beginning of time to his era of history. He used the "day-year principle" in which the word "day" in Biblical prophecy is the equivalent of one year of time in chronology. The series of dates predicted, calculated, and recalculated were as follows: first in the fall of 1843, then in March of 1844, then in April of 1844, and finally, on October 22, 1844. When These dates came and went without manifestation, the event became known as "The Great Disappointment." Many returned to their own lives, some abandoned faith all together, and others came to believe William Miller did indeed discover the "start" of something in 1844, but it was not the Second Coming. These people became known as Adventists. A small group of Adventists believed Miller's discovery was the dating for an end times investigative judgment, coming to fruition at the end of a prophetic period of 2300 days (in chronological time, 2300 years). Now, Seventh-day Adventists believe we are in a period where Christ judges the living and the dead for righteousness in a pre-advent (pre-coming) period. This is known as "cleansing the sanctuary," a second and final phase of Christ's atonement. The ultimate removal of sin and the heavenly sanctuary (of which the earthly sanctuary in the Old Testament is a type) is cleaned, once and for all, with the blood of Christ. Those who are dead in Christ and part of Him shall be judged worthy to have part in the first resurrection. Those who now live for Christ as part of the Seventh-day Adventist movement (keeping the commandments of God) are ready to "translate," or be taken into the everlasting kingdom. Those who believe properly in the faith are vindicated by God's justice, and those who remain loyal shall receive the eternal kingdom. The entirety of this judgment, which is seen as the completion of Christ's ministry, will close before Christ returns. This return of Christ can literally be at any time. The proponents of this theory became the founders of Seventh-day Adventism, especially James (1821-1881) and Ellen Gould White.[4]

As Adventist groups broke away, Ellen Gould White became a central figure within what would become the Seventh-day Adventist movement. Ellen White began having visions shortly after The Great Disappointment (possibly as the result of a head injury, leaving her a frontal lobe epileptic who experienced visions). Throughout her life, she claimed over two thousand in totality. These different visions led to her identity among Adventists as being a prophet, one endowed with a gift of prophecy designed to lead through these times. As a result of these visions, White began writing. Her books remain central to Seventh-day Adventist doctrine, especially the book *Conflict of the Ages*. She depicted the great battle between Jesus and Satan playing out on earth as well as the cosmos, involving the challenges and decisions of humanity. Through another vision, she claimed she saw the Ten Commandments with the fourth commandment (observe the Sabbath day) lit up, more prominent and relevant than all the others. Combined with the influences of the Seventh-day Baptist movement, this led their Adventist community to become Seventh-day Adventists, believing the true day of worship is the Saturday Sabbath rather than Sunday. (They believe Christian worship on Sunday was part of a pagan conspiracy by the Emperor Constantine in the fourth century.) Adventists believe at some point in history it will be illegal to worship on the Saturday Sabbath, as Sunday worship will be the Mark of the Beast (mentioned in the book of Revelation).

Therefore, Seventh-day Adventists, gather for worship on Saturdays rather than Sundays. Their extensive doctrinal beliefs revolve around complex eschatological views, highly influenced by Ellen Gould White. They also believe that certain Old Testament laws, such as the Ten Commandments and various guidelines for health are required practices for believers today.

TRADITIONAL LANGUAGES

English.

ADHERENT IDENTITY

Seventh-day Adventist Church, Seventh-day Adventism; Seventh-day Adventists; Adventists; SDA; Sabbatarians.

SECTS/DIVISIONS

Seventh-day Adventism is, in its essence, a splinter group of Adventism. This has not stopped some of their own members from breaking away from the larger SDA community and starting their own. These groups include:

Branch Davidian flag

- **The Davidians**: Also known as the Davidian SDA, Shepherd's Rod, Branch Davidians, Historic Davidians, and Koreshians. The Davidians are the most notable offshoot of Seventh-day Adventism, founded by Victor Houteff (1855-1955) in 1929. He was the movement's prophet, pushing for reform among the Seventh-day Adventist Church. He believed the church was becoming too lax and, in response, began teaching his own unique interpretation of church doctrine (much of it seen as a blend of New Thought and Adventist eschatology). He was disfellowshipped from his local church in 1930, right before the publication of his book *The Shepherd's Rod.* Determined to promote changes, Houteff refused to leave the church. In 1936, his message was pronounced as heresy. In 1934, the Shepherd's Rod organization came into being. They were later known as the Davidian Seventh-day Adventists. The Branch Davidians were a sect of the main Davidian organization, founded by Benjamin Roden (1902-1978) after the death of Victor Houteff. Roden became the Branch Davidian prophet, claiming he was the modern-day successor of King David. His leadership was followed by his wife, Louis Roden (1916-1986), until the advance of David Koresh (1959-1993) in the 1980s. Today, there are still followers of David Koresh awaiting his return in the resurrection, now known as Koreshians.

- **Seventh-day Adventist Reform**: Seventh-day Adventism has always dealt with challenges related to traditionalism and reform. As the church has sought to develop itself in different waves and movements of examination, there have always been groups resistant to changes or formation as has been presented and accepted by the mainline church. During World War I, there was a wave of such controversy over the role of Seventh-day

Adventists and military involvement, specifically their doctrine of pacifism. In Europe, SDA leaders decided it was all right for members to bear arms and serve in military forces, which conflicted with church authorities. The resulting breakaway group became the Seventh Day Adventist Reform Movement, which later relocated to the United States. It also subsequently led to another group known as the True and Free Seventh-day Adventists. They believed the decisions of European SDA leaders meant the entire denomination had become "Babylon." For the most part, both groups very closely resemble their Seventh-day Adventist origins with slight or minor differences.[5]

Davidian SDA logo

- **Historic Adventism**: Historic Adventists represent conservative ideals with the desire to preserve what is seen as the traditional or "historical" Seventh-day Adventism. Because Adventist doctrine has changed throughout the years, many SDAs believe the systematic changes have moved the church so close to Evangelical Christianity, it has lost its unique identity. Most Historic Adventists take issue with the addition of Trinitarianism, emphasize the essential nature of sanctification, believe Ellen G. White's writings are infallible, and that members of the true church must achieve perfection (spiritual and moral) in this generation. Many are adherents of the King James Only movement, using only the King James Version of the Bible. Historic Adventists don't always break away from the SDA Church, although their relationship with it may be strained or terminated by SDA headquarters. Some Historic Adventist groups include Concerned Brethren, the Adventist Laymen's Fellowship, Hope International, the Hartland Institute, and Remnant Ministries.[6]

- **Progressive Adventism**: In contrast with Historic Adventists, Progressive Adventists are members of the Seventh-day Adventist church that disagree with or advocate a different emphasis on key doctrines within the history of the movement. Specifically in play are the twenty-eight fundamental SDA beliefs (the nature of the Trinity, emphasis on the law, Sabbath observance, nature of Christ, gift of prophecy, or beliefs about creation), the doctrine of the investigative judgment, the belief in global Sunday law to come, and the use of Ellen G. White's writings. Rather than adhering to the traditional church form, many use contemporary Christian music, Evangelical or Charismatic worship structure, and are more mainstream in their style and worship. They tend to be more open to ecumenical activities and are more accepting of Christians of differing denominations. Progressive Adventists aren't an organized group and maintain their membership within the denomination. Examples of Progressive Adventist groups include Adventist Society for Religious Studies, Adventist Forums Conference, Adventists Today Conference, and Spiritual Renaissance Retreat.[7]

NUMBER OF ADHERENTS

There are approximately between 20,000,000 and 25,000,000 Seventh-day Adventists worldwide.[8]

Disputes Within Group

The nature of the SDA movement has three key points to it that make it subject to dispute: the role of Ellen G. White (and subsequently its unique perspectives on prophecy), its perspectives on coming global events as part of its eschatology, and its history of doctrinal change. When an organization believes so keenly that a spiritual gift (such as prophecy) does or can exist only by a localized or central figure, such opens the door for others to come along later, gather a group of disciples, become an almost Messianic-like figure, and claim or follow the same abilities as that original central figure with the intent to restore or bring the group back to its founding principles. When a group is so highly eschatological in nature, there will forever be dispute about the doctrines relating to such because the Bible is not always explicitly clear about what will or will not happen every step of the way, through the end times. With room to question such doctrine and the way the SDA Church has changed its fundamental theologies over the years, splinter groups, internal conflicts, and disputes are inevitable.

As a result, SDA disputes include those over eschatology, historical doctrines of the movement, the role and work of Ellen G. White within the framework of the religion today, the Sabbath, health codes, social prohibitions, current leadership, and the very nature of what it means to be SDA today.

Scriptures

The Holy Bible, Old and New Testaments: the Pentateuch (Genesis, Exodus, Leviticus, Numbers, and Deuteronomy), Historical books (Joshua, Judges, Ruth, 1 Samuel, 2 Samuel, 1 Kings, 2 Kings, 1 Chronicles, 2 Chronicles, Ezra, Nehemiah, Esther), Wisdom books (Job, Psalms, Proverbs, Ecclesiastes, Song of Songs), Prophetic books (Isaiah, Jeremiah, Lamentations, Ezekiel, Daniel, Hosea, Joel, Amos, Obadiah, Jonah, Micah, Nahum, Habakkuk, Zephaniah, Haggai, Zechariah, Malachi), the Gospels (Matthew, Mark, Luke, John), the Acts of the Apostles, the Pauline Epistles (Romans, 1 Corinthians, 2 Corinthians, Galatians, Ephesians, Philippians, Colossians, 1 Thessalonians, 2 Thessalonians, 1 Timothy, 2 Timothy, Titus, Philemon, Hebrews) the General Epistles (James, 1 Peter, 2 Peter, 1 John, 2 John, 3 John, Jude) and Revelation. Most Seventh-day Adventists use the King James Version. Other translations one might use are the New King James Version, New American Standard Bible, the English Standard Version, and the Revised Standard Version.

Seventh-Day Adventist Church logo

There is considerable debate over the exact role of Ellen G. White's writings among Seventh-day Adventists today. Her writings are believed to have been authored under the gift of prophecy (as understood to be the Holy Spirit working through an individual to impart a message through a person). According to the church, there are five tests for a true prophet: dreams and visions, agreement with the

Bible, the witness of Jesus, fulfilled prophecy, and the "orchard test," by which an individual still produces spiritual fruit while scrutinized and examined by others.[9] The church believes White was successful in all five points, and thus her work was guided by divine inspiration. Though some would question the equivalency of Ellen G. White's work in comparison to the Bible, her understanding, interpretation, and extensive literary works are the very shape and understanding of Seventh-day Adventism as we understand it today. Inspired by a variety of sources, including apocryphal works (some of which have a questionable authenticity, such as the Book of Jasher), scientific beliefs popular in that era (many of which have been disproven), and different ideas about health and wellness, also those popular during her lifetime. She authored over two hundred works in her lifetime, most of which are still available today. Some of her major works include:

- ***<u>Steps to Christ</u>***: An introductory primer on how to know Jesus Christ as an individual, examining such topics as repentance, confession, faith, growing into Christ, and personal prayer.

  God does not require us to give up anything that it is for our best interest to retain. In all that He does he has the well-being of his (own) in view. Would that all who have not chosen Christ might realize that he has something vastly better to offer them than they are seeking for themselves. Man is doing the greatest injury and injustice to his own soul when he thinks and acts contrary to the will of God. No real (and lasting) joy can be found in the path forbidden by Him who knows what is best and who plans for the good of his creatures. The path of transgression is the path of misery and destruction.[10]

  It is written that God cursed the ground for man's sake. Genesis 3:17. The thorn and the thistle—the difficulties and trials that make his life one of toil and care—were appointed for his good as a part of the training needful in God's plan for his uplifting from the ruin and degradation that sin has wrought.[11]

- ***<u>Conflict of the Ages Series</u>***: A five-volume work that examines the history of the Bible, from Genesis to the Second Coming of Jesus Christ.[12]

  Volumes I-V are: *Patriarchs and Prophets* (the rebellion of Satan in Heaven to the time of King David), *Prophets and Kings* (King Solomon to Malachi), *The Desire of the Ages* (the life and ministry of Jesus Christ), *Acts of the Apostles* (Great Commission of Matthew 28:19 to the book of Revelation), and *The Great Controversy* (the destruction of Jerusalem in 70 AD through the entirety of church history, including the end of sin and recreation of planet earth). The most popular, and widely circulated, of these books are *The Desire of the Ages* and *The Great Controversy.*

  If intellectual greatness, apart from any higher consideration, is worthy of honor, then our homage is due to Satan, whose intellectual power no man has ever equaled. But when perverted to self-serving, the greater the gift, the greater curse it becomes. It is moral worth that God values. Love and purity are the attributes He prizes most.[13]

  The only defense against evil is the indwelling of Christ in the heart through faith in His righteousness. Unless we become vitally connected with God, we can never resist the unhallowed effects of self-love, self-indulgence, and temptation to sin. We may leave off many bad habits, for the time we may part company with Satan; but without a vital connection with God, through the surrender of ourselves to Him moment by moment, we shall be overcome. Without a personal acquaintance with Christ, and a continual communion, we are at the mercy of the enemy, and shall do his bidding in the end.[14]

given men warning of coming judgments. Those who had faith in His message for their time, and who acted out their faith, in obedience to His commandments, escaped the judgments that fell upon the disobedient and unbelieving. The word came to Noah, "Come thou and all thy house into the ark; for thee have I seen righteous before Me." Noah obeyed and was saved. The message came to Lot, "Up, get you out of this place; for the Lord will destroy this city." Genesis 7:1; 19:14. Lot placed himself under the guardianship of the heavenly messengers, and was saved. So Christ's disciples were given warning of the destruction of Jerusalem. Those who watched for the sign of the coming ruin, and fled from the city, escaped the destruction. So now we are given warning of Christ's second coming and of the destruction to fall upon the world. Those who heed the warning will be saved.[15]

- ***Christ's Object Lessons***: Parable-style teaching (that which uses stories to illustrate spiritual ideas) is a central part of SDA homiletics and instruction. This sets that foundation, examining the different parables of Jesus Christ.

  The great storehouse of truth is the word of God— the written word, the book of nature, and the book of experience in God's dealing with human life. Here are the treasures from which Christ's workers are to draw. In the search after truth they are to depend upon God, not upon human intelligences, the great men whose wisdom is foolishness with God. Through His own appointed channels the Lord will impart a knowledge of Himself to every seeker.[16]

- ***The Ministry of Healing***: A primer for the SDA belief on vegetarian diet.

  Reasons for Discarding Flesh Foods Those who eat flesh are but eating grains and vegetables at second hand; for the animal receives from these things the nutrition that produces growth. The life that was in the grains and vegetables passes into the eater. We receive it by eating the flesh of the animal. How much better to get it direct, by eating the food that God provided for our use![17]

In modern times, the works of Ellen G. White have undergone considerable editing to conform them to more contemporary and social ideas on matters of race, science, and eliminating more controversial ideas from her work. This is a particular issue for Historicist Adventists, as well as those who argue the church is trying to erase, or hide, key aspects of their history for image purposes.

BASIC RELIGIOUS PRACTICES

Seventh-Day Adventism centers around preparing the individual, the world, and the church for the Second Coming of Christ. Worship takes place at a church on the seventh-day Sabbath

(Saturday). Services closely resemble a typical non-liturgical Protestant service, with the service centering around a central scripture text and a sermon given by the leader of the service and local church, the pastor (or another guest minister or elder). Services contain hymns or songs, offering, and prayer. SDA ministers are trained in storytelling akin to parables, to teach the essential nature of church doctrine in a simple, easy-to-understand way.

With its emphasis on education, Seventh-day Adventists value Sabbath School, usually held for about one hour and 40 minutes before Sabbath service. Sabbath School is held for both adults (using the Quarterly, a church publication that examines different doctrinal themes on a rotating schedule) and children (infant through young adult). Sabbath School typically includes a song portion, a mission emphasis, a short talk, and a lesson study.

Most Seventh-day Adventist churches also have a midweek service prayer meeting featuring Bible study and prayer. It is led by a church pastor or elder. Sometimes this midweek service is held in homes, rather than in the church.[18]

Because Seventh-day Adventism upholds complex eschatology, their followers believe in a specific practice of prophetic understanding that supports their doctrine. They have a specified outline of church history from the first coming of Jesus Christ through the millennium by which the righteous will reign in heaven with Christ. Satan shall inhabit a desolate, barren earth until the resurrection and destruction of the wicked, followed by the creation of a new heavens and earth. Prior to the Second Coming of Christ shall be a time of trouble, by which Sunday worship shall be imposed (Sunday worship being the mark of the beast), Sabbath-keeping believers shall be persecuted, and an alliance shall be made between Catholics and Protestants (sometimes identified as the "New World Order"). These general themes are essential aspects of teaching and are often presented in church services and lectures through the instruction of the church's leadership.

All Seventh-day Adventists are required to obey Saturday as the Sabbath day, from Friday night at sundown to Saturday night at sundown. Sabbath observance is seen as a family event, and families are expected to come together to observe the Sabbath, often attending church together. Seventh-day Adventists are prohibited from working on the Sabbath day in any secular job. Instead, the day is considered one for worship (such as attending church) and personal and group devotional practice.

Unique to Seventh-day Adventists is their emphasis on the Ten Commandments, seen as the summary of the greatest principles present in God's law. They are regarded as the standard of God's judgment, binding upon all people, and the basis of divine covenant. Unlike many Christians who believe the Ten Commandments were part of the law and not enforced today or at least not in the same way as under the Old Covenant, SDAs believe the Ten Commandments were in no way changed or non-binding by the saving effort of Jesus Christ. This is part of SDA understanding in the difference between "moral" and "ceremonial" law, believing moral law continues and remains in force, while ceremonial law was completed through the work of Christ.

Followers of Seventh-day Adventism are required to tithe to their church, observe strict dietary guidelines seen as the optimum for health (most are vegetarians), refuse to bear arms or fight in war combat, refrain from wearing jewelry (wedding rings are the exception), maintain modesty in attire, refrain from entertainment venues seen as improper (going to movies or the theater), and abstain from any form of social dancing or modern-day music. They prohibit the use of alcohol, tobacco, and recreational drugs. Members are prohibited from marrying non-members, and adultery, "sexual perversion" (homosexuality is seen as adultery, non-heterosexual sex) are seen as the only acceptable grounds for divorce.

HOLIDAYS

The major focus for Seventh-day Adventists is the weekly Saturday sabbath. SDAs also observe most, if not all, cultural and major religious holidays, such as Christmas, Easter, New Year's Day, Thanksgiving, birthdays and patriotic holidays. These are not special religious events but marked by family and social gatherings.

Seventh-Day Adventist Church in Ore, Hastings, England

VISUAL SIGNS AND SYMBOLS

Open Bible with a central cross on top of the Bible in front of a burning lined flame, representing the work of prophecy in the church intersecting with the resurrection and Second Coming of Christ; writings of Ellen G. White; three angels (representing the message of the three angels in the book of Revelation); the Adventist health system; Saturday worship; *Review and Herald* publications; *Signs* Magazine.

CREEDS, BOOKS, AND LAWS

Adventists of all identities are opposed to the formulation of creeds. As influenced by the teachings and writings of Ellen G. White, Seventh-day Adventists consider their twenty-eight fundamental beliefs of their church to be descriptors of what the church believes and teaches but are not specified criteria for membership. These are:

- The Holy Scriptures
- The Trinity
- The Father
- The Son
- The Holy Spirit
- Creation
- The Nature of Humanity
- The Great Controversy
- The Life, Death, and Resurrection of Christ
- The Experience of Salvation
- Growing in Christ
- The Church
- The Remnant and its Mission
- Unity in the Body of Christ

- Baptism
- The Lord's Supper
- Spiritual Gifts and Ministries
- The Gift of Prophecy
- The Law of God
- The Sabbath
- Stewardship
- Christian Behavior
- Marriage and the Family
- Christ's Ministry in the Heavenly Sanctuary
- The Second Coming of Christ
- Death and Resurrection
- The Millennium and the End of Sin
- The New Earth[19]

Matters of church governance fall in the hands of the Seventh-day Adventist General Conference, which operates thirteen divisions. Division groups together union conferences (self-supporting) and missions. Unions consist of local conferences (self-supporting) and missions, and each local conference and/or mission is composed of local churches. Each congregation has a pastor, elder, deacon, deaconess, church clerk, and treasurer. The conference corporation owns all church property, pays all ministers, and receives financial benefit from each congregation. Decisions, doctrine, and clergy installments are decided at higher levels, rather than congregational levels.[20]

Eclectic Beliefs

As SDAs believe the Second Coming to be imminent, much of their doctrine centers around their specified eschatology of events that have come and are, in their views, soon to come. Much like other groups with connection to Millerite ideas (such as Jehovah's Witnesses), Seventh-day Adventists do not view the promise of a spiritual afterlife in heaven or hell. Instead, SDAs believe in psychopannychy ("soul sleep"), the belief that all dead, whether righteous or not, are "sleeping" in the grave, awaiting final resurrection to judgment. Those who are worthy shall live eternally with Christ. Those who are wicked shall be annihilated, or cease to exist. In connection with this belief, the millennial reign of Christ is said to take place in heaven, where the wicked dead shall remain asleep. The dead in Christ shall rise to heaven, along with those living who are also righteous, to rule and reign with Christ for one thousand years. During this period, Satan will be bound to the earth, which shall become a barren wasteland. After this time, Christ and the righteous shall return to earth, the wicked shall be destroyed, and the earth shall be recreated.

As a cousin of Evangelical Christianity originally forerun in part by the Seventh-day Baptists, the SDA Church regards conversion as accepting Christ and visible through full-immersion water baptism. Individuals baptized as infants must be rebaptized as adults. Seventh-day Adventists also observe communion four times per year, using unfermented grape juice and unleavened bread. SDAs practice open communion (anyone present who is Christian is welcome to partake, even if they are not a member of the Seventh-day Adventist Church).

The Seventh-day Adventist Church is one of the only church systems in the world to operate an entire school system from elementary through college. There are over 5,000 primary schools, 2,400 secondary schools, and over 115 schools of advanced educational learning worldwide. Some of the best-known SDA colleges include Andrews University, Southern Adventist University, and Union College. The church also operates its own healthcare system, Adventist HealthCare, as well as several hospitals, upholding SDA values and ideals in its practice.

When it comes to social issues, Seventh-day Adventists are notoriously conservative in their values. They are opposed to same-sex marriage, abortion (unless the life of the mother is threatened or there is the potential for severe birth defects), and the ordination of women (despite several petitions and votes to change this policy). The church has long taken an interest in political patriotism, believing firmly in values of liberty and freedom of religion.

RELATIONS WITH NON-SDA

Seventh-day Adventists have long stood against the ecumenical movement, believing it is part of prophetic end times arrangement to create a treaty between Protestants and Catholics. To be involved with such is seen as a compromise of the unique doctrines and ideals of the church itself. Over the past few years, the SDA has participated in some activities with some Protestant organizations, but only in the context of discussion and interest. Non-Christian groups, such as Buddhism, Hinduism, Judaism, and Islam, are studied.

HOLY SITES

Seventh-Day Adventist international headquarters, Silver Spring, Maryland; Ellen G. White estate, Silver Spring, Maryland; Hiriam Edson Farm, Clifton Springs, New York; Historic Adventist Village, Battle Creek, Michigan; Joseph Bates home, Fairhaven, Massachusetts; William Miller farm, Whitehall, New York; Avondale College and Sanitarium Health Food Factory, Corranbong, Sunnyside, Australia.

James (1821-1881) and Ellen Gould White (1827-1915)

NOTABLE FIGURES

James (1821-1881) and Ellen Gould White (1827-1915), influential founders; J.N Andrews (1829-1883), author; Magic Johnson (1959-), athlete; Angus T. Jones (1993-), actor; Ben Carson (1951-), politician; DeVon Franklin (1978-), author and preacher; Greg Mathis (1960-), celebrity judge; Archie Moore (c. 1913-1998), athlete; Abel Kirui (1982-), athlete; Clifton Davis (1945-), actor; Cesar Montano (1962-), actor; Grace Daley (1978-), athlete; Edwin Correa (1966-), athlete; Arthur S. Maxwell (1896-1970), author; Little Richard (1932-2020), musician; W.K. Kellogg (1860-1951), inventor.

Notable Groups

The Branch Davidians, founded by Benjamin Roden in 1955, is an apocalyptic-themed breakaway sect from Shepherd's Rod, a sect of Seventh-day Adventism. It was led by Roden himself until his death, and then Roden's wife, Lois Roden, until her death in 1986. The group received its claim to fame during the FBI raid on the Ranch Apocalypse compound in Waco, Texas in 1993. By this time, David Koresh had become leader of this movement (even though Roden's son, George, was the lawful prophet and leader of the group). Koresh secured his position through an affair with Lois Roden prior to her death. He claimed to desire to have a child with her (by this time, she was in her late sixties) to produce a "Chosen One" heir to continue the group. David Koresh claimed to be the "Lamb" of Revelation 5:2 and he desired to create a new lineage of world leaders. His followers were encouraged to regard themselves as "students of the Seven Seals," and many came to be known as Koreshians. The siege ended after a fifty-one-day standoff by which eighty-two members were killed, four ATF agents were killed, and sixteen were wounded. Twelve remaining members were convicted of aiding and abetting in murder of federal officers and unlawful possession of firearms, eight were charged as regards to firearms, five convicted of voluntary manslaughter, and four were acquitted of all charges. Today, there are still Branch Davidians awaiting Koresh's resurrection, along with the followers who were killed. The Branch, The Lord our Righteousness is a breakaway sect connected to the original leadership and now led by Charles Pace (c. 1950-). There are also Branch Davidians who insist they never authorized David Koresh to use their identity, and he was not a true Branch Davidian or proper representative of their organization.[21]

Facts and Figures

Seventh-day Adventists make up one half of 1% of the US Adult population. They are the most racially and ethnic diverse of all American religious groups: 37% are Caucasian, 32% are African-American, 15% are Hispanic, 8% are Asian and 8% are other or mixed race.[22]

Other Important Definitions

- **ABC**: An Adventist Book Center; a bookstore that specializes in SDA literature and also offers health foods.

- **Conditional immortality**: The teaching that all human beings are mortal and will die at the end of their natural lives, but those who come to Christ shall find themselves resurrected to new life, to reign and live forever.

- **Creation**: Seventh-day Adventists believe creation took place in a literal understanding of six twenty-four hour days.

- **The Message**: The teachings and doctrines of the SDA church.

- **New Light**: Additional Biblical truths, or new doctrines and teachings, now part of the denomination that were not observed in prior times.

- **The remnant**: The Seventh-day Adventist Church membership.

- **Three Angels Message**: A reference to Revelation 14:6-12 by which three angels are given a word for the world to prepare them for the second coming. The church believes it is part of this command, to herald the message of the end times to the world.

BELIEVER'S CHARACTERISTICS

Emphasis on the return of Christ and the teachings and revelations of Ellen Gould White; proclamation of an evangelical doctrine with great legalism; emphasis on understandable teaching, learning, dietary health, pacifism, Sabbath observance, tithing, and moral adherence; vegetarianism; isolation from the non-SDA world; emphasis on education; interest in church history and eschatology; belief in soul sleep, with resurrection to come: belief that during the millennium, believers shall reign with Christ in heaven while Satan lives on a desolate world; destruction of the wicked; strict in adherence and world view; historical disagreements; diversity; belief in the special nature and importance of their church's message.

SIKHISM

Even kings and emperors, with mountains of property and oceans of wealth – these are not even equal to an ant, who does not forget God.
(Guru Nanak, Sri Guru Granth Sahib)[1]

THEOLOGY

Belief in one god, an eternal, divine being referred to as AKAL MURAT ("timeless being") or by the name of Waheguru ("wondrous guru"), indescribable, knowable, and perceivable to anyone who is able to surrender their selfishness and meditate upon the oneness found within every bit of creation. The Sikh god is symbolized by Ik Onkar. Sikh deity is formless, beyond time, transcendent, immanent, omnipotent, omnibenevolent, and without gender. Akal Murat has been described in different ways by the different Sikh gurus through their hymns, especially in their holy scriptures. Within the Sikh theology, the major – and most abiding theme – is oneness. Within Sikhism, the concept of the divine is as creator, destroyer, and preserver, all one in literal being.

> *There is only Oankar, and it is called the truth, It exists in all creation, and it has no fear, It does not hate, and it is timeless, universal and self-existent! You will come to know it through the grace of the Guru.*[2]

A merging of Hindu, Muslim, and independent ideas, Sikh theology is best described as both panentheistic (the divine is found pervading and penetrating the universe as well as throughout all space and all time) and monism (deity is the only reality; all things come from that singular source, and return to that singular source). All existing deities and beings are simply reflections of the Universal Being, because Akal Murat is one.[3]

PHILOSOPHY

A fifteenth-century Indian religion founded by Guru Baba Nanak, Sikhism centers around the principle that spiritual ideals and concepts should connect with personal moral conduct, especially in a practical context. Distractions of this world are classified as temporary illusions (*maya*), things that distract from true spiritual pursuit and union with the divine. The ultimate goal of human existence is to reconnect with Akal Murat by overcoming one's personal sense of egoism in order to discover timeless truth found through and in the embodiment of the eternal divine being.[4]

The three pillars of Sikhism are:

- ***Simran*** **and** ***Namm Japo***: The practice of meditating, recalling, and thinking on Akal Murat and chanting the divine name, Waheguru. Sikhs recite the Nintem Banis, a collection of devotional hymns three times daily.

- ***Kirat Karna***: Sikhs believe in the importance of honestly earning one's living. Hard work and personal effort are emphasized. This is part of living in high moral and spiritual virtue.

- ***Vand chhakana***: A principle of charity, Sikhs are to share what they have (such as food and finances) to others, without any consideration to their social caste, creed, race, or sexuality. This emphasizes fellowship, which is central to Sikhs.

The word "Sikh" means "disciple" or "student" and refers to the way in which an adherent seeks to release what they call the Five Vices, so they no longer hold power over an individual. These Five Vices (sometimes called the Five Thieves) are[5]:

- *Kaam* (lust)
- *Krodh* (Anger)
- *Ahenkar* (Ego)
- *Lobh* (Greed)
- *Moh* (attachment)

One overcomes these by focusing the mind on eternal things (those that are seen as being above). To successfully merge, and achieve a oneness with the divine (*Mukti*), Sikhs are to develop the five virtues[6]:

- *Sat* (truth)
- *Daya* (compassion)
- *Santokh* (contentment)
- *Nimrata* (humility)
- *Payyar* (love)

ADHERENT IDENTITY

Sikh, Sikhism.

TRADITIONAL LANGUAGES

Punjabi, Gurmukhi, Sindhi, Sanskrit, Gujarati, Marathi, Hindi.

SECTS/DIVISIONS

There are several Sikh sects. They vary by lineage of accepted gurus, interpretation of the holy texts, believe in a current, living guru, or other concepts that vary from group to group. Some of the details in difference are very minor, and others are more extreme or notable.[7]

- **Namdharis, Nam-Dharis (Kuka Sikhs)**: Emerged in the 1700s believing that in contrast to mainline Sikhism, the line of Sikh Gurus (teachers, instructors) did not end with Guru Gobind Singh. Instead of believing he died, they believe he went into hiding, and lived the remainder of his life in secret. Before his death, they believe he appointed an eleventh guru named Balak Singh to lead their group. In addition to the belief in a continuing guru, Kuka Sikhs (so-called because they are known for ecstatic yelling and expression during their devotional songs) consider the Dasam Granth to be on the same scriptural level as Guru Granth Sahib and include additional hymns from the Chandi di Var as part of their daily recitations. They are notable for wearing white homemade turbans wrapped on their heads.

Namdharis logo

- **Nirankari**: Founded in the nineteenth century by Baba Dyal Das, Nirankari sought to be a Sikh reform movement. The word "Nirankari" means "without form" and describes their belief that Akal Murat cannot represent in any specific form. Thus, their focus is on *nam simaran* rather than any teacher or specific system of devotion. Nirankari refuse any ritual and believe the group should return to the original faith taught by Guru Nanak, and still believes human gurus are necessary to interpret and understand Sikh scriptures. A divided movement, some believe there are additional works relevant as Sikh scriptures, while mainline Sikhs reject this notion.

- **Akhand Kirtani Jatha**: A twentieth century sect that interpret the 5Ks of Guru Gobind Singh differently than mainline Sikhs; they believe male and female Sikhs must wear a small turban (males wear a full turban on top of the smaller ones). They also engage in extensive devotional singing.

Akhand Kirtani Jatha logo

- **Radha Soami Satsang**: Founded in 1861 by Shiv Dayal Singh, this group is a mix of Sikhism and a specific branch of Hinduism known as Vaishnavism. Their name literally means "Krishna's soul" and rejects many conventional Sikh ideas, opting instead that there are living gurus and members present everywhere. Many recite from Adi Granth (a Sikh scripture) during worship and use *sat nam* to describe their deity. They also embrace living gurus and sing communally, as part of their tradition. Otherwise, they significantly vary from traditional Sikh believers.

- **Santan Skihs**: Founded in the 1870s and led by Khem Singh Bedi, this group draws differently – and more strongly – from Hinduism and Islam in its interpretation of belief. Most relevant, Santan Skihs see themselves as a Hindu tradition, rather than a separate belief. They draw on Hindu documents, such as the Vedas and Puranas.

Santan artwork

- **Nirmala**: Started somewhere in the late seventeenth century (most likely by Guru Gobind Singh), the Nirmala are a stricter form of Sikhism that overlaps primarily with Hinduism (especially in their interpretation of Sikh holy writings). Members wear robes, refuse to cut their hair, and continue in the birth and death rituals present within Hinduism. They were among the first mobile missionaries to spread Sikhism throughout India, and also frequently served in the temples.

- **Ravidasi Panth**: Originally part of Sikhism, Ravidassia formed in 2009. Prior, it was considered a Sikh sect. The group represents several different religious ideals and concepts present throughout India, especially during the fourteenth century, when it began. Founded by Ravidas, it was largely an "untouchables" movement as the followers were often discriminated by other Sikh sects. They recognize living gurus and used to acknowledge the Guru Granth Sahib text of Sikhs. Today they use their own text, Amritbani Guru Ravidass Ji.

- **3HO**: Also known as the Sikh Dharma Movement or Sikh Dharma International, it is a western answer to Sikhism. 3HO was founded in 1971 by Yogi Bahajan in New Mexico. 3HO, stands for Healthy, Happy, Holy Organization. Men and women both wear turbans and use the last name Khalsa. They emphasize personal meditation and yoga. Despite a strict code of conduct, the organization is best known for its continuing court cases relating to sexual misconduct, especially in connection with its founder.

3HO logo

NUMBER OF ADHERENTS

There are approximately 27,000,000 Sikhs worldwide. Approximately 83% of the population lives in India. Approximately 76% of all Sikhs live in Punjab in north India.[8]

DISPUTES WITHIN GROUP

The differing disputes among Sikh sects reflect the conflicts often present in religions continuation of teaching or priestly line. At some point, someone deviates from the standard traditional line, introducing something new or changing the lineage in a way deemed heretical or problematic for parts of the membership. As a result, schism becomes inevitable. Modern questions, restrictions on the religion, thoughts about the traditions, and newer sects that reflect conservative Sikh values have added to the conflicting disputes. Beyond this, Sikhism holds to a strong mythological tradition that is easily added to, changed, modified, or adopted in different generations, also making deviation and division possible.

Modern-day Sikhs struggle with the ideas of their religion as present in modern society. In particular, prohibitions on cutting body hair (any hair, anywhere on the body) is considered outdated by many younger Sikhs (especially women who see the ban as preventing hygiene practices). There are also several conflicts between Sikhs and Muslims that have led to violence and persecutions, especially over the past seventy or so years.

SCRIPTURES

The primary Sikh scripture text is the Guru Granth Sahib, (also called the Adi Granth) which means "first scripture." Not just seen as a holy text, the Guru Granth Sahib is seen as their current and perpetual guru, there to lead and guide the Sikh people. Its contents were finalized in 1708 under the leadership of Guru Gobind Singh, who also established it to stand as the ever-living guru and guide for Sikh worship and living. It is used daily in Sikh temples (*gurdwaras*) in specific rituals where it is carried, closed, decorated, and tucked into a bed, as well as reading its contents. The Guru Granth Sahib was authored by thirty-six different contributors to include 5,894 hymns, teachings of the Sikh gurus, and views of other religions, including the writings of two Muslim Sufi poets and thirteen Hindu Bhakti poets. It heralds its own ideals of society, specifically one that holds to their version of divine justice, free from oppression and discrimination.[9,10]

For each and every person, our Lord and Master provides sustenance. Why are you so afraid, O mind? The flamingos fly hundreds of miles, leaving their young ones behind. Who feeds them, and who teaches them to feed themselves? Have you ever thought of this in your mind?[11]

The Kandha, Sikhism's emblem

Burn worldly love,
rub the ashes and make ink of it,
make the heart the pen,
the intellect the writer,
write that which has no end or limit.[12]

There is but One God, His name is Truth, He is the Creator, He fears none, he is without hate, He never dies, He is beyond the cycle of births and death, He is self illuminated, He is realized by the kindness of the True Guru. He was True in the beginning, He was True when the ages commenced and has ever been True, He is also True now.[13]

Realization of Truth is higher than all else. Higher still is truthful living.[14]

The Guru Granth Sahib is divided into thirty-nine chapters and members are forbidden to make any changes within the text. Every single version of it is exactly the same.

A secondary text in Sikhism is the Dasam Granth (Second Scripture). It was authored by Guru Gobind Singh and is controversial within the religion (scriptural by some, questionable by others). It contains hymns, Hindu mythology, a text on the Hindu goddess Durga, sexually-charged stories, an autobiography of Guru Gobind Singh, letters to other people, and discussion of theology and war. It contains over 17,000 verses and is divided into eighteen sections. It is written in old Hindi, Avadhi, Punjabi, and Persian. Authorship is disputed in certain sections.[15]

> *Extend Thy hand to shield me Lord, and all my heart's desires fulfil,*
> *Ever may my mind dwell at Thy feet, deem me Thy own and work my weal,*
> *Slay Thou my enemies one and all, save me from them by Thy hand,*
> *May all the people peace, who serve and do as I command.*
> *May Thine own hand be ever my shield, and all my foes forthwith destroy.*
> *May all my hopes fulfilment find, ever may I crave rapport with Thee.*
> *I may not worship other than Thee, when Thou canst grant me every boon.*
> *Keep my disciples from all harm, and crush my enemies one by one,*
> *Uphold me with Thine own strength, fear of the hotly of death annul.*
> *Be ever Thou on my side O Lord. and take me under Thy banner of steel."* (Benti Chaupai)[16]
>
> *"Whoever was clever in the world established his own sect.*
> *No one tried to unite people in the search for the Creator.*
> *Enmity, contention and pride increased.*
> *All, big and small, flared up and started perishing in their own rivalry.*
> *And none of them tried my way.*
> *They who obtained a little spiritual power struck out their own way.*
> *None of them cared to recognise the Supreme Being,*
> *But became mad, boasting of themselves.*
> *They cared little to recognise the Real Essence.*
> *But each became absorbed in himself and tried to establish his superiority over others."*
> (Bachittar Natak)[17]

Basic Religious Practices

Sikh worship takes place in a Sikh temple, known as a *gurdwara*. Sikhs do not observe a special day (such as Saturday or Sunday) for worship. Instead, they believe in meeting and remaining accessible all days for prayer or worship. In much of the world, *gurdwaras* are open all day, every day, for public prayer or devotion. Attached to each *gurdwara* is a *langar* (a community dining facility). The Guru Granth Sahib Ji must be present in the temple at all times, and is honored in the tradition of a human guru daily: in daily *Prakash* ("light") it is carried in at dawn, taken out of its bedroom, carried on the head, placed and carried in a *palki* (a traditional transport carriage carried by people in procession), brought to its resting place, and after traditional ritual singing and prayers (*ardas*) is opened to a random page. The first complete verse found on the left page is the *vak* (or *mukhawk*) of the day. It is read out loud and then written out to be read throughout the day. At the end of the day, the closing ritual known as the *sukhasan* commences: the devotional narrations and *ardas* conclude, the book is closed, carried on the head, carried in the flower-covered palki with chanting, and bringing it to its own bedroom, then tucking it into bed. Sikh services conclude with the sharing of their holy food (*karah prasad*). It consists of wheat flour, clarified butter, and raw sugar and is distributed to all present.[18]

Sikh community is marked by ritual. Initiation and observance are key to Sikh worship. There are four different rituals that classify as rites of passage as found in the Sikh Rhait Marayada (a manual that outlines the specific responsibilities of Sikh believers). The four rites are: Birth and naming ceremony, *Anand Karaj* ("blissful union," marriage ceremony), *amrit sanskar* (initiation ceremony), and a funeral ceremony. Of these different rites, the most important is the *amrit sanskar*, or Sikh initiation ceremony. Through *amrit sanskar*, a Sikh becomes part of *Khalsa*, their faith community. As part of this rite, male Sikhs take the surname (or sometimes middle name) Singh, meaning "lion." Females take the name kaur, meaning "princess."[19] It is represented by Five "Ks," or *Kakars*, that every sprinkled (sometimes called baptized) (*Amritdhari*) Sikh is required to oblige:

- ***Kesh/Kesi***: Uncut hair for both men and women (members of Sikhism are forbidden to cut their hair; why exactly is a matter of speculation, although there are several theories, including it follows their founder's appearance and hair is a long-standing symbol of holiness).
- ***Kangha***: A wooden comb (symbolizes cleanliness as it keeps the hair tidy).
- ***Karha***: A steel bracelet (symbol of divine eternity, restraint, gentility, and that the Sikh member is linked to the guru).
- ***Kirpan***: A ceremonial sword (seen as a defense of good and the weak in the struggle against injustice in this world; a soldier mentality for the Sikh community).
- ***Kachera***: Special underwear (a boxer-like undergarment worn above the knee as a symbol of chastity).

In addition, Sikhs are required to avoid four specific sins: cutting one's hair, eating *halal* meat (meat slaughtered and prepared according to Muslim practice), having sexual relationships with anyone other than one's spouse, and the use of tobacco. Committing such sins requires a public confession and formal reinitiation. Believers may act in self-defense but should not seek revenge. As a group, Sikhs are to live free from any sort of hate, maintaining their faith in Akal Murat in their personal ethics and conduct.[20]

A Sikh commander

Community and community connection are key in Sikh life, ritual, and worship. When matters are not clearly addressed in the Guru Granth Sahib, the community should gather to make decisions as necessary. It is not uncommon for Sikh families to cohabitate with extended family members rather than as a nuclear family. Each member of a Sikh family is assigned a specific role in the lives of children and in rites that relate to their development and growth. Mothers are seen as first teachers and models of righteous conduct; fathers are involved parents, comparing their relationship between the creator and the child; and grandparents are to deposit Sikh traditions in the new generation.[21]

HOLIDAYS

Sikh festivals are known as *Gurpurb* (Guru's Remembrance Day). They are often held in commemoration of specific gurus, either their births or deaths. The major Sikh holidays include[22,23]:

- **The Birth of Guru Gobind Singh**: Founded the Khalsa and proclaimed Guru Granth Sahib as his successor. Celebrated either in December or January.
- ***Maghi***: Commemorates the martyrdom of forty followers of Guru Gobind Singh who had deserted him, but still fought against forces and were killed in Muktsar (They were blessed as having achieved liberation.) Follows the feat of Lohri (usually around January 14).
- ***Hola Maholla***: Celebrated annually on the Indian feast of Holi (usually in March) in memory of Guru Gobind Singh. Marked with military exercises, staged battles, music, poetry, and processions.
- **Sikh New Year**: The annual New Year observance (March 13 or 14).
- ***Vaisakhi***: The founding anniversary of Khalsa in 1699. Most membership initiations take place on this day. (April 13 or 14).
- **Martyrdom of Guru Arjan**: Marks the anniversary of the fifth guru who was tortured and killed in 1606. (June 16).
- **Celebration of the *Guru Granth Sahib***: Celebrates the completion of the Sikh scripture in 1606. Held on September 1.
- **Diwali**: Hindu festival modified by Sikhs to celebrate the release of the sixth guru, Guru Hargobind, from prison in 1619 (it is known as Bandi Chhor Divas, the Celebration of Freedom). Sikhs light lamps during Diwali every year in memory of this event. Usually observed around October 27.
- **The Birth of Guru Nanak**: November 15. Recognizes the birth of the religion's founder in 1469. (November 15).
- **Martyrdom of Guru Tegh Bahadur**: Marks the anniversary of the execution of the ninth guru, Guru Tegh Bhadur in 1675. (November 24).

- **Martyrdom of the Shaibzade**: A day of remembrance for four young princes martyred in late December. These were the sons of Guru Gobind Singh. These martyrs are remembered on December 21 and 26.

VISUAL SIGNS AND SYMBOLS

Khanda (a double-edged sword); *chakkar* (circle representing God without beginning or end); two crossed *kirpans* (swords); Sikh flag; uncut hair; wooden comb; steel bracelet; Guru Granth Sahib.

A Sikh praying in India

CREEDS, BOOKS, AND LAWS

In Sikhism, there is no higher authority than the Guru Granth Sahib, the Sikh scripture book. In Sikhism, the Guru Granth Sahib is more than just a book; it is seen as the eternal living guru of the Sikh people. It was pronounced to be the last and final guru of the Sikh religion in 1708. Prior to this time, there were ten other Sikh gurus: Guru Nanak Dev Ji, who represents humility (1569-1539); Guru Angad Dev Ji, who represents obedience (1539-1552); Guru Amar Das Sahib Ji, who represents equality (1552-1574); Guru Ram Das Sahib Ji, who represents service (1574-1581); Guru Arjan Dev Ji, who represents self-sacrifice (1581-1606); Guru Har Gobind Sahib Ji, who represents justice (1606-1644); Guru Har Rai Sahib Ji, who represents mercy (1644-1661); Guru Har Krishnan Sahib Ji, who represents purity (1661-1664); Guru Tegh Bahadur Sahib Ji, who represents tranquility (1665-1675); and Guru Gobind Singh Sahib Ji, who represents royal courage (1675-1708). These gurus were seen as divine messengers, individuals who lived the Sikh faith and composed different parts of its scriptural contents, formed the religion, and instructed believers.

Sikhism is seen as a combination of theocratic revelation and governance along with democratic ideals and applications. Outside of their two major books, there is no specific canon law or governing requirements. Sikhs are expected to follow the *rehitnaamas* (edicts) and *tankhaahnaamas* (codes of conduct) that outline right and wrong. In their application (especially in specific matters), the situations by which someone breaks these specific codes of conduct are analyzed on a case-by-case basis. There is no one specified method of problem solving. When individuals are excommunicated, they have the option to re-join, follow corrective measures, and be re-initiated again.

When issues arise, the entire *Khalsa* body is viewed as a "parliament" and matters are handled, voted upon, and decided by the local Sikh community. Motions passed are known as *gurmattas*. When a motion arises, the *Guru Granth Sahib* consulted first, and then the general body discusses and votes on the matter at hand.

ECLECTIC BELIEFS

Most Sikhs live as strict vegetarians, eating no animals or animal byproducts (dairy is fine if it is free from all animal fat). There are some who now eat meat as per a 1980 ruling, but this is not standard practice. They are forbidden from drinking alcohol, using any intoxicants, and the use of tobacco.

Sikhs believe Akal Murat lives in all beings. Through a long series of death and rebirth (up to over eight million), people will be purified and able to return to their god. Karma, or deliberate, intentional actions will help Sikhs to avoid punishments in the eternal cycle. Escaping this cycle and returning to Akal Murat is known as *mukti*. Akal Murat reunites with those he finds pleasing, so Sikhs believe focus and meditation on the divine will bring them to a place where the cycle of death and rebirth can end.

Sikhism does not recognize ordained clergy. Any member of the Sikh community can lead prayers or recite their holy book before the congregation. A *Granthi* (narrator) is a member of any Sikh community who is a ceremonial reader of the Guru Granth Sahib. A *granthi* is approved by five individuals within each Sikh community known as the *Panj Pyare*, who assist in ceremonies (especially the *amrit sanchar*). They are chosen each year by the general body of a Sikh *gurdwara*.[24]

Unique to Sikhism is the *Sahajdhari*, a group of individuals who profess belief in Sikhism but are not initiated into the *Khalsa*. They submit to Sikh gurus but do not always adopt the five symbols of the Sikh faith. They are connected to the *Udasi*, a group of monks that were at one time part of the Sikh faith, but now follow a combination of Sikhism and Hinduism. Also unique is modern Sikhism rejects celibacy in all forms.[25]

Relations with Non-Sikhs

Sikhs believe all religions are valid and reject discrimination against other religions. Having experienced bitter persecutions over the years, the relationship many Indian Sikhs have with Muslims and Hindus is complicated, but does not change the basic Sikh view on other religious practices.

Holy Sites

The Golden Temple (also called the *Harmandir Sahib*) located in Amritsar, India is the holiest site of all Sikh shrines. The city and temple were both built by Guru Arjan to create a spiritual site for all Sikhs to visit and gather.[26]

Sikh children wearing the dastar

Notable Figures

Guru Baba Nanak (1469-1539), founder; Mandip Gill (1988-), actress; Simon Rivers (1978-), actor; Neelam Gill (1995-), model; Ameet Chana (1975-), actor; Kapur Singh (1909-1986), politician; Prem Singh (1943-), artist; Ravi Singh (1969-), humanitarian; Bhagat Puran Singh (1904-1992), humanitarian; Jesse Randhawa (1975-), model; Nanak Singh (1897-1971), writer; Dalip Kaur Tiwana (1935-2020), writer;

Kushwant Singh (1915-2014), writer; Max Arthur Macauliffe (1838-1913), historian; Tom Singh (1949-), businessman; Tosh Masson (1985-) , athlete.

NOTABLE GROUPS

The World Sikh Organization was founded in 1984 and seeks to represent the interests of Sikhs worldwide. It works with Sikh members who live in the Diaspora, outside of the Punjabi in India. Beyond advocating merely for the Sikh community, the World Sikh Organization advocates for religious freedom and supported many other religious groups in their pursuit to practice their religion and express their religious views freely.[27]

FACTS AND FIGURES

Sikhism is the fifth most popular religion in the world. Approximately 99% of people wearing turbans in the United States are Sikhs from India. Sikhs have been in the United States for over one hundred years. There are approximately 700,000 Sikhs in the United States.[28]

OTHER IMPORTANT DEFINITIONS[29,30]

- ***Bani***: An abbreviation of the word *Gurbani*, meaning "verses." Applies to any writings found in the *Guru Granth Sahib*.
- ***Bhagat Bani***: Any writings in the *Guru Granth Sahib* that were not written by the ten gurus themselves.
- ***Dasband***: Also *daswand* or *sasvand*. Ten percent of one's personal income donated to those who are poor or disadvantaged.
- ***Dastar***: A term for the turban worn by Sikh men. Must be tied.
- ***Gatka***: Sikh martial art form.
- ***Gurbani***: Writings of the Sikh gurus.
- ***Gurmukh***: A person who lives to accept the will of Akal Murat in their lives, whether good or bad, without any upset.
- ***Gutka***: A daily prayerbook containing prayers recited every day.
- ***Japi Sahib***: The first eight pages of the *Guru Granth Sahib*; hymns composed by Guru Nanak.

- ***Kurahit kurahat*:** A term for the five "cardinal sins" of the Sikhs: removing or cutting body hair, eating meat, using tobacco or other intoxicants, or committing adultery.

- ***Manmukh*:** The opposite of a *gurmukh*, an individual who is self-centered, and lives according to their own wants rather than the will of Akal Murat.

- ***Mul Mantra*:** A basic statement of belief.

- ***Panj*:** The number five

- ***Patit*:** An apostate, or individual who abandons the Sikh faith.

- ***Shabad*:** Also called *Sabda*, the hymns of Sikhism, found in the *Guru Granth Sahib*.

- ***Sukhmani Sahib*:** Known as the "psalm of peace," it is a specific section of the *Guru Granth Sahib* that speaks on meditation, Sikh holiness, going good, the nature of the mind, avoiding slander, and many other topics. It was authored by Guru Arjan around 1602.

BELIEVER'S CHARACTERISTICS

Emphasis on the Guru Granth Sahib; participation in the local *guardjara*; emphasis on community involvement; accepting of all religious groups; avoidance of the five vices, while focusing on the three pillars; vegetarianism; adaptation of the five *Kharas*; avoidance of alcohol, tobacco, and all drugs; belief in the gurus of Sikhism; Sikh holidays; daily prayers and chants; use of the Dasam Granath; refusal to cut one's hair; wearing the traditional Sikh turban; received the *Amrit Sanskar* ritual; interest in religious freedom.

Taoist Religions

Of all that is good, sublimity is supreme. Succeeding is the coming together of all that is beautiful. Furtherance is the agreement of all that is just. Perseverance is the foundation of all actions.

(*I Ching*)[1]

Theology

A mix of ancient culture, a strong belief in honor, religious practice, animism, polytheism, pantheism, ancestral worship, and nature worship, indigenous far eastern religion (those religions of China, Japan, Korea, and Vietnam) centers around either an impersonal, universal life force or natural essence, called by many names: QI (or KI or CHI), TAO (or DAO); the God of Heaven, seen as comparable to the TAO, along with a number of personal deities, such as family gods or ancestors; a polytheistic number of deities known as *kami*, or nature spirits or gods, which are spirits believed to inhabit all things; a monotheistic religion that embraces the veneration of the ancestors, named CAO DAI, believed to be the creator, God the Father, and the Ultimate Reality found in the universe, along with worship of the Holy Mother and Divine Beings; or atheistic in nature, specifically from far eastern Buddhist practice.

Practitioners of far eastern religion believe it is most advantageous for them to find harmony and balance with both nature and the universe as a whole, and focus on being part of greater flow and harmony within the average ways of life. For them, theology is not the central focus; it is learning to live with the spirits, forces, flow, and ways of existence, adopting an outlook that embraces one's position as part of the larger universe.

Far eastern religion, namely Taoism, Shintoism, Shinism, Confucianism, eastern Buddhism, and Cao Dai all overlap with one another and often borrow from one another in rite, ritual, or symbolism. They are often group labeled as Taoist religions. It is not uncommon to find practitioners of all religions mentioned, who, as part of their culture, incorporate different elements and overlaps into their worship. Eastern religion, in contrast with western understanding, is seldom exclusive of theology, understanding, and practice.

Philosophy

The basic goal of far eastern religion is to find one's place of harmony and balance as part of the universe. Practitioners of eastern religion focus heavily on learning to flow with nature, life, difficulty, a greater spiritual awareness that helps them to be in touch with spiritual forces, aware of natural times and seasons, and connect, on a greater level, with the world around them.

Far eastern religion does not just draw on spiritual ideas, but cultural ones, too. There is an expressed duty to one's ancestors, family, and society, marked by specified roles and actions as one lives out daily life. One is expected not to just pay homage with rite and ritual, but with regular, rigid conduct that helps one remember their place in larger society. Life is not just about one individual person. Personal happiness comes from maintaining honor and obligation. Duty is often found in place of specified moral codes and obligations, with a high focus on personal conduct and reverence.

Far eastern religion has a character of being abstract rather than demonstrative. Some question the veracity of classifying many far eastern religions as proper religions. Many are more influential in ways of thinking, custom, celebration, philosophy, and worldview rather than hardcore religious practice. Practitioners of eastern religion do not practice because they seek eternal salvation, redemption from sin, or to connect with a singular higher power, but to align themselves better, finding their place in a bigger idea of cosmic harmony.

ADHERENT IDENTITY

Taoism (also spelled Daoism), Taoist; Confucianism, Confucian; Shinto, Shintoist; Sindoism, Shinism, Shinist; Zen Buddhism, Zen Buddhist; East Asian Buddhism; East Asian Buddhist; East Asian Mahayana; Cao Dai, Cao Daist.

NUMBER OF ADHERENTS

Exact numbers of practitioners of Taoist religions can be difficult to ascertain, as practitioners of east Asian religion often practice varying forms of other similar religions. One may also practice parts of it, identify more strongly with one than another, or syncretize their practice with a western religion, such as Christianity. It is estimated that combined, all the Taoist religions have approximately 500,000,000 members worldwide.[2]

TRADITIONAL LANGUAGES

Chinese, Korean, Japanese, Vietnamese, Pali, Sanskrit, and Tibetan.

SECTS/DIVISIONS

East Asian religions can be divided by country of origin: China, Korea, Japan, and Vietnam, although the specified religious strains overflow and influence each other, often completely in philosophy, theology, and theory. Due to years of occupation, immigration, and trade with one another, religion is also a shared thread among these nations. Individuals may practice some combined form of Confucianism, Zen Buddhism, Shintoism, and Taoism simultaneously. In modern times, a form of Christianity may be thrown into the overlap.

- **Taoism**: Also spelled Daoism, Taoism is a pantheistic, traditional Chinese philosophy that focuses on one's harmony with the source of everything in existence. This essence (or principle) is known as the Tao (or Dao). One's goal is to be perfectly in sync with this source of all, by being spontaneous, simple, natural, and acting without specific intention (called *wu wei*, often paralleled with the idea of yielding or submissiveness to natural systems). There are three main treasures (or jewels): compassion, frugality, and humility. Recognizing natural cycles, Taoism also embraces the idea that the universe is constantly recreating itself, going through cycles of evolution and change. Humans are considered a small potion, or a microcosm, of the universe. It dates to at least the fourth century B.C. and was largely influenced by the I Ching, an ancient Chinese text that expounds on the connection between human behavior and natural cycles. Theologically, Taoism's pantheism focuses on the idea of an all-encompassing divinity, manifest in many ways, specifically through a pantheon of lesser and higher deities. The major deities are the Three Pure Ones: the pure manifestation of the Tao and the origin of all beings. These Three Beings are: the heavenly or universal chi, the human plane chi, and the earth chi. These three consist of the energy of the entire universe (sort of seen as a personification of impersonal life forces) and are often depicted as elderly Chinese male deities in elaborate robes. Adherents of the religion practice food sacrifice (traditionally animal sacrifice was performed, but not in modern times), burning paper or money to summon ancestors, hold parades, and various forms of divination and mediumship. Laozi is considered the founder of Taoism (although whether he was a literal person or a figurative concept of an ideal teacher is of debate) and the author of the Tao Te Ching, which contains his teachings. It is considered a foundational aspect of Chinese culture and is fundamental in the foundations of Chinese astrology, Zen Buddhism, martial arts, Chinese medicine, and feng shui. Perhaps the best-known symbol of Taoism is the ying and yang, a black and white symbol representing harmony between opposites. Second is the *bagua*, which represents the fundamental Chinese symbols of reality.[3]

Ying Yang

- **Confucianism**: Confucianism is a sixth-century BC system of ancient Chinese hierarchy and behavior attributed to Confucius. The beliefs of Confucianism are not unique to Confucius, but he gathered and turned them into a system. It is often considered a philosophy (a form of primitive humanism) or a "social religion" rather than a formal religious system. It is found throughout the entire religious framework of the far east and is often practiced in connection with the spiritual beliefs of these peoples. Confucianism forms the social code and values principle of Chinese culture, now extending into other far eastern nations, as well. Confucianism looks to "heaven" (*tian*) for the mandate of heaven, the functional equivalent of a general ancestral deity that resided in and with the authority of heaven. To understand such, Confucius advocated self-awareness that came about through an individual's entire life. Proper culture was taught through example and advocated by heaven. Learning is to be lifelong. Connected to Confucianism is the ritual system establishing mutual respect and dependence among families, marriage partners, and other agreements. Authority comes from the mandate of heaven, and proper order within households and society come from a shared vision. Social solidarity is achieved by ritual observance, which comes from filial piety (*xiao*). Performing regular rituals helps to promote mutual understanding and connection among people; through such rites, the invisible realm becomes visible. Confucianism emphasizes social order, with young people in submission to parents and elders, younger siblings in submission to older ones, wives in submission to their husbands, students in submission to their teachers, and citizens in submission to their secular leaders. Friends are considered equal.[4,5] The main texts of Confucianism are known as The Four Books and The Five Classics: The Four books are Great Learning (considered the gateway of learning), Doctrine of the Mean (the way to attain perfect virtue), Analects (speeches and discussions by Confucius and his disciples), and Mencius (conversations with Mencius, a Confucian scholar); the Five Classics are Classic of Poetry (poems, hymns, and eulogies for ceremonies), Book of Documents (the oldest Chinese narrative, containing speeches from rulers and officials of the Zhou period), Book of Rites (outlines rites, social forms, and court ceremonies), I Ching (a divination system known as The Book of Changes), and Spring and Autumn Annals (a historical record of the State of Lu, where Confucius was from).[6]

Image of Confucius

- **Shinto**: The term Shinto literally means "the way of *kami*," a term for the polytheistic spirits, gods, or deities, all of whom work together and are traditionally worshiped in Japan. As the indigenous religion of that nation, Shinto has no set origin, founders, scriptures, or fixed dogmatic principles. Regardless, its general influence on social life and personal outlook have impacted the customs and values of the Japanese people for centuries. It is highly mythological, involving the stories of how the ancient sun goddess Amaterasu Omikami (the ancestor of the Imperial Household) and her descendants unified the people of Japan. There are also stories of the various *kami*, of which there are approximately eight hundred myriads. The three sacred treasures (the mirror, the sword, and the jewels) were first bestowed by the goddess to her grandson. It was a pair of *kami*, known as Izanagi and Izanami, who gave birth to the Japanese islands. Other *kami* became ancestors of the various clans of Japan.

Shinto symbol

There are three different types of Shinto: Shrine Shinto, which has existed since the beginning (functions through shrines operated by Shinto priests, who perform services and ceremonies for adherents); Sect Shinto, which are a group of thirteen Shinto sects that began in the nineteenth century; and Folk Shinto, which is Japanese folk belief that relates to Shinto, without formal structure or doctrinal formulation, found predominately in the rites of agricultural and rural families. These three different types overlap and are interrelated. It is not at all uncommon to find practitioners of all three types. Followers may also practice or have influences from eastern Buddhism, Confucianism, and Christianity (especially Roman Catholicism). Shinto focuses on the *kami*: their creative power, ability to harmonize, and one's ability to remain in the way or will of the *kami* (*makoto*). This is not considered abstract, but present in every moment and encounter an individual has with them. Shinto adherents seek to walk in sincerity, purity of heart, and uprightness (known as *magokoro*); this means they seek to do their best, and in all honesty, in everything. *Magokoro* is considered the ultimate pursuit, as it brings forth other moral virtues. The ultimate goal is continuity and communion (*tsunagri*), which encourages adherents to see both their individuality and continuity with other beings. Adherents visit shrines at their convenience, especially for special rites of passages, beginning when one is a baby, all the way up through youth and marriage. Shinto adherents also have family altars devoted to their personal *kami* and goddess Amaterasu Omikami. Spiritual practices include purification, dance, amulets, divination, and many different festivals and rites of passage. Shinto celebrates several festivals throughout one's life and throughout the year, observe several specialized religious arts (often seen in the design and landscaping of Shinto temples), and are best-known for torii, a special gateway that sits outside Shinto shrines with two stone animals (*komainu* – Korean dogs or *karajishi* – Chinese lions) in front of the shrines. While Shinto does not have scriptures, its sacred books include the Kojiki (Records of Ancient Matters) and Nihon Shoki (Chronicles of Japan). These contain ancient Japanese history, literature, and topography as well as the oral traditions of ancient Shinto belief.[7]

- **Sindoism**: Sindoism literally means "Ways of Gods." It is the indigenous religion of Korea. It is classified as "Korean Shamanism." It is prehistoric in nature. Sindoism (also called Shinism) is a polytheistic and animistic religion focused on the worship of *sin* (specified spirits, nature spirits, and deities). Adherents worship at shrines. Sindo religion is led by the shamans, known as *mu* or *mudang* for females and *basky* for males. These shamans act as intermediaries between the spirits and gods and humanity.[8] Wrapped in complex mythology, the oral mythology of Sindoism is recited during ceremonies. The major deity is Chonjo, also known as Chonjo Sangje, Sangje, or Hanulnim, the "heavenly ancestor" or "supreme emperor Chonjo." He is depicted as a bearded man (dressed in white robes with light blue trim) who emerged from a cosmic egg to create the world and rule in the sky. He is not seen as omniscient or omnipotent but operates as a divine emperor. He receives information from the other gods and has them execute his will. Another major deity is Chonja, the "son of Heaven," born from the sweat of Chonjo's brow after he created earth. He is depicted in like fashion to Chonjo, but younger. He works to help human affairs. Also of relevance is the Yellow Emperor (Hwangje), the product of Chonja and Hwangnyo. He led the first human kingdom and had three sons: the Jade Emperor (Okje), the Stone

Emperor (Sokje), and the Metal Emperor (Kimje). Second rank gods are those who are found in rank after Chonjo and are all regarded as earthly deities (springing forth from the earth during creation). Each one has an opposite force, equal in power. There are three worlds: heaven (seen as good); earth; and the underworld (seen as evil). Known for its elaborate beliefs surrounding the afterlife, Adherents believe death comes when the body can no longer support the soul. After death, the soul is distilled down to its essence, receives purification from any evil, and is either left in the spirit world or ascends to the Divine gate if one is remembered by enough people after death. Bodies are traditionally cremated. Sindo beliefs have undergone substantial changes over the years, and it is possible for a Sindo believer to practice other east Asian religions, or to practice at a Sindo shrine or temple, but not believe in the Sindo gods.[9]

- **Mahayana Buddhism**: We have spoken of Buddhism in depth in a separate section, thus we will not get into the specifications of it here. Mahayana Buddhism is frequently identified as Buddhism practiced in the far east. The purpose of Mahayana Buddhist systems is not so much the establishment of doctrine, but the experience of wisdom as one distances themselves from knowledge that comes by theory or intellect. Rather than looking at Buddhist teaching as a religious doctrine, Mahayana Buddhists see their teachings as guides. Mahayana Buddhist tradition focuses on meditation, especially that practiced for long periods of time, and on statements known as *koans*, which are short, thoughtful ideas for one to focus upon during meditation sessions. They also accept different Buddhist writings, known as the Mahayana sutras, from Chinese, Tibetan, and Sanskrit traditions. Zen Buddhism and Chan Buddhism are examples of Mahayana Buddhism.

Peaceful Buddha

- **Vietnamese folk religion**: A general heading for a few different strains of spirituality unique and indigenous to Vietnam, encompassing a few sets of belief. In themselves, the systems are polytheistic and animistic. They represent any combination of beliefs that incorporate local religion, Buddhism, Confucianism, Taoism, and in some strains, modern elements of Roman Catholicism, Spiritism, and Theosophy. Vietnamese folk religion does not represent an organized, singular religious system, but many different localized spiritual traditions that are devoted to spirits, gods (national deities, ancestral deities, nature deities, personal deities, or community deities), or local powers, identified in Vietnamese as *than*. The religious systems focus on great mythologies, emphasizing the actions of the *than* as well as those

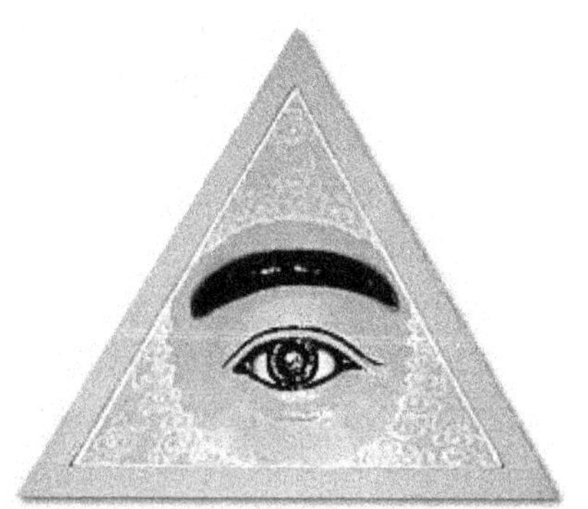
Cao Dai logo

of cultural heroes relevant to the work of the Vietnamese people. Deities are believed to have the power to influence the living by a power known as *linh* (sometimes translated as holy). *Linh* is the means between order (*am*) and disorder (*duong*), with order as the preferred state over creation. It is through *linh* that social transformation takes place, boundaries are set, metaphors are identified, and things are divided or connected. The boundaries are crossed through sacrifice and Vietnamese shamanism. Vietnamese folk deities are representative of four categories: heavenly gods and nature gods, tutelary gods or ancestors, hierarchical pantheons headed by the heavenly emperors, immortals, and sages, and deities of specific Southeast Asian ethnic groups, such as the Cham or Khmer. The most popular are Kinh Duong Vuong and his son, Lac Long Quan, who along with Au Co, are responsible for the Vietnamese people; the Four Immortals (Tan Vien Son Thanh, Thanh Giong, Chu Dong Tu, and Lieu Hanh), and the Four Palace goddesses (Mau Thong Thien, Mau Thong Ngan, Mau Thoai, and Mau Dia Phu). Practitioners attend *mieu*, the Vietnamese term for temples. These shrines may be specifically for deity worship, secondary deity worship, local gods, nature gods, family chapels, or ancestral shrines. In some locations, temple purposes may overlap. Practitioners of Vietnamese folk religion see spirituality as a place to dialogue: between themselves and the spirits or gods, and with them and others. Their spiritual growth seeks to correct or improve (*tu*), self-perfect through meditation (*tu than*), to cultivate gentleness and wisdom (*tu hien*), to correct (*tu sua*), to repair (*chua*), correction (*sua chua*), to rescue (*cuu*), to save souls (*cuu roi*), and to save the country (*cuu nuoc*). The major religions under this heading are Caodiasm, Dao Buu Son Ky Huong, Dao Mau, Dau Tu An Hieu Nghia, Min Duong Trung Tan, and Minh Dao.[10]

DISPUTES WITHIN GROUP

East Asian religion is noted by its syncretism, or the overlap and parallel practice and blend of the different philosophies, theologies, and ideas present in their religious systems. As adherents often practice more than one form of Taoist religion, there aren't any notable things that divide them. There are some differences in the deities worshiped, and both name and language differences, but the systems bear many striking resemblances to one another. While there is no question there are personal disagreements of opinion about matters, for the most part, far eastern religions do not focus on such matters unto conflict.

SCRIPTURES

Far Eastern Religions exist from the earliest times, before modern-day writing and printing. In their origins, traditions and stories were passed down orally, rather than in writing. The concept of writings is, therefore, a later addition to the faith practice. Far eastern religion does not recognize the concept of scripture in the same context as in western religion. Scriptural writings are reflections of the traditions passed down from the ancestors, collections of ideas, sayings, discourses, and writings, or hymns, poems, songs, or other mythologies that relate to the religious tradition at hand. These books are seen more as sacred writings, written works that reflect upon and collect the traditional essences of the historical faith.

- **The I Ching**: Also known as The Book of Changes. While this text is not specific to any one eastern religion exclusively, the I Ching is considered a central text influential in multiple eastern religions (particularly those from China). It is not just considered a religious text, but a foundational Chinese classic writing whose influence has spread worldwide. It is a divination text, meaning its primary use is to foretell the future using a method known as cleromancy (casting of lots, usually with yarrow plant stalks), using random numbers. Six numbers between six and nine are turned into a hexagram, which can then be looked up in the text. They are arranged in what's called the King Wen sequence, which is sixty-four different arrangements of the hexagrams (formed with broken and unbroken lines), each used to represent yin or yang energy. These different arrangements are then interpreted to provide guidance, whether moral or other decisions. Its age is of debate, first written anywhere between the tenth and fourth centuries B.C. It is often attributed to King Wen of Zhou, the Duke of Zhou, and Fu Xi. An important part of the I Ching, known as the Tend Wings, are attributed to Confucius. This addition expounds on the oneness of the universe, provide cosmic authority and influence to the text, and to help the symbolic understanding of the hexagrams. The I Ching is important in Taoism, Confucianism, and Zen Buddhism.[11]

  Man follows Earth, Earth follows Heaven. Heaven follows the Tao. Yet the Tao follows Nature. Tao produced one. One produced two. Two produced Three. Three produced ten thousand beings. Ten thousand beings carry yin and embrace yang; By blending their energies they achieve harmony. Therefore existence and nonexistence produce each other. Difficulty and ease complement each other. Long and short contrast with each other. High and low rely on each other. Sound and voice harmonize with each other. Front and back follow each other. The Tao fulfills its purpose quietly and makes no claim. When success is achieved, withdrawing. The highest good is like water. Water benefits ten thousand beings, Yet it does not contend. Nothing under Heaven is as soft and yielding as water. Yet in attacking the firm and strong, Nothing is better than water.[12]

  If one overshoots the goal, one cannot hit it. If a bird will not come to its nest but flies higher and higher, it eventually falls into the hunter's net. He who in times of extraordinary salience of small things does not know how to call a halt, but restlessly seeks to press on and on, draws upon himself misfortune at the hands of gods and men, because he deviates from the order of nature.[13]

  One should not try to alter natural law by using force. Recognize the situation. In ancient times when there were serious calamities an emperor often issued a "self-blame decree," a mea culpa, to calm people's indignation. Through self-examination and by being central and steadfast, wait for another cycle from Hindrance to Advance.[14]

- **Taoism**: Tao Te Ching (The Way and Its Power) contains the teaching of Lao Tzu, the attributed founder of Taoism. It is eighty-one chapters or sections written in poetic style to encourage different and contradictory interpretations of its content. Its style is ancient rhetoric, consisting of short statements (to create mnemonic association) with intentional contradiction attached (forcing the reader to examine and address obvious contradictions). Also central to Taoism are Zhuangzi, which contains essential Taoist thought, and Daozang, which is classified as the Taoist canon. These sacred writings which address truth, mystery, and divinity are passed down from teacher to student rather than purchased at a bookstore. Also relevant is the Taishang Ganying Pian, which discusses moral issues, especially those of ethics.

A good traveler has no fixed plans
and is not intent upon arriving.
A good artist lets his intuition
lead him wherever it wants.
A good scientist has freed himself of concepts
and keeps his mind open to what is.

Thus the Master is available to all people
and doesn't reject anyone.
He is ready to use all situations
and doesn't waste anything.
This is called embodying the light.

What is a good man but a bad man's teacher?
What is a bad man but a good man's job?
If you don't understand this, you will get lost,
however intelligent you are.
It is the great secret.[15]

Stop thinking, and end your problems.
What difference between yes and no?
What difference between success and failure?
Must you value what others value,
avoid what others avoid?
How ridiculous!

Other people are excited,
as though they were at a parade.
I alone don't care,
I alone am expressionless,
like an infant before it can smile.

Other people have what they need;
I alone possess nothing.
I alone drift about,
like someone without a home.
I am like an idiot, my mind is so empty.

Other people are bright;
I alone am dark.
Other people are sharp;
I alone am dull.

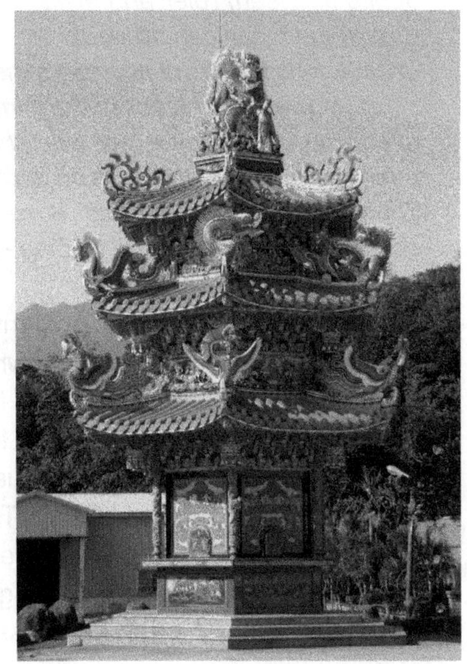
Taoist ghost money urn, Jinshan, Taiwan

Other people have purpose;
I alone don't know.
I drift like a wave on the ocean,
I blow as aimless as the wind.

I am different from ordinary people.
I drink from the Great Mother's breasts.[16]

All streams flow to the sea because it is lower than they are. humility gives it its power. if you want to govern the people, you must place yourself below them. if you want to lead the people, you must learn how to follow them.[17]

- **Confucianism**: The Four Books and The Five Classics create the main body of literature within Confucianism. The Four Books are: Great Learning (considered the gateway of learning), Doctrine of the Mean (the way to attain perfect virtue), Analects (speeches and discussions by Confucius and his disciples), and Mencius (conversations with Mencius, a Confucian scholar). The Five Classics are Classic of Poetry (poems, hymns, and eulogies for ceremonies), Book of Documents (the oldest Chinese narrative, containing speeches from rulers and officials of the Zhou period), Book of Rites (outlines rites, social forms, and court ceremonies), I Ching (a divination system known as the Book of Changes), and Spring and Autumn Annals (a historical record of the State of Lu, where Confucius lived).

The course (of duty), virtue, benevolence, and righteousness cannot be fully carried out without the rules of propriety; nor are training and oral lessons for the rectification of manners complete; nor can the clearing up of quarrels and discriminating in disputes be accomplished; nor can (the duties between) ruler and minister, high and low, father and son, elder brother and younger, be determined; nor can students for office and (other) learners, in serving their masters, have an attachment for them; nor can majesty and dignity be shown in assigning the different places at court, in the government of the armies, and in discharging the duties of office so as to secure the operation of the laws; nor can there be the (proper) sincerity and gravity in presenting the offerings to spiritual Beings on occasions of supplication, thanksgiving, and the various sacrifices. Therefore the superior man is respectful and reverent, assiduous in his duties and not going beyond them, retiring and yielding - thus illustrating (the principle of) propriety.[18]

- **Shinto**: Kojiki (Records of Ancient Matters, also known as Furukotofumi) and Nihon Shoki (Chronicles of Japan, also known as the Nihongi). Kojiki contains myths, legends, songs, genealogies, oral traditions, and historical accounts that pertain to the creation and origin of the Japanese islands. These legends end around the year 641. The mythology of the Kojiki is now used for Shinto rituals, especially their purification ritual. It is considered the oldest literary work in Japan.[19] The Nihon Shoki is a thirty-chapter collection that covers the Japanese version of the creation of the world, the first seven generations of divine beings, and continues on through the eighth century. Its contents include the reigns of forty-two emperors and empresses. It is historical, geographical, and political in nature.[20]

The names of the Deities that were born next were the Earthly-Eternally-Standing-Deity, next the Luxuriant-Integrating-Master-Deity. These two Deities were likewise Deities born alone, and hid their persons. The names of the Deities that were born next were the Deity Mud-Earth-Lord next his younger sister the Deity Mud-Earth-Lady; next the Germ-Integrating-Deity, next his younger sister the Life-Integrating-Deity; next the Deity Elder-of-the-Great-Place, next his younger sister the Deity Elder-Lady-of-the-Great-Place; next the Deity Perfect-Exterior, next his younger sister the Deity Oh-Awful-Lady; next the Deity the Male-Who-Invites, next his younger sister the Deity the Female-Who-Invites.

From the Earthly-Eternally-Standing Deity down to the Deity the Female-Who-Invites in the previous list are what are termed the Seven Divine Generations.[21]

- **Sindo**: There are no scriptures in Sindoism. The most important figure is the shaman.

- **Eastern Buddhism**: Eastern traditions of Buddhism are based on specific, special transmissions of Buddhist tradition outside of the traditional Buddhist scriptures. Practitioners are expected to familiarize themselves with the classical Zen canon: the sutras, especially the Diamond Sutra (A metaphor for thunder or a diamond as a weapon to cut through illusion and get to the true reality), Lankavatara Sutra (a teaching between Buddha and *Mahamati*, which means "great wisdom;" discussion covers the idea that everything in this world is an illusion, a manifestation of our minds), the Vimalakirti Sutra (examines doctrines about the body of Buddha, the illusion of the world, and the superiority of Eastern Buddhist systems over others; it encourages teaching without words, through silence), the Avatamsaka Sutra (a description of the cosmos, specifically containing one another; the Bodhisattva path, the relevance of dharmas, the power of meditation, and the essence of spiritual emptiness), the Heart Sutra (delves into all matter as empty, void of unchanging essence), the Shurangama Sutra (an esoteric eastern Buddhist text that focuses on Buddhist logic), the Mahaparinirvana Sutra (a text that seeks to explore the eternal and indestructible nature of the Buddha), and the Lotus Sutra (another cosmos text, it uses images to proclaim theoretical teachings and essential teachings, in discourses, parables, and practices for believers). The unique writing created by Zen Buddhists is the Platform Sutra. This specific sutra refers to a podium where a Buddhist teacher speaks and presents, and focuses on the true nature of a being, and focuses on the unity of conduct, meditation, and wisdom.

Subhuti, someone might fill innumerable worlds with the seven treasures and give all away in gifts of alms, but if any good man or any good woman awakens the thought of Enlightenment and takes even only four lines from this Discourse, reciting, using, receiving, retaining and spreading them abroad and explaining them for the benefit of others, it will be far more meritorious. Now in what manner may he explain them to others? By detachment from appearances-abiding in Real Truth. -So I tell you-

Thus shall you think of all this fleeting world:

A star at dawn, a bubble in a stream;

A flash of lightening in a summer cloud,

A flickering lamp, a phantom, and a dream.

When Buddha finished this Discourse the venerable Subhuti, together with the bhikshus, bhikshunis, lay-brothers and sisters, and the whole realms of Gods, Men and Titans, were filled with joy by His teaching, and, taking it sincerely to heart they went their ways.[22]

All Buddhas, in all the countless worlds, in the midst of the oceans of mental inclinations of all kinds of sentient beings, urge them to remember the Buddhas . . . they multiply their bodies to go to all worlds in the ten directions to let the sentient beings behold them, meditate on them and contemplate them, attend and serve them, plant roots of goodness, gain the good graces of the Buddhas, and increase the family of Buddhas, all being certain to attain buddhahood.[23]

- **Vietnamese folk religion**: Traditionally, Vietnamese religion focuses on the shaman or priest rather than on written scriptures. Caodaism, as a division of Vietnamese folk religion, does have a variety of Scriptures and draws on a variety of different recitations, especially those from Buddhism. Some of their unique Scriptures include the *Prayers of the Heavenly and Earthly Way*, *The Religious Constitution of Cao Dai Religion*, *The Canonical Codes*, and *The Divine Path to Eternal Life*.

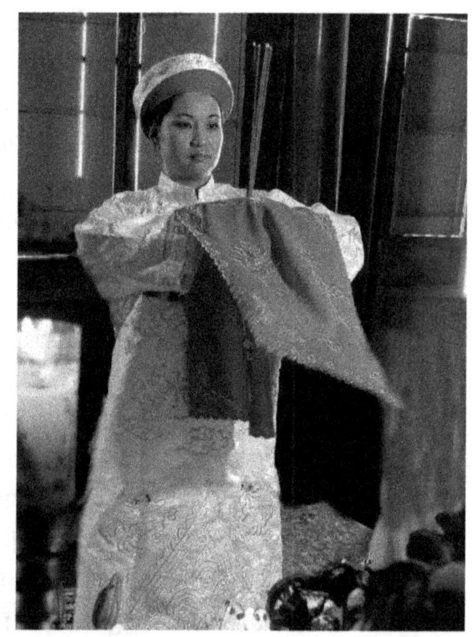

Vietnamese shaman

BASIC RELIGIOUS PRACTICES

Eastern religious worship focuses on individual practice. It is understood that if each individual practitioner of these belief systems adheres to the principles, they will better function as individuals, family members, citizens of society, and with the universe. The goal of these religions is to create flow, helping one better understand their position in life and to embody such. Different eastern religions assist with this process in different ways. Taoism addresses the need for harmony, expounding on the "way," and does such through mediums, divination, festivals, and sacrificial offerings. Confucianism focuses on specified social order, the relevance of ancestors, and essential building blocks within relationships. Shinto focuses on forces behind nature, initiation rites, purity rituals, and seasonal practice. Sindo offers shamanism, supernatural beings, purity rituals, and sacrificial rites. Zen Buddhism offers meditation and enlightenment. Vietnamese folk religion offers forces behind nature, rites, seasonal practices, meditation, and discipline. It is easy to see how these groups have culturally merged, offering different aspects of spiritual practice to practitioners.

There are a few key aspects of far eastern religion that are all essential and basic practices, regardless of the specified branch or religious affiliation. The first, and most key, is ancestor worship. Ancestral worship is an ancient part of far eastern culture. It has, therefore, been adopted into most far eastern systems. Its purpose is to honor those who have gone before adherents, while working to keep the deceased happy and pleased with the living. It is considered a veneration, rather than a specified worship of a deity. Most individuals have a specific ancestral altar in their home, which recalls the deeds of ancestors, may have pictures, and where items are offered, such as burning incense in their memory.

Temples or shrines are also key places of devotion in eastern religious systems. One may go to the temple once per day, a few times per year, for festivals, or exclusively for sacred rites (such as infant dedications or marriages). Individuals go to offer to the gods or spirits, to receive specific rites, participate in the spiritual life of their religious worship, consult with a temple priest or shaman, and to receive instruction, through a direct teacher, of their specified faith.

Meditation, chanting, and disciplinary meditative focuses are often key points within their faith systems. Nature worship is also part of the system, in ways that are seen as helping to honor the spirits or deities that are behind nature's different cycles. In ancient times, politicians such as the king or emperor were also regarded as divine and worthy of worship. Revered and enlightened teachers in various eastern systems are called masters.

Eastern practitioners may also engage in several different practices such as divination, energy channeling or healing, acupuncture, martial arts, or feng shui. Such seek to find eternal balance and harmony with one's environment rather than fighting it.

HOLIDAYS

- **Taoism**: The Lantern Festival celebrates the birth of the Taoist deity, Tianguan, associated with good fortune and positivity (15th day of the first lunar month in February or March); Quingming Festival, Tomb Sweeping Day, ancestor veneration festival (one hundred and four to one hundred and six days after the winter solstice) days after the winter solstice); Duanwu Festival, Dragon Boat Festival, celebrating the life of Qu Yuan of the Zhou, by which people race dragon boats and eat a special kind of riceball (fifth month of the lunisolar Chinese calendar); Chinese New Year, Chinese New Year's Eve to the monthly Lantern Festival, focuses on welcoming the new year with good fortune, visiting temples, parades, and social entertainments (traditional first day of the lunisolar Chinese calendar); and the Hungry Ghost Festival, associated with ghosts and spirits returning from the lower realm, and Buddhists and Taoists alike offer food, incense, and joss paper to keep the deceased happy and avert their sufferings (the fifteenth night in July).[24]

- **Confucianism**: The Birthday of Confucius, a ten-day festival in tribute to Confucius (September 28); Quingming Festival, Tomb Sweeping Day, ancestor veneration festival (104-106 days after the winter solstice); Chongmyo Taeje, honors the kings and queens of the Yi dynasty (first Sunday in May); Chinese New Year, Chinese New Year's Eve to the monthly Lantern Festival, focusing on welcoming the new year with good fortune, visiting temples, parades, and social entertainments.[25]

- **Shinto**: Shogatsu, Shinto/Japanese New Year, celebrating the *kami* of the four directions, prayers for good health, prosperity, and happiness, gifts of money, social games and activities (January 1); Shinto rite for the goddess Izanami, partner of the god Izanagi, creators of nature and the *kami* (January 7); Dosojlm Matsurl, ornaments, decorations, and talisman are gathered and burned in bonfires, with the intent to wish for good health and a rich harvest in the year (January 15); Toshlgol, rite honoring the *kami* and offering prayers for the rice harvest (February 17); Hana Matsurl, the Shinto flower festival, honoring the *kami* (April 8); Shlchl-go-san, festival for three, five, and seven-year olds, which are dressed in traditional clothing and taken to the shrines to receive the protection of the *kami* (October 17); Harvest Festival, prayer for children's growth and for children to be recognized by the gods and nation as members of their society (November 15); Tohl-Talsal, festival to the Sun goddess, Amaterasu (December 22).

- **Sindo**: Seollal, Lunar New Year's Day, most important day of the year, individuals wear their best attire, bow to their elders, eat special soups, and play special games with their families (January 24-26); Children's Day, day dedicated to children (May 5); Chuseok, Korean Thanksgiving Day celebrated with harvest and memorial rituals at the graves of their ancestors (September 30-October 2); National Foundation Day, celebrating the founding of Korea by the god Dangun, acknowledged with a simple shrine throughout Korea (October 3).[26]

- **Eastern Buddhist holidays**: While traditional Buddhism honors several festivals, Zen Buddhists typically observe three. Vesak, or the Buddha's Birthday, usually held in May or June (depending on the lunar cycle); in Japan, it is celebrated April 8; Dhamma Day, on the full moon in July (celebrates the Buddha's teaching of the first Four Noble Truths to reach enlightenment); and Sangha Day, also called Magha Puja, celebrated in February or March (Celebrates a gathering held between Buddha and over twelve hundred of his early disciples; reflects upon the monastic tradition present in Buddhism. Largely celebrated in Cambodia, Laos, Thailand, Sri Lanka, and Myanmar.)[27]

- **Vietnamese folk religion holidays**: Tet Nguyen Dan, Lunar New Year, largest festival of the year, dedicated with religious devotion, fireworks, temple visits, and giving one another flowers (January/February); The Lantern Festival, associated with good fortune and positivity (every fifteenth day of first lunar month, in February or March); Mid-Autumn Festival, harvest festival, street fairs, household altars to honor the full moon (mid-September); Hung King Temple Festival, commemoration of Kinh Duong Vuong, first king of Vietnam (April).

Visual Signs and Symbols

Yin-yang, symbolizing the polarization and balance of the universe, representing male and female, earth and heaven, and light and dark, good and evil; the lotus wheel of Buddhism; lotus flower; statues and images of Confucius, Buddha, and assorted figures in nature, the spirit world, gods and goddesses, and ancestors; a perfect circle; oriental scrolls and writings; shrines and altars; tai symbol of peace; torii gateways; the mirror; the sword; the jewel; western symbolism blended with eastern images; tannegrams; hexagram (I Ching); rising sun; magatama (symbol of good fortune); bagua; Divine Eye.

CREEDS, BOOKS, AND LAWS

Eastern religions are non-credal. They do not establish creeds, nor require creedal statement for membership. Membership in eastern religion is not measured by temple attendance or by theological statements, and has been stated before, it is plausible for members of one eastern religion to practice another. It is also perfectly acceptable for a member to practice their religion independently as part of cultural identity and understanding.

Taoist Shrine in New York City, New York

ECLECTIC BELIEFS

Because eastern religion is ancient and connects to ancient mythologies, customs, and traditions, there is a sense of antiquity within religious practice. In modern times, there have become questions between the ancient and modern, and where exactly these older religions fit within modern society. They are from a time before modern issues were discussed, including abortion, homosexuality, citizen's rights, and encounters with other religious groups. Not making any stand, the religions continue to uphold their ancient customs. They reveal an ancient way of looking at the world; of an indigenous time, as people struggled with the environment, agricultural advances, and other matters that became associated with spiritual progress. Their beliefs represent the evolution of the far Asian culture, from its earliest inceptions in creation myths, down through the ages of governing kings and empires.

RELATIONS WITH NON-EASTERN RELIGIONS

Eastern religion is flexible enough to incorporate many Christian religious systems with its own. Differing religious beliefs are not perceived as threatening.

HOLY SITES

Fushimi Inari Taisha Shrine, Kyoto, Japan; Mount Fuji, Honshu, Japan; South Pututo Temple, Xiamen, China; Kaiyuan Temple, Quanzhou City, China; Temple of the Six Banyan Trees, Guangzhou, China; White Horse Pagoda, Danghe Town, China; Dazu Rock Carvings, Dazu County, China; Jade Buddha Temple, Shanghai, China; Hanshan Temple, Suzhou, China; Chongshan Temple, Taiyuan, China; Confucian Temple, Shandong Province, China; Solitary Joy Temple, Tianjin, China; Yufeng Temple, Lijiang City, China; Lingyin Temple, Hangzhou, China; Siz Harmonies Pagoda, Hangzhou, China; Tianhou Palace, Tianjin City, China; Mount Laoshan, Qingdao, China;

Shaolin Temple, Dengfeng, China; Chengdu Quigyang Gong, Chengdu City, China; Yuantong Temple, Kunming City, China; Golden Temple, Fengming Mountain, China; Qiongzhu Temple, Kunming City, China; Nanshan Temple, Hainan Island, China; Three Pagodas, Dali Ancient City, China; Ji le Temple, Harbin, China; Western Hill and Dragon Gate, Kunming City, China; Famen Temple, Baoji City, China; Thousand Buddha Mountain, Jinan City, China; Wudang Mountains, Shiyan, China; Mount Qingcheng, Dujiangyan, China; Mount Longhu, Yingtan, China; Mount Qiyun, Huangshan, China; Cemetery of Confucius, Qufu, China; Kong Family Mansion, Qufu, China; Emperor Meiji Shrine, Tokyo, Japan; Floating Torii Gate, Miyajima, Japan; Tapsa Temple, Jinan, South Korea; Inwangsan Guksadang, Seoul, South Korea; Sinheungsa Temple, Gangwon-do, South Korea; CaoDai Holy See, Tay Ninh, Vietnam; Temple of Literature and National University, Hanoi, Vietnam; Po Nagar Cham Towers, Nha Trang, Vietnam; Then Mu Pagoda, Hue, Vietnam; One Pillar Pagoda, Hanoi, Vietnam; Mieu Temple, Hue, Vietnam.

Shinto shrine remains, Jinguashi, Taiwan

NOTABLE FIGURES

Confucius, founder of Confucianism; Lao Tzu, teacher of Taoism; Sun Tzu, Chinese governmental figure; Zhuangzi (d. 288 B.C.), philosopher; Alex Anatole (1948-), Taoist priest; Deng Ming-Dao (1954-), author; Benjamin Hoff (1946-), author; Michael R. Saso (1930-), professor; Gia-Fu Feng (1919-1985), translator; Bruce Lee (1940-1973), martial artist and actor; Stephen Russell (1954-2020), "The Barefoot Doctor;" Oguy Sorai (1666-1728), philosopher; Yi I (1536-1584), philosopher; Nguyen Trai (1380-1442), scholar; Wang Fuzhi (1619-1692), scholar; Hirata Atsutane (1776-1843), philosopher; Geoffrey Shugen Arnold (1957-), author; Jan Chozen Bays (1945-), pediatrician; Thich Thien-An (1925-1980), Buddhist monk; Michael O'Keefe (1955-), actor; D.T. Suzuki (1870-1966), author; Ngo Van Chieu (1878-1932), first Caodaist.

NOTABLE GROUPS

Taoism has several schools (sometimes called denominations) within its heading. None claim a sole position of orthodoxy. These different schools typically establish their own specified scriptures that dictate their practice and rites. One of the most famous was the Way of the Five Pecks of Rice, also known as the Way of the Celestial Master. At its height, the group had a theocratic state that was later incorporated into the Kingdom of Wei. Followers were found throughout China. They believed that qi, material energy or life force, was found in everything. To achieve eternal life, one had to have the correct amount of qi in one's body. If one didn't have the right amount, that individual could face illness and death. Sex was seen as a potential source loss of qi. Meditation was used to restore qi balance in the body. It was this movement that allowed

Taoism to first reach the entire population, rather than just wealthy or literate persons.[28]

FACTS AND FIGURES

Approximately 6% of the world population practices a Taoist religious system.[29]

OTHER IMPORTANT DEFINITIONS

- ***Aku***: In Shinto, the association of evil with all things bad, negative, and unfortunate.
- ***Bianhua***: The constant source of change within the world.
- **Dojo**: A place for learning or meditation; often accompanying a Buddhist temple as a formal training for Japanese arts.
- ***Chinju***: The personal *kami* or shrine of an area or Buddhist temple.
- ***Gut***: Also called *kut*. The sacrificial rites performed by Korean shamans involving sacrifices and offerings for ancestors.
- ***Imi***: Something that can be polluting, especially in a ceremony.
- ***Jiao***: Taoist renewal ritual; also refers to "teaching" or "religion" in Confucianism.
- ***Jinja Honcho***: Association of Shinto Shrines in Japan.
- ***Jisha***: A Shinto temple shrine.
- ***Kinhin***: Walking meditation; the practice of walking between long periods of *zazen*.
- **Muism**: Term for Korean Sinism (shamanism).
- **Neo-Confucianism**: A blending of Taoism, Confucianism, and Chinese Buddhism, combining the three together within the backdrop of classic Confucianism.
- **New Confucianism**: Modern Confucianism that adds modern-day democracy, political beliefs, and scientific ideas to Confucianist interpretation.
- ***Onusa***: Wooden wands used in Shinto rituals.
-
- ***Rujiao***: Another term for Confucianism.
- ***Saisen***: Offerings from worshipers.

- ***Samu***: The physical work required as part of participation with a Zen monastery.

- **Sando**: The approach leading from a torii to a shrine; also used in Buddhist temples.

- ***Sanjiao***: "Three teachings;" specifically Buddhism, Taoism, and Confucianism.

- ***Sanzen***: Also known as *nisshitsu*. Going to a Zen Buddhist master for instruction, usually a private meeting held between a student and a master.

- ***Satori***: A term unique to Japanese Buddhism that refers to personal enlightenment.

- ***Sensei***: Also known as *Seonsaeng* or *Xiansheng*. A term that is often used to denote a teacher; also used for professionals in society, such as clergy, lawyers, doctors, or politicians, or individuals who are skilled, such as authors or artists.

- ***Sesshin***: An intense period of meditation at a Zen monastery.

- ***Shintai***: A sacred object.

- ***Shinmyeong***: The Korean shaman rite by which the shaman channels a god or divine being.

- ***Yaza***: Sitting time during *sesshin* that is beyond the normal course of daily routine.

- ***Zazenkai***: A Zen retreat shorter in length than a *sesshin*.

- ***Zazen***: The practice of disciplined, seated Zen meditation. One is required to erase all thoughts and judgments and focus upon the meditative emptiness.

- ***Zendo***: A Japanese meditation hall, where zazen is practiced.

BELIEVER'S CHARACTERISTICS

Emphasis on the right way, proper conduct, and connection with nature and the universe; filial system; ancestral worship and family duty; strong sense of personal responsibility and duty; mixture of eastern religious religions practiced and sometimes western religion too; nature worship; use of statues and prayer chants to diverse gods; meditation; sense of duty and honor; shamans; cultural traditions in worship; temple or shrine visits; use of tai chi, acupuncture, acupressure, reiki, "energy healing," and feng shui; use of ancient eastern scriptures; divination using I Ching, tannegrams, or other ancient methods; emphasis on balance and harmony; separateness; blending of old and new; ancestral festivals; seasonal festivals; belief in many gods or spirits; animism; offerings and sacrifices; superstition; syncretism with many different religious systems.

THEOSOPHY

But in spite of these perhaps too great admissions, I maintain that *Isis Unveiled* contains a mass of original and never hitherto divulged information on occult subjects...I defend the ideas and teachings in it, with no fear of being charged with conceit, since neither ideas nor teaching are mine, as I have always declared; and I maintain that both are of the greatest value to mystics and students of Theosophy.
(Helena Blavatsky)[1]

THEOLOGY

The word "Theosophy" literally means "god-wisdom" or "divine wisdom." Its complicated theological understanding states all that is created (several solar systems) are the product of a Solar Deity or a Logos. Below each of these deities are seven ministers, called planetary spirits, with each of these seven beings in control of spiritual evolution on each planet. Each planet has a seven-fold constitution, called a planetary chain, consisting of a physical globe, two astral bodies, two mental bodies, and two spiritual bodies. Evolution is a process for all life on each planet, from vegetable to spiritual. The universe is seen as an outward reflection from the Absolute, in a belief system known as emanationist cosmology. The world, as is perceived by humanity, is an illusion (called maya). If one sees themselves limited by the present world, one is deluded.

The human being (known as an ego or Monad) emanates from the Solar Deity, to which it will return. Theosophists believe there is an eternal, impersonal force within each human being, called "the Master," the "inner god," and the "higher self." When human beings unite with this inward deity, they will find ultimate wisdom and spiritual enlightenment. Each human being passes through three halls: ignorance, learning, and wisdom. At this point, the human soul merges into the One, the reality of the universe and connected realization.

Theosophists believe in a messianic figure that shall come to earth known as Lord Maitreya or sometimes, the Christ (equated as the Hindu deity Krishna in a previous incarnation and entering Jesus of Nazareth at his baptism). This will usher in a reign of universal peace known as the Age of Aquarius. Later in Theosophy history, Lord Maitreya was introduced as incarnate in a boy from India named Jiddu Krishnamurti (1895-1986).

Also central to Theosophy are the teachings of a group of individuals central to the foundational ideas of the group. They are known as the "masters" (sometimes called the Mahatmas, Adepts, Masters of Wisdom, Masters of Compassion, and Elder Brothers). Together, they form what is called the "Great White brotherhood" or "White Lodge." These are teachers of ancient wisdom, highly evolved individuals who practiced occult ideals (such as clairvoyance or astral projection) during their lifetimes. These masters are the foundations of the world's spirituality, both ancient and modern. The most prominent masters include Koot Hoomi (Kuthumi) and Morya, direct channels during the formation of Theosophy. (There is no evidence any such individuals lived, and many suspect they may have been a hoax to further the work of Theosophy.) These individuals include Abraham, Moses, Solomon, Jesus, Buddha, Confucius, Laozi, Jokob Boheme (1575-1624), Alessandro Cagliostro (1743-1795), and Franz Mesmer (1734-1815).[2]

PHILOSOPHY

While Theosophy does not require a specified set of belief or doctrine, it embraces its own unique ideas about spiritual matters. Theosophy embraces a profound concept of evolution in all life forms and that human evolution is intimately connected with planetary and wider, larger, cosmic evolution. The purpose of human life is to see the human soul emancipated. The human body is seen as having seven parts: body (*rupa*), vitality (*prana-Jiva*), astral body (*linga sarira*), animal soul (*kama-rupa*), human soul (*manas*), spiritual soul (*buddhi*), and spirit (*atma*). The human soul, spiritual soul, and spirit are immortal and eternal. The spiritual soul and spirit do not reside in the human body but are connected to the body through the human soul. Theosophy embraces a belief in reincarnation, believing in karma (the deeds one does in this life affect the way one lives in the next). This explains misery and suffering in the world, seeing difficult or bad circumstances as retribution for things done in past lives.

Modern world religions are believed to have a singular, common foundation known as the "secret doctrine." This secret doctrine was known to Plato and Hindu sages and is the center and focus of every religion. The foundation of this secret is a unity of science and religion. The world has dissected the unity between the two. Throughout history, there have been individuals who preserved the ancient wisdom down to the present day, known as a "secret brotherhood." Only individuals within this special brotherhood understand miracles, the afterlife, psychic powers, and practice and develop paranormal abilities. One day, this ancient religion will be revived and replace the dominant world religions (Christianity, Islam, Judaism, Buddhism, and Hinduism). Ancient texts are considered more relevant than rite and ritual in religious traditions.

Theosophy is about the promotion of this special information and knowledge for the liberation of the soul as humanity moves toward the Age of Aquarius. In this age, Lord Maitreya shall rule in a present incarnation. Secret knowledge will permeate the world. As this knowledge connects to the human soul, the human soul unites to its inner god, thus achieving wisdom and ultimate liberation. It is not so much the intricate practice of occultism (although such is permissible) as the study of and about it.

Their fundamentals are found in *The Secret Doctrine* by Helena Blavatsky (1831-1891), the founder of the movement:

1. *that there is an omnipresent, eternal, boundless, and immutable reality of which spirit and matter are complementary aspects;*
2. *that there is a universal law of periodicity or evolution through cyclic change; and*
3. *that all souls are identical with the universal oversoul which is itself an aspect of the unknown reality.*[3]

ADHERENT IDENTITY

Theosophy, Theosophists, Theosophical Society, Theosophical Temple, United Lodge of Theosophists, Untied Lodge.

NUMBER OF ADHERENTS

There are approximately 30,000 Theosophists in sixty countries worldwide.[4]

TRADITIONAL LANGUAGES

English. Theosophy also contains traces of Sanskrit words.

SECTS/DIVISIONS

- **Theosophical Society – International**: The official headquarters of the Theosophical Society, located in Adyar, in Chennai, India. The Theosophical Society in America is affiliated with it, including around 115 local group branches. It formed after the death of Helena Blavatsky by Henry Steel Olcott (1832-1907) and Annie Besant (1847-1933) due to a faction when William Quan Judge (1851-1896) claimed to be the proper successor for the movement. Some disagreed, and headquarters moved to India in effort to preserve the work. This distinguishes it from other Theosophical lodges that broke away from the official group in the late 1800s.[5]

Theosophy seal

- **Theosophical Society Pasadena**: A breakaway Theosophical group headquartered in Pasadena, California. It claims to be the true Theosophical group founded in 1875, with lineage through the leadership of William Quan Judge. It began in 1895 after the death of Helena Blavatsky. Their major purpose is to further divine wisdom and make Theosophical texts available online.[6]

- **United Lodge of Theosophists (ULT)**: Founded in 1909 by Robert Crosbie (1849-1919), it is an informal Theosophical association. It recognizes five key aspects of the Theosophical movement:

  i. *Recognition of W.Q. Judge as H.P. Blavatsky's colleague and co-worker from the beginning and hence as one of the original founders of the Theosophical Movement*
  ii. *Exclusive adherence to the unaltered works of H.P. Blavatsky and W.Q. Judge along with only those other works that are philosophically in consonance with the aforementioned*
  iii. *Rejection of any other "authorities" in the form of "leaders" or "teachers" and reference to all of its associates as "students" with emphasis on self-reliance*

iv. *Absence of organizational elements such as constitution, by-laws or officers and complete reliance on the "similarity of aim, purpose and teaching," as the only basis of unity*
v. *Anonymity of living persons who write on behalf of ULT to protect against exaltation of personalities and self-advertising*[7]

The ULT focuses on the idea of a lower or illusionary self rather than aggrandizing personalities. Their purpose was to be loyal to the original founders of Theosophy, emphasizing their message without dependence, hierarchy, or organization. They have fifteen lodges worldwide.[8]

- **Arcane School**: Founded by Theosophists, this work was created to usher in the New Age (the Age of Aquarius) in 1923. In 1919, Alice Bailey (1880-1949) believed she was contacted by an Ascended Master named Djual Khul ("The Tibetan") who commissioned her to receive his wisdom via telepathy. From this point, Alice began writing and established an esoteric school with free membership, binding with no pledges or oaths. Her practice was considered unacceptable to the Theosophical society. In 1920, Alice and Foster Bailey disassociated from Theosophy in order to pursue their program. The official publishing company for the Arcane School is the Lucis Trust, and the school now operates the New Group of World Servers (designed to unite people together for the coming civilization) and the Triangles program (to unite people by channeling spiritual energy from the spiritual realm to the world). Their publishing branch is The Theosophy Company.[9,10]

Lucius Trust logo

- **New Age Movement**: Theosophy is considered a key founding point of the modern New Age Movement. Many, if not all New Age groups have some trace or strain of Theosophical idea or doctrine within their ideals, including: the idea of an original secret truths organization that became the foundation of all world religions; a need for focus on the brotherhood of all mankind; the belief in Ascended Masters; and the belief of finding or discovering one's inner deity through invocations, meditation, and visualization. Of specific connection is the I AM Movement, which is an Ascended Masters teaching that started in the 1930s. This specific aspect of the New Age Movement focuses on the idea of Ascended Masters as having achieved the ultimate liberation, no longer bound by reincarnation. It focuses on the idea that the "I AM" (from the ancient Sanskrit term, *So Ham*, which means "I am that I am") presence of the divine is present in each individual person, manifesting as their Higher Self (their "Violet flame"). Every person who calls forth the action of spirit connects to this internal divine power. By tapping into this power, one is fulfilling the teachings of the Ascended Masters and can utilize this power to create justice, life, peace, harmony, and love in one's life. These ideas can be seen in the Church Universal and Triumphant, Ascended Master Teaching Foundation, The Bridge to Spiritual Freedom, City of the Sun Foundation, the Saint Germain Foundation, the Joy Foundation, and Morningland Community, among many others that often teach these beliefs in part, if not in whole.[11]

- **The Liberal Catholic Church**: A group of independent churches that adhere to esoteric understandings of spirituality as part of the Independent Catholic movement. There are two forms of Liberal Catholics: those that embrace the beliefs of Theosophy and those that do not. The Liberal Catholic Church was founded by two individuals, one of whom was Charles Webster Leadbeater (1854-1934), a Theosophist (he was also ordained as a priest in the Old Catholic movement). The group started around 1916 when Leadbeater was given the option to renounce Theosophy or face excommunication. In keeping with Theosophical ideas, the Theosophy branch of the Liberal Catholic Church embraces the unity of all religions, emphasizing their foundations from a common source. They believe they are "catholic" because their concept of a religious unity emphasizes universal principles.[12]

Liberal Catholic Church emblem

- **Rosicrucian Revival**: In the late 1800s and early 1900s several new Rosicrucian-themed secret societies emerged on the scene with modified views from the original group formed in the 1600s. Many of the views present within these societies, though Rosicrucian in nature, inspired by or merged with the ideas of Theosophy. These organizations include the Rosicrucian Fellowship and Lectorium Rosicrucianum.

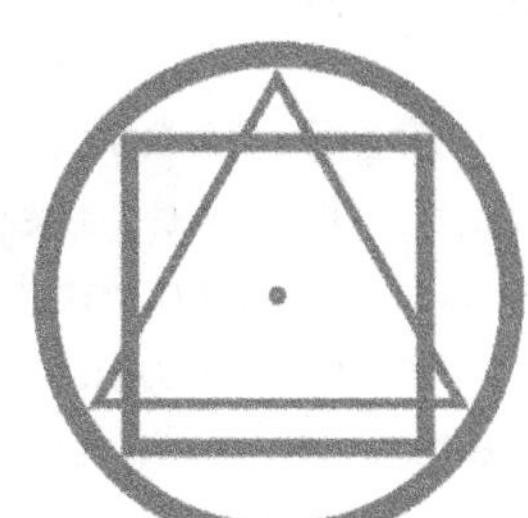

Lectorium Rosicrucianum logo

- **Anthroposophical Society**: Founded in 1923 by Rudolph Steiner (1861-1925), the Anthroposophical Society was an outgrowth of the German branch of the Theosophical Society. The organization within Germany held to their own ideas which eventually became a conflict with the Theosophical society (especially when they rejected the idea of Jiddu Krishnamurti as the reincarnation of Christ). Rudolph Steiner began teaching concepts that linked European philosophy and science with Christian esoterism. Most of the German Theosophical following followed Steiner, which started with fifty-five lodges. It's about developing true knowledge of the spiritual world and cultivating the science of such. It is not considered a secret society, but makes its work public, and its membership open to all. It seeks to discuss the existence of an objective, comprehensible spirit world, accessible by all human existence. Speaking philosophically rather than spiritually, they believe in rational discourse and believe in the use of scientific method for their pursuit. They are best known for their Waldorf Schools, also known as Steiner education. They seek to promote education and practical skill as based in Steiner's philosophical ideals.[13]

Anthroposophical Society logo

DISPUTES WITHIN GROUP

After the death of Helena Blavatsky, the Theosophy movement divided over successorship disputes. The most notable involved William Quan Judge and Henry Steel Olcott and Annie Bessant. While William Judge had been left to oversee the American branch of Theosophy while they operated the organization from India. He felt they deviated from the original teaching of the Great White Brotherhood that inspired the society to begin with; they rejected his accusation. This was not the last time there would be dispute over the veracity of teachings among leaders within the organization. Because the organization relies heavily on the concept of direct revelation from these Masters and does not require any specific belief system or practice, there is ample opportunity for counter beliefs, claims of new or differing revelation, and the establishment of new groups.

SCRIPTURES

Theosophists have no canon of established scriptures. Rather, they recognize all religious texts from the world's major world religions as profound sources of esoteric understanding. They are encouraged to read these texts from their perspective, and understand them in light of secret or hidden knowledge or doctrine. Theosophists also take interest in occult writings throughout history, believing they reveal the secret doctrines found in scripture, but are not always obvious or easy to see.

Writings unique to Theosophy were authored by Helena Blavatsky. Major ones include *Isis Unveiled*, *The Secret Doctrine*, *The Key to Theosophy*, *The Voice of the Silence*, *Gems From the East*, and *Transactions of the Blavatsky Lodge*.

> *Man is a little world–a microcosm inside the great universe. Like a fetus, he is suspended, by all his three spirits, in the matrix of the macrocosmos; and while his terrestrial body is in constant sympathy with its parent earth, his astral soul lives in unison with the sidereal anima mundi. He is in it, as it is in him, for the world-pervading element fills all space, and is space itself, only shoreless and infinite. As to his third spirit, the divine, what is it but an infinitesimal ray, one of the countless radiations proceeding directly from the Highest Cause–the Spiritual Light of the World? This is the trinity of organic and inorganic nature–the spiritual and the physical, which are three in one, and of which Proclus says that 'The first monad is the Eternal God; the second, eternity; the third, the paradigm, or pattern of the universe;' the three constituting the Intelligible Triad.*[14]

> *But it is in the denial of the boundless and endless Entity, possessor of that invisible Will which we for lack of a better term call GOD, that lies the powerlessness of every materialistic science to explain the occult phenomena. It is in the rejection a priori of everything which might force them to cross the boundary of exact science and step into the domain of psychological, or, if we prefer, metaphysical physiology, that we find the secret cause of their discomfiture by the manifestations, and their absurd theories to account for them.*[15]

> *Before the soul can see, the Harmony within must be attained, and fleshly eyes be rendered blind to all illusion.*[16]

Basic Religious Practices

While Theosophy is classified as a religion by experts who analyze the group, Theosophists do not consider themselves to be a religion. By standard definition of religion, they are a combination of a religion and a secret society, opening membership to a broader audience while still incorporating the specified elements of hidden knowledge and initiation. Theosophy centers around the individual and their personal attainment of wisdom and oneness with the divine, encouraging freedom of thought and independence of ideas. There is no specified set of required ethics any in the group must follow. Theosophists meet at lodges, which are formally organized groups with at least seven members. Lodge members study the precepts of Theosophy and present their beliefs and ideals for the public. Study centers consist of at least three members who meet to study Theosophy. There are no prescribed rituals or practices, although some ritual has been introduced by groups connected to Theosophy (such as the Liberal Catholic Church and the United Lodge of Theosophy). Such rituals are often constructs of liturgical form, borrowed from other occult groups and high church religions.[17]

Holidays

There are three specified days within the annual Theosophical calendar: Adyar Day, White Lotus Day, and Founders Day.[18]

Helena Blavatsky (1831-1891)

- **Adyar Day**: Adyar Day was originally known as Olcott Day (because it marked the passing of Henry Steel Olcott). In honor of his death, the president of the society (then Annie Besant) spoke and had religious representatives from the major world religions speak, concluding with an offering of flowers and thanks among those present. In 1923, the day became Adyar Day, a fundraising platform to raise money to continue the expansion and maintenance of the Theosophy headquarters at Adyar. It is a day to give and to remember those of Theosophy who have gone before current members (February 17).

- **White Lotus Day**: Commemoration of the death of Helena Blavatsky in 1891. The day is marked with a special commemorative meeting at headquarters, food given in the name of Helena Blavatsky to poor fishermen in Adyar. The official flag is flown at half-mast. All members meet to express their general love and regard for Helena Blavatsky's memory (May 8).

- **Founder's Day**: This date honors the founding of the organization in 1875 and pays tribute to the original founders: Helena Blavatsky, Henry Steel Olcott, William Quan Judge, and those other original members of the organization (November 17).

VISUAL SIGNS AND SYMBOLS

Theosophy symbol: constructed with a serpent in a circle, biting or swallowing its tail, encompassing a star of David or "seal of Solomon," with the upright triangle white, and the downward triangle black; inside of the seal, one finds an ankh. Near the serpent's head is a small circle, containing a swastika. Around the exterior is the Theosophy motto, "There is no religion higher than truth." Often, at the top, is found the word "OM" in Sanskrit, the sacred word of Hinduism. Theosophists may also incorporate the symbolism of all world religions, and of occult symbolism, into their own personal usage.[19]

CREEDS, BOOKS, AND LAWS

The highest governing hierarchy within Theosophy is the hidden spiritual hierarchy consisting of the Masters of Ancient Wisdom. The organization itself is headed by a president, and its main headquarters is in Adyar, India. It was formed to stand non-sectarian and exists as groups of followers gather under the auspices of headquarters' guidelines for participation. The president is nominated by a General Council and elected by the universal body of members, holding the position for seven years. The only time a president involves in National Section matters is when there is a dispute; otherwise, lodges and National sections (lodges within a nation) are completely autonomous. Members also pay an annual fee and are sponsored by other existing members.[20]

The organization is considered "non-credo," meaning there is no specified creed or stated belief. There are also no specified legal codes or guides for governance. The organization operates by what it calls the Three Objects of Theosophy:

> *To form a nucleus of the universal brotherhood of humanity, without distinction of race, creed, sex, caste, or colour; to encourage the study of comparative religion, philosophy, and science; and to investigate unexplained laws of Nature and the powers latent in human beings.*[21]

ECLECTIC BELIEFS

Central to Theosophy is the belief of reincarnation, as previously mentioned. It is seen as a perfecting cycle, one by which karma and past wrongdoings are worked out and the desire to gain wisdom obtained.

Theosophy sees itself as a bridge between the east and the west, especially in the commonalities of the culture. In the age when Theosophy first formed, Asian culture was new to the west and was seen as foreign. Theosophy also seeks to bridge religious theologies, especially those of the esoteric tradition. Greek and Alexandrian philosophies and religious ideals (especially Gnostic), and Vedanta, Mahayana Buddhism, Kabbalah, and Sufism are seen as central spiritual ideas for exploration and pursuit. It is often considered a religious hybrid by scholars.

RELATIONS WITH NON-THEOSOPHISTS

There is no ban on religious exploration outside of Theosophy. The endeavors of Theosophy encourage the study and exploration of world religion and the incorporation of such ideas in esoteric form. Some Theosophists, given their ideas, aren't as inclined to explore relationships with other religions. Many Theosophists avoid relations with Christians, especially those seen as Fundamentalist or Evangelical.

HOLY SITES

Adayr, Chennai, India.

NOTABLE FIGURES

Helena Blavatsky (1831-1891), founder; Henry Olcott (1832-1907), founder; Annie Besant (1847-1933), founder; William Quan Judge (1851-1896), founder; Jiddu Krishnamurti (1895-1986), believed to be the Lord Maitreya; Charles Webster Leadbeater (1854-1934), founder, Ananda College; Walter Evans-Wentz (1878-1965), anthropologist; Edwin Arnold (1832-1904), writer; Rukmini Devi Arundale (1940-1986), educator; George S. Arundale (1878-1945), president of the Theosophical Society in Chennai, India; Nicholas Camille Flammarion, astronomer and author (1842-1925); Piet Mondrian (1872-1944), artist; Kenneth Morris (1879-1937), writer; J.M Peebles (1822-1922), doctor and spiritualist; L. Frank Baum (1856-1919), author; Alexander Scriabin (1872-1915), musician.

NOTABLE GROUPS

The Theosophical Society – Adyar, located in Chennai, India, is the current headquarters for the worldwide movement. It is known for its "Huddleston Gardens," covering two hundred and sixty acres on the south bank of the Adyar River. The major work of the Theosophical Society takes place here, including publishing (through the Theosophical Publishing House), Olcott Memorial High School (provides free education, uniforms, books, and two daily meals to students), the Besant Scout Camping Centre, the Olcott Education Society, The Olcott Memoria School, and the Theosophical Order of Service, which seeks to engage in relief efforts and charitable work, including medical missions, establishment of schools, feeding programs, work with the disabled, and promotion of vegetarianism.[22,23]

FACTS AND FIGURES

Out of the 30,000 Theosophists worldwide, the highest population is found in India, where there are approximately 10,000 adherents. There are about 5,500 Theosophists in the United States.[24]

OTHER IMPORTANT DEFINITIONS[25]

- **Aaron**: The brother of Moses, seen as the first initiate of a secret Hebrew order.

- **Abhamski**: A mystical term for the four orders of beings: gods, demons, pitris, and men.
- **Abraxas**: A title for divinity, referring to the supreme of seven.
- **Absoluteness**: A universal principle that has no limitations or attributes.
- **Adam Kadmon**: Humanity; archetypal man; created perfect, mythologically depicted as white or caucasian.
- **Adamic Earth**: The primal element in alchemy, one remove from gold.
- **Adept**: The initiation state of occultism, by which one becomes a master of esoterism.
- **Adonai**: A reference to the sun.
- **Aethrobacy**: Levitation.
- **Alexandrian School of Philosophers**: An ancient school of philosophy in Alexandria, Egypt that was known for its extensive library, world-famous scholars, and neo-Platonian ideas.
- **Amenti**: The dwelling of the hidden, secret god, also known as Amen or Amount, as part of the esoteric kingdom of Osiris.
- **Astral body**: The ethereal counterpart, sometimes called a "shadow," of a man or an animal.
- **Astral light**: The invisible source of regional light around earth (and all planets).
- **Baptism**: In Theosophy, baptism is seen as an ancient rite, dating back to Chaldeo-Akkadian theurgy, now adapted as a purification rite or ceremony of initiation.
- **Bodha-Bodhi**: Wisdom-knowledge.
- **Eyes**: The concept of seeing all things within the space of the limitless universe; attaining supreme knowledge.
- **Fire (living)**: Denotes deity; the "One" life.
- **Fire-Philosophers**: A term used to describe Hermetists, alchemists, and Rosicrucians in the Middle Ages.
- **Hair**: A natural receptacle and retainer of one's vital essence, escaping with other eminations of the body; connected and associated with the brain.

- **Heavenly Adam**: The Sephirothal Tree, mixing all the forces of nature and informing of a deific essence, rather than a human one; the image of man as deity.

- **Key**: An emblem representing silence among ancient peoples.

- **Magic**: The great science, inseparable from religion.

- **Mysteries**: Initiations, or rites of initations.

- **OM**: Sometimes translated "Aum," considered the most sacred of all words in Hinduism. It is considered to be an invocation, benedicton, and promise at once; calling upon the three gods of Agni, Varuna, and Martus (Fire, water, and air).

- **Pitris**: The ancestors, or creators of mankind.

- **Planetary spirits**: The rulers or governors of the planets.

- **Pre-existence**: Reincarnation in the past or in the recounting of past lives.

- **Principles**: The elements, or original essences, of which all things are built up and upon.

- **Rings and Rounds**: An explanation of estern cosmogony, explaining evolutionary cycles, including cosmic, geological, or metaphysical.

- **Secret Doctrine**: A general name given to ancient esoteric teachings.

- **Senzar**: A mystical, secret language spoken by all initiates, worldwide.

- **Symbolism**: The visual expression of an idea or thought.

- **Theosophia**: The basis of all world religions and philosophies, taught and practiced by a few, elect beings from the beginning of time.

BELIEVER'S CHARACTERISTICS

Focus on the interest of occultism as a study and investigation, rather than a full practice; emphasis on reincarnation, attainment of spiritual wisdom, finding the divine god within, and universal religious understanding; belief in the idea of truth as a series of universal pursuits for hidden knowledge from the beginning of time; the universe is ordered by the number seven; the seven bodies of the monad; Jesus is merely a being, like all others, who attained perfection, which we too can attain; the focus of the Ascended Masters, or Great White Brotherhood, as they guide and direct through revelation today; interest in a synthesis of eastern and western ideas; focus on ancient schools of thought, philosophies, and religions throughout the ages; esteem of the writings of Helena Blavatsky; desire to see the world's religions unite, by returning to their basic, foundational idea; freethinking ideals; participation in Theosophy lodges or events; interest in what we would classify as occult, or New Age ideals.

Unchurched

It isn't until you come to a spiritual understanding of who you are – not necessarily a religious feeling, but deep down, the spirit within – that you can begin to take control.
(Oprah Winfrey)[1]

Theology

Those who identify as "unchurched" represent a demographic of individuals who do not participate in the world of formal, organized, group-sponsored religious activity. Therefore, they often hold to personalized views of theology, or in some instances, no specified views of theology. A high percentage of the "unchurched" population has a background within organized religion: either as children (often until they are of legal age) or as adults (who reach a point of disillusionment with organized religion or specific beliefs or experiences therein). As a result, the theology of the unchurched often reflects some concept an individual might have believed, been taught, or experienced at some point in their lives. There are also instances where individuals gravitate to the opposite theological position or embody something else entirely.

For the sake of this volume, the classification of "unchurched" is inclusive of those who believe in a higher power or deity without belonging to a religious community. It does not include atheists or agnostics, as they are represented separately. Approximately 68% of the unchurched say they do believe in God, the divine, or a higher power, although they often define what they mean differently.[2]

Philosophy

As a demographic, the unchurched have come to one of two conclusions: either that they do not need to belong to an organized institution to know, believe in, or experience the divine; or believe they do not fit in organized religion and do not feel comfortable, nor welcome, in their spiritual pursuit within any religious organization. Many reject the need for organized religion or the application of it therein. Most come to regard spirituality as a personal pursuit or journey, one that is individualized, applied, controlled, and interpreted by the individual themselves. Most define themselves as "spiritual, but not religious."

Disassociation with organized religion does not mean the unchurched reject spiritual matters, nor pursue independent means of spiritual activity. It simply means they do not pursue such activities through the definitions of an organized religious group or gathering with other believers of like minds. The unchurched are highly suspicious of religious hierarchy, leaders, structure, and church law and regulation. They often adopt parts of religious belief that appeal to them, combine them sometimes with bits and pieces of other belief systems, and create an independent system of belief and practice.

The term "unchurched" does not mean one is not a churchgoer or a Christian (because, in such an instance, it would refer to anyone outside of the Christian faith). The term emerged within American society, using the standard form of organized religion (i.e., church attendance) within American culture as definition for terminology. The unchurched are representative of any individual who has departed from religious belief, choosing instead to practice faith independently, rather than through the experience of a formalized, religious system. Most standards for definition are that an individual is considered "unchurched" if they have not visited nor attended a worship service within the last six months.[3]

ADHERENT IDENTITY

Unchurched; independent spiritual practitioner; spiritual; non-religious; spiritual but not religious; nonreligious, irreligious.

NUMBER OF ADHERENTS

Statistics on the unchurched have remained low over the past twenty to thirty years, although they are slowly on the increase. It is easiest to obtain statics on unchurched individuals within the United States; it is more difficult to find specific numbers elsewhere. Approximately 33% of the American population is "unchurched," somewhere around 100,000,000 people.[4]

TRADITIONAL LANGUAGES

Unchurched individuals, representing a diverse population, do not have a specified language.

SECTS/DIVISIONS

There is no specified organization or dictating group that defines the unchurched. Part of being unchurched is rejecting the idea of outside structure or organization, and this means there aren't formalized groups of unchurched individuals. There are a few basic categorizes of unchurched individuals, regardless:

- **Those who reject organized religion**: The first category consists of those who specifically object to the idea of religion as an organized entity as a philosophical and theological presupposition. While all unchurched do reject organized religion and take issue with religious organizational structure, this group rejects organized religion for the simple reason that it is organized. They are opposed to the idea that spirituality or religion should be regulated, organized, corporate, or institutional. Most take particular issue with things such as church rules, doctrine and dogma, the exclusivity required of spiritual ideas, the need for participation, and financial giving. For this reason, they reject the very concept of organized religion.

- **Those who feel unwelcome**: There are individuals who, due to specific experiences with organized religion feel they are, for whatever reason, unwelcome within organized religion. This may be due to something specific about them that is seen as intolerable or unacceptable within their respective traditions (such as experiencing same-sex attraction, variations in gender identity, political views, income disparity, or positions for women). While such individuals may not be opposed to religion or participating in a religious group, they have not been successful in finding such for themselves and reject participation with all groups, feeling their answers do not lie (at least at this time) with an organized group. Those who feel unwelcome in an organized religious setting may or may not return to a religious group if the right situation presented itself in their lives, but due to current circumstances, they presently do not congregate with a religious group.

- **Hurt by religion**: There are many individuals in this world who, though they do believe or embrace a certain theological belief system, have been hurt by members of a specified religious group, leading them to reject all religious groups. Specific examples can include spiritual, physical, or sexual abuse at the hands of clergy, church members, or growing up in systems that fostered an atmosphere leading to such. Much like those who feel unwelcome, those who have been hurt by religion may not always be opposed to participating with a religious group or with religion in general, but do not feel, based on their experience, as if religion or religious participation is for them. Others may feel religion and organization of religion is the reason for their hurt, and they may reject all religious systems and institutions as a result. The modern Christian deconstruction movement is an example of some of those who have had various experiences with religious hurt and are attempting, in different ways, to process their experience and discern what they now believe.

- **Find their time filled with other things**: Modern society has created the rise of individuals who do not, for any specified reason, feel the need to explore or belong to an organized religious group. When asked, a major reason is that the people are very busy with activities, social engagements, family time, and other things, and do not have the time, nor the need, to belong to an organized religious group and perform the required commitments therein. They may say they believe in God or a higher power and may pray, engage in some religious practices on a private level, observe religious holidays (and possibly visit a worship service on such accompanying days), but do not make the commitment or structured adherence to an organized religious group.

Disputes Within Group

The unchurched do not have a formal, specified set of beliefs or ideas, thus causing a variety of beliefs and ideas about things. Perhaps the major dispute the unchurched community encounters is the question of whether or not to ever belong to an organized religious group.

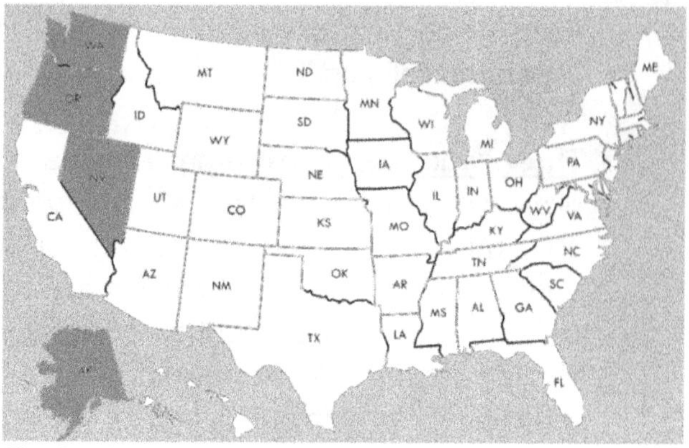

The "Unchurched Belt" of the United States

Scriptures

Unchurched individuals do not use a specified set of scriptures. Some use scriptures, others do not; some explore the scriptures of other or all world religions as a study or interest point. Often, those unchurched who use a scriptural point retain the scriptures of their religious background, whether Jewish, Christian, Muslim, Hindu, Buddhist, or other texts from key world religions. Others might follow New Age writings or find meaning through philosophy, poetry, self-help writing, or classic literature. Some use a combination of many of the aforementioned options.

Basic Religious Practices

As the philosophy of the Unchurched centers around the individual's personal perceptions, ideas, and spiritual encounters, any religious devotions or concepts are practiced privately and with the unique spin of the individual. This encompasses a wide variety of possibilities and expressions of devotion. Some common ones include prayer, especially private prayer, meditation, reading scriptures or sacred writings, watching or listening to religious programming on television or on the internet, or engaging in practices from the New Age Movement or occult that may include yoga, spellcasting, chanting, ceremonial magic, or cultural witchcraft practices.

Holidays

Unchurched individuals do not have, nor observe, any specific or designated holidays. Many observe standard cultural holidays, such as Christmas, Thanksgiving, Easter, and patriotic holidays, in one of two ways: in a family-style embrace, or by visiting an occasional religious service.

Visual Signs and Symbols

The unchurched do not have any specified visual signs and symbols, although they may draw on religious symbols from any world religion or use no symbols at all.

Creeds, Books, and Laws

The unchurched hold to no one official creed or moral guide, and very few writings have been devoted specifically to the unchurched. As most of the unchurched have aversion to the rules, regulations, and required dogma of organized religious institutions, most, if not all, would probably avoid the idea of creeds, rulebooks, guides, and formalized spiritual laws.

ECLECTIC BELIEFS

There are any number of assorted ideas, beliefs, and concepts the unchurched may combine within their own practice or may equally reject as many as they desire.

RELATIONS WITH NON-UNCHURCHED

Many unchurched avoid the mainline religious community due to their perceptions, ideas, or negative experiences. This is not always the case, but it is possible to find religious pessimism among the unchurched. There are some who may find religion a total waste of time, and others still who may be respectful of the beliefs and practices others have, whether inquiring or desiring to learn more about them.

HOLY SITES

There are no specified holy sites of the unchurched, although many take an interest in holy sites found throughout the world. No specific sites except those deemed by the individual. Many unchurched feel a deep connection to things perceived to be spiritual and do indeed seek them out in their lives.

NOTABLE FIGURES

Oprah Winfrey (1954-), talk show host and television producer; Ben Afleck (1972-), actor; Bill De Blasio (1961-), politician; Jessica Simpson (1980-), actress; Helen Mirren (1945-), actress; Justin Timberlake (1981-), musician; Miley Cyrus (1992-), musician.

NOTABLE GROUPS

A large percentage of the unchurched engage in New Age or occult techniques without the regulation or discipline found within occult communities. Many combine multiple religious teachings into one personalized system and add other elements of personal appeal, including philosophy, thinking, disciplines, and writings. The unchurched uniquely create for themselves a personalized and systematic belief structure.

FACTS AND FIGURES

Approximately 35% of the unchurched community is male, aged 18-29. Only 8% of the unchurched are over 65.[5]

OTHER IMPORTANT DEFINITIONS[6]

- **Spiritual but not affiliated**: Abbreviated SBNA, another term for individuals who are unchurched.

- **Spirituality**: Often used as a term to associate the interior spiritual growth and direction of an individual, in contrast with religion, which is seen as an exterior, organizational directive.

BELIEVER'S CHARACTERISTICS

Emphasis on individuality, independence, separateness, and personally devised systems of finding the divine; interest in personal spiritual viewpoints and the rejection of institutional, formal, dogmatic, and established religious views; separation of oneself from a larger body of believers, society, and a reality for the purpose of finding something greater than what exists; pessimism regarding organized religion; distrust of religious clergy and individuals; emphasis on personal and private spiritual practice versus public worship; study and spiritual evolution independently on traditional religion and practice without the religious body; study and spiritual evolution outside of traditional religion, including alternative religion such as paganism, Kabbalah, occult, and New Age; independent practitioners of the New Age Movement, or of practices such as divination methods, meditation, teaching, counseling, or studying.

UNITARIAN UNIVERSALISM

The aim of all worship is to help order the religious consciousness in the individual and the group. It is to help us know and feel how we relate as individuals to ourselves, to the world, to the totality of being. The aim of common worship is to help us face up to our individual and collective limitations and failures, to open us to sources of creative, healing, transforming, and renewing power.
(Commission on Common Worship)[1]

THEOLOGY

Unitarian Universalism stems from two different theological traditions in the history of "free church" (not identifying or associated as a state church) Christianity: Unitarianism and Universalism. Unitarianism originated as a branch of the Anabaptist Movement, one that rejected Trinitarianism. Unitarianism teaches that God is one in number and being. Jesus Christ was a great man, prophet, and savior, but was not God or divine Himself. They reject the doctrines of original sin and the substitutionary atonement of Christ. The Holy Spirit is seen as divine as a spiritual mystery, moving among believers. Unitarians accept the authority of Jesus Christ on issues of morality and also equally accept the role of reason, rationalism, science, and philosophy as coexistent with faith in God. Unitarians believe the Bible can contain error, as the writers were inspired by God but remained human. There are three main forms of Unitarian understanding: Arian (believes in a pre-existence of Christ as Logos, but believes Jesus lived only as a human being); Socinian (believes Christ should be worshiped while denying His divinity), and Strict Unitarian (believes in the divinity of God exclusive to God and there is no Holy Spirit, nor should one worship Christ). Universalism, an eighteenth-century idea, emerged in contrast to Calvinism. Universalists believe that salvation is for everyone, whether they are Christian or not. All humanity will be saved and restored to relationship with God at some point in history.

Although stemming from two theologically based, non-traditional Christian traditions, modern-day Unitarian Universalism can now be classified as non-theistic, meaning the organization takes no official position on deity, the existence of a deity or god, or of the connection between a deity and creation. Belief in a deity is left to the personal discretion of each individual and is not required for membership within the Unitarian Universalist Association. Unitarian Universalists often speak on the existence of the "sacred," which may be defined in many different forms, depending on the individual Unitarian Universalist. Some consider the sacred to be a deity, referred to as GOD, LOVE, MYSTERY, SOURCE OF ALL, THE UNIVERSE, or SPIRIT OF LIFE. Many Unitarian Universalists could be identified as deists: they believe a higher power is somehow in existence (however they may refer to it), but they do not believe that deity has any personality or connection through relationship with anyone or anything in creation.

Unlike other religious groups, theology is not a uniting point or dividing point among Unitarian Universalists. The focus is not common theological foundation or belief, but a belief in the relevance of community, as everyone forges their own way on what is seen as a singular spiritual path, regardless of how it may identify.[2]

Philosophy

Unitarian Universalism centers around the principle that religion, faith, and belief are issues of personal dictate based solely upon experience, whatever that experience may be. Such is not based upon an experience based on a specified, universally required divine revelation. This is summarized as a "free and responsible search for truth and meaning" by which the Unitarian Universalist community comes together in that supportive search, rather than requiring a set establishment of doctrine and understanding to obtain a spiritual purpose.

Unitarian Universalists are interested in activities and work that center on the need of human beings and are often interested in the world of religious humanism, which combines religious rites with the basic concept that human beings are good, with inherent value, focusing on their needs, interests, and abilities.[3] The Unitarian Universalist Association affirms and promotes seven principles:

1. *1st Principle: The inherent worth and dignity of every person;*
2. *2nd Principle: Justice, equity and compassion in human relations;*
3. *3rd Principle: Acceptance of one another and encouragement to spiritual growth in our congregations;*
4. *4th Principle: A free and responsible search for truth and meaning;*
5. *5th Principle: The right of conscience and the use of the democratic process within our congregations and in society at large;*
6. *6th Principle: The goal of world community with peace, liberty, and justice for all;*
7. *7th Principle: Respect for the interdependent web of all existence of which we are a part.*[4]

and six sources:

- *Direct experience of that transcending mystery and wonder, affirmed in all cultures, which moves us to a renewal of the spirit and an openness to the forces which create and uphold life;*
- *Words and deeds of prophetic people which challenge us to confront powers and structures of evil with justice, compassion, and the transforming power of love;*
- *Wisdom from the world's religions which inspires us in our ethical and spiritual life;*
- *Jewish and Christian teachings which call us to respond to God's love by loving our neighbors as ourselves;*
- *Humanist teachings which counsel us to heed the guidance of reason and the results of science, and warn us against idolatries of the mind and spirit;*
- *Spiritual teachings of Earth-centered traditions which celebrate the sacred circle of life and instruct us to live in harmony with the rhythms of nature.*[5]

Unitarian Universalism would be considered a liberal religious organization. It is open and accepting of a divergence of theologies and religious ideas, from liberal Christianity to Wicca and witchcraft, to Satanism and agnosticism, to neo-paganism and atheism. With their focus on open spirituality and humanism, their religious understanding has a strong political component. While many groups see political activity as a secondary point or attempt to avoid it in church all together, Unitarian Universalism sees no contradiction, nor issue, with mixing the realms of faith and politics. It is common to find Unitarian Universalists involved with liberal politics and associated with liberal causes, including immigrant rights, same-sex marriage, polyamory, abortion, anti-war protests, racial issues, worker's rights, education reform, separation of church and state, higher minimum wage standards, and medical research.

TRADITIONAL LANGUAGES

Unitarian Universalism, as an independent movement, has English as its traditional language. The traditional languages of Unitarianism include Polish, Romanian, Hungarian, and English. The traditional language of Universalism is English.

ADHERENT IDENTITY

Unitarian Universalist; Unitarian Universalist Association; Unitarian Universalist Society; Unitarian Universalist Church; UUA; Unitarian; Universalist.

SECTS/DIVISIONS

Unitarian Universalism first came together in 1961 as the merging of two American denominations. Because Unitarian Universalism does not hold to absolutes, their organizations are loosely connected through key points of agreement; namely, those related to seeking, spiritual experience, a lack of absolutes, and humanistic ideals. For the most part, all Unitarian Universalist associations adhere to the same basic points of agreement found in the seven principles and six sources. The major Unitarian Universalist groups are:

Unitarian Universalist Association "flaming chalice" logo

- **The Unitarian Universalist Association**: The original 1961 merger between the American Unitarian Association and the Universalist Church of America. It is headquartered in Boston, Massachusetts and represents most Unitarian Universalism in the United States (and a small number of groups in other countries). UUA representation in Canada is met through The Canadian Unitarian Council. Under the head of the UUA are several small groups, all part of the Unitarian Universalist Association, for specific outreach and interest of specified members. Such groups include the Covenant of Unitarian Universalist Pagans (CUUPs), the Unitarian Universalist Buddhist Fellowship, the Unitarian Universalist Christian Fellowship (UUCF), Church of the Larger Fellowship (CLF), Unitarian Universalist Service Committee, Church of the Younger Fellowship (CYF), Prisoner

Ministry, Unitarian Universalists for Polyamory Awareness, and Leather & Grace – Unitarian Universalists for BDSM Awareness (L&G).

- **General Assembly of Unitarian and Free Christian Churches**: Better known as British Unitarians, the General Assembly of Unitarian and Free Christian Churches is an association for Unitarian, Free Christians, and other liberal religious groups in the United Kingdom and Ireland. The organization itself dates to 1928, although its doctrine has now conformed to modern understanding of Unitarian Universalism.

General Assembly of Unitarian and Free Christian Churches logo

- **The International Council of Unitarians and Universalists**: A large organization of affiliated Unitarian Universalists, Unitarian, and Universalist groups that was started in 1995. While several groups and committees sought to create an affiliated organization, this became possible when the Unitarian Universalist Association started receiving association memberships outside the United States. As a result, the ICUU project is largely funded and overseen by the Unitarian Universalist Association. At present, there are twenty-one full members worldwide.

International Council of Unitarians and Universalists logo

Number of Adherents

There are approximately 800,000 Unitarian Universalists worldwide.[6]

Disputes Within Group

Unitarian Universalism holds no doctrine, officiates, theology or creeds. This means that while on an organizational level Unitarian Universalists seem relatively united, Unitarian Universalists independently hold to whatever they hold to be most important. Disputes and disagreements happen throughout the organization on all levels: personal, local, and governmental, as people disagree on things from their various perspectives. The major area of conflicts within Unitarian Universalist groups relate to governance and just how far they promote and honestly practice their acclaimed views (such as apply to racial diversity in hiring of clergy and church staff).

Scriptures

Historically speaking, Unitarians and Universalists both used the Bible, Old and New Testaments, interpreting it through a highly different method than traditional means. Today, Unitarian Universalists do still use the Bible, but they use it in a very different context. The Bible is not seen as extraordinary or inspired, but as a sacred text, in the same way they see various scripture resources from any and all different religions and traditions (including the Tao-te-King, the Qur'an, the Dhammapada, the Bhagavad Gita, and others): as products of their time in history, never to be interpreted through an exclusive narrative, or thought to be the final word or authority in one's faith or understanding. The writings of the Transcendentalists (such as Ralph Waldo Emerson and Henry David Thoreau) are also often relevant. Additionally, any writing, work, or piece considered of spiritual insight among members is considered valid as a spiritual or historical piece.

> *The poet is the sayer, the namer, and represents beauty. He is a sovereign, and stands on the centre. For the world is not painted, or adorned, but is from the beginning beautiful; and God has not made some beautiful things, but Beauty is the creator of the universe. Therefore the poet is not any permissive potentate, but is emperor in his own right. Criticism is infested with a cant of materialism, which assumes that manual skill and activity is the first merit of all men, and disparages such as say and do not, overlooking the fact, that some men, namely, poets, are natural sayers, sent into the world to the end of expression, and confounds them with those whose province is action, but who quit it to imitate the sayers. The poet does not wait for the hero or the sage, but, as they act and think primarily, so he writes primarily what will and must be spoken, reckoning the others, though primaries also, yet, in respect to him, secondaries and servants; as sitters or models in the studio of a painter, or as assistants who bring building materials to an architect.*[7]

> *I have heard of a man lost in the woods and dying of famine and exhaustion at the foot of a tree, whose loneliness was relieved by the grotesque visions with which, owing to bodily weakness, his diseased imagination surrounded him, and which he believed to be real. So also, owing to bodily and mental health and strength, we may be continually cheered by a like but more normal and natural society, and come to know that we are never alone.*[8]

BASIC RELIGIOUS PRACTICES

Unitarian Universalism centers solely around the individual and their personal perception of spiritual discovery, seeking, awareness, and reality. Services take place on a Sunday, in a meeting hall now known as a society or association (traditionally referred to as a church). The service itself contains features found in a typical Protestant format, such as hymns (from their book, *Singing the Journey* or *Singing the Living Tradition*), readings, a children's lesson, and a sermon, given by a local minister (called Reverend), or a guest speaker. Unique to Unitarian Universalist services is the chalice or candle lighting, which reflects finding or seeking in the dark found as members discern their own spiritual paths. Unitarian Universalism also employs a period of joys and concerns which, although not unique to Unitarian Universalism, may comprise a substantial portion of the service, as it is seen as community-building. Most Unitarian Universalist communities also include a period of meditation or prayer, which may be silent or spoken. At the end of a service, members can "talk back," providing feedback from the message, whether it agrees, disagrees, or with further questions.

Unitarian Universalists have abandoned traditional ideas of sacraments. They do not employ baptism and communion. In their place, Unitarian Universalist churches hold child dedications, presenting and dedicating an infant or young child to search and discover their own spiritual path within Unitarian Universalist's ideals. Unitarian Universalists equivalents of communion are flower communion (members bring flowers to church, assemble them together, and then hand them out to everyone present; usually done in the spring) and water communion (members bring small samples of water from locations special to the participants; the samples are merged together, purified, and then used in special rites throughout the year; usually done in the fall). Many Unitarian Universalist congregations do not hold services in the summer months.

HOLIDAYS

Unitarian Universalists encourage the diversity in exploration and celebration of all religious and secular holidays. As a result, the celebration or observance of holidays is contingent upon the personal ideas and beliefs of the individual practitioner. Unitarian Universalist societies observe all traditional Christian, Jewish, pagan, political, social justice, and nationalist holidays from a secular perspective.

A holiday unique to Unitarian Universalists is Chalica. First introduced in 2005, it merges the concepts of Hanukkah and Kwanzaa with intent to celebrate the seven principles of Unitarian Universalism. Celebrated from the First Monday to the first Sunday in December, each night honors a specific principle. A chalice, typically surrounded by seven candles is lit. Each night, a candle is lit, and a principle read. Participants should honor each principle by doing a specific deed, such as donating to a political cause, or volunteering. Group activities include discussion, songs, and projects. There is also a seven-week version of Chalica that begins in January. Participation varies and is limited among communities.[11]

VISUAL SIGNS AND SYMBOLS

Chalice with flame surrounded by a circle or two overlapping circles (called a flaming chalice); flame within a chalice; flame within a cup; flame within the letter U; symbols incorporating or displaying the representation of all world religions; patriotic symbols (such as the American flag).

CREEDS, BOOKS, AND LAWS

From its inception, Unitarianism has always rejected creeds. Unitarian Universalism does the same, seeing creeds as exclusionary. Instead, they have what is known as a Congregation Covenant, of which there are three major forms used within specified congregations:

Love is the doctrine of this church,
The quest of truth is its sacrament,
And service is its prayer.
To dwell together in peace,
To seek knowledge in freedom,
To serve human need,
To the end that all souls shall grow into harmony with the Divine-
Thus do we covenant with each other and with God.[9]

Love is the spirit of this church,
and service is its law.
This is our great covenant:
To dwell together in peace,
To seek the truth in love,
And to help one another.[10]

In the freedom of truth,
And the spirit of Jesus,
We unite for the worship of God
And the service of all.[12]

Unitarian Universalist Church, Nashua, New Hampshire

The only laws that exist within Unitarian Universalist organizations relate to the operation and oversight of financial governance. Local congregations are associated via affiliation and are independently governed.

ECLECTIC BELIEFS

Unitarian Universalism could be defined in its essence as a set of eclectic beliefs. Because each individual seeks their own path and own ideas, there is no one singular set of values, doctrines, or ideas held by the organization as a whole. Religious services, experiences, rituals, and rites of passage have been secularized or turned into general services that anyone, of any persuasion, can participate in or receive. It is not unusual to meet a Unitarian Universalist who accepts beliefs traditionally considered counterculture, such as witchcraft or Satanism. Atheism and agnosticism, long-considered antithetical to religious experience, are welcomed and accepted. It is not uncommon to meet a UUA who embraces socially unconventional ideas. Lawmaking and social activism are seen as the answer to solve all problems in society.

One unique aspect of Unitarian Universalists is their "Coming of Age" religious education program for young adults. Young members are paired with adult mentors to serve as guides for questions and issues as they mature into adulthood. They are encouraged to participate in community service and worship services through their local UUA. As part of this project, young members are brought to a diversity of religious services. When they are done, each participant creates their own "credo statement," one that outlines their own beliefs and ideas acquired throughout the experience.

RELATIONS WITH NON-UNITARIAN UNIVERSALISTS

As Unitarian Universalism believes everyone is on the same spiritual path, seeking the same things, and heading in the same direction, it is a champion in interfaith activity. However, UUAs tend to be highly intolerant of denominations and religious groups that disagree with UUA attitudes of tolerance and universal acceptance of all religious groups and faiths. There is also some question about those who accept conservative politics or social views, even though Unitarian Universalism makes no specific requirement that members must adhere to liberal politics or social ideas.

Holy Sites

The Unitarian Universalist Association headquarters, Boston, Massachusetts; other sites would vary, as deemed sacred by individual society members.

Notable Figures

Albert Schweitzer (1875-1965), physician and humanitarian; Christopher Reeve (1952-2004), actor; Arthur J. Altmeyer (1891-1972), creator of the Social Security system; Roger Nash Baldwin (1884-1981), founder of the American Civil Liberties Union; John Bardeen (1908-1991), physicist; Christopher C. Bell (1933-), author; Lee Carter (1987-), politician; Brock Chisholm (1896-1971), director of the World Health Organization; Buckminster Fuller (1895-1983), inventor; Greta Gerwig (1983-), actress; Gary Gygax (1938-2008), creator of Dungeons and Dragons; Naomi King (1970-), minister; W.M. Kiplinger (1891-1967), publisher; Ashley Montagu (1905-1999), anthropologist; Paul Newman (1925-2008), actor; Laura Pedersen (1965-), author; Melissa Harris-Perry (1973-), political commentator; Pete Seeger (1919-2014), musician; Margaret Sutton (1903-2001), author; Kurt Vonnegut (1922-2007), author; Joanne Woodward (1930-), actress.

Notable Groups

Interweave was a membership organization that worked in areas related to sexual orientation and gender identity. It was politically driven in nature and operational in assisting individuals identifying as queer in their local communities. At its height, it held events at the General Assembly as well as their own annual Convocation and supported a national network, through different UUA congregations. The national organization, Interweave Continental, disbanded in 2016.[13]

Facts and Figures

Approximately 88% of Unitarian Universalists are white, with 43% having a household income of $100,000 a year or more. 20% believe in a deity with absolute certainty, while 27% do not believe in a god. 49% of members seldom or never pray.[14]

Other Important Definitions[14]

- **Chalice lighters**: Individuals who support the creation of Unitarian Universalist congregations through financial donations.

- **Friend**: An individual who agrees with the precepts of Unitarian Universalism and may support or attend a congregation, but does not become a member of any congregation.

- **Our Whole Lives**: Known as the OWL program, it is the major curriculum for Unitarian Universalist Youth. It addresses issues such as sexual education, gender issues, and the UUA's views on spirituality.

- **Small group ministries**: Also called "chalice circles." Small groups of no more than ten people who gather to discuss aspects of their faith from the UUA perspective.

- **Memorial fund**: When a monetary donation is made to the church after a person dies, with no specified direction as to what the money should cover.

- **Welcoming Congregation**: A term originating in the 1980s to describe communities that were accepting of the LGBTQ community.

BELIEVER'S CHARACTERISTICS

Interest in the "searching" aspect of spirituality; emphasis on personal perceptions of experience, personal opinion, and personal belief; lack of foundational doctrine and teaching; no specified scriptural knowledge or understanding; emphasis on the oneness of all mankind, the universal search, and the universal destination; embrace of all beliefs, with the exception of conservative viewpoints, including Satanism, paganism, New Age, and occult; emphasis and interest in education, especially higher education; liberal political beliefs; lack of ability to justify beliefs outside of opinion; humanist views of life and faith; secular church services; use of a variety of religious texts; political activism; encouragement of non-belief, atheism, and agnosticism.

Utopianism

Tis a gift to be simple, 'tis a gift to be free,
'Tis a gift to come down where we ought to be,
And when we find ourselves in the place just right,
'Twill be in the valley of love and delight.
Where true simplicity is gain'd,
To bow and to bend we shan't be ashm'd,
To turn, turn will be our delight
Till by turning, turning we come round right.
(Elder Joseph)[1]

Theology

While the specific deities of utopian groups vary (as they can form the thoughts of any religious background or any atheistic ideals), utopian groups espouse one of three possible theologies on utopianism. The first is a belief in universalism, that eventually all people on earth will be saved from the evils of this world. In that light, peoples of the world need to come together to learn the value of community. The second is a form of salvation of the elect, believing only certain individuals (most likely, those of the specific community) will be saved from coming tribulation and trial. They should come together as a community to edify and encourage one another until that time. The third ideal is that utopia begins and ends with the actions of human beings. The possibility of creating a perfect society (whether seen as a divine or a strictly human institution) is present within the power of changing ideals. These ideals may come in the form of creating one's own society or reforming society as a whole, believing different laws, policies, governances, and the ideas of humanity will bring about a perfect societal state.

Based more in philosophical ideas about how the world should be than actual theology, Utopianism can merge with any spiritual ideal or stand on its own without any theological basis. It can be about preparing or ushering the Kingdom of God, about promoting the basic ideals of any religious group in communal form, or about promoting a form of humanism by which society is seen as having the potential to transform into the best it can be. In modern times, utopianism is often seen as a political ideal, obtainable through specified work to legislate humanity in the desired direction.

Philosophy

Utopianism centers around the singular principle of somehow attaining a perfect society free from injustice, pain, and suffering. A utopist isn't necessarily interested in the complexities of theological salvation, especially that which establishes the idea of salvation's benefits coming at a later point in time (such as after death or in a world to come, such as after Jesus returns), but more interested in working towards the absence of worldly suffering. The goal is to create a perfect society. Utopists believe if the rest of society would follow their set of precepts, they could achieve an end to the ills that are often part of life and living with others.

By definition of the word, "utopia" does not exist. It, by definition, literally means "no place." In other words, one could say that the idea of utopia, as admirable as it might be, is unobtainable. This has not stopped people throughout history from pursuing its ideals. Historically, utopianism could be classified as experimental communal living, based in a belief that to find the perfect society, one had to create the perfect society. This idea was particularly present in the late 1800s; society would progress toward better things, and creating such communities would help society to move toward perfection that much faster.

Utopists could be considered experimenters in communal living and believe that if all in the world would adopt their methods of social approach, utopia would exist. When the world, as they predict, comes around to their thinking, utopia will reign supreme on earth. Even though experimental community living is not nearly as common as it was once upon a time, utopian communities do still exist, as do utopian ideals. Whether the goal is to create a literal community today or to transform the world through greater legislation, utopianism is still an ideal held by many worldwide.[2]

Number of Adherents

It is unknown how many utopian advocates exist today. Individuals may advocate for utopianism without being part of a larger community, while those who belong to utopian communities are often small in number. At the peak of experimental utopian communities, there were groups that numbered below 10,000 members, with most groups substantially smaller.

Traditional Languages

English, French, German.

Adherent Identity

Utopian, utopianism, identities associated with specific groups, such as the United Society of Believers in Christ's Second Appearing, Shakers; Oneida Community; Aurora Colony, Aurora Mills; Bruderhof Communities, Bruderhof; Hutterian Brethren, Hutterite Church, Hutterites; Amish, Old Order Amish; Icarians; Owenism, Owenites; Fourierism, Fourierist; Society of the Woman in the Wilderness; Brook Farm Community; Sojourners Community, Sojourners; Ephrata Cloister, Ephrata Community; Brotherhood of the New Life, Fountain Grove; Harmony Society, Rappites; Society of Separatists of Zoar; Koinoina Farm; Padanaram Settlement; Reba Place Fellowship; Gloriavale Christian Community, Cooperites; Jesus Christians; Jesus People USA; The Farm (Tennessee); the Findhorn Foundation; Buddhafield; Branch Davidians; Children of God; Twelve

Tribes; People's Temple, and others that are too numerous to list.

SECTS/DIVISIONS

While there are many communities that may live or dwell together, not every communal group adheres to utopian ideology. Utopian communities typically emerge in the wake of social, religious, or political upheaval, causing people to seek something better than the standard way of living general society has to offer. Except for a small number of groups, most utopian experiments do not survive beyond a few generations. There are exceptions, but many of those mentioned in this list are now defunct.

- **Anabaptist communities**: The communities with the longest – and strongest – histories in utopianism, Anabaptist utopian groups have existed since the sixteenth century. Founded upon strong religious values of Anabaptist Bible-based community living, baptizing only after a profession of faith, plain dress, strong traditional family ties, traditional roles for men and women, and community self-sufficiency. These communities include the Hutterian Brethren, Amish, Bruderhof Communities, and in some instances, Mennonites (although this is not typical for all Mennonite communities).

- **Shakers**: Formally known as The United Society of Believers in Christ's Second Appearing, the Shakers were nicknamed due to intense religious fits by which they would quake or shake during worship services. The group gathered believing the return of Christ would be within their lifetime; first in Britain, and then in the Americas (with the first settlement in Watervliet, New York). Founded by Ann Lee (1736-1784) in 1747, this Quaker breakaway sect is best-known for its egalitarianism, pacifism, and celibacy (Adam's first sin was seen as an impure sexual act rather than disobedience). All members were required to abstain from sex, even those who were married (the group would take in orphans and homeless individuals in the hopes they would eventually adopt the lifestyle). In their communities, men and women lived separately, with the entire community contributing to its support and upkeep. They lived simply, adopted their own version of plain dress, and became known for their worship, work, high-quality goods, unique lifestyle, and design, which is seen in furniture and architecture today.

  Ann Lee was seen as the first among many in the movement to completely embody the spirit of Jesus Christ. They recognized God as both male and female. She was believed to be the manifestation of the second Christian church, which was completed in the Shaker movement. As a unique millennial community, they believed themselves to be the embodiment of Christ's second coming within themselves, rather than waiting for Christ to return physically. A strongly mystical movement, their lively worship resulted in over ten thousand penned songs, dance movements, marching, speaking in tongues, and spiritual visions.[3]

  The Shaker movement peaked around the mid-nineteenth century. At one time, there were about 6,000 Shakers across approximately 20 communities. Their numbers began to dwindle after the 1850s, with most Shaker communities closing by the 1920s. Across the United States, many former Shaker communities are now museums dedicated to their history. Today, there are approximately three living Shakers dwelling together at a village community used as a preservation of Shaker living, in Sabbathday Lake, Maine. They now identify as more of a religious vocation with an acceptance process, requiring members to be between the ages of 18 and 50, unmarried, celibate, and without dependents.[4]

- **Oneida Community**: Also known as Perfectionists or Bible Communists, the Oneida Community was founded by John Humphrey Noyes (1811-1886) and thrived in Oneida, New York in 1847. As another millennialist community of the belief that the Second coming of Christ had already happened, the Oneida Community believed one was free of sin after conversion and that sexual relationships were essential, but monogamy was not. This practice was known as "complex marriage" and was bound by the idea that every woman was the wife of every husband and every husband of every wife. The community employed regulations on sexual control, carefully pairing couples for procreation and requiring others engaging in sexual activity to practice the "withdrawal method." Children born in the community remained with their mothers until they were able to walk but were then raised by the community in a common nursery. The group embraced an extended family system, believing it could create perfection worldwide.

The Oneida Community

  The Oneida Community employed a form of Christian socialism, believing that socialism couldn't survive without religious beliefs. Women and men worked together, in the same positions. Women wore pants and cut their hair short for practical purposes, although both were uncustomary for the time.

  The community was a success for about 30 years. After coming under public criticism for their sexual practices and socialist ideals, John Noyes sought to reorganize the community, abandoning their traditional system. Some moved to Canada (including Noyes), while others created Oneida Community, Ltd. Today, this company is known for its silver-plated goods, such as tableware. The community itself is no longer in existence.[5]

- **Radical Pietist/Separatist communes**: Pietism was both a Lutheran movement and later an Anabaptist movement devoted to personal religious practice and Christian living. The goal was to avoid sin and devote oneself to Christ as one followed the precepts of the

Bible. Pietism was a controversial ideal. While it was an influential movement in the formation of religious groups (such as Congregationalists, Baptists and Methodists) and voting rights in the United States and Britain, the Pietists suffered persecution in Germany. Separatists were British Calvinists who also experienced persecution in Europe, also leading them to the United States. This led to the formation of Pietist and Separatist communities in the United States, including the Harmony Society, Labadists, Society of the Separatists of Zoar, the Society of the Woman in the Wilderness, the Ephrata Cloister, and the Amana Colonies, who are now known for the formation the Amana Corporation. None of these groups are in existence today.[6]

- **Jesus Movement communes**: The Jesus Movement of the 1960s created an intersection between Evangelical Christianity and the hippie counterculture. This unique crossing caused young Christians to incorporate Christian values into the communal living and community ideals of the secular hippie movement. While most adopted Evangelical ideas, there were those who were part of the peace movement (anti-Vietnam War), neo-Orthodoxy, Christian socialism, and other ideas associated with more liberal political or theological views. The result was communal communities, some of which still exist. Such groups include Jesus Christians, Jesus People USA, and the Sojourners Community (which no longer exists in communal form but does exist as a ministry and media organization).

- **Evangelical communes**: In modern times, many Evangelical Christians feel the world is becoming too secular or inhospitable to their values. In response, communes that espouse more "traditional" Christian values are sometimes seen as a viable option. While the specific beliefs of each community vary, they are typically conservative in nature: traditional roles for men and women, opposition to same sex marriage, strict disciplines for children, limited access to television and internet, anti-government, labor, midwifery, and home births, and in some instances, uniforms (although not all follow this practice). Some of these communities have come under fire in recent years for sexual abuse scandals or for cultlike practices. Such groups include Gloriavale Christian Community and Padanaram Settlement.

- **New Age communes**: An outgrowth of the hippie movement subculture in the 1960s, New Age communes promoted the ideas of anti-war, drug subculture, mind expansion, shared property, and New Age values along with communal living. Many of these experiences worked initially but did not have the infrastructure to remain so informally governed long-term. Many disbanded while others restructured themselves to continue. Such groups include the Findhorn Foundation and The Farm.

- **Political communes**: There are utopian groups that specifically existed or do now exist to make a statement against politics. Whether they were formed to prove politics wrong (that different groups of people can work together), to make certain political statements (such as offering political asylum or equality of the sexes), Political groups may or may not have a spiritual formation attached to them. Such groups include the Icarians, Fourierism, Owenism, Koinoina Farm, and Reba Place Fellowship.

- **Communal cults**: Not all cults are communal in nature, but most only take notice of a cult when such is the case. Communal cults vary in their doctrinal structure but all focus on the emphatic need to create a perfect society built around their doctrine. Members may live communally in one house, on a compound in a series of houses, and often pool resources or exercise disbursement of funds as controlled by a leader. Such groups include Buddhafield, Twelve Tribes, People's Temple (now defunct), and the Branch Davidians (mostly defunct).

Shakers during worship

DISPUTES WITHIN GROUP

Utopian communities all vary from one another, outside of their dedicated devotion to creating a perfect society. Among different groups, there is disagreement on how to bring about this perfect world. However, not all things are perfect within utopian societies. Disputes do arise. Examination of the history of such groups shows most utopian communities begin to face challenges within the first generation of their existence. Often their views, unconventional living style, financial management, and personal beliefs create conflict rather than eliminating it. The point of communal living within utopian communities is often that it is hard. Through its difficulties, it's believed that individuals are able to attain a better sense of perfection. No matter how hard they may try or how communal a community may be, however, disputes still result.

SCRIPTURES

Utopian groups vary in their belief of sacred text. Christian utopian groups universally use the Bible in one form or another. Interpretation widely varies. New Age communities use any variety of New Age texts, or in some instances, rely solely on the leadership of a group to guide them in spiritual understandings. Political groups may or may not have texts that inspired them; much of the time, they are based on the central ideas of the founder or founders. While such ideas might have been documented as a sort of "canon" for the community, they are not considered to be on par with scripture.

BASIC RELIGIOUS PRACTICES

While the specifics of utopian practices vary, utopian communities vary from traditional religious groups in one central way: they are community-focused, seeing the entirety of their belief system as a way of life. Often systematic in approach, utopianism focuses on the "parts" of the process to create a whole society. This means such communities view their religious or philosophical practice as a daily thing, engaging the idea of community work, discipline, and social practice and engagement as part of building a whole, bigger than the individual. Every individual is required to help the community to run efficiently and at its full capacity. Utopian communities, therefore, have an extended family feel to their structure and nature.

Group gatherings serve multiple functions. Utopian groups often meet for meals, social activities, and worship services, if such is part of the community's code. The purpose of such services is community worship, communication with one another, and to continually reignite the ethics and mores of the community. Most times of worship included or include prayer, song, reading of scripture, and community preaching. Groups that are more politically minded may engage in political actions or debates, either among themselves or by promoting legislative change.

Amish children riding in the back of a buggy

HOLIDAYS

Utopian communities vary in their holiday practices, especially those that no longer exist. While standard religious and secular holidays (such as Christmas and Easter) might be a general practice, in some instances, utopian communities have observed their own holidays, such as a Founder's Day or day of relevance among the group. Some utopian groups, focusing more on their immediate work, did not or do not recognize holidays, at all.

VISUAL SIGNS AND SYMBOLS

Most utopian societies mentioned no longer exist. In the days they did, most did not employ logos or branding as we do today. Among those that do, many groups (especially those from Anabaptist and Evangelical tradition) shun logos and visual images. More modern groups might use their community's name as part of branding or have a small, nondescript symbol to place on goods.

Utopian societies are more noted for their members and their communities, as the community's symbols, rather than actual logos in place for their identities. In some communities (such as Anabaptist), members adopt plain unadorned clothing and women wear a veil over their hair. Such is not the case with every group.

Robert Owen (1771-1858)

CREEDS, BOOKS, AND LAWS

Utopian communities are typically highly regulated and governed. Days, work, and activities are often structured. In communities where members work outside of the group, agreements are formed on involvement with outside activities and financial arrangements.

Utopian communities often function by agreements, sometimes called articles of association, contracts, or covenants (or in the older Anabaptist orders, *ordnung*) which are signed, pledged, or verbally stated conditions for group membership. These specified agreements outline the responsibilities of each community member and clearly state the requirements each member must meet to join the community. Some groups also have a community handbook, rule, or guidebook that is part of group rule and order.

Most utopian groups employ some semblance of congregational or democratic rule, with community discussions, votes, and plans to keep all members informed of changes, issues, and communal regulations.

ECLECTIC BELIEFS

Even when such is not stated as part of obvious doctrine or concept, perfectionism is a strong principle of utopian communities. If one believes the perfect society is an obtainable idea, then attaining perfection, both individually and as a group, are also concepts members must, in some way, espouse.

Outside of these specifics, utopian groups have specified governances related to their unique communities. As can be seen from group descriptions, there are several ways a utopian community can exist: some are celibate, some endorse partner swapping, some manage with all their own goods, some are staunchly religious, some endorse family life, most require all share goods and finances communally. Each group fits the vision of perfection that it believes can be obtained.

RELATIONS WITH NON-UTOPIAN GROUPS

Utopian communities vary in their approach to relationships with outsiders. In earlier times, utopian communities were self-sufficient and self-sustaining, frequently out of necessity (due to persecution or disapproval of the community's ways). In modern times, utopian groups find it nearly impossible to survive without some relationship with the outside world. Whether it is the tourism of Amish country or The Farm's community store, most modern utopian groups are forced to open their facilities and lives for the sake of financial profit. In some instances, members of a group may work off-site in a secular job, as well.

When it comes to religious discussion, most utopian groups aren't included in ecumenical or interfaith dialogue. They aren't large enough, or considered relevant enough, to be included in such discussions. There have been historical exceptions to this rule, but overall, the utopian focus is on the group, rather than discussing or explaining things to the outside world.

HOLY SITES

Utopian members would embrace each one of their immediate community sites as holy.

NOTABLE FIGURES

Ephrata Cloister, Ephrata, Pennsylvania

Ann Lee (1736-1784), founder, the Shakers; Stephen Gaskin (1935-2014), founder, the Farm; John Humphrey Noyes (1811-1886), founder, the Oneida Community; Eberhard Arnold (1883-1935), founder, the Bruderhof Community; Jacob Hutter c. 1500-1536), founder, Hutterian Brethren; Jakob Ammann (1644-c. 1730), founder, Amish; Jean de Labadie (1610-1674), founder, Labadists; Joseph Bimeler (1778-1853), founder, Society of Separatists of Zoar; Johannes Kelpius (1667-1708), founder, Society of the Woman in the Wilderness; Johann Conrad Beissel (1691-1768), founder, Ephrata Cloister; Dave and Cherry McKay, founders, Jesus Christians; Jim Wallis (1948-), founder, Sojourners; Neville Cooper (-2018), founder, Gloriavale Christian Community; Daniel and Lois Wright, founders, Padanaram Settlement; Johann Georg Rapp (1757-1847), founder, Harmony Society; Etienne Cabet (1788-1856), founder, the Icarians; Robert Owen (1771-1858), founder, Owenism; Clarence and Florence Jordan and Martin and Mabel England, founders, Koinonia Farm; Anne F. Beiler (1949-), founder, Auntie Anne's.

NOTABLE GROUPS

The Farm, founded by Stephen Gaskin in 1971 outside of Summertown, Tennessee, began as an experimental living community. Its roots are found in the founder's teachings and lectures in the 1960s. After one particular tour, Stephen and his friends led a vehicle caravan across the United States, finally deciding at the end to buy land collectively.

Members of The Farm took vows of poverty, promising to invest in no personal property (aside from things such as clothing and tools), although some of these restrictions have now laxed. Man-made psychotropics (marijuana and LSD were both frequently used), birth control, alcohol, tobacco, and animal products were also forbidden. Housing structures were initially unconventional, but over time, became more substantial. The group's spirituality is strictly New Age and their members embrace a vegan diet. The Farm is also best known as the seat of the modern midwifery movement. While Stephen Gaskin was originally the sole leader of the group, The Farm is now governed by a board of directors.

The Farm experienced several challenges in its early years, including a boom in interest and population without the needed resources and infrastructure to handle the group's collective needs. The group does still exist today, with notable changes from its early days. There are approximately two hundred members, most who have been there since its early days. It has its own electrical crew, composting crew, farming crew, communications, construction crew, clinic, laundromat, and ambulance service, among other outreaches that help the group function. The Book Publishing Company is known for printing the teachings of Gaskin and other members of the organization.[7]

FACTS AND FIGURES

Utopian communities peaked in the nineteenth century, with many experimental living communities continuing to exist until the twentieth century. There are different reasons why communities fell apart, but the primary reasons were conflicts within the communities themselves coupled with changes from the outside world.[8]

OTHER IMPORTANT DEFINITIONS

- **Associationism**: The basic doctrine of political and economic ideas of Charles Fourier, namely, that communal living was a futuristic endeavor, found in his Fourierism communities.

- **Conscientious objector**: An individual who refuses to participate in military service on religious grounds. Anabaptist utopians continue this practice to this day.

- **Divine Economy**: A concept within the Harmony Society that would establish a perfect dwelling place for God upon earth.

- **Egalitarian**: The belief in the equality of the sexes, as seen in the Icarian and Shaker utopian communities.

- **Era of Manifestations**: A period of Shaker revivals that resulted in spiritual outpouring and conversions to the faith. It lasted from around 1837 until 1850.

- ***Gelassenheit***: Often translated as "submission," the Amish practice of not drawing attention to one's self.

- **Intentional community**: An optional community designed to thrive around communal living.

- **Nonresistance**: A classic Anabaptist doctrine, practiced in all Anabaptist utopian communities, which forbids members to participate in military activities, wearing a military uniform, or, in original times, paying taxes that would fund military efforts and wars.

- ***Ordnung***: The Amish order of the church, consisting of regulations every member must obey. Such pertains to everyday life, attire, use of modern conveniences, and community participation.

- **Pacifism**: The value that one is against war. Such is present in many utopian communities, including the Harmony Society, the Shakers, and modern-day Anabaptist communities.

- **Plain dress**: The Anabaptist tradition of wearing clothing that is not form-fitting, is made durable for work, and contains no adornment or modern conveniences, such as zippers.

- ***The Schleitheim Confession***: An Anabaptist statement of faith from 1527 on which the Hutterian Brethren are founded.

BELIEVER'S CHARACTERISTICS

Emphasis on creation of a utopia, a perfect society, free from injustice, poverty, pain, and suffering; communal living; communal work; austere religious practices; activism; plain dress; communal religious devotion; patriarchy; egalitarianism; religious or political socialism; discipline; structure; community distribution of goods and funds; self-sufficiency; experimental living; strong, central leadership; perfectionism; group activities; traditional beliefs; new age beliefs; Christian socialism; ideas about the changing of the world; apocalyptism; cultic tendencies.

Zoroastrianism

God bears in mind all prayers made to him, past, present, and future; those made by ordinary people as well as the believers in many gods.
(The Avesta, Yasna 29:4)[1]

Theology

Zoroastrianism is a complex religion with an equally complex theology. It focuses on two dualistic entities, one good, and one evil, in conflict with one another: AHURA MAZDA (Wise Lord), seen as the supreme being, transcendent, universal, all good, one, and uncreated creator; and ANGRA MAINYU (the destructive spirit). Truth and cosmic order (*Asha*) originate as powerful life forces from Ahura Mazda. Such stand against *Druj* (falsehood and deceit). The destructive forces are born from *Aka Manah* (evil thoughts) and stand against Spenta Mainyu (creative spirit). Ahura Mazda is depicted as having an escort of entities (the power of all other existing gods in existence) who also battle and work against evil forces for the purpose of good. Their deity operates through the seven *Amesha Spentas*, direct spiritual emanations from him: Spenta Mainyu (holy, creative spirit), Vohu Manah (Good/purpose), Asa Vahista (best truth/righteousness), Xsaora Vairya (desirable dominion), Spenta Armaiti (holy devotion), Haurvatat (wholeness), and Ameretat (immortality). These beings are how Ahura Mazda accomplished the work of creation. The exemplified characteristics of the *Amesha Spentas* are desirable qualities that all practitioners of Zoroastrianism should practice throughout their lives, rather than seeing them as distant, unobtainable beings.[2] In addition to the *Amesha Spentas*, Zoroastrians also recognize the *Yazata* (worthy of worship or veneration), divine entities worthy of worship because they are holy beings. They may serve as either manifested specified beings or concepts and ideas. Such includes plants with a healing or medicinal nature, ancient creatures, the spirits of the dead or unborn, and prayers that have a holy or powerful identity in and of themselves. The dualistic nature of divine forces manifests in cosmic conflict between the values each represents: good and evil and truth and falsehood, with adherents called to be good for the sake of goodness, spreading happiness through charity.[3]

Zoroastrian theology does not have one identifiable label. It contains elements of monotheism, dualism, henotheism, monism, and polytheism. There is no specific unity of theology or philosophy throughout the ages. There are both ancient and modern understandings of the belief system, creating more complications in identifying the exact theological nature of the religious system. The religion itself reflects several thousand years of tradition, additions, and theological definitions, all of which contribute to its complex nature.[4]

Philosophy

Zoroastrianism (known as Mazdayasna to its adherents) centers around a prophetic figure named Zarathustra (Zoroaster in Greek, Zartosht and Zardosht in Persian, and Zaratosht in Gujarati). Scholars disagree about when he lived (estimates range from the sixth millennium BC to the sixth to seventh century BC). He received a spiritual enlightenment by the Daitya River at the age of thirty after a vision of Vohu Manah. Vohu Manah took Zoroaster into the presence of Lord Ahura Mazda, where he was taught the true religion. This true religion consists of a few key points: first, Zoroastrianism is the true religion, teaching true spiritual enlightenment. Second, due to the eternal conflict between Lord Mazda and Angra Mainyu, the entire universe (including humanity) must choose which way they follow (either good or evil). To pursue good, Zoroastrians must follow the threefold path of Asha: *Humata* (good thoughts), *Huxta* (good words), and *Huvarshta* (good deeds). Good deeds come from good thoughts (such keeps evil and malice away). They must practice charity, which aligns one's soul to Asha, recognize the spiritual equality and duty of both male and female, and be good for the sake of goodness (without expectation of hope for reward). Nature is sacred and natural elements should be preserved, especially water, earth, fire, and air. As practitioners of the religion preserve these ways, one participates in their understanding of free will, choosing to obey and follow the ways of the true deity and the right religion.

Central to the Zoroastrian faith are purification rites. Fire (*atar*) and water (*aban*) are the major agencies of ritual purity, as they were the first and last elements created. According to scripture, they believe fire originated from water, connecting and purifying the two in a deeply cosmic way. Fire is a conduit for wisdom and spiritual insight and water is the source of the wisdom. Both fire and water are represented in Zoroastrian temples known as fire temples (*dar-e-mar* or *agiyari*). The traditions surrounding fire worship date back to the ninth century BC and are synchronous with the founding of the religion. These centers are essential places of worship for practitioners of the faith.

Zoroastrians believe the spirit of evil will be destroyed at the end of time and good will reign in all. This shall occur by a process known as *Frashokereti*, a total cosmic regeneration. This era shall be ushered by a figure known as the Saoshyant (one who brings benefit), a messianic-like individual who shall bring a great and lasting benefit to the cosmos.[5]

Adherent Identity

Zoroastrianism; Mazdaism: Parsiism; Mazdayasna; Fire Worshiper.

Number of Adherents

At one time, Zoroastrianism was the official religion of the Persian Empire. Today it is in serious decline. Persecutions, relocations, war, and trauma in the Middle East and Asia have changed

Faravahar

the backdrop of worship for this community, turning it into a minority religion. It has not helped that Indian adherents (Parsis) refuse to proselytize, and many Middle Eastern practitioners are prohibited from doing so by law. Estimates place the worldwide community between 100,000 and 200,000.[6]

Traditional Languages

Avestan (also called Zend), Dari, Pahlavi, and Gujarati.

Sects/Divisions

Zoroastrianism has a long list of traditions and influences throughout its history. Many believe it's an influence for Judaism, Gnosticism, Christianity, and Islam, as all these religions overlapped with it at some point in history. Today, it has two main sects: reformists and traditionalists. As the community often no longer exists in its native origins (most Zoroastrian communities are found in India and North America with few communities still in Persia), there are questions about how the religion can adapt to its changing world. The reason for the change is obvious: the religion will not survive if thought is not given to its evolution through the next generations. The religion itself has no specified religious hierarchy and is governed by small councils and high priests who exert local authority (some choose not to accept the rulings of their local councils). The major differing point between reformists and traditionalists is the issue of conversion.

- **Reformists**: Also called "liberals," Reformists are interested in interpreting their faith through a modern lens, specifically with the understanding that the community is often no longer in its native territory much of the time. Modern-day Zoroastrians, in a diversity of places, are now exposed to varying faith traditions, cultures, and differing ideas about religion. In attempt to adjust to changing surroundings, Reformist Zoroastrians believe in the acceptance of any individual person, whether born into the religion or not, to freely practice Zoroastrianism. They see the decision to practice the religion as an act of free will, and do not consider such to be proselytism as such carries an association of force or pressure to convert. Reformists are more tolerant of sharing and welcoming others to practice the faith, interfaith marriage and accepting the children therein, a greater ethnic diversity in the religious community, and a broader interpretation of the rituals and rites of Zoroastrianism.

- **Traditionalists**: Traditionalists believe the Reformist interpretation of Zoroastrian history and doctrine is heretical and threatening to its purity and accuracy. Traditionalists forbid proselytizing and do not accept converts (individuals who are not members of the religion by their birth into a practicing family). To be a true member of the community, one must be born to two Zoroastrian-practicing parents who both also met the same requirements at birth. Individuals who marry outside the faith are considered apostate, and children born to such are classified as illegitimate, and therefore, ineligible to be members of the religion. As a patriarchal tradition, this is especially true for children born to a woman who marries outside of the faith. Such children are often shunned (children of Zoroastrian men who intermarry may, in some instances, be accepted). Traditionalists see Zoroastrianism as more than just a general religion, but as the religion of a specific, ethnic culture. Intermarriage and conversions destroy the ethnic identity and strength of the religion. Ethnicity and faith are seen as permanently linked, believing the religion should be observed by only a single ethnic group. Those who follow this faith must maintain their purity, as the original followers did so when they abandoned previous religious beliefs.[7]

Disputes Within Group

As discussed above, the major dispute within Zoroastrianism relates to proselytizing and embracing converts. As a dying community, the solutions to resolve this issue from within are not simple. Some see the issue as greater devotion and exclusivity to the religion, while others believe a more diverse and open approach is needed. This has created great disagreement within the faith community.

Scriptures

The scriptural text of Zoroastrianism is the Avesta, also known as the Zend-Avesta. The text is divided into five parts: the Gathas, a collection of sacred hymns, which are believed to be the literal words of Zoroaster (seen as the very central liturgical aspect of the scriptures); the Yasna, which details a rite of preparation and sacrifice of a sacred plant called *haoma*; the Visp-rat, with a number of liturgical tributes to different Zoroastrian spiritual figures; the Vendidad (Videvdat), which covers Zoroastrian ritual and civil law, as well as a creation myth and story of the first man, known as Yima; the Yashts, which are a collection of twenty-one hymns to *yazatas* (angels) and ancient heroic figures; and the Khurda Avesta (little Avesta), which covers hymns, prayers, and minor texts for specific rites and occasions.

> *May Ahura Mazda be pleased. In the name of God, the Beneficent, the Forgiver, the Kind. May there be praise for the name of Ahura Mazda, who has always existed, exists, and will always exist. One of his names is God, the Beneficent Spirit, the most Spiritual among the spiritual ones. One of His names is Ahura Mazda (the Omniscient Lord). He is the Lord, great, mighty, wise, creator, nourisher, protector, supporter, righteous, forgiver, holy dispenser of good justice, all powerful.*[8]
>
> *My) gratitude to the Highest among the existent, who creates (things) and brings (them) to an end. He has, by His existence at all times, and by His strength and wisdom, created the six superior Ameshaspands, several great Yazatas, the brilliant paradise Garothman, the revolving sky, the brilliant sun, the splendid moon, the stars of various kinds, the wind, the air, the water, the fire, the land, the trees, the cattle, the metal and mankind.*
>
> *Praise and homage to the righteous God, who, by (the gift of) speech, elevated man over all creatures of the world, and who gave him the power of reasoning, the power of rising superior to time, and the gift of ruling over the creations for the purpose of fighting, warring against, and shunning Daevas (evil influences).*[9]

> *Ahura Mazda has created for the benefit of mankind several virtues such as innate wisdom, acquired wisdom, good discipline, hope, contentedness ...... The nature of contentedness is this: to keep one's body free from improper desires; to keep him disgusted with discontentment; to make him afraid of dishonesty; not to let him do that which is to cause him sorrow at the end; to make him attain things worthy of acquirement; and not to trouble and injure himself for things that cannot be avoided.*[10]

Other writings of historical importance include the Denkard, Bundahishn, Menog-i Khrad, Selections of Zadspram, Jamsap Namag, Epistles of Manucher, Rivayats, Dadestan-i-Denig, and Arda Viraf Namag. These texts are not scripture, but have played a heavy role in shaping the religion from the ninth and tenth centuries onward.

> *Be it known that, the governor, over the body which the Creator of unbounded creation, God, has given to man, is his own soul. In the body, the obtaining of the assistance of the yazads, is through Bud. And through it the reasoning faculty becomes a wisher for, and obtainer of; strength. (Man) is a possessor of strength and a keeper-of-himself-durable through Hosh. Through reason man is a finder-out of falsehood, a distinguisher, and a doer of every deed. Owing to much connection with the yazads, through (the faculty named) Akho, a path is found to the mind by wisdom, purity and gladness that have an eye for the Invisible. Again, seven other bodily things have been created, giving complete embellishment to the body from without; among these are the five senses. These are spoken of; by those who have knowledge regarding them, as the senses of sight, hearing, taste, smell, and touch, the windows connected with which are placed outside the body; and the nerves in the dwelling are the proper carriers of his messages to the owner of the dwelling-house. Again, there is a description-giving sense-the tongue, which is the bringer out of knowledge regarding the owner of the body from within the body and is the publisher of whatever may be his wishes and thoughts. In this manner every man is made to personally govern his body, for the freedom of his wishes. Hence, (this is) like the kings of the world who are rulers according to their will over people, and, are considered good rulers over the body of the people, by managing the kingdom with wisdom, through the good use of their powers; and, such rule gives to many unworthy persons relations with the Kingdom of Light; and, consequently, such a king becomes happy and respected in the invisible world; but if he be a misuser of his powers, of evil understanding, and an injurer, then, owing to that, his kingdom is at once subverted, and he remains despised and possessed of evil reward, in the ever-harassing hell. Among the people of this world, the nature which is in itself like to the nature of the Creator Ohrmazd, is the nature of holy men, who are keepers of the principle of good thought in Akho, givers of place in their hearts to the service of the Spenamino, keepers in their minds of (the commands of) Srosh, sufferers in a sufficient manner, and givers of authoritative decisions to God's creatures and obeyers of the law. The nature of that holy man, whose senses possess, in the body, the powers of the soul, is, – for the purpose of (giving) to the people of the world, through Hosh, knowledge regarding God, – like to that of the holders of relations with heavenly ways; and is, – in obtaining true wisdom by means of the faculty of reason, – as if possessing the brilliancy of fire; (and) is, through the understanding a giver of much admonition for (the doing of) wise deeds and things; as also a raiser to superior rank by imparting knowledge regarding the good religion, and eager to tell and do things calculated for its (religion's)*

greater purity, and for fuller thought regarding it; and is, – owing to the higher power [residing] in his body, – courageous, not afraid of any one, and a remover [of evil], in the midst of all beholders. Again, [the nature of that holy man] is, – owing to keeping a benignant outlook through the eyes, – like that of Khwarshed; – owing to hearing what is good through the ears, – like that of Srosh; – owing to being a truth-teller through the tongue, – like that of Rashn; and, owing to doing good work with the hands and being a mover-about with the feet for righteousness, – a worker for eternity; as also, without evil, by means of the soul and other powers of the body.[11]

In propitiation of the creator Ohrmazd and all the angels – who are the whole of the heavenly and earthly sacred beings [yazdan] – are the sayings of Ervad Zadspram, son of Yudan-Yim, who is of the South, about the meeting of the beneficent spirit and the evil spirit.

It is in scripture thus declared, that light was above and darkness below, and between those two was open space. Ohrmazd was in the light, and Ahriman in the darkness; Ohrmazd was aware of the existence of Ahriman and of his coming for strife; Ahriman was not aware of the existence of light and of Ohrmazd. It happened to Ahriman, in the gloom and darkness, that he was walking humbly [fro-tanu] on the borders, and meditating other things he came up to the top, and a ray of light was seen by him; and because of its antagonistic nature to him he strove that he might reach it, so that it might also be within his absolute power. And as he came forth to the boundary, accompanied by certain others, Ohrmazd came forth to the struggle for keeping Ahriman away from His territory; and He did it through pure words, confounding witchcraft, and cast him back to the gloom.

For protection from the fiend [druj] the spirits rushed in, the spirits of the sky, water, earth, plants, animals, mankind, and fire He had appointed, and they maintained it [the protection] three thousand years. Ahriman, also, ever collected means in the gloom; and at the end of the three thousand years he came back to the boundary, blustered [patistad], and exclaimed thus: 'I will smite thee, I will smite the creatures which thou thinkest have produced fame for thee – thee who art the beneficent spirit I will destroy everything about them.'

Zoroaster

Ohrmazd answered thus: 'Thou art not a doer of everything, O fiend!'

And, again, Ahriman retorted thus: 'I will seduce all material life into disaffection to thee and affection to myself.'

Ohrmazd perceived, through the spirit of wisdom, thus: 'Even the blustering of Ahriman is capable of performance, if I do not allow disunion [la barininam] during a period of struggle.' And he demanded of him a period for friendship, for it was seen by him that Ahriman does not rely upon the intervention of any vigorous ones, and the existence of a period is obtaining the benefit of the mutual friendship and just arrangement of both; and he formed it into three periods, each period being three millenniums. Ahriman relied upon it, and Ohrmazd perceived that, though it is not possible to have Ahriman sent down, ever when he wants he goes back to his own requisite, which is darkness; and from the poison which is much diffused endless strife arises.

And after the period was appointed by him, he brought forward the Ahunwar formula; and in his Ahunwar these kinds of benefit were shown: – The first is that, of all things, that is proper which is something declared as the will of Ohrmazd; so that, whereas that is proper which is declared the will of Ohrmazd, where anything exists which is not within the will of Ohrmazd, it is created injurious from the beginning, a sin of a distinct nature. The second is this. that whoever shall do that which is the will of Ohrmazd, his reward and recompense are his own; and of him who shall not do that which is the will of Ohrmazd, the punishment at the bridge owing thereto is his own; which is shown from this formula; and the reward of doers of good works, the punishment of sinners, and the tales of heaven and hell are from it. Thirdly, it is shown that the sovereignty of Ohrmazd increases that which is for the poor, and adversity is removed; by which it is shown that there are treasures for the needy one, and treasures are to be his friends; as the intelligent creations are to the unintelligent, so also are the treasures of a wealthy person to a needy one, treasures liberally given which are his own. And the creatures of the trained hand of Ohrmazd are contending and angry (ardik), one with the other, as the renovation of the universe must occur through these three things. That is, first, true religiousness in oneself, and reliance upon a man's original hold on the truly glad tidings (nav-barham), that Ohrmazd is all goodness without vileness, and his will is a will altogether excellent; and Ahriman is all vileness without goodness. Secondly, hope of the reward and recompense of good works, serious fear of the bridge and the punishment of crime, strenuous perseverance in good works, and abstaining from sin. Thirdly, the existence of the mutual assistance of the creatures, or along with and owing to mutual assistance, their collective warfare; it is the triumph of warfare over the enemy which is one's own renovation.

By this formula he (Ahriman) was confounded, and he fell back to the gloom; and Ohrmazd produced the creatures bodily for the world first, the sky; the second, water; the third, earth the fourth, plants; the fifth, animals; the sixth, mankind. Fire was in all, diffused originally through the six substances, of which it was as much the confiner of each single substance in which it was established, it is said, as an eyelid when they lay one down upon the other.

Three thousand years the creatures were possessed of bodies and not walking on their navels; and the sun, moon, and stars stood still. In the mischievous incursion, at the end of the period, Ohrmazd observed thus: 'What advantage is there from the creation of a creature, although thirstless, which is unmoving or mischievous?' And in aid of the celestial sphere he produced the creature Time (zurvan); and Time is unrestricted, so that he made the creatures of Ohrmazd moving, distinct from the motion of Ahriman's creatures, for the shedders of perfume (boi-dadan) were standing one opposite to the other while emitting it. And, observantly of the end, he brought forward to Ahriman a means out of himself, the property of darkness, with which the extreme limits (virunako) of Time were connected by him, an envelope (posto) of the black-pated and ash-colored kind. And in bringing it forward he spoke thus: 'Through their weapons the cooperation of the serpent (azho) dies away, and this which is thine, indeed thy own daughter, dies through religion; and if at the end of nine thousand years, as it is said and written, is a time of upheaval (madam kardano), she is upheaved, not ended.'

At the same time Ahriman came from accompanying Time out to the front, out to the star station; the connection of the sky with the star station was open, which showed, since it hung down into empty space, the strong communication of the lights and glooms, the place of strife in which is the pursuit of both. And having darkness with himself he brought it into the sky, and left the sky so to gloom that the internal deficiency in the sky extends as much as one-third over the star station.[12]

Basic Religious Practices

Zoroastrians practice their religion independently, rather than corporately, at fire temples. Their practice centers around the Fire Ceremony, as fire is the symbol of Lord Mazda. These temples house the sacred fire that burns within them. There are three grades of fire that may burn in a Zoroastrian temple: *Atash Dadgah* (consecrated in a few hours by two priests who receive the Yasna liturgy; a lay member may tend the fire when there are no services); *Atash Adaran* (the "fire of fires," which requires a gathering of hearth fire from the *asronih* [priesthood], *ratheshtarih* [soldiers and civil servants], *vastaryoshih* [farmers and herdsmen]. And *hutokshih* [artisans and laborers]; eight priests consecrate this fire, and the process takes two to three weeks); and *Atash Behram* ("fire of victory," involves gathering fire from sixteen different sources including lightning, a cremation pyre, and hearths; each are purified, and then joins the others; thirty-two priests are required for the consecration ceremony, which takes a year to complete). When an adherent gathers at the temple, they offer a sweet-smelling wood to the fire through the celebrant priest. Priests wear a cloth mask over nose and mouth to prevent any sort of breath from contaminating the fire and use a pair of tongs to then offer the wood in the fire. Special white ash is then offered to the adherent from the fire, who dabs it on their forehead and eyelids. Some ashes are then often taken home for a *Kushti* ritual, which may be done at home as part of ceremonial dress.

Zoroastrian priests do not publicly teach or preach, but specifically work to tend the fire. There are three levels of the Zoroastrian priesthood: the chief priest of the temple is a *dastur*, an ordinary priest is a *mobad* (transferred through patrineal lines), and an *herbad* or *ervad* assists the *dastur* and *mobad* in ceremony.

Central rituals include the *Yasna*, a recitation of the liturgical text as found in the *Avesta* and the sacrificial ritual involving *Haoma*. Zoroastrians are also known for local festivals that have emerged through cultural traditions which may incorporate elements such as shamanism, herbal healing, hallucinogenic aids, or drinking fortified wine. All Zoroastrians are encouraged to pray the *gahs* (watches) five times daily, pray with their hands outstretched, cover their heads in prayer, and celebrate holy festivals.

Zoroastrians are also known for two very important outward symbols of their faith: the *sedreh*, which is an undergarment, and the *Kushti*, which is a girdle. The *Sudreh* is worn to protect adherents from evil, as a spiritual shield. It contains a small pocket in the front which is a collection spot for good deeds. The *Kushti* is a sacred girdle worn by Zoroastrians around their waist. It is made of seventy-two (symbolizing the chapters in the *Yasna*) white, wool threads, tied twice in a double knot in the front and back. The *Kushti* is tied and untied several times a day in a ritual known as the *Nirang-i Kushti*. When practiced, the adherent must stand still, in one spot, and refrain from speaking to anyone else.[13]

Zoroastrians prefer what is called "next of kin" or "cousin marriage," believing that marrying within one's religion is essential to perform the necessary social responsibilities. Marriage must be completed with certain specified rituals. All marriages are registered with the Registrar of Zoroastrian Marriages. Fathers and husbands are the head of households. All in a household must submit to whatever his will may be. Women are expected to care for their children and households, although many have entered the workforce in modern times. Households may be extended or nuclear. It is considered of primary Zoroastrian duty to marry and have children. Rites are performed on newborns, steeping the child's lips in the juice of *haoma*. Children become full members of Zoroastrianism at age seven, with a nine-day initiation ceremony known as *sedre-pushun* or *Navjote*. At this time, a child learns the important prayers found in Zoroastrian Scripture and is given their own *Sedreh* and *Kushti*.

Members of Zoroastrianism commit themselves to their three-fold path of good thoughts, good words, and good deeds as they promote the equality of the sexes, the importance of cleanliness in the environment, hard work and charity, the condemnation of oppression of human beings, condemnation of cruelty against animals, and the condemnation of sacrifice of animals.[14]

HOLIDAYS

Zoroastrians use three versions of ancient and traditional calendars for ceremonial purposes. They are much like the Armenian and Mayan *Haab* calendars, dividing their time into years, months, weeks, days, and watches. Days begin at dawn, and each day is divided into five watches: *Hawan* (sunrise to noon), *Rapithwin* (noon to 3 PM), *Uzerin* (3 PM to sunset), *Aiwisruthrem* (sunset to midnight), and *Ushahin* (midnight to sunrise). There are twelve months of the calendar, with corresponding intersections of festival days, special for worship. These are divided into seasonal festivals, name-day feasts, and other holiday days.[15,16]

- **Seasonal festivals**: Known as *gahanbars* (proper season), these are associated with Ahura Mazda's creation of the *Amesha Spentas* and special aspects of creation (sky, earth, water, plants, animals, and human beings). They are celebrated for five days; *Hamaspathmaidyem Gahanbar* is celebrated for ten days. It used to be that such festivals were celebrated at their actual dates, but now may be celebrated at other times when the modern and ancient calendars are irreconcilable. These festivals are: *Maidyozarem Gahanbar* ("Midgreening;" mid-spring festival); *Maidoyshahem Ghanbar* (midsummer, summer solstice festival); *Paitishahem Gahanbar* (bringing in the corn, harvest festival); *Ayathrem Gahanbar* (bringing home the herds, end of autumn festival); *Maidyarem Gahanbar* (mid-year, winter solstice festival); *Hamaspathmaidyem Gahanbar* (festival of mankind, specifically remembering the souls of the deceased).

- **Name-day feasts**: There are fifteen different name-day feasts, specifically to be held at the time when a specified *yazata* intersects.

- **Jashan of Dadvah**: Four days of the tenth month (first, eighth, fifteenth, and twenty-third) dedicated to Ahura Mazda, as *Dae* Creator (observed in December and January).

- **Jashan of Bahman**: Second day of the eleventh month, celebrating the creation of animals (usually observed on January 16).

- **Jashan of Spendarmad**: Fifth day of the twelfth month, celebrating the earth (usually observed on February 18).

- **Jashan of Farvardin**: celebrates the *Fravashis*, nineteenth day of the first month (usually observed on April 8).

- **Jashan of Adravisht**: Third day of the second month, celebrating fire and luminaries (usually observed on April 22).

- **Jashan of Hordad**: Sixth day of the third month, celebrating water (usually observed on May 25).

- **Jashan of Tir/Tiregan**: Celebrates *Tishtrya*, a fertility spirit and the rains, thirteenth day of fourth month (usually observed on July 1).

- **Jashan of Amurdad**: Seventh day of the fifth month, celebrating plants (usually observed on July 25).

- **Jashan of Shahrevar**: Fourth day of the sixth month, celebrating metals and minerals (usually observed on August 21).

- **Jashan of Aban.Abanegan**: Celebrates *Apas* (water), the waters of Aredvi Sura Anahita, an Indo-Iranian cosmic fertility figure associated with water; ninth day of the eighth month (usually observed on October 26)

- **Jashan of Adar/Adaregan**: Celebration of *Atar* (fire) on the tenth day of the ninth month (usually observed on November 24).

- **Jashan of Mihr/Mehregan**: Celebration of Mithra, the deity of light and oath, on the sixteenth day of the seventh month (usually observed on October 2).

- **Other holy days**: *Nouruz* (Zoroastrian New Year, on the date of the spring equinox or in July or August); *Pateti* (Day of Penitence, on the last day or five days of the calendar years); *Sadeh* (a midwinter festival, celebrated one hundred days and nights before New Year's Day; observed with a bonfire); *Zartosht No-Diso* (death anniversary of Zarathushtra, celebrated on the eleventh day of the tenth month, usually around December 26); and Khordad Sal (the birthday of Zoroaster, the sixth day of the first month, usually around March 26).

VISUAL SIGNS AND SYMBOLS

Fire; the *Faravahar* (disc with wings representing a sun with wings, and a human torso, with a bearded face, representing humanity; represents Ashur, the god of war, showcasing the battle of good and evil; decked out in feathers, showing as a guardian angel, watching over humanity and aiding in the struggle for goodness, to face Ahura Mazda); Zoroaster; the number five; *Sudre* and *Kusti*, cypress tree, *Avesta*, Tower of Silence; Zoroastrian fire temples.

CREEDS, BOOKS, AND LAWS

Zoroastrianism derives its civil and religious law from the Avestas, specifically the Vendidad (Videvdat). The Vendidad is an ecclesiastical code relating to specific aspects of a Zoroastrian's life: hygiene, care for the dead, cleansing, disease, mourning for the dead, death ritual and renumeration of deeds after death, sanctity and invocations for fire, earth, water, and stars; wealth, charity, marriage, physical effort, unacceptable social behavior, breach of contract, assault, worthiness of priests, and care for bulls, dogs, otters, the *Sraosha* bird, and the *haoma* tree. There is also a specific section on penance for violations of the law. The regulations of the Vendidad are not presented as moral absolutes, universally necessary, mandatory, or spiritual in nature. More than anything, it is a presentation of desired social laws, customs, and culture present among those who follow the religion.[17]

> *Make thy own self pure, O righteous man! any one in the world here below can win purity for his own self, namely, when he cleanses his own self with good thoughts, words, and deeds.*[18]

ECLECTIC BELIEFS

Zoroastrianism has a complex cosmology which states the entire creation was set to operate by Ahura Mazda's plan. Violations of this order are violations of Ahura Mazda and are known as *druj*. *Druj* include chaos, natural decay, and lies. It is the spiritual duty of every created thing to defend Ahura Mazda. Adherents are to reflect deeds that align with their creator with the inherent goodness that is to flow with creation's principles of order. These deeds manifest as social and familial obligations and remaining faithful to responsibilities. Focusing on free will, all beings are seen as having the conscious ability to choose, and human beings are responsible for their situations, how they act, and the results therein.

Sacred fire

The material universe was created to ensnare evil. Its design was as a floating, egg-shaped universe, first the spiritual, and later, the physical. The archetypical man was Gayomard, and Gavaevodata was the primordial bovine, or bull.

In contrast to Ahura Mazda, Angra Mainyu counter-created demons and annoying creatures (ants, flies, snakes). For every good being created, Angra Mainyu created an opposite, evil being. When it came to humans, he was unable to create a suitable match. His response was to invade the universe, inflicting with suffering and death. Those evil forces were now trapped in the universe, unable to leave. Gayomard and Gavaevodata both released seeds, saved by the Moon (*Mah*). From the seeds of the bull, all beneficial plants and animals of the earth were born; from the man's seed came the first human couple. Evil present in the world is the result of Angra Mainyu's spiritual attack on creation.

Each individual must face the Chinvat Bridge (bridge of judgment) at death. Forced to cross it, humans are judged by the *Yazatas* Mithra, Sraosha, and Rashnu for their deeds. One is either met by a sweet-smelling young woman or an ugly, old smelly woman, representative of good or bad deeds. The young woman leads the dead across the bridge to paradise toward what is called the House of Song. The old woman leads the dead toward a razor's edge and abyss toward the House of Lies. The House of Lies is a temporary place to handle punishments just for crimes. It is packed tightly and smells bad, although people there believe they are in isolation. Those who are balanced between good and bad go to *Hamistagan*, a neutral waiting place. Souls here can relive their lives and do better deeds while they await final judgment.

The world exists in three phases: creation, the present world, a three-thousand-year period mixed with good and evil, and the final state, where good and evil will be separated. A final battle shall ensue to accentuate this struggle, and it shall focus on the battle of good and evil. Total chaos shall ensue during the final evil assault: the sun and moon will fail to give light, casting the whole world into a state of winter, and people shall lose their respect for religion, elders, and family members. A savior (*Saoshyant*) will be born of a virgin, impregnated by the prophet Zoroaster while bathing in a lake. The dead shall be raised, the world shall be judged twice (spiritually and physically), and the wicked shall return to hell, purged of sin. All shall be purified through a river of molten metal. Good will triumph over evil, and all souls will be redeemed at the final judgment.

Unique to Zoroastrianism is its death rite. Death rites take place at a Tower of Silence, which are large, circular structures built for the process of excarnation (dead bodies are exposed to vultures). Each roof is divided by three concentric rings. The body of men are found in the outer ring, women in the middle ring, and children in the internal ring. Bodies are left for decay. After the bones are bleached by the elements, they are collected in an ossuary pit to disintegrate. All that remains is washed out to sea. Such is to keep the body from contaminating anything, as dead bodies are viewed as pollutants.[19]

Zoroastrianism views on contemporary issues tend to vary. Homosexuality has traditionally been seen as a form of demon worship, but some modern interpretations reject this notion. Issues such as abortion and birth control are also unclear or variable among believers.[20]

Relations with Non-Zoroastrians

Although Zoroastrian mystical aspects have been absorbed into other religious traditions and is also the product of syncretism as relates to several systems of ancient deities, Zoroastrians, with their emphasis on separateness and purity, remain very much unto themselves, with little interest of other religions. Some of this is a desire to preserve their culture, as Zoroastrians have experienced persecution (especially from Muslims) throughout history. In some parts of the western world, Zoroastrians are more interested in converts and coexisting with other groups. As a religious entity, they have always sought to live peacefully and respectfully with others.

HOLY SITES

Pir-e Sabz (Chak-Chak) shrine, near Ardakan, Iran; Seti Pir, near Yazd, Iran; Pir-e NNarestuneh, Yazd, Iran; Pir-e Banu-{ars, near Sharifabad, Iran; Pir-e Naraki, Mt. Nareke, Iran; Pir-e Herisht, near Sharifabad, Iran; Shekaft-e Yazdan, near Zardju, Iran; Mt. Ushi-darena, Iran; Mt. Asnavant (mt. Ushenai), Iran; Mt. Hara-Berezaiti (Mt. Alborz), the Daitya River.

NOTABLE FIGURES

Zoroaster, founder of Zoroastrianism; Cyrus the Great (c. 600-530 B.C.), founder of the first Persian Empire; Darius the Great (550-486 B.C.), fourth Persian king of the Achaemenid Empire; Jamshid Bahman Jamshidian (1850-1932), modern banking pioneer; Feroze Gandhi (1912-1960), publisher; John Abraham (1972-), actor; N.H. Wadia (1925-2016), neurologist; Behramji Malabari (1853-1912), author; Cyrus Broacha (1971-), MTV India VJ; Diana Penty (1985-), actress; Freddie Mercury (1946-1991), musician; Dolly Nazir (1935-), athlete; Gary Lawyer (1959-), musician; Kaizad Gustad (1968-), film director; Mehr Jesia (1968-), model; Nina Wadia (1968-), comedian and actress; Perizaad Zorabian (1973-), actress; Rohinton Mistry (1952-), writer; Sanjay Gandhi (1946-1980), politician; Sam Piroj Bharucha (1936-), politician; Jehangir Sabavala (1922-2011), painter.

NOTABLE GROUPS

Parsi Zoroastrians are followers of Zoroastrianism (Iranian descent) in India. According to the tradition, a group of Iranian followers of Zoroaster left Persia (between 785 and 936) when given the choice to convert to Islam or leave. They opted to maintain their own religious traditions. The Parsis sought a new home in Gujarat, a state in India. The group travelled by boat across the Arabian Sea and were suspect to be turned away via a cup of milk, a symbol fearing their presence would cause their populations to overflow beyond capacity. The Parsis returned the cup of milk with some sugar, proving that not only would they not cause overpopulation, but they would sweeten the population of people present in Gujarat by blending in with their presence. Their community has remained in India ever since. Today, there are approximately 60,000 Parsi in India.[21]

FACTS AND FIGURES

Approximately 11,000 Zoroastrians live in the United States and 6,000 in Canada.[22]

OTHER IMPORTANT DEFINITIONS[23]

- ***Afrin***: A blessing or benediction.

- ***Nafrin***: A curse.
- ***Ahriman***: Another term for Anra Mainyu, literally meaning "destructive spirit."
- ***Ahunwar***: The holiest prayer of the religion.
- ***Amahraspand***: The highest spiritual beings created by Ahura Mazda.
- ***Ashavan***: A righteous or just person or being.
- ***Az***: Demon of greed.
- ***Bedhin***: A lay person, a person of the "Good Religion" (i.e. Zoroastrianism).
- ***Hadish***: A sacred being.
- ***Hamazor***: Ritual greeting.
- ***Juddin***: A term for someone who is not a Zoroastrian.
- ***Margarzan***: A mortal sin.
- ***Mashye-Mashyane***: The first human couple, born of the seed of Gayomard.
- ***Nahn***: A ritual washing of the entire body.
- ***Ohrmazd***: Another term for the supreme being, echoed on the first day of the month on the Zoroastrian religious calendar.
- ***Pahlavi***: Middle Persian language by which many Zoroastrian writings are preserved.
- ***Padyab***: A ritual washing of the exposed parts of the body (such as the hands).
- ***Panchayat***: A local association, or group, of Zoroastrians.
- ***Ram***: Joy; name of a Yazad.
- ***Spenta Mainyu***: Holy spirit.
- ***Urvan***: Soul
- **Wad**: Wind; also can mean atmosphere.

- ***Zam***: Earth
- ***Zot***: Officiating priest

BELIEVER'S CHARACTERISTICS

Emphasis on teachings of Zoroaster as true religion; purity in belief; focus on the battle of good and evil; equal power between the divine and evil forces; fire ceremonies; fire temples; traditional family roles; patrilineal lines; refusal to accept converts; embrace of the *Avesta*; complex cosmology; belief in the three ages of the world; pronounced eschatology that promotes the idea of all evil purged, and all living once again, without the pull or power of evil; emphasis on doing right; use of the *Sedreh* and *Kushki*; embrace of Zoroastrian rites; separateness; specified ethnicity (Persian or Parsi) in practice; independent worship; practice of daily prayer, five times per day, with hands extended; coming great battle of good vs. evil; awaiting the day of *Saoshyant*.

References

Epigraph

[1]Vasudevan, Sreeram. "Religion." *Poemhunter.com.* August 23, 2009. https://www.poemhunter.com/poem/religion/. Accessed March 2, 2023.

Agnosticism

[1]"Agnosticism Quotes." https://www.goodreads.com/quotes/tag/agnosticism. Accessed June 8, 2020.

[2]"Agnosticism." https://www.britannica.com/topic/agnosticism. Accessed June 15, 2020.

[3]"Demographics of Atheism." https://en.wikipedia.org/wiki/Demographics_of_atheism. Accessed June 15, 2020.

[4]Hume, David. *Enquiry Concerning Human Understanding, The.* https://www.goodreads.com/work/quotes/300449-an-enquiry-concerning-human-understanding. Accessed November 2, 2022.

[5]"What Did Darwin Believe?" https://www.darwinproject.ac.uk/commentary/religion/what-did-darwin-believe. Accessed June 15, 2020.

[6]Darwin, Charles. *Origin of the Species, The.* https://www.goodreads.com/work/quotes/481941-on-the-origin-of-species-by-means-of-natural-selection-or-the-preservat. Accessed November 2, 2022.

[7]"Bertrand Russell Quotes." https://www.goodreads.com/quotes/111905-as-a-philosopher-if-i-were-speaking-to-a-purely. Accessed November 2, 2022.

[8]"Leslie Weatherhead Quotes." https://libquotes.com/leslie-weatherhead. Accessed November 2, 2022.

[9]"North Texas Church of Freethought." https://en.wikipedia.org/wiki/North_Texas_Church_of_Freethought. Accessed June 15, 2020,

[10]Shermer, Michael. "Number of Americans with No Religious Affiliation is Rising, The: The Rise of the Atheists." https://www.scientificamerican.com/article/the-number-of-americans-with-no-religious-affiliation-is-rising/. Accessed June 15, 2020.

[11]Robinson, Ashley. "What Does it Mean to be Agnostic?" https://blog.prepscholar.com/agnostic-definition. Accessed June 15, 2020.

Armstrongism

[1]"True Humility – NOT!" *The Painful Truth – Herbert W. Armstrong's Worldwide Church of God.* https://herbertwarmstrong.com/2019/06/08/true-humility-not/#more-13855. Accessed November 15, 2022.

[2]"Armstrongism." https://en.wikipedia.org/wiki/Armstrongism. Accessed December 7, 2020.

[3]"Grace Communion International." https://en.wikipedia.org/wiki/Grace_Communion_International. Accessed December 7, 2020.

[4]Armstrong, Herbert W. "Introduction: How the Seven Mysteries Were Revealed." *Mystery of the Ages.* https://www.thetrumpet.com/literature/read/35-mystery-of-the-ages/28. Accessed November 2, 2022.

[5]"Armstrongism." https://en.wikipedia.org/wiki/Armstrongism. Accessed December 10, 2020.

[6]Armstrong, Herbert W. *Plain Truth, The.* March 1938, p. 8. "A Sampling of Herbert W. Armstrong's Prophetic Record." https://hwarmstrong.com/hwa-prophetic-record.htm. Accessed November 2, 2022.

[7]Armstrong, Herbert W. *Plain Truth, The.* January 1939, p. 4. "A Sampling of Herbert W. Armstrong's Prophetic Record." https://hwarmstrong.com/hwa-prophetic-record.htm. Accessed November 2, 2022.

[8]Armstrong, Herbert W. *Plain Truth, The.* August 1952, Pp. 1 and 10. "Herbert Armstrong Ministry 1930-1986. https://exitsupportnetwork.com/herbert-armstrong-ministry-1930-1986/. Accessed November 2, 2022.

9 Armstrong, Herbert W. *Co-Worker Letter*, January 10, 1958. "The Plain Truth About Mr. Herbert W.

Armstrong, Part 1." https://hwarmstrong.com/plain-truth-hwa.htm. Accessed November 2, 2022.
[10]Armstrong, Herbert W. *Plain Truth, The.* August 1949, p.3. "The Plain Truth About Mr. Herbert Armstrong, Part 1." https://hwarmstrong.com/plain-truth-hwa.htm. Accessed November 2, 2022.
[11]Armstrong, Herbert W. *Co-Worker Letter,* May 22, 1953. "Did Herbert Armstrong Set Dates?" https://exitsupportnetwork.com/did-herbert-armstrong-set-dates/. Accessed November 2, 2022.
[12]Weinland, Ronald. "Is Christ About to Return?" *False Prophet Ronald Weinland.* https://fprw.wordpress.com/. Accessed November 2, 2022.
[13]Flurry, Gerald. *Philadelphia Trumpet, The,* January 2021. https://www.thetrumpet.com/23193-why-donald-trump-will-remain-americas-president. Accessed November 2, 2022.
[14]"Armstrongism." https://en.wikipedia.org/wiki/Armstrongism. Accessed December 10, 2020.
[15]"Living Church of God." https://en.wikipedia.org/wiki/Living_Church_of_God. Accessed December 10, 2020.
[16]https://silenced.co/_sections/dangers/. Accessed December 10, 2020.

ATHEISM

[1]"Atheism." https://www.goodreads.com/quotes/tag/atheism/ Accessed August 12, 2020.
[2]"Atheism." https://en.wikipedia.org/wiki/Atheism. Accessed August 12, 20208/12/2020
[3]Ibid.
[4]"Demographics of Atheism." https://en.wikipedia.org/wiki/Demographics_of_atheism. Accessed August 12, 2020.
[5]"Practical Atheism." https://en.wikipedia.org/wiki/Practical_atheism. Accessed August 14, 2020.
[6]"Implicit and Explicit Atheism." https://en.wikipedia.org/wiki/Implicit_and_explicit_atheism. Accessed August 13, 2020.
[7]"Secular Humanism." https://en.wikipedia.org/wiki/Secular_humanism. Accessed August 14, 2020.
[8]Nitezsche, Friedrich. "Atheist Quotes." https://www.goodreads.com/quotes/tag/atheism?page=1. Accessed November 3, 2022.
[9]Dawkins, Richard. "Atheist Quotes." https://www.goodreads.com/quotes/tag/atheism?page=1. Accessed November 3, 2022.
[10]Hitchens, Christopher. https://www.goodreads.com/quotes/tag/atheism?page=1. Accessed November 3, 2022
[11]Dawkins, Richard. "Atheist Quotes." https://www.goodreads.com/quotes/tag/atheism?page=1. Accessed November 3, 2022.
[12]Rand, Ayn. "Ayn Rand Quotes." https://www.goodreads.com/author/quotes/432.Ayn_Rand. Accessed December 30, 2022.
[13]"Atheist Creed." https://www.pinterest.com/pin/133771051403522426/. Accessed August 14, 2020.
[14]"American Atheists." https://en.wikipedia.org/wiki/American_Atheists. Accessed August 145, 2020.
[15]"Madalyn Murray O'Hair." https://en.wikipedia.org/wiki/Madalyn_Murray_O%27Hair. Accessed August 15, 2020.
[16]Ibid.
[17]Lipka, Michael. "10 Facts About Atheists." https://www.pewresearch.org/fact-tank/2019/12/06/10-facts-about-atheists/. Accessed August 15, 2020.
[18]"Atheism Terms Definitions and Distinctions." http://rationalrazor.com/2016/08/24/atheism-terms-definitions-and-distinctions/. Accessed August 15, 2020.
[19]"Atheism Terminology." http://www.eoht.info/page/atheism+terminology. Accessed August 15, 2020.

BAHÁ'Í FAITH

[1]Effendi, Shoghi. *The Unfolding Destiny of the British Bahá'í Community,* p. 457. https://bahaiquotes.com/subject/dark-thoughts. Accessed September 17, 2020.
[2]"Bahá'í Faith." https://en.wikipedia.org/wiki/Bah%C3%A1%CA%BC%C3%AD_Faith. Accessed September 17, 2020.
[3]Hokhoyan. Anush. "Armenia and Followers of the Bahá'í Faith." https://www.evnreport.com/arts-and-culture/armenia-and-followers-of-the-bahai-faith. Accessed September 17, 2020.
[4]"People of Bayan or Bayanis." https://www.thesectsofbahais.com/bayanis.html. Accessed September 17, 2020.

[5]"Daheshists." https://www.thesectsofbahais.com/daheshists.html. Accessed September 17, 2020.
[6]"Essence of the Bahá'í Faith." https://www.thesectsofbahais.com/thirdm.html. Accessed September 17, 2020.
[7]"Those who Believe in Continuation of Guardianship." https://www.thesectsofbahais.com/guardian.html. Accessed September 17, 2020.
[8]"Heterodox Bahá'ís" https://www.thesectsofbahais.com/hetex.html. September 17, 2020.
[9]"Universal House of Guardianship Followers of Five Elders." https://www.thesectsofbahais.com/elders.html. Accessed September 17, 2020
[10]"Aqdas Bahá'í Faith." https://www.thesectsofbahais.com/aqdasis.html. Accessed September 17, 2020.
[11]"Bahá'í Holy Texts." https://www.bbc.co.uk/religion/religions/bahai/texts/texts.shtml. Accessed September 17, 2020.
[12]Introduction, *Bahá'í Scriptures: Selections from the Utterances of Bahá'u'lláh and 'Abdu'l-Bahá*, Page v-vi, Bahá'í Committee on Publications, 1928. https://bahai-library.com/holley_bahai_scriptures. Accessed November 17, 2022.
[13]Ibid., Chapter 1 pg. 14-16. Accessed November 17, 2022.
[14]"Bahá'í Faith." https://en.wikipedia.org/wiki/Bah%C3%A1%CA%BC%C3%AD_Faith#Summary. Accessed September 17, 2020.
[15]"Universal House of Justice." https://en.wikipedia.org/wiki/Universal_House_of_Justice. Accessed September 18, 2020.
[16]"Bahá'í Faith." https://en.wikipedia.org/wiki/Bah%C3%A1%CA%BC%C3%AD_Faith. 9/18/2020
[17]"Bahá'í International Community." https://en.wikipedia.org/wiki/Bah%C3%A1%CA%BC%C3%AD_International_Community. Accessed September 18, 2020.
[18]"Statistics." https://bahaipedia.org/Statistics. Accessed September 18, 2020.
[19]Winters, Jonah. "Short Glossary of Bahá'í Terms." https://bahai-library.com/winters_bahai_glossary. Accessed September 18, 2020.

BLACK IDENTITY MOVEMENT

[1]Farrakhan, Louis. Saviours' Day speech, Chicago, Illinois, February 26, 2012. https://www.adl.org/education/resources/reports/nation-of-islam-farrakhan-in-his-own-words. Accessed October 1, 2020.
[2]"Black Hebrew Israelites." https://en.wikipedia.org/wiki/Black_Hebrew_Israelites. October 15, 2020.
[3]"Extremist Sects Within the Black Hebrew Israelite Movement." https://www.adl.org/resources/backgrounders/extremist-sects-within-the-black-hebrew-israelite-movement. Accessed October 21, 2020.
[4]"Moorish Sovereign Citizens." https://www.splcenter.org/fighting-hate/extremist-files/group/moorish-sovereign-citizens. Accessed October 16, 2020.
[5]"Nation of Islam." https://en.wikipedia.org/wiki/Nation_of_Islam. Accessed October 20, 2020.
[6]Muhammad, Elijah. *Message to the Blackman in America.* https://www.goodreads.com/work/quotes/283678-message-to-the-blackman-in-america 11/17/2022
[7]Ibid.
[8]Ibid.
[9]Ibid.
[10]Ali, Drew. *The Holy Koran of the Moorish Science Temple of America.* https://hermetic.com/moorish/7koran. November 17, 2022.
[11]"Nation of Islam." https://en.wikipedia.org/wiki/Nation_of_Islam. Accessed October 20, 2020.
[12]"Hebrew Roots." https://en.wikipedia.org/wiki/Hebrew_Roots. Accessed June 8, 2020.
[13]"Moorish-American Holidays." https://sites.google.com/site/moorishsciencetemple75inc/wwwmoorishsciencetempleofamericainc75com. Accessed October 20, 2020.
[14]Muhammad, Elijah. "What the Muslims Want." *Message to the Blackman in America.* https://www.noi.org/muslim-program/. Accessed October 21, 2020.

[15]"Five Percent Nation." https://www.britannica.com/topic/Five-Percent-Nation. Accessed October 21, 2020.
[16]"Who are the Black Israelites at the Center of the Viral Standoff at the Lincoln Memorial?" https://www.washingtonpost.com/religion/2019/01/22/who-are-black-israelites-center-viral-standoff-lincoln-memorial/. Accessed October 21, 2020.
[17]"Extremist Sects Within the Black Hebrew Israelite Movement." https://www.adl.org/resources/backgrounders/extremist-sects-within-the-black-hebrew-israelite-movement. Accessed October 21, 2020.
[18]Gordon, Bill. "Nation of Islam." https://www.namb.net/apologetics/resource/nation-of-islam/. Accessed October 21, 2020.

BUDDHISM

[1]"Dalai Lama Quotes." https://www.brainyquote.com/quotes/dalai_lama_108821. Accessed April 11, 2020.
[2]"Buddhist Deities." https://en.wikipedia.org/wiki/Buddhist_deities. Accessed April 11, 2020.
[3]"The Four Types of Buddhism." https://exploringyourmind.com/four-types-buddhism/. Accessed April 13, 2020.
[4]Marino, Lee Ann B. *Understanding Demonology, Spiritual Warfare, Healing and Deliverance: A Manual for the Christian Minister*. Charlotte, North Carolina: Apostolic University Press, 2017. Pp. 171-174.
5 "Aleph Cult." https://en.wikipedia.org/wiki/Aleph_(Japanese_cult). Accessed April 13, 2020.
6"Buddhists." *The Global Religious Landscape*. https://www.pewforum.org/2012/12/18/global-religious-landscape-buddhist/. Accessed April 13, 2020.
7 http://buddhasutra.com/files/brahmana_sutta.htm 11/21/2022
8 https://www.dhammatalks.org/vinaya/bmc/Section0006.html 11/21/2022
9 https://www.wisdomlib.org/buddhism/book/dhammasangani/d/doc3725.html 11/21/2022
10 https://www.onelittleangel.com/wisdom/quotes/book.asp?mc=8 11/21/2022
11 https://en.wikipedia.org/wiki/Buddhist_holidays 4/13/2020
12 https://en.wikipedia.org/wiki/Refuge_(Buddhism) 4/14/2020
13 https://en.wikipedia.org/wiki/Buddhist_pilgrimage_sites 4/14/2020
14 https://en.wikipedia.org/wiki/Soka_Gakkai_International 4/14/2020
15 https://www.pewresearch.org/fact-tank/2019/04/05/5-facts-about-buddhists-around-the-world/ 4/13/2020

CHINESE CHRISTIANITY

[1]"Watchman Nee Quotes." https://quotefancy.com/watchman-nee-quotes. Accessed July 9, 2021.
[2]"Christianity in China." https://en.wikipedia.org/wiki/Christianity_in_China. Accessed May 19, 2022.
[3]Clark, Colin. "What Christianity in China is Really Like." https://www.thegospelcoalition.org/article/what-christianity-in-china-is-really-like/. Accessed May 19, 2022.
[4]"Christianity in China." https://en.wikipedia.org/wiki/Christianity_in_China. Accessed May 19, 2022.
[5]"Three-Self Patriotic Movement." https://en.wikipedia.org/wiki/Three-Self_Patriotic_Movement. Accessed May 19, 2022.
[6]"China Christian Council." https://en.wikipedia.org/wiki/China_Christian_Council. Accessed May 19, 2022.
[7]"Chinese Patriotic Catholic Association." https://en.wikipedia.org/wiki/Chinese_Patriotic_Catholic_Association. Accessed June 2, 2022.
[8]"Chinese Orthodox Church." https://en.wikipedia.org/wiki/Chinese_Orthodox_Church. Accessed June 2, 2022.
[9]"Christianity in China." https://en.wikipedia.org/wiki/Christianity_in_China. Accessed June 7, 2022.
[10]"Bible Translations into Chinese." https://en.wikipedia.org/wiki/Bible_translations_into_Chinese. Accessed June 2, 2022.
[11]Enos, Olivia and Childs, Emma. "Preserving the Integrity of the Bible in China." https://www.heritage.org/religious-liberty/commentary/preserving-the-integrity-the-bible-china. Accessed June 2, 2022.
[12]Johnson, Eme. "How Does China Celebrate Christmas?" *Travel Tomorrow*. https://traveltomorrow.com/how-does-china-celebrate-christmas/. Accessed June 2, 2022.
[13]"Christianity in China." https://en.wikipedia.org/wiki/Christianity_in_China. Accessed June 7, 2022.
[14]Albert, Eleanor and Maizland, Eleanor. "Religion in China." *Council on Foreign Relations*.

https://www.cfr.org/backgrounder/religion-china. Accessed June 7, 2022.
[15]"China Gospel Fellowship." https://en.wikipedia.org/wiki/China_Gospel_Fellowship. Accessed June 7, 2022.
[16]"China Gospel Fellowship Able to Worship Openly." https://thealabamabaptist.org/china-gospel-fellowship-able-to-worship-openly/. Accessed June 7, 2022.
[17]McKay, Hollie. "Conservative Church Claims South Korea's Government is Persecuting Them By Blaming Members for Coronavirus Spread." *Fox News*. https://www.foxnews.com/world/south-korea-church-coronavirus-spread. Accessed July 8, 2021.
[18]"Shincheonji: Korean Sect Leader Found Not Guilty of Breaking Virus Law." *BBC News*, https://www.bbc.com/news/world-asia-55642653. Accessed July 8, 2021.
[19]"Christianity in China." https://en.wikipedia.org/wiki/Christianity_in_China. Accessed June 7, 2022

CHRISTIAN IDENTITY MOVEMENT

1 https://web.archive.org/web/20141128063716/https://www.cjccan.org/ 8/15/2020
2 https://en.wikipedia.org/wiki/Christian_Identity 8/21/2020
3 https://kingidentity.com/doctrine.htm 8/17/2020
4 https://en.wikipedia.org/wiki/Christian_Identity 8/17/2020
5 https://en.wikipedia.org/wiki/Christian_Identity 8/17/2020
6 https://www.splcenter.org/fighting-hate/extremist-files/group/kingdom-identity-ministries 8/17/2020
7 https://en.wikipedia.org/wiki/Church_of_Israel 8/19/2020
8 https://www.splcenter.org/fighting-hate/extremist-files/group/kingdom-identity-ministries 8/20/2020
9 https://www.splcenter.org/fighting-hate/extremist-files/ideology/christian-identity 8/20/2020
10 https://www.splcenter.org/fighting-hate/intelligence-report/2015/what-sovereign-citizen 8/20/2020
11 https://www.splcenter.org/fighting-hate/extremist-files/ideology/sovereign-citizens-movement 8/20/2020
12 https://www.splcenter.org/fighting-hate/extremist-files/individual/richard-butler 11/21/2022
13 https://israelect.com/ChurchOfTrueIsrael/comparet/comp27.html 11/21/2022
14 https://www.nytimes.com/2002/11/17/books/chapters/the-terrorist-next-door.html 11/21/2022
15 https://en.wikiquote.org/wiki/William_Luther_Pierce 1/21/2022
16 https://www.adl.org/hate-symbols 8/21/2020
17 https://www.adl.org/education/references/hate-symbols/14-words 8/21/2020
18 https://en.wikipedia.org/wiki/88_Precepts 8/21/2020
19 https://en.wikipedia.org/wiki/Christian_Identity 8/21/2020
20 https://en.wikipedia.org/wiki/Northwest_Territorial_Imperative 8/21/2020
21 https://en.wikipedia.org/wiki/Elohim_City,_Oklahoma 8/21/2020
22 https://en.wikipedia.org/wiki/Aryan_Brotherhood 8/21/2020
23 https://www.adl.org/education/resources/glossary-terms/defining-extremism-white-supremacy 8/22/2020

CHRISTIAN SCIENCE

[1]"Mary Baker Eddy Quote." https://www.quotes.net/quote/49711. Accessed May 15, 2020.
[2]Buttner, Marguerite Emily. "Seven Synonyms For God." *Christian Science Journal, The*. January 1963. https://journal.christianscience.com/shared/view/10j33ukrufw. Accessed May 15, 2020.
[3]"What's Christian Science?" http://csnyc.com/whats-christian-science/. Accessed May 15, 2020.
[4]Hanna, Septimus J. "Trinity, The." *Christian Science Journal, The*. July 1915. https://journal.christianscience.com/shared/view/17f7qholobc. Accessed May 15, 2020.
[5]Bergenheim, Richard C. Holy Ghost and Healing, The. *Christian Science Journal, The*. August 1995. https://journal.christianscience.com/shared/view/pp63a9bvh8. Accessed May 15, 2020.
[6]"Christian Science." https://en.wikipedia.org/wiki/Christian_Science. Accessed May 15, 2020.
[7]Baker, Mary Eddy. *Science and Health With Key to the Scriptures* 18:1-19:11. https://www.christianscience.com/the-christian-science-pastor/science-and-health/chapter-ii-atonement-and-eucharist. Accessed November 21, 2022.
[8]Ibid., 9:16-27 https://www.christianscience.com/the-christian-science-pastor/science-and-health/chapter-xi-some-objections-answered?citation=SH%20342:16-342:20. Accessed November 21, 2022.

[9]Ibid., 15:9-12 https://www.christianscience.com/the-christian-science-pastor/science-and-health/chapter-xv-genesis?citation=SH%20510:9-510:12. Accessed November 21, 2022.
[10]"Tenets of Christian Science." *Beliefs and Teachings.* https://www.christianscience.com/what-is-christian-science/beliefs-and-teachings. Accessed May 15, 2020.
[11]"Manual of the Mother Church." https://en.wikipedia.org/wiki/Manual_of_The_Mother_Church. Accessed May 15, 2020.
[12]""Christian Science."
https://en.wikipedia.org/wiki/Christian_Science#Establishing_the_church,_move_to_Boston. Accessed May 15, 2020.
[13]"Christian Science Reading Room." https://en.wikipedia.org/wiki/Christian_Science_Reading_Room. Accessed May 15, 2020.
[14]"Christian Science Publishing Society." https://en.wikipedia.org/wiki/Christian_Science_Publishing_Society. Accessed May 15, 2020.
[15]Barrett, Stephen. "Christian Science Statistics: Practitioners, Teachers, and Churches in the United States." March 13, 2016. https://quackwatch.org/related/cs/. Accessed May 15, 2020.
[16]"Glossary of Christian Science Terminology." *Ex-Christian Scientist, The.*
https://exchristianscience.com/index/glossary/. Accessed May 15, 2020.

CULTS

[1]"Philip Zimbardo Quotes." http://www.morefamousquotes.com/quotes/2781876-many-cults-start-off-with-high-ideals.html. Accessed December 12, 2020.
[2]"Unification Movement." https://en.wikipedia.org/wiki/Unification_movement. Accessed December 17, 2020.
[3]Schneider, Nathan. "Short Discourse on Cult Terminology." *Killing the Buddha.* May 30. 2009.
https://killingthebuddha.com/ktblog/short-discourse-on-cult-terminology/. Accessed December 17, 2020.

EASTERN CHURCH MOVEMENTS

[1]"Unification Church Quotes." https://www.azquotes.com/quotes/topics/unification-church.html. Accessed December 22, 2020.
[2]"Unification Church." https://en.wikipedia.org/wiki/Unification_Church. Accessed June 28, 2021.
[3]"Eastern Lightning." https://en.wikipedia.org/wiki/Eastern_Lightning. Accessed June 28, 2021.
[4]"World Mission Society Church of God."
https://en.wikipedia.org/wiki/World_Mission_Society_Church_of_God#Beliefs_and_practices. Accessed June 28, 2021.
[5]"Shincheonji Church of Jesus." https://en.wikipedia.org/wiki/Shincheonji_Church_of_Jesus. Accessed June 28, 2020.
[6]"Unification Church." https://en.wikipedia.org/wiki/Unification_Church#Beliefs. Accessed June 28, 2021.
[7]"Organizations Controlled By And/Or Associated With Moon." https://culteducation.com/unif121.html. Accessed June 29, 2021.
[8]Blake, Mariah. "Fall of the House of Moon, The." *New Republic, The.* November 12, 2013.
https://newrepublic.com/article/115512/unification-church-profile-fall-house-moon. Accessed June 29, 2021.
[9]"Eastern Lightning." https://en.wikipedia.org/wiki/Eastern_Lightning 6/29/2021
[10]"What is the Church of Almighty God?" https://www.gotquestions.org/Church-of-Almighty-God.html. Accessed June 29, 2021.
[11]"World Mission Society Church of God." https://en.wikipedia.org/wiki/World_Mission_Society_Church_of_God. Accessed June 30, 2021.
[12]"About Us." *WMSCOG East Coast.* https://wmscog.com/about-the-world-mission-society-church-of-god/. Accessed June 30, 2021.
[13]"What is the World Mission Society Church of God, and What Do They Believe?"
https://www.gotquestions.org/World-Mission-Society-Church-of-God.html. Accessed July 2, 2021.
[14]Harris, Chris. "Former Members Allege New Jersey Church, South Korea-Based World Mission Society Church of God, is Actually a Cult." *People.* December 10, 2015. https://people.com/celebrity/ex-followers-say-south-korean-church-is-mind-control-cult/. Accessed June 30, 2021.

[15]"World Mission Society Church of God." *World Religions and Spirituality Project.* https://wrldrels.org/2017/10/13/world-mission-society-church-of-god/ 7/2/2021
[16]"Olive Tree (Religious Movement)." https://en.wikipedia.org/wiki/Olive_Tree_(religious_movement). Accessed July 2, 2021.
[17]"Shincheonji Chuch of Jesus." https://en.wikipedia.org/wiki/Shincheonji_Church_of_Jesus. Accessed July 1, 2021.
[18]"Shincheonji Church of Jesus – Cult of Christianity." https://www.apologeticsindex.org/14298-shincheonji-cult-of-christianity. Accessed June 8, 2021.
[19]"Shincheonji Church of Jesus." https://en.wikipedia.org/wiki/Shincheonji_Church_of_Jesus 7/1/2021
[20]"Frequently Asked Questions." https://www.scjus.org/faq/. Accessed June 1, 2021.
[21]"Four Korean Heresies." *From Pastor Bhjraj Bhatta.* February 23, 2016. https://vojraj.blogspot.com/2016/02/four-korean-heresies.html. Accessed June 1, 2021.
[22]"Evangelical Baptist Church of Korea." https://en.wikipedia.org/wiki/Evangelical_Baptist_Church_of_Korea. Accessed June 1, 2021.
[23]"Good News Mission." https://en.wikipedia.org/wiki/Good_News_Mission. Accessed July 1, 2021.
[24] Moon, Sung Myung. *Exposition of the Divine Principle.* Chapter 7, 4.12, 4.13, 4.2, 1996 Translation. https://www.unification.net/dp96/dp96-1-7.html#Chap7. Accessed November 22, 2022.
[25]Xiangbin, Yang. *Word Appears in the Flesh, The.* Chapter 26. https://www.holyspiritspeaks.org/interpretation-of-the-twenty-sixth-utterance/. Accessed November 22, 2022.
[26]Kwak, Chung Hwan. *Holy Days and Holidays.* Tradition, Book One, The. http://www.tparents.org/Library/Unification/Books/Tt1/TT1-14.htm. Accessed July 6, 2021.
[27]"Resurrection Day." *WMSCOG East Coast.* https://wmscog.com/resurrection-day/. Accessed July 7, 2021.
[28]"Pledge of the Families and My Pledge." *About Unification Church Tradition.* http://www.tparents.org/Library/Unification/Topics/Traditn/PLEDGE.htm. Accessed July 7, 2021.
[29]Wilson, Andrew. "New Authorized Translation of the Family Pledge, The." *About Unification Church Tradition.* http://www.tparents.org/Library/Unification/Topics/Traditn/FAMPLEDG.htm. Accessed July 7, 2021.
[30]"Lee Man-hee." https://en.wikipedia.org/wiki/Lee_Man-hee. Accessed July 8, 2021.
[31]McKay, Hollie. "Conservative Church Claims South Korea's Government is Persecuting Them by Blaming Members for Coronavirus Spread." *Fox News.* https://www.foxnews.com/world/south-korea-church-coronavirus-spread. Accessed July 8, 2021.
[32]"Shincheonji: Korean Sect Leader Found not Guilty of Breaking Virus Law." *BBC News.* January 13, 2021. https://www.bbc.com/news/world-asia-55642653. Accessed July 8, 2021.
[33] "Unification Church." https://religionfacts.com/unification-church. Accessed July 8, 2021.
[34]Ibid.
[35]Ibid.
[36]"Religious Texts used by the Church of the Almighty God (Eastern Lightning)." https://www.refworld.org/docid/546486eb4.html. Accessed July 8, 2021.
[37]Ibid.
[38]"World Mission Society Church of God – WMSCOG." https://www.apologeticsindex.org/659-world-mission-society-church-of-god. Accessed July 8, 2021.
[39]Ibid.
[40]"What is the Shincheonji Church of Jesus and Who are its Members? And More Importantly, What are its Links to the Coronavirus? *Korea JoongAng Daily.* March 17, 2020. https://koreajoongangdaily.joins.com/news/article/article.aspx?aid=3075027. Accessed July 8, 2021.
[41]Ibid.
[42]Ibid.

EVANGELICAL CHRISTIANITY

[1]"Evangelical Quotes." https://www.azquotes.com/quotes/topics/evangelical.html. Accessed March 29, 2020.
[2]"Church of God (Seventh-Day)." https://en.wikipedia.org/wiki/Church_of_God_(Seventh-Day). Accessed June 4, 2020.
[3]"Evangelicalism." https://en.wikipedia.org/wiki/Evangelicalism. Accessed March 31, 2020.

[4]Riley, Jennifer. "NIV Bible Tops List By Evangelical Leaders." *Christian Post, The.* April 11, 2008. https://www.christianpost.com/news/niv-bible-tops-list-by-evangelical-leaders.html. Accessed March 31, 2020.
[5]Patrick, Mimi. "VBS Pledges: Bible, American, & Christian Flag." *Ministry-to-Children.com.* https://ministry-to-children.com/vbs-pledges-bible-christian-and-american-flag/. Accessed November 22, 2022.
[6]"James C. Dobson Quotes." https://www.goodreads.com/author/quotes/1060839.James_C_Dobson 11/222/2022.
[7]"Rick Warren Quotes." https://www.goodreads.com/author/quotes/711.Rick_Warren. Accessed November 22, 2022.
[8]"Billy Graham Quotes." https://www.goodreads.com/author/quotes/40328.Billy_Graham?page=5. Accessed November 22, 2022.
[9]"Franklin Graham Quotes." https://www.goodreads.com/author/quotes/91937.Franklin_Graham. Accessed November 22, 2022.
[10]"Tim LaHaye Quotes." https://www.christianquotes.info/quotes-by-author/tim-lahaye-quotes/. Accessed November 22, 2022.
[11]"Liberty University." https://en.wikipedia.org/wiki/Liberty_University. Accessed April 1, 2020.
[12] "Evangelical Christianity." http://www.religioustolerance.org/chr_prac2a.htm. Accessed April 1, 2020. 4/1/2020
[13]"Evangelicalism." https://en.wikipedia.org/wiki/Evangelicalism. Accessed March 31, 2020.

Fictitious/Parody Religion

[1]"Gospel of the Flying Spaghetti Monster Quotes, The." https://www.goodreads.com/work/quotes/43552-the-gospel-of-the-flying-spaghetti-monster. Accessed June 9, 2022.
[2]"Parody Religion." https://en.wikipedia.org/wiki/Parody_religion. Accessed July 7, 2022.
[3]Ibid.
[4]"Gospel of the Flying Spaghetti Monster Quotes, The." https://www.goodreads.com/work/quotes/43552-the-gospel-of-the-flying-spaghetti-monster. Accessed November 23, 2022.
[5]"The Dude de Ching Quotes." https://www.goodreads.com/work/quotes/10171113-the-dude-de-ching. Accessed November 23, 2022.
[6]Parry, James. "Kibo's Happynet Manifesto." https://enjoymutable.com/home/kiboshappynetmanifesto. Accessed November 23, 2022.
[7]"Book of the SubGenius Quotes." https://www.goodreads.com/work/quotes/168543-the-book-of-the-subgenius-the-sacred-teachings-of-j-r-bob-dobbs. Accessed November 23, 2022.
[8]"Principia Discordia Or How I Found Goddess and What I Did to Her when I Found Her Quotes." https://www.goodreads.com/work/quotes/86801-principia-discordia-or-how-i-found-goddess-and-what-i-did-to-her-when. Accessed November23, 2022.
[9]"Dudeist Holidays." https://dudeism.com/holidays/. Accessed July 14, 2022.
[10]"Discordian Calendar." https://en.wikipedia.org/wiki/Discordian_calendar. Accessed June 14, 2022.
[11]"Days of Significance." *Temple of the Jedi Order.* https://www.templeofthejediorder.org/40-information/2318-days-of-significance-and-monthly-reflections. Accessed June 14, 2022.
[12]"Matrixism." https://en.wikipedia.org/wiki/. Accessed June 14, 2022.
[13]"X-Day (Church of the SubGenius)." *Holidays That Might Get Overlooked.* July 5, 2016. https://www.facebook.com/HTMGO/posts/x-day-church-of-the-subgenius-x-day-is-a-traditional-part-of-the-church-of-the-s/1088023637924958/. Accessed June 14, 2022.
[14]"The Aerican Empire: Calendar." https://www.aericanempire.com/calendar.html. Accessed June 14, 2022.
[15]Tricycle. "Dudeism=Buddhism?" *Tricycle: The Buddhist Review.* June 10, 2010. https://tricycle.org/trikedaily/dudeismbuddhism/ 6/14/2022
[16]"Church of the SubGenius." https://en.wikipedia.org/wiki/Church_of_the_SubGenius. Accessed June 14, 2022.
[17]"Missionary Church of Kopimism." https://en.wikipedia.org/wiki/Missionary_Church_of_Kopimism. Accessed June 14, 2022.
[18]Cusack, Carole. "Discordianism." *World Religions and Spirituality Project.* https://wrldrels.org/2016/10/08/discordianism/. Accessed June 14, 2022.
[19]"Doctrine of the Order." *Temple of the Jedi Order.* https://www.templeofthejediorder.org/doctrine-of-the-order.

Accessed June 14, 2022.
[20]"Jedi Creed." *Star Wars Fanon*. https://swfanon.fandom.com/wiki/Jedi_Creed. Accessed June 14, 2022.
[21]Doctrine of the Order." *Temple of the Jedi Order*. https://www.templeofthejediorder.org/doctrine-of-the-order. Accessed June 14, 2022.
[22]"Maxims of Jediism." *Temple of the Jedi Order*. https://www.templeofthejediorder.org/40-information/38-21-maxims-of-jediism. Accessed June 14, 2022.
[23]"Matrixism." https://en.wikipedia.org/wiki/. Accessed June 14, 2022
[24]"Iglesia Maradoniana." https://en.wikipedia.org/wiki/Iglesia_Maradoniana. Accessed June 14, 2022.
[25]"Church of Euthanasia." *Church of Euthanasia*. https://www.churchofeuthanasia.org/. Accessed June 14, 2022.
[26]"Commandments." *United Church of Bacon*. https://unitedchurchofbacon.org/our-beliefs/. Accessed June 14, 2022.
[27]"These Five Rituals Will Help You You Shine on Saint Stupid Day, Also Called April Fool's Day." *Interesly*. March 31, 2017. https://www.interesly.com/saint-stupid-april-fools-day/. Accessed June 14, 2022.
[28]"Flying Spaghetti Monster." https://en.wikipedia.org/wiki/Flying_Spaghetti_Monster. Accessed June 14, 2022.
[29]"Jedi Census Phenomenon." https://en.wikipedia.org/wiki/Jedi_census_phenomenon. Accessed June 14, 2022.
[30]"Discordianism." https://en.wikipedia.org/wiki/Discordianism. Accessed June 14, 2022.
[31]"Church of the SubGenius." https://en.wikipedia.org/wiki/Church_of_the_SubGenius. Accessed June 14, 2022.
[32]Ibid.
[33]"Discordianism." https://en.wikipedia.org/wiki/Discordianism. Accessed June 14, 2022.
[34]Ibid.
[35]"Church of Euthanasia." https://en.wikipedia.org/wiki/Church_of_Euthanasia. Accessed June 14, 2022.
[36]"Frequently Asked Questions About 'Intelligent Design.' *ACLU*. https://www.aclu.org/other/frequently-asked-questions-about-intelligent-design. Accessed June 14, 2022.
[37]"Omphalos Hypothesis." https://en.wikipedia.org/wiki/Omphalos_hypothesis#Criticisms. Accessed June 14, 2022.
[38]"Discordianism." https://en.wikipedia.org/wiki/Discordianism. Accessed June 14, 2022.
[39]"Poe's Law." https://en.wikipedia.org/wiki/Poe%27s_law. Accessed June 14, 2022.
[40]"Russell's Teapot." https://en.wikipedia.org/wiki/Russell%27s_teapot. Accessed June 14, 2022.

GNOSTICISM/NEO-GNOSTICISM

[1]*The Gospel of Philip*. http://gnosis.org/naghamm/gop.html. Accessed September 19, 2020.
[2]"Gnosticism." https://en.wikipedia.org/wiki/Gnosticism. Accessed September 22, 2020.
[3]"Mandaeism." https://en.wikipedia.org/wiki/Mandaeism. Accessed September 22, 2020.
[4]"Hermeticism." https://en.wikipedia.org/wiki/Hermeticism. Accessed September 22, 2020.
[5]"Gnosticism." https://en.wikipedia.org/wiki/Gnosticism. Accessed September 22, 2020.
[6]"Naassene Fragment." https://en.wikipedia.org/wiki/Naassene_Fragment. November 23, 2022.
[7]"Apocryphon of James, The." *Gnostic Society Library, The*. http://gnosis.org/naghamm/jam.html. Accessed November 23, 2022.
[8]"Sophia of Jesus Christ, The." *Gnostic Society Library, The*. http://gnosis.org/naghamm/sjc.html. Accessed November 23, 2022.
[9]"Acts of Peter and the Twelve Apostles, The." *Gnostic Society Library, The*. http://gnosis.org/naghamm/actp.html. Accessed November 23, 2022.
[10]"Hypostasis of the Archons, The." *Gnostic Society Library, The*. http://gnosis.org/naghamm/hypostas.html. Accessed November 23, 2022.
[11]"Hymn of the Pearl." https://en.wikipedia.org/wiki/Hymn_of_the_Pearl. Accessed November 23, 2022.
[12]"On the Origin of the World." *Gnostic Society Library, The*. http://gnosis.org/naghamm/origin.html. Accessed November 23, 2022.
[13]Mabry, John R. "Considering the Gnostic Sacraments." http://www.apocryphile.org/jrm/articles/gnostic.html. Accessed September 28, 2020.
[14]"Creeds of Gnostic Churches." *Hermetic Library*. https://hermetic.com/dionysos/creed. Accessed September 19, 2020.
[15]Bell, Matthew. "These Iraqi Immigrants Revere John the Baptist, but They're not Christians." *World, The*. October

6, 2016. https://www.pri.org/stories/2016-10-06/these-iraqi-immigrants-worship-john-baptist-theyre-not-christians. Accessed September 29, 2020.
[16]Meithras, T. "Glossary of Gnostic Terms, A." *Ecclesia Gnostica Universalis.* https://www.ecclesiagnosticauniversalis.org/a-glossary-of-gnostic-terms/. Accessed September 30, 2020.

HINDUISM

[1]Subramuniyaswami, Satguru Sivaya. "Hinduism, the Greatest Religion in the World." *What is Hinduism?* https://www.himalayanacademy.com/media/books/what-is-hinduism/web/ch01a.html. Accessed April 21, 2020.
[2]"Hinduism." https://en.wikipedia.org/wiki/Hinduism. Accessed April 18, 2020.
[3]Subramuniyaswami, Satguru Sivaya. "Hinduism, the Greatest Religion in the World." *What is Hinduism?* https://www.himalayanacademy.com/media/books/what-is-hinduism/web/ch01a.html. Accessed April 21, 2020.
[4]"Vaishnavism." http://www.religionfacts.com/vaishnavism. Accessed April 18, 2020.
[5]"Shaivism." http://www.religionfacts.com/shaivism. Accessed April 18, 2020.
[6]"Shaktism." *Encyclopedia Britannica.* https://www.britannica.com/topic/Shaktism. Accessed April 20, 2020.
[7]"Hindu Denominations." https://en.wikipedia.org/wiki/Hindu_denominations. Accessed April 20, 2020.
[8]Ibid.
[9]"Sikhs." https://en.wikipedia.org/wiki/Sikhs 4/16/2020
[10]"Vedas, The." Hinduism. https://www.sacred-texts.com/hin/. Accessed April 20, 2020.
[11]"Wisdom of the Rig Veda, The." https://www.onelittleangel.com/wisdom/quotes/book.asp?mc=291. Accessed November 30, 2020.
[12]"Agama." *Encyclopedia Britannica.* https://www.britannica.com/topic/Agama-Hindu-literature. Accessed April 20, 2020.
[13]"Bhagavad Gita Quotes." https://www.goodreads.com/author/quotes/8126474.Bhagavad_Gita. Accessed November 30, 2022.
[14]Ibid.
[15]"Hindu Texts." https://en.wikipedia.org/wiki/Hindu_texts. Accessed April 23, 2020.
[16]"3 Seriously Relevant Life Lessons We Can Learn From the Bhagavad Gita." *Youaligned.* https://www.yogiapproved.com/om/3-life-lessons-we-can-learn-from-the-bhagavad-gita/. Accessed April 23, 2020.
[17]Veylanswami, Satguru Bodhinatha. "Importance of the Agamas. Willpower and Cognition, The." https://www.himalayanacademy.com/view/bd_2011-01-21_importance-of-agamas. Accessed November 30, 2022.
[18]"Holi." https://en.wikipedia.org/wiki/Holi. Accessed April 20, 2020.
[19]"Maha Shivaratri." https://en.wikipedia.org/wiki/Maha_Shivaratri. Accessed April 20, 2020.
[20]"Raksha Bandhan." https://en.wikipedia.org/wiki/Raksha_Bandhan. Accessed April 20, 2020.
[21]"Ganesh Chaturthi." https://en.wikipedia.org/wiki/Ganesh_Chaturthi. Accessed April 20, 2020.
[22]"Vijayadashami." https://en.wikipedia.org/wiki/Vijayadashami. Accessed April 20, 2020.
[23]"Krishna Janmashtami." https://en.wikipedia.org/wiki/Krishna_Janmashtami. Accessed April 20, 2020.
[24]"Hindu Symbols." https://www.ancient-symbols.com/hindu-symbols.html. Accessed April 20, 2020.
[25]"Hinduism: Hinduism and the Family." https://family.jrank.org/pages/768/Hinduism-Hinduism-Family.html. Accessed April 20, 2020.
[26]"Monasticism." https://en.wikipedia.org/wiki/Monasticism. Accessed April 20, 2020.
[27]Subramuniyaswami, Satguru Sivaya. "Hinduism, the Greatest Religion in the World." *What is Hinduism?* https://www.himalayanacademy.com/media/books/what-is-hinduism/web/ch01a.html. Accessed April 22, 2020.
[28]Holy Cities of Hinduism, The." *WorldAtlas.* https://www.worldatlas.com/articles/the-holy-cities-of-hinduism.html. Accessed April 20, 2020.
[29]"International Society for Krishna Consciousness." https://en.wikipedia.org/wiki/International_Society_for_Krishna_Consciousness. Accessed April 20, 2020.
[30]"Hinduism By Country." https://en.wikipedia.org/wiki/Hinduism_by_country. Accessed April 20, 2020.

[31]"Key Terms in Hinduism." https://www.wabashcenter.wabash.edu/syllabi/r/robbins/1JM8Q-PHIL203/HinduTerms.html. Accessed April 20, 2020.
[32]"Glossary of Hindu Terms, A." http://www.mmiweb.org.uk/publications/glossary/glossaries/hindglos.html. Accessed April 20, 2020. 4/20/2020
[33]"Japamala." https://en.wikipedia.org/wiki/Japamala. Accessed April 20, 2020.
[34]"Key Terms in Hinduism." https://www.wabashcenter.wabash.edu/syllabi/r/robbins/1JM8Q-PHIL203/HinduTerms.html. Accessed April 20, 2020.
[35]"Vedanga." https://en.wikipedia.org/wiki/Vedanga. Accessed April 20, 2020.

INDIGENOUS RELIGION

[1]"First Nations Quotes." https://www.goodreads.com/quotes/tag/first-nations. Accessed July 26, 2022.
[2]"Native American Religion." https://en.wikipedia.org/wiki/Native_American_religion. Accessed July 27, 2022.
[3]"Traditional Folk Religions: Indigenous Belief Systems." https://libguides.spsd.org/worldreligions/folk. Accessed July 27, 2022.
[4]"Indigenous Peoples." https://en.wikipedia.org/wiki/Indigenous_peoples. Accessed August 2, 2022.
[5]"List of Indigenous Peoples." https://en.wikipedia.org/wiki/List_of_Indigenous_peoples#Circumpolar. Accessed August 4, 2022.
[6]"Henotheism." https://en.wikipedia.org/wiki/Henotheism. Accessed August 9, 2022.
[7]"Monotheism." https://en.wikipedia.org/wiki/Monotheism. Accessed August 9, 2022.
[8]"Shamanism." https://en.wikipedia.org/wiki/Shamanism. Accessed August 10, 2022.
[9]"Neoshamanism." https://en.wikipedia.org/wiki/Neoshamanism. Accessed August 11, 2022.
[10]"First Nations Version: An Indigenous Translation of the New Testament." https://www.amazon.com/First-Nations-Version-Indigenous-Translation/dp/0830813500. Accessed August 11, 2022.
[11]"Alaska Native Religion." ttps://en.wikipedia.org/wiki/Alaska_Native_religion. Accessed August 11, 2022.
[12]"Indigenous Peoples." https://www.worldbank.org/en/topic/indigenouspeoples. Accessed August 11, 2022.
[13]"Native American Religion." https://en.wikipedia.org/wiki/Native_American_religion. Accessed August 11, 2022.
[14]Ibid.
[15]Ibid.
[16]"Native American Church." https://en.wikipedia.org/wiki/Native_American_Church. Accessed August 11, 2022.
[17]"Definition of Smudging, A." *Indigenous Corporate Training, Inc.* February 16, 2017. https://www.ictinc.ca/blog/a-definition-of-smudging. Accessed August 11, 2022.
[18]"Sweat Lodge." https://en.wikipedia.org/wiki/Sweat_lodge. Accessed August 11, 2022.
[19]Smith, Derek G. "Religion and Spirituality of Indigenous Peoples in Canada." *Canadian Encyclopedia, The.* December 4, 2011. https://www.thecanadianencyclopedia.ca/en/article/religion-of-aboriginal-people. Accessed August 11, 2022.
[20]Ibid.
[21]Ibid.

ISLAM

[1]ul-Bari, Fath. "Hadith Quotes." Page 102, Vol. 1.
[2]"Islam." https://en.wikipedia.org/wiki/Islam. Accessed April 7, 2020.
[3]"Islamic Sects: Major Schools, Notable Branches." *Information is Beautiful.* https://informationisbeautiful.net/visualizations/islamic-sects-schools-branches-movements/. Accessed April 7, 2020.
[4]"Sufism." https://en.wikipedia.org/wiki/Sufism. Accessed April 7, 2020.
[5]"Druze." *Encyclopedia Britannica.* https://www.britannica.com/topic/Druze. Accessed April 9, 2020.
[6]"Bábism." https://en.wikipedia.org/wiki/B%C3%A1bism. Accessed April 9, 2020.
[7]"Nation of Islam." *Encyclopedia Britannica.* https://www.britannica.com/topic/Nation-of-Islam. Accessed April 7, 2020.
[8]"Islam By Country." https://en.wikipedia.org/wiki/Islam_by_country. Accessed April 7, 2020.

[9]"Quran." https://en.wikipedia.org/wiki/Quran. Accessed April 7, 2020.
[10]Surah Fatiha 1:1-7. https://myislam.org/surah-fatiha/. Accessed November 30, 2022.
[11]Surah Mursalat 77:1-50. https://myislam.org/surah-mursalat/, Accessed November 30, 2022.
[12]"Islam." https://en.wikipedia.org/wiki/. Accessed April 9, 2020.
[13]An-Nawawi's 40 Hadith, Hadith No, 2. https://sunnah.com/nawawi40. Accessed November 30, 2022.
[14]"Laylat al-Qadr." https://en.wikipedia.org/wiki/Laylat_al-Qadr. Accessed April 9, 2020.
[15]"Sharia." https://en.wikipedia.org/wiki/Sharia. Accessed April 9, 2020.
[16]El-Zibdeh, Nour. "Understanding Muslim Fasting Practices." *Today's Dietician*. Vol. 11, No. 8 P. 56. https://www.todaysdietitian.com/newarchives/072709p56.shtml. Accessed April 9, 2020.
[17]Eardley, Nick. "What is Halal Meat?" *BBC News*. May 12, 2014. https://www.bbc.com/news/uk-27324224. Accessed April 9, 2020.
[18]"Islam by Country." https://en.wikipedia.org/wiki/Islam_by_country. Accessed April 9, 2020.

JAINISM

[1]"Jainism Quotes." https://www.goodreads.com/quotes/tag/jainism. Accessed November 2020, 2020.
[2]"Janism." https://en.wikipedia.org/wiki/Jainism. Accessed November 20, 2020.
[3]"Lord Mahavir and Jain Religion." https://www.angelfire.com/co/jainism/mahavir.html Accessed November 30, 2020.
[4]"Jainism." https://en.wikipedia.org/wiki/Jainism#Asceticism_and_monasticism. Accessed November 30, 2020.
[5]"Jainism." *Encyclopedia Britannica*. https://www.britannica.com/topic/Jainism. Accessed November 30, 2020.
[6]Ibid.
[7]"Digambara." https://en.wikipedia.org/wiki/Digambara. Accessed November 30, 2020.
[8]Ibid.
[9]"Jainism." *Encyclopedia Britannica*. https://www.britannica.com/topic/Jainism/Festivals#ref59025. Accessed November 30, 2020.11/30/2020
[10]"Mahavira Quotes." https://www.brainyquote.com/authors/mahavira-quotes. Accessed November 30, 2022.
[11]"Digambara." https://en.wikipedia.org/wiki/Digambara. Accessed November 30, 2020.
[12]"Jainism." *Encyclopedia Britannica*. https://www.britannica.com/topic/Jainism. Accessed November 30, 2020.
[13]"Holy Kalpa Sutra." https://www.ishwar.com/jainism/holy_kalpa_sutra/texts02.html. Accessed November 30, 2022.
[14]Holy Kalpa Sutra." https://www.ishwar.com/jainism/holy_kalpa_sutra/texts07.html. Accessed November 30, 2022.
[15]"12 Vows." https://sites.fas.harvard.edu/~pluralsm/affiliates/jainism/jainedu/12vows.htm. Accessed November 30, 2020.
[16]Ibid.
[17]"Holidays." Jainism. https://aboutjainism.weebly.com/holidays.html. Accessed December 1, 2020.
[18]"Paryushana." https://en.wikipedia.org/wiki/Paryushana. Accessed December 1, 2020.
[19]"Jain Law." https://en.wikipedia.org/wiki/Jain_law. Accessed December 1, 2020.
[20]"Jainism." *New World Encyclopedia*. https://www.newworldencyclopedia.org/entry/Jainism. Accessed December 1, 2020.
[21]"Jainism." *New World Encyclopedia*. https://www.newworldencyclopedia.org/entry/Jainism. Accessed December 1, 2020.
[22]Ibid.
[23]Ibid.
[24]"Svetambara." https://en.wikipedia.org/wiki/%C5%9Av%C4%93t%C4%81mbara. Accessed December 1, 2020.
[25]"Janism." https://en.wikipedia.org/wiki/Jainism. Accessed December 1, 2020.
[26] Perkins, McKenzie. "Jainism Glossary: Definitions, Beliefs, Practices." *Learn Religions*. March 25, 2019. https://www.learnreligions.com/glossary-of-jainism-definitions-beliefs-practices-4583999. Accessed December 1, 2020.

JEHOVAH'S WITNESSES

[1]*Knowledge that Leads to Everlasting Life.* Chapter 5, "Whose Worship Does God Accept?" Brooklyn, New York: The Watchtower Bible and Tract Society of New York, Inc., 1995. p. 51

[2]What is the Holy Spirit? https://www.jw.org/en/bible-teachings/questions/what-is-the-holy-spirit/. Accessed April 24, 2020.

[3]"Charles Taze Russell." https://en.wikipedia.org/wiki/Charles_Taze_Russell. Accessed April 27, 2020.

[4]"Jehovah's Witnesses Splinter Groups."
https://en.wikipedia.org/wiki/Jehovah%27s_Witnesses_splinter_groups. Accessed April 27, 2020.

[5]Ibid.

[6]"God's Kingdom Society." *Investigator 170*, September 2016.
http://ed5015.tripod.com/JwGKSGodsKingdomSociety170.html. Accessed April 27, 2020.

[7]"Jehovah's Witnesses Splinter Groups."
https://en.wikipedia.org/wiki/Jehovah%27s_Witnesses_splinter_groups. Accessed April 27, 2020.

[8]Baldas, Tresa. "Ex-Jehovah's Witnesses Break Silence on Shunning: My Mother Treats Me Like I'm Dead.'" *Detroit Free Press.* Accessed March 18, 2018.
https://www.freep.com/story/news/local/michigan/2018/03/18/jehovahs-witnesses-murder-suicide-keego-harbor/409695002/. Accessed April 27, 2020.

[9]John 1:1-2. https://www.jw.org/en/library/bible/study-bible/books/john/1/. Accessed December 15, 2022.

[10]John 8:58. https://www.jw.org/en/library/bible/study-bible/books/john/8/. Accessed December 15, 2022.

[11]Colossians 1:15-20. https://www.jw.org/en/library/bible/study-bible/books/colossians/1/. Accessed December 15, 2022.

[12]"Watchtower, The." https://en.wikipedia.org/wiki/The_Watchtower. Accessed April 28, 2020.

[13]"Jehovah's Witnesses Practices." https://en.wikipedia.org/wiki/Jehovah%27s_Witnesses_practices. Accessed April 28, 2020.

[14]Ibid.

[15]"Organizational Structure of Jehovah's Witnesses."
https://en.wikipedia.org/wiki/Organizational_structure_of_Jehovah%27s_Witnesses. Accessed April 29, 2020.

[16] *Watchtower, The.* June 1, 1952. p 338. https://towerwatch.com/about-jehovahs-witnesses/the-ever-changing-beliefs-of-the-watchtower/. Accessed December 15, 2022.

[17] *Watchtower, The.* August 1, 1965. p. 479 https://towerwatch.com/about-jehovahs-witnesses/the-ever-changing-beliefs-of-the-watchtower/. Accessed December 15, 2022.

[18] *You Can Live Forever in Paradise on Earth.* Brooklyn, New York: The Watchtower Bible and Tract Society of Pennsylvania, 1989. https://towerwatch.com/about-jehovahs-witnesses/the-ever-changing-beliefs-of-the-watchtower/. Accessed December 15, 2022.

[19] "Honor the Son, Jehovah's Chief Agent." *Watchtower, The.* February 1, 1991. p. 17.
https://towerwatch.com/about-jehovahs-witnesses/the-ever-changing-beliefs-of-the-watchtower/. Accessed December 15, 2022.

[20]"A Corresponding Ransom for All." *Watchtower, The.* February 15, 1991. p. 14. https://towerwatch.com/about-jehovahs-witnesses/the-ever-changing-beliefs-of-the-watchtower/. Accessed December 15, 2022.

[21]Russell, Charles Taze. *Studies in Scriptures Series , Vol, 4: The Day of Vengeance.* (1897 ed.). p.621.
https://www.jwfacts.com/watchtower/failed-1914-predictions.php. Accessed December 19, 2022.

[22]Russell, Charles Taze. *Studies in the Scriptures, Vol. 2: The Time is At Hand* (1911 ed.). p.239.
https://www.jwfacts.com/watchtower/failed-1914-predictions.php. Accessed December 19, 2022.

[23]Russell, Charles Taze. *Studies in the Scriptures, Vol. 2: The Time is At Hand* (1889 ed.) pp. 77-78.
https://www.jwfacts.com/watchtower/failed-1914-predictions.php. Accessed December 19, 2022.

[24]Russell, Charles Taze. *Studies in the Scriptures, Vol. 3: Thy Kingdom Come* (1891 ed.) p.153.
https://www.jwfacts.com/watchtower/failed-1914-predictions.php. Accessed December 19, 2022.

[25]*Zion's Watch Tower.* July 15, 1894. p.226 (reprints 1677). https://www.jwfacts.com/watchtower/failed-1914-predictions.php Accessed December 19, 2022.

[26]Russell, Charles Taze. *Studies in the Scriptures, Vol. 2: The Time is At Hand* (1911 ed.) p.99.
https://www.jwfacts.com/watchtower/failed-1914-predictions.php Accessed December 19, 2022.

[27]*Zion's Watch Tower.* June 15, 1911, p.190 (reprints p.4842). https://www.jwfacts.com/watchtower/failed-

1914-predictions.php. Accessed December 19, 2022.
[28]Russell, Charles Taze. *Studies in the Scriptures, Vol. 3: Thy Kingdom Come* (1911 ed.)
https://www.jwfacts.com/watchtower/failed-1914-predictions.php, Accessed December 19, 2022.
[29]Russell, Charles Taze. *Studies in the Scriptures, Vol. 4: The Day of Vengeance* (1911 ed.). p.547.
https://www.jwfacts.com/watchtower/failed-1914-predictions.php. Accessed December 19, 2022.
[30]*Zion's Watch Tower* July 15, 1894, p.226. https://www.jwfacts.com/watchtower/failed-1914-predictions.php. Accessed December 19, 2022.
[31]*Millions Now Living Will Never Die*, International Bible Students Association, 1920. P. 105
https://www.jwfacts.com/watchtower/failed-1914-predictions.php. Accessed December 19, 2022.
[32]*Life Everlasting—In Freedom of the Sons of God*. Brooklyn, New York: Watch Tower Bible & Tract Society of Pennsylvania, 1966. Pp. 28,29.
https://www.jwfacts.com/watchtower/failed-1914-predictions.php. Accessed December 19, 2022.
[33]Doyle, D. John. "Jehovah's Witnesses and Artificial Blood." *Canadian Medical Association Journal*, December 5, 2000. 163(5): pp. 495-496. https://www.ncbi.nlm.nih.gov/pmc/articles/PMC80440/. Accessed April 30, 2020.
[34]"Jehovah's Witnesses and Congregational Discipline."
https://en.wikipedia.org/wiki/Jehovah%27s_Witnesses_and_congregational_discipline. Accessed April 30, 2020.
[35]"Corporations of Jehovah's Witnesses."
https://en.wikipedia.org/wiki/Corporations_of_Jehovah%27s_Witnesses. Accessed April 30, 2020.
[36]Lipka, Michael. "Closer Look at Jehovah's Witnesses Living in the US, The." *Pew Research Center*. April 26, 2016. https://www.pewresearch.org/fact-tank/2016/04/26/a-closer-look-at-jehovahs-witnesses-living-in-the-u-s/. Accessed April 30, 2020.
[37]Whyte, Lloyd N. Jehovah's Witnesses: Glossary Words and Concepts." *North American Mission Board*. April 1977. https://www.namb.net/apologetics-blog/jehovaha-s-witnesses-glossary-words-and-concepts/. Accessed April 30, 2020.
[38]"Jehovah's Witnesses Glossary." https://rationalwiki.org/wiki/Jehovah%27s_Witnesses_glossary. Accessed April 30, 2020.
[39]Whyte, Lloyd N. Jehovah's Witnesses: Glossary Words and Concepts." *North American Mission Board*. April 1977. https://www.namb.net/apologetics-blog/jehovaha-s-witnesses-glossary-words-and-concepts/. Accessed April 30, 2020.
[40]Nuccio, Sylvanie. "55 Loaded Language Terms ONLY Jehovah's Witnesses Use and Understand." January 12, 2018. https://medium.com/@SylvianeNuccio/55-loaded-language-terms-only-jehovahs-witnesses-use-and-understand-2e89e8a906dd. Accessed April 30, 2020.
[41]Ibid.
[42]"Jehovah's Witnesses Glossary." https://rationalwiki.org/wiki/Jehovah%27s_Witnesses_glossary. Accessed April 30, 2020.

JUDAISM

[1]Dayan, Moshe. *Jerusalem Report* (1998).
https://www.jewishvirtuallibrary.org/moshe-dayan-quotes-on-judaism-and-israel. Accessed 2/20/2020.
[2]Genesis 12:1-3. https://www.chabad.org/library/bible_cdo/aid/8176. Accessed December 20, 2022.
[3]"Samaritans." https://en.wikipedia.org/wiki/Samaritans. Accessed June 15, 2022.
[4]"2018 Word Jewish Population." Berman Jewish Databank. https://www.jewishdatabank.org/databank/search-results/study/1060. Accessed February 21, 2020.
[5]"Jewish Holidays." https://en.wikipedia.org/wiki/Jewish_holidays#Rosh_Chodesh%E2%80%94The_New_Month. Accessed June 9, 2020.
[6]"Jewish Holidays & Celebrations – List." Peninsula Jewish Community Center. https://pjcc.org/jewish-life/jewish-holidays-explained/. Accessed June 9, 2020.
[7]Deuteronomy 6:4. https://www.chabad.org/library/bible_cdo/aid/9970. Accessed December 21, 2022.
[8]Tractate Moed Katan: Chapter 2 (Regulations Concerning Labor, Mourning, and Buying and Doing Business in that way, and Also in the Intermediate Days. *Mishna, Gemara*. Jewish Virtual Library.

https://www.jewishvirtuallibrary.org/tractate-moed-katan-chapter-2. Accessed December 21, 2022.
[9]Tractate Bava Metzia, Chapter 2: Laws Relating to Found Articles, Which may or may not be Kept Without Proclmation, and how Found Articles Shall be Cared for, etc." *Mishna VI, Gemara.* Jewish Virtual Library. https://www.jewishvirtuallibrary.org/tractate-bava-metzia-chapter-2. Accessed December 21, 2022.
[10]Chapter X: Sundry Regulations Concerning the Sabbath. https://www.sacred-texts.com/jud/t02/eru14.htm#page_227. Accessed December 21, 2022.
[11]"Key Findings From the Global Religious Futures Project." *Pew Research Center.* December 21, 2022. http://www.globalreligiousfutures.org/religions/jews. Accessed February 24, 2020.
[12]"Study Finds Orthodox Have Most Synagogues in US." August 16, 2002. https://www.jweekly.com/2002/08/16/study-finds-orthodox-have-most-synagogues-in-u-s/. Accessed February 24, 2020.

LIBERAL CHRISTIANITY

[1]McGrath, James F. "Year in Quotes on Posters, The." *Religion Prof: The Blog of James F. McGrath.* December 30, 2012. https://www.patheos.com/blogs/religionprof/2012/12/the-year-in-quotes-on-posters.html. Accessed June 7, 2022.
[2]"Liberal Christianity." https://en.wikipedia.org/wiki/Liberal_Christianity. Accessed July 6, 2022.
[3]Todd, Douglas. "Liberal Christianity: Ten Things to Know About This 'Middle Way.' Vancouver Sun. June 7, 2014. https://vancouversun.com/news/staff-blogs/liberal-christianity-ten-things-worth-knowing-about-this-third-way. Accessed June 6, 2022.
[4]"Liberal Christianity." https://en.wikipedia.org/wiki/Liberal_Christianity. Accessed June 8, 2022.
[5]"Liberation Theology." https://en.wikipedia.org/wiki/Liberation_theology. Accessed June 8, 2022.
[6]"Progressive Christianity." https://en.wikipedia.org/wiki/Progressive_Christianity. Accessed June 8, 2022.
[7]"Walter Rauschenbusch Quotes." https://en.wikiquote.org/wiki/Walter_Rauschenbusch. Accessed December 21, 2022.
[8]"Harry Emerson Fosdick Quotes." https://www.brainyquote.com/authors/harry-emerson-fosdick-quotes. Accessed December 21, 2022.
[9]"John Shelby Spong Quotes." https://www.goodreads.com/author/quotes/45659.John_Shelby_Spong. Accessed December 21, 2022.
[10]"John Dominic Crossan Quotes." https://www.goodreads.com/author/quotes/43692. Accessed December 21, 2022.
[11]"Hans Kung Quotes." https://www.goodreads.com/author/quotes/50004.Hans_K_ng. Accessed December 21, 2022.
[12]"Marcus J. Borg Quotes." https://www.goodreads.com/author/quotes/22721.Marcus_J_Borg. Accessed December 21, 2022.
[13]"Robin Meyers Quotes." https://www.goodreads.com/author/quotes/15501.Robin_Meyers. Accessed December 21, 2022.
[14]"Gustavo Guiterrez Quotes." https://www.goodreads.com/author/quotes/151379.Gustavo_Guti_rrez. Accessed December 21, 2022.
[15]"Riverside Church." https://en.wikipedia.org/wiki/Riverside_Church. Accessed June 9, 2022.
[16]"Liberals Who are Christian." *Pew Research Center.* https://www.pewresearch.org/religion/religious-landscape-study/christians/christian/political-ideology/liberal/. Accessed June 9, 2022.

MORMONISM

[1]*Teachings of the Prophet Joseph Smith,* sel. Joseph Fielding Smith (1976), p. 98. https://history.churchofjesuschrist.org/faq/joseph-smith/quote-index?lang=eng. Accessed May 8, 2020.
[2]Lund, John L. "Council in Heaven." https://eom.byu.edu/index.php/Council_in_Heaven. Accessed May 8, 2020.
[3]"Adam and Eve (Latter-Day Saint Movement." https://en.wikipedia.org/wiki/Adam_and_Eve_(Latter_Day_Saint_movement). Accessed May 8, 2020.
[4]"Restoration Branches." https://en.wikipedia.org/wiki/Restoration_branches. Accessed May 13, 2020. 5/13/2020
[5]"Community of Christ." https://en.wikipedia.org/wiki/Community_of_Christ. Accessed May 13, 2020.

[6]"Mormon Fundamentalism."
https://en.wikipedia.org/wiki/Mormon_fundamentalism#Independent_Mormon_fundamentalists. Accessed May 13, 2020.
[7]"New Almanac Offers Look at the World of Mormon Membership."
https://www.washingtonpost.com/national/religion/new-almanac-offers-look-at-the-world-of-mormon-membership/2014/01/13/7beb7888-7c86-11e3-97d3-b9925ce2c57b_story.html. Accessed May 13, 2020.
[8]"Restoration Branches." https://en.wikipedia.org/wiki/Restoration_branches. Accessed May 13, 2020.
[9]"Mormons" https://en.wikipedia.org/wiki/Mormons. Accessed May 13, 2020.
[10]Alma 7:23-24. "7 Best book of Mormon Quotes (& Answers to Life's Questions.)" *Or So She Says...* June 15, 2022. https://oneshetwoshe.com/best-book-of-mormon-quotes/. Accessed December 21, 2022.
[11]Helaman 5:12. Ibid.
[12]Moroni 10:3-5. Ibid.
[13]"Doctrine and Covenants of the Church of Jesus Christ of Latter-Day Saints Quotes, The."
https://www.goodreads.com/work/quotes/2978666-the-doctrine-and-covenants-of-the-church-of-jesus-christ-of-latter-day-s. Accessed December 21, 2022.
[14]"Pearl of Great Price (Latter-Day Saints), The."
https://en.wikipedia.org/wiki/Pearl_of_Great_Price_(Latter_Day_Saints). Accessed May 13, 2020.
15 Matthews, Robert J. "Why Don't We Use the Inspired Version of the bible in the church? Would it be Helpful to Me to Read it?" *The Church of Jesus Christ of Latter-day Saints.*
https://www.churchofjesuschrist.org/study/new-era/1977/04/q-and-a-questions-and-answers/why-dont-we-use-the-inspired-version-of-the-bible-in-the-church?lang=eng. Accessed May 13, 2020.
[16]"Pearl of Great Price Quotes." https://www.goodreads.com/work/quotes/1374254-pearl-of-great-price. Accessed December 21, 2022.
[17]Holy Books of the Church of Jesus Christ of Latter-day Saints, The." *BBC.* October 8, 2009.
https://www.bbc.co.uk/religion/religions/mormon/texts/holybooks.shtml. Accessed May 13, 2020.
[18]Genesis 1:1-5, *Inspired Version* (Joseph Smith, Jr.). https://www.centerplace.org/hs/iv/genesis.htm. Accessed December 21, 2022.
[19]"Melchizedek Priesthood (Latter-Day Saints)."
https://en.wikipedia.org/wiki/Melchizedek_priesthood_(Latter_Day_Saints)#Priesthood_leadership_callings. Accessed May 13, 2020.
[20]"Endowment (Mormonism." https://en.wikipedia.org/wiki/Endowment_(Mormonism). Accessed May 13, 2020.
[21]"Mormon Holy Days." *BBC.* October 6, 2009.
https://www.bbc.co.uk/religion/religions/mormon/holydays/holydays_1.shtml. Accessed May 14, 2020. 5/14/2020
[22]Olaveson, Breanna. "20 Most Popular LDS Symbols and Images." *UtahValley 360.* February 20, 2014.
https://utahvalley360.com/2014/02/20/20-popular-lds-images-from-stripling-warriors-to-forget-me-nots/. Accessed May 14, 2020.
[23]"Mormon Articles of Faith in Full, Describing Mormon Beleifs, The." *BBC.* October 2, 2009.
https://www.bbc.co.uk/religion/religions/mormon/beliefs/articles.shtml. Accessed May 14, 2020.
[24]"Church of Jesus Christ of Latter-Day Saints, The."
https://en.wikipedia.org/wiki/The_Church_of_Jesus_Christ_of_Latter-day_Saints. Accessed May 14, 2020.
[25]"Mormonism and Christianity." https://en.wikipedia.org/wiki/Mormonism_and_Christianity. Accessed May 14, 2020.
[26]"Apostolic United Brethren." https://en.wikipedia.org/wiki/Apostolic_United_Brethren. Accessed May 14, 2020.
[27]Goodman, Stephen. "How Many Practicing Members of the Church of Jesus Christ of Latter-Day Saints are there in the World?" *Quora.* https://www.quora.com/How-many-practicing-members-of-the-Church-of-Jesus-Christ-of-Latter-day-Saints-are-there-in-the-world. Accessed May 13, 2020.
[28]"Atonement." *Mormonism Research Ministry.* https://www.mrm.org/atonement-definition. Accessed December 21, 2022.
[29]"Mormon Lingo 101: Top Basic Words and Phrases Unique to Mormonism." *Grace for Grace.* August 30, 2012.
https://graceforgrace.com/2012/08/30/mormon-lingo-101-top-basic-words-and-phrases-unique-to-

mormonism/. Accessed December 21, 2022.
[30]"Church of the Devil Definition." *Mormonism Research Ministry.* https://www.mrm.org/church-devil. Accessed December 21, 2022.
[31]"Creation Definition." https://www.mrm.org/creation. Accessed December 21, 2022.
[32]"Mormon Lingo 101: Top Basic Words and Phrases Unique to Mormonism." *Grace for Grace.* August 30, 2012. https://graceforgrace.com/2012/08/30/mormon-lingo-101-top-basic-words-and-phrases-unique-to-mormonism/. Accessed December 21, 2022
[33]"Hosanna Shout." *Mormonism Research Ministry.* https://www.mrm.org/hosanna-shout. Accessed December 21, 2022.
[34]"New Jerusalem." *Mormonism Research Ministry.* https://www.mrm.org/new-jerusalem. Accessed December 21, 2022.

NEW AGE MOVEMENT
[1]Slick, Matt. "Interesting Quotes from New Age Sources." *CARM.* December 5, 2008. https://carm.org/new-age-interesting-quotes. Accessed May 27, 2020.
[2]"Astrological Age." https://en.wikipedia.org/wiki/Astrological_age. Accessed May 28, 2020.
[3]"I AM Activity." https://en.wikipedia.org/wiki/%22I_AM%22_Activity. Accessed May 28, 2020.
[4]"Human Potential Movement." https://en.wikipedia.org/wiki/Human_Potential_Movement. Accessed May 28, 2020.
[5]"Transcendental Meditation Cost." https://www.thumbtack.com/p/transcendental-meditation-cost. Accessed May 28, 2020.
[6]"Transcendental Meditation." https://en.wikipedia.org/wiki/Transcendental_Meditation. Accessed May 28, 2020.
[7]"What is the TM Technique?" *TM.* https://www.tm.org/#what-is-tm. Accessed May 28, 2020.
[8]"Realizing the New Age." *Encyclopedia Britannica.* https://www.britannica.com/topic/New-Age-movement/Realizing-the-New-Age. Accessed May 30, 2020.
[9]"New Age Movement."
https://en.wikipedia.org/wiki/New_Age#Decline_or_transformation?:_1990%E2%80%93present. Accessed May 30, 2020.
[10]"Course in Miracles, A." https://en.wikipedia.org/wiki/A_Course_in_Miracles. Accessed May 30, 2020.
[11]"Course in Miracles Quotes, A." https://www.goodreads.com/work/quotes/167753-a-course-in-miracles. Accessed December 22, 2022.
[12]"Urantia Book, The." https://en.wikipedia.org/wiki/The_Urantia_Book. Accessed May 30, 2020.
[13]"Paper 99: The Social Problems of Religion (99:0.1-3)." *Urantia Book, The.* https://en.wikiquote.org/wiki/The_Urantia_Book. Accessed December 22, 2022.
[14]"Paper 101: The Real Nature of Religion." (101:4.2) *Urantia Book, The.* https://en.wikiquote.org/wiki/The_Urantia_Book. Accessed December 22, 2022.
[15]"Aquarian Gospel of Jesus the Christ, The."
https://en.wikipedia.org/wiki/The_Aquarian_Gospel_of_Jesus_the_Christ. Accessed May 30, 2020.
[16]"Sec 3, Gimel, Chapter 7:1-28." *Aquarian Gospel of Jesus the Christ, The.* https://www.sacred-texts.com/chr/agjc/agjc010.htm. Accessed December 22, 2020.
[17]"Oahspe: A New Bible." https://en.wikipedia.org/wiki/Oahspe:_A_New_Bible#influence. Accessed May 30, 2020.
[18]"Oahspe Quotes." https://www.goodreads.com/work/quotes/25787760-oahspe. Accessed December 22, 2022.
[19]"Aleister Crowley Quotes." https://www.goodreads.com/author/quotes/3948.Aleister_Crowley. Accessed December 22, 2022.
[20]"Emanuel Swedenborg." https://www.goodreads.com/author/quotes/36217.Emanuel_Swedenborg. Accessed December 22, 2022.
[21]"Annie Besant Quotes." https://www.brainyquote.com/authors/annie-besant-quotes. Accessed December 22, 2022.
[22]"Celestine Prophecy Quotes, The." https://www.goodreads.com/work/quotes/2603195-the-celestine-

prophecy. Accessed December 22, 2022.
[23]"Eckhart Tolle Quotes." https://www.goodreads.com/author/quotes/4493.Eckhart_Tolle. Accessed December 22, 2022.
[24]"Deepak Chopra Quotes." https://www.goodreads.com/author/quotes/138207.Deepak_Chopra, Accessed December 22, 2022.
[25]"Great Invocation, The." https://www.lucistrust.org/the_great_invocation. Accessed June 1, 2020.
[26]"Church Universal and Triumphant." https://en.wikipedia.org/wiki/Church_Universal_and_Triumphant. Accessed June 2, 2020.
[27]"Members of the New Age Movement." Pew Research Center. https://www.pewforum.org/religious-landscape-study/religious-family/new-age/. Accessed June 2, 2020.
[28]"New Age Glossary." *North American Mission Board*. https://www.namb.net/apologetics-blog/new-age-glossary/. Accessed June 2, 2020.

NEW THOUGHT MOVEMENT

[1]Cady, H. Emilie. *Lessons in Truth*. http://www.unityhawaii.org/wp-content/uploads/2017/03/LESSONS-IN-TRUTH.pdf. Accessed September 9, 2020.
[2]"New Thought." https://en.wikipedia.org/wiki/New_Thought. Accessed September 12, 2020.
[3]"Unity Church." https://en.wikipedia.org/wiki/Unity_Church. Accessed September 14, 2020.
[4]"Religious Science." https://en.wikipedia.org/wiki/Religious_Science. Accessed September 14, 2020.
[5]"Church of Divine Science." https://en.wikipedia.org/wiki/Church_of_Divine_Science. Accessed September 14, 2020.
[6]"Seicho-no-Ie." https://en.wikipedia.org/wiki/Seicho-no-Ie. Accessed September 14, 2020.
[7]"Jewish Science." https://en.wikipedia.org/wiki/Jewish_Science. Accessed September 14, 2020.
[8]"Father Divine." https://en.wikipedia.org/wiki/Father_Divine. Accessed September 14, 2020.
[9]"Huna (New Age)." https://en.wikipedia.org/wiki/Huna_(New_Age). Accessed September 14, 2020.
[10]"Charles Filmore Quotes." https://www.azquotes.com/author/4806-Charles_Fillmore. Accessed December 30, 2022.
[11]"Emmet Fox Quotes." https://www.goodreads.com/author/quotes/88582.Emmet_Fox. Accessed December 30, 2022.
[12]"H. Emilie Cady Quotes." https://www.goodreads.com/author/quotes/134953.H_Emilie_Cady. Accessed December 30, 2022.
[13]"New Thought." https://en.wikipedia.org/wiki/New_Thought. Accessed September 16, 2020.
[14]"Glossary of New Thought Terms." https://en.wikipedia.org/wiki/Glossary_of_New_Thought_terms. Accessed September 16, 2020.

OCCULT

[1]"Aleister Crowley Quotes." https://www.goodreads.com/quotes/15604-do-what-thou-wilt-shall-be-the-whole-of-the. Accessed January 3, 2023.
[2]Marino, Lee Ann B. "Occult Foundations." Chapter 5: The Occult. *Understanding Demonology, Spiritual Warfare, Healing, and Deliverance: A Manual for the Christian Minister*. Cary, North Carolina: Apostolic University Press, 2017.
[3]"Arcadia or the Gospel of the Witches Quotes." https://www.goodreads.com/work/quotes/1283294-aradia-or-the-gospel-of-the-witches. Accessed January 5, 2023.
[4]"Coming Forth by Night, as Received by Michael Aquino (Text w/out Illustrations), The." *Sanguine Woods, The*. June 27, 2020. https://thesanguinewoods.wordpress.com/2020/06/27/the-coming-forth-by-night-as-received-by-michael-aquino-text-w-out-illustrations/. Accessed January 5, 2023.
[5]"Magik in Theory and Practice Quotes." https://www.goodreads.com/work/quotes/835451-magick-in-theory-and-practice. Accessed January 5, 2023.
[6]"Dogme et Rituel de la Haute Magie Quotes." https://www.goodreads.com/work/quotes/293672-dogme-et-rituel-de-la-haute-magie. Accessed January 5, 2023.
[7]"Third Key, the Verses 8-18." *Six Keys of Eudoxus, The*. https://www.sacred-texts.com/alc/eudoxus.htm. Accessed January 5, 2023.

[8]"Morals and Dogma of the Ancient and Accepted Scottish Rite of Freemasonry Quotes." https://www.goodreads.com/work/quotes/6117935-morals-and-dogma-of-the-ancient-and-accepted-scottish-rite-of-freemasonr. Accessed January 5, 2023

[9]"Tertium Organum or the Third Canon of Thought and a Key to the Enigmas Quotes." https://www.goodreads.com/work/quotes/1232346-tertium-organum-or-the-third-canon-of-thought-and-a-key-to-the-enigmas. Accessed January 5, 2023.

[10]"Ordo Templi Orientis." https://en.wikipedia.org/wiki/Ordo_Templi_Orientis. Accessed August 4, 2020.

[11]Ibid.

[12]"Astrological Aspect." https://en.wikipedia.org/wiki/Astrological_aspect. Accessed August 5, 2020.

[13]"Baphomet." https://en.wikipedia.org/wiki/Baphomet. Accessed August 5, 2020.

[14]"Alchemy." https://en.wikipedia.org/wiki/Classical_planet#Alchemy. Accessed August 5, 2020.

[15]"Elemental." https://en.wikipedia.org/wiki/Elemental. Accessed August 5, 2020.

[16]"Grimoire." https://en.wikipedia.org/wiki/Grimoire. Accessed August 5, 2020.

[17]"Thelema." https://en.wikipedia.org/wiki/Thelema. Accessed August 5, 2020.

ORTHODOXY

[1]Maximus the Confessor and Brianchianinov, Ignatius. "Suffering Cleanses." *Ascetic Experience, The.* https://asceticexperience.com/2016/09/suffering-cleanses/. Accessed March 20, 2020.

[2]"Byzantine Rite." https://en.wikipedia.org/wiki/Byzantine_Rite. Accessed March 19, 2020.

[3]"Eastern Orthodox Church Organization." https://en.wikipedia.org/wiki/Eastern_Orthodox_Church_organization. Accessed March 20, 2020.

[4]"Orthodox Churches (Oriental)." *World Council of Churches.* https://www.oikoumene.org/en/church-families/orthodox-churches-oriental. Accessed March 20, 2020.

[5]"Eastern Orthodox Church." https://en.wikipedia.org/wiki/Eastern_Orthodox_Church. Accessed March 20, 2020.

[6]"Nestorians." http://factsanddetails.com/world/cat55/sub392/entry-5792.html. Accessed March 20, 2020.

[7]"Lectionary." https://orthodoxwiki.org/Lectionary. Accessed March 21, 2020.

[8]"On Living Soberly." *Monastery of Christ in the Desert.* https://christdesert.org/prayer/desert-fathers-stories/on-living-soberly/. Accessed January 12, 2023.

[9]"On Doing Nothing for Show." *Monastery of Christ in the Desert.* https://christdesert.org/prayer/desert-fathers-stories/on-doing-nothing-for-show/. Accessed January 12, 2023.

[10]"On Love." *Monastery of Christ in the Desert.* https://christdesert.org/prayer/desert-fathers-stories/on-love/. Accessed January 12, 2023.

[11]"On Unceasing Prayer." *Monastery of Christ in the Desert.* https://christdesert.org/prayer/desert-fathers-stories/on-unceasing-prayer/. Accessed January 12, 2023.

[12]"Saints of the Orthodox Church, The." *Greek Orthodox Archdiocese of America.* https://www.goarch.org/-/the-saints-of-the-orthodox-church. Accessed March 23, 2020.

[13]"Liturgical Year." https://en.wikipedia.org/wiki/Liturgical_year. Accessed March 23, 2020.

[14]"Canon Law: Eastern Orthodox Churches." *University of Iowa Law Library, The.* https://libguides.law.uiowa.edu/c.php?g=103191&p=668525. Accessed March 23, 2020.

[15]"Nicene Creed." https://stgregorioscathedral.com/nicene-creed. Accessed January 16, 2023.

[16]"Eastern Orthodoxy." *Encyclopedia Britannica.* https://www.britannica.com/topic/Eastern-Orthodoxy/The-sacraments. Accessed March 23, 2020.

[17]"Nun." https://en.wikipedia.org/wiki/Nun. Accessed March 23, 2020.

[18]Radu, Sintia. "Increasingly Unorthodox World, An: Leaders in the Orthodox Church say the Religion may need to Adapt to Contemporary Times to Remain Relevant." *U.S. News & World Report.* December 6, 2017. https://www.usnews.com/news/best-countries/articles/2017-12-06/orthodoxism-is-declining-in-the-overall-christian-population. Accessed March 24, 2020.

PAGANISM/NEO-PAGANISM

[1]"Margot Adler Quotes." https://www.goodreads.com/author/quotes/8023.Margot_Adler. Accessed November 10, 2020.

[2]Wigington, Patti. "Gods of the Celts." *Learn Religions*. December 24, 2018. https://www.learnreligions.com/gods-of-the-celts-2561711. Accessed November 10, 2020.
[3]Wigington, Patti. "Norse Deities." *Learn Religions*. March 28, 2019. https://www.learnreligions.com/norse-deities-4590158. Accessed November 10, 2020.
[4]Wigington, Patti. "Gods of the Ancient Greeks." *Learn Religions*. March 28, 2019. https://www.learnreligions.com/gods-of-the-ancient-greeks-4590177. Accessed November 10, 2020.
[5]Wigington, Patti. "Deities of Ancient Egypt." *Learn Religions*. June 10, 2018. https://www.learnreligions.com/deities-of-ancient-egypt-2561794. Accessed November 10, 2020.
[6]"How Many Pagans Are There?" *Patheos Library of World Faiths & Religions*. https://www.patheos.com/library/answers-to-frequently-asked-religion-questions/how-many-pagans-are-there. Accessed November 12, 2020.
[7]"Paganism." https://en.wikipedia.org/wiki/Paganism. Accessed November 12, 2020.
[8]"Druidry (Modern)." https://en.wikipedia.org/wiki/Druidry_(modern). Accessed November 12, 2020.
[9]"Heathenry (New Religious Movement.)" https://en.wikipedia.org/wiki/Heathenry_(new_religious_movement). Accessed November 12, 2020.
[10]"Hellenism (Religion)." https://en.wikipedia.org/wiki/Hellenism_(religion). Accessed November 12, 2020.
[11]"Kemetism." https://en.wikipedia.org/wiki/Kemetism. Accessed November 12, 2020.
[12]"Sacred Texts." *Religion Library: Paganism*. https://www.patheos.com/library/pagan/origins/scriptures. Accessed November 14, 2020.
[13]"Wheel of the Year." https://en.wikipedia.org/wiki/Wheel_of_the_Year#Autumn_Equinox_(Mabon). Accessed November 17, 2020.
[14]Gardner, Gerald. "The Charge: Lift Up the Veil. *Gardnerian Book of Shadows, The*. https://www.sacred-texts.com/pag/gbos/gbos02.htm. Accessed January 16, 2023.
[15]"Wicca: A Guide for the Solitary Practitioner Quotes." https://www.goodreads.com/work/quotes/503350-wicca-a-guide-for-the-solitary-practitioner. Accessed January 16, 2023.
[16]"Neopaganism in the United States." https://en.wikipedia.org/wiki/Neopaganism_in_the_United_States. Accessed November 17, 2020.
[17]"A to Z Pagan Glossary, The." *Flying the Hedge: A Modern Approach to Hedgecraft*. February 15, 2016. https://www.flyingthehedge.com/2016/02/the-to-z-pagan-glossary.html. Accessed November 17, 2020.

PENTECOSTAL CHRISTIANITY

[1]"Jesus Quotes and God Thoughts." March 28, 2015. https://quotesthoughtsrandom.wordpress.com/2015/03/28/is-it-counterfeit/. Accessed April 2, 2020.
[2]Acts 2:17-21. *King James Version of the Holy Bible*, Public Domain.
[3]1 Corinthians 12:1-12. Ibid.
[4]"Church of God With Signs Following." https://en.wikipedia.org/wiki/Church_of_God_with_Signs_Following. Accessed April 3, 2020.
[5]"Way International, The." https://en.wikipedia.org/wiki/The_Way_International. Accessed June 9, 2020.
[6]"Charismatic Christianity." https://en.wikipedia.org/wiki/Charismatic_Christianity. Accessed April 3, 2020.
[7]"NAE Statement of Faith." https://denverseminary.edu/about/who-we-are/nae-statement-of-faith/. Accessed January 17, 2023.
[8]Baer, Robert. "Quotes about Pentecostal." https://quotlr.com/quotes-about-pentecostal. Accessed January 17, 2023.
[9]Wigglesworth, Smith. Ibid.
[10]Stott, John. Ibid.
[11]Mott, John. Ibid.
[12]"Yoido Full Gospel Church." https://en.wikipedia.org/wiki/Yoido_Full_Gospel_Church. Accessed April 4, 2020.
[13]"Pentecostalism." https://en.wikipedia.org/wiki/Pentecostalism. Accessed April 3, 2020.

PROTESTANT CHRISTIANITY

[1]"Protestantism Quotes." https://www.goodreads.com/quotes/tag/protestantism. Accessed March 26, 2020.
[2]Fairchild, Mary. "How Many Christians are in the World Today?" Learn Religions. April 16, 2020.

https://www.learnreligions.com/christianity-statistics-700533. Accessed March 26, 2020.
[3]"Lutheranism by Region." https://en.wikipedia.org/wiki/Lutheranism_by_region. Accessed March 26, 2020.
[4]Michaelson, Jay. "Anglicans Demote Episcopalians as Global Christianity Gets More Polarized." *Daily Beast, The*. April 13, 2017. https://www.thedailybeast.com/anglicans-demote-episcopalians-as-global-christianity-gets-more-polarized. Accessed March 26, 2020.
[5]"United Methodist Church." https://en.wikipedia.org/wiki/United_Methodist_Church. Accessed March 26, 2020.
[6]"Anabaptism." https://en.wikipedia.org/wiki/Anabaptism. Accessed March 26, 2020.
[7]"Calvinism." https://en.wikipedia.org/wiki/Calvinism. Accessed March 26, 2020.
[8]"Unitarianism at a Glance." BBC. January 16, 2004.
https://www.bbc.co.uk/religion/religions/unitarianism/ataglance/glance.shtml. Accessed March 26, 2020.
[9]"List of Bible Translations by Language." https://en.wikipedia.org/wiki/List_of_Bible_translations_by_language. Accessed March 26, 2020.
[10]"Preface. *First Book of Common Prayer, The*. https://www.bcponline.org/. Accessed January 23, 2023.
[11]"Comprehensive Summary, Foundation, Rule, and Norm." *Formula of Concord – Solid Declaration, The*. https://bookofconcord.org/solid-declaration/. Accessed January 23, 2023.
[12]"Chapter 3: Of God's Eternal Decree." *Westminister Confession of Faith, The. Ligonier Ministries*. May 12, 2021. https://www.ligonier.org/learn/articles/westminster-confession-faith. Accessed January 23, 2023.
[13]"Basic Pattern of Worship, The." *Book of Worship*. https://www.umcdiscipleship.org/book-of-worship/the-basic-pattern-of-worship. Accessed January 23, 2023.
[14]*Schleitheim Confession of Faith, 1527*.
https://courses.washington.edu/hist112/SCHLEITHEIM%20CONFESSION%20OF%20FAITH.htm. Accessed January 23, 2023.
[15]Serveto, Michael. Book 1: "Argument." *On the Errors of the Trinity*.
http://www.teleiosministries.com/pdfs/Doctrines_of_Men/errors_trinity_servetus.pdf. Accessed January 23, 2023.
[16]"Ecumenical Creeds: Apostle's Creed." *Protestant Reformed Churches in America*.
https://www.prca.org/about/official-standards/creeds/ecumenical/apostles. Accessed January 23, 2023.
[17]"Ecumenical Creeds: Nicene Creed." *Protestant Reformed Churches in America*.
https://www.prca.org/about/official-standards/creeds/ecumenical/nicene. Accessed January 23, 2023.
[18]"Athanasian Creed." https://en.wikipedia.org/wiki/Athanasian_Creed. Accessed January 23, 2023.
[19]"Preterism." https://en.wikipedia.org/wiki/Preterism. Accessed March 28, 2020.
[20]"Protestant Statistics." *Introduction to Protestantism: Exploring the Protestant Faith*.
http://protestantism.co.uk/protestant-statistics. Accessed March 28, 2020.
[21]Chapter 2: religious Switching and Intermarriage. *Pew Research Center*. May 12, 2015.
https://www.pewforum.org/2015/05/12/chapter-2-religious-switching-and-intermarriage/. Accessed March 28, 2020.

ROMAN CATHOLICISM

[1]"Roman Catholic Quotes." https://www.azquotes.com/quotes/topics/roman-catholic-church.html. Accessed March 19, 2020.
[2]Matthew 16:18-19. *New American Bible (Revised Edition)*.
https://www.biblegateway.com/passage/?search=Matthew+16%3A18-19&version=NABRE
[3]"Byzantine Rite." https://en.wikipedia.org/wiki/Byzantine_Rite. Accessed March 19, 2020.
[4]"How Many Roman Catholics are There in the World?" BBC News. March 14, 2013.
https://www.bbc.com/news/world-21443313. Accessed March 19, 2020.
[5]"Catholic Bible." https://en.wikipedia.org/wiki/Catholic_Bible. Accessed March 19, 2020.
[6]"Catechism of the Catholic Church Quotes." https://www.goodreads.com/work/quotes/106769-catechismus-catholic-ecclesi. Accessed January 24, 2023.
[7]Ibid.
[8]Ibid.
[9]Ibid.

[10]Ibid.
[11]Ibid.
[12]"Apostle's Creed." United States Conference of Catholic Bishops. https://www.usccb.org/prayers/apostles-creed. Accessed January 24, 2023.
[13]"Catholic Nicene Creed, The." https://www.beginningcatholic.com/catholic-nicene-creed. Accessed January 24, 2023.
[14]"Chalcedonian Creed." https://www.theopedia.com/chalcedonian-creed. Accessed January 24, 2023.
[15]"Athanasian Creed, The." https://www.beginningcatholic.com/athanasian-creed. Accessed January 24, 2023.
[16]"Opus Dei." https://en.wikipedia.org/wiki/Opus_Dei. Accessed March 20, 2020.
[17]Kuruvilla, Carol. "Fewer Catholics of All Ages are Attending Mass, Gallup Study Finds." *HuffPost*. April 11, 2018. https://www.huffpost.com/entry/catholics-attending-mass-gallup-study_n_5acd082ae4b06a6aac8c7506. Accessed March 20, 2020.
[18]Ibid.
[19]Ghose, Tia. "By the Numbers: Who are Catholics in America?" *LiveScience*. September 21, 2015. https://www.livescience.com/52236-who-are-american-catholics.html. Accessed March 20, 2020.
[20]Ibid.
[21]Ibid.

SACRED NAME/HEBREW ROOTS MOVEMENTS

[1]*Sacred Name, The*. Garden Grove, California: Qadesh La Yahweh Press. 2002. http://yahweh.org/publications/sny/sacrednm.pdf. Accessed June 4, 2020.
[2]"Hebrew Roots." https://en.wikipedia.org/wiki/Hebrew_Roots. Accessed June 6, 2020.
[3]"British Israelism." https://en.wikipedia.org/wiki/British_Israelism. Accessed June 8, 2020.
[4]"Grace Communion International." https://en.wikipedia.org/wiki/Grace_Communion_International#Related_denominations. Accessed June 8, 2020.
[5]"Sacred Name Groups." *Encyclopedia.com*. https://www.encyclopedia.com/religion/encyclopedias-almanacs-transcripts-and-maps/sacred-name-groups-0#A. Accessed June 8, 2020.
[6]O'Neil, Lorena. Hebrew Roots Rising: Not Quite Christians, Not Quite Jews." *USA Today*. March 13, 2014. https://www.usatoday.com/story/news/nation/2014/03/13/ozy-hebrew-roots-movement/6373671/. Accessed June 8, 2020.
[7]Leviticus 23:2. *Tree of Life Version*. https://www.biblegateway.com/passage/?search=Leviticus+23%3A2&version=TLV. Accessed January 25, 2023.
[8]"Hebrew Roots." https://en.wikipedia.org/wiki/Hebrew_Roots. Accessed June 8, 2020.
[9]"Why Biblical Law?" *Yahweh's Assembly in Yahshua*. https://yaiy.org/literature/BibicalLaw.html. Accessed January 24, 2023.
[10]"What is 119 Ministries?" https://www.gotquestions.org/119-Ministries.html. Accessed June 9, 2020.
[11]"House of Yahweh." https://en.wikipedia.org/wiki/House_of_Yahweh. Accessed June 9, 2020.

SATANISM

[1]"Satanic Bible Quotes, The." https://www.goodreads.com/work/quotes/1039648-the-satanic-bible. Accessed June 16, 2020.
[2]"Theistic Satanism." https://en.wikipedia.org/wiki/Theistic_Satanism. Accessed June 16, 2020.
[3]"Satanism." https://en.wikipedia.org/wiki/Satanism. Accessed June 16, 2020.
[4]Ibid.
[5]"Our Lady of Endor Coven." https://en.wikipedia.org/wiki/Our_Lady_of_Endor_Coven. Accessed June 18, 2020.
[6]"Satanism." *History*. https://www.history.com/topics/1960s/satanism. Accessed June 18, 2020.
[7]"Satanic Bible, The." https://en.wikipedia.org/wiki/The_Satanic_Bible. Accessed June 19, 2020.
[8]"Satanic Bible Quotes, The." https://www.goodreads.com/work/quotes/1039648-the-satanic-bible. Accessed January 25, 2023.
[9]Ibid.

[10]Ibid.
[11]Ibid.
[12]"F.A.Q. Holidays." Church of Satan. https://www.churchofsatan.com/faq-holidays/. Accessed June 19, 2020.
[13]"Walpurgis Night." https://en.wikipedia.org/wiki/Walpurgis_Night. Accessed June 19, 2020.
[14]LaVey, Anton Szandor. "Nine Satanic Statements, The." *Church of Satan*. https://www.churchofsatan.com/nine-satanic-statements/. Accessed June 19, 2020.
[15]Lavey, Anton Szandor. "Eleven Satanic Rules of the Earth, The." *Church of Satan*. https://www.churchofsatan.com/eleven-rules-of-earth/. Accessed June 19, 2020.
[16]LaVey, Anton Szandor. "Nine Satanic Sins, The." *Church of Satan*. https://www.churchofsatan.com/nine-satanic-sins/. Accessed June 19, 2020.
[17]"Satanic Temple, The." https://en.wikipedia.org/wiki/The_Satanic_Temple. Accessed June 19, 2020.
[18]"Satanism." https://en.wikipedia.org/wiki/Satanism. Accessed June 19, 2020.

SCIENTOLOGY

[1]"Scientology Quotes." https://www.wiseoldsayings.com/scientology-quotes/#ixzz6L8TaUJdT. Accessed April 30, 2020.
[2]"3.1 Read: The Eight Dynamics." *Lesson Number 3*. https://www.scientology.org/fot/lesson-3/eight-dynamics.html. Accessed April 30, 2020.
[3]Kuroski, John. "Five of the Strangest Things Scientologists Actually Believe." All That's Interesting. May 9, 2016. https://allthatsinteresting.com/scientology-beliefs. Accessed April 30, 2020.
[4]"Scientology." https://en.wikipedia.org/wiki/Scientology#Theological_doctrine. Accessed April 30, 2020.
[5]"Does Scientology Have a Concept of God?" *Scientology Beliefs*. https://www.scientology.org/faq/scientology-beliefs/what-is-the-concept-of-god-in-scientology.html. Accessed April 30, 2020.
[6]"Schisms and Sects." *Religion Library: Scientology*. https://www.patheos.com/library/scientology/historical-development/schisms-sects. Accessed May 2, 2020.
[7]"Process Church of the Final Judgment." https://en.wikipedia.org/wiki/Process_Church_of_the_Final_Judgment. Accessed May 2, 2020.
[8]"Free Zone (Scientology)." https://en.wikipedia.org/wiki/Free_Zone_(Scientology). Accessed May 2, 2020.
[9]Ortega, Tony. "Scientologists: How Many of Them Are There, Anyway?" *Village Voice, The*. July 4, 2011. https://www.villagevoice.com/2011/07/04/scientologists-how-many-of-them-are-there-anyway/. Accessed May 2, 2020.
[10]"Sacred Texts." *Religion Library: Scientology*. https://www.patheos.com/library/scientology/origins/scriptures. Accessed May 2, 2020.
[11]"L. Ron Hubbard Quotes." https://www.goodreads.com/author/quotes/33503.L_Ron_Hubbard. Accessed January 25, 2023.
[12]Ibid.
[13]"L. Ron Hubbard." https://en.wikiquote.org/wiki/L._Ron_Hubbard. Accessed January 25, 2023.
[14]Ibid.
[15]Ibid.
[16]Ibid.
[17]Ibid.
[18]Nededog, Jethro. "How Scientology Costs Members up to Millions of Dollars, According to Leah Remini's Show." *Insider*. December 14, 2016. https://www.businessinsider.com/scientology-costs-leah-remini-recap-episode-3-2016-12#scientologists-allegedly-spend-thousands-of-dollars-to-purchase-every-book-written-by-founder-l-ron-hubbard-1. Accessed May 2, 2020.
[19]"Prices uo to OT8 and Beyond." http://www.xenu.net/archive/prices.html. Accessed May 2, 2020.
[20]"OT VIII." https://en.wikipedia.org/wiki/OT_VIII. Accessed May 2, 2020.
[21]"Operating Thetan." https://en.wikipedia.org/wiki/Operating_Thetan 5/2/2020
[22]Nededog, Jethro. "How Scientology Costs Members up to Millions of Dollars, According to Leah Remini's Show." *Insider*. December 14, 2016. https://www.businessinsider.com/scientology-costs-leah-remini-recap-episode-3-2016-12#scientologists-allegedly-spend-thousands-of-dollars-to-purchase-every-book-written-by-founder-l-ron-hubbard-1. Accessed May 2, 2020.

[23]Boyd, Kayla. "Tom Cruise & Scientology: How Much Does it Cost Him?" *CafeMom.* April 5, 2018. https://thestir.cafemom.com/celebrities/211635/tom-cruise-scientology-how-much-does-it-cost-him/226324/according_to_bankrate_tom_cruise_has_a_net_worth_of_about_550_million_but_how_much_of_that_fortune_goes_toward_his_faith/2. Accessed May 2, 2020.
[24]"Prayer for Total Freedom, A." *Scientology.* https://www.scientology.org/what-is-scientology/scientology-religious-ceremonies/a-prayer-for-total-freedom.html. Accessed May 2, 2020.
[25]"What are Scientology Sunday Services?" *Scientology.* https://www.scientology.org/faq/inside-a-church-of-scientology/what-are-scientology-sunday-services.html. Accessed May 2,2020.
[26]"Scientology Holidays." https://en.wikipedia.org/wiki/Scientology_holidays. Accessed May 22, 2020.
[27]"List of Symbols of Scientology." https://en.wikipedia.org/wiki/List_of_symbols_of_Scientology. Accessed May 4, 2020.
[28]"Creed of the Church of Scientology, The." *Scientology.* https://www.scientology.org/what-is-scientology/the-scientology-creeds-and-codes/the-creed-of-the-church.html. Accessed May 2, 2020.
[29]"Code of Honor, The." *Scientology.* https://www.scientology.org/what-is-scientology/the-scientology-creeds-and-codes/the-code-of-honor.html. Accessed May 4, 2020.
[30]"Piercing the Corporate Veil: The True Structure of Scientology." http://www.cs.cmu.edu/~dst/Cowen/essays/corporate.html. Accessed May 4, 2020.
[31]"Sea Org." *Ex-Scientology Kids.* https://exscientologykids.com/sea-org-2/. Accessed May 4, 2020.
[32]"Scientology Policy Directive." Issue 1. August 22, 2000. https://scientologymoneyproject.com/wp-content/uploads/2014/06/scientology-policy-directive-waivers.pdf. Accessed May 4, 2020.
[33]Knapp, Dan. "Group That Once Criticized Scientologists now Owned by One." *CNN Interactive.* December 19, 1996. http://www.cnn.com/US/9612/19/scientology/index.html. Accessed May 5, 2020.
[34]Jacobsen, Jonny. "Counting Scientology 5. Reality Check." *medium.com.* https://medium.com/how-many-scientologists-are-there-really/5-factoring-in-reality-3f0bb2d4e4cf. Accessed May 5, 2020.
[35]"Scientology Critical Information Directory.: http://www.xenu-directory.net/glossary/glossary_a.htm. Accessed May 5, 2020.

SEVENTH-DAY ADVENTISM

[1]"Ellen G. White Quotes." https://www.azquotes.com/author/15567-Ellen_G_White. Accessed May 19, 2020.
[2]"What Adventists Believe About the Trinity." *Seventh-Day Adventist Church.* https://www.adventist.org/beliefs/fundamental-beliefs/god/trinity/. 5/19/2020
[3]"Seventh-day Adventist Theology." https://en.wikipedia.org/wiki/Seventh-day_Adventist_theology. Accessed May 19, 2020.
[4]"Heavenly Sanctuary." https://en.wikipedia.org/wiki/Heavenly_sanctuary. Accessed May 20, 2020.
[5]"True and Free Seventh-Day Adventists." https://en.wikipedia.org/wiki/True_and_Free_Seventh-day_Adventists. Accessed May 25, 2020.
[6]"Historic Adventism." https://en.wikipedia.org/wiki/Historic_Adventism. Accessed May 25, 2020.
[7]"Progressive Adventism." https://en.wikipedia.org/wiki/Progressive_Adventism Accessed May 25, 2020.
[8]"Seventh-Day Adventist Church." https://en.wikipedia.org/wiki/Seventh-day_Adventist_Church. Accessed May 25, 2020.
[9]"Authentic Gift of Prophecy, The: 5 Ways to Know." https://www.adventist.org/articles/the-gift-of-prophecy/. Accessed May 25, 2020.
[10]"Steps to Christ Quotes." https://www.goodreads.com/work/quotes/2508972-steps-to-christ. Accessed January 28, 2023.
[11]Ibid.
[12]"Conflict of the Ages." https://en.wikipedia.org/wiki/Conflict_of_the_Ages. Accessed May 25, 2020.
[13] "Desire of Ages, Quotes, The." https://www.goodreads.com/work/quotes/730495-the-desire-of-ages. Accessed January 28, 2023.
[14]Ibid.
[15]Ibid.
[16]"Christ's Object Lessons Quotes." https://www.goodreads.com/work/quotes/1689923-christs-object-lessons. Accessed January 28, 2023.

[17]"Ministry of Healing Quotes, The." https://www.goodreads.com/work/quotes/2508940-the-ministry-of-healing. Accessed January 28, 2023.
[18]"Sabbath School." https://en.wikipedia.org/wiki/Sabbath_School. Accessed May 25, 2020.
[19]"28 Fundamental Beliefs." https://szu.adventist.org/wp-content/uploads/2016/04/28_Beliefs.pdf. Accessed May 25, 2020.
[20]"Polity of the Seventh-day Adventist Church." https://en.wikipedia.org/wiki/Polity_of_the_Seventh-day_Adventist_Church. Accessed May 25, 2020.
[21]"Branch Davidians." https://en.wikipedia.org/wiki/Branch_Davidians. Accessed May 25, 2020.
[22]Lipka, Michael. "Closer Look at Seventh-Day Adventists in America, A." *Pew Research Center*. November 3, 2015. https://www.pewresearch.org/fact-tank/2015/11/03/a-closer-look-at-seventh-day-adventists-in-america/. Accessed May 25, 2020.

SIKHISM

[1]"Sikhjsm Quotes." https://www.goodreads.com/quotes/tag/sikhism 4/14/2020
[2]"Ang 1." *Sri Guru Granth Sahib*. Accessed January 1, 2023.
[3]"God in Sikhism." https://en.wikipedia.org/wiki/God_in_Sikhism. Accessed April 14, 2020.
[4]Ibid.
[5]"Five Virtues." https://en.wikipedia.org/wiki/Five_Virtues. Accessed April 16, 2020.
[6]"Three Pillars of Sikhism." https://en.wikipedia.org/wiki/Three_pillars_of_Sikhism. Accessed April 16, 2020.
[7]"Sects of Sikhism." https://en.wikipedia.org/wiki/Sects_of_Sikhism. Accessed April 16, 2020.
[8]"Sikhs." https://en.wikipedia.org/wiki/Sikhs. Accessed April 16, 2020.
[9]"Sikh Scriptures." https://en.wikipedia.org/wiki/Sikh_scriptures. Accessed April 16, 2020.
[10]"Writers of Guru Granth Sahib." https://en.wikipedia.org/wiki/Writers_of_Guru_Granth_Sahib. Accessed April 16, 2020.
[11]"Guru Nanak Quotes." https://www.goodreads.com/author/quotes/333495.Guru_Nanak. Accessed January 30, 2023.
[12]Ibid.
[13]Ibid.
[14]Ibid.
[15]"Dasam Granth." https://en.wikipedia.org/wiki/Dasam_Granth. Accessed April 16, 2020.
[16]"Bani of Guru Gobind Singh." https://www.sikhiwiki.org/index.php/Bani_of_Guru_Gobind_Singh. Accessed January 30, 2023.
[17]Ibid.
[18]"Guru Granth Sahib." https://en.wikipedia.org/wiki/Guru_Granth_Sahib. Accessed April 16, 2020.
[19]"Sikhism." https://www.britannica.com/topic/Sikhism/Sikh-practice. Accessed April 16, 2020.
[20]"Five Ks, The." BBC. September 29, 2009.
https://www.bbc.co.uk/religion/religions/sikhism/customs/fiveks.shtml. Accessed April 17, 2020.
[21]Khalsa, Sukhmandir. "All About the Sikh Family: The Role of Family Members in Sikhism." *Learn Religions*. March 28, 2019. https://www.learnreligions.com/all-about-the-sikh-family-4590164. Accessed April 17, 2020.
[22]"Sikhism Holidays." http://www.religionfacts.com/sikhism/holidays. Accessed April 17, 2020.
[23]"List of Sikh Festivals." https://en.wikipedia.org/wiki/List_of_Sikh_festivals. January 30, 2023.
[24]"Sikh Beliefs." *BBC*. https://www.bbc.co.uk/bitesize/guides/z77634j/revision/3. Accessed April 17, 2020.
[25]"Udasi." https://en.wikipedia.org/wiki/Udasi. Accessed April 17, 2020.
[26]Fosco, Molly. "Holiest Place in Sikhism Explained, The." Seeker. Jul 23, 2015. https://www.seeker.com/the-holiest-place-in-sikhism-explained-1501524888.html. Accessed April 17, 2020.
[27]"World Sikh Organization." https://en.wikipedia.org/wiki/World_Sikh_Organization. Accessed April 17, 2020.
[28]"Who are Sikhs? What is Sikhism?" Sikhnet. https://www.sikhnet.com/pages/who-are-sikhs-what-is-sikhism. Accessed April 17, 2020.
[29]"Glossary of Sikhism." https://en.wikipedia.org/wiki/Glossary_of_Sikhism. Accessed April 17, 2020.
[30]"Sukhmani Sahib." https://en.wikipedia.org/wiki/Sukhmani_Sahib. Accessed April 17, 2020.

TAOIST RELIGIONS

[1]"I Ching Quotes." https://www.quotes.net/authors/I+Ching. Accessed August 26, 2020.
[2]"Eastern Religions." https://en.wikipedia.org/wiki/Eastern_religions. Accessed August 31, 2020.
[3]"Taoism." https://en.wikipedia.org/wiki/Taoism. Accessed August 31, 2020.
[4]"Confucianism." *Encyclopedia Britannica*. https://www.britannica.com/topic/Confucianism. Accessed September 1, 2020.
[5]"Confucianism." https://en.wikipedia.org/wiki/Confucianism. Accessed September 1, 2020.
[6]"Four Books and Five Classics." https://en.wikipedia.org/wiki/Four_Books_and_Five_Classics. Accessed September 1, 2020.
[7]"Shinto." Encyclopedia Britannica. https://www.britannica.com/topic/Shinto/Types-of-shrines. Accessed September 1, 2020.
[8]"Korean Shamanism." https://en.wikipedia.org/wiki/Korean_shamanism. Accessed September 1, 2020.
[9]"Sindoism." https://iiwiki.us/wiki/Sindoism#Core_beliefs_and_principles. Accessed September 1, 2020.
[10]"Vietnamese Folk Religion." https://en.wikipedia.org/wiki/Vietnamese_folk_religion. Accessed September 2, 2020.
[11]"I Ching." https://en.wikipedia.org/wiki/I_Ching. Accessed September 3, 2020.
[12]"I Ching or Book of Changes Quotes, The." https://www.goodreads.com/work/quotes/521797-y. Accessed February 1, 2023.
[13]Ibid.
[14]Ibid.
[15] "Tao Te Ching Quotes." https://www.goodreads.com/work/quotes/100074. Accessed February 1, 2023.
[16]Ibid.
[17]Ibid.
[18]"Book of Rites, The." https://www.goodreads.com/work/quotes/41422067-the-book-of-rites. Accessed February 1, 2023.
[19]"Kojiki." https://en.wikipedia.org/wiki/Kojiki. Accessed September 3, 2020.
[20]"Nihon Shoki." https://en.wikipedia.org/wiki/Nihon_Shoki. Accessed September 3, 2020.
[21]"Sect. II: The Seven Divine Generations. *Kojiki, The*. https://www.sacred-texts.com/shi/kj/kj009.htm. Accessed February 1, 2023.
[22]"Diamond Sutra Quotes, The." https://www.goodreads.com/work/quotes/139176-vajracchedik-praj-p-ramit-s-tra. Accessed February 1, 2023.
[23]"Quotes of the Avatamsaka Sutra, The." World Spiritual Heritage. https://www.onelittleangel.com/wisdom/quotes/saint.asp?mc=112. Accessed February 1, 2023.
[24]"Taoism." https://daoismreligion.weebly.com/special-days-of-celebration.html. Accessed September 7, 2020.
[25]"Key Holidays and Festivals." https://10cpconfucianism.weebly.com/holidays-and-festivals.html. Accessed September 7, 2020.
[26]"Public Holidays." Visit Korea. https://english.visitkorea.or.kr/enu/TRV/TV_ENG_1_1.jsp. Accessed September 7, 2020.
[27]"Traditions and Holy Days." https://sites.google.com/site/zenreligion/traditions-and-holy-days. Accessed September 7, 2020.
[28]"Way of the Five Pecks of Rice." https://en.wikipedia.org/wiki/Way_of_the_Five_Pecks_of_Rice. Accessed September 8, 2020.
[29]"Geography of Religion, The." http://www.geography.hunter.cuny.edu/courses/geog247_grande/fall2017/17-2017-PP17%20Religion1.pdf. Accessed September 8, 2020.

THEOSOPHY

[1]"My Books." *Theosophy Trust Memorial Library*. https://www.theosophytrust.org/482-my-books. Accessed August 6, 2020.
[2]"Theosophy." https://en.wikipedia.org/wiki/Theosophy. Accessed August 6, 2020.
[3]"Theosophical Mysticism." https://en.wikipedia.org/wiki/Theosophical_mysticism. Accessed August 8, 2020.
[4]Szymczak, Patricia M. "Theosophists Study Religion and More." *Chicago Tribune*. March 10, 1989. https://www.chicagotribune.com/news/ct-xpm-1989-03-10-8903250661-story.html. Accessed August 6,

2020.
[5]"Theosophical Society Adyar." https://en.wikipedia.org/wiki/Theosophical_Society_Adyar. Accessed August 7, 2020.
[6]"Theosophical Society Pasadena." https://en.wikipedia.org/wiki/Theosophical_Society_Pasadena. Accessed August 7, 2020.
[7]"United Lodge of Theosophists." https://en.wikipedia.org/wiki/United_Lodge_of_Theosophists. Accessed August 7, 2020.
[8]Ibid.
[9]"Arcane School." https://theosophy.wiki/en/Arcane_School. Accessed August 7, 2020.
[10]"Arcane School." Encyclopedia.com. https://www.encyclopedia.com/science/encyclopedias-almanacs-transcripts-and-maps/arcane-school. Accessed August 7, 2020.
[11]"I AM Movement." https://en.wikipedia.org/wiki/%22I_AM%22_Activity. Accessed May 28, 2020.
[12]"Liberal Catholic Church." https://en.wikipedia.org/wiki/Liberal_Catholic_Church. Accessed August 7, 2020.
[13]"Anthroposophical Society." https://en.wikipedia.org/wiki/Anthroposophical_Society. Accessed August 7, 2020.
[14]"Isis Unveiled Quotes." https://www.goodreads.com/work/quotes/1043355-isis-unveiled-volumes-1-and-2. Accessed February 1, 2023.
[15]Ibid.
[16]"Voice of the Silence Quotes, The." https://www.goodreads.com/work/quotes/385158-the-voice-of-the-silence. Accessed February 1, 2021.
[17]"Find a Local Group." https://www.theosophical.org/membership/connect/find-a-local-group. Accessed August 8, 2020.
[18]Rajan, Ananya S. "Three Special Days Celebrated in the Theosophical Societys Calendar." *Theosophy World Resource Centre*. https://www.theosophy.world/resource/three-special-days-celebrated-theosophical-societys-calendar. Accessed August 8, 2020.
[19] "Theosophical Symbols." *Blavatsky.net*. https://www.blavatsky.net/index.php/theosophical-symbols. Accessed August 8, 2020.
[20]"Theosophy." *Encyclopedia Britannica*. https://www.britannica.com/topic/theosophy. Accessed August 6, 2020.
[21]"Theosophical Society Adyar." https://en.wikipedia.org/wiki/Theosophical_Society_Adyar. Accessed August 8, 2020.
[22]Ibid.
[23]"Theosophical Order of Service." https://en.wikipedia.org/wiki/Theosophical_Order_of_Service. Accessed August 8, 2020.
[24]Szymczak, Patricia M. "Theosophists Study Religion and More." *Chicago Tribune*. March 10, 1989. https://www.chicagotribune.com/news/ct-xpm-1989-03-10-8903250661-story.html. Accessed August 6, 2020
25 Blavatsky, H.P. *Theosophical Glossary, The*. Glosshttp://www.theosophy.org/Blavatsky/Theosophical%20Glossary/Thegloss.htm. Accessed August 8, 2020.

UNCHURCHED

[1]"Oprah Winfrey Quotes." https://www.azquotes.com/author/15820-Oprah_Winfrey/tag/spirituality. Accessed October 28, 2020.
[2]"Spiritual but not Religious." https://en.wikipedia.org/wiki/Spiritual_but_not_religious. Accessed October 27, 2020.
[3]"Unchurched Population Nears 100 Million in the US." *Barna Research Group*. https://www.barna.com/research/unchurched-population-nears-100-million-in-the-u-s/. Accessed October 26, 2020.
[4]Ibid.
[5]"Spiritual but not Religious." https://en.wikipedia.org/wiki/Spiritual_but_not_religious. Accessed Ocrober 2, 2020.
[6]Ibid.

Unitarian Universalism

[1]"What Worship Means to Us." *Commission on Common Worship, Unitarian Universalist Association*, 1983. http://peopleschurch.net/visitors/what-worship-means-to-us/. Accessed May 26, 2020.
[2]"Existence of a Higher Power in Unitarian Universalism." *Unitarian Universalist Association*. https://www.uua.org/beliefs/what-we-believe/higher-power. Accessed May 27, 2020.
[3]"Religious Humanism." https://en.wikipedia.org/wiki/Religious_humanism. Accessed May 27, 2020.
[4]"Seven Principles, The." *Unitarian Universalist Association*. https://www.uua.org/beliefs/what-we-believe/principles. Accessed May 27, 2020.
[5]"What We Believe." *Unitarian Universalist Association*. https://www.uua.org/beliefs/what-we-believe/sources. Accessed May 27, 2020.
[6]"Unitarian Universalism." https://en.wikipedia.org/wiki/Unitarian_Universalism. Accessed May 27, 2020.
[7]"Transcendentalism Quotes." https://www.goodreads.com/quotes/tag/transcendentalism?page=1. Accessed February 6, 2023.
[8] Ibid.
[9]Williams, L. Griswold. 'Congregational Covenants." *Unitarian Universalist Association*. https://www.uua.org/re/tapestry/adults/river/workshop7/175905.shtml. Accessed May 27, 2020.
[10]Blake, James Vila. "Congregational Covenants." *Unitarian Universalist Association*. https://www.uua.org/re/tapestry/adults/river/workshop7/175905.shtml. Accessed May 27, 2020.
[11]Marino, Lee Ann B. "Ten December Holidays You Probably Don't Know About." *Leadership on Fire*. https://www.patheos.com/blogs/leadershiponfire/2023/12/ten-december-holidays-you-probably-dont-know-about/. Posted December 11, 2023. Accessed May 18, 2024.
[12]Ames, Charles Gordon. "Congregational Covenants." *Unitarian Universalist Association*. https://www.uua.org/re/tapestry/adults/river/workshop7/175905.shtml. Accessed May 27, 2020.
[13]"Interweave." *Unitarian Universalist Association*. https://www.uua.org/offices/organizations/interweave. Accessed May 27, 2020.
[14]"Unitarians." *Pew Research Center*. https://www.pewforum.org/religious-landscape-study/religious-denomination/unitarian/. Accessed May 27, 2020.
[15]"Glossary of Unitarian Universalist Terms." Unitarian Universalist Church of Tampa. https://uutampa.org/glossary-of-unitarian-terms/. Accessed May 27, 2020.

Utopianism

[1]"Simple Gifts." https://en.wikipedia.org/wiki/Simple_Gifts. Accessed June 14, 2022.
[2]Budds, Diana. "What I Learned from a Year in Utopias." *Curbed*. December 23, 2019. https://archive.curbed.com/2019/12/23/21032132/failed-utopias-2019-nice-try. Accessed June 15, 2022.
[3]"Shakers." https://en.wikipedia.org/wiki/Shakers. Accessed June 22, 2022.
[4]"Sunday Meeting." Shaker Village. https://www.maineshakers.com/about/. Accessed June 22, 2022.
[5]"Oneida Community." *Encyclopedia Britannica*. https://www.britannica.com/topic/Oneida-Community. Accessed June 22, 2022.
[6]"Pietism." https://en.wikipedia.org/wiki/Pietism. Accessed June 23, 2022.
[7]"Farm (Tennessee), The." https://en.wikipedia.org/wiki/The_Farm_(Tennessee). Accessed June 23, 2022.
[8]"Utopias in America." National Park Service. https://www.nps.gov/articles/utopias-in-america.htm. Accessed June 23, 2022.

Zoroastrianism

[1]"Wisdom and teachings of Zoroastrian Religion." *World Philosophical Heritage*. https://www.onelittleangel.com/wisdom/quotes/religion.asp?mc=57. Accessed August 22, 2020.
[2]"Amesha Spenta." https://en.wikipedia.org/wiki/Amesha_Spenta. Accessed August 24, 2020.
[3]"Zoroastrianism." https://en.wikipedia.org/wiki/Zoroastrianism. Accessed August 24, 2020.
[4]"Zoroastrianism." *Encyclopedia Britannica*. https://www.britannica.com/topic/Zoroastrianism/Beliefs-and-mythology. Accessed August 24, 2020.
[5]"Zoroastrianism." https://en.wikipedia.org/wiki/Zoroastrianism. Accessed August 24, 2020.
[6]"Zoroastrianism." *History*. October 8, 2019. https://www.history.com/topics/religion/zoroastrianism. Accessed

August 24, 2020.
[7]"Conversion: To the Zoroastrian Faith in the Modern Period." *Encyclopedia Iranica*. https://iranicaonline.org/articles/conversion-vii. Accessed August 24, 2020.
[8]"Ahura Mazda." https://ramiyarkaranjia.com/quotes-from-zoroastrian-texts/#_Toc524450267. Accessed February 6, 2023.
[9]Ibid.
[10]Ibid.
[11]"Exposition in the Good Religion Regarding State and Religion." *Denkard, The*: Book 3. http://www.avesta.org/denkard/dk3s1.htm#chap58. Accessed February 6, 2023.
[12]"Chapter 1: The Original State of the Two Spirits." *Selections of Zadspram*. http://www.avesta.org/mp/zadspram.html#chapter1. Accessed February 6, 2023.
[13]"Kushti." https://en.wikipedia.org/wiki/Kushti. Accessed August 25, 2020.
[14]"Zoroastrians – Marriage and Family." Countries and their Cultures Forum. https://www.everyculture.com/Africa-Middle-East/Zoroastrians-Marriage-and-Family.html. Accessed August 25, 2020.
[15]"Zoroastrian Calendar." https://en.wikipedia.org/wiki/Zoroastrian_calendar. Accessed August 25, 2020.
[16]"Zoroastrian Festivals." https://en.wikipedia.org/wiki/Zoroastrian_festivals. Accessed August 25, 2020.
[17]"Venidad." https://en.wikipedia.org/wiki/Vendidad. Accessed August 25, 2020.
[18]"Quotes of the Avesta, The." *World Spiritual Heritage*. https://www.onelittleangel.com/wisdom/quotes/saint.asp?mc=214. Accessed February 6, 2023.
[19]"Zoroastrianism." https://en.wikipedia.org/wiki/Zoroastrianism. Accessed August 25, 2020.
[20]"Tower of Silence." https://en.wikipedia.org/wiki/Tower_of_Silence. Accessed August 25, 2020.
[21]"Zoroastrianism." *History*. October 8, 2019. https://www.history.com/topics/religion/zoroastrianism. Accessed August 25, 2020.
[22]Goodstein, Laurie. "Zoroastrians Keep the Faith, and Keep Dwindling." *New York Times, The*. September 6, 2006. https://www.nytimes.com/2006/09/06/us/06faith.html. Accessed August 25, 2020.
[23]"Glossary and Standardized Spelling of Zoroastrian Terms." http://www.avesta.org/zglos.html. Accessed August 25, 2020.

ABOUT THE AUTHOR

DR. LEE ANN B. MARINO, PH.D., D.MIN., D.D. (she/her) is "everyone's favorite theologian" leading Gen X, Millennials, and Gen Z with expertise in leadership training, queer and feminist theology, general religion, and apostolic theology. She has served in ministry since 1998 and was ordained as a pastor in 2002 and an apostle in 2010. She founded what is now Sanctuary Apostolic Fellowship Empowerment (SAFE) Ministries in 2004. Under her ministry heading Dr. Marino is founder and Overseer of Sanctuary International Fellowship Tabernacle (SIFT) (the original home of National Coming Out Sunday) and The Sanctuary Network, and Chancellor of Apostolic Covenant Theological Seminary (ACTS).

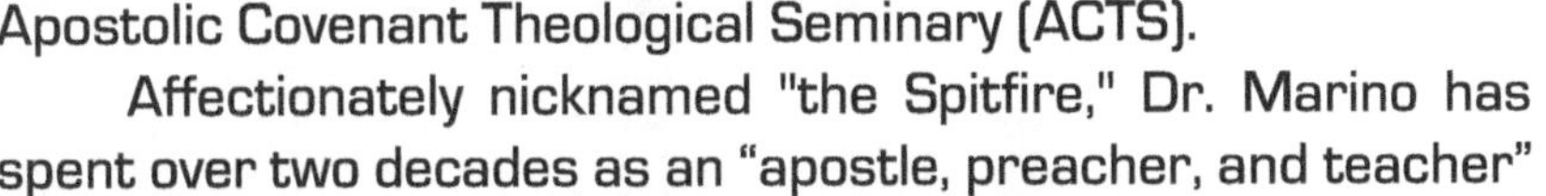

Affectionately nicknamed "the Spitfire," Dr. Marino has spent over two decades as an "apostle, preacher, and teacher" (2 Timothy 1:11), exercising her personal mandate to become "all things to all people" (1 Corinthians 9:22). Her embrace of spiritual issues (both technical and intimate) has found its home among both seekers and believers, those who desire spiritual answers to today's issues.

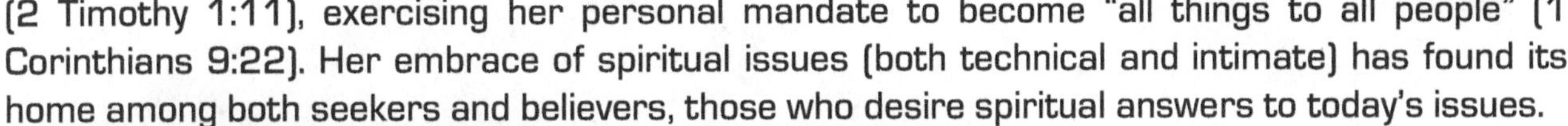

Dr. Marino has preached throughout the United States, Puerto Rico, and Europe in hundreds of religious services and experiences throughout the years. A history maker in her own right, she has spent over two decades in advocacy, education, and work for and within minority spiritual communities (including African American, Hispanic, and LGBTQ+). She has also served as the first woman on all-male synods, councils, and panels, as well as the first preacher or speaker welcomed of a different race, sexual orientation, or identity among diverse communities. Today, Dr. Marino's work extends to over 150 countries as she hosts the popular *Kingdom Now* podcast, which is in the top 20 percentile of all podcasts worldwide. She is also the author of over 35 books and the popular Patheos column, *Leadership on Fire*. To date, she has had five bestselling titles within their subject matter: *Understanding Demonology, Spiritual Warfare, Healing, and Deliverance: A Manual for the Christian Minister*; *Ministry School Boot Camp: Training for Helps Ministries, Appointments, and Beyond*; *Discovering Intimacy: A Journey Through the Song of Solomon*; *Fruit of the Vine: Study and Commentary on the Fruit of the Spirit*; and *Ministering to LGBTQ+ (and Those Who Love Them): A Primer for Queer Theology* (and its accompanying workbook).

As a public icon and social media influencer, Dr. Marino advocates healthy body image (curvy/full-figured), representation as a demisexual/aromantic, and albinism awareness as a model. Known to those she works with, she is a spiritual mom, teacher, leader, professor, confidant, and friend. She continues to transform, receiving new teaching, revelation, and insight in this thing we call "ministry." Through years of spiritual growth and maturity, Dr. Marino stands as herself, here to present what God has given to her for any who have an ear to hear.

For more information, visit her website at kingdompowernow.org.

www.ingramcontent.com/pod-product-compliance
Lightning Source LLC
Chambersburg PA
CBHW080407270326
41929CB00018B/2929

* 9 7 8 1 9 4 0 1 9 7 7 2 2 *